Amphibians

second

and Reptiles

edition

in Colorado

Horned lizard on 700-year-old pottery from Mesa Verde (Montezuma County, Colorado).

Amphibians

second

and Reptiles

edition

in Colorado

Geoffrey A. Hammerson

University Press of Colorado
& Colorado Division of Wildlife
1999

Copyright © 1999 by the University Press of Colorado

Published by the University Press of Colorado
245 Century Circle, Suite 202
Louisville, Colorado 80027

Printed in the United States of America

The University Press of Colorado is a cooperative publishing enterprise supported, in part, by Adams State College, Colorado State University, Fort Lewis College, Mesa State College, Metropolitan State College of Denver, University of Colorado, University of Northern Colorado, University of Southern Colorado, and Western State College of Colorado.

The paper used in this publication meets the minimum requirements of the American National Standard for Information Sciences—Permanence of Paper for Printed Library Materials. ANSI Z39.48–1984

Library of Congress Cataloging-in-Publication Data

Hammerson, Geoffrey A.
   Amphibians and reptiles in Colorado / Geoffrey A. Hammerson. —
2nd ed.
   p. cm.
   Includes bibliographical references (p.) and index.
   ISBN 0-87081-521-0 (alk. paper). — ISBN 0-87081-534-2 (pbk. :
alk. paper)
   1. Reptiles—Colorado. 2. Amphibians—Colorado. I. Title.
QL653.C6H35   1999
597.9'09788—dc21   99-10312
      CIP

With gratitude for twenty years of generosity and kindness,
and with my deepest affection and admiration,
I dedicate this book to Hobart M. Smith.

Contents

Illustrations

Plates

Figures

Maps

Distribution Maps

Tables

Acknowledgments

I received financial support for some of my field and museum studies from the Walker Van Riper Fund of the University of Colorado Museum, the Kathy Lichty Memorial Fund of the Department of EPO Biology at the University of Colorado, Colorado Natural Heritage Inventory (now Colorado Natural Heritage Program), the Colorado Field Office of The Nature Conservancy, and the Colorado Division of Wildlife. The large number of color photographs was made possible through the generous financial support of the Colorado Division of Wildlife. Through the encouragement of Larry Master and Deborah Jensen, the conservation science department of The Nature Conservancy supported part of the final stages of manuscript preparation. I did the majority of the research and writing in my spare time, without any financial support.

The efforts of Chuck Loeffler of the Colorado Division of Wildlife were critical in bringing this book from concept to reality—many thanks to you, Chuck. I am grateful to Luther Wilson of the University Press of Colorado for taking an interest in this project, and I thank Laura Furney and Debbie Korte for efficiently handling the production and editorial responsibilities.

I was fortunate to have Steve Corn, Lauren Livo, Chuck Loeffler, Steve Mackessy, Hobart M. Smith, and James M. Walker review sections of the manuscript as it neared completion. They made many useful suggestions for corrections, additions, clarifications, and other improvements to the book. I am particularly grateful to Hobart Smith and Lauren Livo for their many and diverse contributions to this project. Some errors likely remain among the thousands of pieces of information included here, but these are solely my responsibility.

I regret that cannot adequately acknowledge all of those who facilitated my studies over the years. All I can do here is express my sincere appreciation to Dave Armstrong; Kyle Ashton; Karolis Bagdonas; George Baxter; Audrey and Jim Benedict; Jim Bennett; Robert Bezy; Carl Bock; Marty Bolt; Bill and Louise Bradley; Russ Bromby; Eldon Brown; Richard Bunn; Bruce Bury; Steve Busack; John Carothers; Alan Carpenter; Charles Carpenter; Dave Chiszar; Robert Cohen; Joseph Collins; Steve Corn; Ronald Crombie; Alex Cruz; William Degenhardt; Alan de Queiroz; James Dixon; Mark Dodero; William Duellman; Max Dutton; Jim Fitzgerald; Jerry Freeman; Sandy Frimel; J. E. Gillis; Anna Goebel; Michael Grant; Harry Greene; Donald Hahn; Kay Hammerson; Loreé Harvey; Charles Haynes; Jim Heckers; John Hess; Justin Hobert; Donald Hoffmeister; J. E. Hogue; Dee Holladay; Richard Holland; Rosanne Humphrey; Crawford Jackson; Michelle King; Arnold Kluge; Garry Knopf; Dave Langlois; Beth Lapin; Peter LaRochelle; John Legler; Alan Leviton; Lauren Livo; Chuck Loeffler; Mark Lomolino; Willard Louden; Mark Ludlow; John Lynch; Tom Lytle; Steve Mackessy; Robert F. Martin; Hyman Marx; T. Paul Maslin; Larry Master; Terry Matthews; Michael McCoid; C. J. (Jack) McCoy, Jr.; Liz McGhee; Peter Meylan; Paul Miller; Chad Montgomery; Doyle Mosier; Toby Mourning; Charles Myers; Betsy Neely; Tom

Nesler; George Oliver; Elizabeth Owen; Gary Packard; Chris Pague; Marty Pancak; Steve Petersburg; David Pettus; Phil Pister; Douglas Post; Andrew Price; Horace Quick; Cindy Ramotnik; Leah Ramsay; Matt Rand; Robert Reese; Felix Revello; Holly Richter; Jose Rosado; Douglas Rossman; Stan Roth; Robert Sanz; Cecil Schwalbe; John Scott; Mike Scott; Judy Sheppard; Mike Sherman; John Simmons; Hobart Smith; Greg Snyder; Kenneth Soltesz; Albert Spencer; Robert C. Stebbins; Barbara Stein; Adrienne Stolfie; John Suhay; Tom Swain; Wilmer Tanner; Walter Tordoff; John Torres; Fred Truxal; W. Thomas Turner; Randy Vaeth; Larry Valentine; Heidi and Mark Van Everen; Richard Vogt; David Wake; James M. Walker; Robert Webb; Steve Wilcox; Olwen Williams; John Wright; Shi-Kuei Wu; Mike Wunder; and Robert Zweifel. In addition, I express my thanks to all of the ranchers and other landowners throughout Colorado who permitted me to search for amphibians and reptiles on their property. I am especially grateful to my colleagues who unselfishly shared their observations and data with me and by doing so fostered a satisfying atmosphere of cooperation. I enjoyed sharing the sense of fun and mystery that comes from studying these intriguing animals.

The distribution maps in this book benefited greatly from the existence of well-managed museums. Museums provide a permanent record of materials and information that is critical to biologists and conservationists. The following museums/institutions contributed to the accuracy and completeness of my distribution maps by allowing me to examine reptile and amphibian specimens in their care or by providing information on their herpetological collections: American Museum of Natural History (AMNH), Brigham Young University Monte L. Bean Life Science Museum (BYU), California Academy of Sciences (CAS), Carnegie Museum of Natural History (CM), Colorado National Monument (COLM), Colorado State University (later incorporated into the BS/FC collection, now at MSB), Field Museum of Natural History (FMNH), Harvard University Museum of Comparative Zoology (MCZ), Los Angeles County Museum of Natural History (LACMNH), Louisiana State University Museum of Zoology (LSUMZ), National Museum of Natural History (USNM), New Mexico State University (NMSU), San Diego Natural History Museum (SDSNH), Texas A & M University (TCWC), Texas Memorial Museum (TNHC), University of Arizona (UAZ), University of California Museum of Vertebrate Zoology (MVZ), University of Colorado Museum (UCM), University of Florida Museum of Natural History (UF-FSM), University of Illinois Museum of Natural History (UIMNH), University of Kansas Museum of Natural History (KU), University of Michigan Museum of Zoology (UMMZ), University of Nebraska State Museum (UNSM), University of New Mexico Museum of Southwestern Biology (MSB), University of Northern Colorado Museum of Natural History (UNC-MNH), University of Oklahoma Stovall Museum of Zoology (UOMZ), University of Texas at El Paso (UTEP), and University of Utah (UU).

I especially thank Sandy, Kay, Ursa, and Rudy for their loving support and patience during the many months when my attention and time were absorbed in the preparation of this book.

Introduction

The day was dry and dusty, and the sun, alone in a cloudless sky, bore down on the broad canyon bottom. Animal life seemed absent, but it was simply hidden from view in the cooler confines of shaded crevices and burrows. Even with the setting sun, the parched heat lingered. Then, in the west, against the horizon, a mound of clouds, small and barely noticeable at first, began growing rapidly. As it loomed closer, it was accompanied by an east wind that seemed determined to draw me into the towering thunderhead. After a brief pause, the wind reversed direction and began to blow hard, and the sky became a dense, dark blanket of gray as the temperature plummeted several degrees within a few minutes. The evening rain began with scattered splats but quickly became an unrelenting torrent. Dry depressions turned to ponds and small lakes, and a waterless arroyo transformed into a raging river 15 feet deep and 100 feet wide.

After 30 minutes, the rain subsided, and in the growing darkness I headed out to observe the aftermath. In this formerly quiet, parched landscape, where it seemed inconceivable that an amphibian could live, there were now hundreds of toads of several species hopping around and beginning a vocal cacophony that lasted well into the next morning. Individuals that had not shed eggs or sperm for many months—perhaps years—at last were able to reproduce. Some of Colorado's most secretive, rarely observed snakes emerged into the open and crawled toward new destinations. The physical and biological world was remarkably transformed by this sudden chance addition of water.

This event, which occurred in June 1979 in southeastern Colorado, illustrates a basic characteristic of amphibians and reptiles in Colorado—extreme daily, seasonal, and annual variation in behavior and populations, resulting from predictable and unpredictable changes in the physical environment. This dynamism makes field study of amphibians and reptiles exceptionally interesting, challenging, and at times puzzling. I have learned to be ready for surprises. Even after decades of investigation, I have to admit that I find amphibians and reptiles rather mysterious. But this mystery makes them all the more fun to study and is the major reason why I embarked on the research that resulted in this book.

Amphibians and Reptiles in Colorado contains information on the identification, distribution, conservation status, habitat, behavior, and life history of each reptile and amphibian species known to inhabit this state. Nearly all of the amphibians and reptiles of Wyoming, eastern Utah, northern New Mexico, and western Kansas are included here as well. The area covered by the book encompasses primarily the west-central Great Plains, the southern Rocky Mountains, and the canyons, mesas, and plains of the upper Colorado River basin.

My studies of Colorado amphibians and reptiles began in 1977 and continued, with a few interruptions, through early 1999. I attempted to review available information on the amphibians and reptiles occurring in Colorado and adjacent states, including published literature as well as numerous theses, dissertations, and other unpublished reports. Biologists, friends, and acquaintances throughout the region supplied me with much useful information. An examination of approximately 20,000 specimens in the collections of 16 museums and a survey and evaluation of the records of several additional museums yielded a wealth of distributional and biological data and allowed me to detect and correct several published distribution records based on incorrectly identified specimens. My own field surveys throughout the state and region over more than two decades generated thousands of pages of notes on distribution, abundance, habitat preferences, behavior, and life histories, plus scores of memorable personal experiences and inadvertent adventures. I conducted field studies in all of Colorado's 63 counties, and I gained field experience with every species of amphibian and reptile known to currently inhabit the state. However, over the years, I have become increasingly aware of how little we know about most aspects of the lives and populations of these animals.

My studies of amphibians and reptiles in Colorado began at a time when these animals were largely ignored by the vast majority of wildlife biologists, who were preoccupied with game birds, mammals, and sport fishes. It has been particularly satisfying to see growing interest in the amphibians and reptiles of this region, especially within the conservation and resource management communities, and to know that the first edition of this book helped spark it. I hope that this second edition will help biologists of the new millennium explore the mysteries of the natural world and take action to protect these animals, who fill unique ecological and biological roles and continue to fascinate Colorado's many human residents and visitors.

Regarding herpetology, the study of amphibians and reptiles, readers should bear in mind that these two groups are as different from each other as birds are from mammals. Nevertheless, for historical and practical reasons, they often are studied together. Early naturalists did not see the differences between amphibians and reptiles as important and treated them as a single group. Biologists today recognize that amphibians and reptiles constitute two distinct classes of vertebrates (animals with a backbone), though they continue to study them together because research methods are quite similar.

Herpetology comes from the Greek word *herpes,* referring to a creeping or crawling thing. For informal simplicity in oral communication, amphibians and reptiles frequently are referred to collectively as "herps." *Herptiles,* an ugly word, is an inappropriate term for amphibians and reptiles and should be avoided. *Herpetofauna* refers to the assemblage of amphibian and reptile species in a particular area.

Amphibians

second

and Reptiles

edition

in Colorado

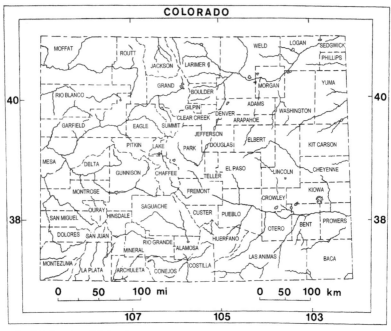

Map 0.1. Counties of Colorado.

Chapter 1

History of Herpetology in Colorado

This book is devoted mainly to species accounts summarizing the lives of Colorado's amphibians and reptiles. But first I wish to describe important events in the history of Coloradan herpetology and to acknowledge the people and publications that helped shape our knowledge of the field. To keep this review relatively brief, I have omitted some significant contributions. Many of these, however, are mentioned in the species accounts. The scientific names in this book are those currently in use; please keep in mind that authors cited in text may refer to the same species by different names.

The first recorded observations of amphibians and reptiles in Colorado were made in pre-Columbian times in southwestern Colorado. Native American rock art created prior to the arrival of Europeans in Colorado often depicts amphibians and reptiles. Inhabitants of the area now known as Mesa Verde decorated stoneware and pottery with images of lizards, including one recognizable as a short-horned lizard (see frontispiece).

Most of the well-known early explorations of Colorado left no record of amphibians or reptiles. The Franciscan fathers Domínguez and Escalante traveled through western Colorado during August and September 1776, but their journal includes no reports of amphibians or reptiles. The journal of Zebulon Pike, whose famous expedition crossed southeastern Colorado during the fall and winter of 1806–1807, also fails to mention amphibians and reptiles, though this is hardly surprising, given the cold weather.

The first scientific account referring to amphibians or reptiles in Colorado (James 1823) is based primarily on the observations of zoologist Thomas Say, who accompanied Major Stephen Long's Colorado expedition. Captain John R. Bell's journal, recorded during this same expedition (Fuller and Hafen 1957), also contains several herpetological observations.

Long and his party entered Colorado along the South Platte River in late June 1820 and traveled to areas now known as Denver, Pikes Peak, Pueblo, and the Royal Gorge. The expedition split up, and the group of which Say was a member left Colorado by way of the Arkansas River sometime after July 29, 1820. Say collected specimens of amphibians and reptiles in Colorado, but his notes and some of the specimens were lost when three members of the expedition deserted the group at the end of August. Other specimens, deposited in the Peale Museum in Philadelphia, later were destroyed or lost (Dundee 1996).

Say's account includes the original descriptions of three taxa collected in Colorado: Great Plains toad, diploid checkered whiptail, and a subspecies of the coachwhip. Say also recorded the first Coloradan observations of a horned lizard (probably the short-horned lizard) in what is now El Paso or Pueblo County (Dundee 1996) and of the western rattlesnake. The expedition's accounts of "miliary rattlesnakes" in northeastern Colorado and *"Crotalus tergeminus"* (massasauga) from an unspecified location (but placed in the northeastern Colorado section of the narrative, which also includes observations of the species from an area east of Colorado), in addition to *"Crotalus confluentus"* (western rattlesnake), are enigmatic. Dundee (1996) concluded that the expedition did encounter massasaugas in northeastern Colorado, where presently they do not occur. I agree with Gloyd (1940) that it is more likely that only *C. viridis* was seen in northeastern Colorado and that massasaugas were picked up farther south later in the trip, possibly in Colorado or somewhere to the southeast, or perhaps earlier in Iowa.

Compilation of the expedition narrative was hampered by the loss of the original notes, which resulted in some errors and confusions. For example, a description of a two-legged amphisbaenid (wormlike reptile) supposedly collected in northeastern Colorado is included in Say's account. However, the description of the animal's behavior ("They were so active, that it was not without some difficulty that we succeeded in obtaining a specimen" [James 1823, p. 70]) cannot be realistically applied to an amphisbaenid, which is a slow-moving, burrowing animal, and lessens the credibility of the record (see Appendix A).

Emory (1848) made the next contribution to Colorado herpetology. He mentioned an 1846 observation of a Texas horned lizard near the junction of the Arkansas River and Big Sandy Creek. Hallowell (1857) described the many-lined skink from material apparently collected in Colorado.

Spencer Baird (1859) listed species of amphibians and reptiles collected during the railroad surveys of the mid-nineteenth century. Several of Baird's records were based on specimens that may have been collected in Colorado. If so, the first records for Colorado included the tiger salamander, Wood-house's toad, collared lizard, short-horned lizard (if not previously recorded by Say), Great Plains skink, and western hognose snake. That same year, Tierney (1859) also reported observing a larval tiger salamander ("torpedo") at Bijou Creek in eastern Colorado. Conner (1970) made observations of a rattlesnake, horned lizard, and what probably was a bullsnake (imaginatively described as 10 feet long, with red eyes and a head as big

as the closed fist of a man) in Bent County around 1859.

Yarrow (1875) reported on amphibians and reptiles collected in the southwestern United States during the early 1870s. Collections were made in Colorado during 1873–1874 at Pagosa Springs, the San Luis Valley, Twin Lakes, South Park, Fairplay, Denver, Colorado Springs, and Pueblo by J. Yarrow, H. C. Yarrow, J. T. Rothrock, H. W. Henshaw, C. E. Aiken, E. D. Cope, and others. Species recorded from Colorado for the first time included the mountain toad, western chorus frog, northern leopard frog, lesser earless lizard, plateau lizard, racer, bullsnake (discounting the record of Conner mentioned earlier), and western terrestrial garter snake. Dubious records listed by Yarrow included Woodhouse's toad, lesser earless lizard, and tree lizard from Twin Lakes, Lake County, and common garter snake from the San Luis Valley (see accounts of these species for explanation). Also, Yarrow's record of the checkered garter snake *(Thamnophis marcianus)* was based on a specimen of the plains garter snake (see Cope 1900). White (1878) related an observation of a garter snake, probably *Thamnophis sirtalis* (Smith and Chiszar 1988), which if true was the first valid record of that species in Colorado. The famous traveler Isabella Bird visited Colorado in 1873 and observed various reptiles, including species she referred to as rattlesnakes, moccasin snakes, carpet snakes, green racers, water snakes, tree snakes, and mouse snakes (Bird 1879).

Yarrow's (1882) checklist of North American reptiles and amphibians included numerous records of specimens from Colorado, most of which reiterated his 1875 records. The only undoubtedly valid addition to the Coloradan herpetofauna was the striped whipsnake. All other new records of species supposedly collected in Colorado in the 1882 checklist are dubious or outright erroneous. His "Colorado" records of the desert iguana *(Dipsosaurus dorsalis),* brush lizard *(Urosaurus graciosus),* sidewinder *(Crotalus cerastes),* and shovelnose snake *(Chionactis occipitalis)* undoubtedly were based on specimens collected along the Colorado River valley southwest of Colorado, as may have been a record of the common kingsnake. These obvious errors suggest that his "Colorado" and "Colorado River" records of the collared lizard, longnose leopard lizard, tree lizard, and side-blotched lizard also were not collected in Colorado. In addition, Yarrow's records of the massasauga and the western ribbon snake from the "headwaters of Colorado" presumably were based on snakes from along the Colorado River in Texas.

The first indisputable Colorado records of the tree lizard and plateau striped whiptail were included in Cope's (1900) monograph on the crocodilians, lizards, and snakes of North America. Several of Yarrow's inaccurate records were repeated. Cope also incorrectly listed specimens of the Texas horned lizard from Colorado; these same specimens were listed under the short-horned lizard earlier in his publication. The museum numbers and collection data correspond exactly with Yarrow's (1882) records of the short-horned lizard.

Two other species were added to the known herpetofauna of Colorado during the opening decade of the 1900s. Dickerson (1906) reported the first record of the plains spadefoot. Ruthven's (1908) study of the garter snakes included the first Colorado record of the common garter snake (or the second record, if White's [1878] record is credible).

The extraordinary zoologist T.D.A. Cockerell (1910) published the herpetological results of a 1909 University of Colorado Museum expedition to northwestern Colorado and included some records from elsewhere in the state. Species previously unreported included the northern water snake and milk snake. Cockerell's erroneous record of the common garter snake from northwestern Colorado was based on the western terrestrial garter snake.

Merrit Cary's (1911) account of his 1905–1909 biological survey of Colorado was the first major contribution to Colorado herpetology since Yarrow's (1875) report. Cary provided the first state records of the Great Basin spadefoot, sagebrush lizard, side-blotched lizard, six-lined racerunner, western whiptail, and smooth green snake.

Cary also provided descriptions of the Colorado distributions and habitats of numerous amphibian and reptile species. The only questionable record in Cary's account was that of a tree lizard from Arboles in Archuleta County (see species account).

The first comprehensive account of the herpetofauna of Colorado was published in 1913 by Max Ellis and Junius Henderson of the University of Colorado Museum. They included descriptions and localities for all taxa then believed to occur in Colorado, based on previously published records and specimens in museums in Boulder, Denver, and Greeley. Arthur E. Beardsley and Horace G. Smith were important contributors of museum specimens mentioned in the publication. The Ellis and Henderson report included the first documented state records for the green toad, northern cricket frog, canyon treefrog, plains leopard frog, snapping turtle, yellow mud turtle, painted turtle, spiny softshell, ringneck snake, ground snake, plains black-headed snake, and massasauga (discounting the uncertain record of James [1823]). Most of these were based on specimens collected by Beardsley and deposited in the museum at State Teacher's College (now the University of Northern Colorado) in Greeley. That collection no longer exists, but the museum register of specimens does. Ellis and Henderson, too, repeated some of Yarrow's erroneous records; other records I regard to be invalid as natural occurrences include the American toad, eastern box turtle, roundtail horned lizard (but see species account), and western diamondback rattlesnake, plus the Texas horned lizard from Boulder and Denver and the Great Plains skink from Weld County (Hammerson 1984; Livo, Hammerson, and Smith 1998). The brown snake (Storeria dekayi) was reported from Las Animas County, but this record never has been confirmed by additional specimens (but see Appendix A).

A short addition to the Ellis and Henderson account was published in 1915. The red-spotted toad, bullfrog, and blackneck garter snake were reported from Colorado for the first time, and additional records for other species were listed.

Not until the 1920s did anyone produce a substantial natural history account based on a field study of an amphibian or reptile in Colorado. The groundbreaker was Gilmore (1924), who published a study of the life history of the plains spadefoot in the Colorado Springs area.

In 1925, Helen Gaige of the University of Michigan collected extensively in the San Luis Valley and in the vicinity of Walsenburg and became the first woman to make a substantial contribution to Colorado herpetology. At the Spanish Peaks, she collected the type specimens of the smooth green snake *Liochlorophis vernalis blanchardi* (Grobman).

Burnett (1926) published new distributional records for several Colorado amphibians and reptiles, including the first state record for the New Mexico spadefoot and a somewhat questionable record of the northern cricket frog from Weld County (see species account). Charles Burt traveled through Colorado in 1928 and published additional distributional records (Burt and Burt 1929).

In 1930, the renowned snake student Laurence Klauber described a new subspecies of the western rattlesnake, *Crotalus viridis decolor* (now considered a junior synonym of *Crotalus viridis concolor* Woodbury), based on specimens collected in western Colorado in 1900. Beginning in 1936 and continuing through the 1940s, Klauber published extensively on a series of more than 850 rattlesnakes collected by C. B. Perkins at prairie-dog towns near Platteville, Weld County.

Lewis T. Barry of the Denver Museum of Natural History made important contributions to Colorado herpetology during the early 1930s (Barry 1932a, 1932b, 1933a). He recorded the first state records of the longnose leopard lizard, desert spiny lizard, night snake, and western ribbon snake.

Charles Burt again collected in Colorado during the early 1930s and published (1933a, 1933b, 1935) numerous new distributional records. Burt (1932) also showed that Burnett's (1932) Colorado record of the five-lined skink *(Eumeces fasciatus)* was based on a specimen of the many-lined skink.

Jones-Burdick (1939) published a brief guide to the snakes of Colorado; a few of Yarrow's (1882) erroneous records persisted in the account.

Predictably, the war years of the early 1940s yielded few new publications. Woodbury and Woodbury (1942) described *Elaphe laeta intermontana (Elaphe guttata intermontana)* based partly on specimens from western Colorado, providing the first state record for the species. In 1943, Hugo Rodeck published the short *Guide to the Amphibia of Colorado.*

A new era in Colorado herpetology began in the mid-1940s with the arrival of T. Paul Maslin. Maslin began collecting amphibians and reptiles in Colorado in 1946 while at what is now Colorado State University in Fort Collins. Soon after, he became curator in herpetology at the University of Colorado Museum in Boulder, where he remained until his retirement in 1978. Maslin was largely responsible for building the museum's herpetology collection into one of national importance. His early contributions include the first published record of the wood frog in Colorado (1947c; see Hammerson 1982a), a brief guide to the lizards of Colorado (1947b), and notes on range extensions for several species (1947a).

Other significant publications of the 1940s include the first Colorado record of the glossy snake in Klauber's (1946) description of the subspecies *blanchardi,* and Swenson and Rodeck's (1948) first state records of the longnose snake and lined snake. Robert C. Stebbins traveled through Colorado in 1946 and 1949 and included some of his observations in his outstanding 1951 book *Amphibians of Western North America.*

Popular guides and taxonomic revisions involving Colorado species were published in the 1950s. Rodeck (1950) published a guide to the turtles of Colorado. Burger (1950) described a new subspecies of western whiptail, *Cnemidophorus tigris septentrionalis,* and designated a specimen from Garfield County as the holotype. During the 1950s, Maslin evaluated the taxonomic status in Colorado of the coachwhip (1953) and many-lined skink (1957), and he described the lizard *Sceloporus undulatus erythrocheilus* (1956) based on material largely from Colorado.

The herpetological highlight of the 1950s was the appearance of Maslin's (1959) annotated checklist of Colorado amphibians and reptiles. He included nearly all published references pertaining to Colorado herpetology and listed catalog numbers and localities for all Colorado specimens in the University of Colorado Museum. The dubious records of Yarrow (1882) and Ellis and Henderson (1913) were discussed.

The 1960s were a productive period. Clarence J. (Jack) McCoy, Jr., then of the University of Colorado, published several papers based primarily on his extensive fieldwork in western Colorado during the early 1960s. McCoy, Knopf, and Walker (1964) published the first state record of the southwestern black-headed snake. Benjamin Banta and his students at Colorado College carried out extensive pitfall trapping in southeastern Colorado and published several brief but valuable accounts of the herpetofaunas of the Black Forest, Wet Mountains, Phantom Canyon, and the prairie east of Colorado Springs.

As with Maslin's arrival in the 1940s, Hobart M. Smith's move from Illinois to Colorado in the early 1960s was a major catalyst for further herpetological study. The field activities of Smith, Robert Reese, Robert Brown, Richard Holland, and the herpetology classes at the University of Colorado yielded a wealth of new distributional information summarized by Smith, Maslin, and Brown (1965). Maps depicting the occurrence of species among the 63 counties of Colorado were the basic reference for distributional information until the early 1980s.

Valuable studies of the herpetofauna of southwestern Colorado were published by Dean and Stock (1961), Harris (1963), and Douglas (1966). Donald Hahn collected extensively in the San Luis Valley from 1960 to 1965; his unpublished master's thesis (1968) is an important contribution from that region.

Intensive field studies of single species of Coloradan amphibians and reptiles, accomplished primarily by graduate students of David Pettus of Colorado State University and T. Paul Maslin of the University of Colorado, began to increase during the 1960s. Dissertations and theses focused on species such as the tiger salamander (Reese 1969), plains spadefoot (Woody 1967), western chorus frog (Spencer 1964a; Hess 1969a; Tordoff 1967; Matthews 1968), wood frog (Bagdonas 1968), checkered whiptail (Knopf 1966), and western whiptail (McCoy 1965). Among various other studies, Donald Johnson (1966) summarized the diets of lizards in Montezuma County, Post and Pettus (1966) demonstrated the occurrence of two species of leopard frogs in Colorado, McCoy (1967) described the natural history of the longnose leopard lizard in Mesa County, and Donald Tinkle (1967) reported on the population biology of the side-blotched lizard in Mesa County. At the close of the 1960s, Kenneth Porter (1969b) described the wood frogs of the Southern Rocky Mountains as a new species, *Rana maslini.* However, Bagdonas and Pettus (1976) later demonstrated that Porter's basis for recognizing the Colorado wood frog as a distinct species was invalid.

Two species were added to the known herpetofauna in the 1970s. Spencer (1974) and Kappel (1977a, 1977b) reported the common kingsnake from southwestern and southeastern Colorado, respectively. Livo (1977) reported the first Colorado record of the Couch's spadefoot.

Distributional information for the state was reported in a new format by Langlois (1978). Langlois presented a coded summary of the habitat associations and distributions of amphibians and reptiles in 28 "latilong" blocks (units of 1° latitude by 1° longitude).

Graduate student research contributed significantly to Coloradan herpetology during the 1970s. Species studied most intensively included the tiger salamander (Bizer 1977, 1978; Sexton and Bizer 1978), mountain toad (Campbell 1970a, 1970b, 1970c, 1970d, 1971, 1976), western chorus frog (Hoppe 1978), northern and plains leopard frogs (Post 1972; Gillis 1975a,

1979), wood frog (Bagdonas 1971), plateau lizard (Ferner, 1974, 1976; Turner 1974), and western terrestrial garter snake (Scott 1978). Tinkle and Ballinger (1972) conducted research on plateau lizard populations in Mesa County.

Native Colorado amphibians and reptiles became popular subjects for laboratory research in the 1970s. David Norris of the University of Colorado and Gary Packard and David Pettus of Colorado State University, together with their students, published extensively on topics in physiology, endocrinology, and genetics. David Chiszar of the University of Colorado began an ongoing program of research on rattlesnake feeding behavior.

To my knowledge, conservation efforts directed specifically at Colorado's amphibians and reptiles began when R. D. Zortman (1968) proposed that the Bridge Canyon area in extreme southwestern Colorado be designated a natural area because of its rich reptile fauna. Subsequently, the Bureau of Land Management established the 443-acre McElmo Rare Lizard and Snake Area, which must be one of the most unusual preserves ever created in Colorado. The area, now known as the McElmo Research Natural Area, was fenced in 1986 to keep out grazing livestock.

In 1973 the Colorado state legislature enacted the Nongame, Endangered, or Threatened Species Conservation Act and authorized the Colorado Wildlife Commission to establish regulations pertaining to collection, possession, sale, and transportation of nongame wildlife, including amphibians and reptiles. The state legislature passed the Colorado Natural Areas Act in 1977, creating a program to identify and protect ecosystems, ecological communities, and other natural features such as habitat for rare or endangered plants and animals through a statewide system of designated natural areas. One of these, the Mexican Cut Preserve in Gunnison County, acquired for protection in 1966 by The Nature Conservancy (TNC), was established in part to protect an ecologically interesting system of ponds inhabited by the tiger salamander.

By the end of the 1980s, Colorado's key academic herpetologists (T. Paul Maslin, David Pettus, and Hobart Smith) had retired and were succeeded in their departments by biologists with nonherpetological, out-of-state, or laboratory-oriented research interests, signaling a potential decline in herpetological field study at Colorado's major universities. Nevertheless, the 1980s and 1990s saw continued research on the distribution, conservation, and taxonomy of the state's amphibians and reptiles, conducted by personnel from both academia and natural resource agencies. Pierce (1980) and Pierce and Mitton (1980) examined genetic variation in the tiger salamander. Haynes and Aird (1981) summarized their studies on Colorado's disjunct population of wood frogs. Livo (1981b) studied northern leopard frog reproduction in Boulder County. Aird (1984a) studied morphological and genetic variation in the western rattlesnake in Colorado, Wyoming, and Utah. Wiese (1985, 1990) reported on bullfrog populations and ecology in northeastern Colorado. Recognition of a decline in certain amphibian populations in the southern Rocky Mountains (e.g., Corn and Fogelman 1984) led to increased study of the status and biology of montane amphibians (e.g., Corn, Stoltzenburg, and Bury 1989; Hammerson 1989a, 1992; Kiesecker 1991, 1996; Livo 1995a; Corn, Jennings, and Muths 1997; Corn 1998), spearheaded to a large degree by Steve Corn. Corn and Bury (1986) demonstrated that the proposed split of the racer into two species was unwarranted. Doctoral research by Kocher (1986) and Rand (1991) yielded, respectively, valuable information on taxonomically relevant genetic variation in the tiger salamander and behavioral biology of *Sceloporus undulatus erythrocheilus*. Goebel's (1996) doctoral thesis documented patterns of genetic variation in *Bufo boreas* in the southern Rockies, setting the stage for a taxonomic revision of the species. Jim Walker, Harry Taylor, and colleagues expanded our knowledge of unisexual populations of whiptail lizards, and Walker, Cordes, and Taylor (1997) recognized the triploid and diploid populations of the checkered whiptail as distinct species.

Snyder and Hammerson (1993) reported on the water balance and behavior of canyon treefrogs in Mesa County.

Field surveys of amphibian and reptile distribution throughout Colorado continued during the 1980s and 1990s. In addition to studies of montane amphibians already mentioned, Hobart Smith, David Chiszar, Lauren Livo, and others published many new county distributional records. Larry Valentine was a source of valuable distributional information on reptiles and amphibians in western Colorado. Jerry Freeman and Loreé Harvey (unpublished data) surveyed the amphibian fauna of the San Luis Valley in 1991. In the mid-1990s biologists from the University of Northern Colorado conducted intensive field surveys of the herpetofauna of southeastern Colorado (Mackessy 1998), and Division of Wildlife personnel surveyed northwestern Colorado (Mourning 1997). Hobert's (1997) master's thesis on the massasauga in southeastern Colorado provided valuable information on the distribution and biology of that species, as did Montgomery's (1998) thesis on the Texas horned lizard. In 1997, David Schmidt and Cindy Ramotnik astounded the herpetological community by confirming the existence in northwestern Otero County of a highly disjunct population of roundtail horned lizard (Ramotnik 1998).

The 1990s saw the rejuvenation of the Colorado Natural Heritage Program (CNHP) under the leadership of Chris Pague. Now affiliated with Colorado State University, CNHP has become a major repository of information and a significant research program for imperiled and rare plants, natural communities, and animals, including amphibians and reptiles. One outcome of CNHP research was the rediscovery of the canyon treefrog in southeastern Colorado. The Colorado Field Office of TNC, led by Mark Burgett and Betsy Neely, emerged as a frontrunner in producing, assembling, and using scientific data for the identification and protection of natural areas of high conservation value. A major protection effort for the amphibians, reptiles, and other

fauna and flora of the shortgrass prairie ecosystem, which encompasses the Great Plains region of eastern Colorado, was initiated by TNC in 1997. Major conservation areas have been identified, including nearly all of the most significant ones for amphibians and reptiles. A plan for ensuring adequate protection of the sites has been established, and initial efforts for carrying out the plan are underway.

In the mid-1990s, the Colorado Division of Wildlife consolidated amphibian and reptile research and management, which for years had been administered by different units, under the direction of Chuck Loeffler. Loeffler encouraged and supported much-needed research on the status of amphibians and reptiles and promoted the publication of this book. The mountain toad was a focus of attention within the Division of Wildlife in the mid- to late 1990s, and a conservation/recovery team worked to improve our knowledge of and the status of that species (Goettl 1997).

My own involvement in Colorado herpetology began in 1977, when I enrolled at the University of Colorado to study with Hobart Smith. I soon became interested in the local herpetofauna and reported on the distribution and conservation status of various species in several minor publications. These included the first state records of the Great Plains narrowmouth toad (1980) and Texas blind snake (1982). For my doctoral thesis (1981), I analyzed patterns of distribution of the state's herpetofauna. The first edition of *Amphibians and Reptiles in Colorado* was published in 1982 and reprinted in 1986. Subsequently, I co-authored several papers on various aspects of Colorado herpetology and created for the Colorado Division of Wildlife an amphibian and reptile distributional database, which serves as a primary source of documentation for the maps appearing in this book. Most recently, I have devoted myself to research for this book, focusing on obtaining additional information on amphibian and reptile distribution, population status, habitat, ecology, life history, and behavior.

Chapter 2

Environmental Relationships

Colorado, a roughly rectangular state whose boundaries coincide with latitudes of 37° and 41° north and longitudes of approximately 102° and 109° west, encompasses an area of about 268,000 square km (104,000 square miles). The state lies at the southern end of the Rocky Mountain chain and straddles the Continental Divide, the high mountain crest that separates the Pacific and Atlantic drainage systems. Colorado is perhaps best known for the rugged mountains that cross the central part of the state, but the gently sloping plains to the east and the plateaus, canyons, and basins to the west occupy an even greater area (Map 2.1). The following sections on the physiography, hydrography, climate, and habitats of Colorado summarize the environmental context and relationships of the state's herpetofauna.

PHYSIOGRAPHIC REGIONS

The following description of the physiographic features of Colorado is organized according to Fenneman's (1931) classification and is based largely on Fenneman; Chronic and Chronic (1972); Larson, Ozima,

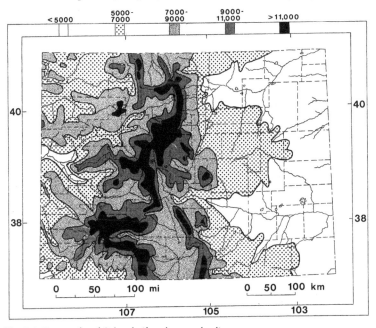

Map 2.1. Topography of Colorado (feet above sea level).

and Bradley (1975); Lipman and Mehnert (1975); Scott (1975); Steven (1975); Taylor (1975); and Tweto (1975, 1979). For a more detailed yet readable description of the physiography and landscape evolution of Colorado, I recommend Chronic (1980) and Benedict (1991).

Colorado encompasses five major physiographic provinces (Map 2.2) of diverse geological makeup (Map 2.3). Prominent physiographic features are identified in Map 2.4. Geological terms are defined in the Glossary.

Great Plains

High Plains. The High Plains region is relatively flat and featureless (but nonetheless beautiful) and ranges in elevation from less than 3,500 feet (1,070 m) to slightly more than 5,000 feet (1,525 m) along the Platte-Arkansas Divide in east-central Colorado. It is covered by Upper Tertiary sediments consisting mostly of loose- to well-cemented sand and gravel. Much of this layer is overlain by wind-deposited dune sands of Quaternary age. A notable exception to the flatness of most of the High

Plains is Two Buttes, a double-pointed cone of intrusive igneous rock dating from the middle Tertiary.

Colorado Piedmont. The Upper Tertiary sedimentary cover is absent from this part of the Great Plains, eroded away by the Platte and Arkansas rivers and their tributaries. The major rocks now exposed are largely Cretaceous shales, but older Tertiary sedimentary rocks are extensively exposed at the western part of the Platte-Arkansas Divide and across the northern part of the piedmont. In many areas there is a surface layer of Quaternary gravels, alluvium, and wind-deposited sands. Especially prominent are the sandhills along the southern edges of the South Platte River, Arkansas River, and Big Sandy Creek.

The western border of the Piedmont abuts the Front Range of the Rocky Mountains and varies in elevation from 5,000–7,000 feet (1,525–2,135 m). Steep, eastward-dipping Paleozoic and Mesozoic sedimentary rocks, one layer of which forms the notable Dakota hogback, characterize this western boundary. The Piedmont extends to an elevation of about 3,350 feet (1,020 m) near

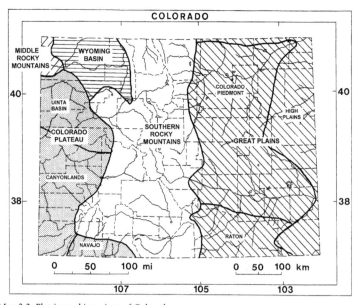

Map 2.2. Physiographic regions of Colorado.

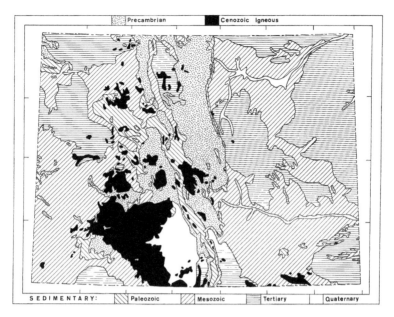

Map 2.3. Geological features of Colorado (based on a 1967 map by Oetking, Feray, and Refro).

the Kansas-Colorado border. Relief is gradual, though the crest of the Platte-Arkansas Divide rises as much as 1,500 feet (460 m) above the major valley bottoms at the same longitude.

Raton Section. This area, named for its highest mesa, consists of several mesas, dissected plateaus, deep canyons cut through the Dakota sandstone, and volcanic mountains, providing extensive rocky habitat that is absent in most of the Great Plains in Colorado. The mesas (e.g., Raton Mesa, Mesa de Maya, Fowler Mesa, Tecolote Mesa, and Carrizo Mountain) are capped by thick layers of Miocene-Pliocene basalt and reach elevations of 5,000–9,600 feet (1,525–2,930 m). The Tertiary sedimentary cover of the high plains is missing here, though a highland (7,000–8,500 feet [2,135–2,590 m]) of late Cretaceous and early Tertiary sedimentary rocks lies between the Rocky Mountains and Raton Mesa. The resurfacing of the erosion-resistant Dakota sandstone is notable, in that this layer dips strongly downward from its exposed position at the western

edge of the Great Plains and is 2,000 feet (610 m) beneath Cheyenne Wells near the Kansas border to the north. Deep canyons have formed where streams, such as the Purgatoire, Apishapa, and Cucharas rivers, have cut through the sandstone into softer underlying sediments. Where the strata overlying the sandstone have not been eroded, flat plains may exist, sometimes marked with perched limestone cuestas.

The Spanish Peaks (rising to more than 13,500 feet [4,115 m]) are a prominent feature of volcanic origin (early Miocene) in the western part of the Raton Section. From the east they appear to be part of the Rocky Mountains, but actually they are a plains feature; the usual hogback of Mesozoic sedimentary layers runs between them and the Rockies.

The Great Plains region, particularly the Colorado Piedmont and the Raton Section, supports the highest diversity of amphibians and reptiles in Colorado (Figure 2.1), including nearly 80 percent of the species occurring in the state and many species not occurring in other regions of Colorado.

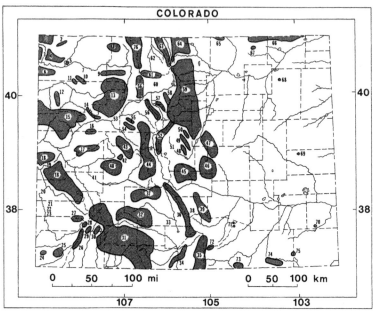

Map 2.4. Prominent physiographic features of Colorado: (1) O-wi-yu-kuts Plateau, (2) Vermillion Bluffs, (3) Lodore Canyon, (4) Uinta Mountains, (5) Cross Mountain, (6) Yampa Plateau, (7) Axial Basin, (8) Elkhead Mountains, (9) Williams Fork Mountains, (10) Danforth Hills, (11) Gray Hills, (12) Cathedral Bluffs, (13) White River Plateau, (14) Grand Hogback, (15) Roan Plateau, (16) Battlement Mesa, (17) Grand Mesa, (18) Uncompahgre Plateau, (19) Unaweep Canyon, (20) Paradox Valley, (21) Dry Creek Basin, (22) Big Gypsum Valley, (23) Disappointment Valley, (24) Sleeping Ute Mountain, (25) La Plata Mountains, (26) La Plata Mountains, (27) San Miguel Mountains, (28) Rico Mountains, (29) West Needle Mountains, (30) Needle Mountains, (31) San Juan Mountains, (32) La Garita Hills, (33) San Luis Valley, (34) San Luis Hills, (35) Culebra Range, (36) Sangre de Cristo Range, (37) Cochetopa Hills, (38) Wet Mountain Valley, (39) Wet Mountains, (40) West Elk Mountains, (41) Black Canyon of the Gunnison, (42) Ruby Mountains, (43) Elk Mountains, (44) Sawatch Range, (45) Arkansas Hills, (46) Pikes Peak Massif, (47) Rampart Range, (48) Puma Hills, (49) Tarryall Mountains, (50) Kenosha Mountains, (51) South Park, (52) Mosquito Range, (53) Glenwood Canyon, (54) Red Table Mountain, (55) Hardscrabble Mountain, (56) Gore Range, (57) Williams Fork Mountains, (58) Blue Ridge, (59) Front Range, (60) Middle Park, (61) Rabbit Ears Range, (62) North Park, (63) Medicine Bow Mountains, (64) Laramie Range, (65) Chalk Bluffs, (66) Peetz Table, (67) Pawnee Buttes, (68) Fremont Butte, (69) Twin Buttes, (70) Two Buttes, (71) Rattlesnake Buttes, (72) Spanish Peaks, (73) Raton Mesa, (74) Mesa de Maya, (75) Carrizo Mountain, (76) Park Range.

Southern Rocky Mountains

The Southern Rocky Mountains traverse central Colorado in belts running roughly north-south. The mountains rise abruptly from the Great Plains to the east and interdigitate with the Colorado Plateau to the west. Essentially, the Southern Rockies constitute a peninsula of coniferous forest extending south from the boreal forest of Alaska and Canada into the mainly treeless landscape of the Great Basin and Great Plains.

Eastern granitic belt. This belt includes several high mountain ranges (with many peaks of 12,000–13,000 feet [3,660–3,960 m]) extending from Wyoming to the Sangre de Cristo and Culebra ranges. These ranges consist largely of Precambrian crystalline rocks. Paleozoic and Mesozoic sedimentary rocks that once covered them have been eroded and now exist as flanking strata

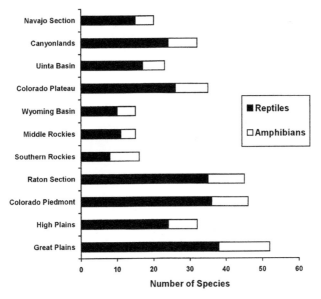

Fig. 2.1. Number of species of amphibians and reptiles occurring in the physiographic regions of Colorado.

forming foothill hogbacks, though the Sangre de Cristo Range is flanked on the east by complexly folded sedimentary rocks of Upper Paleozoic age. Oligocene volcanic rocks are present as a discontinuous cover on the western slope of the Wet Mountains and also form the Arkansas Hills north of the Arkansas River. Glaciation is evident throughout most of the Eastern Granitic Belt, with the exception of the Wet Mountains. Between the Wet Mountains and the Sangre de Cristo Range lies the prominent lowland of the Wet Mountain Valley, a Neogene graben deeply filled with Tertiary sediments and Pleistocene glacial deposits.

Western granitic belt. This belt comprises another series of mountains running mainly north-south and extending from the Park Range in the north (elevations up to 12,200 feet [3720 m]) to the Sawatch and Mosquito ranges in the south. The Sawatch Range includes a cluster of the highest peaks in Colorado, with several exceeding 14,000 feet (4,270 m). The Sawatch and Mosquito ranges, which both have numerous intru-

sions of igneous rocks, are separated by a deep, late Tertiary graben occupied by the Arkansas River. Many of these mountains are beautifully rugged and have been heavily glaciated.

Mountains west of the granitic belts. West of the granitic mountains are several mountain ranges that lack extensive exposures of Precambrian crystalline rocks. Following are descriptions of some of the region's major ranges.

The White River Plateau (10,000–12,000 feet [3,050–3,660 m]) is a flat-topped, steep-sided dome consisting mainly of a thick layer of Paleozoic and Mesozoic sedimentary rocks. Precambrian rocks are exposed only in deep canyons. The Flat Tops in the northern part of the plateau are covered by Tertiary basalts. The western and southwestern sides of the plateau are flanked by sharply upturned Mesozoic and Lower Cenozoic rocks forming the Grand Hogback, a ridge marking the boundary between the Rocky Mountains province and the Colorado Plateau province.

The Elk Mountains, west of the Sawatch Range, consist of folded and faulted Paleozoic and Mesozoic sedimentary rocks extensively intruded by Oligocene igneous rocks. Several peaks exceed 14,000 feet (4,270 m), and most show evidence of severe glaciation.

Southwest of the Elk Mountains are the West Elk Mountains, bordered on the south by the Gunnison River. The northern part of the West Elk Mountains consists largely of intrusive rocks of middle Tertiary age surrounded by the Cretaceous sandstone and shale that once covered them. The southern part of the range is composed of eroded Oligocene volcanic breccia. The isolated peaks of these mountains range from 11,500–12,500 feet (3,500–3,810 m).

South of the Gunnison River is a vast volcanic area whose peaks are known collectively as the San Juan Mountains. They are dominated by volcanic rocks of Tertiary age. The San Miguel, Rico, and La Plata mountains in the western part of this area consist of Paleozoic conglomerates, shales, and limestones intruded by masses of Tertiary igneous rock. The Needle Mountains, deeply cut by the Animas River, comprise an area of exposed Precambrian metamorphic rocks surrounded by volcanic and sedimentary layers. Elevations of many peaks exceed 13,000 feet (3960 m), and some rise more than 14,000 feet.

Intermontane basins. The late Cretaceous to Eocene orogenic events that gave rise to the north-south mountain belts also created a structural basin between them. North Park and Middle Park occupy this basin, which today is divided by the Rabbit Ears Range, formed of volcanic rocks of Oligocene and possibly Miocene age. These volcanic rocks rest upon the Upper Cretaceous and Lower Tertiary sediments that fill the basin. The floor of North Park is broad and flat (averaging about 8,000 feet [2,440 m]), but folding and faulting in Middle Park has obscured its basinlike nature. Like North and Middle parks, South Park (mainly 8,500–10,000 feet [2,590–3,050 m]) consists of a structural depression between the two major granitic mountain belts. The upper South Platte River flows through South Park.

The San Luis Valley in south-central Colorado is the largest intermontane basin in the state. It is a graben produced by late Tertiary faulting, though faulting has continued through the Holocene. Total displacement between the bedrock floor of the graben and the crest of the bordering Sangre de Cristo Mountains may be as much as 15 km. The graben is filled with up to 10 km of volcanic and clastic sediments. Most of the valley, formerly occupied by a lake, is flat, averaging 7,500–8,000 feet (2,290–2,440 m).

A low range of Oligocene volcanic rocks, the San Luis Hills, occupies the southern end of the valley. The northern end of the valley, now an enclosed basin without natural external drainage, was continuous with the southern end of the upper Arkansas River valley during Miocene times. The connection was offset by subsequent faulting and volcanic activity.

The Southern Rocky Mountains province is depauperate in reptiles but has nearly as many amphibian species as the High Plains and Colorado Plateau (Figure 2.1). It includes two species, the mountain toad and wood frog, that are restricted, or nearly restricted, to the province. Three of the eight amphibian species and most of the reptiles are restricted to the San Luis Valley.

Middle Rocky Mountains

The Middle Rocky Mountains are represented in Colorado by the eastern flank of the west/east-trending Uinta Mountains, which extend about 30 miles (50 km) into the extreme northwestern corner of the state. The Uinta Mountains represent an uplift exposing Precambrian sedimentary rocks. In Colorado, Paleozoic and Mesozoic sediments formerly covering the Precambrian rocks have been eroded and now flank the range only along its southern side. Elsewhere, the margins of the range are buried beneath Tertiary sediments. The Green River has cut a gorge 3,000 feet (915 m) deep where it crosses the mountains at Lodore Canyon. The Yampa Plateau is an associated uplift whose Precambrian rocks still lie buried beneath the sediments. Within Colorado, elevations in the Middle Rocky Mountains generally range from 7,000–8,500 feet (2,135–2,590 m), with a few peaks exceeding 9,000 feet (2,745 m). The Middle Rocky Mountains province constitutes a small portion of the state and is inhabited by relatively few species of amphibians and reptiles.

Wyoming Basin

The mountainous terrain of the Southern and Middle Rocky Mountains is interrupted by the Wyoming Basin, a sediment-filled depression extending between the Uinta Mountains and the Park Range. The basin links the Great Plains with the Colorado Plateau, grading into the plateau just north of the White River. In Colorado, the Wyoming Basin consists of broad areas with little relief except for a few scarps and dissected cuestas. The Elkhead Mountains in the eastern part of the basin are capped by Oligocene basalt that has protected the underlying sediments from erosion. The flat-topped summits of the mountains rise 2,000–3,000 feet (610–915 m) above the adjacent basin. The Wyoming Basin province, a small area of the state, supports relatively few species of amphibians and reptiles.

Colorado Plateau

Most of west-central and southwestern Colorado is characterized by high mesas and plateaus dissected by rocky canyons. This topography results from the interaction of resistant sedimentary rocks, a dry climate, and abundant water streaming down from the mountains to the west.

Uinta Basin. This northern portion of the Colorado Plateau consists largely of a dissected plateau capped mainly by Eocene sedimentary layers. The Roan Plateau rises to more than 8,000 feet (2,440 m) before descending 3,000 feet (915 m) to the Colorado River in the south. The Book Cliffs prominently mark this descent. To the south and east, the flat Pliocene basalt caps of Grand Mesa and Battlement Mesa

overlie thick layers of Tertiary sandstone and shale. These mesas rise to more than 11,000 feet (3,350 m) and 9,000 feet (2,745 m) respectively. Moraines and hundreds of rock-basin lakes are conspicuous results of Pleistocene glaciation on Grand Mesa.

Canyonlands. The Colorado, Gunnison, and Uncompahgre rivers have eroded Tertiary sediments down to the more resistant Mancos shale (Cretaceous) to form broad valleys along the northwestern boundary of this section. To the south, the eastern margin skirts the western edge of the San Miguel and La Plata mountains and extends into New Mexico between the Mancos and La Plata rivers.

A prominent feature of this section is the Uncompahgre Plateau, a southeast/northwest-trending uplift rising to more than 9,000 feet (2,745 m). Mesozoic sediments draped over a Precambrian core are exposed on the uplift. A late Tertiary uplift caused the old Colorado-Gunnison River to abandon its course through Unaweep Canyon, which transects the northern end of the plateau. The plateau includes a series of basins separated by low ridges of Mesozoic strata.

Farther south is the Great Sage Plain, a relatively flat region approximately 6,500–7,000 feet (1,980–2,135 m) in elevation, extending southwest from the Dolores River to New Mexico. This plain, formed on the strong Dakota sandstone, is dissected by canyons along the state's western border.

The gentle topography of extreme southwestern Colorado is interrupted by two prominent features, Sleeping Ute Mountain and Mesa Verde. Sleeping Ute Mountain consists of intrusive igneous rocks of Laramide age, rising to nearly 10,000 feet (3,050 m) at Ute Peak. To the east, the south-dipping cuesta of Mesa Verde rises to more than 8,500 feet (2,590 m) at its northern end, 2,000 feet (610 m) above the adjacent Mancos River Valley. The Cretaceous Mesa Verde sandstone is much dissected at the southern end of the cuesta.

Navajo Section. This section, east of the La Plata River and south of the San Juan Mountains, consists primarily of a structural depression (the San Juan Basin) deeply filled with Tertiary sediments. Late Cretaceous rocks are exposed around the basin's edges. Plateaus dissected by south-flowing streams are typical, and elevations range from about 6,000–8,500 feet (1,830–2,590 m).

The Colorado Plateau, especially the Canyonlands section, supports a high number of reptile species and has a particularly rich lizard fauna, many species of which are restricted in Colorado to this region (Figure 2.1).

DRAINAGE SYSTEMS

Water draining from Colorado west of the Continental Divide ultimately mingles with that of the Pacific Ocean via the Gulf of California. East of the Divide, drainage systems ultimately lead to the Atlantic Ocean by way of the Gulf of Mexico.

All of western Colorado is included in the Colorado River basin. Within the state,

tributaries of the Colorado River include the Green, Yampa, White, Gunnison, Dolores, and San Juan rivers (Map 2.5). Of these, all but the Green arise in the mountains of Colorado. Sharp contrasts in terrain occur along these rivers. On its short curving path through Colorado, the Green River flows through the open basin of Browns Park then transversely through the Uinta Mountains in the deep, narrow Lodore Canyon. The Yampa River occupies a broad valley through much of its course before entering a sinuous canyon in western Moffat County. Along most of its length, the White River flows through a valley without deep canyons.

Gore Canyon and Glenwood Canyon are two prominent features carved by the Colorado River. Elsewhere, this river, arising in the vicinity of Rocky Mountain National Park, generally occupies broad valleys, the most prominent of which is Grand Valley, west of the confluence of the Colorado and Gunnison rivers. The deep chasm of the

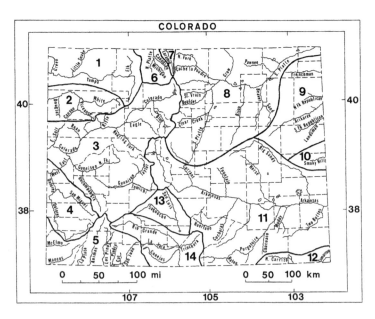

Map 2.5. Major streams and drainage areas of Colorado: (1) Yampa River drainage, (2) White River drainage, (3) Colorado River drainage, (4) Dolores River drainage, (5) San Juan River drainage, (6) North Platte River drainage, (7) Laramie River drainage, (8) South Platte River drainage, (9) Republican River drainage, (10) Smoky Hill River drainage, (11) Arkansas River drainage, (12) Cimarron River drainage, (13) Saguache Creek drainage, (14) Rio Grande drainage.

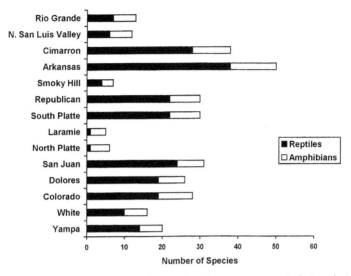

Fig. 2.2. Number of species of amphibians and reptiles known to occur in drainage basins in Colorado.

Black Canyon of the Gunnison is a well-known feature cut by the Gunnison River, but it is atypical of much of the stream's course, which generally occupies a valley. The Dolores River flows through canyons along most of its path through Colorado. A notable exception occurs where the river flows transversely across the Paradox Valley. The San Juan River and the lower portions of its tributaries generally occupy broad valleys or wide canyons.

The major tributaries of the Colorado River converge in western Colorado and eastern Utah and, after passing through a bewildering array of deeply incised canyons in southern Utah and northern Arizona, flow through low, hot desert into the Gulf of California.

Major streams draining eastern Colorado typically emerge from the eastern edge of the mountains through deep canyons. Prominent examples include Poudre Canyon, Big Thompson Canyon, Boulder Canyon, Clear Creek Canyon, Platte Canyon, and the Royal Gorge. After leaving the mountains, these streams typically occupy broad valleys. An exceptional area lies south of the Arkansas River, where several streams, including the Purgatoire,

Apishapa, and Huerfano rivers have cut deep canyons through the strong horizontal surface of the Dakota sandstone. Streams in the high plains of eastern Colorado are largely ephemeral due to the porosity of the Tertiary rock and rapid absorption of water. Perennial streams such as the North and South Forks of the Republican River occur where the Tertiary cover has been eroded, exposing the less absorbent Cretaceous formations.

All of eastern Colorado and North Park ultimately drain into the Gulf of Mexico via the Mississippi River. The North Platte and Laramie rivers converge in southeastern Wyoming and join the South Platte river in western Nebraska. Streams of the Republican River drainage converge in southwestern Nebraska and merge with the Smoky Hill River in eastern Kansas. All of these streams eventually drain into the Missouri River and later the Mississippi River before entering the Gulf of Mexico. The Arkansas River is joined by the Cimarron River before reaching the Mississippi. Streams leaving eastern Colorado flow through relatively flat country of increasing humidity and temperature on their way to the Gulf of Mexico.

The southern part of the San Luis Valley in south-central Colorado is drained by the Rio Grande, which, after emerging from the San Juan Mountains, flows southward on the flat floor of the valley. The river traverses a group of volcanic hills and occupies a shallow rocky gorge in the southern part of the valley. The Rio Grande flows south between north/south-trending mountain ranges in New Mexico, then crosses the arid country of the Texas-Mexico border before reaching its outlet in the Gulf of Mexico. In the northern part of the San Luis Valley, Saguache and San Luis creeks occupy an enclosed basin without exterior drainage.

The Arkansas River drainage and the Cimarron River drainage (despite its small size in Colorado) have the richest amphibian and reptile faunas in Colorado (Figure 2.2). The relatively few species in the Smoky Hill drainage reflect, in part, its small size but also a lack of adequate study of that area. In western Colorado, amphibian diversity is highest in the Colorado River drainage, whereas the San Juan River drainage supports the largest number of reptile species. Overall, few species are restricted to a single drainage system.

ELEVATION

Colorado is the highest state, with an average elevation of about 6,800 feet (2,075 m) above sea level. Elevations range from 14,443 feet (4,403 m) on the top of Mt. Elbert in central Colorado to about 3,350 feet (1,020 m) at the Colorado-Kansas border along the Arkansas River. At the abrupt junction of the mountains and western edge of the Great Plains, elevations generally are 4,500–6,000 feet (1,370–1,830 m). The high plateaus of western Colorado range from average elevations of about 11,000 feet (3,355 m) (White River Plateau) to 7,000 feet (2,135 m) (Mesa Verde). Elevations along the western margin of the state can be as low as 4,500–5,000 feet (1,370–1,525 m) along the major rivers.

In general, most amphibian and reptile species in Colorado occur at the lower ele-vations (Table 2.1 and Figure 2.3). About 70 percent of the amphibian species

in Colorado do not venture above 8,000 feet (2,440 m). Some 50 percent of the reptile species do not occur above 6,000 feet (1,830 m), and around 75 percent are not found above 8,000 feet (2,440 m). Amphibians and reptiles that range across the breadth of Colorado reach higher elevations in the southern part of the state. North-south differences in the upper elevational limits may be 2,000–3,000 feet (600–900 m) or more. Some species, such as the plains spadefoot and Great Plains toad, exhibit a distinct discontinuity in their elevational ranges, occurring generally at elevations of 7,500–8,000 feet (2,285–2,440 m) in the San Luis Valley and generally below 6,000 feet (1,830 m) elsewhere. A fairly large number of species found in the lowlands of eastern Colorado do not occur at the lowest elevations (3,000–4,000 feet [915–1,220 m]) of the Great Plains region, probably due to lack of suitable habitat.

Elevation exerts its influence on amphibian and reptile distribution primarily through differences in climate. However, elevational differences in the concentration of atmos-pheric gases also may be significant. Low partial pressures of oxygen at high elevations may make highland areas uninhabitable for egg-laying species by inhibiting the supply of oxygen to developing embryos (see Guillette et al. 1980). Thus, all else being equal, a lowland area would provide suitable conditions for more species (egg-layers and live-bearing) than would a highland area, where egg-layers are at a dis-advantage. The fact that the only snake and lizard species inhabiting areas above 10,000 feet (3,050 m) in Colorado (Phrynosoma hernandesi and Thamnophis elegans) are both live-bearing supports this idea. The soils of high-elevation environments may not provide suitably warm egg-laying sites, but pregnant females can warm the developing young by shuttling among sun-heated sites.

CLIMATE

The varied topography and unique geographic position of Colorado interact to produce an unusually diverse array of

	3,000-4,000	4,000-5,000	5,000-6,000	6,000-7,000	7,000-8,000	8,000-9,000	9,000-10,000	10,000-11,000	11,000-12,000	12,000+
Tiger Salamander	x	x	x	x	x	x	x	x	x	
Couch's Spadefoot	x	x								
Plains Spadefoot	x	x	x	x	x					
Great Basin Spadefoot		x	x	x						
New Mexico Spadefoot		x	x	x						
Mountain Toad						x	x	x	x	
Great Plains Toad	x	x	x		x					
Green Toad		x	x							
Red-spotted Toad		x	x	x						
Woodhouse's Toad	x	x	x	x	x					
Northern Cricket Frog	x									
Canyon Treefrog		x	x	x						
Western Chorus Frog	x	x	x	x	x	x	x	x	x	x
Narrowmouth Toad		x								
Plains Leopard Frog	x	x	x							
Northern Leopard Frog	x	x	x	x	x	x	x	x	x	
Wood Frog						x	x			
Snapping Turtle	x	x	x							
Painted Turtle	x	x	x	x	x					
Ornate Box Turtle	x	x	x							
Yellow Mud Turtle	x	x								
Spiny Softshell	x	x	x							
Collared Lizard	x	x	x	x	x					
Longnose Leopard Lizard		x	x							
Lesser Earless Lizard	x	x	x							
Texas Horned Lizard	x	x	x							
Short-horned Lizard		x	x	x	x	x	x	x		
Roundtail Horned Lizard		x								
Sagebrush Lizard		x	x	x	x	x				
Desert Spiny Lizard		x	x							
Plateau and Prairie Lizards	x	x	x	x	x	x	x			
Tree Lizard		x	x	x	x					
Side-blotched Lizard		x	x	x						
Triploid Checkered Whiptail		x	x	x						
Six-lined Racerunner	x	x	x	x	x					
Diploid Checkered Whiptail		x	x	x						
Western Whiptail		x	x							
Plateau Striped Whiptail		x	x	x	x					
Variable Skink			x	x	x					
Many-lined Skink	x	x	x							
Great Plains Skink	x	x	x	x	x					
Texas Blind Snake		x								
Glossy Snake	x	x								
Racer	x	x	x	x	x					
Ringneck Snake		x	x							
Great Plains Rat Snake	x	x	x							
Western Hognose Snake	x	x	x							
Night Snake	x	x	x	x	x					
Common Kingsnake		x	x							
Milk Snake	x	x	x	x	x					
Smooth Green Snake			x	x	x	x				
Coachwhip	x	x	x	x	x					
Striped Whipsnake			x	x	x					
Northern Water Snake	x	x	x							
Bullsnake/Gopher Snake	x	x	x	x	x	x				
Longnose Snake	x	x								
Ground Snake	x	x	x							
SW. Black-headed Snake		x	x	x						
Plains Black-headed Snake	x	x	x	x						
Blackneck Garter Snake	x	x	x	x						
W. Terrestrial Garter Snake		x	x	x	x	x	x	x	x	x
Western Ribbon Snake		x								
Plains Garter Snake	x	x	x	x						
Common Garter Snake	x	x	x							
Lined Snake	x	x	x							
Western Rattlesnake	x	x	x	x	x	x	x			
Massasauga	x	x	x							

Table 2.1. Elevational distribution (feet above sea level) of native amphibians and reptiles in Colorado. Some marginal or atypical elevational occurrences are not indicated.

climatic conditions (Table 2.2). In mountainous sections, climate varies greatly over short distances. One can descend 8,000 feet (2,450 m) from the icy environs of a glacier to an oppressively hot river valley in only 20 airline miles (32 km). Average monthly temperature in summer generally decreases about 3°F (1.7°C) per 1,000-foot (305-m) increase in elevation. At any given elevation, the soils on south-facing slopes have less moisture and higher temperatures than do north-facing slopes.

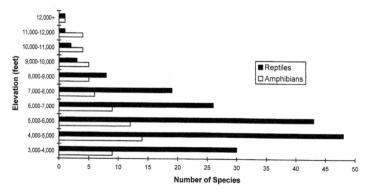

Fig. 2.3. Number of species of amphibians and reptiles occurring at different elevations in Colorado. A few marginal occurrences of species in certain elevational categories are not included. Between 6,000 and 8,000 feet (1,830 and 2,440 m), the number of species decreases by about 60 percent in amphibians and 80 percent in reptiles.

Weather Station	Elevation (m)	Average Annual Precipitation (cm)	Mean Minimum Temperature in January (°C)	Mean Minimum Temperature in July (°C)
West				
Rangely	1,590	24	-17	12
Grand Junction	1,478	23	-9	18
Montrose	1,777	23	-10	14
Cortez	1,894	34	-10	13
Mountains				
Estes Park	2,286	35	-9	8
Aspen	2,417	50	-14	7
Telluride	2,670	55	-17	5
Alamosa	2,298	18	-19	9
Western Plains				
Fort Collins	1,525	37	-10	11
Denver	1,610	39	-9	15
Pueblo	1,428	28	-10	16
Trinidad	1,752	31	-9	15
Eastern Plains				
Sterling	1,201	38	-12	15
Wray	1,090	43	-11	16
Burlington	1,270	39	-9	16
La Junta	1,277	28	-10	18

Table 2.2. Climatological characteristics of selected locations throughout Colorado. Data are based on the period 1951–1980. Within each geographic group, stations are listed from north to south.

In summer, maximum daily temperature averages in the low to mid-90°s (32° to 35°C) over most of the eastern plains and in the low river valleys of western Colorado (Map 2.6). The highest temperatures often occur when southwesterly winds bring hot, dry air over the state. In mountain towns, summer temperatures generally do not exceed the low 80°s (26° to 28°C). In summer, southeastern Colorado and the Grand Valley of Mesa County have the warmest nighttime temperatures (Map 2.7).

In winter, nighttime temperatures typically fall to about 8° to 20°F (–13° to

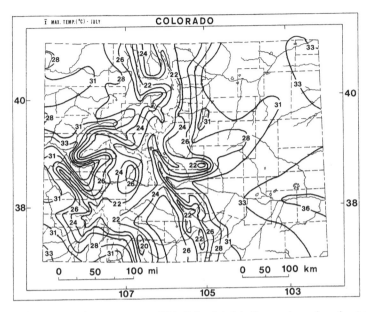

Map 2.6. Mean maximum temperature (°C) in Colorado in July. Lines are drawn through points of approximately equal value.

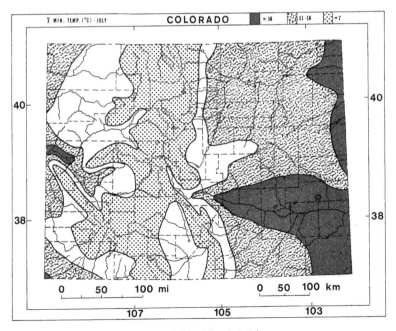

Map 2.7. Mean minimum temperature (°C) in Colorado in July.

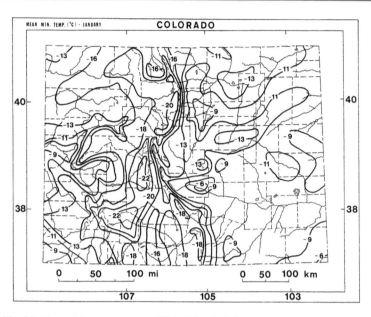

Map 2.8. Mean minimum temperature (°C) in Colorado in January.

–7°C) on the eastern plains (warmest in the low valleys) and western valleys and plummet to near or below 0°F (–18°C) in most mountain towns (Map 2.8). Relatively mild winter temperatures along the eastern base of the Rocky Mountains result from warm westerly winds called chinooks. These downslope winds typically bring dramatic increases in temperature. Winter winds usually are strong in eastern Colorado and frequently result in dry soil conditions. Winter winds are most severe in the mountains. A high-pressure area often forms over western Colorado in winter, resulting in clear, cool days and cold nights. Masses of frigid polar air frequently move south into the plains in winter, bringing the coldest temperatures. These cold air masses usually do not significantly affect temperatures in western Colorado.

The growing season, or frost-free period, is longest in southern Colorado and the low western valleys (up to 160 days or more) and shortest in the mountains (generally not more than 60 days; at high elevations freezing temperatures can occur in any month) (Map 2.9).

Seasonal precipitation varies greatly in different areas of the state. When a polar air mass contacts warm moist air moving north from the Gulf of Mexico, heavy snows typically occur in eastern Colorado, especially in fall and spring. Western Colorado receives most of its winter precipitation when east-moving air masses from the Pacific coast cool as they rise over the mountains and release their moisture as snow. Much of the mountainous portion of Colorado is deeply blanketed with snow in winter. Average annual snowfall is nearly 300 inches (762 cm) in some areas, decreasing to less than 25 inches in some parts of the intermountain San Luis Valley.

Eastern Colorado receives most of its precipitation during the growing season. Warm, moist air from the Gulf of Mexico often moves into the state during spring and summer, bringing heavy rains and intense thunderstorm activity to the plains region. Summer thunderstorms and afternoon showers also are common in the mountains. Eastern Colorado and the mountains have the state's greatest amount of warm-weather precipitation (Map 2.10).

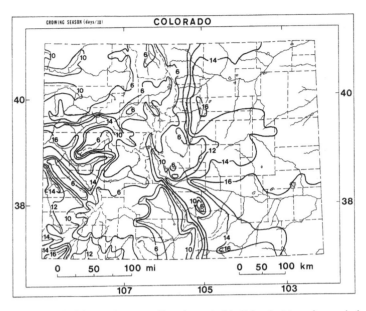

Map 2.9. Length of the growing season (frost-free period) in Colorado. Map value equals the number of days divided by 10.

In contrast, summers in the lowlands of western Colorado are relatively dry, as are those in the San Luis Valley, which sits in the rain shadow of the San Luis Mountains. In western Colorado, June usually is the driest month; precipitation may be totally absent. Summer rains typically are heaviest during August. Throughout the state, humidity is usually low and evaporation rapid.

These variations in temperature and moisture have significant effects on the distribution of amphibians and reptiles. Most amphibians and reptiles cannot live in a cold environment. They require relatively warm body temperatures for feeding and reproduction but are unable to generate their own body heat. Unless there is an adequate external heat source, they languish and ultimately die.

A cool climate may prohibit survival and reproduction even in areas with abundant food resources. Foraging and larval development are inhibited if there are too few hours of suitably warm temperature during the year. Consistently deep, long-lasting snow cover in the mountains can render habitat unsuitable if the activity season is too short for successful reproduction (though some snow cover may be important in protecting hibernating amphibians and reptiles from lethal subfreezing temperatures).

Among a large array of environmental and geographical variables, the July mean overnight low (Map 2.7) is the best predictor of the number of reptile and amphibian species living in a particular area, though it is more effective in predicting the former than the latter (Figure 2.4 and see Hammerson 1981). Elevation, though a fairly accurate predictor of climate, is not as good a predictor of the number of species. Many species of frogs, toads, and snakes forage primarily at night and are active only when nighttime temperatures are relatively high. Areas with low nighttime temperatures in summer probably do not provide suitable habitat for some of these nocturnal species. For reptiles, the number of species is greatly reduced in areas with a July mean minimum temperature below 50°F (10°C);

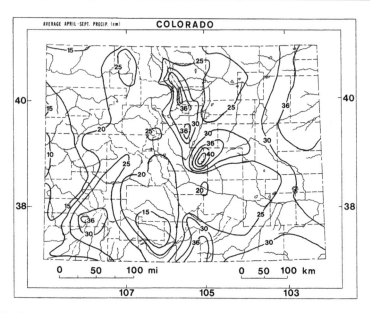

Map 2.10. Mean warm-season (April-September) precipitation (cm) in Colorado.

approximately 60°F (15.5°C) also appears to be a pivotal temperature.

However, the scatter of points in Figure 2.4 indicates that factors other than summer nighttime temperature influence the distributions of amphibians and reptiles. For example, the number of lizard species in an area does not strongly correlate with mean minimum temperature in July, as might be predicted in view of the absence of nocturnal lizard species in Colorado. In addition, cold winter temperatures may kill individuals that select hibernacula too shallow to avoid freezing. Predictably, areas in Colorado with severe winter conditions are inhabited by fewer species of amphibians and especially reptiles than areas with relatively mild winter temperatures. And, of course, geohistory, habitat, ecological interactions, precipitation, and other factors also affect the composition and diversity of local herpetofaunas.

In addition, feeding and breeding activities are strongly influenced by the occurrence of warm-season rainfall. Some toads breed only after heavy rains, and spring and summer showers may stimulate the activity of various amphibians and snakes. One might therefore expect more species to occur in areas with higher precipitation, all else being equal. However, my studies (Hammerson 1981) reveal that precipitation variables do not explain much of the variation in number of amphibian or reptile species. For amphibians, this may be because many toads are highly adapted to semiarid conditions and can survive with minimal rainfall. Also, species thriving in more mesic conditions may have their requirements met by streams flowing through areas with low rainfall. Reptiles appear to be associated with areas that receive relatively little warm-season precipitation (Hammerson 1981), perhaps because in Colorado these areas tend to be lowland areas with favorably warm temperatures.

HABITATS

Habitat is the set of ecological conditions in which a species lives. Aquatic and wetland habitats commonly are differentiated by criteria such as depth, rate of flow,

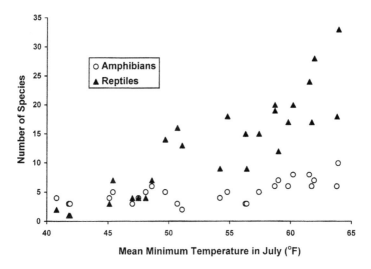

Fig. 2.4. Relationship between summer climate and the number of species of amphibians and reptiles in 26 locations throughout Colorado.

clarity, temperature, extent, and permanency of the water, as well as by the types of plants present. Vegetation, topography, soils or substrate, moisture, temperature, and sun exposure often are used to distinguish different kinds of terrestrial animal habitats. Frequently, vegetation is the primary descriptor for terrestrial habitats (Map 2.11).

Because amphibians and reptiles in Colorado depend little on plants for food or reproduction, categorizing reptile and amphibian habitats based on vegetation might seem a questionable practice. However, vegetation affects important aspects of the physical microenvironment such as temperature, surface moisture, sun exposure, and wind and in doing so may impact the distribution of amphibians and reptiles. Also, vegetation, which varies in response to climate, soil, and other conditions, is a good indicator of the general environment and therefore a useful descriptor in the classification of animal distribution.

In the following paragraphs, the term *locally* indicates that the species occurs in the applicable habitat only within certain geographic areas.

Terrestrial (Upland) Ecosystems

Alpine tundra. Alpine tundra, dominated by long-lived, low-growing perennial plants and interrupted by expanses of glacier-carved rock, occurs above the upper limit of tree growth (usually 11,500–12,000 feet [3,305–3,660 m]) on the highest mountains in Colorado. It is a cold, windswept environment with a short growing season. This beautiful ecosystem typically is devoid of amphibians and reptiles, though the tiger salamander, mountain toad, western chorus frog, and western terrestrial garter snake occur in the lower elevations of the tundra in a few areas, especially in the vicinity of water.

Subalpine forest/woodland. Extensive subalpine forests of often densely spaced conifers dominate the high mountains below the alpine zone. Englemann spruce *(Picea englemannii),* subalpine fir *(Abies lasiocarpa),* and lodgepole pine *(Pinus contorta)* are the primary subalpine conifers. Lodgepole pine is scarce in the Sangre de Cristo Range and absent from the mountains of southwestern Colorado. Stands of aspen *(Populus tremuloides),* a broad-leaved,

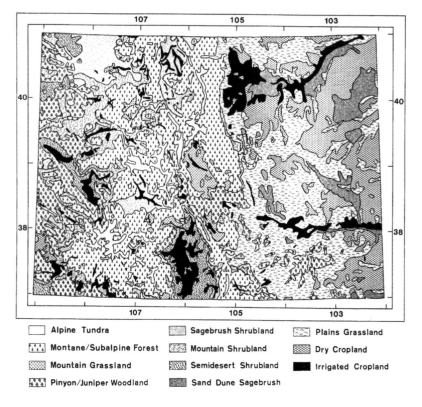

Map 2.11. Vegetation of Colorado. Based on "Major land resource area and generalized land use map—Colorado" (U.S. Department of Agriculture, Soil Conservation Service, 1969).

deciduous tree, also are present throughout the subalpine region, with the largest and tallest stands occurring in central and southwestern Colorado. Subalpine conifers may invade and replace aspen stands in the absence of fires. The lower limit of subalpine forest varies considerably but usually falls at about 8,200–9,500 feet (2,500–2,900 m). Subalpine forest provides favorable habitat for few amphibians and reptiles (Figure 2.5). Some species, such as the tiger salamander, mountain toad, wood frog, and western terrestrial garter snake may forage in the forest or hibernate there, but these species are more closely associated with subalpine wetlands.

Montane forest/woodland. The lower mountains of Colorado are forested by broad-crowned conifers, of which ponderosa pine *(Pinus ponderosa)* and Douglas-fir

(Pseudotsuga menziesii) are most common, the former mainly on warmer sites and the latter in cooler areas with more moisture. Ponderosa pine is a less conspicuous component of montane forest in northern and western Colorado than in other areas. In southern Colorado, shrubby patches of Gambel oak *(Quercus gambellii)* often occur between openly spaced pines. A broken tongue of montane forest known locally as the Black Forest departs from the main mountain chains and extends eastward along the Platte-Arkansas Divide between Denver and Colorado Springs. Aspen and lodgepole pine transgress the arbitrary boundary between the montane and sub-alpine forest types.

Montane forest/woodland is inhabited by a relatively small number of amphibians and reptiles, especially in northern Colorado. Typical species include the plateau lizard (in rocky areas), sagebrush lizard (in western Colorado), variable skink, milk snake, bullsnake, western terrestrial garter snake, and western rattlesnake. Tiger salamanders may occur in forest areas adjacent to lakes, ponds, or wetlands. Additional species, including the variable skink and short-horned lizard, are found in this habitat in southern

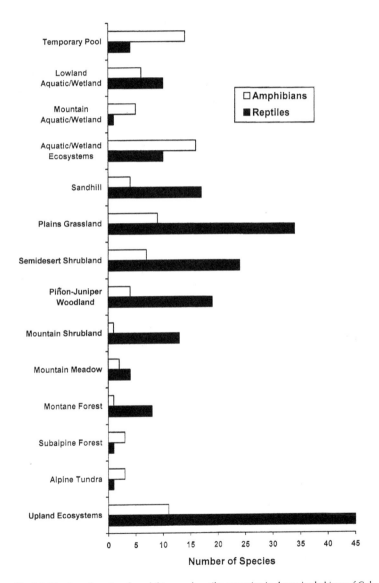

Fig. 2.5. Number of species of amphibians and reptiles occurring in the major habitats of Colorado. Riverine and lacustrine habitats are here included in the composite aquatic/wetland habitat type. Species occurring in riparian habitats are not enumerated because they largely comprise those occurring in adjacent aquatic, wetland, and upland habitats.

Plate 2.1. Grassland and rocky mountain shrubland habitats of the Dakota Hogback at the Great Plains-Rocky Mountains junction in Douglas County. Common species here include the orange-lipped plateau lizard, six-lined racerunner, racer, bullsnake, and western rattlesnake.

Colorado. All of these species exist primarily in woodlands or along forest edges or openings, not in dense stands of trees that produce extensive shading.

Mountain meadow. The well-drained meadows that occur throughout the subalpine and montane forest zones typically are sparsely inhabited by amphibians and reptiles unless associated with a body of water or wetland area (see wetland and aquatic ecosystem descriptions). For example, western chorus frogs regularly occupy upland meadows near their breeding ponds, as do tiger salamanders, especially in areas riddled with rodent burrows (used by both species for hibernation and shelter). Most of the montane forest/woodland species also can be found in some mountain meadows.

Mountain shrubland. Shrublands dominated by deciduous Gambel oaks and other shrubs occur throughout the foothills and lower mountains of Colorado. Montane stands of sagebrush extend over a wide elevational range to above 10,000 feet (3,050 m) on warm slopes in the mountains and occupy extensive areas in northwestern Colorado, North and Middle parks, and the Gunnison basin. Mountain shrubland dominated by mountain mahogany (*Cercocarpus*

spp.) occurs as a narrow foothills belt between montane forest and plains grassland along the eastern base of the Rocky Mountains. Overall, mountain shrublands are most extensive in western Colorado. Among the typical inhabitants of this ecosystem are the plateau lizard and western rattlesnake, which favor exposures of broken rock, plus the sagebrush lizard, milk snake, smooth green snake (locally), bullsnake/gopher snake, and western terrestrial garter snake.

Piñon-juniper woodland. Relatively open stands of small, shrubby conifers cover extensive areas of western and southern Colorado, mainly at elevations of about 6,000–8,500 feet (1,830–2,590 m). Piñon pine *(Pinus edulis)* dominates at higher elevations, whereas junipers (*Juniperus* spp.) are most common at lower elevations and north of the Colorado River in western

Plate 2.2. Piñon-juniper woodland in Mesa County. Typical inhabitants include the collared lizard, sagebrush lizard, northern plateau lizard, tree lizard, side-blotched lizard, western whiptail, plateau striped whiptail, night snake, striped whipsnake, bullsnake, and western rattlesnake.

Plate 2.3. Semidesert shrubland in Mesa County. One of a few areas inhabited by the longnose leopard lizard.

Colorado. In the western part of the state, these woodlands generally occur on shallow soils of rocky slopes immediately above semidesert shrubland ecosystems that occupy deeper alluvial soils. Montane forest or mountain shrubland typically interdigitates with piñon-juniper woodland at its upper margin. In southeastern Colorado, piñon-juniper ecosystems occupy rocky canyons or slopes of broken basalt within areas otherwise dominated by plains grassland. Reptiles, especially lizards, are conspicuous residents. Among the more typical species are the collared lizard, sagebrush lizard, plateau lizard, tree lizard, side-blotched lizard (locally along arroyos), western whiptail, striped plateau lizard, night snake, striped whipsnake, bullsnake, and western rattlesnake. Red-spotted toads commonly range into these woodlands near intermittent streams.

Semidesert shrubland. These shrublands occur on deep soils of lowland areas generally below 7,000 feet (2,130 m) in western Colorado, and in extensive areas of the San Luis Valley at about 7,500–8,000 feet (2,285–2,590 m). Saline soils with a high water table are dominated by greasewood *(Sarcobatus vermiculatus)*. Saltbush *(Atriplex* spp.) is common on drier, less alkaline soils. Stands of big sagebrush, best developed on deep, well-drained alluvium, often occur near greasewood stands, and rabbitbrush is common along intermittent stream courses. Shrubs often are rather openly spaced.

Semidesert shrublands support a large number of reptile species. In summer, a walk through these shrublands in western Colorado might yield longnose leopard lizard (locally), sagebrush lizard, side-blotched lizard (locally, especially along arroyos), western whiptail, striped whipsnake, and bullsnake/gopher snake. Where exposures of rock occur, the collared lizard, plateau lizard, and tree lizard usually are common. Various toads inhabit these shrublands and can be observed most readily at night, especially after rains.

Plains grassland. The gently sloping Great Plains of eastern Colorado are dominated by sod-forming grasses, of which blue grama *(Bouteloua gracilis)* and buffalo grass *(Buchloe dactyloides)* are most common. Yucca *(Yucca glauca)* and, especially south of the Platte-Arkansas Divide, cactus *(Opuntia* spp.) are conspicuous elements of the vegetation. Under the usual grazing regime, plains grassland is maintained as a dense, short turf, often interrupted by patches of bare soil. Taller grasses characteristic of the prairie east of Colorado occur in limited areas with ample moisture and protected from grazing in extreme eastern Colorado and the Black Forest area on the western crest of the Platte-Arkansas Divide. Much of this ecosystem has been converted to dryland and irrigated farmland (Map 2.11). The remaining unplowed prairie (Map 2.12) supports an exceptionally diverse amphibian and reptile fauna. Protection of these vulnerable native grasslands is by far the number one conservation need of the Colorado herpetofauna. Some of the more typical species of plains grassland are the tiger salamander, plains spadefoot, Woodhouse's toad, Texas horned lizard, lesser earless lizard, prairie lizard, ornate box turtle, glossy snake, coachwhip, bullsnake, and western rattlesnake. The amphibians are most common in grasslands near ponds or streams or in broad valleys.

Plate 2.4. Semidesert shrubland degraded by thick growth of exotic cheatgrass in Mesa County. Lizard diversity and abundance are reduced in such areas.

Plate 2.5. Semidesert shrubland in Montezuma County. One of a few areas inhabited by the longnose leopard lizard and desert spiny lizard.

Plate 2.6. Semidesert shrubland and riparian zone along the San Juan River in Montezuma County. The lesser earless lizard, desert spiny lizard, glossy snake, and common kingsnake are among the notable reptile species in the area.

Plate 2.7. Semidesert shrubland at the Great Sand Dunes in the San Luis Valley. Habitat of a population of unusually small short-horned lizards.

Plate 2.8. Plains grassland at Pawnee Buttes in Weld County. Typical inhabitants include the plains spadefoot, lesser earless lizard, short-horned lizard, bullsnake, and western rattlesnake.

Plate 2.9. Plains grassland, juniper-covered canyon rim, and lowland riparian habitats in Baca County. Areas such as this in southeastern Colorado support the state's highest diversity of amphibians and reptiles.

Plate 2.10. Sandhill habitat in Weld County. Typical species include the ornate box turtle, northern prairie lizard, six-lined racerunner, many-lined skink, western hognose snake, milk snake, bullsnake, and western rattlesnake.

Plate 2.11. Mountains of Boulder County with alpine tundra, subalpine forest, mountain marsh habitats. Mountain toads were common here before most of the wetlands were inundated by the reservoir.

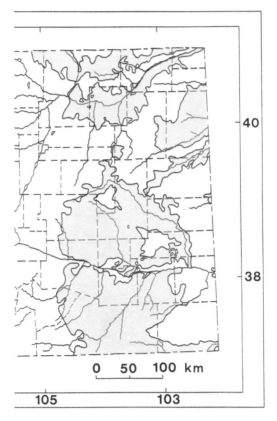

Map 2.12. Untilled landscapes of the central shortgrass prairie ecoregion of eastern Colorado, determined through satellite imagery. Yellow areas indicate landscapes dominated by untilled prairie. These areas include some of the state's best amphibian and reptile habitats. Adapted from a map produced by Heidi Van Everen for The Nature Conservancy.

Sandhills. Sand sagebrush *(Artemisia filifolia)* and a variety of grasses are the prevalent plants on the low, rolling sandhills of the Great Plains. The largest areas of this ecosystem occur along the South Platte River, in Yuma County, along Big Sandy Creek, along the Arkansas River, in southern Baca County, and in El Paso County east of Colorado Springs. The sandy soils of this ecosystem provide good habitat for the plains spadefoot, Woodhouse's toad, Great Plains toad, ornate box turtle, lesser earless lizard, prairie lizard, six-lined racerunner, many-lined skink, western hognose snake, bullsnake, milk snake, and western rattlesnake.

Palustrine (Wetland) Ecosystems

Mountain riparian. Riparian ecosystems include streamside areas that may be briefly flooded but generally are not marshy. The extent of the riparian zone is defined by the distribution of moisture-loving plants (e.g., cottonwood, willow, blue spruce) that do not occur in the adjacent upland habitat. Typical amphibians and reptiles of mountain riparian zones above 7,000 feet (2,135 m) include the variable skink (locally), smooth green snake, and milk snake, and most of those species occurring in adjacent upland habitats.

Lowland riparian. Lowland riparian zones below 7,000 feet (2,135 m) may be occupied by narrow or wide stands of cottonwood trees, lines of willows, or only a low, sparse cover of sedges, rushes, and other herbaceous plants. In western and southern Colorado, the introduced salt-cedar or tamarisk (*Tamarix* sp.) is a well-established riparian species, often forming dense, nearly impenetrable thickets. Lowland riparian zones (and associated floodplains) are used by a large number of species, including essentially all of those occurring in adjacent aquatic, marsh, and upland habitats. Some of the species most closely associated with riparian corridors include the northern cricket frog, plains and northern leopard frogs, smooth green snake, northern water snake, and common garter snake. Many species occurring in associated upland areas may be more abundant in riparian areas. The red-spotted toad and canyon treefrog occur primarily in riparian zones in rocky canyon bottoms.

Mountain marsh. I include in this category marshes, lake shallows, small ponds, marshy stream backwaters, and wet meadows in the mountainous regions of Colorado. These waters and wetlands provide breeding and feeding habitat for several amphibians, including the tiger salamander (ubiquitous), mountain toad (formerly widespread, now scarce), western chorus frog (ubiquitous), northern leopard frog (locally), and wood frog (locally), plus the western terrestrial garter snake (ubiquitous). Mountain wetlands support relatively few species of amphibians but are the primary habitat for the mountain toad and wood frog.

Lowland marsh. Lowland marsh habitats as here defined encompass marshes, shallow ponds, and the marshy edges of streams, deep ponds, and reservoirs occurring at elevations below 7,000 feet (2,135 m). These habitats may have cattails, bulrushes, or any of a large variety of other wetland plants. The tiger salamander, Woodhouse's toad, western chorus frog, plains and northern leopard

Plate 2.12. Mountain marsh habitat in Jackson County. Habitat of the mountain toad, western chorus frog, northern leopard frog, wood frog, and western terrestrial garter snake.

Plate 2.13. Old beaver pond in Chaffee County. Breeding site of the mountain toad.

frogs, bullfrog, snapping turtle, painted turtle, northern water snake, bullsnake, and garter snakes are the species most often encountered.

Temporary pool. Temporary pools form in depressions or along intermittent streams. These pools may include herbaceous upland plants, spikerushes *(Eleocharis),* or sedges, or they may be relatively barren. In lowland areas (and in intermontane basins such as the San Luis Valley) these pools generally form after heavy rains or as a result of flooding. Temporary pools may not seem significant, but these fishless bodies of water are critical as the only suitable breeding habitat for a large number of amphibians (Figure 2.5). Lowland pools that last a month or longer are important breeding sites for four species of spadefoot toads, the Great Plains toad, green toad, Woodhouse's toad, plains leopard frog, and Great Plains narrowmouth toad. Tiger salamanders frequently are found in them,

and yellow mud turtles commonly use them in limited areas in eastern Colorado. The red-spotted toad and canyon treefrog breed only in pools along intermittent streams. In the mountains, temporary pools may result from rainfall, snowmelt, or groundwater fluctuations. The mountain toad, western chorus frog, and wood frog breed with variable success in these impermanent waters. Garter snakes commonly visit and prey on amphibians in temporary pools in both lowland and upland areas.

Riverine Ecosystems

Riverine ecosystems include rivers and creeks, collectively termed streams. Colorado streams include several big rivers and thousands of creeks of varying size. Streams in the state, particularly in the lowlands, are markedly dynamic and typically undergo dramatic seasonal fluctuations in

Plate 2.14. South Platte River in Weld County. Typical species include the snapping turtle, painted turtle, spiny softshell, northern water snake, and common garter snake.

Plate 2.15. Lowland marsh habitat in Yuma County sandhills. Habitat of the yellow mud turtle, common garter snake, and many more-widespread species.

Plate 2.16. Carrizo Creek in canyon habitat in southeastern Colorado. Native stream-associated species include the red-spotted toad, plains leopard frog, blackneck garter snake, and plains garter snake. The plains leopard frog was the most numerous frog species along the stream when this photograph was taken in 1978. In the mid-1990s, the stream was degraded by large amounts of cattle manure, exotic bullfrogs were extremely abundant, and leopard frogs were scarce or absent.

size, flow volume, temperature, and other physical characteristics. Some stream courses, especially in the Great Plains province, regularly are dry in summer. The western terrestrial garter snake, tiger salamander, mountain toad, western chorus frog, northern leopard frog, and wood frog sometimes occur in mountain streams, but generally they avoid cold flowing water, favoring instead warmer quiet waters, wetlands, or moist uplands. Below about 7,000 feet (2,135 m), most of the species occurring in lowland wetland ecosystems (marshes) commonly use stream backwaters. Open, flowing waters of some permanent lowland streams are used by reptiles such as the garter snakes, northern water snake, snapping turtle, painted turtle, yellow mud turtle, and spiny softshell.

Lacustrine (Lake) Ecosystems

Lacustrine ecosystems include large, relatively deep lakes. Shallow lakes (less than 2 m deep), ponds and lakes smaller than 20 acres (8 ha) (unless deeper than 2 m), and the marshy shallows of deep lakes are ecologically quite similar to marshes and thus are regarded as wetland ecosystems (see Cowardin et al. 1979). In pre-Columbian times, lakes were numerous only in the high mountains, where cold, clear waters are trapped behind glacial moraines or fill glacier-scoured basins. Natural mountain lakes are inhabited by the tiger salamander, mountain toad, western chorus frog, northern leopard frog, wood

frog, and western terrestrial garter snake, all of which tend to use the warmer shallow waters along the edge. Mountain reservoirs (impounded waters behind dams) are usually steep-sided and undergo a substantial decrease in water level during the summer; these bodies of water lack warm marshy shallows and typically support few if any amphibians and reptiles. In lowland areas, where lakes formerly were almost nonexistent, dams on major rivers have created many large reservoirs. These are used by minimal numbers of various species typical of lowland wetlands, though the shallows of reservoirs filling in spring sometimes are used by substantial numbers of amphibians that breed in temporary pools.

ECOLOGICAL VERSATILITY, HABITAT DIVERSITY, AND THE DISTRIBUTION AND DIVERSITY OF AMPHIBIANS AND REPTILES

Some species, such as the tiger salamander, short-horned lizard, plateau and prairie lizard, gopher snake, western terrestrial garter snake, and western rattlesnake occur in a wide variety of habitats, whereas many others are far more restricted. Not surprisingly, the species with the greatest ecological flexibility tend to have the broadest distributions.

One might expect areas with greater habitat diversity to support more species of amphibians and reptiles. Areas with substantial topographic relief tend to have more species of birds and mammals than

Plate 2.17. Temporary pool in semidesert shrubland in Moffat County. Breeding site of the Great Basin spadefoot.

SPATIAL PATTERN OF AMPHIBIAN AND REPTILE DIVERSITY

The relationships discussed in the preceding sections result in a bold pattern of amphibian and reptile diversity: certain portions of southeastern and southwestern Colorado are inhabited by far more species than other areas, particularly the northern and central portions of the state (Figures 2.6 and 2.7). In a well-chosen area of a few square kilometers in the moderate elevations of the Rocky Mountains of north-central Colorado, one might find five species of amphibians and one snake, but no lizards or turtles. In contrast, an area of equal size in the Raton Section of Otero County in southeastern Colorado could yield 10 amphibian species, four kinds of turtles, nine species of lizards, and 19 snakes. This portion of southern Otero County stands out not only for its exceptionally diverse herpetofauna but also as an area to which several species

more homogeneous areas. This probably reflects the greater diversity of habitats in topographically heterogeneous areas. To determine the relationship between habitat diversity and the number of species of amphibians and reptiles, I statistically examined for each county of Colorado the relationship between the number of species and the amount of topographic relief (the difference between the lowest and highest elevations, up to a maximum elevation of 10,000 feet [3,050 m], beyond which amphibians and reptiles generally are scarce or absent). My analyses (Hammerson 1981) indicate that, on a statewide basis, the number of species in a county has no consistent relationship with topographic relief or, presumably, habitat diversity. Evidently, other factors such as climate are more important than habitat diversity. However, within areas with favorable climate, habitat heterogeneity clearly contributes to the number of species present. For example, in the species-rich regions of southwestern and southeastern Colorado, areas encompassing dry plains, floodplains, and rocky canyons support many more species than any of these habitats do individually.

Plate 2.18. Canyon-bottom pools in Mesa County. Breeding site of the Great Basin spadefoot, red-spotted toad, Woodhouse's toad, and canyon treefrog. The canyon bottom and slopes support a diverse and abundant lizard fauna, including the collared lizard, sagebrush lizard, northern plateau lizard, side-blotched lizard, tree lizard, western whiptail, and plateau striped whiptail.

are restricted or nearly restricted, and it is the only place where diploid and triploid speciation stages of any of the parthenogenetic *Cnemidophorus* complexes in North America are known to coexist.

BIOGEOGRAPHIC CONTEXT

What is the relationship between the herpetofauna of Colorado and those of other regions of North America? One might suppose that the mountain herpetofauna of the Colorado Rocky Mountains is similar to those of other North American mountain ranges, such as the Sierra Nevada or the Appalachian Mountains. However, there is very little overlap. Despite some corresponding current environmental conditions, differenc-

es in Cenozoic and Pleistocene conditions have led to the establishment of divergent biotas. The herpetofauna of montane Colorado resembles most closely those of the Wasatch Mountains of Utah, the Middle Rockies, and boreal Canada. The herpetofaunas of the nonmountainous areas west and east of the Continental Divide in Colorado are quite dissimilar due to long isolation from each other by the inhospitable high mountains of the Rocky Mountain chain. The amphibians and reptiles of western Colorado are a subset of those widespread in the Great Basin and Sonoran Desert, whereas the herpetofauna of eastern Colorado primarily is composed of ecologically versatile members of the Great Plains and Chihuahuan Desert herpetofaunas.

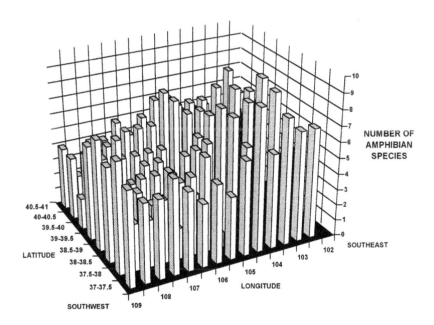

Fig. 2.6. Amphibian species density in Colorado, based on the number of species occurring in 128 blocks of approximately 0.5° latitude by 0.5° longitude. Species density is highest in southeastern Colorado.

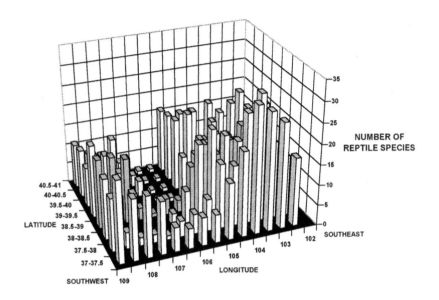

Fig. 2.7. Reptile species density in Colorado, based on the number of species occurring in 128 blocks of approximately 0.5° latitude by 0.5° longitude. Species density varies greatly across the state and is highest in southeastern Colorado.

Chapter 3

Relationship to Humans

IMPACTS OF HUMANS

Human activities often have devastating consequences for native wildlife. Some effects are obvious, but some of the more disastrous impacts are subtle.

In Colorado, residential and commercial development has been extensive along the western edge of the Great Plains. Natural plains grasslands supporting a rich flora and fauna have been replaced by human communities wherein chiefly exotic species thrive. Amphibians and reptiles have been largely eliminated from these areas, and the few species that remain in undeveloped tracts usually do not survive long in the presence of humans. For example, thousands, probably tens of thousands, of amphibians and reptiles are killed by vehicles each year as they attempt to cross roads linking the ever-growing urban and commercial areas. Similar losses of amphibian populations have occurred along the Wasatch Front in Utah, where breeding sites are surrounded by housing developments and new roads (Hovingh 1986).

Intensive agriculture, especially farming in which no native vegetation is allowed to remain, has exterminated amphibians and reptiles over large areas of eastern Colorado, the San Luis Valley, and the Grand Valley of Mesa County. These areas are readily seen in satellite images of the state, and the enormous extent of impact in eastern Colorado is particularly impressive. In many areas, amphibians and reptiles have been completely eliminated over miles of terrain, and individuals survive only in undisturbed refuges along streams or topographic breaks.

Fortunately, significant tracts of untilled prairie still remain in eastern Colorado (Map 2.12). These unplowed landscapes, plus unplowed valley lands in western Colorado, include the amphibian and reptile habitats most sorely in need of long-term protection, which usually can be accomplished by maintaining a regime of light-to-moderate livestock grazing.

Heavy pesticide use on croplands and rangelands may reduce the food supply for insectivorous species and may contaminate amphibian breeding ponds, killing embryos or causing deformities; some pesticides can kill adults outright. On the other hand, rodent-infested fields and ranch buildings provide favorable habitat for mammal-eating snakes. Bullsnakes are notable for their persistence in agricultural areas despite massive habitat change. Water retention and diversion structures in irrigated areas provide places to live for aquatic or amphibious species in areas where ponds and wetlands naturally were scarce. Throughout the rangelands and farming areas of Colorado, snakes, lizards, and toads devour enormous numbers of rodents and insects each year. Farmers and ranchers who protect amphibians and reptiles and their habitats reap the economic (and aesthetic) benefits of these natural pest-control agents.

Mineral extraction has altered large areas in some parts of Colorado (e.g., the molybdenum mine at Climax). Massive disruption of the land surface by mining typically directly eliminates all amphibians and reptiles. Only extraordinary and unlikely reclamation procedures, not simple smoothing of the land and revegetation, could restore a habitable environment for many species that are closely restricted to specific substrate textures and depend both daily and seasonally on access to subterranean retreats of particular thermal characteristics. Mining often creates holes and depressions that fill with water and may contain hazardous concentrations of metals. In northwestern Colorado, mine-spoils ponds that were 10–30 years old apparently remained uninhabited by amphibians or reptiles (Canton 1982).

However, the greatest mining threat to amphibians and reptiles is not posed by digging but rather by toxic concentrations of minerals draining from mines and mine tailings into streams, ponds, and lakes. Porter and Hakanson (1976) found that mine drainage in Clear Creek County had concentrations of hydrogen ion, iron, copper, and zinc all individually much greater than the tolerance levels of tadpoles of the mountain toad. Only after the water was diluted approximately 1,000 times could the tadpoles survive in it.

Energy resource development continues to cause significant alterations to the landscape. Strippable coal deposits exist in both western and eastern Colorado. Rich deposits of oil shale occur in the northwestern part of the state. Uranium is widespread in southwestern Colorado and exists in isolated localities throughout western and central portions of the state. Gas and oil resources are extensive in both eastern and western Colorado. Development of these resources poses a significant threat to the habitats of amphibians, reptiles, and other wildlife.

Timber resources are abundant in Colorado, and logging is a common activity in montane and subalpine forests. Removal of trees from the vicinity of mountain ponds may result in increased pond temperature and sun exposure, and under certain circumstances these changes could negatively affect the reproduction of amphibians. The major impacts of logging on amphibians in Colorado are indirect. For example, amphibian reproduction is adversely impacted when eggs are covered by sediments resulting from excessive erosion. Hence, logging, mining, overgrazing, road building, and

other activities that destroy soil-holding vegetation often are detrimental to amphibian populations.

Water development projects have significantly affected many areas. Most major rivers and numerous smaller tributary streams have been dammed, forming large and small reservoirs both in the mountains and in lowland areas. Spring runoff that normally would flood streamside lowlands now is held behind dams for gradual release throughout the summer, reducing in some areas the availability of seasonal floodplain breeding habitats for amphibians. On the other hand, fields are regularly flooded by irrigation water during the summer, when dry conditions normally would prevail. Even the Continental Divide has been crossed in the quest for more water; tunnels and pipelines carry Western Slope water underneath it to eastern Colorado. On a smaller scale, thousands of ponds have been created to water cattle on rangelands throughout the state.

One result of all this water manipulation has been a substantial increase in the area and seasonal availability of aquatic and wetland habitats in many lowland areas of Colorado, especially in the South Platte and Arkansas River valleys and the San Luis Valley. In general, these habitats are widely inhabited by amphibians and aquatic and amphibious reptiles. However, creation of these environments probably has not greatly impacted the overall geographic distribution of most native species within the state. The effect has been to increase the habitable portion of the general area already occupied. However, non-native bullfrogs have colonized and spread throughout much of Colorado, due largely to the availability of human-created permanent ponds, and northern leopard frogs evidently expanded their range in eastern Colorado as a result of human-augmented habitat availability (Gillis 1975). Reese (1973) suggested that certain distributional phenomena in tiger salamander subspecies may be explained by the transport of individuals in water diversion structures. Livo (pers. comm.) observed six box turtles, a yellow mud turtle, and a plains garter snake trapped in a dry section of a concrete-lined irrigation ditch in Yuma County. Such structures can be significant barriers to local amphibian and reptile movement patterns and in some circumstances may act as death traps to the animals that wander into them.

Water resource development in Colorado has not been restricted to water retention and redistribution projects. In an attempt to increase the amount of precipitation that falls on the state, winter clouds over the mountains frequently have been seeded. The ecological impact of snowpack augmentation on mountain-dwelling amphibians and reptiles is unknown, but Campbell (1976: 289) suggested that the mountain toad would be adversely affected because "dates of snowmelt, availability of melt water, and changes in snowfall in general would have a significant effect on recruitment to the local adult populations."

It is disturbing that major water diversion and storage projects with huge potential environmental consequences continue to be proposed. Fortunately, the detrimental impacts of these large-scale developments are now well recognized (by some), and ecologically destructive schemes may not be so readily undertaken as they have been in the past.

Severe automobile-exhaust air pollution, consisting mainly of carbon monoxide, photochemical oxidants, nitrogen dioxide, and particulates, has been a by-product of urbanization in the Denver metropolitan area. The direct effects of air pollution on amphibians and reptiles are unknown. Indirect effects through acid precipitation may be significant. Oxides of nitrogen and sulfur (the latter is not a problem in Colorado), commonly emitted as industrial and vehicular pollutants, combine with water in the atmosphere to form acids that fall to earth in rain or snow and acidify bodies of water. Some wetland areas in the Mt. Zirkel Wilderness in north-central Colorado may have experienced significant acidification from nearby power plants. Lake acidification has been correlated with the disappearance of aquatic life in eastern North America and Europe, but the best available evidence indicates that the present extent of acidification

is probably not directly harming amphibians in our region.

Activities related to the development of recreational fishing frequently have been harmful to native amphibian populations. In the mountains, many wetlands and small ponds and lakes formerly harboring healthy populations of amphibians have been inundated as a result of dam and reservoir construction (one justification for these projects has been the enhancement of fishing opportunities). These reservoirs rarely provide favorable habitat for amphibians and reptiles and are typically stocked with non-native game fishes such as trout or (in lowlands) various warm-water game fishes. These predatory fishes may devastate salamander and frog populations by eating eggs, larvae, or adults. Amphibians survive only where shallow, vegetation-choked areas provide sufficient cover. Unfortunately, these important vegetated shallows often are eliminated, along with the amphibians, under typical reservoir management or when pools are deepened prior to stocking them with trout. Treatment of aquatic habitats with rotenone or other toxicants, such as commonly occurs in conjunction with fisheries management, can be lethal to amphibian larvae and softshell turtles (Fontenot, Noblet, and Platt 1994). Tiger salamander populations locally may be depleted through excessive harvest of larvae for use as fishing bait.

The introduction and subsequent population growth and range expansion of the bullfrog apparently has had a harmful impact on native amphibians. Tiger salamanders rarely are found in ponds inhabited by bullfrogs, even if other conditions are favorable (Reese 1969). Bullfrogs appear to be replacing or to have replaced native leopard frogs in some areas of eastern Colorado (Hammerson 1981), but it is uncertain whether this has been due to bullfrog predation on leopard frogs, competitive interactions, habitat changes favoring bullfrogs, differential impacts of exotic game fishes, or other factors.

Various non-native amphibians and reptiles are introduced periodically in or near cities in Colorado when people liberate their pets. Other species arrive in the state as waifs accidentally transported via interstate commerce (Livo, Hammerson, and Smith 1998). Most of these animals languish and die because suitable environmental conditions for them do not exist in Colorado. Individuals accustomed to captivity may soon die if released into the wild, even if local temperature and moisture conditions are suitable, because they can no longer fend for themselves. In the event that liberated individuals do survive, they may transmit diseases contracted in captivity to native populations. And if a breeding population of an exotic species is established, it is highly probable that the introduced species will negatively impact native wildlife through predation or competition. Even the transfer of a native species from one portion of its range to another can be harmful through the disruption of locally adapted gene pools. For these reasons, amphibians and reptiles should never be released in areas from which they were not obtained, and long-term captives never should be turned loose in the wild, even in the places where they were captured.

At least one exotic plant clearly has a negative impact on native lizards. Cheat-grass *(Bromus tectorum),* an early-season annual widely established in Colorado, forms a dense ground cover in areas that under natural conditions would have a sparse growth of forbs and/or scattered clumps of bunch grasses. Cheatgrass thickets are virtually impenetrable by many lizards and exclude them from otherwise suitable habitat. Even if accessible, the deep shade and obstruction of vision make these cheatgrass thickets unfavorable for lizards, except perhaps as escape cover adjacent to more suitable areas with native vegetation.

Future human threats to amphibians and reptiles in Colorado are uncertain but ominous. Massive disruption of the landscape by energy development and population growth, with its associated urban-suburban sprawl, could create a bleak future for amphibians, reptiles, and other wildlife (as well as humans) unless ecosystem protection is adequately incorporated into the growth and development process.

IMPACTS ON HUMANS

In general, amphibians and reptiles are innocuous animals that rarely cause any harm to humans or their property. Sometimes they prey on species that are hunted by humans—snapping turtles may kill young waterfowl in ponds, bullsnakes may eat duck eggs, and garter snakes, water snakes, and turtles may occasionally catch a sport fish (probably a sick or injured one)—but the impact is hardly significant, and we can easily afford to share these food resources with our fellow predators, which, after all, depend on them more than we do.

Only rattlesnakes (two species in Colorado) pose any threat to human safety. Rattlesnakes are indeed dangerous, but they are not as deadly as many would believe. In the United States, more than ten times as many people die each year from bee stings or lightning strikes than rattlesnake bites (less than 1 percent of these injuries are fatal). Among humans, most snake bites result from careless behavior in handling captives or attempting to capture or kill a snake found in the wild. Very rarely is someone fatally bitten during an unexpected encounter with a rattlesnake (Straight and Glenn 1993). Livestock that have been bitten may experience swelling and become sick, but they rarely die.

The educational and aesthetic values of amphibians and reptiles should not be overlooked. Various species make ideal subjects for learning about physiology, genetics, ecology, behavior, conservation, and other topics. Observation of frog or lizard behavior in the field is no less rewarding than bird or mammal study. Few experiences in nature study are as thrilling as a nighttime visit to a pond in which hundreds of frogs and toads are singing.

Chapter 4

Conservation Status Ranks and State Regluations

CONSERVATION STATUS RANKS

The following global and state conservation-status ranking system was devised by The Nature Conservancy and is used by natural heritage programs, conservation data centers, and many natural resource agencies throughout the United States, Canada, and much of Latin America. The codes for the species conservation-status ranks begin with a letter, G or S, referring to the global (G) or state (S) conservation status, followed usually by a numeral, 1–5. The numeric codes for each rank are defined as follows:

1 = critically imperiled because of few (1–5) occurrences or few remaining individuals or other factors making it especially vulnerable to extinction (or extirpation within a state).

2 = imperiled because of rarity (generally 6–20 occurrences) or few remaining individuals or other factors making it vulnerable to extinction (or extirpation within a state).

3 = vulnerable throughout the global or state range or occurring locally within a restricted range; generally 21–100 occurrences.

4 = apparently secure; more than 100 occurrences, but may be rare in some parts of the range.

5 = demonstrably secure, though may be rare in some parts of the range.

In some cases, a letter code may follow the G or S. H indicates a historical species: GH signifies a species that has not been observed anywhere in the world for many years, and SH signifies a species that has not been detected anywhere in the state for many years. X indicates a species that is known to be or most likely is extinct (GX) or extirpated from the state (SX). SR denotes species that have been reported from the state and that may have been established at one time but for which recent confirmation of their presence here is lacking. SE refers to introduced (exotic) species with established populations.

Though the number of occurrences, or distinct populations, may suggest a certain numeric rank, a species that is declining or facing significant threats to its continued existence in a substantial portion of its range may be elevated in rank (for instance, a species with 12 occurrences but a declining population may be elevated from G2 to G1). A rank of G4S2 indicates that the species is apparently secure on a global scale but imperiled within the state (for example, a species may be common in other states but rare in Colorado). These coded conservation ranks are used to help prioritize conservation actions.

Table 4.1 indicates the global and state conservation status ranks (as of 1998) for all amphibian and reptile species known from Colorado, excluding fossils and introduced species without established populations. In the table, some ranks indicating uncertainty of status have been simplified in favor of higher conservation concern (e.g., G3G4 becomes G3). State of Colorado status also is coded as follows: E = endangered (in immediate jeopardy of becoming extirpated from Colorado); T = threatened (may become endangered in Colorado in the foreseeable future). Conservation status ranks may change over time; contact the Colorado Natural Heritage Program and the Colorado Division of Wildlife for current information. A previous account of so-called threatened species in Colorado compiled by Ashton (1976) was based on inadequate (and in some cases erroneous) information and

	Global Status								State Status							
	GX	GH	G1	G2	G3	G4	G5		SX	SH	S1	S2	S3	S4	S5	SR	SE
Tiger Salamander							x								x		
Couch's Spadefoot							x				x						
Plains Spadefoot							x								x		
Great Basin Spadefoot							x						x				
New Mexico Spadefoot							x							x			
Mountain toad			?								E						
Great Plains Toad							x							x			
Green Toad							x					x					
Red-spotted Toad							x							x			
Woodhouse's Toad							x								x		
Northern Cricket Frog							x			x							
Canyon Treefrog							x					x					
Western chorus frog							x								x		
Gr. Pl. Narrowmouth Toad							x					x					
Plains Leopard Frog							x						x				
Bullfrog							x										x
Northern Leopard Frog							x						x				
Wood Frog							x						x				
Snapping Turtle							x							x			
Painted Turtle							x								x		
Ornate Box Turtle							x								x		
Yellow Mud Turtle							x					x					
Spiny Softshell							x							x			
Collared Lizard							x								x		
Longnose Leopard Lizard							x					x					
Lesser Earless Lizard							x								x		
Texas Horned Lizard						x							x				
Short-horned Lizard							x								x		
Roundtail Horned Lizard							x					x					
Sagebrush Lizard							x								x		
Desert Spiny Lizard							x					x					
Plateau and Prairie Lizards							x								x		
Tree Lizard							x							x			
Side-blotched Lizard							x							x			
Diploid Checkered Whiptail							x					x					
Six-lined Racerunner							x								x		
Triploid Checkered Whiptail				x								x					
Western Whiptail							x							x			
Plateau Striped Whiptail							x							x			
Variable Skink							x					x					
Many-lined Skink						x								x			
Great Plains Skink							x							x			
Texas Blind Snake							x			x							
Rubber Boa							x									x	
Glossy Snake							x						x				
Racer							x								x		
Ringneck Snake							x					x					
Great Plains Rat Snake							x						x				
Western Hognose Snake							x							x			
Eastern Hognose Snake							x									x	
Night Snake							x						x				
Common Kingsnake							x					x					
Milk Snake							x								x		
Smooth Green Snake							x							x			
Coachwhip							x								x		
Striped Whipsnake							x							x			
Northern Water Snake							x							x			
Bullsnake/Gopher Snake							x								x		
Longnose Snake							x					x					
Ground Snake							x							x			
Brown Snake							x									x	
SW. Black-headed Snake							x					x					
Plains Black-headed Snake							x						x				
Blackneck Garter Snake							x					x					
W. Terrestrial Garter Snake							x								x		
Western Ribbon Snake							x			x							
Plains Garter Snake							x								x		
Common Garter Snake							x							x			
Lined Snake							x							x			
Western Rattlesnake							x								x		
Massasauga					x							x					

Table 4.1. Conservation status of Colorado amphibians and reptiles as of 1998.

cannot be used as a basis for comparison with current status.

With a few exceptions, the amphibian and reptile species occurring in Colorado are demonstrably secure on a global scale, but a substantial portion of the state's amphibian and reptile fauna is of significant conservation concern. In most cases, the conservation concern stems from a species' restricted range in the state, which results in relatively high vulnerability to extirpation by localized events. The mountain toad is an example of a species that once was widespread and common but now is restricted and relatively rare.

REGULATIONS PERTAINING TO AMPHIBIANS AND REPTILES IN COLORADO

The Colorado Wildlife Commission, recognizing that amphibians and reptiles are important components of natural ecosystems, and seeking to prevent the loss of any portion of the state's wildlife heritage, has enacted regulations designed to protect these species from excessive exploitation and other threats. The following regulations were in effect as of July 1998.

Tiger salamander *(Ambystoma tigrinum).* Persons with a valid fishing license may harvest or possess not more than 50 larvae for use as bait. The season is open all year. The maximum number of metamorphosed, adult salamanders that may be possessed is six.

Mountain toad (*Bufo boreas* complex). This toad is classified as an endangered species by the state; federal listing under the U.S. Endangered Species Act has been determined by the U.S. Fish and Wildlife Service to be warranted but so far has been precluded by activities of higher priority. Collection or possession of this amphibian is unlawful without a valid scientific collection license.

Bullfrog *(Rana catesbeiana).* Daily bag and possession limit is 10 frogs. A valid fishing license is required for harvest. The season is open all year.

Snapping turtle *(Chelydra serpentina).* This turtle is classified as a game reptile. Anyone with a valid Colorado small-game or fishing license may take snapping turtles from April 1 through October 31. There is no bag or possession limit. State statutes also provide that snapping turtles may be killed on private property by the owner or leaseholder of such property if the turtles are causing "damage to crops, real or personal property, or livestock."

Western (prairie) rattlesnake *(Crotalus viridis).* Rattlesnakes of this species, with the exception of those in Garfield, Mesa, Delta, and Montrose counties (e.g., the midget faded rattlesnake, *C. v. concolor*), are classified as small game and may be taken from June 15 through August 15 by holders of a valid small-game license. The daily bag limit is three, with a possession limit of six. On private property they may be killed if they are creating a nuisance or causing damage to property.

Amphibians and reptiles that may be possessed without a special license. Up to 4 individuals of the following species may be taken annually and held in captivity, provided that no more than 12 in the aggregate are possessed at any time: plains spadefoot, Woodhouse's toad, western chorus frog, painted turtle, ornate box turtle, lesser earless lizard, sagebrush lizard, tree lizard, side-blotched lizard, prairie and plateau lizard, western whiptail, racer, western hognose snake, bullsnake, western terrestrial garter snake, and plains garter snake. These and their progeny may be disposed of by gift or as authorized by the Division of Wildlife. They may be released into the wild, provided they have not come into contact with amphibians and reptiles from other geographic regions and they are released as close as possible to, but no farther than 10 miles from, their place of origin.

All other amphibians and reptiles. Taking or possession is prohibited without a special license for scientific collecting, rehabilitation, education, or propagation.

Chapter 5
How to Observe and Photograph Amphibians and Reptiles

Many people have remarked that reptiles and amphibians seem scarce in much of our area. Indeed, the secretive habits of most species can make them difficult to observe. But a little patience, knowledge of the animals' behavior and habitats, and a few observational techniques will greatly increase the chances of finding them, especially if the constraints of season and weather are considered. A wide variety of species can be observed in Colorado's national parks, monuments, and grasslands (see Appendix B).

Most reptiles and amphibians in our area can be observed most readily from April to October, the period when most activity occurs. Late spring and early summer are especially good times. Warm sunny mornings and warm evenings (particularly after heavy summer rains) also bring out many species. Cold weather and wind tend to inhibit activity.

A daytime visit to a marshy area or a pond or lake with shallow, weedy margins usually yields various frogs, snakes, and turtles. Walk slowly along the edge and listen carefully—many species are heard before they are seen. Don't forget to look closely in the water for larvae. Once you find an animal, don't pounce on it in an effort to catch it. Some of the most interesting observations are made by sitting or standing quietly and simply watching.

Another productive daytime technique is to search under rocks, logs, boards, and other debris on the ground. This is one of the best ways to find species that are secretive. Under ideal conditions, nearly every other rock or log might shelter an amphibian or reptile. But sometimes you won't find anything. One day I kept track of my success as I looked for snakes on a rocky hillside in southeastern Colorado; I lifted 92 rocks 30–60 cm in diameter before I found a single snake. On other days, all it took was one rock or piece of wood. An object that has been overturned should be returned carefully to its original position so that the hiding place is preserved for future use. Reptiles and amphibians are most often found under objects that have been in contact with the soil for some time; a rock or log that has been newly turned is not as attractive a hiding place. An animal found under a heavy rock or log should be released at the edge of the object after it has been repositioned. This allows the animal to crawl into the hiding place without danger of being crushed.

Conspicuous rock exposures are good places to find several kinds of lizards, especially during late morning or late afternoon (activity is reduced at midday during hot weather). Approach slowly and quietly to within about 20 feet or so. If you sit quietly and use binoculars, you may get a good view of feeding, courtship, or territorial behavior. Certainly, you will notice a lot more going on than if you focus solely on capture.

One of the best ways to find frogs and toads is to listen for their calls at night in spring or after heavy summer rains. Once a chorus is heard, a cross-country hike with flashlight in hand may lead to one of the most enjoyable spectacles in the animal world. The beam of the flashlight (ideally with a red filter) usually causes little disturbance as the males call and joust with one another in an effort to attract the attention of females. When several species are breeding simultaneously, the result can be a visual and aural extravaganza.

Snakes often can be found by walking or driving slowly (15–20 mph) on little-traveled blacktop roads on warm nights. As the air cools, snakes crossing the road tend to linger on the heated pavement, where they readily can be seen on the plain, dark surface. Unfortunately, this habit results in thousands of snakes being crushed by cars each year. Searching roads can be especially productive during and immediately after heavy spring and summer rains, which stimulate many snakes and amphibians to roam.

Road-hunting by car is an effective way to find reptiles and amphibians but can be quite dangerous. I would not recommend trying it on roads traveled by more than one car every few minutes. When an animal is found, pull onto the shoulder of the road and park. Don't forget to close the doors on the road side of the car when retrieving the animal. An animal captured on the road (or anywhere else) should be released off the road in the area where it was found. Animals that are released elsewhere may die for lack of suitable habitat or may, in certain circumstances, adversely impact other species in the area of release.

PREPARING FOR FIELD STUDIES

I hope this book will inspire you to begin your own field studies of reptiles or amphibians. Anyone can make valuable scientific contributions if a study is carefully planned and executed. The most efficient approach is to study a species that lives nearby. What you study is limited only by your imagination. It makes sense to begin by reading everything you can about a species or topic of interest to you, but do not accept everything you read (including information in this book!) as the final word. In fact, it is worthwhile to investigate a situation where your field observations do not conform with published information or do not seem to be addressed in the literature. It is beyond the scope of this book to review field study methods, but I recommend that prospective researchers begin by reading works on marking methods, sampling techniques, and life-history study methods by Ferner (1979), Corn and Bury (1990), and especially Heyer et al. (1994) and Olson, Leonard, and Bury (1997), as well as *Guidelines for Use of Live Amphibians and Reptiles in Field Research,* published by the Society for the Study of Amphibians and Reptiles in 1987. Survey methods for montane amphibians were discussed by Livo (1995b).

The urgent but unanswered questions in biology do not concern biochemical or molecular processes but rather the dynamics of natural populations and the relationship between population viability and patterns and processes in the landscape. In particular, we need to know how to assure the persistence of wildlife populations in the face of a growing human population and shrinking natural habitats. We desperately need long-term studies of marked populations living under a wide range of environmental conditions. I particularly encourage potential researchers to employ study methods that harm neither the habitat nor the animals.

SALVAGING DEAD REPTILES AND AMPHIBIANS

Reptiles and amphibians that are found dead can yield valuable information on geographic variation, distribution, food habits, activity patterns, reproduction, and other life-history characteristics. If you do not have access to suitable chemical preservatives, dead specimens should be wrapped in aluminum foil or several layers of plastic and placed on ice (or in a freezer if chemical preservation cannot be undertaken soon). Proper chemical preservation generally entails hardening the specimen in buffered 10 percent formalin for a day, then storing it in 70 percent ethanol (except amphibian larvae, which should be stored in 10 percent formalin). The formalin should be injected into all thick parts of the body or allowed to seep inside through cuts in the body wall. Further details can be found in Duellman (1962).

If the specimen cannot be salvaged, take one or more close photographs of it, pre-ferably with a macro lens. The following information should be recorded for each specimen or photograph: exact location where found (include topographic map coordinates, if possible), date when found, collector's name, habitat, and other biological information such as stomach contents and number of eggs or young in the reproductive tract of females. Write the information in pencil or permanent ink and place it with the specimen (attach it to the specimen, if possible) or write the data on the back of each photograph or on the frame around color slides. This information is crucial; specimens unaccompanied by collection data have relatively little scientific value.

Frozen or chemically preserved salvaged specimens and photographs should be donated to a major natural history museum. To deposit a specimen or photograph, contact the University of Colorado Museum (Boulder), which is the state's major repository of reptiles and amphibians. This will ensure that the material will be properly cared for and that researchers will have ready access to it.

PHOTOGRAPHY

The camera equipment and procedures used to create the photographs in this book are relatively simple. Other equipment and methods may work as well or better, but the following are effective, reasonably inexpensive, and suitable for opportunistic field use.

I carried with me a standard 35-mm single-lens-reflex camera equipped with a 50-mm macro lens. For most photographs, taken with an electronic flash unit, I used slow (ISO 64) color slide film, though some were taken with faster (ISO 100 or 200) film.

The fundamental dilemma in photographing reptiles and amphibians is that the subject, which the photographer hopes will pose with regal demeanor, is intent only on escape. Except in ponds at night, I usually had to capture my subjects by hand prior to photographing them. I captured some lizards with the aid of a small noose tied to the end of a fishing pole or stick. Sometimes careful stalking allowed me to get close enough to photograph undisturbed subjects, but usually they hopped, ran, or crawled away and had to be captured. Some individuals calmed down if held for a few minutes before being set down gently and photographed. Others would not sit still for even a single photograph. I coaxed some of these "hyperactive" animals to relax by letting them crawl beneath some object such as my hat or hand. Thus hidden and shaded, the animal often became immobile and could be photographed after the cover was carefully lifted. Some photographers calm their reptile or amphibian subjects by chilling them in an ice chest or refrigerator. This makes the animals lethargic and easier to photograph but also often changes or dulls their colors and prevents them from maintaining a normal posture. Sometimes the method produces good results if the animal is then placed in the sun and allowed to warm.

To my eye, the best photographs of amphibians and reptiles are those taken in the animal's natural habitat. Technically, it is not very difficult to obtain high-quality, unobscured photographs of these animals in their natural surroundings, but physically it can be rather awkward, as I can attest from my experiences photographing frogs at night as I sank into the soft mud bottom of a marsh or attempting to take close-ups of lizards while kneeling among sharp rocks or cactus.

When the sun is out and high magnifications are not required (i.e., the subject is fairly large), excellent photographs can be taken with natural light. For sharp prints, shutter speed should not be less than 1/250 second. However, many amphibians and reptiles are small, and they may not sit still in direct sunlight, or there may not be any sunlight available. In such cases, close-up photography using only natural light usually results in pictures that lack sharpness or in which a substantial portion of the subject is out of focus. This is because the shutter speed must be too slow or the aperture too large in order to compensate for inadequate light. High-speed color films may alleviate the problem somewhat but at the cost of reduced color intensity. Use of a tripod may allow sharp photos by minimizing camera movement at slow shutter speeds, but many amateur photographers dislike lugging a tripod into the field. Hence, a flash unit may be the best way to attain photographs with maximum sharpness, richness of color, and depth of focus. The flash allows you to use a small aperture (maximizing depth of focus) and to employ very high effective shutter speeds (maximizing sharpness). I took most of the photographs in this book with an aperture setting of f/22, with the camera held in one hand and the flash unit in the other. Flash-to-subject distance, which depends on the magnification of the photo and the light output of the flash (as well as on the film speed and aperture setting), was determined using the calculations and tables in Blaker (1976: 310–322) or by simple experimentation.

Chapter 6

Explanation of Species Accounts

The species accounts in this book contain information on the identification, distribution, conservation status, habitat, life history, and taxonomy of each species of amphibian and reptile occurring in Colorado. Only species with populations currently or formerly established within the state are included in the main accounts. Species possibly native to Colorado but known from single specimens or observations are discussed in Appendix A. Amphibians and reptiles regarded as having been introduced by humans and without documented established populations in the state (Livo, Hammerson, and Smith 1998) are not included. In addition, the Texas rat snake *(Elaphe obsoleta lindheimeri)* found in Kiowa County and reported without qualification by Montgomery, Childers, Manzer, et al. (1998b) was likely a non-natural occurrence. It was probably translocated in association with interstate movement of agricultural equipment (Mackessy 1998).

Photographs. Each species is illustrated by at least one color photograph. Variation between sexes, ages, or individuals from different areas is illustrated in some cases. I took the photographs, unless they are otherwise credited.

Recognition. I have not included a complete description for each species but rather have focused on the characteristics that together distinguish each species from any other species in Colorado. Major differences between sexes, ages, and individuals from different areas are described where appropriate. Maximum sizes are based mostly on Stebbins (1985) and Conant and Collins (1991), except as indicated. Abbre-

viations used in this section are defined in the Glossary.

Most adult amphibians and reptiles can be readily identified using the photographs and recognition characteristics in conjunction with the distribution maps. For more difficult cases, consult the detailed identification keys in Appendix C. *It is important to bear in mind that characteristics for identifying larvae pertain to individuals in the later stages of development;* hatchlings may look quite different. Advice on identifying larvae and an explanation of labial tooth row formulas are included at the beginning of the "Key to Amphibian Larvae" in Appendix C. Egg sizes mentioned in this section refer to oviductal or freshly laid eggs. Morphological characteristics of amphibians and reptiles are illustrated in Appendix C and defined in the Glossary.

Most frogs and toads can be identified readily by their vocalizations, which I describe in this section of the species accounts. Davidson (1996) provided a useful collection of recordings of the voices of anurans from our region.

Distribution. The total range of each species is briefly stated, followed by a description of the geographic and elevational distribution in Colorado.

Maps. Detailed maps show the distribution of each species in Colorado. Black dots indicate places where the species is known to occur or to have occurred historically. Many dots represent two or more closely adjacent localities. The mapped occurrences reflect distributional records documented by museum collections (see Acknowledgments for museum acronyms used in the species accounts), scientific literature, some unpublished reports, my own field observations, and the field notes of selected highly experienced herpetologists. I carefully evaluated the authenticity of each distributional record before accepting it as valid. Specific locality data for each dot are available in my files. Doubtful records of occurrence and occurrences believed to represent introduced specimens without established breeding populations are not included. A map of the counties of Colorado is included on page xxviii).

With few exceptions, the distinction between present and former occurrences is unimportant at the scale I have used for mapping. This is true because each dot on the map covers an area about 10 km in diameter, and most extirpations in Colorado are quite localized. Generally, extirpated populations are within 10 km of an extant population of the same species, so the dot would not be removed in mapping present occurrences. Though the expanding Denver metropolitan area and large-scale agriculture in eastern Colorado have eliminated certain amphibians and reptiles over areas several miles across, distinguishing between the probably extant and probably extirpated occurrences of these species would not greatly alter the distributional patterns depicted on the maps. In the distribution section of the species accounts, I have mentioned a few particular cases in which regional declines in distribution or significant-though-localized extirpations have occurred.

Conservation Status. This section discusses trends in distribution and abundance, factors that have affected these attributes, management issues, and available information on population density.

Habitat, Activity, Reproduction and Growth, Food and Predators, Remarks. These sections summarize what is known about the habitat, activity patterns, movements, reproduction and growth, diet, predators, populations, and other aspects of the lives of Colorado's amphibians and reptiles. For amphibians that differ in breeding and nonbreeding habitats, nonbreeding habitat is described under "Habitat" and breeding habitat is described under "Reproduction

and Growth." The focus is on Colorado and adjacent states, but, lacking local observations, or for comparative purposes, I sometimes included information from other areas.

Taxonomy and Variation. This section covers taxonomic issues, particularly relating to the population units I have chosen to recognize as species. For some species I describe patterns of morphological or genetic variation.

Taxonomy and systematics, the disciplines of naming and classifying the products of evolution, attempt to be objective but in reality are highly subjective. Even with adequate data, different people often reach different conclusions about which populations should be joined as a single species. Scientists face the subjective task of choosing which taxonomic arrangement to adopt and hence which names to use. The common and scientific names in this book generally follow what I regard as those most widely used or those upheld by recent taxonomic revisions with adequate supporting data. Most of the names conform with Collins (1997). Derivations of scientific names are discussed in Appendix D.

Scientific names for familiar species are becoming less stable as increasing numbers of taxonomists adopt the phylogenetic species concept (PSC) or similar evolutionary species concept (ESC). The PSC and ESC emphasize evolutionary history, especially as reflected in genetic and morphological differentiation of populations, and allow limited interbreeding between the units recognized as species. Many taxonomists are abandoning strict adherence to the biological species concept (BSC), which generally lumps all interbreeding units as a single species, regardless of patterns of genetic and morphological differentiation. The basic taxonomic result of this trend is a tendency toward recognition of a greater number of species by proponents of the PSC and ESC (often through the elevation of subspecies to species).

I agree that it may be appropriate to recognize as distinct species those differentiated populations that exhibit very small zones of interbreeding (as reflected in patterns of variation) relative to the size of the ranges of the species in question. In other words, if members of a population unit are recognizable as such throughout a broad range, except in a narrow zone along a margin, then one might recognize that unit as a species (if adequate data are available for determining the pattern of variation). The unit represents an evolutionary lineage, as reflected in its unique characteristics. An illustrative example is perhaps provided by the plateau lizard subspecies *Sceloporus undulatus erythrocheilus*. This lizard is well differentiated from its close relatives—all individuals are readily identifiable as *erythrocheilus*. In very small areas at the edge of the range, it rather abruptly grades (via individuals with intermediate characteristics) into an adjacent subspecies. Hence it could be regarded as a distinct species *(Sceloporus erythrocheilus)* under the PSC but is considered a subspecies and conspecific with its intergrading neighbor under the BSC.

What, then, is a subspecies? Subspecies are geographical subdivisions of species, defined by various arbitrary characteristics. Subspecies usually differ from one another in *average* color, scalation, body proportions, or other characteristics, but not all individuals of a subspecies are necessarily recognizably different from those of other subspecies. Subspecies interbreed with adjacent subspecies of the same species, unless they are geographically isolated. Isolated subspecies generally exhibit average but not absolute differences in characteristics. Where two subspecies meet and interbreed, they are said to intergrade. Intergrading subspecies may be intermediate in appearance between the two subspecies or may contain some individuals that resemble one subspecies, some that look like the other,

and some that are intermediate. When the area of intergradation is large, boundaries between subspecies become indistinct and subspecific names rather meaningless.

Most subspecific names derive from an early era in taxonomy when we knew relatively little about patterns of geographic variation and every variant was described as a distinct taxon. Modern biologists generally do not recognize subspecies within species exhibiting clinal patterns of variation (i.e., characteristics that change gradually over a relatively large area). Also, taxa defined by environmentally induced characteristics and taxa that tell us nothing about the evolutionary history of the population are disregarded as invalid. For example, scale arrangements and counts and body size and shape of reptiles are influenced to some degree by temperature conditions during development. Some taxonomists feel that most or all subspecies are unworthy of taxonomic recognition, whereas others regard subspecific names as useful for cataloguing distinctive patterns of variation within a species (Smith, Chiszar, and Montanucci 1997). Recent studies have shown that patterns of genetic variation often correspond poorly with currently named subspecies.

Units of Measurement. Throughout this book, linear measurements are reported as millimeters (mm), centimeters (1 cm = 0.39 inches), meters (1 m = 3.28 feet), or kilometers (1 km = 1.6 miles), except in the case of elevation, where both metric (m) and English (feet) units are provided. Area is given as hectares (1 ha = 2.47 acres), square meters (1 m^2 = 10.8 square feet), or square kilometers (1 km^2 = 247 acres or 0.39 square miles). Mass is reported as grams (28.35 g = 1 ounce) or kilograms (1 kg = 2.2 pounds).

Chapter 7

Amphibians

Amphibians (class Amphibia) first appeared during the late Devonian period some 400 million years ago. The first amphibians were much larger than those alive today, but all of these ancient species are now extinct.

Today's amphibians include 4,780 species in three groups—caecilians, salamanders, and frogs. The caecilians (order Gymnophiona, about 165 species) are wormlike burrowing or aquatic animals restricted to tropical regions. The salamanders (order Caudata) and frogs (order Anura) are characterized in detail in this chapter.

Skin and Color. Amphibians are distinguished by moist, glandular, naked skin. Unlike that of fishes, reptiles, birds, and mammals, amphibian skin has no covering of scales, feathers, or hair. The skin contains numerous glands of two major kinds, mucous and poison. Mucous gland secretions keep the skin moist and sometimes quite slippery, facilitating escape from predators. In some species, the mucus is toxic and functions as an antipredator device. Poison glands are contained within a capsule of smooth muscle and often are aggregated, forming warts or glandular ridges in the skin. These glands secrete during stressful stimulation (e.g., attempted predation). The secretion often is noxious (sometimes toxic) and serves as a deterrent to predation. Predators that ingest these secretions may experience stronger heartbeat, weakened respiration, general muscular paralysis, and nausea. Enhanced protection from diving beetle predation in various metamorphic amphibian larvae is associated with development of the poison glands. Amphibian skin secretions also may protect against microbial infections.

Many amphibians, especially frogs, can readily change the brightness or intensity of their skin color. Color change results from movement of pigment within certain color cells (chromatophores), structural changes in other kinds of chromatophores, and movements of the chromatophores. Chromatophores are arranged in layers in the dermis, where scattered pigment granules also may be present. Color is affected by temperature, light, background color, and stress. Cold generally darkens color. Even at constant temperature, some frogs can change color to match their background. Color changes are primarily under hormonal control and may be brief or long-lasting. The unusual blue coloration of certain frogs results from a genetic mutation in which one of the chromatophore layers is missing. In certain arboreal South African frogs, dense layers of chromatophores appear to reduce water loss.

Amphibians shed the outer layer of skin at intervals of several days to several weeks. In many frogs, the skin comes off in irregular pieces. In other species, it is shed whole. Frogs and toads may eat all or part of the skin as it is shed. Skin derivatives such as true claws are lacking in amphibians, but horny clawlike growths sometimes are present.

Temperature, Metabolism, and Respiration. Amphibians are ectothermic, deriving their body heat from the external environment, and are not especially tolerant of very hot or cold conditions. They are unable to produce their own body heat. The thick layer of dead, keratinized cells that acts as a water-repellent outer covering in other land-dwelling vertebrates is very thin in amphibians. Consequently, amphibians constantly lose water from the portion of the skin that is exposed to air. The rate of water loss is inversely proportional to the humidity, and most amphibians dehydrate rapidly when exposed to dry conditions (however, see species account of the canyon treefrog). Terrestrial species lose water less rapidly than more aquatic ones.

When active, frogs tend to have higher body temperatures than salamanders. The earliest embryonic stages of amphibians are the most susceptible to death from overheating, but generally larvae are tolerant of higher temperatures than adults of the same species. Amphibian temperature tolerance increases to a certain degree from spring to summer. Tadpoles of lowland species tolerate higher temperatures than do species from cooler mountain climates.

Amphibians in temperate regions such as Colorado avoid the long cold winters and dry midday heat of summer by taking refuge in buffered microenvironments such as underground burrows, crevices beneath rocks, or bodies of water. The period of inactivity may last only several hours each day in summer, but in winter the animals may be confined to their hibernacula for five successive months or more.

Some amphibians are active early in the spring, when freezing nighttime temperatures are not uncommon. These amphibians generally breed in aquatic habitats and avoid freezing by submerging in the water. At least some of these species also can survive freezing weather even in relatively exposed sites on land. For example, the wood frog and western chorus frog overwinter beneath leaf litter, logs, and other surface objects. In some of these sites, the frogs may be subjected to subfreezing temperatures. Both species are able to survive the formation of ice within the body. Apparently, the blood and extracellular fluids freeze completely, whereas intracellular water remains unfrozen; hence cells are not damaged. Heartbeat and breathing cease in frozen frogs. After freezing, the tissues and urine of the frogs

contain elevated levels of glycerol and/or glucose, which may act as antifreeze or possibly prevent damage to temporarily frozen cells. Synthesis of these compounds apparently occurs in the liver only after exposure to subfreezing temperatures. In contrast to the wood frog and western chorus frog, the northern leopard frog, which overwinters underwater, and spade-foot toads and true toads, which spend winter in underground burrows, apparently cannot survive body freezing. Salamanders also are killed by internal freezing. Probably all Coloradan amphibians supercool a few degrees below 0°C without ice forming in the body and thus can survive some freezing conditions to which they may be exposed. Solutes in the blood reduce the freezing point in the same way that salt in water does.

Temperature has a great effect on the physiology and development of amphibians. In general, energy requirements are quite low, and amphibians can survive long periods without eating. Metabolic rate speeds up greatly with increasing temperature. Compared to mammals or birds, the metabolic rate of amphibians is quite low. For example, the metabolic rate of a warm 10-gram frog is only one-tenth that of a mammal of the same weight. The rate of embryonic and larval development and speed of locomotion (including frog jumping ability) also increase with rising temperature.

Because amphibian skin is moist and relatively well supplied with blood, it functions as a respiratory surface. Probably all amphibians obtain at least some of their oxygen through the skin. The lungs, the lining of the mouth, and the gills of larval stages also are respiratory tissues. Some salamanders (family Plethodontidae, not known to occur in Colorado) have no lungs and rely solely on the skin and mouth lining for oxygen exchange.

Amphibians and Water. Amphibians regain the water lost during terrestrial excursions by absorbing it through the skin while sitting in a pool of water or on damp soil. Water also is obtained from food. Amphibians do not drink in the usual sense. When submerged, they experience a problem opposite that they encounter on land.

Water constantly is absorbed through the skin and must be eliminated by producing large volumes of dilute urine.

Amphibians live almost exclusively in freshwater or terrestrial environments. All but a few are intolerant of saline conditions. The kidneys cannot produce hypertonic urine, in which solutes are more concentrated than in the blood. Nitrogen wastes are eliminated mostly as ammonia in larvae and aquatic species, mostly as less toxic urea in terrestrial species. A few arboreal tropical and subtropical frogs produce mostly uric acid. Urine flows into the cloaca first and then into the bladder. As a result of their ectothermy and poor resistance to dehydration, amphibians and their activities are greatly influenced by weather.

Senses. Most amphibians have good vision, though caecilians and some salamanders do not. The eye is focused by changing the position of the lens (as opposed to changing the shape of the lens in mammals). Color vision is poor or nonexistent. Eyelids are absent in larvae and in permanently aquatic species. In ranid frogs exposed to bright light at night, the pupil closes slowly, reaching minimum size after 10–20 minutes; it takes several hours to redilate.

Some amphibians are capable of extraoptic photoreception. The frontal organ and pineal body, located in the dermis between the eyes, act as photoreceptors. In some ranid frogs, neither the eyes nor the parapineal photoreceptors are essential for positive response to light. Extraoptic photoreceptors detect light but do not form an image. They are involved in color change, synchronization of daily activity patterns, and spatial orientation.

Amphibians have a dual sound-receptor system. A unique inner ear papilla acts as a low-frequency sound receptor. Sound is transmitted through the forelimb and shoulder girdle to the opercular bone and then to the inner ear. This system results in high sensitivity to ground vibrations. Frogs have an additional inner ear papilla (a forerunner of the cochlea of mammals) that is a high-frequency sound receptor. Sound travels from the eardrum (tympanum) to the columella (stapes) and then to the inner ear.

At least some amphibians also receive sound at the eardrum via the wall of the body next to the lung. Salamanders and caecilians have no tympanum or middle ear cavity and have poor hearing ability.

Olfaction (sense of smell and taste) is well developed in amphibians. Smell receptors are present in the nasal chambers. The vomeronasal (Jacobson's) organ (paired blind sacs opening into the nasal cavity and innervated by the olfactory nerve) function in chemoreception. Available evidence indicates that most or all species can detect food by odor alone. In experimental situations, *Bufo* toads and *Rana* frogs can recognize and orient to odors of their home pond water, even after a two-month absence.

A lateral-line organ, sensitive to motion, is present in aquatic forms.

Reproduction and Growth. The melting ice and snow and warming days of early spring hail the onset of the amphibian breeding season in Colorado. Beginning with the northern leopard frog and western chorus frog in March, breeding of various species may extend through August. Generally, the breeding season of each species is restricted to a rather short portion of the spring and summer months (some exceptions are described in the various species accounts). Breeding entails the aggregation of individuals in ponds, lakes, marshes, or other bodies of water. Generally, males are the first to arrive. In Colorado, all amphibians lay their eggs in the water, generally in warm, quiet shallows.

The fertilized eggs of amphibians (see introductory accounts of salamanders, frogs, and toads) initially develop within a string, sphere, or mass of jellylike mucoid material that absorbs water and swells after oviposition. The shell that envelops the eggs of reptiles and birds is absent, and placental connections between the mother and her developing young, such as those that occur in mammals and some reptiles, are lacking. The eggs, usually pigmented on the upper surface, are enclosed in spherical chambers within the jelly. The jelly, secreted by the oviduct, helps protect the ova from predation, injury, and fungi, and it also serves as a mechanism by which the eggs can be attached to various objects. Experiments have shown that the jelly capsule is necessary for successful fertilization. Enzymes secreted by the sperm head digest the jelly capsule.

After a few days or weeks, a tiny amphibian emerges from each egg and adopts an independent aquatic existence. At this point, the amphibian is called a larva (plural, larvae). None of the amphibians in Colorado are known to care for their eggs or offspring. Frog larvae have gills that become hidden internally soon after the larva hatches. The gills are supplied with oxygen carried by water passing into the mouth, through the gills, and out an opening called the spiracle. In Coloradan frogs, the spiracle is on the left side, except in the narrowmouth toad, in which it is ventral to the anus. Conspicuous limbs develop late in the larval stage, soon before metamorphosis.

Amphibian larvae in Colorado live in the water for weeks, months, or even a year or more, depending on the species. Eventually, they undergo a remarkable change called metamorphosis. During this process, which is controlled by thyroid hormones, the gills are resorbed (all amphibians, including those without an aquatic stage, have gills at some point during their development), eyelids develop, and the tail fin becomes smaller (tiger salamander) or entirely disappears (frogs). Frog larvae quickly develop strong limbs, and the small beaklike mouth is replaced by a wide, gaping mouth. The animal then becomes more amphibious or primar-ily terrestrial.

The reproductive tracts (gonads and associated ducts) of amphibians in Colorado exhibit seasonal cycles of activity and size, enlarging prior to breeding and shrinking after the breeding season. Fat bodies associated with the gonads provide fuel for reproduction. In Colorado, adult females of most or all species lay a maximum of one clutch of eggs per year (though the eggs of a clutch may not be laid in a single mass).

Feeding. Metamorphosed amphibians of all groups, as well as larval salamanders, eat invertebrates, and some species also eat small vertebrates. Larvae initially live off stored yolk in the gut before soon switching to exogenous foods (invertebrates for salamanders, minute organic material for frogs). Many amphibians depend on vision to detect and capture food, and movement of the prey often is an important stimulus for the feeding response. However, as previously mentioned, most or all species can detect food by odor alone, especially if they have previous experience with prey of that odor. The mouth parts of adult amphibians are adapted for grasping prey but not for chewing. Food typically is swallowed whole. Amphibian teeth generally are of the same size and shape throughout the mouth (homodont) and may be replaced several times during an individual's life. The tongue is best developed in land-dwelling species.

Predation and Mortality. Amphibians in a temperate climate such as Colorado's experience high mortality rates in the larval and juvenile stages, largely due to stresses posed by the physical environment. The vast majority of young die before reaching maturity, most in their first year. Predation sometimes takes a large toll. The predators of metamorphosed amphibians include a wide range of carnivorous vertebrates, and these, in addition to large predatory insects such as diving beetles and water bugs, also eat amphibian larvae.

Salamanders

Most salamanders (order Caudata) are four-legged, long-tailed amphibians. The vast majority are small, but an aquatic Japanese species sometimes exceeds 5 feet (1.5 m) in total length. The approximately 410 species inhabit much of the Northern Hemisphere, and one family ranges into the New World tropics as far as northern South America. About 150 species occur in the United States and Canada (Collins 1997). Salamanders exist in the fossil record as far back as the late Jurassic.

Salamanders differ from frogs in that fertilization of the eggs occurs inside the body of the female in most species, including all those in the western United States. The male deposits a small mound of jelly capped by a packet of sperm. The female picks up the sperm with the lips of her cloaca and stores the sperm in her body until the eggs are laid. One of the advantages of internal fertilization is that it allows flexibility in the choice of an egg-laying site. Because males need not be present when the eggs are deposited, females can more easily select conditions favorable for embryonic development. External fertilization occurs in some aquatic salamanders, such as the hellbender *(Cryptobranchus allegheniensis)* and sirens *(Siren* spp.) of the central and eastern United States. In contrast to frogs, salamanders breed in silence, and their courtship behavior often includes chemical communication. Depending on the species, salamander eggs may be laid on land or in the water (as in Colorado's single species).

MOLE SALAMANDERS
Family Ambystomatidae

Mole salamanders are a North American group comprising approximately 33 species, about half of which occur in the United States. Many of these broad-headed, stout-bodied salamanders are found in the eastern United States, but the family ranges from southeastern Alaska and Labrador south to southern Mexico. The Mexican axolotl, *Ambystoma mexicanum,* is one of the famous members of the family, but it does not occur in Colorado. Until recently, the eight species in the families Dicamptodon-tidae (giant salamanders) and Rhyacotri-tonidae (torrent salamanders) were included in this group. Two formerly recognized gynogenetic species are now regarded as hybrids not warranting species status. The largest species of mole salamander is the tiger salamander, sole representative of this family in Colorado.

Plate 7.1. Adult tiger salamander (Boulder County, Colorado).

Tiger Salamander
Ambystoma tigrinum (Green, 1825)

Recognition. Skin smooth, somewhat slimy; tail long; four toes on each forefoot; maximum TL about 34.6 cm. Color pattern ranges from black with yellowish bars or spots to pale or dark with dark spots or mottling (see "Taxonomy and Variation"). *Metamorphosed adult:* stocky, 11-14 costal grooves, head broad, eyes small, tubercles on bottom of feet. *Mature male:* large dark papillae posterior to vent during breeding season; tail relatively long. *Larvae:* hatchlings about 9-14 mm long, initially lack limbs; front limbs develop first, and hind limbs develop after larvae reach about 25 mm TL (Tanner, Fisher,

and Willis 1971); large larvae (usually less than 13 cm TL but up to 35 cm TL) have three conspicuous pairs of gills and four gill slits on each side of neck; tail fin extends forward to about shoulder region; variable coloration. *Eggs:* laid singly or in short rows or small clusters; egg 2–4 mm in diameter, brown on upper surface, surrounded by jelly covering of thin, dense inner coats and a thick soft outer coat; after oviposition, inner capsule surrounding egg liquefies, allowing egg to rotate.

Map 7.1. Distribution of the tiger salamander in Colorado.

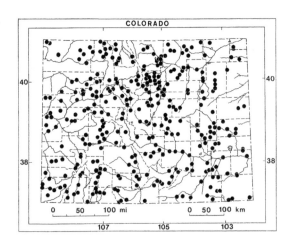

Plate 7.2. Adult tiger salamander (Jackson County, Colorado).

found that fish absence was the most important factor influencing tiger salamander presence in Gunnison County and vicinity, and Corn, Jennings, and Muths (1997) reported that trout and tiger salamanders rarely occur together in Rocky Mountain National Park. Trout and tiger salamanders do coexist in some lakes (Dartt 1879; Blair 1951), especially where vegetated shallows provide habitat not easily accessible to the fishes. Levi and Levi (1955) surmised that trout may conflict with paedomorphic salamanders but not with metamorphosing populations.

Some have suggested that breeding-pond acidification related to atmospheric pollution may cause periodic failure of tiger salamander reproduction in the mountains of Colorado (Harte and Hoffman 1989, 1994). Low pH, even if not fatal to salamander larvae, may result in reduced growth rates and ultimately could diminish salamander populations through decreased survival or feeding success (Kiesecker 1996). However, recent water chemistry data, together with information on acid tolerances of salamander larvae, suggest that eggs and embryos in the wild do not experience harmful levels of acidification (Corn, Stoltzenburg, and Bury 1989; Corn and Vertucci 1992; Wissinger and Whiteman 1992; Vertucci and Corn 1994).

Under certain conditions, larval populations may be vulnerable to bacterial infections associated with livestock grazing. In the mountains of Utah, Worthylake and Hovingh (1989) observed recurrent mass mortality of larvae associated a bacterial infection and suggested that increased nitrogen levels due in part to sheep grazing may have been involved. Bryant (1995) observed a mass mortality event in the summer of 1993 that appeared to be associated with an opportunistically pathogenic bacterium. In Arizona, similar die-offs, apparently associated with bacterial pathogens, have

Distribution. Southern Canada from British Columbia to Manitoba, Great Lakes region, and southern New York south to southwestern United States, central Mexico, and U.S. Gulf Coast. Occurs throughout Colorado at elevations up to about 12,000 feet (3,660 m) in the southwestern mountains.

Conservation Status. Tiger salamanders occur throughout their historical range in Colorado. They remain easy to find and locally abundant in suitable habitat statewide. Ponds often contain up to several thousand larvae. Recent surveys found no evidence of significant declines in distribution or abundance (Corn, Stoltzberg, and Bury 1989; Hammerson 1989a, 1992; Corn, Jennings, and Muths 1997). A local decline in numbers over several years, reported by Harte and Hoffman (1989), turned out to be a temporary fluctuation from which the population subsequently recovered (Wissinger and Whiteman 1992). Hovingh (1986) reported that tiger salamanders remain quite common in aquatic systems in glaciated portions of the Uinta Mountains in northeastern Utah. The widespread creation of small, fishless artificial bodies of water has provided much suitable habitat where previously there was little, and these salamanders have been quick to colonize it (Norris 1973; pers. obs.).

Many mountain lakes formerly inhabited by tiger salamanders now have few or none of these amphibians due to the stocking of trout, which easily consume and deplete the larval populations (e.g., Blair 1951; pers. obs.). Geraghty and Willey (1992)

been reported (Pfennig, Loeb, and Collins 1991). Cannibal morphs seemed particularly vulnerable, probably due to their feeding on diseased larvae. Again, fecal contamination of ponds by introduced livestock was suggested as a possible cause of the fatal outbreaks. In contrast to these reports, larvae sometimes do thrive in large numbers in manure-laden ponds in Colorado (see "Habitat"). Nevertheless, die-offs of larvae, apparently associated with pathogenic bacteria, have been observed in Colorado. In 1991 in a pool on Grand Mesa, Delta County, I saw two 8-cm-TL larvae swimming upside down, which was associated with the presence of air in the intestines and probably caused by bacterial infection. Whether fecal contamination by livestock was involved is unknown.

In view of the recent plethora of news reports of amphibians having extra limbs, I note that Bishop and Hamilton (1947) found 19 tiger salamanders (17 larvae and 2 adults) with extra digits and limbs in Muskee Lake in Boulder County in 1946 and 1947. Such malformities appear to be rare in Colorado tiger salamanders.

Habitat. Tiger salamanders occur in virtually any habitat within their elevational range, provided there is a suitable body of water nearby for breeding. They inhabit ponds, lakes, and impoundments ranging in size from a few meters in diameter to several acres. Suitable habitat in the mountains includes the clear waters of lakes, glacial kettle ponds, and beaver ponds, though many beaver ponds with cold flowing water are devoid of salamanders (Burger 1950).

In some areas, the salamanders occur in abundance in sewage sedimentation ponds and turbid ponds badly polluted with cattle manure (Smith, Maslin, and Brown 1965). Tiger salamanders are most common in permanent or semipermanent ponds, but they also use ephemeral ponds that may appear and disappear as moisture conditions change over a period of years (Costello 1969:171–172; Carter 1992). Many inhabit small, human-dug ponds. Vegetation may or may not be present in the water. Sunny, mud-bottomed ponds at least 18–24 inches (46–61 cm) deep with a shallow beachlike shore seem to be preferred (Reese 1969). Tiger salamanders generally are scarce or absent in waters inhabited by predatory fishes (Burger 1950; Willey 1980; Corn, Jennings, and Muths 1997), bullfrogs, turtles, and crayfish (Reese 1969), though I found many large larvae in a small Boulder County lake that contained abundant crayfish (*Cambarus diogenes,* possibly introduced in this lake).

Tiger salamanders in Colorado tolerate a wide range of water temperatures, ranging from near freezing to above 30°C. Depending on their habitat, they generally do not tolerate water temperatures above about 36–39°C, with mountain salamanders being the least heat tolerant (Delson and Whitford 1973). Feder et al. (1982) reported that temperatures of larvae in Colorado in August ranged from 13–26°C. In the mountains, large numbers of larvae often aggregate in sun-warmed shallows under cover of shoreline vegetation. When the shallows cool at night, larvae move into deeper water (Prosser 1911; Heath 1975; pers. obs). Tiger salamanders in ponds sometimes form dense aggregations of hundreds of individuals independent of where the warmest temperatures are (Willey 1990).

Plate 7.3. Vent region of adult male tiger salamander (Hinsdale County, Colorado).

Metamorphosed salamanders usually spend the winter in rodent burrows, which are important retreats in summer as well. In eastern Colorado, winter retreats often are on gentle slopes south of the breeding ponds (Reese 1969). Vaughan (1961) reported numerous instances of tiger salamanders using burrows still occupied by pocket gophers in eastern Colorado, and on Grand Mesa he saw an adult burrowing into a freshly plugged pocket gopher burrow in July. Costello (1969) mentioned the use of prairie-dog burrows. It may be no coincidence that the largest salamander populations often are in ponds with evidence of substantial nearby populations of burrowing rodents. Salamanders sometimes dig their own burrows in loose soil or hide in moist crevices in dried mud but do not overwinter in these shallow temporary shelters. Tiger salamanders sometimes appear in old cellars, old wells, and basement window wells in residential areas near breeding ponds, and these sites may be used for hibernation. Sometimes they occur in caves in Colorado (Parris 1973).

Activity. Metamorphosed adults are active primarily from March through November. Larvae also are most active at this time but may be observed year-round on some pond bottoms if viewing conditions are suitable. Terrestrial activity occurs primarily at night, though salamanders may be abroad during daylight hours in wet weather. Spring and summer rains often stimulate aboveground activity by metamorphosed adults. Larvae appear to be mainly diurnal, moving about in shallow, sunny areas. When startled, they quickly swim for deep water or into thick vegetation; sometimes they attempt to burrow into the substrate, frequently coming to rest with only the head hidden. The larvae often surface briefly to breathe air, particularly in warm water with low oxygen availability. In hand, both larvae and metamorphosed individuals sometimes produce soft vocal sounds.

Metamorphosed adult tiger salamanders in Colorado sometimes exhibit certain apparent defensive postures when closely approached by a person (or, presumably, a potential predator). The posture involves flexing the head downward and raising the tail, which may be undulated or lashed. These postures make it likely that a predator will contact the distasteful secretions of the integumentary poison glands. When probed with my finger, two adults (95–110 mm SVL) found on land at night in rainy weather in Morgan and Pueblo counties quickly curled the tail forward and over the head. Both produced sticky skin secretions and smelled of roasted nuts (much like spadefoot toads). During a rainstorm, Livo (pers. comm.) observed several salamanders assuming a similar posture as vehicles passed over them on a busy highway in eastern Colorado. Parallel behavior has been observed in tiger salamanders in Missouri (D. Smith 1985).

Reproduction and Growth. In spring, adult tiger salamanders leave their winter retreats and migrate distances of up to several hundred meters to their breeding ponds. Migrations in the plains region often occur during or after rains once daytime temperatures have warmed to about 10°C (Reese 1969). Migrations may be interrupted by dry, windy weather. In the mountains, movements to the breeding ponds may occur anytime from April to July, depending on when winter ice and snow melt (Hamilton 1949; Reese 1969). In the mountains of Gunnison County (9,200–11,500 feet [2,800–3,500 m]), breeding ponds become free of ice between late May and mid-July (Sexton and Bizer 1978). Males generally arrive at the ponds before females. Breeding aggregations may include a few or up to several hundred adults. In Colorado, breeding individuals probably are at least in their third calendar year. Typically, salamanders breed in the same pond from year to year, but individual adults may not breed every year.

Mating activity occurs underwater. Courtship consists of a period of nuzzling and butting, at the conclusion of which the male deposits a spermatophore, a cone of jelly with a small packet of sperm at its tip. The spermatophore, the jelly of which is produced by glands that open into the cloaca, is attached to some object in the water. The female picks up the sperm with the lips of her cloacal opening and stores it

Plate 7.4. Eggs of tiger salamander (La Plata County, Colorado). *Lauren Livo and Steve Wilcox.*

temporarily in a structure that opens into her cloaca. Fertilization occurs as the eggs pass through her cloaca just before they are laid. If the female has picked up sperm from more than one male, the offspring from one clutch of eggs could have multiple fathers.

Typically, a female lays her eggs within two days of picking up a spermatophore (Anderson 1970; Wilbur 1977). The female, unaccompanied by the male, attaches the eggs to vegetation or other objects about 5–25 cm below the surface of the water (Hamilton 1949; Reese 1969). The jelly of eggs from clear mountain ponds sometimes contains symbiotic green algae that consume carbon dioxide produced by the embryos and supplies them with oxygen when light is available. Clutch size varies with the size of the female; larger females lay up to 1,000 eggs. Norris (1973) found that females from a pond in Boulder County contained an average of 414 eggs.

In the Great Plains, eggs may be laid from mid-March to mid-August (Reese 1969). In the mountains, oviposition occurs from April (Hamilton 1949) through early August, with the latest clutches being laid at the highest elevations. Egg-laying occurs from mid-April to at least mid-June in much of western Colorado (Reese 1969). However, in a given pond or region, the period of egg-laying may more restricted. At 5,600 feet (1,700 m) in Boulder County, spawning takes place from March through May (Norris 1989). In the mountains of Gunnison and Pitkin counties, eggs are laid from late May through at least late July and probably early August (Sexton and Bizer 1978; Wissinger and Whiteman 1992). Small larvae less than 5 cm TL often coexist with much larger ones in mountain ponds in late August (pers. obs.). Breeding season in a pond may vary from year to year, depending on when suitable conditions exist. In Colorado, this may be most characteristic of the drier lower elevations, where water may be available in early spring and then again after summer rains. Late-season breed-

ing also has been observed in adjacent states (Tanner, Fisher, and Willis 1971; Allison, Brunkow, and Collins 1994). As is typical of pond-breeding salamanders, the eggs receive no parental care.

After breeding, metamorphosed salamanders in the mountains may leave the ponds for the terrestrial portion of their home range for the summer, fall, and winter, or they may not return to land until late summer (Reese 1969; Heath 1975; Whiteman, Wissinger, and Bohonak 1994). In the mountains of Gunnison County, movements of breeders from their breeding ponds to land or to other ponds (usually from permanent to semipermanent waters) and movements of nonbreeders into ponds occur during rainy periods in July and early August (Whiteman, Wissinger, and Bohonak 1994). Metamorphosed adults commonly are found in mountain ponds through at least late August (pers. obs.). Adults in the Great Plains frequently spend the summer in the water of their breeding ponds. Staying in aquatic habitats in the summer allows the salamanders to avoid the usually dry, harsh conditions that characterize terrestrial environments in both lowland and mountainous areas of Colorado.

Eggs hatch 2–5 weeks after being laid, taking the longest in the coolest mountain ponds (Sexton and Bizer 1978). In the mountains of Gunnison County, hatchlings first appear as early as late June in some ponds and not until late August in others (Sprules 1972; Sexton and Bizer 1978). Larvae develop large lungs fairly early, allowing habitation of water with little oxygen.

The length of the larval period varies greatly. Sexually immature larvae may metamorphose before their first winter, 2–5 months after hatching. This occurs commonly at low elevations and in warmer mountain ponds. Mass migrations of the newly metamorphosed salamanders from plains breeding ponds commonly take place on rainy nights in August but may extend through November if conditions are favorable (Reese 1969). Metamorphosis typically happens in August in the mountains. Salamanders sometimes leave the ponds before metamorphosis is complete, especially when drying of the ponds stimulates the animals to begin metamorphosis earlier than usual (Reese 1969). These salamanders often have short gill stubs and open branchial slits. On

a road in the San Luis Valley, Hahn (1968) found a metamorph (52 mm SVL) with traces of gills remaining in early August.

Size at metamorphosis is highly variable. Reese (1969) reported that metamorphosis occurs at an average size of 131 mm TL and 74 mm SVL, whereas Roth, Roth, and Smith (1991) found a gill-less metamorph, lacking gill clefts, only 57 mm TL (36 mm SVL). In the mountains of Gunnison County, size at metamorphosis averaged 54–83 mm SVL in several different ponds (Sexton and Bizer 1978). Four metamorphic individuals with short gill stubs found in Saguache and San Miguel counties were 88–90 mm SVL and 155–180 mm TL; larger fully gilled larvae were present in the same ponds (pers. obs.). In western Texas, metamorphosis occurs at 10–14 cm SVL (Kenney and Rose 1974).

Some tiger salamanders do not metamorphose until they are one or two years old. This delayed metamorphosis takes place in cool mountain ponds, in plains ponds where egg-laying occurred late in summer, and

Plate 7.5. Larval tiger salamander (Weld County, Colorado).

Plate 7.6. Larval tiger salamander (Jackson County, Colorado).

Plate 7.7. Sexually mature larval tiger salamander (Boulder County, Colorado).

even in ponds adjacent to those in which salamanders metamorphosed before their first winter (Sprules 1972; DeBoer 1973; Rodda 1975). Larvae overwinter in the ponds below the ice. In the mountains, they metamorphose and leave the ponds from late July to early September. In some ponds, there seems to be a two-year interval between the production of significant numbers of metamorphs, apparently because the older larvae eat most of the younger larvae before the former metamorphose at an age of just over two years.

Larvae sometimes become sexually mature before metamorphosis and begin breeding when 1–2 years old, never having left the water. This phenomenon, called paedomorphosis or neoteny, seemingly occurs rather haphazardly but of course requires permanent or nearly permanent ponds. As in Arizona (Collins 1981), paedomorphic larvae in Colorado may occur at both high and low elevations and in the same ponds as, or in ponds adjacent to, those containing nonpaedomorphic larvae. Large sexually mature male larvae may court and mate with metamorphosed females. In Gunnison County, Whiteman (1997) found that males were more likely to become paedomorphic and females were more likely to metamorphose. Paedomorphic males breed more frequently than do metamorphosed males. Paedomorphic males apparently tolerate lower levels of food resources in permanent ponds but maximize their mating opportunities by their consistent presence in breeding areas, whereas females that metamorphose and are able to move to temporary ponds experience enhanced nutrition that may help support energy-expensive egg production (see "Food and Predation"). In Texas, morphs of two sizes have been observed among larvae, with one metamorphosing readily at a small size and the other metamorphosing at a large size and often becoming sexually mature in the larval stage (Rose and Armentrout 1976). Paedomorphosis has been attributed to low pond temperature (Bizer 1978), pond depth, and vulnerability to drying or freezing solid (Sprules 1972), and to the nature of the bottom of the pond (soft versus rocky) (DeBoer 1973), but much work remains to be done before we can explain fully this intriguing phenomenon.

Breeding success in a given pond may vary with fluctuations in climate. During droughts, drying of breeding ponds sometimes results in mass mortality of the larvae before they can metamorphose. In the mountains, deep snow in some years may block light from ponds, resulting in oxygen depletion and death of larvae (Bradford 1993; Vertucci and Corn 1994). In western Colorado, Carter (1992) found that larval tiger salamanders in some ponds are killed when ponds dry in summer. In other ponds, larvae do not survive the winter. Some pond basins that are dry in summer may contain water and larvae the following year.

Food and Predators. The tiger salamander has small teeth along the edge of the upper and lower jaws and across the roof of the mouth. Prey capture involves a quick lunge and snap of the jaws. The tongue of the adult is broad and fleshy but does not play an important role in food capture. Food items held in the jaws are maneuvered down the throat by jerky motions of the head, by pushing the projecting end of the prey against some object, or by actions of the tongue. The salamander may shake the prey in its jaws or walk backward as it begins to swallow. Tiger salamanders can detect and locate food by using either vision or sense of smell (Lindquist and Bachmann 1982).

In the water, metamorphosed salamanders eat snails, copepods, cladocerans, fairy shrimp, bugs, beetles, and the larval stages of mayflies, dragonflies, caddisflies, midges, and other insects. In Gunnison County, metamorphosed adults in permanent ponds eat mainly bottom-dwelling aquatic insects such as caddisflies, hemipterans, beetles, and chironomids, as well as terrestrial insects that fall into the water (Whiteman, Wissinger, and Bohonak 1994). In nonpermanent ponds, fairy shrimp *(Branchinecta coloradensis)* may dominate the diet (Whiteman, Wissinger, and Bohonak 1994; Whiteman, Wissinger, and Brown 1996). In fact, after breeding, metamorphosed adults selectively move to nonpermanent ponds containing the easy-to-catch fairy shrimp and depart the ponds when fairy shrimp populations decline or disappear. These ponds also tend to have fewer salamander larvae, which lessens competition for food resources. The stomachs of adults found on land often are empty (Reese 1969), but the diet includes just about any small animal that can be captured and swallowed, though very tiny animals generally are ignored.

Larvae feed opportunistically on aquatic invertebrates and some small vertebrates (primarily the eggs and larvae of amphibians, including tiger salamander) (e.g., Norris 1989). Small larvae in Gunnison County may focus on phantom midge pupae and large zooplankton such as water fleas (cladocerans), copepods, and larval midges (Chironomidae) (Dodson and Dodson 1971; Sprules 1972). Large larvae eat just about anything they can catch and swallow, including snails, large zooplankton, fairy shrimp, amphipods, aquatic insect larvae, diving beetles, leeches, tadpoles of mountain toad and northern leopard frog, amphibian eggs, and smaller salamander larvae (Burger 1950; Reese 1969; Koerwitz 1973). In Gunnison County, Whiteman, Wissinger, and Brown (1996) found that paedomorphic larvae feeding on prey other than fairy shrimp (not available in permanent ponds) grow more slowly than do metamorphosed

individuals that were to able to feed on the easily captured fairy shrimp in nonpermanent ponds. In Boulder County, Norris (1989) found one paedomorphic larva that had eaten 44 tiger salamander eggs. Feeding may occur on the bottom or while the larvae are suspended or swim anywhere within the water column (buoyed by their lungs) (Lannoo and Bachmann 1984a), including just beneath the surface in daytime. Benthic feeding may involve pushing the mouth into soft bottom substrates. Hungry larvae are not averse to biting a baited fishing hook.

Cannibalism occurs frequently among the larvae, especially where hatchlings coexist with older larvae. Cannibalistic larvae may undergo moderate to pronounced morphological changes (Reese 1969, 1975; Snow 1978; Pedersen 1991). The body may increase in bulk and length, the head may double in width to 65 mm, the teeth in the roof of the mouth and in the lower jaw may disproportionately increase in length and number, and the lateral line system may become hypertrophied. The longest known tiger salamander from Colorado was a cannibal measuring 34.6 cm TL. The heaviest was a Boulder County cannibal with a mass of 434 g (Snow 1978). These impressive, massive cannibals may be either male or female, but the females have enlarged cloacal glands and externally resemble males. The cannibalistic morph has been found in Colorado and in several adjacent states (Collins and Holomuzki 1984) at both high and low elevations. Broad-headed cannibals usually are found in paedomorphic populations, which provide a continual supply of high-quality food (smaller salamander larvae, which dominate the diet). They exhibit high growth rates (Lannoo and Bachmann 1984b) and possibly may metamorphose earlier than their noncannibal cohorts, an advantage in ponds that may be drying. After they metamorphose, they eventually become rather ordinary-looking salamanders. Pierce and Mitton (1980) found no evidence of genetic differentiation between paedomorphic and metamorphosing salamanders, and there is evidence that diet and larval density contribute to the development of the cannibal morphological traits that appear in certain *Ambystoma* larvae (Powers 1907; Collins and Cheek 1983; Walls, Belanger, and Blaustein 1993).

Tiger salamanders can tolerate severe physiological hardship when unable to eat or drink or access moisture. Adults from Wyoming tolerated water losses of up to 35–40 percent of their initial body mass (Romspert and McClanahan 1981).

Known predators of the tiger salamander in Colorado include the raccoon *(Procyon lotor);* coyote *(Canis latrans);* aquatic turtles; western terrestrial garter snake; plains garter snake; bullfrog; fishes such as cutthroat trout *(Oncorhynchus clarki),* other trouts, and bass *(Micropterus* spp.); American white pelican *(Pelecanus erythrorhynchos);* ring-billed gull *(Larus delawarensis);* black-crowned night heron *(Nycticorax nycticorax);* green heron *(Butorides virescens);* snowy egret *(Egretta thula);* American kestrel *(Falco sparverius);* ducks; common raven *(Corvus corax)* (I saw one tear off the front half of a metamorphosed individual and eat it); crayfish; and giant water bug *(Lethocerus americanus)* (Reese 1969; D. Langlois, pers. comm.; D. and J. Ward, pers. comm.; pers. obs.). Doubtless they are taken by various other water birds, carnivores, and invertebrate predators, including adult and larval diving beetles (*Dytiscus* spp.), which easily prey on small amphibian larvae. Holomuzki (1986) found that larvae in Arizona retreat to deeper water at night, when diving beetles are active in shallow areas. Ballinger, Lynch, and Cole (1979) reported heavy predation by the plains garter snake in western Nebraska.

Aquatic salamanders in all stages sometimes are parasitized by leeches. On Grand Mesa, I found a fully gilled 12-cm-long larva on the shore of a lake. Apparently, the salamander was attempting to rid itself of the several leeches attached to its neck and belly. Metamorphosed adults found by Michelle King (pers. comm.) in a pond in Park County in early July were heavily infested with large leeches on the underside.

Remarks. Rogers (1985) examined Pleistocene remains of tiger salamanders in the San Luis Valley and found that paedo-

morphic populations were associated with older deposits representing warmer waters with few fishes, whereas younger deposits contained primarily metamorphosing salamanders and trout.

H. M. Smith (1990) described the interesting life of Robert Reese, who contributed greatly to our knowledge of the tiger salamander in Colorado.

Taxonomy and Variation. The tiger salamander exhibits fascinating and bewildering patterns of color variation in our area. The broad geographic patterns of color variation are as follows. Specimens from the Great Plains region (subspecies *mavortium*) usually have yellowish or greenish bars or spots on a dark background; spotted individuals are more common in southeastern Colorado, whereas the barred pattern is more common in areas to the north. Adult tiger salamanders in North Park, Middle Park, and northwestern Colorado (south to the Grand Junction area) generally have black spots or irregular blotches on a dark gray to dark cream (usually dark olive) background. Reese (1972) assigned these to the subspecies *melanostictum.* In the remainder of western and central Colorado, where subspecies *nebulosum* is represented (Reese 1972), metamorphosed adults are uniformly dark gray or dark brown, or have a reticulation of black spots or an intermingling of different shades of brown on a dark background, or have evenly dispersed round black spots on a plain gold or olive background. Clearly, the subspecies *melanostictum* and *nebulosum* are hard to differentiate on this basis, and, unfortunately, better criteria for distinguishing these taxa are not available in the literature.

Color variation in *nebulosum* (and probably in other subspecies) is to some degree influenced by the environment (Fernandez and Collins 1988). Though each individual appears to have a unique color pattern, coloration can change relatively quickly (over 2–3 hours) as the skin pigment aggregates or disperses, depending on the color of the salamander's surroundings, or it may change gradually throughout an individual's life as the number of chromatophores and amount of pigment vary in response to changes in the environment and as part of the normal aging process (metamorphosed adults tend to become paler as they grow older) (Fernandez and Collins 1988).

Unusual color patterns are not uncommon in our area. These local variations sometimes make it difficult to categorize tiger salamanders according to subspecies. Smith and Reese (1970) found atypical salamanders mixed with normal ones in ponds in northeastern Colorado. The atypical individuals included larvae with light-centered dark spots and a golden sheen. After metamorphosis, the atypical specimens had round dark spots on a light background or small light spots on a dark background; metamorphosis occurred at a larger size than in normal specimens. Transportation of larvae from one area as fishing bait or through water diversions probably accounts for some of the unusual color pattern variations observed in Colorado (though this may not apply to the example just mentioned).

These various color patterns grade into one another in some areas. Intermediates between the typical *mavortium* and *nebulosum* patterns are especially evident across a rather broad area along the eastern Rocky Mountains in southern and central Wyoming and in central Colorado, including the San Luis Valley and South Park (Dunn 1940; Reese 1972; Kocher 1986). Considering the apparently broad area of intergradation (based on color pattern variation), the ranges of these two subspecies should not be characterized as meeting abruptly along a very narrow contact zone (compare Collins, Mitton, and Pierce 1980; Pierce and Mitton 1980). However, differing concepts of the variability within each subspecies may lead to different conclusions on the geographic relationships of the two taxa.

Pierce and Mitton (1980) addressed the relationship between *mavortium* and *nebulosum* by examining enzymatic variability in 17 populations: 14 in Colorado, 2 in New Mexico, and 1 in Texas. They found that significant genetic changes occurred across the Front Range in the area of *mavortium-nebulosum* intergradation as defined by Reese (1972). However, the pattern of variation was rather complicated. In a principal components analysis, some samples from the mountains clustered with samples closer to the plains near Boulder (i.e., closer to *mavortium*) than with other mountain *(nebulosum)* samples. Samples from within the range of *mavortium* in Colorado more closely resembled samples from within the range of *nebulosum* than those from within the range of *mavortium* in Texas. Significant genetic differences occurred even among closely adjacent ponds within a very small area on the Enchanted Mesa in Boulder; some of these populations were genetically less similar to each other than they were to populations near Ward, high in the mountains to the west, or near Limon, in the Great Plains far to the east. Though these results could be interpreted as consistent with the hypothesis of intergradation between and conspecificity of *mavortium* and *nebulosum*, Pierce and Mitton (1980) emphasized the general pattern of genetic differences between populations of *mavortium* and *nebulosum*, and Collins, Mitton, and Pierce (1980) even cautiously suggested the possibility that *mavortium* and *nebulosum* may be different species.

Some of the difficult-to-explain patterns of variation found by Pierce and Mitton (1980) may result from artifacts. For example, some samples may have encompassed only a small part of the variation actually present in a population, and other samples perhaps were genetically "contaminated" by salamanders introduced from other areas by humans. Subsequent studies by Kocher (1986) and Jones and Collins (1992) demonstrated that clinal genetic continuity exists between subspecies *mavortium* and *nebulosum* in a broad zone across southern Colorado and along an interdigitating contact zone in New Mexico.

A study of mitochondrial DNA (mtDNA) variation in the tiger salamander complex by Shaffer and McKnight (1996) found low levels of genetic differentiation over vast geographic areas. One interesting finding from a Colorado perspective was that two populations from the San Juan Mountains of Conejos and San Juan counties in

Colorado stood significantly apart from all others sampled in the Rocky Mountains and Great Plains. Unfortunately, few samples from the region were studied and no morphological correlations were described, so the geographic extent of this entity, which could be a distinct species, remains unknown. The apparent uniqueness of the San Juan Mountains population may result from genetic contamination by introduced salamanders. Elsewhere in Colorado and adjoining areas, populations exhibited extremely little divergence. There was no indication that the recognized subspecies in the Rocky Mountains and Great Plains represent distinct evolutionary lineages (monophyletic entities). Irschick and Shaffer (1997) examined morphological variation in larvae of 60 populations of four subspecies of *A. tigrinum* and found that subspecies *mavortium, nebulosum,* and *melanostictum* are almost indistinguishable from one another.

In view of all of the morphological and allozyme data, I believe that for now, all tiger salamanders in Colorado are best regarded as conspecific, though the taxonomic status of the San Juan Mountains population requires further study. Most of the results described in the preceding paragraphs suggest that the existing subspecific nomenclature for tiger salamanders is inade-quate and inappropriate for characterizing the geographic pattern of variation in Colorado and elsewhere in the region. These subspecies have been distinguished on the basis of postmetamorphic color pattern, but color pattern may be influenced strongly by natural selection in different environments and may not be concordant with certain genetic patterns of variation (Kocher 1986). More comprehensive genetic and morphological analyses are needed before a phylogenetically coherent taxonomic arrangement can be devised. In the meantime, it seems appropriate to avoid the use of subspecific names for tiger salamanders in Colorado.

There is some question as to whether tiger salamanders of eastern North America (subspecies *tigrinum*) are conspecific with those in Colorado and elsewhere in central and western North America. The issue revolves around the relationship between populations usually assigned to the eastern subspecies *tigrinum* and those assigned to the Great Plains subspecies *mavortium.* The mtDNA data of Shaffer and McKnight (1996) indicate that *tigrinum* represents one of several (weakly) differentiated groups in the *A. tigrinum* complex. However, existing data (Kocher 1986; Routman 1993) show that *tigrinum* and *mavortium* clearly exhibit genetic continuity over a broad zone of 50–100 km (Kocher's data encompass southeastern Nebraska and adjacent Iowa and Missouri). Irschick and Shaffer (1997) examined larval morphology and found relatively little phenotypic differentiation. Nevertheless, Shaffer and McKnight (1996) and Irschick and Shaffer (1997) supported the view that subspecies *tigrinum* is not the same species as the tiger salamanders of the central and western United States, based largely on the maintained historical integrity of the subspecies away from the hybrid zone and on the authors' acceptance of the phylogenetic species concept, which focuses on the evolutionary history of differentiated entities and minimizes the importance of hybridization. Irschick and Shaffer (1997:44) did acknowledge the problem of the broad zone of intergradation/ hybridization between subspecies *tigrinum* and *mavortium,* describing the classification of these populations as "a vexing and largely unresolved issue." If these taxa are not conspecific, then the eastern tiger salamander retains the name *Ambystoma tigrinum,* whereas tiger salamanders in Colorado and elsewhere in the central and western United States and southern Canada become *Ambystoma mavortium* Baird 1850 (except in California, where *A. californiense,* formerly included in *A. tigrinum,* occurs). However, I interpret existing data as showing that *mavortium* and *tigrinum* are conspecific, and thus I continue to regard the species in Colorado as *A. tigrinum.*

Frogs and Toads

Frogs and toads (order Anura) are tailless amphibians (as adults) with elongate hind limbs. There is no technical distinction between frogs and toads; *frog* can be used as a general term for both the smooth-skinned jumpers commonly known by that name and the warty-skinned hoppers known as toads. The features associated with excellent jumping ability in many species include lengthy hind limbs with elongate ilia (hip bones). Ranid frogs and treefrogs (hylids) are among the best jumpers, often covering 1 m or more in a single leap, whereas *Bufo* toads make only short jumps of about 4–5 body lengths, though they are rather tireless hoppers. The urostyle (a section of fused tail vertebrae), hidden between the long hip bones, is a unique characteristic of anurans.

The evolution of most groups of frogs was closely associated with the history of the southern Mesozoic supercontinent Gondwanaland. *Triadobatrachus* (order Proanura) of the lower Triassic of Madagascar may represent a sister group of the anurans. *Vieraella* of the early Jurassic in Argentina is the earliest known frog.

Today frogs have a nearly worldwide distribution, being absent only from the extreme northern part of the globe, Antarctica, and some isolated islands. They are most diverse in the tropics. Globally, there are approximately 4,200 species, of which about 95 occur in the United States and Canada, with 17 inhabiting Colorado.

Frogs are notable for their often conspicuous mating behavior. With the exception of one species (mountain toad), breeding aggregations of frogs in Colorado are easy to locate because the males mark their arrival with loud vocalizations. Often several frog species may call simultaneously from one pond, and the resulting chorus can be oppressively loud to a human in their midst. Inflatable pouches that lie under the skin of the throat or neck, and the eardrums in at least the bullfrog, act as sound resonators. The sacs are inflated with air from the lungs, which enters through one or two tiny openings in the mouth cavity. Frequent calling is an energy-expensive activity that results in a huge increase in the frog's metabolic rate. Each species gives a distinctive call that attracts females of the same species and, in some species, functions in male-male territorial or dominance interactions. The male's advertisement call is made with the mouth closed (some frogs produce an open-mouthed distress scream). In some species, different parts of the call have different functions. In chorus frogs *(Pseudacris),* the pulse repetition rate is the only component necessary for females to distinguish between the calls of closely related species.

The hearing of female frogs is tuned to the calls of their own species. However, this does not mean that the frogs cannot hear certain other sounds outside the frequency range of the call. The eardrums are critical for females attempting to locate males. This can be demonstrated by applying grease to one of the female's eardrums. Greased females hop around in circles, whereas ungreased females orient toward calling males with high precision.

In some species, such as bullfrogs, territorial male frogs can recognize particular individuals by differences in their calls. Bullfrog males are more likely to move toward or attack strangers than adjacent territory holders (with whom they already have established a dominance relationship).

In frogs, mating begins when a female that is ready to breed approaches a male. He immediately pounces on her and clasps his front legs around her waist (spadefoots) or chest (other Colorado frogs). The pair is then said to be in amplexus, which may last several hours. Sometimes a male clasps another male who comes too close. He realizes his mistake by the relatively slender (not egg-laden) body and distinctive protest or release calls and vibrations of the clasped male, which is soon freed. Release calls can be evoked by grasping a male toad in an amplexuslike way; the response may wane after the breeding season is over. Sometimes, males amplex frogs of other species or inanimate objects that bump into them. Males cling tenaciously to receptive females, which generally are larger than the males. Dark, nonslip pads on one or more inner digits of the forelimbs help them grip the slippery females. The pads represent highly keratinized patches of modified mucous glands.

Mature male frogs generally also are characterized by robust forelimbs and loose, dark-colored throat/neck skin. Males of some species (e.g., wood frogs, spadefoot toads) swim around when calling and may search actively for females. Male toads and spadefoots sometimes wrestle each other and attempt to displace other amplexing males.

Frogs native to Colorado lay their eggs in water. As the female deposits her eggs, the male sheds sperm over them while embracing her. Afterward, the male and female go their separate ways. The externally fertilized eggs (characteristic of all but a few frog species worldwide) are left to develop on their own. Most North American frogs lay their eggs in the water, but quite diverse egg-laying behavior occurs in various tropical and subtropical species.

Males of many frog species have rudimentary oviducts (Mullerian ducts) as adults. They are often quite well developed in the northern leopard frog *(Rana pipiens)*. A few African frogs are able to change sex from female to male.

For the most part, metamorphosed frogs eat invertebrates. The tongue of metamorphosed anurans, especially toads of the genus *Bufo,* is often highly adapted for capturing such prey. It is attached at the front of the mouth, and the free rear portion can be flipped rapidly forward. The tip of the tongue may be coated with a sticky substance derived from the intermaxillary gland in the roof of the mouth. A quick flip of the sticky-tipped tongue secures the prey. Some species use the forelimbs to push food into the throat. When swallowing, frogs often depress their eyeballs, causing them to bulge into the mouth cavity, which helps push food down the throat. Teeth are present in the upper jaw of many frogs, but true toads *(Bufo)* have no teeth. Frogs generally assimilate a high proportion (two-thirds or more) of the calories they ingest.

The feeding apparatus of larval frogs differs greatly from that of adults. Tadpoles of most species have horny, beaklike mouthparts and rows of denticles. Larvae of most species feed indiscriminately on material suspended in the water or graze on the pond bottom on submerged objects, ingesting bacteria, diatoms, cyanobacteria, green algae, protozoa, microscopic arthropods, their own fecal pellets, and a wide variety of organic and inorganic debris. Sometimes larvae feed on animal carcasses. The larvae of spadefoots occasionally are cannibalistic. During metamorphosis, the long, coiled gut of frog larvae, adapted for a basically vegetarian diet, changes to a relatively short and simple one adequate for the carnivorous diet of adults.

SPADEFOOT TOADS AND RELATIVES
Family Pelobatidae

The 90 living species are terrestrial/fossorial and occur in North America, Europe, western Asia, northern Africa, southeastern Asia, and Indonesia, though the number of species and geographic range of Pelobatidae are more restricted by some definitions of the family. The species in Asia and Indonesia bear little resemblance to those occurring in North America. This section focuses on characteristics of the six North American species, four of which inhabit Colorado.

Spadefoots have "cat eyes," with vertically elliptical pupils that may open to a rounded shape in darkness. Some species have a boss (lump) between the eyes. Some have parotoid glands behind the eyes. All have teeth only in the upper jaw. Compared to true toads, spadefoots have rather thin skin, and when moving quickly (e.g., across a road), they jump higher than true toads.

Spadefoots are well adapted to arid conditions. They enter water only to breed, avoiding dry conditions on land by burrowing (rear-end first) into the soil using a spadelike metatarsal tubercle on each hind foot. Spadefoots spend most of their time buried in the soil, often continuously for 8–10 months. During this time, they live off lipids stored mainly in coelomic fat bodies. In winter, they may be buried at depths of 1 m or more. In summer, they are usually found within the first 10 cm of the soil.

Spadefoots are better able to extract water from relatively dry soil than are aquatic frogs. The New Mexico spadefoot can absorb water from soil containing just a few percent water. Spadefoots store urea in their body fluids; the high concentration (not tolerated by most frogs) helps reduce water loss in low-moisture soils. These toads also are better able to tolerate desiccation (up to about 50 percent of their body mass) than are aquatic frogs. A large volume of water (up to 30 percent of standard body weight) can be stored in the bladder and utilized if necessary.

Late spring and summer rainfall is the primary stimulus bringing spadefoots to the surface. Even when temperature conditions are favorable, these toads may pass several weeks of dry summer weather buried in the soil before a thunderstorm brings the soaking rains that prompt their activity. In summer, buried toads may keep their burrows open at the surface even if they do not emerge to feed.

Unlike many amphibians, spadefoots do not require a habitat with permanent water. In fact, they avoid most permanent bodies of water (but may use springs or semipermanent waters that fluctuate greatly in size). Breeding typically occurs in temporary pools that form after heavy spring or summer rains or after floods in the absence of local rain. Sometimes the toads call from pools that dry up within a day or two. In a given location, spadefoots do not breed if rains are inadequate to form breeding ponds. Breeding typically involves a large number of individuals (sometimes hundreds in a single pool) and lasts 1–3 nights, with most mating taking place the first night. Males call vigorously and loudly and may actively search for females, which generally are moderately to greatly outnumbered by the males in any given pond. Males grasp females around the waist during amplexus.

After breeding, adults disperse up to several hundred meters into surrounding terrestrial habitats. Embryonic and larval development can be very fast, especially in ponds that shrink rapidly. This is advantageous, for if ponds dry up before metamorphosis is complete, the larvae will be killed. Temperature tolerance of the larvae is relatively high. Because large lungs develop early, the larvae are tolerant of anoxic water, in which they frequently come to the surface to gulp air. Just as the lungs develop early, so does the spade on each rear foot. These spades are visible well before major metamorphic changes have occurred. Typically, spadefoots leave the water before the tail is fully resorbed. This may be a response to predation by younger larvae on metamorphosing ones, which move awkwardly and are vulnerable to attack. Newly emerged toadlets use moist microhabitats near the breeding pond.

Spadefoots produce skin secretions that may smell like roasted nuts, popcorn, or garlic and may cause sneezing, runny nose, and watery eyes in humans. If secretions come in contact with the human eye, they may produce a burning sensation but otherwise are not harmful. Presumably, these secretions deter predation, but few pertinent observations are available.

Formerly, spadefoots all were assigned to the genus *Scaphiopus*. Here I follow Wiens and Titus (1991) in placing North American spadefoots in two genera, *Spea* and *Scaphiopus*. However, Hall (1998) argued that this split is unwarranted. Studies by Wiens and Titus (1991) and others indicate that among currently recognized species in the genus *Spea*, *S. bombifrons* and *S. intermontana* are each other's closest relative and are more closely related to *S. hammondii* of California than to *S. multiplicata*.

Plate 7.8. Adult female Couch's spadefoot (Otero County, Colorado).

Couch's Spadefoot
Scaphiopus couchii (Baird, 1854)

Recognition. Pupil vertically elongate in bright light; a single hard, black, sickle-shaped spade on each hind foot; parotoid glands present but indistinct; frontoparietal fontanelle absent (dissection required); adult SVL often 6–7 cm, rarely up to 9 cm. *Mature male:* greenish yellow with scattered dark spots; dark patches on the inner three digits of forelimbs of mature individuals during breeding season; expanded vocal sac large and evenly rounded; breeding call a croaking "yeow." *Female:* greenish yellow; coarse dark mottling of juveniles becomes a finer dark reticulation in adults. *Larvae:* dorsum usually bronze, dark brown, or dark gray to black (black in preservative); body typically wider in rear than in front; tail fin clear with fine scattered dark dots and lines that are most numerous in dorsal fin; eyes dorsal; intestine visible through skin; jaws serrated, never cusped; lower mandible striated; labial tooth rows usually 4/4, 4/5, or 5/5 (Bragg and Hayes 1963); oral papillae completely encircle mouth (narrow dorsal gap may be present); no keratinized area on roof of mouth; anus on midline at front end of ventral tail fin; usually not more than 3.5 cm TL. *Eggs:* black above, whitish below, diameter 1.3–1.6 mm, surrounded by one jelly envelope, deposited in a cluster, cylindrical mass, or string of several to more than 100 (Livezey and Wright 1947; Stebbins 1951; Zweifel 1968).

Distribution. Southwestern United States and much of northern Mexico. Known to occur in southeastern Colorado at elevations of about 3,800–4,500 feet (1,160–1,370 m).

Conservation Status. Due in part to its erratic activity and cryptic behavior, Couch's spadefoot is one of the most poorly understood amphibians in Colorado. First detected in 1977 (Livo 1977, 1981a), it has been observed in only a few sites but likely is more widespread, though still highly localized. All known populations were detected because they occur in accessible areas along roads. Undoubtedly, some populations exist away from public roads and remain undiscovered. Recent extensive field surveys have revealed a few new occurrences (Mackessy 1998; Montgomery, Sifert, et al. 1998; pers. obs.), but clearly this spadefoot is not as prevalent as the plains spadefoot and New Mexico spadefoot, which breed in the same type of habitat.

Population dynamics in Colorado are little known. Local populations observed in Colorado in 1977–1979 (Livo 1977; pers. obs.) were still present in the same areas in the mid-1990s (Mackessy 1998; pers. obs.).

No significant threats have been identified in Colorado, though no specific study has been conducted. The toads inhabit prairie areas currently used for cattle grazing. Known populations probably will be secure as long as cultivation and pesticide use are excluded.

Habitat. Couch's spadefoot inhabits the shortgrass prairie ecosystem in Colorado. It spends most of its life burrowed in the soil and is exceptional among toads in being able to survive long periods there, even in extreme desert conditions (Mayhew 1965). Patches of dead dry skin, which may retard water loss, have been found on individuals newly emerged from the soil in California. Recently metamorphosed juveniles may hide in moist cracks between or under plates of drying mud.

Activity. Active toads have been observed in Colorado from May through early October. These toads perhaps may be active in late April if warm rains occur then. Activity takes place at night during and after spring and summer rains. Dimmitt and Ruibal (1980b) found that the sound or vibration caused by falling rain is the stimulus for emergence from the soil (as long as the weather is warm enough). In Colorado, I have found this species active at night at air temperatures of 16–18°C.

An adult female that I found in Otero County produced creaking groans when handled.

Reproduction and Growth. Breeding occurs only after heavy rains fill depressions and small reservoirs (stock ponds) with water. Breeding aggregations have been observed in Colorado in mid-May (Livo 1977, 1981a) and June (pers. obs.); breeding undoubtedly occurs in July and probably August in some years. In Arizona and Texas, temperatures of at least 17–18°C are needed

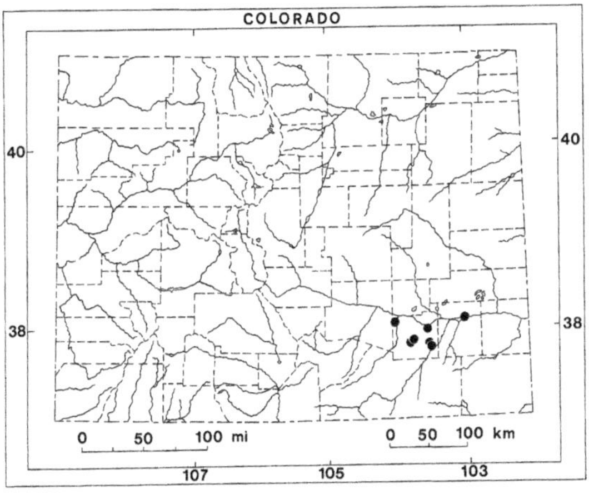

Map 7.2. Distribution of Couch's spadefoot in Colorado.

to stimulate breeding (Wasserman 1957; Zweifel 1968). With adequate rains and temperature, toads emerge from the ground and move quickly to the pools. Males that I observed in Otero County began vigorous breeding calls about an hour after a torrential evening rain began. I heard them calling all night long; they did not quiet until about 10:00 A.M. the following morning. Each rendition of the breeding call lasts less than a second, and the call may be repeated many times in succession. In New Mexico, breeding adults most often were found in grass clump habitats in water less than 12 cm deep (Creusere and Whitford 1976). Males in breeding aggregations sometimes wrestle with one another and may attempt to displace other males from amplexus (Woodward 1982a). Among six breeding aggregations studied by Woodward (1984b) in New Mexico, the largest included 72 females.

Reproduction of this toad has not been studied in detail in Colorado. Elsewhere,

females lay eggs on vegetation in water usually less than 15 cm deep. Bragg (1962) reported that in Oklahoma, *S. couchii* breeds in water that tends to be shallower than that used by *S. bombifrons*. Eggs hatch in 1–3 days, depending on temperature (Justus et al. 1977). Temperatures of 15°C or higher apparently are needed for successful embryonic development (Hubbs and Armstrong 1961). In New Mexico, the average number of mature eggs per adult female varied from about 1,500–4,025 in four breeding aggregations (Woodward 1987a, 1987b).

The larval stage passes quickly. In Texas, it lasted 8–16 days (Newman 1989). Bragg (1964) reported that development from egg to metamorphosis lasted 14–15 days in Oklahoma. Average size of newly metamorphosed toadlets (9–13 mm SVL) varies under different conditions (larval density, pond duration) (Newman 1989).

This toad may successfully reproduce in a quick-drying pond as long as metamorphosis

Plate 7.9. Calling male Couch's spadefoot (Arizona).

Plate 7.10. Juvenile Couch's spadefoot (Otero County, Colorado).

occurs before the water evaporates totally, but in Texas most breeding pools dried before any larvae could metamorphose, resulting in 100 percent mortality (Newman 1987). Species that breed in the same ponds with Couch's spadefoot in Colorado include the New Mexico spadefoot and the green toad.

Food and Predators. Foods eaten in Colorado are not known. Elsewhere, this toad feeds opportunistically on termites, ground and scarab beetles, ants, grasshoppers, crickets, caterpillars, seed bugs, spiders, and other small arthropods (Whitaker, Rubin, and Munsee 1977; Punzo 1991). The toads are capable of gorging themselves, filling the stomach with food amounting to half their prefeeding body mass. On a diet of high-fat termites, they can consume enough energy in a single feeding to last them for more than a year (Dimmitt and Ruibal 1980a).

Predators undoubtedly include various mammals, birds, and snakes. Larvae in some Texas ponds incurred high rates of predation by yellow mud turtles, spotted skunks (*Spilogale* sp.), and hydrophilid beetle larvae (Newman 1987). The turtles and skunks decimated some populations. In Oklahoma, Bragg (1962) found that larvae of the plains spadefoot sometimes prey on the larvae of Couch's spadefoot; predation by *Spea* larvae probably occurs in Colorado as well.

Remarks. In Arizona, an internal blood parasite *(Pseudodiplorchis americanus)* drains energy from toads during their long hibernation period (Tocque 1993). The parasite infects the toads when they enter water to breed.

Taxonomy and Variation. No subspecies have been described.

Plate 7.11. Adult plains spadefoot (Weld County, Colorado).

Plains Spadefoot
Spea bombifrons (Cope, 1863)

Recognition. Pupil vertically elongate in bright light; a single hard, wedge-shaped spade on each hind foot; hard lump between eyes, slightly forward of an imaginary line crossing the middle of both eyes; dorsum often with a roughly hourglass-shaped marking (four light lines; often absent in smaller individuals); anterior ends of the arched frontoparietal bones elevated and rough/pitted (dissection required); maximum SVL about 6 cm. *Mature male:* dark patches on inner 2–3 digits of forelimbs during the breeding season; expanded vocal sac slightly bilobed; breeding call a brief snore, much faster than the long, stuttering snore of the New Mexico spadefoot. *Larvae:* dorsum brown or green to whitish, or mottled gray and dull olive yellow, usually of pale appearance, sometimes with bluish iridescence; dorsal fin clear or with sparse yellowish and gray mottling/flecks; ventral fin clear or mainly clear with sparse yellow flecks; body globular; eyes dorsal; belly iridescent golden, gut coil not visible (large larvae); mandibles frequently cusped, lower mandible not striated; jaw muscles sometimes greatly hypertrophied and may bulge from the sides of the face in front of the eyes; labial tooth rows 0/0 to 6/6, mostly 4/4 or 3/4 (Bragg and Bragg 1958); oral papillae completely encircle mouth (dorsal gap may be present); anus on midline at front end of ventral tail fin; usually up to 7 cm TL, sometimes up to 9.5 cm. *Eggs:* black above, white below, diameter 1.5–1.6 mm (Zweifel 1968), surrounded by two jelly envelopes, in elliptical masses of about 10–250.

Distribution. Great Plains from southern Canada to northern Mexico, west in the Southwest to eastern Arizona. Occurs throughout the plains of eastern Colorado, generally below 6,000 feet (1,830

m) but up to 6,250 feet (1,910 m) in Fremont County; also occurs disjunctly in the San Luis Valley at elevations of about 7,500–8,000 feet (2,290–2,440 m). Tanner (1989:505) stated that *S. bombifrons* occurs "in the San Juan River basin of southern Colorado" but provided no supporting evidence. In San Juan County, Utah, the species is found within shouting distance of the western edge of Montezuma County, Colorado, but as yet there is no documentation of its occurrence in southwestern Colorado. Records of *S. bombifrons* from La Plata County (Harris 1963) pertain to *S. multiplicata.*

Conservation Status. The plains spadefoot is widespread and locally abundant in many areas in the Great Plains region of eastern Colorado. Recent surveys by Jerry Freeman and Loreé Harvey (unpublished data) indicate that the San Luis Valley population also is doing well.

Intensive agriculture undoubtedly has eliminated spadefoots from certain areas, but the terrestrial habitat in some locales is too dry or too far from water for large-scale agricultural development. Some populations have been lost to residential and commercial development along the western margin of the Great Plains between Fort Collins and Trinidad. Large numbers are killed by vehicles on roads near breeding ponds. However, populations overall appear to be secure and no major widespread threats are known to exist.

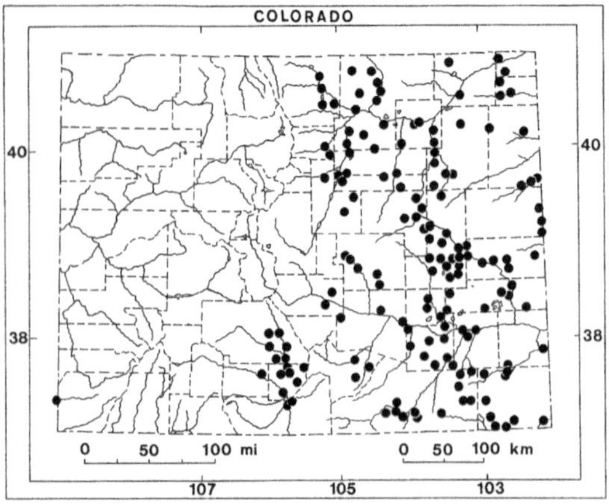

Habitat. This is a characteristic toad of the grasslands and sandhills of eastern Colorado. It is common in areas with soft sandy/gravelly soils along stream floodplains. This toad inhabits semidesert shrublands in the San Luis Valley.

Plains spadefoots dig their own burrows in the soil and also use rodent burrows. Rodents do not

Map 7.3. Distribution of the plains spadefoot in Colorado.

Plate 7.12. Adult plains spadefoots (Morgan County, Colorado).

Plate 7.13. Burrowing adult plains spadefoot (Weld County, Colorado).

Plate 7.14. Hind foot of adult plains spadefoot (Weld County, Colorado).

always welcome them. In Baca County, Smith, Maslin, and Brown (1965) observed a spotted ground squirrel *(Spermophilus spilosoma)* attacking a spadefoot, apparently evicting the toad from a burrow. Vaughan (1961) found a spadefoot in the soil plug of a pocket gopher burrow in Weld County. Smith, Maslin, and Brown (1965) occasionally found spadefoots under tin or boards during the day. Juveniles may hide in moist cracks between or under plates of drying mud.

Activity. In Colorado, activity occurs mainly from late April or May through the end of August, with some activity in September and infrequently into early October. Most individuals still active after August are juveniles or small adults. Activity takes place mostly at dusk and at night in air temperatures usually between about 12–26°C, but breeding may occur day or night, and active toads sometimes can be seen after sunrise (Burt 1933b).

Defensive responses I have observed in Colorado include puffing up with air and squatting low with the head bent downward. In hand, these toads often release fluid from the vent, and males often vocalize (the sound rhymes with "oh" or "bat") with the mouth open or closed. Some individuals produce a strong to faint odor that reminded me of roasted nuts, buttered popcorn, corn chips, or garlic. When removed from the water, large larvae may produce clicking sounds with the mouth parts.

Reproduction and Growth. Breeding of the plains spadefoot was studied in El Paso County by Gilmore (1924) and Goldsmith (1926) and in Yuma County by Woody (1967) and Woody and Thomas (1966, 1968). The following information is based largely on these studies and my own field observations.

The breeding habitat consists of flooded areas and temporary pools formed by heavy rains. Breeding pools may be muddy or clear and vary in depth from a few centimeters to 1 m or more.

Breeding aggregations generally form after rains of 18 mm or more and at air temperatures of at least 10°C (the water is usually warmer than this). In Colorado, I found that calling tends to be most vigorous and persistent at air temperatures above 12°C. Bragg and Smith (1942) found that in Oklahoma, breeding ordinarily does not occur at air temperatures below about 11°C. Minimum temperatures associated with breeding in southern Arizona typically are higher (Zweifel 1968).

In Colorado, breeding has been observed from May through mid-August, though probably it takes place primarily from May through July. Once spadefoots emerge, breeding proceeds rapidly, with mating occurring as soon as an hour after dark on the day of a heavy rain. Males call from the edges of the pools or while floating in shallow water. In New Mexico, breeding adults most often occupy sparsely vegetated areas in water more than 12 cm deep (Creusere and Whitford 1976). Breeding ponds average

perhaps two dozen calling males, though some have many more. Males in breeding aggregations sometimes wrestle with one another and may attempt to displace other males from amplexus (Woodward 1982a). Large choruses can be heard from a distance of 3 km or more.

Mating and egg-laying may be completed in a particular pool in only 2–3 days. Eggs are attached to submerged vegetation or other objects in the water. Each female may lay several egg masses during a single breeding event. The mean number of mature eggs per female was 1,600 in southern New Mexico (Woodward 1987a, 1987b) and 2,626 in Iowa (range 1,572–3,844) (Mabry and Christiansen 1991). Adults usually leave the water immediately after the eggs are laid but may linger for several days if rains continue. Adults may move 60–150 m during each of 1–2 nights as they leave the breeding pools and move upland.

Eggs hatch in 2–3 days. Larvae develop rapidly and commonly complete metamorphosis in 36–40 days. In some ponds, metamorphosis may take place 21 days after the eggs are laid; in other ponds, not until 75 days or more after hatching. King (1960) found that plains spadefoots in Oklahoma may progress from egg to metamorphosis in as few as 13–14 days. In a laboratory study, Bragg (1966) determined that the larval stage can persist up to at least 21 weeks after the eggs are laid.

Rains occurring after those initiating the first breeding event may result in a second emergence of toads, presumably those that did not breed earlier. Thus, multiple breeding events may occur at a given pool each year. Based on the sizes of spadefoots found active in and away from breeding pools, I suspect that plains spadefoots in Colorado typically breed for the first time when they are about two years old. Young from spring breeding events may breed in the summer of their second calendar year, whereas those that metamorphose in late summer may not breed until their third calendar year; however, this remains to be verified. In Iowa, males mature at about 31–38 mm SVL, females at 32–40 mm (Mabry and Christiansen 1991). Breeding

Plate 7.15. Larval plains spadefoot (Weld County, Colorado).

plains spadefoots in Colorado generally are 40–60 mm SVL.

Food and Predators. The adult diet consists primarily of various invertebrates. Major foods in Yuma County include adult moths, caterpillars, carabid beetles, and other small arthropods (Whitaker, Rubin, and Munsee 1977). Richard Bunn informed me that he found a plains spadefoot with a *Peromyscus* mouse in its mouth in southeastern Colorado.

Larvae sometimes depart from their usual diet of minute organic material and prey on fairly large invertebrates (such as fairy shrimp and insect larvae) and other tadpoles, including their own species, especially the injured or dead. Predatory tadpoles may develop large beaked jaws powered by enlarged muscles; expression of these characteristics may be moderate to extreme. Bragg and Bragg (1959) and Bragg (1962) reported that predatory larvae grow rapidly and may be among the first to metamorphose, an advantage in the ephemeral breeding pools. Also, the predatory larvae tend to become more robust juveniles, another survival advantage. Both predatory and nonpredatory larvae may coexist in a single pond.

In Oklahoma, Bragg and King (1960) described "boiling aggregations" of larvae, apparently feeding on food material that they had stirred up from the pond bottom. They also observed slowly swimming schools of feeding larvae.

Various predators sometimes eat these toads. Sexton and Marion (1974) watched several Swainson's hawks *(Buteo swainsoni)* catching spadefoots as the toads swam in ponds in Lincoln County. Plumpton and Lutz (1993) found a few spadefoots in the diet of burrowing owls *(Athene cunicularia)* in Adams County. Tom Strong (pers. comm.) reported that a young black-crowned night heron *(Nycticorax nycticorax)* had eaten an adult spadefoot in Weld County. In Las Animas County, I found a western terrestrial garter snake that had eaten three plains spadefoot tadpoles. Stabler (1948) found a plains spadefoot in the stomach of a western rattlesnake near Colorado Springs. Ballinger, Lynch, and Cole (1979) reported predation on larvae by the plains garter snake in western Nebraska.

Remarks. The plains spadefoot and New Mexico spadefoot breed simultaneously in the same ponds in several areas in southeastern Colorado. Females of both species are able to discriminate between the calls of their own and the other species, but genetic, morphological, and behavioral evidence indicates that the two species hybridize in some areas (Hughes 1965; Forester 1969, 1973; Sattler 1980, 1985; Simovich 1994), probably as a result of inadvertent encounters between females and the non-discriminating males of the other species. Interspecific amplexus rarely has been observed in Colorado (R. Bunn, pers. comm.; pers. obs.).

Taxonomy and Variation. Pierce (1976) reported that *S. bombifrons* is represented by an atypical fast call type in the area from southeastern Arizona to western Texas, including Mexico. The two known call types (fast and slow) both occur in New Mexico and Texas but have not been observed together. Sattler (1980) found no allozyme differences between individuals of the two call types. Limited allozyme evidence did suggest that the population of *S. bombifrons* in southern Texas may be a cryptic species (Sattler 1980).

Plate 7.16. Adult male *(left)* and female *(right)* Great Basin spadefoots in amplexus (Moffat County, Colorado).

Great Basin Spadefoot
Spea intermontana (Cope, 1883)

Recognition. Pupil vertically elongate in bright light; a single hard, wedge-shaped spade on each hind foot; glandular lump directly between eyes (lump is not as far forward as in the plains spadefoot); fronto-parietal bones arched (elevated in middle) and ridged along orbital margin, fontanelle relatively small (dissection required, see Zweifel 1956) or absent (Hall 1998); usually less than 6.5 cm SVL, adults average about 5–6 cm SVL. *Mature male:* dark patches on inner three digits of forelimbs during breeding season; expanded vocal sac slightly bilobed; breeding call a nasal "waah" (rhymes with "laugh"). *Larvae:* dorsum brown to blackish, large individuals appearing relatively pale; fins mainly clear or may have sparse dark scrawls or fine dark suffusion except on basal part of ventral fin; eyes dorsal; both mandibles serrated; lower mandible not striated; carnivore morph has a broadened head, a cusp on the upper mandible, and a notch in the

lower mandible; labial tooth rows 2–4/1–4, usually 3/4 or 4/4; oral papillae completely encircle mouth (narrow dorsal gap may be present); anus on midline at front end of ventral tail fin; hatchlings average about 1 cm TL (Washington [Brown 1989]); large larvae often 5–6 cm TL, up to at least 8.5 cm in Colorado (pers. obs.). *Eggs:* deposited in small strings, sheets, or clusters up to about 2 cm in diameter, generally 10–40 eggs per cluster (see Hall 1998).

Distribution. Throughout the Great Basin and adjacent regions from northern Arizona to southern British Columbia and west to southwestern and central Wyoming and northwestern Colorado; not known to occur southeast of the Colorado River in Utah or Arizona (Hall 1998). Occurs north of the Uncompahgre Plateau in western Colorado at elevations below 7,000 feet (2,135 m). A record from San Miguel County (Secoy and Brown 1968) is based on *S. multiplicata* (Hammerson 1982b). Maslin (1959) reported metamorphosing specimens of this species from Moffat County as *Bufo woodhousii* (Hammerson 1982b).

Conservation Status. This toad is widespread in northwestern Colorado, where it

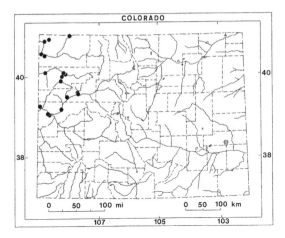

COLORADO

Map 7.4. Distribution of the Great Basin spadefoot in Colorado.

After being handled for a few minutes, toads found in British Columbia produced an odor that smelled like peanuts (Waye and Shewchuk 1995). Some individuals tilted the head downward upon capture and/or secreted a cream-colored substance from the parotoid glands. Two regurgitated when held for an extended period. I have smelled a roasted nut odor in both males and females in Colorado, and some individuals tilted the head downward, greatly inflated the lungs, and tucked the feet under the body in response to probing.

is known from several scattered locations. Because it has been relatively easy to find new populations (under suitable conditions of temperature and moisture), it is likely that additional populations will be discovered. The habitat remains relatively intact, and no major threats are known to exist, so the population trend probably is stable.

Habitat. In Colorado, the Great Basin spadefoot inhabits piñon-juniper woodlands, sagebrush, and semidesert shrublands. It ranges from the bottoms of rocky canyons to broad dry basins and stream floodplains. Cary (1911) caught this toad in mid-August in mousetraps among beds of prickly pear cactus on a sandy knoll in Garfield County. Inactive periods are spent burrowed in the soil. Juveniles may hide in moist cracks between or under plates of drying mud.

Activity. Active toads have been found in Colorado from May through September. Probably they are active in April as well, when warm temperatures and rains coincide. Like other spadefoots, the Great Basin spadefoot is, for the most part, nocturnally active during and after spring and summer rains.

Reproduction and Growth. In Colorado, breeding occurs in temporary pools formed by heavy rains, pools along intermittent stream courses, and floodwaters along permanent streams. Calling males generally sit, partially float, or cling to objects in shallow water. Eggs are attached to rocks, plant material, or the pond bottom. Each female may deposit several hundred eggs divided among multiple egg clusters. In Moffat County, I found larvae in pools that also contained fairy shrimp, clam shrimp, and tadpole shrimp (see Graham 1995). Based on habitats used elsewhere, this species may also breed in the permanent pools of springs

Plate 7.17. Defensive posture of adult female Great Basin spadefoot (Moffat County, Colorado).

and in the absence of rain (Stebbins 1951; Zweifel 1956; Hovingh, Benton, and Bornholdt 1985). I found breeding spadefoots in Moffat County in mid-June (air temperature 13°C, water temperature 15°C). In Colorado and Utah, breeding seems to occur most frequently in May, June, and July, though Hardy (1939) reported breeding as early as April in east-central Utah. Larvae hatch within about two days and metamorphosis begins a few weeks later (Hall, Larsen, and Fitzner 1997; Hall 1998). Spadefoots in various stages of metamorphosis have been found in Moffat County in early to late June.

In western Utah, breeding takes place from April to early June in reservoirs with fluctuating water levels and in spring systems, often in human-made or -modified habitats (Hovingh, Benton, and Bornholdt 1985). Breeding adults average about 6 cm SVL, compared to 5 cm in Idaho, Nevada, and the Colorado River basin in Utah. Most metamorphose by early July, at 16–38 mm SVL, but larvae may be found in some

springs as late as August and September. In British Columbia, most completed metamorphosis by late July, when some had only small limbs (Harestad 1985). Newly metamorphosed toads average about 25 mm SVL in British Columbia (Harestad 1985) and 21 mm in Washington (Brown 1989). Hall (1998) reported that laboratory-raised spadefoots complete metamorphosis at 20 mm SVL.

Just after metamorphosis, the young may aggregate for a while (Arnold and Wassersug 1978) but soon disperse from the natal ponds. In British Columbia, small toadlets were captured 110 m from the breeding pond on a dry, south-facing hill in early August (Harestad 1985).

Food and Predators. No information is available for Coloradan toads, which undoubtedly eat various arthropods. Tanner (1931) found that the stomachs of a few individuals from Utah contained ants, beetles, a grasshopper, a wasp, and a cricket. A toad in British Columbia regurgitated

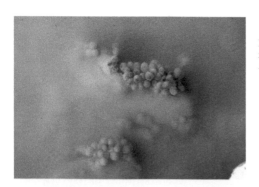

Plate 7.18. Eggs of Great Basin spadefoot (Mesa County, Colorado). *Lauren Livo and Steve Wilcox.*

Plate 7.19. Larval Great Basin spadefoot and tadpole shrimp (Moffat County, Colorado).

several caterpillars and a beetle (Waye and Shewchuk 1995). Larvae usually feed on detritus, plant material, algae, and other minute organic material, but sometimes they become predaceous and develop beaked jaws and bulging jaw muscles (Hall 1998).

Predators are poorly known. Larvae sometimes are eaten by the western terrestrial garter snake (Wood 1935). In southern British Columbia, Harestad (1985) observed common crows *(Corvus brachyrhynchos)* catching and eating larvae. Gleason and Craig (1979) and Green et al. (1993) reported predation on adults by the burrowing owl *(Athene cunicularia)* in Idaho and the Pacific

Northwest, though the toads may not have been entirely eaten because of their noxious skin secretions.

Taxonomy and Variation. Limited allozyme data indicate that Great Basin spadefoots from Oregon and Colorado apparently are not sister taxa (Wiens and Titus 1991). A sample from Mesa County in Colorado was genetically more similar to a sample of *S. bombifrons* than it was to *S. intermontana* from Oregon. Further study is needed to determine whether the Great Basin spadefoot as presently defined actually consists of two or more species. The Great Basin spadefoot and New Mexico spadefoot hybridize in eastern Utah (Hall 1998).

Plate 7.20. Adult New Mexico spadefoot (Las Animas County, Colorado).

New Mexico Spadefoot
Spea multiplicata (Cope, 1863)

Recognition. Pupil vertically elongate in bright light; a single hard, wedge-shaped spade on each hind foot; no lump between eyes; upper surface gray or brown with numerous scattered dark spots (no stripes); frontoparietal bones flat, separated by

extensive fontanelle (dissection required); maximum SVL about 6.5 cm. *Mature male:* dark throat and dark patches on the three inner digits of forelimbs during breeding season; expanded vocal sac slightly bilobed; breeding call a stuttering croak about one second long (duration decreases with increasing temperature). *Larvae:* dorsum pale brown to gray; eyes dorsal; lower mandible not striated; carnivore morph has a broadened head due to hypertrophied jaw muscles, a cusped upper mandible, and relatively short intestine of only a few coils (Pfennig 1992b); labial tooth rows variable, 2–5/3–4; oral papillae completely encircle mouth (narrow dorsal gap may be present); anus on midline at front end of ventral tail fin; usually less than 7 cm TL. *Eggs:* 1.0–1.6 mm in diameter, each surrounded by two jelly envelopes, deposited in small clusters of up to several dozen (Livezey and Wright 1947; Zweifel 1968).

Distribution. Southeastern Utah, southern Colorado, and southwestern Kansas south through Arizona, New Mexico, and western Texas to central Mexico. Occurs north to the Arkansas River valley in southeastern Colorado at elevations generally below 6,000 feet (1,830 m). Occurs south of the Uncompahgre Plateau at elevations below 6,500 feet (1,980 m) in southwestern Colorado. A record for Kiowa County (Chiszar and Smith 1995a) is based on a difficult-to-identify mangled specimen of *Spea bombifrons.* Juvenile spadefoots resembling this species have been collected in the northern San Luis Valley, where *S. bombifrons* is the only documented spadefoot. However, juvenile *S. bombifrons* and *S. multiplicata* can be difficult to distinguish, and further surveys are needed to determine whether *S. multiplicata* occurs in that area. Mackessy (1998) reported *S. multiplicata* in Crowley, Kiowa, and Lincoln counties, north of previous localities in southeastern Colorado, but I have not personally confirmed these identifications.

Conservation Status. The distribution and abundance of the New Mexico spadefoot in Colorado appear unchanged over the last several decades. Past agricultural development probably eliminated some populations. Local populations near roads likely have been depleted as a result of mortality caused by vehicles. However, the species is locally abundant in both southwestern and southeastern Colorado, and no significant threats currently exist. The species can be regarded as secure within its somewhat limited range in the state.

Habitat. This toad lives in plains grassland in southeastern Colorado. It occurs in sagebrush and semidesert shrubland in basins and floodplains of streams in western Colorado. Typical of spadefoots, it enters water only to breed and spends most if its life buried in the soil. Burnett (1926) found one of these toads in the entrance of a prairie-dog burrow in Montezuma County. Juveniles may hide in moist cracks between or under plates of drying mud.

Activity. Active individuals have been found in Colorado from May through September. Most activity takes place at night, often but not always in association with rain. I have found individuals active at air temperatures of 10–24°C.

When handled, these toads may release fluid from the vent, inflate the lungs, and produce sticky skin secretions that smell like buttered popcorn or garlic. A 37-mm-SVL individual held in my hand repeatedly vocalized ("eh, eh, eh, eh, eh") with the mouth closed and the vocal sac partially inflated. A 43-mm-SVL female filled her lungs with air and produced a similar vocalization.

Livo, Chiszar, and Smith (1997) described and illustrated an immobile defensive posture

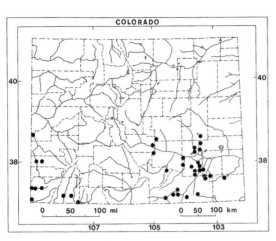

Map 7.5. Distribution of the New Mexico spadefoot in Colorado.

assumed by a toad that had been handled and doused with water. The head was lowered, with the eyes nearly closed. The elbows were extended outward, and the hind limbs were tightly folded. I observed similar behavior in this and the other *Spea* species in Colorado.

Reproduction and Growth. Temporary pools are used for breeding, which in Colorado occurs primarily in June and July, though choruses may form after heavy rains as late as mid-August (Bury 1977). Breeding activities may take place both day and night during and immediately after heavy rains. In western Texas, Long (1989) observed activity from late March through mid-September and breeding from late May through mid-August. Throughout the range, breeding most often occurs at water temperatures of about 18–24°C (sometimes higher) (Brown 1967, 1976; Zweifel 1968), but Gehlbach (1965) found spadefoots laying eggs in water at 12°C in northwestern New Mexico. Breeding at temperatures below

18°C also occurs in Colorado (pers. obs.). Breeding males usually are about 4–5 cm SVL; reproductive females may reach or exceed 6 cm SVL. Among three breeding aggregations studied by Woodward (1984a) in New Mexico, the largest included 105 females and 1,560 males.

Males call while floating and swimming or from shoreline areas. In New Mexico, breeding adults generally are found in open water more than 12 cm deep (Creusere and Whitford 1976). Males in breeding aggregations sometimes wrestle with one another and may attempt to displace other amplexing males (Woodward 1982a). In Arizona, Sullivan (1985b) found that silent males near calling males sometimes successfully intercept and mate with females approaching the calling male. In southeastern Colorado, the New Mexico spadefoot has been observed breeding simultaneously in the same ponds with the plains spadefoot and with Couch's spadefoot (but not with both of these species in the same pond).

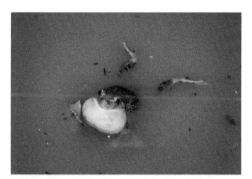

Plate 7.21. Calling male New Mexico spadefoot (Arizona).

Plate 7.22. Defensive posture of adult New Mexico Spadefoot (Otero County, Colorado). *Lauren Livo and Steve Wilcox.*

Eggs are attached to objects in the water. In New Mexico, the number of mature eggs per adult female averaged about 805–1,410 in three breeding aggregations (Woodward 1987a, 1987b). Adults leave the water very soon after breeding.

Eggs hatch within about two days. In Arizona, larvae metamorphose at an age of 2–6 weeks and 12–29 mm SVL (Pfennig, Mabry, and Orange 1991). Metamorphosing individuals have been found in Colorado in mid-August, but the process surely occurs at least as early as July in some years.

Food and Predators. Metamorphosed individuals feed opportunistically on ground-dwelling arthropods. An adult female found in San Miguel County had eaten a spider. In Texas, the diet includes beetles, grasshoppers, crickets, ants, termites, spiders, and other invertebrates as available (Punzo 1991). Dimmitt and Ruibal (1980) determined that this toad may require seven feedings a year to survive.

Pfennig (1990) found that a carnivorous larval morph develops as a consequence of eating of fairy shrimp. Apparently, thyroid hormone in the prey induces development of the carnivorous morph (Pfennig 1992b). Because the shrimp are most abundant in pools that are most ephemeral, and carnivorous tadpoles develop faster than omnivorous ones, the association of carnivory with shrimp ingestion allows the spadefoot to respond adaptively to its short-lived breeding environment (Pfennig 1990). On the other hand, omnivorous larvae in longer-lasting pools develop larger fat reserves and survive better after metamorphosis than do carnivorous morphs (Pfennig 1992a).

Mackessy (1998) reported an instance of predation on this toad by the plains garter snake in Las Animas County.

Remarks. The possibility of hybridization between *S. bombifrons* and *S. multiplicata* in Colorado is discussed in the account of *S. bombifrons.*

Taxonomy and Variation. The western spadefoot *(Spea hammondii)* of California and Baja California formerly was included in this species, but *S. hammondii* and *S. multiplicata* exhibit morphological and behavioral differences (Brown 1976) and clearly are genetically distinct (Sattler 1980; Wiens and Titus 1991). Though most herpetologists do not recognize any subspecies of *S. multiplicata,* Tanner (1989) concluded, on the basis of cranial characteristics and skin tuberculation, that certain populations in Mexico represented a different subspecies than that occurring throughout most of the range. In Tanner's arrangement, Colorado populations would be subspecies *stagnalis.* Tanner regarded *S. hammondii* and *S. multiplicata* as conspecific, but as mentioned earlier, existing data indicate that they are not.

TRUE TOADS
Family Bufonidae

This large family of about 400 species (more than 200 in the genus *Bufo* alone) occurs nearly worldwide (but is not native to Australia, Madagascar, New Guinea, or isolated marine islands). The largest species, *Bufo blombergi* of South America, reaches 25 cm SVL. Five of the approximately 20 species in the United States and Canada are found in Colorado.

Toads are chunky, short-limbed hoppers. Most are terrestrial/fossorial. Adult toads of some species are accomplished burrowers, using paired tubercles on each hind foot

Plate 7.23. Embryos of New Mexico spadefoot (Montezuma County, Colorado). *Lauren Livo and Steve Wilcox.*

to dig into the soil. Other species do not burrow but instead use existing shelters. Juvenile toads apparently cannot burrow very well and probably find abandoned burrows in which to overwinter. Adults of most species are mainly nocturnal, but small juveniles often are active day and night.

Toads lack teeth but have a well-developed tongue, as is usual in terrestrially feeding amphibians. The skull is well ossified, and the head skin is co-ossified in most species.

Most have thick glandular skin and numerous warts. Warts and the large lumps (parotoid glands) behind the eyes of toads are aggregations of poison glands. Pressure, such as a bite to the neck, causes the white, sticky poison to squirt or ooze out of the parotoid gland (this is easily demonstrated by squeezing a parotoid gland between your thumb and finger). The distasteful parotoid gland secretions of *Bufo* are toxic to birds and mammals if ingested in quantity. Bird and mammal predators that eat toads often reject the parotoid glands and dorsal skin and eat only the viscera. Toad eggs also are toxic. Larval toads of at least some species initially are unpalatable to various insect and vertebrate predators, then become palatable before again becoming noxious at the end of metamorphosis as the warty aggregations of poison glands develop. Humans have used toad skin secretions as a mind-altering drug. Handling toads does not cause warts in humans.

When threatened, metamorphosed toads typically crouch motionless or hop away. If actually grasped, toads inflate the body by filling the well-developed lungs with air. Presumably this makes it harder for a predator to handle and swallow the toad.

Toads are tolerant of rather extreme dehydration, surviving losses of 40–45 percent of their initial empty-bladder body mass. To recover moisture losses, toads absorb water through a well-vascularized patch on their posterior ventral skin. The bladder may hold a large amount of dilute urine (about 20–30 percent of the total weight in a fully hydrated Great Plains toad) from which water can be reabsorbed during dry periods. When roughly handled, toads generally release fluid from the bladder and/or the cloaca.

With the possible exception of the mountain toad, true toads in Colorado have a lek-like mating system in which males aggregate and produce vocal displays and females select mates from among the singers. All Coloradan toads exhibit external fertilization of eggs and have aquatic larvae. The eggs of most species are laid in two strings, one from each ovary/oviduct. Elsewhere, a few toad species (e.g., African *Nectophrynoides*) exhibit internal fertilization and give birth to fully formed toadlets. The lungs of toad larvae do not develop until metamorphosis.

Bidder's organ, representing ovarian tissue at the anterior end of each gonad (including the testes of males), is unique to bufonid toads. These organs possibly serve an endocrinogenic function in both males and females, and under natural conditions they produce viable eggs in females of some species but not others (see Roessler, Smith, and Chiszar 1990).

Plate 7.24. Adult mountain toad (Garfield County, Colorado).

Mountain Toad
Western Toad, *Bufo boreas* complex

Recognition. Skin warty; parotoid glands oval; cranial crests absent or indistinct; usually a light stripe along middle of back (most prominent in mature females); tarsal fold well developed; tubercles on underside of hind foot lack sharp cutting edge; foot tubercles yellowish in juveniles; females rarely greater than 11 cm SVL, males rarely exceed 9.5 cm SVL. The mid-dorsal stripe may be absent or inconspicuous in juveniles (which may have reddish warts). *Mature male:* dark patch on the inner surface of the innermost digit on the forefeet during breeding season; vocal sac absent; may produce repeated chirping sounds if grasped by hand (females usually are silent or emit few chirps). *Larvae:* body and tail (including fins) black or dark brown; eyes about halfway between dorsal midline and lateral edge of head; labial tooth rows 2/3; oral papillae restricted to sides of mouth; anus on midline at front end of ventral tail fin; measurements of fully developed larvae: head-body length about 14–17 mm, tail length about 16–20 mm, tail height about 6–8 mm, maximum TL about 34–37 mm (Burger and Bragg 1947; Blair 1951; pers. obs.). *Eggs:* black, about 1.5–1.8 mm in diameter, occurring in 1–3 rows (often 2 rows that appear to be a single zigzagging row) in long strings of double-layered jelly.

Distribution. This species belongs to the *Bufo boreas* group, which occurs throughout much of western North America, except the arid Southwest, ranging from southeastern Alaska to northern Baja California, Utah (Ross et al. 1995), and northern New Mexico (Campbell and Degenhardt 1971; Degenhardt, Painter, and Price 1996). The mountain toad is restricted to the southern part of the Rocky Mountains (see "Taxonomy and Variation"). Historically, the mountain toad occurred throughout most of the mountainous portion of Colorado but apparently not in the Sangre de Cristo Range, Wet Mountains, or Pikes Peak region. The elevational range is mainly 8,500–11,500 feet (2,600–3,500 m), with higher and lower occurrences in some areas (Campbell 1970c). Campbell (1976) reported toads occurring as high as 11,860 feet (3,615 m) in the San Juan Mountains, and Livo and Yeakley (1997) reported an occurrence at 11,940 feet (3,640 m) in Clear Creek County. Toads at the highest elevations tend to be females (Campbell 1970d). An old record from Pagosa Springs (elevation not specified, but possibly 7,100 feet [2165 m]) (AMNH 6936) and a series from "3 mi. E, 4 mi. S Collbran" (KU 39187–39198, identification confirmed by W. E. Duellman) may represent unusual low-elevation occurrences, if the collection data are accurate. I suspect that the specimen reported from Pagosa Springs probably was collected near that city at a higher elevation. The locality near Collbran evidently is at 6,800 feet (2,075 m), based on a collection of *Sceloporus undulatus* made at that elevation at precisely the same location (Legler 1960a); this strongly suggests that the toad data are erroneous—the elevation is much too low, and the mountain toad and *S. undulatus* never have been found together in Colorado. A low-elevation record of the mountain toad from T5N R70W Section 27, Larimer County (UCM 1379), within the range of *B. woodhousii,* undoubtedly represents a transposition of data with a specimen of *B. woodhousii* (UCM 1380) supposedly collected in the Estes Park area, where the expected species is the mountain toad. The mountain toad and Woodhouse's toad appear to be completely allopatric in Colorado. The only area where they possibly occur together is in northern Archuleta County (see Harris 1963).

Conservation Status. The mountain toad is listed by the Colorado Division of Wildlife as endangered in Colorado. It is included in the Southern Rocky Mountain population of the *Bufo boreas* group, which is a candidate for federal protection under the U.S. Endangered Species Act (USFWS 1995). This signifies that the toad is to be listed when actions of higher priority are completed.

Once very common in the mountains of Colorado (e.g., Ellis and Henderson 1915; Burt 1933b; Burger and Bragg 1947; Blair 1951), the mountain toad underwent a severe decline in distribution and abundance that likely began in the early 1970s and extended into the 1990s in some areas. Local declines had been observed in the 1970s but were not reported until the 1990s (Carey 1993). Toads were widespread and abundant in the mountains of Boulder County in the 1960s but were scarce or localized by the end of the next decade. In the late 1970s, toads were easy to find in the Park Range and San Juan mountains; today they are scarce in those areas. That a widespread decline had occurred was not apparent until the 1980s (Corn, Stoltzenburg, and Bury 1989). Toads disappeared completely from some areas and became rare in others, yet at the same time, they remained locally numerous in a few places. The decline encompassed populations throughout the Southern Rocky Mountains of southern Wyoming, Colorado, and northern New Mexico. Surveys in New Mexico in the late 1980s and early 1990s revealed no toads at the three locations where toads formerly occurred (Stuart and Painter 1994; Degen-hardt, Painter, and Price 1996), though subsequent surveys indicated that the species

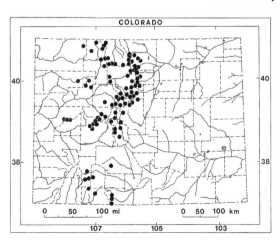

Map 7.6. Distribution of the mountain toad in Colorado, 1900–1998.

may not be completely gone from New Mexico (Goettl 1997). In the Medicine Bow Mountains, Sierra Madre, and Pole Mountains in Wyoming, a known distribution of two dozen sites in the late 1980s and early 1990s shrank to just one site in 1996 (Boreal Toad Conservation Strategy Team [BTCST] 1997). Ross et al. (1995) and Ross and Fridell (1997) reported that in Utah *B. boreas* had disappeared from several historical montane sites, but they found this toad in several new localities in both lowland areas and the mountains.

In Colorado, recent surveys of several hundred potential breeding sites within the historic range indicate that the toad has completely disappeared or declined to extreme rarity in most of the state (Corn, Stoltzenburg, and Bury 1989; Hammerson 1989a, 1992; Carey 1993; Livo 1995a). The largest populations now occur along the North Fork of the Big Thompson River in Rocky Mountain National Park (Corn, Jennings, and Muths 1997), the Cottonwood Creek drainage in the San Isabel National Forest in Chaffee County (pers. obs.), the Snake River/Ten-Mile Creek area of Summit County, and the Clear Creek/Henderson Mine area in Arapaho National Forest and Clear Creek County (BTCST 1997). As of the early 1990s, the two largest populations known to exist in the Southern Rocky Mountains occurred in Rocky Mountain National Park; each included approximately 200 males, with 8–35 egg masses deposited annually at each site (Corn, Jennings, and Muths 1997), though a decline may have taken place in at least one of these populations in the mid-1990s (L. Livo, pers. comm.). With scattered other populations recently observed, these areas amount to just a few dozen known breeding sites, compared to the (probably) thousands that existed several decades ago. It is likely that additional populations remain to be discovered, as this toad lacks a conspicuous breeding call and thus is unusually difficult to detect.

Several factors may have contributed to the decline of the mountain toad and other amphibians of mountainous western North America, including damaging effects of increased ultraviolet (UV-B) light on embryos (e.g., Blaustein, Hoffman, et al. 1994, 1995; Anzalone, Kats, and Gordon 1998); acidification and heavy-metal contamination of water (Porter and Hakanson 1976; Harte and Hoffman 1989, 1994; BTCST 1997); habitat destruction and degradation, such as may result from water management, minerals management, road construction, livestock management, timber and fire management, and recreation (BTCST 1997); impacts of introduced trout; an apparently introduced infectious fungal disease (Berger et al. 1998; Cunningham 1998); pathogen-induced mortality resulting from suppressed immune systems caused by some undetermined environmental stressor (Carey 1993, 1997); climate change (Corn and Fogleman 1984; Corn 1994); and predation (Corn 1993). None of these is satisfactory as a complete explanation for the existing pattern of toad distribution and abundance. Likely, multiple factors are involved. Certainly, habitat alteration has played a role, as some natural mountain wetlands formerly inhabited by toads have been flooded by reservoirs (e.g., Campbell 1970d). For example, the filling of Lefthand Reservoir in Boulder County flooded toad habitat and forced hundreds of toads to become concentrated around the margin of the newly formed lake (Campbell 1970d). These inundated wetlands, which tend to be in the wettest areas available in a given drainage basin, formerly may have served as important (or the only) breeding areas during periods of drought, when marginal breeding sites would be dry. Hence the relationship between reservoir construction and toad decline may not be obvious, because the impact of reservoir construction may not become apparent until decades later. Also, most reservoirs undergo large fluctuations in water level, and many of them provide little or no shallow-water larval habitat (but see Corn, Jennings, and Muths 1997). In addition, reservoirs in Colorado generally have flooded and eliminated much wet-meadow toad foraging habitat. In some areas, such as on Grand Mesa, algal blooms, apparently the result of nutrient enrichment caused by poorly

Map 7.7. Known breeding sites of the mountain toad in Colorado, 1990–1997.

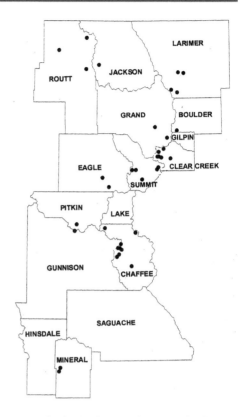

functioning septic systems, have degraded some lakes formerly inhabited by mountain toads.

Acid tolerances of larvae, pH characteristics of breeding sites, and the timing of breeding together indicate that anthropogenic water acidification currently is not a major threat (Corn, Stoltzenburg, and Bury 1989; Corn and Vertucci 1992; Vertucci and Corn 1996), though local exceptions may exist (BTCST 1997). Carey (1997) stated that low pH alone is unlikely to cause increased vulnerability to infection by pathogenic bacteria. Organochlorine pesticides also appear to be unrelated to the toad decline (Carey 1997). Toad larvae in some areas have high whole-body concentrations of heavy metals, and current research is attempting to determine how this may affect growth and survival (Carey 1997). Experimental studies by Corn (1998) yielded no evidence that UV-B levels are directly responsible for the toad decline. Fungal infections that may cause mortality of toad embryos (Blaustein, Hokit, et al. 1994) have not been observed in the Rocky Mountains (Corn, Jennings, and Muths 1997).

Exotic and native trout species have been introduced throughout nearly all mountain lakes in Colorado, but their effects on the mountain toad are poorly known. The larval stages of some *Bufo* species are unpalatable to various fish predators, at least during part of their development (Voris and Bacon 1966; Licht 1968, 1969; Campbell 1970d:61; Brodie and Formanowicz 1987, Kats, Petranka, and Sih 1988). Preliminary observations suggest that trout are not important predators on toad larvae in Colorado (M. S. Jones, J. P. Goettl, and L. J. Livo, unpublished observations), but the relationship between trout and the mountain toad

in the Southern Rocky Mountains has not been exhaustively examined. Alterations (e.g., dredging) designed to improve trout habitat may degrade toad breeding habitat. Toxicants such as antimycin, widely used in fisheries management, may be lethal to larval toads, although a large mountain toad population currently exists in at least one lake that was treated with antimycin in 1986 (Corn, Jennings, and Muths 1997).

Native predators such as the common raven *(Corvus corax)* and dytiscid beetle larvae may cause significant mortality (see "Food and Predators") but are unlikely to be responsible for the widespread decline in the toad population. Introduced bullfrogs, implicated in native anuran declines in several areas of western North America, do not occur in mountain toad habitat in the Southern Rockies.

Livestock and humans may have direct impacts on toads. In southeastern Idaho,

Bartelt (1998) observed that hundreds of newly metamorphosed *Bufo boreas* were trampled to death by a group of several hundred sheep. The increasing numbers of hikers in Colorado's mountains may have had impacts, at least locally. At Red Rock Lake in Boulder County, a heavily used recreation area where mountain toads are now extirpated, Campbell (1970d) observed several dead toads that evidently had been trampled.

The bottom line is that toads definitely have declined in the Southern Rockies, but we do not know why. For most of the factors potentially involved in this decline, indirect and sublethal detrimental impacts are poorly known. Hopefully, research now in progress will shed some light on the situation.

A recovery plan for the toad has been drawn up (Goettl 1997), and implementation has begun. Management includes captive propagation and reintroduction. Such actions pose the risk of harmful genetic alterations and disease transmission and must be undertaken only with extreme caution. Scherff-Norris (1997) described methods for propagating mountain toads in captivity.

Habitat. In Colorado, the mountain toad typically lives in damp conditions in the vicinity of marshes, wet meadows, streams, beaver ponds, glacial kettle ponds, and lakes interspersed in subalpine forest (lodgepole pine, Englemann spruce, subalpine fir, and aspen). In southern Colorado and locally northward, toads sometimes have been found where ponderosa pine is present. In late spring and early summer, toads frequently are observed in the water, at its edge, or atop partially submerged logs. Later in summer, they may become more terrestrial, though generally the habitat is damp, and many individuals stay close to water. However, Campbell (1976) reported that females, in contrast to males, tend to move to drier, more densely vegetated areas after the breeding season, and I have seen juveniles on the

dry floor of subalpine forest. Ellis and Henderson (1913) found large numbers of these toads under streetlights and along irrigation ditches at Buena Vista (7,955 feet [2,425 m]) in Chaffee County. They also observed mountain toads in the warm waters of Hortense Hot Springs, Chaffee County, though the hot springs acted as death traps for some toads.

When inactive, mountain toads hide beneath rocks or logs or in rodent burrows. Unlike certain other toads in Colorado, they do not burrow deeply into the soil. At Rabbit Ears Pass, Burnett (1926) found toads in moist ground under decayed stumps and logs. Campbell (1970b) reported that toads moved 900 m (and 95 m lower in elevation) from their summer habitat and spent the winter in natural, rock-lined chambers near a creek in subalpine forest in Boulder County. At least 30 toads hibernated in five chambers along 30 m of creek. Flow of groundwater kept the site from freezing. The toads moved very little during winter. The mass of one newly emerged toad in May was 82 percent of its mass the previous July. In Clear Creek County, several toads fitted with radios hibernated in ground squirrel *(Spermophilus lateralis)* burrows (Jones and Goettl 1998). Beaver lodges and dams also may serve as hibernation sites (Goettl 1997). In early spring, Livo (pers. comm.) observed on a beaver dam in Chaffee County numerous toadlets that had metamorphosed the previous season, suggesting that they had spent the winter in the dam, where flowing water would maintain air temperatures above freezing.

Plate 7.25. Juvenile mountain toad (Chaffee County, Colorado).

Activity. Mountain toads emerge from their hibernation sites in May and begin returning to them in late August and early September. Most individuals cease activity by the end of September, though some basking near the entrances of wintering sites may occur in September and October (Goettl 1997). In summer, activity often takes place in daytime but may occur at twilight and night if temperatures are mild or favorable microclimates are present. On Grand Mesa, Burt (1933b) found numerous young and adults in the grass at a pond's edge at noon in early August; others were inactive under rocks or wood; one adult was floating in the water. (Note: the Grand Mesa population now appears to be extirpated.) Early and late in the season, activity occurs primarily in daytime.

Mountain toads in Colorado are active over a wide range of temperatures. Toads are most active at air temperatures of 12–20°C, though activity has been observed as low as –2°C (body temperature 3.1°C) on rare occasions (Campbell 1970d). For 165 toads studied by Campbell (1970d), the mean body temperature was 20.8°C (range 0.6–30.8°C), a few degrees warmer than air, substrate, and water temperatures. Carey (1976) found that body temperatures generally range from 0–10°C during nighttime activity and 15–33°C during daytime activity. My data for daytime body temperatures of active toads (13–26°C, average 19°C) are consistent with these data. At Rabbit Ears Pass, Brattstrom (1963) recorded generally higher body temperatures of 22–30°C (average 26°C) in early August.

Toads can elevate their body temperature above air temperature by basking in the sun (especially in the morning), by squatting low on warm substrates, and by entering water during sudden cold snaps (Campbell 1970d). On a June morning, Muths and Corn (1997) observed basking by individual adult male toads and amplexed pairs at a snowbound breeding site in Rocky Mountain National Park. Basking toads had body temperatures averaging about 23°C, far above the average air temperature of 13°C. Nonbasking amplexed pairs in the water had an average body temperature of 13°C, close to the water temperature. The authors suggested that higher body temperatures resulting from basking may be beneficial by increasing the rate of digestion, facilitating sperm production, and allowing earlier breeding and hence more time for larval and postmetamorphic growth before winter.

Campbell (1976) found that mountain toads exhibit highly variable movement patterns. Sometimes a toad stays in the same spot for several days but occasionally may move more than 50 m from one day to the next. An individual may move up to 4 km or more between breeding and nonbreeding habitats (Steve Corn, unpublished data).

Mountain toads make only short hops and thus progress slowly compared to frogs. When disturbed near water, they may hop into the water and swim. In hand, males may chirp, and both sexes may release fluid from the vent. Prolonged handling may result in the secretion of a whitish substance from one or more of the warts on the dorsal skin.

Reproduction and Growth. Breeding occurs in still or barely flowing water in marshy areas with sedges and shrubby willows and along gently sloping edges of large and small lakes, beaver ponds, glacial kettle ponds, roadside ditches, ponds resulting from excavations by humans, and even small puddles (Burger and Bragg 1947; pers. obs.). Successful breeding (i.e., larval development through metamorphosis) generally requires permanent or semipermanent water, though breeding also takes place in temporary ponds. In Gunnison County, Burger and Bragg (1947) occasionally found toad larvae associated with larvae of the northern leopard frog.

These toads differ from all others in Colorado because they lack a loud breeding call. In mature males, the inflatable vocal sac and dark throat skin that typifies adult males of other species are absent. At most, breeding males emit a soft chirping sound, especially when grasped or touched by another male. The call also may be emitted without such contact and may function in the formation of male aggregations at breeding sites and in attracting females. Groups of males sometimes form chirping aggregations that can be heard many dozens of meters away (Campbell 1970d; Black and Brunson 1971). Males in breeding aggregations may attempt to amplex any nearby toad, including other males (Marco, Kiesecker, and Chivers 1998).

Breeding begins as the winter snowpack starts to thaw—May in areas with early snowmelt, as late as July or early August in other localities. In a given site, breeding may extend over several weeks, though a definite peak typically occurs. Oviposition may take place in ice-rimmed pools or ponds with relatively warm water (Campbell 1970d). Eggs are deposited in water generally not more than 6 inches (15 cm) deep, often just deep enough to submerge the eggs, usually in areas most exposed to the sun (e.g., north shores). Frequently, eggs are laid in the open on detritus-covered bottoms, or they may become tangled among submerged vegetation. On muddy bottoms, the jelly may become covered with silt or fine organic debris. In Gunnison County, Carey (1976)

found that typical clutches include about 3,200–8,700 eggs (average 5,200). Three egg strings in Rocky Mountain National Park included 7,035, 7,993, and 10,872 eggs (Steve Corn, pers. comm.). Adults may linger at breeding sites for up to several weeks. Eventually, they disperse, mainly into nearby wetlands and sometimes into forested uplands.

In Gunnison County, Carey (1976) found that individual females tend to breed every other year. Studies of a PIT-tagged population in Clear Creek County indicate that females frequently require two or more years before returning to breeding sites (Mark Jones, pers. comm.).

Larval development takes two months or more, with the shortest periods occurring in the warmest sites. At the highest elevations, or where late snowmelt and cooler temperatures result in late breeding and slower development, larvae may not metamorphose before the ponds freeze. Campbell (1970d) reported that these larvae overwinter

Plate 7.26. Eggs of mountain toad (Chaffee County, Colorado).

Plate 7.27. Larvae of mountain toad (Chaffee County, Colorado).

Plate 7.28. Aggregation of newly metamorphosed mountain toads (Clear Creek County, Colorado). *Lauren Livo and Steve Wilcox.*

beneath the ice and metamorphose in their second summer; however, overwintering of larvae was not actually observed, but inferred from the presence of larvae of two size classes, which could result from early and late breeding in a single year rather than from larval overwintering. Tadpoles too small to transform before the onset of winter have been observed at numerous sites in Colorado, but despite recent regular monitoring of toad breeding sites, overwinter survival of larvae never has been observed (Fetkavich and Livo 1998). Campbell (1970d, 1972) found that toad reproduction generally is unsuccessful (i.e., metamorphosis not attained) at elevations above 11,000 feet (3,385 m).

Larvae commonly are present in the breeding pools into August, and in some areas remain less than full grown in mid-August. Metamorphosis occurs primarily in August but may take place as early as late July or as late as mid-September in some locations. Burger and Bragg (1947) and Blair (1951) found that metamorphosis occurs in the Elk Mountains in late July and early August. In the same area, Lillywhite and Wassersug (1974) reported that more than 50 newly metamorphosed toads formed an aggregation several individuals deep on the mud bank of a pond in late morning in mid-August. Hahn (1968) observed metamorphosing toads in early August in the San Juan Mountains.

Recently metamorphosed toadlets typically are about 10–16 mm SVL (Blair 1951; pers. obs.) but occasionally reach 16–20 mm (average 18 mm) (L. J. Livo, pers. comm.). Newly metamorphosed toadlets can be numerous in sunny areas along the shores of breeding sites. They may disperse from their natal sites and move into nearby wetlands or simply overwinter along the border of the pools where they developed. Juveniles

(usually 20–35 mm SVL) often can be found in wetlands adjacent to breeding sites.

As is true of most amphibians, larval and juvenile mountain toads experience rather severe mortality, but individuals that survive their youth may live long lives. Campbell (1976) reported that mountain toads in Colorado may live nine years or more. Breeding adult males generally are 55–93 mm SVL, and females usually reach about 75–115 mm SVL (Campbell 1970d; Carey 1976). Minimum age of breeders is about four years in males and six years in females (Carey 1976).

Food and Predators. Mountain toads in Colorado eat a wide variety of invertebrates, including grasshoppers, various beetles, mosquitoes, crane flies, stink bugs, damsel bugs, water striders, backswimmers, alderflies, moths/caterpillars, black flies, deer flies, muscid flies, ants, wasps, bees, mites, daddy longlegs, spiders, and snails (Burger and Bragg 1947; Campbell 1970a). Near Buena Vista in Chaffee County, Ellis and Henderson (1915) observed juveniles at midday frequently capturing spiders and small diptera among grass stems along a creek.

Known predators on adult toads in Colorado include the raccoon *(Procyon lotor),* red fox *(Vulpes vulpes),* domestic dog, and common raven *(Corvus corax)* (Corn 1993; Jones, Goettl, and Livo, unpublished). The uneaten remains of adults often include the head, limbs, skin, and ovaries, tissues likely to be high in toxins. Predation events sometimes remove a significant proportion of the local toad breeding population (Corn

1993). Documented predators of larvae and metamorphosing and newly metamorphosed individuals in Colorado and southern Wyoming include the mallard *(Anas platyrhynchos),* spotted sandpiper *(Actitis macularia),* American robin *(Turdus migratorius),* gray jay *(Perisoreus canadensis),* Steller's jay *(Cyanocitta stelleri),* western terrestrial garter snake, tiger salamander larvae, and dytiscid beetle larvae (Reese 1969; Campbell 1970d; David Pettus, in Campbell 1970d; Beiswenger 1981; Goettl 1997; Livo 1998a; Jones, Goettl, and Livo, unpublished). Some instances of predation on young toads can be severe, as in the case of a spotted sandpiper that ate 21 newly metamorphosed toadlets in approximately 30 seconds (Jones, Goettl, and Livo, unpublished). Under laboratory conditions, larvae may be alerted to predation on conspecific larvae through the release of substances from injured individuals and may avoid areas with these cues (Hews 1988).

Wood frog larvae in eastern North America are effective predators on the eggs and hatchlings of *Bufo* toads, and toads avoid laying eggs in ponds inhabited by wood frog larvae (Petranka et al. 1994). Mountain toads in Colorado also infrequently lay their eggs in wood frog breeding ponds.

James and Maslin (1947) described a Jackson County toad that was parasitized by fly larvae. Metamorphosed individuals sometimes are parasitized by leeches (pers. obs.).

Remarks. Scherff-Norris and Livo (unpublished) found pea clams *(Pisidium)* attached to the toes of two newly metamorphosed toadlets in Boulder County, suggesting that this toad sometimes may act as a dispersal agent for the clam.

Taxonomy and Variation. The mountain toad is a member of the *Bufo boreas* complex. Burger and Bragg (1947) and Hubbard (1972) described several morphological, biochemical, and vocal differences between toads of the *Bufo boreas* complex in the Southern Rocky Mountains and those in the Pacific Northwest. In recent decades, toads from both regions have been regarded as members of the subspecies *Bufo boreas boreas* Baird and Girard, 1852. Goebel (1996) examined mtDNA variation in toads of the *Bufo boreas* group throughout western North America and found that various populations in the southern Rocky Mountain region are genetically distinctive and may warrant recognition as one or more different species. Hence it is possible that the scientific name of the Colorado population will change in the near future. If all populations in Colorado are regarded as conspecific with those in central Utah, the scientific name for these likely would become *Bufo pictus* Cope, 1875. However, until a change is formally proposed and supported by published data, I choose to refer to the toads inhabiting the mountains of Colorado as members of the *Bufo boreas* complex and provisionally adopt the appropriate English name "mountain toad." A literal translation of *pictus* might suggest the English name "painted toad" for this species, but this name makes little sense for the species in Colorado. "Boreal toad" logically should be reserved for populations to the northwest that (in the event of a taxonomic revision) would retain the name *Bufo boreas* (type locality is near Puget Sound), and "western toad," or some other name, should be used for other populations in Pacific coastal North America.

Plate 7.29. Adult female Great Plains toad (Otero County, Colorado).

Great Plains Toad
Bufo cognatus (Say, 1823)

Recognition. Skin with numerous small warts; cranial crests prominent, diverge posteriorly from hard lump on top of snout; parotoid glands elongate; dorsum with somewhat symmetrical pattern of large, light-edged dark spots; often a sharp-edged tubercle and a smaller dark-tipped tubercle on underside of hind foot; females up to 114 mm SVL, males usually less than 95 mm SVL. *Mature male:* dark, loose throat skin and dark patch on inner surface of innermost digit of forefeet during breeding season; expanded vocal sac large, elongate, may extend upward in front of face; breeding call a long, continuous trill or pulsating ringing sound (at close range, similar to ear-splitting sound of jackhammer) lasting at least several seconds; varies somewhat with temperature and size of male (Krupa 1990); loud nasal quacks sometimes precede trill (San Luis Valley, pers. obs.). *Juvenile:* warts reddish. *Larvae:* dorsum initially blackish, then becomes paler and mottled brown and gray dorsally (Bragg 1936); under magnification,

dark dorsum may have an overlying golden suffusion (Weld County, pers. obs.); dorsal pattern of large paired blotches appears before metamorphosis is complete; eyes dorsal; dorsal fin highly arched; fins clear with some black dendritic lines, mainly in upper fin, sometimes extensively mottled in upper and lower fins (Bragg 1957); dorsal fin heavily pigmented, ventral fin clear or very sparsely pigmented (Weld County, pers. obs.); tail musculature lacks an unpigmented band along the lower margin; anus on midline at front end of ventral tail fin; upper mandible strongly arched; labial tooth rows usually 2/3; third tooth row on lower lip (i.e., the one farthest from mandibles) considerably shorter than first row on lower lip; oral papillae restricted to sides of mouth; in Oklahoma, TL usually about 26–29 mm, seldom more than 30 mm (Bragg 1940), but up to at least 35 mm in Colorado (pers. obs.). *Eggs:* black above, whitish below, about 1.1–1.2 mm in diameter, usually in a single row in long strings of two-layered jelly that is constricted between the eggs; partitions separate eggs from each other (Bragg 1937; Zweifel 1968).

Distribution. Throughout the Great Plains (north to southern Alberta, Saskatchewan, and Manitoba in Canada; east to Missouri), southwestern United States (west to southeastern California), and much of the northern half of Mexico. Occurs throughout most of eastern Colorado, generally below 6,000 feet (1,830 m) and in the San Luis Valley at 7,500–8,000 feet (2,285–2,440 m). There are no known documented occurrences in the western part of the Arkansas River drainage in eastern Colorado. However, Hahn (1968) stated that the Great Plains toad occurs in the Wet Mountain area of Fremont and Custer counties, citing unpublished information from Benjamin Banta. A record from Colorado Springs, based on Yarrow (1875) and assigned to this species by Maslin (1959), is unsubstantiated by any specimens in the U.S. National Museum collection upon which Yarrow reported; all of the specimens from Colorado Springs are *Bufo woodhousii*. In the San Luis Valley, the Great Plains toad occurs primarily in the internal drainage basin in the northern part of the valley, but it also inhabits the Rio Grande drainage. An old record from Fort Garland, Costilla County (Yarrow 1875, not shown on Distribution Map 7.8), probably represents the point from which the specimens were shipped, not the precise collection locality.

Conservation Status. The Great Plains toad apparently still is widespread in its historical range in eastern Colorado (Mackessy 1998; pers. obs.) and the San Luis Valley

(Freeman and Harvey, unpublished data). It is difficult to judge whether abundance has changed over time, but the toad currently is locally common in some areas. The single Boulder County population that I discovered in 1978 now apparently is extirpated as a result of large-scale residential and commercial development in Louisville. Intensive cultivation and pesticide use probably have reduced populations in some areas, but the severity of these threats is unknown. Many toads are killed on roads adjacent to breeding pools. In general, the Colorado population appears to be relatively stable and unthreatened, but this toad is much more localized and far less numerous than the sympatric Woodhouse's toad.

Habitat. The Great Plains toad inhabits plains grassland, sandhills, and agricultural areas in eastern Colorado, especially along floodplains of streams where soils are relatively soft. Habitat in the San Luis Valley consists of sandy semidesert shrublands. This toad normally enters water only to breed. Inactive periods are spent burrowed in the ground or, in summer, sometimes under rocks or wood or in cracks of drying mud (juveniles). During the active season, daytime burrows are only a few centimeters deep (Bragg 1937).

Activity. In Colorado, most activity is nocturnal from May to September, especially when conditions are mild and moist. Daytime activity may occur during breeding events.

Toads active away from breeding pools usually have body temperatures of 15°C or higher (pers. obs.). As is true of amphibians in general, toads active on land have lower body temperatures than the surrounding air temperature. For example, four adults active on a lakeshore at 9:00–9:35

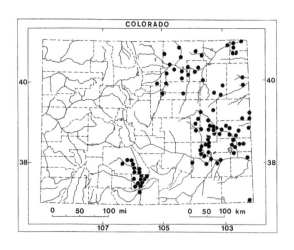

Map 7.8. Distribution of the Great Plains toad in Colorado.

Plate 7.30. Calling male Great Plains toad (Alamosa County, Colorado).

P.M. in the San Luis Valley had body temperatures of 16.8–19.4°C at an air temperature of 21°C; one toad in the water matched the water temperature of 17.0°C (Livo 1990). Toads acclimated to 15°C die if their body temperature reaches 41–42°C (Paulson and Hutchison 1987).

In hand, these toads often release fluid from the vent. Adult males may emit a repeated quacking chirp if grasped by the body.

Reproduction and Growth. Primary breeding habitat in Colorado includes reservoirs that fluctuate greatly in size and areas temporarily flooded by heavy rains. Usually, the water is clear or slightly turbid. Other amphibians known to breed in pools with the Great Plains toad in Colorado include the plains spadefoot, Woodhouse's toad, western chorus frog, and plains leopard frog.

Here, and elsewhere in the range (see Krupa 1994), the breeding season corresponds with the occurrence of warm rains that result in pond formation or flooding, rather than with a particular date. If early breeding takes place, breeding after rains later that year at the same site is rare; likewise, late breeding happens mainly in years when the first spring rains fall relatively late in the season (Krupa 1994). The amount of rain needed to stimulate breeding may be as little as 0.4 cm (mean 4.4 cm); breeding rarely if ever occurs in the absence of rain (Krupa 1994).

In Colorado, the male's breeding call may be heard under appropriate conditions from May to July. I have heard these toads calling when air temperature was as low as 7°C, but these individuals were in water of 11°C. Bragg (1940) found that breeding in Oklahoma requires air temperatures of at least 12°C. Ballinger and McKinney (1966) found breeding choruses at water temperatures of 15–28°C. Temperature requirements for breeding may be higher in southern Arizona (Zweifel 1968).

In Oklahoma, breeding may take place on many consecutive nights early in the season, but later it may be restricted to only one or two nights; peak breeding generally occurs during the first two nights after a rainstorm (Krupa 1994). In Arizona, Sullivan (1985b) found that breeding events last an average of 2–3 nights.

Calling males may sit along the shoreline or brace themselves on submerged plants. Females are more likely to mate with males that call frequently (Sullivan 1985a). Silent males near calling males sometimes successfully intercept and mate with approaching females (Sullivan 1982a). Male calling and female arrivals at breeding sites typically happen during the first few hours after sunset (Krupa 1994), but I observed several calling males and gravid females in shallow water under cloudy skies in midafternoon in late May in the San Luis Valley. Krupa (1994) found that amplexed pairs hide in dense vegetation until morning, then swim to open shallow areas where egg-laying occurs after an average of 13–14 hours of amplexus. In contrast, Bragg (1937) reported that oviposition often does not take place until the afternoon of the following day.

Mature females lay up to 45,000 eggs but usually fewer than 10,000 (Krupa 1994). Some females are capable of laying multiple clutches in a single season (Krupa 1986). Several females may deposit their clutches in a small area.

Eggs hatch in 2–3 days. Larval development proceeds rapidly under suitably warm conditions. In Oklahoma, the period from egg deposition to complete metamorphosis lasts 4–5 weeks in early spring but only 18

	San Luis Valley	Eastern Colorado	Oklahoma
Male snout-vent length	46 (41-51) (n = 18)	75 (55-81) (n = 13)	75 (56-98) (n = 758)
Female snout-vent-length	52 (47-57) (n = 10)	87 (80-98) (n = 10)	80 (60-115) (n = 91)

Table 7.1. Snout-vent length (mean, range, sample size) (mm) of adult *Bufo cognatus* in Colorado (Hammerson 1981) and Oklahoma (Krupa 1994). Data for Colorado are based on preserved specimens; Oklahoma toads were measured alive.

days in June (Krupa 1994). Hahn (1968) found metamorphosed toadlets only 17 days after the eggs were laid in a pool in the San Luis Valley. In Oklahoma, high larval densities and cool temperatures, resulting in reduced growth rate, and pond desiccation in warm weather often cause larval mortality before metamorphosis (Krupa 1986). Recently metamorphosed toadlets may be as small as 1 cm SVL and grow rapidly to 2 cm (Bragg 1940; Hahn 1968; Graves, Summers, and Olmstead 1993; pers. obs.). Newly metamorphosed individuals have been observed in the San Luis Valley in late July (Hahn 1968; pers. obs).

In years with abundant spring and summer rainfall, large numbers of toadlets may be produced, and they may move together across the land. Bragg and Brooks (1958) described a massive movement of juveniles that occurred in the northern Great Plains in the summer of 1941. A study by Graves, Summers, and Olmstead (1993) indicated that aggregation may occur independent of habitat features and that vision and olfaction are involved in the aggregation response. Perhaps toads in aggregations are more likely to survive if predators are confused or overwhelmed by sheer numbers, but on the other hand, aggregations may attract predators and incur heavy predation. Of course, aggregations might result from other factors, such as regulation of body temperature or water loss.

Estimates of age at onset of breeding range from 2–5 years. However, using skeletochronological methods, Rogers and Harvey (1994) found that among a sample of 79 toads from a breeding aggregation in the San Luis Valley, none was older than two years. Data from Oklahoma also suggest a short breeding life—only 7–8 percent of 184

marked adults were recaptured in subsequent years (Krupa 1994).

Food and Predators. This toad is an effective enemy of many agricultural pests. The usual diet includes moths, caterpillars, flies, beetles, ants, and other small arthropods (e.g., Smith and Bragg 1949). A toad that I found in Weld County defecated beetle remains for 3–4 days. Smith and Bragg (1949) found that weevils (curculionid beetles) regularly survived passage through the digestive tract of the Great Plains toad. Dimmitt and Ruibal (1980) determined that this toad requires 11–22 feedings per year to survive.

Predators are not well known. In South Dakota, Graves, Summers, and Olmstead (1993) found that the stomachs of plains garter snakes sometimes contain nothing but *Bufo cognatus* toadlets. Stuart (1995) documented predation on a 7-cm-SVL Great Plains toad by an 18-cm-SVL bullfrog in New Mexico. Known predators on larvae include spadefoot tadpoles and diving beetle larvae (Bragg 1940). Crows *(Corvus brachyrhynchos)* may eat metamorphic individuals (Bragg 1940).

Remarks. Sullivan (1990) recorded a natural hybrid between the Great Plains toad and red-spotted toad in central Arizona.

Taxonomy and Variation. Breeding individuals in the San Luis Valley are much smaller than those elsewhere in the Great Plains (Table 7.1). Similarly, Hahn (1968) found that sexually mature adults in the San Luis Valley were only 41–60 mm SVL. Rogers and Harvey (1994) sampled a breeding aggregation in the San Luis Valley and found a similar size in males, but females were smaller (mean SVL near 46 mm). However, values for two-year-old females (mean SVL about 51 mm) were close to those I recorded.

One-year-old males (mean SVL about 35 mm) generally were smaller than females (mean SVL 37 mm) of the same age. In addition to being relatively small, individuals in the San Luis Valley have a relatively shorter, more rounded parotoid gland. Hahn believed that the San Luis Valley population probably warrants subspecific status. A rangewide study of morphological and genetic variation is needed to clarify the taxonomic status of the San Luis Valley population. (Note: Living individuals are larger than preserved material just described. For example, six calling males in the San Luis Valley were 54–62 mm SVL [average 56 mm], and two females found near these males were 56 and 62 mm SVL. Living females in eastern Colorado attain a size of at least 11 cm SVL.)

The original description of *Bufo cognatus* was based on a specimen collected along the Arkansas River in southeastern Colorado (Say, in James 1823), probably a few miles west of Holly in Prowers County (Dundee 1996).

Plate 7.31. Adult green toad (Baca County, Colorado).

Green Toad
Bufo debilis (Girard, 1854)

Recognition. Dorsum green with numerous small black spots and irregular lines; underside immaculate or with few small black marks on chest or throat; parotoid glands large and broad (shaped like a kidney bean), low on shoulders; cranial crests weak or absent; head and body distinctly flattened; maximum SVL about 51 mm. *Mature male:* dark throat with loose skin during breeding season; expanded vocal sac evenly rounded; breeding call a flat buzz lasting about 2–8 seconds. *Larvae:* stippled with black, with golden patches on dorsum and tail musculature, relatively pale compared to most *Bufo* larvae; underside black and golden laterally, with no black pigment on throat and midbelly regions; dorsal fin clear initially, later pigmented with dark dots or lines; ventral fin with sparse dark pigment at end of development; labial tooth rows usually 2/2 (unique among toads in Colorado); tooth row closest to mandible on upper lip with wide gap in middle; tooth rows on lower lip continuous and shorter than anterior row on upper lip; oral papillae restricted to sides of mouth; anus on right side at front end of ventral tail fin; 3.1–3.4 mm TL at hatching, maximum TL about 25 mm (10 mm body, 15 mm tail) at stage 36 (Arizona, Zweifel 1970). *Eggs:* yellowish with dark pigment at one end, about 1 mm in diameter, deposited in small clusters (Zweifel 1970).

Distribution. Southeastern Colorado and western Kansas south through New Mexico, southeastern Arizona, and Texas to central Mexico. Known from several locations in southeastern Colorado at elevations of about 4,000–5,000 feet (1,220–1,525 m). Found "near Trinidad" (6,000 feet [1,830 m]), Las Animas County, in 1883 (Ellis and Henderson 1913; UNC-MNH museum register). Records from extreme west-central Kansas (Collins 1993) suggest that the green toad may occur in extreme east-central Colorado between the Arkansas and Republican River drainages.

Conservation Status. The green toad is known from relatively few sites in Colorado, with each site yielding no more than about 25 adults at any one time (Mackessy 1998; L. Livo, pers. comm.; pers. obs.). However, finding this toad is difficult except after spring and summer rains, even in sites where it is known to occur. Though it is likely that at least several populations remain undiscovered in the ample supply of suitable habitat in southeastern Colorado, numerous surveys in the region indicate

that this species probably exists only in a limited number of scattered locations. There are no known existing threats of major significance. Populations should be secure as long as cattle ranching remains the primary land use in green toad habitat.

Habitat. This toad lives in areas of short-grass prairie, in gently rolling plains and canyon bottoms. Inactive periods are spent in crevices between rocks and in burrows. The flattened shape of these toads facilitates squeezing into small spaces. Green toads have weak limbs and feet and do not dig their own burrows. In New Mexico, Creusere and Whitford (1976) found adults in ant-nest chambers; juveniles took refuge in rodent burrows or in cracks between plates of drying mud.

Activity. Known records of activity in Colorado extend from June to early September, but activity certainly takes place at least as early as May. Activity is primarily nocturnal, during and after rains. Some daytime activity (e.g., calling) occurs during breeding events. I have found active individuals in Colorado at air temperatures as low as 11°C.

Reproduction and Growth. In Colorado, breeding takes place in temporary ponds and in pools along intermittent streams after heavy rains in late spring and summer. I have heard calling males from early to late June in Colorado. Two 45-mm-SVL females found dead on roads in early June had already laid their eggs. In the absence of earlier rains, breeding events occur as late as mid-August (Mackessy 1998; L. Livo, pers. comm.). The few breeding pools I observed in Colorado had muddy water and a rocky/muddy bottom. In New Mexico, breeding sites usually have sparse to dense vegetation (Creusere and Whitford 1976). Breeding pools in Col-

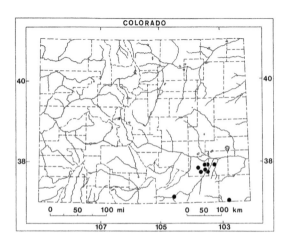

Map 7.9. Distribution of the green toad in Colorado.

orado are shared with the New Mexico spadefoot and Couch's spadefoot.

Calling males occupy shoreline areas, usually partially hidden in vegetation, or sit in shallow water, often among vegetation. Calling males may aggregate in certain sections of large breeding pools and do not actively search for females, waiting instead for a female to touch them (Sullivan 1984). Calling is most vigorous at night but may continue until midmorning after heavy evening rains. Stebbins (1951) and Zweifel (1968) recorded calling males at water temperatures of 19–22°C, corresponding with my limited data for Colorado. In southeastern Arizona and adjacent New Mexico, Sullivan (1984) found that choruses last only 1–3 nights.

In Arizona and New Mexico, Sullivan (1984) found that calling males are 37–46 mm SVL. Of pairs in amplexus, males average 42 mm SVL, females 50 mm.

Food and Predators. Food consists primarily of small arthropods. In a sample of three adult toads that I found dead on roads in Colorado, one stomach contained several dozen black ants (2–3 mm) and one 3-mm beetle; the others contained only ants. Stuart (1995) documented predation on a 42-mm-SVL green toad by a 18-cm-SVL bullfrog in New Mexico.

Taxonomy and Variation. The subspecies in Colorado is *Bufo debilis insidior* Girard, 1954. However, the green toad has not been the subject of a modern analysis of geographic variation throughout its range, so the validity of the named subspecies is unknown.

Plate 7.32. Adult red-spotted toad (San Miguel County, Colorado).

Red-spotted Toad
Bufo punctatus (Baird and Girard, 1852)

Recognition. Dorsum gray or brown with orange or red warts; head and body flattened; parotoid glands circular or somewhat oval; cranial crests inconspicuous; maximum SVL about 7.6 cm (usually about 4–6 cm). *Mature male:* throat dusky during breeding season; expanded vocal sac evenly rounded; breeding call a high, ringing trill lasting about 3–12 seconds, sometimes varying in pitch, emitted up to several times per minute. Juveniles of Woodhouse's toad have red spots and sometimes are mistaken for this species. *Larvae:* Head-body more or less ovoid; dorsum blackish; venter dark with much gold spotting; throat unpigmented; eyes dorsal; head relatively broad (snout end of body not as pointed as in Woodhouse's toad larvae when viewed from above); dorsal fin with much dark pigment, ventral fin mainly clear (mature larvae); upper mandible with thin extension on each side; labial tooth rows 2/3; tooth row farthest from mandible on lower lip nearly as long as tooth row closest to mandible on lower lip; oral papillae restricted to sides of mouth; anus on midline at front end of ventral tail fin; usually less than 40 mm TL, often 30–32 mm TL. *Eggs:* black above, whitish below, 1.0–1.3 mm in diameter, surrounded by single jelly envelope, deposited individually or in small clusters of a few eggs.

Distribution. Southern Nevada, southern Utah, southern Colorado, and southwestern Kansas south to southern Baja California and central mainland Mexico. Occurs in southeastern Colorado principally south of the Arkansas River at elevations below 6,000 feet (1,830 m) and in southwestern Colorado mainly south of the Colorado River at elevations below 7,000 feet (2,135 m). I have unconfirmed reports that this toad inhabits southern La Plata County. An unsubstantiated report of *Bufo punctatus* from Boulder County (Tonn 1961:841) undoubtedly was based on juvenile specimens of *B. woodhousii.*

Conservation Status. The red-spotted toad lives in rough terrain that generally is not suitable for intensive development, so habitat loss has not been a problem. Most populations exist away from roads and do not incur much mortality from vehicles. The toad remains plentiful in many locations, and there is no evidence that the distribution and abundance have changed over the past several decades. There are no known existing threats of any significance in Colorado.

Habitat. In Colorado, the red-spotted toad usually is associated with rocky canyons, but in some places it occurs along streams and in canyon bottoms where large rocks are absent in the immediate vicinity. Junipers and shrubs usually are scattered over the slopes of these canyons. The red-spotted toad may wander widely at night in wet weather. In the heat of the day and during the cold season, it hides in crevices, rodent burrows, or under rocks. Its flattened head and body facilitate squeezing into tight spaces. Burnett (1926) found an individual in a prairie-dog burrow in late July in Montezuma County. I found six adults under a single rock 15 m from a temporary canyon-bottom rain pool in the same county. In summer, a retreat may be used by the same toad on several consecutive days (Weintraub 1974).

Activity. Active individuals have been found in Colorado from May through October. Most activity occurs at night, often beginning about 30–60 minutes after sunset (Weintraub 1974), but it is not unusual to find these toads hopping along canyon-bottom streams in the morning or late afternoon. Infrequent recaptures of marked toads suggest that individuals are not active every night, even if conditions are suitable (Weintraub 1974). Various studies in south-

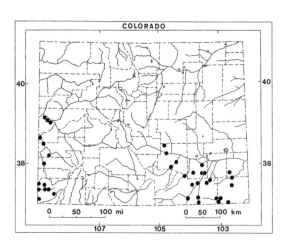

Map 7.10. Distribution of the red-spotted toad in Colorado.

ern California (Turner 1959; Tevis 1966; Weintraub 1974) indicate that home range size varies with local conditions; the largest home ranges (up to several hundred meters long) are found where fluctuating moisture availability along stream courses allow the toads to travel large distances.

In August in southern California, Moore and Moore (1980) found that toads active in the open at night had a lower average body temperature (24°C, range 19–34°C) than did toads hidden during the day in rodent burrows (one toad maintained a temperature near 35°C throughout the day). Similarly, in Colorado, several toads that I found active at night had body temperatures of 18–21°C, whereas a few found under rocks in daytime had temperatures of 24–28°C. The lowest body temperature at which red-spotted toads are active usually is from 14–18°C (Tevis 1966; Zweifel 1968) (but see Gehlbach 1965). Dehydrated red-spotted toads exhibit a well-developed water-absorption response

that involves placing the thin-skinned pelvic region on a damp substrate (Brekke, Hillyard, and Winokur 1991) (see account of true toad family).

Individuals disturbed near pools may hop into the water, dive to the bottom, and often come to rest unhidden. In San Miguel County, a 55-mm-SVL adult male flattened its body and bent its head downward when I reached toward it. In hand, it exhibited second-long silent body vibrations similar to those associated with release calls. Another adult found in Montrose County exhibited the same behavior.

Reproduction and Growth. Temporary pools, spring-fed pools, large bedrock potholes, and permanent plunge pools along small intermittent streams are the primary breeding habitat in Colorado. Sometimes breeding occurs along river bottomlands in habitats used by the Woodhouse's toad (McCoy, Smith, and Tihen 1967). Breeding pools often are bounded by large rocks, may have a layer of sand or silt on the

Plate 7.33. Calling male red-spotted toad (Baca County, Colorado).

Plate 7.34. Male and female red-spotted toads in amplexus (Mesa County, Colorado).

bottom, and usually are clear, greenish, or slightly turbid during the period of larval development.

Males call nocturnally while sitting on bare rock at the edge of breeding pools or on the pool bottom in shallow water. Males commonly call during daylight hours while hidden in rock crevices near the breeding pools. Males sometimes wrestle with each other or move to new locations between periods of calling. Breeding aggregations generally include fewer than 20 calling males (frequently fewer than 10) at a single pool.

Initial amplexus and oviposition often occur in different locations. In Arizona, one male vocalized until a female made contact with him, then he clasped her and the pair moved out of the chorus area, after which the female laid her eggs (Sullivan 1984, 1985b). In Mesa County, I found a pair in amplexus at 10:00 P.M. under a rock 1 m from a tiny stream; two additional males

were grasping portions of the female's body, but they released her and fled soon after I lifted the rock.

Breeding in Colorado takes place from about mid-May through August, with most egg deposition in late May and early June, at least in Mesa County. A female found dead on the road in Las Animas County in late May was full of eggs. In Mesa County, I found that most egg-laying occurs after the majority of Woodhouse's toads have bred, though there is some overlap. Breeding may take place over a prolonged period in a particular location. At several ponds in Arizona, Sullivan (1985b) found that breeding lasts an average of about three weeks.

In northwestern New Mexico, Gehlbach (1965) found a breeding chorus at relatively low temperatures (water about 12°C, air about 9°C). Higher temperatures (most often 20–29°C) seem to be required for breeding in southern California and southern Arizona (Turner 1959; Tevis 1966; Zweifel 1968).

Plate 7.35. Defensive posture of red-spotted toad (San Miguel County, Colorado).

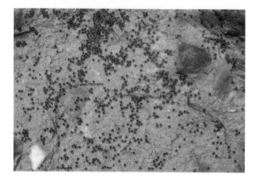

Plate 7.36. Eggs of red-spotted toad (San Miguel County, Colorado).

Eggs are laid on the bottoms of pools and often loosely cover large areas in a single layer. Newly metamorphosed individuals have been observed in Colorado as early as July 2. Luepschen (1981) reported finding albino larvae in late August in Mesa County; one of these larvae had not yet metamorphosed on October 7 (however, larval identification characteristics were not mentioned, and apparently no voucher specimens were saved, so it is impossible to verify the identity of the larvae). Newly metamorphosed young that I found on August 11 in Mesa County were 15 mm SVL (plus a 1-mm tail stub); a 25-mm-SVL juvenile found on the same day may have metamorphosed a month earlier.

At Mesa Verde, Montezuma County, Douglas (1966) found recently hatched larvae on August 2. By mid-August, the legs were beginning to develop. On October 6 the larvae had metamorphosed, and the toadlets (about 15 mm SVL) were in grassy areas beside the breeding pools.

In Colorado, the presence of non-breeding juveniles (27–35 mm SVL) during the late-May breeding season indicates that participation in breeding occurs no sooner than the third calendar year.

Breeding often is unsuccessful. Hot weather commonly results in drying of the breeding pools before the larvae complete metamorphosis. Embryos and larvae sometimes are killed when heavy rains cause sudden high stream flows that wash eggs or larvae out of the breeding pools and into areas that quickly dry (Douglas 1966; pers. obs.).

Food and Predators. Red-spotted toads feed opportunistically on bugs, beetles, ants, bees, and other arthropods (Tanner 1931; Smith 1934, 1956).

In San Miguel and Mesa counties, I observed several dead adults that had been preyed upon, with only the head and neck (parotoid glands) remaining, indicating predation by mammals or birds. Creusere and Whitford (1976) reported that spadefoot larvae in New Mexico eliminated red-spotted-toad larvae through predation.

Remarks. McCoy, Smith, and Tihen (1967) found hybrids (sterile males) between the red-spotted toad and Woodhouse's toad in Mesa County in 1963. I observed a 44-mm-SVL hybrid toad in the same canyon complex in 1990 and found another probable hybrid along the Dolores River in Mesa County in 1988. McCoy, Smith, and Tihen believed that irrigation in the Grand Junction area allowed expansion of Woodhouse's toad into the range of the red-spotted toad, resulting in hybridization between the formerly habitat-separated species. Malmos, Reed, and Starret (1995) reported hybridization between these same species in the Grand Canyon region of Arizona.

Taxonomy and Variation. No subspecies have been described.

Plate 7.37. Adult Woodhouse's toad (Weld County, Colorado).

Woodhouse's Toad
Bufo woodhousii (Girard, 1854)

Recognition. Dorsum yellowish brown, grayish, or olive, with asymmetrical pattern of small dark spots that generally contain 1–2 warts; typically a light stripe along middle of back; cranial crests (supraorbital ridges) more or less parallel between eyes; parotoid glands about twice as long as wide; maximum SVL about 12.7 cm; females grow much larger than males. *Mature male:* during breeding season, throat dark and dark patches present on inner surfaces of first and second digits of front feet; expanded vocal sac spherical or slightly elongated; breeding call a loud "waaaaaah" lasting about 1–4 seconds and emitted up to several times per minute. *Juvenile:* mid-dorsal stripe absent or inconspicuous, usually some warts reddish, often misidentified as red-spotted toad. *Larvae:* dorsum brown or dark gray, often with light mottling/dense gold flecking; head narrow when viewed from above (snout end more pointed and overall body shape more triangular than in red-spotted toad); belly gold with black mottling; eyes dorsal; fins mainly clear with sparse pigment flecks, more in upper fin than in lower fin; tail musculature dark with light mottling/gold flecking, pale along lower margin; labial tooth rows 2/3; oral papillae restricted to sides of mouth; anus on midline at front end of ventral tail fin; maximum TL at least 35 mm in Colorado. *Eggs:* black above, tan below, 1.0–1.5 mm in diameter, deposited in a single or double row within a single-layer jelly string.

Distribution. Great Plains from Montana and North Dakota south through New Mexico, northern Mexico, and Texas; west of the Great Plains, ranges north to Utah and western Colorado and disjunctly to Idaho, eastern Oregon, and southeastern Washington; and southwest (disjunctly) to southeastern California and northeastern Baja California. Fowler's toad *(Bufo fowleri),* formerly included in *B. woodhousii,* is found in eastern North America. Woodhouse's toad occurs throughout Colorado at elevations below 7,000 feet (2,135 m), though it reaches 7,900 feet (2,410 m) in the Wet Mountains. The highest occurrences in northwestern Colorado are at about 6,000 feet (1,830 m). A disjunct population occurs in the San Luis Valley at elevations of about 7,500–8,000 feet (2,285–2,440 m).

Museum records of *Bufo woodhousii* from Estes Park in Larimer County (UCM), Twin Lakes in Lake County (USNM), and South Park in Park County (MCZ) are based on very old records that never have been confirmed by later collections. I regard the data or identifications for these high-elevation occurrences as erroneous. A record from Grand County (Maslin 1959) is based on a misidentified specimen of *Bufo boreas* (Hammerson 1984).

The mountain toad and Woodhouse's toad occupy complementary areas in Colorado. The only place where they reportedly coexist is in northern Archuleta County (Harris 1963).

Conservation Status. Woodhouse's toad is widespread and abundant in many places in Colorado and easily is the state's most commonly encountered amphibian. It is an adaptable species, often tolerant of irrigated agricultural development and cattle ranching. These toads frequently forage at night on roadways, and traffic is a significant cause of mortality. In some areas near major breeding complexes, vehicles may kill hundreds of individuals every year. It amazes me that the toads persist in these areas. Dams and water diversions probably have negatively impacted this toad by reducing the extent and frequency of stream flooding and thus the availability of suitable breeding habitat. Despite these impacts, the distribution of Woodhouse's toad does not appear to be shrinking, and the species can be regarded as secure, due in part to the contribution of many human-created bodies of water that function as breeding sites.

At Wellsville Warm Spring in Fremont County, Brown (1979) observed that two of four immature individuals found in the main pool lacked eyes, but developmental anomalies are rarely observed in this species.

Habitat. Woodhouse's toad is associated primarily with deep friable soils in river valleys and floodplains. It commonly inhabits irrigated agricultural areas. Hot midday periods are spent burrowed in the soil, under rocks or other cover, or on damp soil in shade or partial sun. In Douglas County, an adult female occupied a three-inch-deep chamber on a grassy slope in the morning for at least two successive days; the toad's head was visible at the burrow opening. Presumably, winter is spent burrowed deep in the soil.

Activity. Emergence from winter retreats generally occurs in April or early May. Engeman and Engeman (1996) observed that an adult trapped for many years in a window well of a house in a suburban area near Denver emerged in March in five of nine years and in April or May in the other years; the early emergence may be related to warmer-than-natural conditions in this artificial setting. Most toads end the year's activity in September or October. Activity is primarily nocturnal but sometimes occurs through late morning or even in mid-afternoon. Temperatures of 15°C or higher are

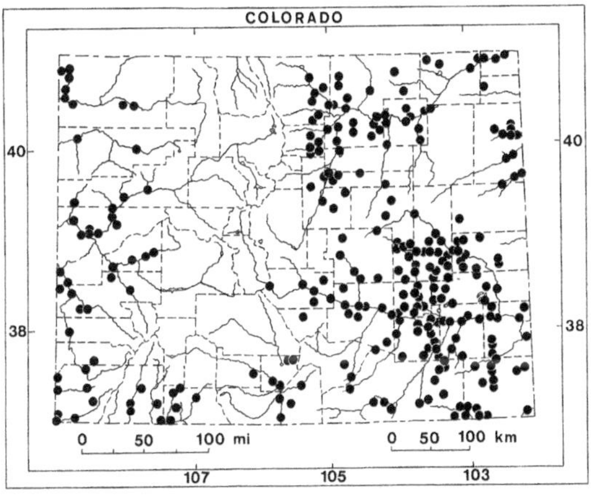

Map 7.11. Distribution of Woodhouse's toad in Colorado.

most favorable for nocturnal activity, though on rare occasions activity takes place at air temperatures as low as 8°C (pers. obs.). Nineteen individuals that I found active on land in Colorado had body temperatures of 15–30°C (average 21°C). Activity may occur during, or in the absence of, rainfall.

Large individuals are capable of relatively long jumps (up to at least 60 cm). When disturbed near water, these toads may jump into the water, dive to the bottom, and become immobile in full view. When grasped, they often inflate the lungs with air, and males typically chirp, vibrate (sometimes accompanied by a grunt), and release fluid from the vent; sometimes they partially inflate the vocal sac.

Reproduction and Growth. Woodhouse's toad breeds in marshes, rain pools, ponds, lakes, reservoirs, flooded areas, stream backwaters, and other bodies of water with a shallow margin and without a strong current. Breeding pools may be clear or muddy, sometimes contain extensive growths of algae or other vegetation, and may vary in size from 1 m or so across to several hectares.

In Colorado, breeding usually takes place in April, May, or June, often after rains when the air temperature is 12°C or higher. Breeding in a particular location may occur over a period of about 3–7 weeks (Sullivan 1985b, 1986; Woodward 1982b, 1984b), and larvae of different sizes commonly are found in a single pond. Gehlbach (1965) observed that breeding occurred after both spring and summer rains in northwestern New Mexico.

Males call while sitting in shallow water. Calling seems to be most vigorous during the first few hours after sunset but may take place day or night. Most choruses include fewer than 30 males. Individual males do not participate in chorus activity every night. For example, in New Mexico, individual males spent an average of about two nights

Plate 7.38. Calling male Woodhouse's toad (Weld County, Colorado).

Plate 7.39. Eggs of Woodhouse's toad (Mesa County, Colorado).

in the pond, females one night (Woodward 1982b, 1984b). In Texas, Thornton (1960) found some females in amplexus twice in the same breeding season, but it is likely that most females breed only once per year. Males in breeding aggregations sometimes wrestle with one another and may attempt to displace other males from amplexus (Woodward 1982a).

Eggs are laid in shallow water and may become tangled in submerged vegetation. The largest females lay the most eggs. In New Mexico, the number of mature eggs contained in adult females averaged 10,469 (Woodward 1987b). A large (10-cm-SVL) female in Oklahoma laid a clutch of 28,500 eggs (Krupa 1995).

Eggs hatch after a few days, and the larval period generally lasts about 4–7 weeks. Large numbers of newly metamorphosed toadlets about 10–13 mm SVL often are present in Colorado in June and July. I have found metamorphosing toadlets as early as the second week of June in Yuma County and in late May in southeastern Utah (San Juan County). Newly metamorphosed toadlets may double in SVL in their first month out of the water (Flowers and Graves 1996). Burt (1933b) found juveniles 15–18 mm SVL on August 10 in Montrose County. Similarly, Gehlbach (1965) observed that recently metamorphosed individuals in northwestern New Mexico were 13–19 mm SVL in early August.

In Colorado, the presence of nonbreeding juveniles (25–45 mm SVL) in early June indicates that reproductive activity occurs no sooner that the third calendar year. Probably,

males attain sexual maturity a year sooner than females. Engeman and Engeman (1996) observed a toad that remained trapped in a window well in the Denver area from 1978 to at least 1996, indicating the long potential lifespan of this species.

Long (1988) found that male Woodhouse's toads in northern Texas possessed Mullerian ducts (rudimentary oviducts).

Food and Predators. The known diet includes isopods, scorpions, mites, spiders, centipedes, springtails, grasshoppers, crickets, moths, caterpillars, flies, maggots, bugs, beetles, ants, and bees, with beetles, caterpillars and ants among the most common prey items (Smith 1934; Smith and Bragg 1949; Stebbins 1951; Flowers and Graves 1996; pers. obs.). Small juveniles eat small prey about 1–5 mm long (Flowers and Graves 1996). The stomach of an adult can hold quite a bit of food—a 100-mm-SVL female that I found dead on a road in Morgan County contained two 27-mm beetles, two 20-mm beetles, 18 smaller beetles, one isopod, two 20-mm spiders, eight 35-mm cutworms, and one 25-mm maggot. Flowers and Graves (1996) found that newly metamorphosed juveniles in South Dakota contained up to 62 prey items. Van Riper (1957) photographed and described the method by which food is captured with the tongue.

The blackneck garter snake sometimes preys on these toads in Colorado, and other garter snakes, the western hognose snake, northern water snake, bullsnake, and bullfrog also may eat metamorphosed individuals (Bragg 1940b; Ballinger, Lynch, and Cole 1979; Jones, Ballinger, and Nietfeldt 1981). Larvae may be eaten by spadefoot toad larvae, garter and water snakes, and predaceous insects. Predators undoubtedly also include certain birds and mammals, evidenced by commonly observed eviscerated carcasses with the head, parotoid glands, and dorsal skin left

Plate 7.40. Larval Woodhouse's toad (Weld County, Colorado).

Plate 7.41. Probable hybrid between a Woodhouse's toad and a red-spotted toad (Mesa County, Colorado).

behind. Woodward and Mitchell (1990) observed that skunks and possibly raccoons *(Procyon lotor)* sometimes prey on and disembowel Woodhouse's toad in New Mexico, with males more likely to be attacked than females. However, at one site, no predation was observed in 4 of 12 years of study.

Remarks. See "Remarks" regarding hybridization in the account of the red-spotted toad.

Taxonomy and Variation. Toads from throughout Colorado usually have been assigned to the subspecies *Bufo woodhousii woodhousii* Girard, 1854 (Maslin 1959; Smith, Maslin, and Brown 1965). Conant and Collins (1991) indicated that specimens from south-central Colorado are intergrades between the subspecies *woodhousii* and *australis*. However, these subspecies were distinguished by minor coloration differences of doubtful taxonomic significance in a species that exhibits a great deal of local variation.

Compared to populations elsewhere in Colorado, populations from the San Luis Valley tend to have a less distinct dorsal pattern, a greater percentage of individuals with dark ventral pigmentation, and a more pronounced tendency toward hypertrophy of the cranial crests and development of a raised interorbital boss (hard lump between the eyes). Hahn (1968) described other distinctive features of the San Luis Valley population.

Sanders (1987) divided *Bufo woodhousii* into multiple species, based largely on cranial characteristics, as follows: *B. woodhousii* (Utah, Arizona, New Mexico, Texas), *B. antecessor* (southeastern Washington, Oregon, Idaho, Utah, western Colorado, part of New Mexico), *B. planiorum* (northern and central Great Plains, including eastern Colorado), *B. hobarti* (= *B. w. fowleri* of most authors, excluding northeastern United States), and *B. fowleri* (restricted mainly to

southern New England). Sanders (1986) also elevated *Bufo woodhousii velatus* to species status. Dundee and Rossman (1989) regarded *velatus* as a racial variant of *woodhousii* produced from various gene introgressions from other toad species. Most herpetologists have ignored Sanders's work, probably because of its difficult-to-digest descriptive approach and lack of quantitative population comparisons. Nevertheless, Sanders revealed some interesting patterns of variation that warrant further consideration.

Sullivan, Malmos, and Given (1996) examined advertisement-call variation and concluded that *B. fowleri,* formerly regarded as a subspecies of *B. woodhousii,* should be recognized as a distinct species and that subspecies *australis* and *woodhousii* should continue to be regarded as western forms of the *B. woodhousii* complex.

TREEFROGS
Family Hylidae

Treefrogs inhabit the Americas, the West Indies, temperate Eurasia, extreme northern Africa, the Japanese archipelago, and the Australia–New Guinea region, with some 755 species worldwide. The treefrogs of the Australia–New Guinea region may represent an independent lineage. Appearance and size of treefrogs vary. Many treefrogs have long, slender limbs. Though some are ground-dwelling and do little climbing, most members of the family are arboreal and have distinctive toe pads that, through surface tension, allow them to climb well and adhere to smooth surfaces. An intercalary cartilage between the last and second-to-last phalanges of each digit allows flat placement of the toe pad. Worldwide, treefrogs exhibit diverse modes of reproduction, but those in North America have a typical frog life history that includes aquatic eggs and larvae. In contrast to true toads, the lungs of treefrog larvae develop and become functional early in the larval period.

Of the 26 species of treefrogs in the United States and Canada, 3 inhabit Colorado. Of these, only the canyon treefrog is an adept climber.

Plate 7.42. Adult northern cricket frog (Yuma County, Colorado). This specimen, photographed in September 1979, was the last observed in the state.

Northern Cricket Frog
Acris crepitans (Baird, 1854)

Recognition. Dark triangle between eyes; large webs between hind toes; whitish marks on upper lip; dorsum usually grayish with small irregular dark marks; eardrum small and indistinct; dark stripe on rear of thigh; maximum SVL about 38 mm, adults average about 26–27 mm SVL. *Mature male:* throat yellowish or dusky; innermost digit of forefeet with thickened pad on inner side during breeding season; expanded vocal sac evenly rounded; breeding call an accelerating then decelerating "gick-gick-gick" lasting up to 30 seconds and sounding like stones being tapped together. *Larvae:* dorsum olive to brown with black mottling; eyes dorsolateral, slightly inside outer margin of head when viewed from above; tail long with low fins (greatest tail height about 10–11 mm), fin with bold dark markings and sometimes with dark tip; narrow dark line along upper edge of tail musculature; belly white to yellowish, with intestinal coil visible; labial tooth rows 2/2 or 2/3; oral papillae extend below lower labial tooth row, not much indented at sides of mouth; anus on right side at front end of ventral tail fin; maximum TL about 4–5 cm. *Eggs:* blackish above, tan below, 1.0–1.2 mm in diameter, enclosed in two jelly envelopes, deposited singly or in small clusters.

Distribution. The northern cricket frog occurs in much of the central and eastern United States (and, at least formerly, extreme southern Ontario, Canada), north to the southern Great Lakes region, east to southern New York and western Florida, south to the Gulf Coast and extreme northern Mexico, and west to eastern New Mexico and eastern Colorado (perhaps formerly to southeastern Arizona [Frost 1983a]). It is abundant in many areas. In Colorado, it is known from the North Fork and South Fork of the Republican River in Yuma County (about 3,500–3,600 feet [1,070–1,100 m]) and perhaps also from the South Platte River drainage in Weld and Morgan counties (see "Conservation Status").

Conservation Status. The following information is a condensed version of Hammerson and Livo (1999).

The presence of this frog in Colorado was first documented by Ellis and Henderson (1913), who reported the collection of two juveniles (18–20 mm [UCM 195]) from the North Fork Republican River drainage at Wray, Yuma County, by Max Ellis on October 26, 1912. The next Yuma County record comprised nine individuals collected two miles east of Wray on July 10, 1948 (UCM). Additional specimens were collected in this area and in the South Fork Republican River drainage at Bonny Reservoir in the 1950s.

Northern cricket frogs evidently remained fairly common in these areas of Yuma County through the 1960s and 1970s. I made the last known observation of this species in Colorado along the North Fork Republican River on September 20, 1979.

Occurrences of cricket frogs in the South Platte River drainage are few and questionable. Burnett (1926) reported that a specimen was found at the entrance of a prairie-dog burrow near Briggsdale, Weld County, on May 27, 1922; the specimen (number 4843), no longer in existence, was deposited in the collection of the Colorado Agriculture College (now the University of Northern Colorado). This record may be based on a misidentified *Pseudacris triseriata,* which I have observed in exactly the same circumstances in the same area, but Burnett's report included records of *Pseudacris,* suggesting that he was able to distinguish between the two species. On the other hand, he did publish an erroneous record of an incorrectly identified lizard (Burnett 1932; Burt 1932). A record from the southern half of Weld County (Hammerson 1982c) was based on an unpublished species list by an experienced herpetologist, but no documentation of the occurrence is available, and searches in the area both at the time of the report and later yielded no observations of this species, so I removed the dot from Map 7.12. A record of the northern cricket frog from Morgan County (Fitzgerald 1978; Hammerson 1982c) is based on specimens collected in June 1971 (University of Northern Colorado collection). One additional specimen in the South Platte River drainage, from Varsity Lake on the University of Colorado campus in Boulder (July 25, 1957, UCM, not mapped), was obtained

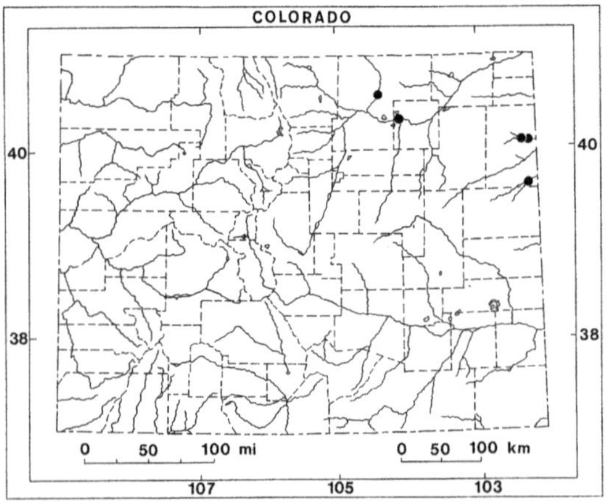

Map 7.12. Distribution of the northern cricket frog in Colorado.

from a short-lived introduced population that was extirpated when the lake was drained (T. P. Maslin, pers. comm., 1978).

In the 1980s and 1990s, Lauren Livo and I made several field surveys at the historical localities in Colorado and in other areas of apparently suitable habitat in Yuma County, but these yielded no additional observations of cricket frogs, nor did our surveys in Weld and Morgan counties. The species remains present along the South Fork Republican and Smoky Hill rivers in extreme western Kansas, is common in central Kansas and central Oklahoma, and exists as small isolated populations along the Platte River in central Nebraska, but no records more recent than 1977 are known for the North Fork Republican River in Nebraska, and in Oklahoma cricket frogs apparently do not occur within about 150 kilometers of Colorado (Hammerson and Livo, 1999).

In summary, the northern cricket frog was fairly common in the Republican River drainage in Colorado through at least the late 1970s, and it may have occurred in the Platte River drainage in Weld and Morgan counties through at least the early 1970s. Subsequent surveys indicate that the species has declined in distribution and may be extirpated from Colorado. Conspicuous breeding calls make this species easy to locate, so it is unlikely that the frog still occurs in the recently surveyed locations within the historic range. However, localized populations, especially away from public roads on private land, are easily missed. Additional field surveys, directed specifically at this species, are needed in the Platte, Republican, and intervening drainages in eastern Colorado.

What accounts for the decline of the northern cricket frog in Colorado? It may be the result of normal fluctuations at the margins of the species' range due to climatic changes (e.g., see Regan 1972). However, the frogs still were locally common in Colorado after the exceptionally cold winter of 1978–1979, when the average temperature in January was 6.8°C below normal (NOAA data).

Among anthropogenic factors that may have reduced or eliminated northern cricket frog populations, habitat change, estab-

lishment of exotic species, and chemical contaminants warrant consideration. Over the past two decades, some changes in the habitat of northern cricket frogs have occurred in Colorado, but the extent of primary breeding habitat (ponds with shallow, marshy edges) seems little altered, and land use within the historic range apparently has remained relatively stable in recent decades.

The non-native bullfrog *(Rana catesbeiana)*, a well-known predator on small frogs (Bury and Whelan 1984), including the northern cricket frog (Lewis 1962; Tyler 1978; Perrill and Magier 1988), is now abundant within the historic range of *Acris* in Colorado, but it was present and may have been abundant in some areas at least as early as the 1940s and 1950s, so it is difficult to attribute the cricket frog's more recent decline to the impact of the bullfrog.

Chemicals associated with agricultural activity in the historic range of *Acris* in Colorado could have caused a decline through excessive mortality in adults and/or embryos, but information is insufficient for adequate evaluation of this possibility.

At present, the decline of the cricket frog in Colorado is inexplicable but parallels a similar puzzling decline in the Midwest, where the species has largely disappeared from the northern portion of its range in the southern Great Lakes region (Harding 1997; Lannoo 1998). Factors responsible for the decline in the Midwest remain speculative, but vegetation succession, climatic fluctuations (e.g., drought), predation by exotic and native species, competition from other frog species, and water pollution caused by pesticides and/or other chemicals associated with agriculture possibly are significant. However, further study is needed before any reliable conclusions can be reached on the cause(s) of northern cricket frog decline in the northern and northwestern margins of its range. This frog's short lifespan may make it vulnerable to extirpation by short-duration phenomena. The species remains common in much of the south-central and southeastern United States.

Habitat. In Colorado, the northern cricket frog occurs (or occurred) along the sunny, muddy, or marshy gently sloping edges of permanent or semipermanent ponds, reservoirs, and streams, and along irrigation ditches, in pastures, and in sand-hill country. When disturbed, cricket frogs leap into the water and may hide under plants or debris; if unmolested, they usually return to shore quickly. Winter habitat is poorly known, but they may hide underwater or in rodent burrows or other underground sites. Dillenbeck (1988) seined a cricket frog from a small stream in eastern Kansas in late January. Burnett (1926) reported one collected in late May from the opening of a prairie-dog burrow in Weld County, but whether that represented a wintering site (or even an actual observation of this species) is unknown.

Nevo (1973) demonstrated that the relatively large body size of cricket frogs in the western part of the range is associated with enhanced resistance to desiccation in a dry environment. This may be most important in winter, for in summer the frogs are closely tied to moist environments, even in the dry portion of the range. However, adults may cease activity in wetlands in midsummer and may then be exposed to relatively dry conditions if they move to terrestrial sites.

Activity. Active cricket frogs have been observed in Colorado from May to October, but undoubtedly the annual period of activity begins as early as April (perhaps even March, if the weather is warm). Individuals active in late summer and early fall are primarily young of the year. Most activity occurs during daylight hours and on warm summer evenings. Burkett (1984) found that cricket frogs in eastern Kansas usually are relatively sedentary, though they sometimes disperse widely during mild, moist weather.

Cricket frogs are remarkable leapers for their size. Under experimental conditions, they can leap up to 38 times their SVL (average maximum is about 28 times); some jumps cover more than 80 cm (Zug 1978). In contrast, *Bufo* toads generally cover only about five times their body length.

Reproduction and Growth. Males call on warm days and nights from the shoreline or while perched on mats of algae or other aquatic vegetation. Specific information on reproduction in Colorado is not available, but a synthesis of information from elsewhere in the range suggests that the following may apply in the state. Calling may begin in April (and on warm days in March) and continues through July or August (late-summer calling is stimulated by rains), but actual breeding probably does not begin until higher temperatures arrive in May. Breeding probably ends in July.

Females prefer males that call often at a relatively low pitch (Perrill and Lower 1994). Sometimes males perch silently near calling males and intercept and mate with approaching females. Compared to calling males, the silent males conserve energy and may avoid detection by predators (Perrill and Magier 1988).

Eggs float or stick to submerged plants. Each female may lay about 150–400 eggs that hatch after a few days. The larval period generally lasts about 10–15 weeks in eastern Kansas (Burkett 1984). Newly metamorphosed individuals, about 10–15 mm SVL, have been observed in Colorado in early July. Metamorphosis probably extends through late summer. In eastern Kansas, all breeders were approximately one year old (Burkett 1984). Potential longevity is at least five years, but few live that long. In Kansas, Burkett (1984) reported that less than 0.1 percent of individuals alive in early September survive through the following September-October.

Food and Predators. Cricket frogs eat various small invertebrates obtained on shore or in the water. Typical food items in Kansas and Nebraska include beetles, beetle larvae, midge larvae, flies, water boatmen, leaf hoppers, and other bugs, as well as Hymenoptera, Lepidoptera, Orthoptera, crustaceans, spiders, and springtails (Jameson 1947; Burkett 1984).

Typical predators probably include bullfrogs, amphibious snakes, and various predatory birds, mammals, and aquatic arthropods. Known predators in Kansas include fishing spiders, largemouth bass *(Micropterus salmoides)*, northern water snake, common garter snake, great blue heron *(Ardea herodias)*, green heron *(Butorides virescens)*, and raccoon *(Procyon lotor)* (see Burkett

1984). Caldwell (1982) suggested that the conspicuous black tip on the tail of some larvae, mostly in pond habitats, may attract the attacks of larval dragonflies to that expendable part of the body.

Taxonomy and Variation. The northern cricket frog exhibits variable dorsal coloration (gray, brown, reddish, green, olive, and/or blackish). Gray is by far the most common color in Colorado and western Kansas, where gray individuals constituted 98 percent of a sample of 91 adults (Gorman 1986). Cricket frogs in western Kansas (and presumably eastern Colorado) are less variable genetically than are populations in eastern Kansas (Gorman and Gaines 1987). The subspecies in Colorado is *Acris crepitans blanchardi* Harper, 1947.

Plate 7.43. Adult canyon treefrog showing "flash" colors (Mesa County, Colorado).

Canyon Treefrog
Hyla arenicolor (Cope, 1866)

Recognition. Toe tips paddle-shaped; dorsum light brown or gray, often matching color of rock, becoming chalky in individuals in full sun at midday; hind toes with extensive webbing; rear of thighs and groin orange-yellow; maximum SVL about 57 mm. *Mature male:* throat skin loose and dusky during breeding season; expanded vocal sac bilobed; breeding call a loud, nasal, rapid, stuttering "ah-ah-ah-ah-ah" lasting usually about 0.75–2.0 seconds, sometimes sounding like an engine turning, a woodpecker drumming, or a machine gun.

Larvae: dorsal coloration brownish, paler than blackish *Bufo* larvae that often occur in the same pools but somewhat darker than large *Spea* larvae; tail fin relatively high, mainly clear with scattered dark squiggles mostly in upper fin and fin tip (sometimes more heavily speckled in large larvae); tail musculature with dark bars or spots; belly gold/cream-colored; gut coil visible; throat dark; eyes widely separated, just inside outer margin of head when viewed from above; labial tooth rows 2/3; tooth row closest to mandible on upper lip has narrow gap in middle; tooth row farthest from mandible on lower lip almost as long as other rows on lower lip; oral papillae encircle mouth except for most of section above anterior tooth row of upper lip; anus on right side at front end of ventral tail fin; maximum TL at least 54 mm in Colorado. *Eggs:* dark above, pale below, enclosed in single jelly envelope, deposited individually or in small clumps.

Distribution. Southern Utah and southern Colorado south through Arizona, New Mexico, and western Texas to central Mexico. Occurs in western Colorado along the southern edge of the Colorado River valley east to Grand Junction and along the Dolores River and its tributaries from near the Utah border south into San Miguel County, mainly at elevations of about 4,500–6,300 feet (1,370–1,920 m).

Arthur E. Beardsley collected this frog at Mesa de Maya in southeastern Colorado in 1886 (Ellis and Henderson 1913; University of Northern Colorado museum register), but a lack of subsequent observations and the fact that the specimen was lost or destroyed cast some doubt on the authenticity of this disjunct record. However, based on Beardsley's other collections of amphibians and reptiles previously undiscovered in Colorado—collections that took a long time to confirm—I suggested (1982a) that the Mesa de Maya record of *Hyla* be taken seriously. The recent rediscovery of the canyon treefrog on private land at Mesa de Maya, after a lapse of more than 100 years, was an exciting and satisfying tribute to Beardsley's excellent reliability. There is an unconfirmed report of an occurrence of this frog in Bent Canyon, Purgatoire River drainage, northern Las Animas County.

Conservation Status. Finley (1953) reported the first record of this frog from western Colorado (Mesa County). Soon thereafter, several other populations were discovered to the north in and near Colorado National Monument in Mesa County. These remained the only known populations until 1992, when Tom Beck of the Colorado Division of Wildlife transported me by raft to several locations along the Dolores River drainage in Montrose and San Miguel counties, allowing me to confirm his earlier observations of treefrogs in those areas. Subsequent surveys in the early and mid-1990s demonstrated that the canyon treefrog still exists in good numbers in historical and additional localities in Mesa County. Thus, the conservation status of this frog appears to be secure and the species less threatened in Colorado than previously believed. Treefrogs occur mainly on public lands.

Annual reproductive success varies with rainfall (see "Reproduction and Growth") and undoubtedly contributes to significant population fluctuations, but local populations of the canyon treefrog nevertheless can persist for decades. Humans probably constitute the greatest existing threat. In spring and early summer, adult treefrogs perch out in the open on rocks during daylight hours and are extremely vulnerable to excessive human exploitation . A single visit by an overzealous collector can have enormous impact on a local population. Fortunately, there is relatively little demand for these frogs in the pet trade, and many sites are protected by their remoteness. However, increased recreational activity in Colo-

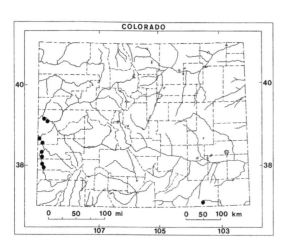

Map 7.13. Distribution of the canyon treefrog in Colorado.

rado National Monument and neighboring public lands is creating greater potential for detrimental human impacts.

Habitat. The canyon treefrog occurs along intermittent streams in deep, rocky canyons. Scattered cottonwood trees often grow along inhabited stream courses. Piñon-juniper woodland usually covers the canyon slopes. Except on warm rainy nights, canyon treefrogs in Colorado do not range far from the permanent canyon-bottom pools. Despite their name, canyon treefrogs in Colorado do not climb trees. Generally, they perch or feed on solid rock surfaces within a single leap of the water or move about on the ground between pools. During the cold season or periods of drought, they retreat to rock crevices not far from their breeding sites.

Activity. Most activity takes place at night from May to September. During this period, particularly in late spring and early summer, these frogs often perch quietly in the sun on dry, steeply sloped rocks. I studied such behavior in Mesa County in late spring and early summer and found that both male and female frogs usually spend the entire daylight period in one spot, an average of 1 m from a pool of water (Snyder and Hammerson 1993). If undisturbed, they do not visit water at all during the day and tolerate conditions that certainly would be fatal to a typical aquatic frog. They frequently use the same perch site on successive days. Perched frogs tuck their limbs beneath the body and maintain a head-down posture. At midday, when sun-loving phrynosomatid lizards retreat to the shade, these treefrogs remain in the sun and maintain a body temperature of about 29–31°C. Preest, Brust, and Wygoda (1992) made similar observations in Arizona. Evaporation of water from the skin keeps the frogs much cooler than a dry-skinned lizard would be under the same conditions. I was unable to determine whether egg-laden

females might be more thermophilic than females without developing eggs. Dorsal coloration at midday may be quite pale and often closely matches the rocks upon which the frogs are perched. During the day, the frogs I observed lost about 25 percent of their body mass through evaporation, an amount equivalent to their bladder water reserves (Snyder and Hammerson 1993).

At dusk or soon after dark, the treefrogs become mobile, often move higher up on rocks, and roam while feeding. By dawn, they return to their daytime perches. Some individuals, perhaps all, visit pools of water, submerge their rear end, and rehydrate during the predawn or early morning hours before assuming their daytime perch. Canyon treefrogs sometimes do not perch in the open but rather sit at the entrance of or within holes or crevices in rocks above pools; the frogs withdraw from the opening if disturbed (pers. obs.; L. Livo, pers. comm.).

Canyon treefrogs successfully exploit warm, dry microhabitats because their skin is much more resistant to water loss than that of a more aquatic frog, such as a leopard frog (Snyder and Hammerson 1993). Basking and maintaining relatively warm body temperatures may speed digestion and growth and perhaps aid in combating parasites and bacterial infection (see brief literature review by Preest, Brust, and Wygoda 1992).

Individuals flushed from perches often leap into the water and dive to the bottom, where they typically remain visible while at rest. When grasped, these frogs usually release fluid from the vent and may produce a

Plate 7.44. Calling male canyon treefrog (Mesa County, Colorado).

sticky skin secretion. Adult males that I captured in Mesa County smelled like buttered popcorn or roasted nuts, as do spadefoot toads. Males in hand may emit a quacking sound.

Reproduction and Growth. Breeding takes place in canyon-bottom stream pools that often are bounded by solid rock. Males sometimes call from deep plunge-pool "tanks" in bedrock. Calling is most vigorous and frequent during early evening and at night, but daytime calling is not uncommon during the height of the breeding period. Calling males generally perch on rocks near pools. In southeastern Arizona and southwestern New Mexico, calling occurred at body and water temperatures of 21–25°C (Zweifel 1968).

Calling and breeding seem to peak after rains in May-June. On June 10 in Mesa County, I watched a gravid female approach a male each time he called. Eventually, she touched him with her forefoot, whereupon he climbed on her back and amplexed her.

On the same day in the same area, a female laid eggs in water that was 13.8°C. My observation of a single 46-mm-TL larva in late May suggests that some breeding may occur in April, as it is unlikely that the larva overwintered. Larvae of different sizes commonly are found in the same pool, indicating multiple local breeding events. Breeding may take place as late as July if spring conditions are exceptionally dry. Some treefrogs may breed after heavy rains in summer, regardless of the occurrence of spring breeding in the same locations. In northwestern New Mexico (7,800 feet [2,380 m]), Gehlbach (1965) found metamorphosing frogs (17–20 mm in body length) in early July and freshly laid eggs two weeks later in the same pond.

Eggs generally are attached to objects at the bottom of pools. Few details are known of the larval development of this frog. In Arizona, Zweifel (1961) observed metamorphosis 50–60 days after oviposition. Metamorphosing canyon treefrogs have been

Plate 7.45. Basking canyon treefrogs (Mesa County, Colorado).

Plate 7.46. Larval canyon treefrog (Mesa County, Colorado).

observed in Colorado from late July through late August. Newly metamorphosed individuals were 15–25 mm SVL in southeastern Arizona (Zweifel 1961) and 22–28 mm SVL (average 25 mm) in northwestern New Mexico (Gehlbach 1965). Young treefrogs in Colorado are similar in size to the New Mexico sample. In Colorado, adult males typically are 42–52 mm SVL (mode 45 mm); breeding females usually are 45–55 mm SVL (most are larger than 50 mm). The presence of apparent subadults (34–35 mm SVL) in June suggests that breeding first occurs no sooner than the third calendar year.

Food and Predators. In a sample of fecal pellets collected in Mesa County, I found the remains of weevils and various other beetles, ants, and a small scorpion (only species with hard exoskeletons were evident in the pellets, so soft-bodied prey probably escaped detection). Elsewhere, known foods include beetles, ants, caterpillars, bugs, caddisflies, centipedes, spiders, and worms (Stebbins 1951; Painter 1985). The straight or slightly curved, cylindrical-to-ovoid fecal pellets are mostly 9–23 mm long and up to 7 mm (usually not more than 5 mm) in diameter. Larvae ingest minute organic material obtained from rock surfaces, bottom detritus, leaves of vascular plants, and submerged filamentous algae. Sometimes they feed at the surface on floating material.

Predators on treefrogs are poorly known but may include various carnivorous mammals, birds, and snakes. Tanner (1929) found a treefrog in the stomach of a night snake in southern Utah. The frogs clearly rely on cryptic coloration and immobil-ity as their primary means of avoiding detection by diurnal predators. Despite the frogs' cryptic color and behavior, a human can easily learn to spot them. One would think that ravens *(Corvus corax)* and other corvids would find and eat them, but the number of treefrogs sitting out in the open indicates that they seldom, if ever, do. Perhaps the frogs' skin secretions make them unpalatable. On several occasions, I have found dead, dry, or decaying, nearly intact individuals that apparently had been discarded by a predator. I once saw a treefrog jump into the water just as an ash-throated flycatcher *(Myiarchus cinerascens)* landed in the tree above it; perhaps the frog was responding to a perceived potential predation attempt.

The bright orange-yellow flash colors on the rear surface of the thighs and in the groin area may startle or confuse a predator. The bright color is exposed only when the legs are extended during a leap and disappears from view when the frog lands and perches with its legs folded. The perched frog usually blends with its background and may be difficult to locate when sitting motionless. This color pattern and behavior is analogous to the bright colors of the expanded wings of certain flying grasshoppers that are cryptically colored when perched.

Larvae presumably are vulnerable to various invertebrate predators, as well as generalist vertebrate predators. Adults that I found in Mesa County sometimes were attacked by mosquitoes.

Taxonomy and Variation. No subspecies have been described.

Plate 7.47. Adult female western chorus frog (Jackson County, Colorado).

Western Chorus Frog
Pseudacris triseriata (Wied, 1838)

Recognition. Dark lateral stripe extending from snout to groin; dorsum variable—green, brown, reddish, or reddish and green, with green or brown stripes or spots; hind toes not distinctly webbed; maximum SVL about 37 mm. *Mature male:* throat skin loose and yellowish or dark during breeding season; expanded vocal sac evenly rounded or slightly flattened; breeding call a stuttering "preeep" that ascends in pitch. *Larvae:* dorsum olive to blackish; tail fin tall, strongly arched, finely stippled or squiggled with brown; eyes at outside margin of head when viewed from above; gut more or less visible through pale golden belly skin; labial tooth rows usually 2/3; oral papillae encircle mouth except for wide gap above upper mandible; more papillae at sides of mouth than elsewhere, marginal papillae not indented at sides of mouth; anus on right side at front end of ventral tail fin; hatchlings 4.8–5.4 mm in Fort Collins (5,000 feet [1,525 m]), 5.9–6.5 mm at Chambers Lake (9,300 feet [2,835 m]) (Pettus and Angleton 1967);

maximum TL about 52 mm (pers. obs.), usually 35–38 mm TL in Gunnison County (Blair 1951). *Eggs:* pigmented over more than half of surface, pigmentation heaviest at higher elevations; diameter larger at higher elevations (1.04–1.32 mm, Chambers Lake) than at lower elevations (0.76–0.85 mm, Fort Collins) (Pettus and Angleton 1967); deposited in loose, irregular, or elongate clusters of several to more than 150.

Distribution. Northern central Canada south through much of the United States to central Arizona, central New Mexico, and the Gulf Coast; absent from Pacific coast states, Nevada, Florida peninsula, and most of New York and New England. Occurs throughout much of Colorado, ranging from below 3,500 feet (1,065 m) in eastern Colorado to above 12,000 feet (3,670 m) in Hinsdale County (Spencer 1971); localized and uncommon in much of western and southeastern Colorado. A record from Las Animas County (Livo, Chiszar, and Smith 1995) is documented by misidentified larvae of *Bufo woodhousii;* however, chorus frogs were calling at the site, so the record remains valid.

Conservation Status. Though some local populations seem to have dwindled

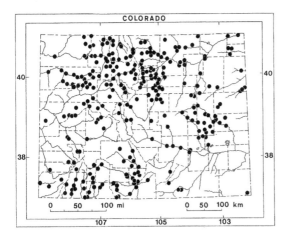

Map 7.14. Distribution of the western chorus frog in Colorado.

populations that included as few as 37 adults. The largest population studied by Hess (1969) totaled about 36,000 individuals.

Habitat. Chorus frogs in lowland areas of Colorado usually remain in or very near a nonflowing body of water, such as a marshy pond, for most of the spring and summer. In the mountains, chorus frogs occur along the edges of bodies of water and also range into wet meadows, usually within about 700 m of their breeding sites, sometimes crossing a few hundred meters of upland habitat (Spencer 1964a). Periods of inactivity may be spent in water, among thick wetland vegetation, under objects on the ground, or in rodent burrows. On August 30 in Rocky Mountain National Park, Livo (pers. comm) heard two males calling faintly from within a dry meadow containing pocket gopher *(Thomomys talpoides)* workings. The meadow was a considerable distance from any breeding pond and may have been a wintering site. In spring in Weld County, I found a chorus frog at the entrance of a prairie-dog *(Cynomys ludovicianus)* burrow, another possible wintering site.

Activity. Emergence from wintering sites typically takes place in March in lowland areas. Activity extends into September and October, with some individuals remaining active into November, even after cold spells. In general, these frogs tend to be relatively inconspicuous in lowland areas in summer. Spring emergence in the mountains may not occur until May. Spencer (1964a) found that chorus frogs at high elevations may remain active even after September snowstorms, but in other places or years, they may disappear by mid-September, even if warm weather continues.

In the mountains at 9,700 feet (2,955 m), most activity takes place between 10:00 A.M.

in recent decades, the western chorus frog remains widespread and common in many areas (Hammerson 1989a, 1992; Corn, Stoltzenburg, and Bury 1989; Livo 1995a; Corn, Jennings, and Muths 1997). There are thousands of breeding sites in Colorado. The species recently has been documented as being more widespread in southeastern Colorado than previously known (Livo, Hammerson, Smith, et al. 1998), and this may reflect both actual range expansion and increased survey effort. Gillis (1975) described a range expansion of chorus frogs into southeastern Colorado along Big Sandy Creek, an expansion evidently made possible by the creation of artificial ponds in the area. This frog remains common in aquatic systems in glaciated portions of the Uinta Mountains in northeastern Utah (Hovingh 1986).

Local habitat destruction has affected some populations, but there are no known existing threats of widespread significance. Occasionally, newly metamorphosed individuals with eye or limb malformations are observed in Colorado (Livo 1998b), but a small number or periodic incidence of developmental deviations is to be expected in any population and should cause no alarm.

Populations of chorus frogs often consist of separate, nearly isolated colonies (Spencer 1964a) and vary tremendously in size. Tordoff (1980) found mountain

Plate 7.48. Western chorus frog (Jackson County, Colorado).

and 3:00 P.M., though calling may extend late into the night during the breeding season (Spencer 1964a). Activity in lowland areas tends to be diurnal in early spring and fall, nocturnal or crepuscular during warm spring and summer weather.

Reproduction and Growth. Chorus frogs breed in marshes, rain pools, snowmelt pools, bog ponds, glacial kettle ponds, beaver ponds, marshy edges of lakes and reservoirs, flooded areas, and other bodies of water with little or no current. Usually, these frogs do not breed in mountain pools kept cool by large influxes of stream water, and larvae do not tolerate temperatures greater than about 38–39°C (Hoppe 1978). Breeding pools usually contain aquatic or wetland plants and submerged terrestrial vegetation. Spencer (1971) found chorus frogs breeding in boggy ponds bordered by sedges and willows at and above the upper limit of forest in the San Miguel and San Juan mountains at 11,800–12,040 feet (3,600–3,670 m), and two lone males were calling at 12,200 feet (3,720 m). Both permanent and temporary waters are used, and eggs commonly are laid in ponds that dry up before the tadpoles metamorphose. Frogs using temporary ponds that persist long enough for completion of larval development may benefit from the typically low numbers and varieties of predators in such environments (Skelly 1996).

In lowland areas, males begin calling usually in late March or April, generally when air temperature is above 10°C. Chorusing continues through spring and early summer. In Kansas, noncalling adult males sometimes sit near calling males and attempt to intercept approaching females; calling and noncalling males do not necessarily maintain those roles (Roble 1985). Calling may come to a temporary halt by late spring but may begin again in summer (as late as August [Burt 1933b]) after heavy rains or when fields are flooded with irrigation water.

In the Great Plains region of Colorado, most oviposition takes place in April, May, and June. Little is known about the incidence of egg deposition during the choruses that occur in lowland areas after June. Corn (1980) reported that egg-laying females were present in a pond in the foothills of Larimer County from April 24 to June 4. Hahn (1968) observed breeding chorus frogs at moderate elevations in the San Luis Valley (about 7,500–8,000 feet [2,285–2,440 m]) from late April to early July.

At high elevations (above 9,000 feet [2,900 m]), breeding begins immediately after the spring thaw in late May or early June (Matthews and Pettus 1966). Non-breeding yearlings emerge from their winter retreats a week or two after breeding has begun. Spencer (1964a) observed breed-

Plate 7.49. Adult male western chorus frog (Boulder County, Colorado).

ing from June 10 to June 20 and from May 14 to June 4 in two different years in the mountains of Larimer County. He observed vigorous chorusing and recently hatched larvae in July at elevations above 11,800 feet (3,600 m) (Spencer 1971). Calling (but not oviposition) is common through late August at high mountain breeding sites and in adjacent meadows. Some of the males calling in August appear to be young of the year, as small as 21 mm SVL. Late-summer calls tend to have a coarse quality in comparison to calls at breeding sites.

Eggs usually are attached to vegetation in shallow water. Each female may lay several egg clusters. Pettus and Angleton (1967) found that females from mountain and lowland areas in Colorado lay an average of 450 eggs (range 137–793) that develop best at temperatures of 20–24°C. Clutch size increases with size of the female (Pettus and Angleton 1967). Hatching may occur within a few days (Ellis and Henderson 1915). Eggs from Kansas

hatched in 5–8 days at 17–25°C (mean 21°C) (Heinrich 1985).

Metamorphosis occurs as early as early June in lowland areas but takes place primarily during July and August (but sometimes as late as early September) in the mountains (Blair 1951; Stebbins 1951; Harris 1963; Spencer 1964a, 1971; pers. obs.). Chenoweth (1950) reported recently metamorphosed individuals (13–14 mm SVL) on July 13 at 9,200 feet (2,805 m) in northwestern New Mexico. Newly metamorphosed frogs in Colorado typically are about 13–16 mm SVL (pers. obs.), though Blair (1951) reported that metamorphosing individuals in Gunnison County were 7–8 mm SVL in a beaver pond and 10–12 mm SVL in a glacial pond. Young usually leave the water before the tail is fully resorbed.

Breeding populations at low elevations are composed only of individuals that hatched the previous year (Spencer 1964a; Hess 1969; Miller 1977). Mountain males do not breed until they are about two years

Plate 7.50. Eggs of western chorus frog (Boulder County, Colorado). *Lauren Livo and Steve Wilcox.*

Plate 7.51. Larval western chorus frog (Larimer County, Colorado). *Lauren Livo and Steve Wilcox.*

old, females not until they are three years old (Spencer 1964a; Matthews 1971).

In a lowland population, Miller (1977) estimated that survival from egg to metamorphosis was about 30 percent. Frogs in this population reached average adult size about 78 days after metamorphosis. Spencer (1964a) determined that the breeding of each mountain female resulted in 12–20 frogs that survive through metamorphosis. Mortality is most severe in the younger stages. Matthews (1968) found the annual death rate in a mountain population to be 31 percent in adults, 45 percent in yearlings, and 90–94 percent in juveniles; only about 1 percent of the eggs laid produced an adult frog. For a mountain population, Tordoff and Pettus (1977) estimated that two-thirds of the adults were newly recruited into the breeding population each year, indicating substantial mortality among adults. However, at least some individuals in the mountains live for five years or more (Spencer 1964a).

Food and Predators. The diet includes a wide variety of invertebrates. Christian (1976) found spiders, daddy longlegs, mites, isopods, springtails, Orthoptera, thrips, bugs, beetles, Neuroptera, caddisfly larvae, caterpillars, flies, ants, a centipede, a worm, and snails in the stomachs of lowland frogs. Not surprisingly, larger individuals ate larger prey (Christian 1982).

Known predators in Colorado include the pied-billed grebe *(Podilymbus podiceps),* great blue heron *(Ardea herodias),* black-crowned night heron *(Nycticorax nycticorax),* American robin *(Turdus migratorius),* gray jay *(Perisoreus canadensis),* western terrestrial garter snake, plains garter snake, common garter snake, tiger salamander (larvae prey on larvae), and bass *(Micropterus* sp.) (Matthews and Pettus 1966; Bagdonas 1968; Miller 1977; Kiesecker 1996; Livo, Hammerson, Smith, et al. 1998; R. Ryder, pers. comm.; D. and J. Ward, pers. comm.). In Larimer County, Miller (1977) found two adult common garter snakes that each had eaten at least five juvenile chorus frogs. A plains garter snake in Lincoln County contained one adult and three larval chorus frogs (Livo, Hammerson, Smith, et al. 1998). On Grand Mesa, I found a larva

that had been captured by a large diving beetle *(Dytiscus)* larva. Ballinger, Lynch, and Cole (1979) reported predation on larvae by the plains garter snake in western Nebraska.

Remarks. Corn (1986) found albinistic chorus frogs in two populations in Larimer County. Albino eggs and larvae had scarcely any dark pigment, and metamorphosed individuals had a reddish dorsal coloration and faint dorsal striping. Embryos, larvae, and juveniles developed normally.

Spencer (1964c) found that small clams occasionally were attached to the toes of chorus frogs in the mountains of Larimer County. The frogs evidently sometimes serve as a dispersal vector for the clams.

Taxonomy and Variation. Frog watchers familiar only with the tiny males from lowland areas often are surprised at the size this frog attains in the mountains. For example, in Larimer County, average SVL of adult males at an elevation of 4,900 feet (1,500 m) is about 24 mm (19–28 mm), whereas at 10,350 feet (3,155 m) the average is 34 mm (30–36 mm) (Pettus and Spencer 1964). The increase in body size as elevation rises is somewhat clinal.

Coloration is another easily observed variable characteristic of western chorus frogs. The dorsum may be brown, green, red, or red and green, and the spots or stripes may be brown or green (Matthews and Pettus 1966; Hoppe and Pettus 1984). In the mountains of Larimer County, brown dorsum with brown spots was the most common coloration in one population, whereas red dorsum with brown spots was most common in another population. No frogs in either population had a green or red-and-green dorsum combined with brown spots, but all other color combinations were observed in one population or the other (Tordoff, Pettus, and Matthews 1976). Tordoff and Pettus (1977) found that the frequencies of dorsal color phenotypes remained stable from year to year within populations, but consistent and significant differences in color phenotype frequencies existed among different populations. In the plains region of Larimer County, chorus frogs are brown with brown spots, or brown with green spots (Hess 1969). Members of the various phenotypes may differ in their reproductive behavior (e.g., time of arrival and duration of stay in breeding ponds) (Corn 1980).

The dorsal coloration may consist of solid stripes, rows of spots, small spots lacking a definite arrangement, or intermediate patterns. The dorsolateral stripes may be straight-edged or wavy-edged and may fuse in places with the mid-dorsal stripe. In a population in Weld County and another in the plains region of Boulder County, two-thirds of the frogs had a continuous left dorsolateral stripe, one-fourth had one break in the stripe, and the remainder had two breaks, three breaks, or an irregularly spotted dorsum (Hammerson 1981).

Chorus frogs in Colorado were assigned to the subspecies *P. t. maculata* by P. Smith (1956), based primarily on their relatively short hind legs, though the difference between subspecies *maculata* and the adjacent subspecies *triseriata* in tibia/body-length ratio amounts to only a few percent (P. Smith 1956), and other reported differences between these two subspecies are relatively minor. Whether morphological variation is paralleled by concordant genetic variation in these two subspecies is unknown. Because Smith's large pooled samples come from vast geographic areas, it is impossible to determine whether the pattern of variation across the ranges of *maculata* and *triseriata* might be clinal (clinal variation generally is inconsistent with the designation of subspecies). Smith assigned chorus frogs from Arizona and New Mexico to subspecies *triseriata*, with the exception of a single specimen from northeastern New Mexico that was considered an intergrade between *triseriata* and *maculata*. However, Gehlbach (1965) found that the relative hind limb length of specimens from northwestern New Mexico placed them as *triseriata-maculata* intergrades. Neither of these areas of intergradation was shown by Conant and Collins (1991), and Degenhardt, Painter, and Price (1996) did not attempt to distinguish the two subspecies in their distribution map for New Mexico. Jones, Ballinger, and Nietfeldt (1981) mentioned a relatively broad area of intergradation

between the subspecies *triseriata* and *maculata* in Nebraska.

Platz (1989) examined the calls and morphology of western chorus frogs (nominal subspecies *maculata* and *triseriata*) in the Great Plains region from South Dakota to Oklahoma and in one montane population in Colorado (no morphological data were presented for Colorado samples). He reported that two call types were present and that call type appeared to correspond with morphological variation. Platz (1989) suggested that two species are present in the Great Plains, including eastern Colorado, and that they correspond with the taxa *maculata* and *triseriata*. However, this interpretation is questionable for the following reasons: (1) the data presented on call characteristics (Platz's Figures 3 and 4) seem to suggest a continuum rather than two discrete call types (though the difference between the ends of the continuum is impressive); (2) the different calls might represent variation among or within individuals of a single species; (3) if two species are present, some sites should contain both (no habitat or breeding season differences were noted), yet no syntopic breeding was reported despite broad geographic overlap; (4) the response of females to call variations is unknown, so the possible significance of call variation as a possible reproductive isolating mechanism cannot be ascertained; (5) the morphological data do not convincingly demonstrate the presence of two species because some populations assigned to *maculata* are more similar to some *triseriata* populations than to certain other populations designated as *maculata* (Platz's Figure 5); (6) all of the morphological characters used mainly reflect overall body size, rather than truly independent attributes; (7) no genetic data were presented that might clarify the relationships among the sampled populations (Hedges 1986, Highton 1991, and Cocroft 1994 analyzed genetic data for *Pseudacris* but did not include *maculata-triseriata* comparisons in their samples); and (8) montane populations, which exhibit striking morphological, physiological, and life history differences from plains populations (e.g., Pettus and Spencer 1964; Pettus and Angleton 1967; Miller 1977), were not adequately represented in the samples, thus leaving their systematic position unresolved. In summary, though western chorus frogs exhibit significant variation, and Platz's results indicate intriguing vocal variation, existing data do not clearly indicate that two species are present in the Great Plains or in Colorado. Morphological data indicate that *maculata* and *triseriata* are joined by extensive intergradation (P. Smith 1956; Conant and Collins 1991). Accordingly, Vogt (1981) and Oldfield and Moriarty (1994) did not present any evidence that two species might be present in Wisconsin and Minnesota, where extensive intermediacy between *triseriata* and *maculata* occurs. The overall pattern of morphological variation in western North American *Pseudacris* suggests that *maculata* and *triseriata*, as presently defined, may roughly represent northern and southern ends of an ecomorphic cline rather than meaningful taxonomic entities. I concur with Degenhardt, Painter, and Price (1996) and continue to refer to chorus frogs throughout this region as a single species, *Pseudacris*

triseriata, until a robust, fine-grained pattern of genetic discontinuity is demonstrated. Further study integrating genetic, morphological, and vocal variation is needed.

NARROWMOUTH TOADS AND RELATIVES
Family Microhylidae

This family of some 315 species is widespread, occurring from southern North America to South America, and in Africa, Southeast Asia, Indonesia, and northern Australia. The few U.S. species are diminutive, squat, small-headed frogs. Elsewhere, some resemble treefrogs. All microhylids in the United States are secretive and spend much of their time underground or beneath rocks. Most species, including those in the United States, are toothless. In some microhylids, the young develop directly into frogs in a terrestrial site, but North American species have an aquatic larval stage.

Plate 7.52. Adult Great plains narrowmouth toad (Baca County, Colorado).

Great Plains Narrowmouth Toad

Gastrophryne olivacea (Hallowell, 1856 [1857])

Recognition. Fold of skin across back of head in adult; snout pointed; toes unwebbed; eardrum not evident; gray or brown dorsal skin smooth and thick, with or without scattered dark spots; head and body flattened; maximum SVL about 42 mm in females, 37 mm in males. *Mature male:* during breeding season, throat skin loose, yellowish or dark; small tubercles on lower mandible and chest; expanded vocal sac pea-sized and spherical; breeding call a nasal buzz lasting 1–4 seconds, usually preceded by a short, distinct whistle ("whit"); several toads calling vigorously sound like a squadron of toy airplanes (or bees or distant sheep). *Larvae:* dorsum grayish brown to blackish, venter spotted and streaked (Bragg 1957); tail fin low, tip usually dark; eyes on outside margin of head when viewed from above; keratinized beak, labial teeth, and oral papillae absent; upper lip is a flap with notch in middle; single spiracle opens at midventral line well back on body, immediately ventral to medial anus; maximum TL about 37 mm. *Eggs:* heavily pigmented on top and sides, 1.2–1.4 mm in diameter (Stebbins 1951), enclosed in a single jelly envelope that is flattened on one side and 3–4 mm in diameter, with envelopes easily separated from one another; deposited in flat, floating surface films usually less than 7 cm across and containing dozens to hundreds of eggs.

Distribution. Missouri, extreme southern Nebraska, extreme southeastern Colorado, southwestern and probably northeastern New Mexico (Degenhardt, Painter, and Price 1996), and southern Arizona (Sullivan et al. 1996) south through Kansas, Oklahoma, western Arkansas, and Texas to central Mexico. Occurs in southeastern Colorado at elevations of about 4,000–5,000 feet (1,220–1,525 m).

Conservation Status. This small toad was first detected in Colorado in 1979, when I found it in four locations in Baca County (Hammerson 1980). Since then, the range has expanded slightly to include adjacent Las Animas County (Boback et al. 1997). Populations appear to be small and localized, and they are almost impossible to detect, except after heavy spring or summer rains or unless mild moist conditions exist at the soil's surface. Additional populations likely remain undiscovered, but overall geographic range and habitat considerations, together with the results of a good number of surveys in southeastern Colorado over the past two decades by Livo, personnel of the Colorado Natural Heritage Program, Mackessy (1998), and me, suggest that significant enlargements of the known range in Colorado are unlikely.

Existing habitat appears to be stable, and no significant existing threats have been identified. Barring major climatological changes, the species probably will remain secure in Colorado as long as livestock grazing continues to be the primary land use in the areas of southern Baca and

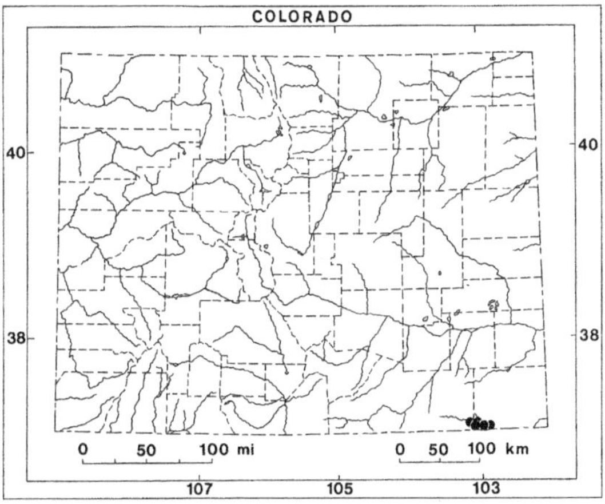

Map 7.15. Distribution of the Great Plains narrowmouth toad in Colorado.

Las Animas counties occupied by this toad. However, pesticide application on rangelands is a potential threat, due to possible toxicity to eggs and larvae and impacts on adult food resources.

Habitat. In Colorado, narrowmouth toads inhabit areas dominated by low grasses and forbs in the bottoms of rock-rimmed canyons and on slopes with numerous flat rocks partially imbedded in the soil. Under suitable conditions, the toads can be found day or night under rocks and at the edge of rain pools and stock ponds. Narrowmouth toads occupy burrows and other underground sites in winter.

Activity. Most activity occurs after spring or summer rains have moistened the soil and when air temperatures are above 16°C. Fitch (1956a) found that these toads are exceptionally tolerant of warm temperatures, with body temperatures of 17–38°C (usually 24–31°C) during activity. Narrowmouth toads have been found in Colorado from May to August.

Fitch (1956a) determined that home range size in Kansas generally was less than 120 m in diameter (often much less) and that individuals sometimes move through unsuitable habitat from their home range to breeding ponds.

Reproduction and Growth. Breeding in Colorado takes place in temporary pools and in larger semipermanent ponds behind earthen dams. Breeding pools that I observed in Baca County had rocky or muddy bottoms and muddy or slightly turbid water and usually were ringed by sunflowers. Mackessy (1998) reported that two males were calling in a deep, shaded pond in Las Animas County.

Males call while floating or with the front feet braced on vegetation (Nelson 1973) and the snout pointed upward in shallow water at the edge of the pond, often hidden in low vegetation or tumbleweeds. Calling occurs day or night and is most vigorous in darkness. Sometimes individual males participate in multiple breeding events in the same year (Fitch 1956a). Females are secretive and relatively difficult to find in breeding ponds. Breeding seems to occur during brief periods (a few days at most) after heavy warm summer rains. In Kansas, Fitch (1956a) found that from late May through August, large choruses usually form only after 5 cm or more of rain has fallen over several days; heavy rains before June are less likely to stimulate breeding than summer rains. In one year, rains in early June and early August each yielded breeding and successful production of metamorphosed offspring at the end of each of those months. Choruses have been observed in Colorado in June, July, and August (Hammerson 1980; Mackessy 1998), and I found a newly laid raft of eggs in a small pool next to a larger pond on July 18. Calling males that I observed in Colorado were in water that was 23–24°C. In southern New Mexico, calling has been observed from late June to late August (Degenhardt, Painter, and Price 1996). Glands on the belly of the male secrete a sticky substance that helps him cling to the female during amplexus, which is axillary.

Each breeding female deposits up to several hundred eggs, which hatch in about two days. Larval development from hatching to metamorphosis typically requires 3–4 weeks (Fitch 1956a). Newly metamorphosed toadlets are approximately 15–16 mm SVL and disperse from the ponds when rain

Plate 7.53. Juvenile Great Plains narrowmouth toad (Baca County, Colorado).

facilitates overland travel (Fitch 1956a). Breeding males are at least 29 mm SVL; breeding females average a few millimeters larger. In eastern Kansas, males may mature within one year after metamorphosis (Fitch 1956b). In Colorado's shorter growing season, first-time breeders probably are about two years old. In the wild, very few live as long as 7–8 years (Fitch 1956b).

Food and Predators. Feeding apparently occurs under cover (Fitch 1956a). Narrowmouth toads that I observed in Baca County defecated the remains of ants, which dominate the diet throughout the range of this species. Larvae feed on suspended organic material.

In laboratory trials, water snakes, garter snakes, snapping turtles, and night herons often rejected eastern narrowmouth toads *(G. carolinensis)* after biting them, apparently due to unpalatable skin secretions; the same predators rarely rejected spring peepers *(Pseudacris crucifer)* or cricket frogs *(Acris crepitans)* (Garton and Mushinsky 1979). However, based on evidence from other states (Fitch 1956a; Collins 1993), shrews, bullfrogs, leopard frogs, garter snakes, and other predators probably do occasionally prey on *G. olivacea* in Colorado. Shrews ate *G. olivacea* only after removing and discarding the skin and feet (Fitch 1956a), suggesting that this species is distasteful. Secretions and thick skin may protect these toads from ant attacks.

Remarks. Blair (1936) reported the occurrence of usually 1–3 but up to 9 narrowmouth toads in most tarantula burrows that he examined in Oklahoma. Hunt (1980) found up to five narrowmouth toads in tarantula burrows in Texas. Disturbed toads hid beneath the tarantula. Blair pointed out the thermal and moisture advantages for toads in tarantula burrows and suggested that tarantulas may serve an antipredator function. Hunt similarly proposed that the spider may protect toads from foraging snakes, and the toads reciprocate by keeping marauding ants from bothering the tarantula and its eggs and offspring. Tarantulas are not uncommon in southeastern Colorado, so it would not be surprising if a toad-tarantula association also occurs in Colorado.

McAllister and Tabor (1985) discussed animal associates found under rocks with narrrowmouth toads.

Taxonomy and Variation. Prior to De Carvalho's (1954) revision, this species was included in the genus *Microhyla.* Some authors have recognized two subspecies *(olivacea* and *mazatlanensis),* but Nelson (1972) concluded that the recognition of subspecies is unwarranted.

TRUE FROGS
Family Ranidae

About 710 species of true frogs are distributed throughout the world, absent only from southern South America, the Australian region, oceanic islands, and the West Indies, except where bullfrogs have been introduced. Ranids are the most common frogs in Africa and Eurasia. Size and shape in this family vary. Some members are fossorial, some toadlike, and others arboreal. The largest species, *Conraua goliath* of Africa, sometimes grows to 30 cm SVL. In North America, all true frogs are comparable in general appearance (long legs, webbed feet, relatively smooth skin), and most are more or less aquatic. All species in the United States have teeth only in the upper mandible. Four of the 26 species in the United States inhabit Colorado. Metamorphosed individuals of the three native Coloradan species have prominent dorsolateral ridges.

Amplexus is axillary in all North American ranids. Breeding males have noticeably more muscular forelimbs than do adult females, most of which deposit large masses of numerous eggs in quiet, temporary, or permanent water. Species that breed in cold water early in the year lay submerged, globular masses. Flat egg masses that initially float are typical of late spring/early summer breeders. Globular egg masses enhance heat retention in cool water, whereas flat sheets of eggs facilitate oxygen uptake and heat dissipation in warm, low-oxygen water (Ryan 1978).

The larvae of most species have beaks,

denticles, and a single spiracle on the left side. As in treefrogs, the lungs develop and are inflated early. In different species, the duration of the larval stage ranges from a few months to more than a year. In some species (none in the United States), the young develop directly into frogs (with no aquatic larval stage) on terrestrial sites.

Plate 7.54. Adult plains leopard frog (Baca County, Colorado).

Plains Leopard Frog
Rana blairi (Mecham et al. 1973)

Recognition. Dorsum brown, with large rounded or oval dark spots that usually have a light border; skin somewhat rough or nodulated; eardrum usually with distinct light spot; dorsolateral folds inset toward midline on rump; hind toes with extensive webbing; rear of thigh with dark reticulation; vestigial oviducts absent in male (dissection required); maximum SVL about 11 cm, adults usually about 7–10 cm SVL. *Mature male:* base of innermost digit on forefeet swollen during breeding season; expanded vocal sacs, one on each side, extend above forelimbs; breeding call a series of short "clucks" followed by a few low chuckling or grunting sounds, together lasting usually less than two seconds. *Larvae:* dorsum brown, olive, or gray, paler than northern leopard frog; dorsal spots circular and rear surface of thighs with transverse dark bars near metamorphosis (Post and Pettus 1966; Dunlap and Kruse 1976); snout rounded in dorsal view; oral disc subterminal (Korky 1978); eyes dorsal, iris medium-gold, with no dorsal or ventral dark spots (Scott and Jennings 1985); tail fin high, 70–90 percent of body length; labial tooth rows 2-3/3 (tooth row closest to mandible on upper lip may consist of just a few labial teeth on one or both sides of mandibles); oral papillae surround mouth except for wide gap above mandibles, papillae usually dense lateral to mandibles; anus on right side at front end of ventral tail fin; large larvae average around 6 cm TL. *Eggs:* black above and whitish below, surrounded by 2–3 jelly envelopes, deposited in rounded clusters often 5–15 cm in diameter and including up to several hundred eggs (masses smaller than those of northern leopard frog).

Distribution. Southwestern South Dakota south to central Texas; east through Iowa, Missouri, and Illinois to west-central Indiana; southeast along the Mississippi River to southeastern Missouri; west to eastern Colorado, New Mexico, and (disjunctly) southeastern and north-central Arizona (Clarkson and Rorabaugh 1989; Conant and Collins 1991; Brown 1992). Occurs in the Great Plains portion of the Arkansas River drainage in southeastern Colorado and in the Republican River drainage in northeastern Colorado at elevations principally below 5,000 feet (1,525 m) but reaching 6,000 feet (1,830 m) in the southwestern portions of Las Animas and Pueblo counties.

The distribution of the plains leopard frog in Colorado largely is complementary to that of the northern leopard frog. Limited areas of sympatry have been found along portions of the Big Sandy Creek drainage in Cheyenne and Kiowa counties, the Arkansas River near Pueblo (see "Remarks"), the Huerfano River in southern Pueblo County, and along Fountain Creek in southern El Paso County, though *Rana pipiens* apparently disappeared from most or all of the Big Sandy Creek region between 1975 and 1986 (Cousineau and Rogers 1991). Smith et al. (1993b) reported specimens from the 1940s indicating possible sympatry along the Arkansas River in Bent County as well (see discussion in account of northern leopard frog).

Records of the plains leopard frog from Weld County are questionable. Post and Pettus (1966:478, Table 1) reported specimens

of the "DF complex" *(Rana blairi)* from 14 km east of Greeley, but I suspect this was a typographical error because the authors' distribution map does not show *Rana blairi* in Weld County. I have examined specimens (UCM 5935–5937) of *R. blairi* from 3 km west of Milton Reservoir, Weld County, but must conclude that the frogs were introduced artificially or that the collection data are in error; all other specimens of leopard frogs from that area are *R. pipiens.* Another specimen (UMMZ 62196) of *Rana blairi* supposedly was collected at Monte Vista, Rio Grande County, but all other specimens from that area and from the entire San Luis Valley are *R. pipiens.* The collectors of the specimen found leopard frogs in *Rana blairi* range three days later on the same expedition, so it is likely that the specimen was mislabeled.

Conservation Status. The plains leopard frog remains widely distributed within its historic range in eastern Colorado (Mackessy 1998; pers. obs.), but lack of adequate data make it difficult to determine whether overall abundance has changed. The frogs are common in at least some locations. Local populations may include up to several hundred metamorphosed individuals at a single pond (Gillis 1975). In some areas inhabited by non-native bullfrogs, *Rana blairi* has become scarce or absent (Hammerson 1982d). For example, in the 1970s the plains leopard frog was common along a Baca County section of Carrizo Creek characterized by pools of clean water and the absence or scarcity of bullfrogs. By the 1990s, that creek section had thick growths of algae, increased cover of cattails, a heavy load of cattle manure, and was abundantly inhabited by bullfrog larvae, juveniles,

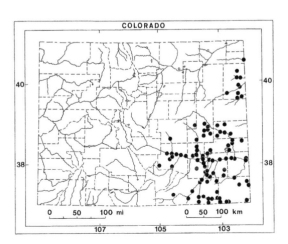

Map 7.16. Distribution of the plains leopard frog in Colorado.

Plate 7.55. Adult plains leopard frog
(Baca County, Colorado).

and adults; plains leopard frogs
were scarce. The change in habitat conditions makes it difficult
to know whether the decline in
leopard frog abundance was due
to impacts of the bullfrog or to
physical or biological environmental changes favoring the bullfrog. Bullfrog larvae may be less
vulnerable to fish predation than
are leopard frog larvae (Kruse and Francis
1977), and bullfrog larvae readily eat the
eggs and larvae of the plains leopard frog,
at least under captive conditions (Ehrlich
1979). Large overwintered bullfrog larvae
could greatly reduce leopard frog reproductive success. However, plains leopard frogs
can persist in the presence of bullfrogs for
decades (e.g., in Picture Canyon in Baca
County). The plains leopard frog's ability to
reproduce in bodies of water that may dry up
in summer, something the bullfrog cannot
do, may help explain the leopard frog's ability to persist in areas inhabited by bullfrogs,
even if bullfrogs can eliminate or reduce
leopard frog populations in permanent
waters through competition, predation, or
other direct interactions. Though the plains
leopard frog remains widespread and locally
common in its range in Colorado, better
information on its population dynamics and
interactions with bullfrogs is needed.

Habitat. The plains leopard frog inhabits
the margins of streams, natural and artificial
ponds, reservoirs, creek pools, irrigation
ditches, and other bodies of water in plains
grassland, sandhills, stream valleys, or
canyon bottoms. Lynch (1978) found general habitat differences between the plains
and northern leopard frogs in Nebraska.
Rana blairi occurred mainly along turbid
streams in areas of loess soils, whereas
Rana pipiens typically was associated with
clear streams in areas of sandy soils. *Rana
blairi* may disperse and feed far from water
during mild, wet conditions. Winter is spent
underwater at the bottom of ponds and deep
pools.

Activity. The primary activity period
in Colorado extends from March or April
through October, and probably warm periods
in November as well. In late September and
October, large numbers may gather at certain
bodies of water favored as overwintering
sites (Gillis 1975; pers. obs.). Activity may
occur day or night.

These frogs are capable of long dispersal
movements. Gillis (1975) found that from
one year to the next, some plains leopard
frogs moved up to 8 km between ponds; one
Rana blairi–Rana pipiens hybrid moved 14
km.

Plains leopard frogs leap higher and
farther than do bullfrogs of the same size.
In Colorado, individuals that are disturbed
at the edges of ponds often flee landward
to shrubs or weeds or hide under rocks, if
such cover is available. This behavior also
has been observed in New Mexico (Degenhardt, Painter, and Price 1996). Sometimes
they leap into emergent vegetation such as
cattails, sometimes into the water. Frogs that
flee into lakes or rivers generally return to
shore quickly, perhaps reflecting the risk of
consumption by large predatory fishes. Gillis
(1975) observed that *Rana pipiens* often emitted an alarm call at the approach of danger,
but no such call was observed in *Rana blairi.*

Reproduction and Growth. Breeding
occurs in permanent, semipermanent, and
temporary ponds, and in stream pools and
backwaters in sites lacking a strong current.
The breeding season varies greatly from
year to year and from place to place. South
of the Arkansas River, breeding takes place
in May, June, or July (Post 1972). I heard

calling males from late May to mid-June in Baca County and found fresh egg masses in May and early June in Las Animas and Bent counties. North of the Arkansas along Big Sandy Creek, breeding may occur from early April (Post 1972) to late August (Gillis 1975). During one year along Big Sandy Creek, breeding took place April 9–24 in some areas, but not until June 5–11 at another site (Post 1972). Gillis (1975) found that breeding along Big Sandy Creek often coincides with heavy rains. In the Republican River drainage in Yuma County, breeding occurs as soon as early April or late March. For example, on April 3 in Yuma County, Livo (pers comm.) observed nine egg masses (most in neural fold stage), several calling males, and a pair in amplexus at an air temperature of 12.5°C and a water temperature of 11°C. Post (1972) reported that the breeding season along the Arkansas River in Pueblo County lasted from June

22 to July 10, June 21 to June 29, June 19 to July 3, and June 11 to June 27 in four consecutive years. More than one breeding event may take place each year at a given pool; freshly laid eggs and large tadpoles sometimes are found together.

Clusters of approximately 200–600 eggs are attached to vegetation in shallow water (often 10–20 cm deep). Larvae may metamorphose anytime during summer, the date depending on when the eggs were laid. I found metamorphosing larvae and newly metamorphosed frogs from late June to early September in Bent and Las Animas counties. Early spring clutches yield newly metamorphosed frogs by the end of June. Gillis (1975) found that tadpoles from eggs laid in late August overwinter in the ponds and metamorphose the following spring. Size distributions of breeding and nonbreeding individuals indicate that most first-time breeders are at least two years old.

Plate 7.56. Egg mass of plains leopard frog (Bent County, Colorado).

Plate 7.57. Larval plains leopard frog (Baca County, Colorado).

Food and Predators. The diet includes various invertebrates and probably occasional small vertebrates. The stomach of a frog I found dead on a road in Prowers County was full of grasshoppers.

On three occasions, I have been alerted to predation on these frogs by their loud distress screams. In each case, a western terrestrial garter snake or a blackneck garter snake held the frog in its jaws. The larvae are vulnerable to predation by fishes such as centrarchids (Kruse and Francis 1977). The eggs and larvae may be eaten by bullfrog larvae (Ehrlich 1979).

Remarks. Hybridization between the plains and northern leopard frogs has been documented in the area along Big Sandy Creek in Cheyenne and Kiowa counties (Post 1972; Gillis 1975). Gillis (1975) suggested that sympatry and hybridization of leopard frogs in the Big Sandy Creek drainage were relatively recent phenomena resulting in part from the creation of artificial ponds through sand and gravel excavation in the 1950s and 1960s. These ponds provided suitable semipermanent breeding habitat for the northern leopard frog in an area formerly inhabited solely by the plains leopard frog, which can breed in more ephemeral waters (Gillis 1975). Gillis (1975) suggested that periodic flooding may have transported eggs, larvae, or metamorphosed *Rana pipiens* downstream into areas inhabited by *Rana blairi.* By the late 1980s, most of these ponds were dry, and only *Rana blairi* and hybrids were found in the area (Cousineau and Rogers 1991).

In Pueblo County, Post and Pettus (1967) and Post (1972) found that plains and northern leopard frogs occur sympatrically but breed at different times (northern breeds earlier) and in different habitats (northern in permanent water, plains in ephemeral pools) and are not known to hybridize. However, I examined Pueblo County specimens whose morphological characteristics suggested hybridization. Kruse and Dunlap (1976) used serum albumins to reveal instances of leopard frog hybridization in portions of the Great Plains and concluded that external morphological characteristics can be used to identify hybrids. Lynch (1978) described zones of sympatry and infrequent hybridization between *Rana blairi* and *Rana pipiens* in Nebraska.

Gillis (1979) described various physiological and behavioral characteristics that allow the plains leopard frog to exploit drier habitats than does the northern leopard frog. Adult *Rana blairi* tolerate slightly higher levels of body water loss than do adult *Rana pipiens* (36 percent and 33 percent, respectively). When exposed to sunlight, juvenile *Rana blairi* lose water at a significantly lower rate than do *Rana pipiens* juveniles, in part due to the chunkier body shape of *blairi.* In dehydration trials, *Rana blairi* assumed a crouched, legs-tucked, water-conservation posture sooner than did *Rana pipiens.* Both species exhibited vigorous escape-attempt behavior as they approached a lethal level of dehydration.

Taxonomy and Variation. No subspecies are recognized.

Plate 7.58. Adult male bullfrog.

and young); throat yellow in breeding season; base of innermost digit on forefeet swollen; expansion of the internal vocal sac causes a bulging of the throat; breeding call a deep bellowing "um-rum" or "um-er-rum" or similar vocalization; also produces other calls (see "Activity"). *Juvenile:* green with many scattered small black dots on dorsum. *Larvae:* in large individuals, upper surface green with small, black sharp-edged dots (dots also on tail fin); dorsum black with gold crossbands in individuals less than 2.5 cm TL (Altig 1970); labial tooth rows 1–3/3; oral papillae encircle mouth except for wide gap above mandibles; anus on right side at front end of ventral tail fin; maximum TL about 18 cm, commonly more than 10 cm. *Eggs:* black above, whitish below, 1.2–1.7 mm in diameter (average 1.3 mm) (Livezey and Wright 1947), deposited in flat jelly masses up to more than 1 m in diameter and containing thousands of eggs (mass initially floats at surface of water but soon sinks).

Bullfrog
Rana catesbeiana (Shaw, 1802)

Recognition. Dorsum green or brown, usually with dark spots or mottling (but not large rounded spots); eardrum large, with fold of skin curving around top and rear edges; hind toes fully webbed; dorsolateral folds absent. Record size is an Oklahoma female that was 20.4 cm SVL and 909 g (Lutterschmidt, Marvin, and Hutchison 1996), but such large individuals are quite rare. An adult male from Baca County measured 17 cm SVL, with a 6.7-cm-wide mouth and 28-cm-long hind legs (groin to tip of toe) (this was a preserved specimen that would have been somewhat larger while living). *Mature male:* eardrum usually distinctly larger than eye (same diameter in female

Distribution. Native to eastern and central North America; introduced and established worldwide, including Colorado and many other areas of western North America. In Colorado, the bullfrog is most widespread in the Great Plains region but is enlarging its range through continued inadvertent and intentional (illegal) introductions and subsequent expansion from established populations.

Conservation Status. Game species covered by fishing regulations. The bullfrog apparently is not native to Colorado. None of the several accounts of the herpetofauna of Colorado published in the 1800s mentioned the occurrence of bullfrogs. Arthur

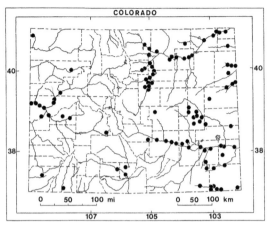

Map 7.17. Distribution of the bullfrog in Colorado.

24 counties (Hammerson 1982c). Wiese (1989) searched for bullfrogs in eastern Colorado and found them in 44 sites, 32 of which supported moderate-to-large bullfrog populations. Currently, bullfrogs are known from at least 36 counties. There is no evidence that bullfrogs have disappeared from any of the counties where they have been reported—populations appear to persist once established.

E. Beardsley collected throughout eastern Colorado in the 1800s and found several species of amphibians that are rare and localized in the state (Hammerson 1982a), but evidently he did not collect any bullfrogs on these expeditions—at least they were not mentioned in the museum register where his other collections were recorded.

Ellis and Henderson (1913, 1915) knew of no native populations and stated that introductions of bullfrogs into several ponds and reservoirs in the upper South Platte River valley during the early 1900s were not very successful. Rodeck (1943) reported that bullfrogs were then known only from Kit Carson County. Swenson and Rodeck (1948) added Denver and the Cimarron River to the areas known to be inhabited. Maslin (1950) stated that the bullfrog was well established in the vicinity of Wray, Yuma County, in the Cimarron River drainage, and in the Arkansas River valley as far west as Pueblo. In addition to previously known sites, Maslin (1959) recorded bullfrogs from near Fort Morgan in Morgan County and from the vicinity of Two Buttes Reservoir in Baca County.

Since 1959, the number of areas known to be inhabited by bullfrogs has increased greatly. Smith, Maslin, and Brown (1965) listed records in 12 counties where bullfrogs had not previously been recorded. I mapped all known occurrences statewide and indicated a distribution encompassing

The presence of bullfrogs in Colorado undoubtedly is a result of introductions and the creation of naturally rare favorable habitat. Prior to settlement by humans of European descent, permanent lakes and ponds were scarce in lowland areas of Colorado. Today there are thousands of them, created in response to agricultural, domestic, and recreational needs, and for flood control. These bodies of water were rapidly colonized by native northern and plains leopard frogs that probably had been restricted to stream pools and seasonally flooded areas along streams. Ellis and Henderson (1915:258) reported that leopard frogs were "very abundant near all of the ponds and lakes in eastern Colorado." Now these ponds support numerous bullfrogs.

The mechanism by which bullfrogs became widely established in Colorado is not well documented. Currently, the Colorado Division of Wildlife does not actively propagate or introduce bullfrogs, but some introductions have been performed in the past (Jim Bennett, pers. comm.). It is possible that bullfrogs were inadvertently introduced during fish-stocking operations; bullfrogs commonly invade and do well in warm-water fish hatchery ponds (Corse and Metter 1980) and could end up with fishes that are routinely stocked in various ponds and reservoirs. Bullfrog larvae can survive among predatory game fishes, which under certain circumstances are averse to eating them (Kruse and Francis 1977). Probably some bullfrogs were introduced by private citizens hoping to establish a local huntable population. Overall, however, introductions likely have been infrequent, due to the lack of favorable habitat in many regions and a low level of recreational interest in the species. Based on the rapid population expansion of the bullfrog in Colorado, and the presumably low level of introductions, it appears that once a bullfrog population becomes established in an area, the frogs may quickly colonize adjacent bodies of water, including ones isolated by large expanses of uplands. In eastern Colorado, I have found bullfrogs in recently rain-filled temporary stock ponds more than 1.6 km from the nearest permanent water.

Concurrent with the establishment and expansion of the bullfrog in Colorado have been declines in the distribution and abundance of the northern and plains leopard frogs (Hammerson 1982d) and the northern cricket frog (Hammerson and Livo, in press). The declines are discussed in the accounts of these species. Bullfrogs have been implicated strongly in the decline of certain native frogs in western North America (e.g., see Hayes and Jennings 1986; Schwalbe and Rosen 1988; Lanoo et al. 1994; Rosen and Schwalbe 1995; Fisher and Shaffer 1996; Kiesecker and Blaustein 1997; Kupferberg 1997). In their native range in eastern North America, bullfrogs may suppress local green frog *(Rana clamitans)* populations (Hecnar and M'Closkey 1997).

Bullfrogs may impact other frog species through intense predation, predatory or competitive larval interactions, and the transmission of parasites or pathogens (Ehrlich 1979; Werner 1994; Werner, Wellborn, and McPeek 1996; Kiesecker and Blaustein 1997; Kupferberg 1997; Goldberg, Bursey, and Cheam 1998). Inhibitory effects of bullfrog larvae on larval leopard frogs described by Rose (1960) and Licht (1967) may be primarily a laboratory artifact (Biesterfeldt, Petranka, and Sherbondy 1993).

Available evidence does not conclusively demonstrate that the bullfrog is the cause

of the leopard frog decline in Colorado. Habitat change and/or introduced predatory fishes are among the other factors potentially responsible for the decline of leopard frogs in the lowlands of Colorado (Hammerson 1982d). Bradford (1989) documented that predatory fishes and viable populations of native frogs did not coexist in the high Sierra Nevada of California. Hayes and Jennings (1986) concluded that fish predation was the most compelling explanation for declines of native ranids, but they emphasized that existing data are insufficient to distinguish adequately among bullfrogs, introduced fishes, and habitat change as the cause in any particular case. Also, northern leopard frogs have declined in areas where bullfrogs are absent (Corn, Stoltzenburg, and Bury 1989; pers. obs.).

Despite the lack of definitive evidence of their impact on leopard frogs, bullfrogs in Colorado nevertheless are an exotic species in the state and should be regarded as ecologically undesirable. Efforts should be made to contain or reduce their distribution and abundance whenever possible. Unfortunately, this will be extremely difficult to accomplish where bullfrogs are well-established in large complexes of favorable permanent aquatic habitat.

Habitat. Typical habitat consists of permanent ponds, reservoirs, quiet stream pools, and large, deep marshes. Flowing streams and irrigation ditches also are inhabited if the current is not too swift. Primary habitat generally includes some areas of deep water, stands of cattails, and often woody vegetation overhanging the water's edge. Bullfrogs frequently coexist with predatory game fishes. They often sit in the sun or under shoreline vegetation or on thick mats of algae. Only rarely are bullfrogs observed more than a leap or two from water, but they do leave it occasionally and quickly colonize temporary or newly created bodies of water hundreds of meters from permanent streams or ponds. Winter typically is spent at the bottom of a body of water. Larvae generally rest and feed on the bottom, and often occupy warm shallows when the remainder of the water is cool (e.g., in spring and fall). Wiese (1985)

Plate 7.59. Newly metamorphosed bullfrog (Gunnison County, Colorado).

discussed bullfrog habitats in northeastern Colorado.

Bullfrogs appear to be relatively tolerant of polluted water. In eastern North America, Rowe et al. (1996) found that bullfrog larvae may occur in abundance in coal-ash settling ponds with various metal contaminants. However, these larvae exhibit oral deformities that under certain conditions may negatively affect food procurement and growth.

Activity. Most activity occurs from March through October. Warm weather may result in earlier and later activity. Smaller individuals are more likely to be active in early spring than are mature adults. Activity may take place day or night during the warmer months. When sufficient sun is available, active adults maintain body temperatures of 26–33°C (mean 30°C) (Lillywhite 1970). In the hot climate along the lower Colorado River in Arizona-California, Clarkson and deVos (1986) observed adults exposed along shorelines only at night. Bullfrogs appear to be relatively sedentary, though some individuals may move up to a few kilometers within a single summer (Bury and Whelan 1984).

When startled along shoreline areas, bullfrogs, especially the young, emit a squawk or bleat as they leap into the water. Some flee with a rapid series of skittering, splashy jumps. When grasped, some individuals become limp, feigning death. Eventually, they "recover" and attempt to escape.

Bullfrogs may produce several types of vocalizations in addition to the well-known breeding call of the adult male (see Bury and Whelan 1984). One of the most remarkable of these is an open-mouthed scream lasting up to several seconds. This distress call may be emitted by a frog held in hand. Other calls include a brief cluck or grunt that sounds like the top of an empty can being struck and a soft vibrating growl lasting 1–2 seconds.

Reproduction and Growth. Breeding occurs in permanent bodies of water that typically contain thick growths of algae and rooted aquatic plants such as cattails. Breeding pools usually are rich in aquatic animal life and have a soft mud bottom. Bullfrogs generally are lowland inhabitants because they require warm water for breeding. However, they thrive in one site in the mountains of Gunnison County at 9,000 feet (2,745 m) where the warm waters of Hot Spring Creek enable them to reproduce in an otherwise-too-cold area.

Actual dates of breeding in Colorado are not well known. The bellowing calls of the males can be heard from May through August or even early September, but calling seems to be most vigorous in June and early July, which may be peak breeding season. Lauren Livo (pers. comm.) found newly hatched tadpoles as late as early September in eastern Boulder County. Mature males may form choruses (breeding aggregations), the location of which may change as temperature, vegetation, or other conditions alter (Howard 1978). Calling males are able to recognize one another by voice (Davis 1987). Apparently, bullfrog calls are broadcast mostly through the eardrums (Purgue 1997).

Large mature males defend territories, usually along shorelines or next to vegetation mats (Howard 1978). Adult females often stay hidden along the shoreline until they become sexually receptive (Emlen 1977). They initiate amplexus by making physical contact with an adult male. Amplexus and oviposition generally last from 15 minutes to

2.5 hours and occur between about midnight and dawn in the male's territory (Howard 1978), near the male's calling site (Ryan 1980), though in some studies bullfrogs have been found to mate and lay eggs in areas outside the sites defended by calling males (Emlen 1968, 1976). Water depth at the site of oviposition may be greater than 1 m. Adult males may push and wrestle with each other between bouts of calling. Some small adult males may not call at all but rather linger near larger, calling males and attempt to intercept approaching females (Howard 1978).

Bullfrogs produce large numbers of eggs. In New Mexico, the number of mature eggs contained in adult females averaged 11,126 (Woodward 1987b). A 7-inch (18-cm) female laid 47,840 eggs (McAuliffe, cited by Krupa 1995). Some older (larger) females produce two clutches of eggs each year, one early and another a few weeks later; younger adult females generally oviposit in the latter part of the breeding season (Emlen 1977).

Eggs develop normally at temperatures of about 15–32°C (Moore 1942) (higher temperatures result in abnormalities or death) and hatch in about 2–5 days.

The larval period is longer than for any other anuran in Colorado. Early spring populations in at least some areas of the state include very large larvae as well as much smaller individuals of various sizes, suggesting that larvae overwinter once or twice and metamorphose during their second or third summer. Little or no growth takes place in winter. Larvae in different stages of metamorphosis have been observed in Colorado from March to September. Newly metamorphosed bullfrogs, usually about 35–55 mm SVL but sometimes as small as 25 mm SVL or as large as 60 mm SVL (Collins 1979), are most abundant in late summer and early fall. Under ideal conditions in captivity, bullfrogs can reach metamorphosis as soon as three months after the egg was laid, and males may begin calling as early as six months after metamorphosis, at about

Plate 7.60. Larval bullfrog beginning metamorphosis.

Plate 7.61. Metamorphosing bullfrogs.

10 cm SVL (Starrett and Bazilian 1996). However, development takes much longer under natural conditions.

Shirose et al. (1993) provided information on reproduction and growth in an area with a short growing season in southeastern Canada. Breeding males formed aggregations that lasted 4–6 weeks. The smallest male captured in a breeding chorus was 90 mm SVL (estimated age of three years post-metamorphosis); the smallest female found in a breeding assemblage was 94 mm SVL (four years post-metamorphosis). Breeding adults averaged about 11 cm SVL. Other studies done in warmer climates have estimated that bullfrogs attain sexual maturity 1–3 years after metamorphosis. In Colorado, sexual maturity probably is attained no sooner than 2–3 years after metamorphosis. Minimum size at maturity (at least 9 cm SVL) seems to be fairly consistent throughout the range, taking into consideration a lack of standard criteria for judging maturity. Few bullfrogs in the wild live more than 8–10 years after metamorphosis.

Food and Predators. Bullfrogs generally sit quietly and pounce on nearly any approaching animal that is small enough to be captured and swallowed, including various aquatic and terrestrial invertebrates, fishes, amphibians (larvae and adults, including other bullfrogs), reptiles, and small birds and mammals (Bury and Whelan 1984; Clarkson and deVos 1986). Sometimes they ingest vegetation, probably incidental to feeding on animals. Insects are an important food item, as are crayfish and smaller frogs when available (Bury and Whelan 1984). Mackessy (1998) reported that a sample of bullfrogs from southeastern Colorado ate various flying and aquatic insects, crayfish, the plains leopard frog and plains garter snake, and a deer mouse *(Peromyscus maniculatus)*. Wiese (1986) reported that small bullfrogs account for a large portion

of the diet of adult bullfrogs in northeastern Colorado. Stuart and Painter (1993) found that juvenile and larval bullfrogs dominated the diet of adult bullfrogs in a high-density population in New Mexico. Stuart (1995) documented predation by a 18-cm-SVL bullfrog on a 7-cm-SVL Great Plains toad, a 4.2-cm-SVL green toad, a mouse, a centipede, and beetles in New Mexico. In Kansas, adult bullfrogs were highly attracted to the distress calls of immature bullfrogs and leopard frogs, especially at night (Smith 1977). Smith suggested that a frog emitting the distress call might benefit if a bullfrog, attracted to a potential meal, interferes with another predator's attack on the frog. Larvae eat algae, detritus, carrion, minute animals associated with vegetation, and amphibian eggs and larvae (Ehrlich 1979).

Many kinds of predatory animals eat bullfrogs (Bury and Whelan 1984). Snapping turtles sometimes prey on males calling in deep water. In Colorado, known predators include great blue heron *(Ardea herodias)* (D. and J. Ward, pers. comm.) and Swainson's hawk *(Buteo swainsoni)* (R. Ryder, pers. comm.). There is contradictory evidence regarding the palatability of bullfrog larvae to predatory fishes. For example, Kruse and Francis (1977) found that largemouth bass *(Micropterus salmoides)* in experimental tanks ate bullfrog tadpoles only if other foods were not available, and black bullheads *(Ameiurus melas)* would not eat the larvae at all, whereas Lewis and Helms (1964) found that largemouth bass and smallmouth bass *(Micropterus dolomieu)* in ponds readily consumed small bullfrog lar-

Plate 7.62. Newly metamorphosed bullfrog with extra limbs (Weld County, Colorado).

vae. Small larvae may succumb to predatory invertebrates such as beetles, water bugs, and dragonfly nymphs; larvae of any size may be killed by viral and bacterial infections (Cecil and Just 1979). Leeches sometimes prey on developing bullfrog embryos.

Remarks. In Weld County, I found a recently metamorphosed bullfrog that had two extra hind limbs. In Illinois, Lopez and Maxson (1990) found a healthy young bullfrog with 10 extra hind limbs. Abnormal

development associated with exposure to agricultural chemicals likely were involved in both instances.

Taxonomy and Variation. Bullfrog populations exhibit low levels of genetic variation and divergence (Wiese 1990). Newly established populations derived from a small number of introduced individuals apparently are not subject to adverse effects associated with small population size (Wiese 1990). No subspecies are recognized.

Plate 7.63. Northern leopard frog (Weld County, Colorado).

Northern Leopard Frog
Rana pipiens (Schreber, 1782)

Recognition. Dorsum green or brown, with large rounded or oval spots; skin smooth; eardrum usually lacks distinct light spot; dorsolateral folds not inset toward midline on rump; hind toes with extensive webbing; rear of thigh with dark spotting; vestigial oviducts usually present in male (dissection required) (Pace 1974); maximum SVL about 11 cm. *Mature male:* base of innermost digit on

forefeet swollen during breeding season; expanded vocal sacs, one on each side, extend above forelimbs; typical breeding call a prolonged snore lasting 2–3 seconds followed by 2–3 series of stuttering croaks or chuckles (sometimes the chuckles are given without the introductory snore and vice versa). *Larvae:* dorsum dark brown or olive to gray; snout pointed in dorsal view, oral disc terminal (Korky 1978); eyes dorsal, iris gold, surrounded by dark spots (Scott and Jennings 1985); intestinal coil often visible through skin; tail fin moderately high, 65–80 percent of body length, with sparse pigment; labial tooth

Map 7.18. Distribution of the northern leopard frog in Colorado.

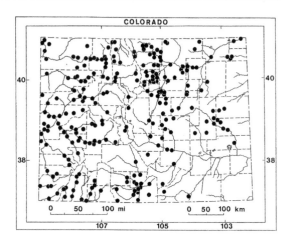

rows 2/3 or, rarely, 3/3; oral papillae surround mouth, with wide gap above mandibles, papillae sparse lateral to the mandibles; anus on right side at front end of ventral tail fin; large larvae average about 6 cm TL; maximum TL in Colorado at least 10 cm (pers. obs.); larvae near metamorphosis with elongate dorsal spots, rear surface of thighs with mottled dark bars (Post and Pettus 1966, Dunlap and Kruse 1976). *Eggs:* black above, whitish below, diameter averaging 1.3–2.3 mm in different clutches (Livo 1981b), enclosed in 2–3 jelly envelopes; deposited in large, somewhat flattened globular masses 5–15 cm in maximum diameter and including up to several thousand eggs.

Distribution. Southern Canada and northern United States south to Maryland, West Virginia, Kentucky, northern Illinois, extreme northwestern Missouri, Nebraska, New Mexico, Arizona, and eastern California (Stebbins 1985; Conant and Collins 1991). Occurs throughout Colorado, excluding most of the southeastern and east-central portions of the state. Elevational range extends from below 3,500 feet (1,065 m) in northeastern Colorado to above 11,000 feet (3,355 m) in southern Colorado.

Specimens of *Rana pipiens* (UCM 47599–47600) from the vicinity of Two Buttes Reservoir (not mapped), Baca County, in an area far from other *R. pipiens* populations, may represent introductions or a data error. Another record from southeastern Colorado along the Arkansas River in Bent County (not mapped) and records from Yuma County (Smith et al. 1993b, not mapped) also are difficult to interpret. It is unknown whether several specimens of *R. pipiens* collected with *R. blairi* in 1947 in Bent County reflect a natural or introduced

population or whether this population still exists. Post and Pettus (1966) and Post (1972) did not map the Bent County record as *R. pipiens* or *R. blairi,* despite the existence of the specimens in the collection at Colorado State University, where Pettus and Post were employed; apparently, they were unaware of the specimens or perhaps viewed the data as questionable. The identity of these specimens recently was determined to be *R. pipiens* by experienced herpetologists, but I have not personally verified the identifications. The Yuma County records of *R. pipiens* are based on three specimens collected by Pettus and Post in 1967, yet Post (1972:61a) did not include any Yuma County records of *R. pipiens* on his distribution map, and no *R. blairi* records were mapped in the indicated locality. He did map two sites in Phillips County (just north of Yuma County) that were not included on the earlier map in Post and Pettus (1966). Perhaps these are the actual localities for the 1967 collections, or perhaps they represent (not quite accurately placed) UCM and UIMNH specimens collected in Phillips County in 1963 and 1964 (e.g., see Smith, Maslin, and Brown 1965). Further study of leopard frog distribution in Phillips and Yuma counties is needed to clarify the situation.

Conservation Status. The formerly abundant northern leopard frog has become scarce in many areas of Colorado. Some populations have disappeared due in least in part to changes in habitat. Breeding sites, such as those along streams and in mountain glacial kettles, change in suitability in response to climatic variation and flooding; though some sites may become unusable, others may be created by these events. From 1973–1982 in Larimer County, Corn and Fogleman (1984) documented the extirpation of nine populations at elevations of 7,760–8,265 feet (2,365–2,520 m). Six populations disappeared due to drought-related drying of breeding ponds; the others may have succumbed to random events that befall small populations. I suspect that local extirpation and (re)colonization are normal features in the ecology of the northern leopard frog in the drought-prone climate of Colorado. However, some of the northern leopard frog disappearances in the mountains of the Front Range (Corn, Stoltzenburg, and Bury 1989, 1997; Hammerson 1989a, 1992; Livo 1995a) have no satisfactory explanation.

In some lowland areas, reduced or extirpated leopard frog populations are associated with the presence of the increasingly abundant bullfrog (Hammerson 1982d), the larvae and adults of which may negatively impact leopard frogs (see account of bullfrog). Northern leopard frogs are now greatly outnumbered by bullfrogs in many stream courses, ponds, reservoirs, and wetlands in eastern Colorado. At Sawhill Ponds in Boulder County, where many years ago I described a leopard frog decline that was simultaneous with a bullfrog population increase (Hammerson 1982d), bullfrogs have remained abundant, whereas northern leopard frogs have managed to persist and breed successfully in low numbers in one or two ponds, especially the one that is semipermanent and often unfavorable for bullfrog reproduction and for the predatory fishes that are stocked in many ponds. In some areas, human alterations of wetlands have increased water depth and permanence, resulting in the replacement of leopard frogs by bullfrogs and fishes, especially near large rivers and other permanent bodies of water. It may be no coincidence that the sites in eastern Colorado where northern leopard frogs occur in greatest abundance are small,

relatively isolated reservoirs that have not been colonized by or stocked with bullfrogs or predatory fishes.

Declines in lowland areas of Colorado are not always associated with the presence of bullfrogs. The northern leopard frog apparently expanded its range in the Big Sandy Creek drainage of eastern Colorado after artificial ponds were created through sand and gravel excavation in the 1950s and 1960s (Gillis 1975), but *Rana pipiens* seems to have disappeared from most or all of the Big Sandy Creek region between 1975 and 1986 (Cousineau and Rogers 1991). The cause of the decline is uncertain but is not attributable to bullfrog impacts. Flood control measures and diversion of water for irrigation probably have reduced the availability of breeding habitat along floodplains in the lowland segments of some streams. Though northern leopard frogs have disappeared from many natural breeding sites in Colorado, they still occur in many human-created habitats, both in the lowlands and in the mountains. The degree to which natural habitat loss has been offset by the addition of artificial habitat is unknown.

Leopard frog conservation in lowland areas of Colorado probably is best accomplished through the creation and protection of habitats that favor leopard frog reproduction but limit or prohibit successful breeding by bullfrogs and predatory fishes. Specifically, periodic dewatering or large water-level reductions in late summer after leopard frogs have metamorphosed might be beneficial. Establishment of semipermanent wetlands among permanent wetlands may allow the persistence of leopard frogs in areas where bullfrogs and exotic predatory fishes cannot be eliminated without unacceptable damage to other wetland resources. In addition, northern leopard frog refuges could be established in isolated bodies of water, such as foothills ponds, far from permanent deepwater habitats inhabited by bullfrogs and fishes.

Malformed leopard frogs with limb and eye abnormalities have been observed in eastern North America and, rarely, in Colorado (Livo 1998b). Rosine (1952) reported polydactylism in a Boulder County population that is now extirpated, leaving us to wonder whether the unknown factor(s) causing the polydactylism may have contributed to the population decline.

Habitat. Typical habitats include wet meadows and the banks and shallows of marshes, ponds, glacial kettle ponds, beaver ponds, lakes, reservoirs, streams, and irrigation ditches. Usually, leopard frogs are found at the water's edge, but they may roam far from permanent water in wet meadows or during mild wet weather. Winter is spent at the bottom of a body of water such as a pond or stream. In a Canadian river in winter, juvenile and adult northern leopard frogs were observed hibernating beneath rubble, generally where water depth was greater than 85 cm (Cunjak 1986). The frogs were dark-colored, had closed eyes, and were torpid but capable of swimming.

Activity. In the plains region, emergence from winter retreats typically occurs in March. Activity continues until October or November, when cold weather forces the frogs into dormancy. However, Hahn (1968) found active leopard frogs in January and February in pools formed by warm artesian wells in the San Luis Valley. Activity may take place day or night.

These frogs sometimes move long distances. Gillis (1975) marked a northern leopard frog in a pond in Cheyenne County and found the same individual 3 km away at another pond the following year.

Approached by a person, leopard frogs may crouch motionless or leap away into water or dense vegetation. Sometimes they leave the water to hide in shoreline vegetation. Frogs flushed from lakeshores in San Miguel County jumped into the water and immediately returned to shore if no vegetative cover was available in the water. This response probably was related to the danger of predation by trout—frogs that jumped into cover of aquatic vegetation stayed there. Adults can move well over 1 m in a single leap.

Plate 7.64. Unusual blue variant of northern leopard frog (Weld County, Colorado).

Plate 7.65. Defensive posture of northern leopard frog (Jackson County, Colorado).

Plate 7.66. Eggs of northern leopard frog (Boulder County, Colorado).

Leopard frogs sometimes exhibit defensive postures. In Jackson County, a 62-mm-SVL frog that I tapped on the dorsum lowered its head and extended its elbows outward, with the forefeet close to the head. A newly metamorphosed frog in Hinsdale County exhibited the same response.

Reproduction and Growth. Breeding occurs in the shallow, quiet areas of permanent bodies of water, in beaver ponds, and in seasonally flooded areas adjacent to or contiguous with permanent pools or streams. Breeding sites typically contain vegetation, mats of algae, and fairly clear water.

At low elevations in Colorado, males begin calling on warm, sunny days in March or April. In eastern Boulder County, I found calling males in water that was 14–23°C. Males call while floating at the surface and frequently wrestle with each other between calls. In favorable habitat, 20–25 or more males may be present in a 20 m x 20 m area. Kruse (1981) found that female *Rana pipiens* were attracted to the mating call of *Rana pipiens* but not to that of *Rana blairi* or a presumed hybrid. The chuckle in the call may function in territorial interactions. When grasped by a male attempting amplexus, males and unreceptive females emit distinctive release calls, lasting a few tenths of a second (McClelland and Wilczynski 1989). Reproductively active males sometimes clasp inanimate objects (Livo 1981b). Calling in eastern Boulder County usually wanes in April but sometimes occurs in May or early June. I heard northern leopard frogs calling vigorously after a heavy rain in late May at 5,000 feet (1,525 m), but whether oviposition occurred is unknown.

The secretive females start laying eggs a few days after calling begins. Most females in the plains region of Boulder County lay their eggs by mid-April, sometimes by the end of March if warm weather arrives early. Along the Arkansas River in Pueblo County, Post (1972) found that the breeding season lasted from April 15 to May 20, April 24 to May 7, and April 12 to May 16 in three consecutive years. Along Big Sandy Creek in eastern Colorado one year, the season extended from April 9 to April 30. Females evidently produce one clutch per season.

Egg masses are attached to vegetation just below the surface in relatively warm shallows typically about 3–10 inches (7–25 cm) deep. In eastern Boulder County, midday water temperatures adjacent to several freshly laid egg masses were 12–23°C. At elevations of 5,150–8,265 feet (1,570–2,520 m) in Colorado and southern Wyoming, egg masses average about 3,000 eggs (range 645–6,272) (Corn and Livo 1989), with larger females laying more eggs (Livo 1981b). There is no evident relationship between clutch size and elevation.

In the plains region of Boulder County, eggs hatch in 4–15 days (Livo 1981b). Egg masses deposited in late March often are covered with tiny hatchlings by mid-April (pers. obs.). Early clutches may hatch before later clutches are deposited (Livo 1981b). Females often lay their eggs in distinct aggregations within the breeding site (Livo, pers. comm.). Hatchlings in eastern Boulder County are 5.5–8.4 mm TL (Livo 1981b).

I found numerous newly metamorphosed individuals in late June and early July in eastern Boulder County. Size at metamorphosis is about 21–36 mm SVL. Frogs do not begin breeding before their second spring.

Breeding males generally are larger than 5 cm SVL (average near 7 cm); females are larger than 6 cm SVL (average 7–8 cm).

At moderate elevations (6,680–7,760 feet [2,035–2,365 m]) in Larimer County, eggs are laid in late May and early June; metamorphosis takes place from mid-July through mid-September after a larval period averaging 10–12 weeks (the shortest was 58 days, the longest, occurring at the highest elevation, was 105 days) (Corn 1981). At elevations of 6,680–8,265 feet (2,035–2,520 m) in northern Colorado and southern Wyoming, breeding begins between early and late May (Corn and Livo 1989). In the San Luis Valley (7,500 feet [2,285 m]), calling may continue until at least late June (pers. obs.). Hahn (1968) observed newly metamorphosed individuals in the San Luis Valley on July 24. At 7,200 feet (2,195 m) in northwestern New Mexico, Gehlbach (1965) observed large numbers of recently metamorphosed young (9–25 mm SVL, mean 21.6 mm) on August 21–23.

Information on reproduction at high elevations is sketchy. I observed metamorphosing and newly metamorphosed individuals (26 mm SVL) in early August at 8,870 feet (2,705 m) in Jackson County and nearly metamorphosed young (34 mm SVL, 9 mm tail) in mid-August at 8,400 feet (2560 m) in Hinsdale County. At 9,000 feet (2,745 m) in Jackson County, I found many sizeable larvae lacking enlarged hind limbs in early August, and in the same area Stebbins (1951) found tadpoles on August 23. Blair (1951) reported that leopard frogs in the Elk Mountains (9,500 feet [2,895 m]) did not metamorphose before August 12. Hahn (1968) observed metamorphosing leopard frogs on August 2 at 10,500 feet (3,200 m) in southern Colorado. Brattstrom (1963) observed larvae (erroneously reported as bullfrogs) on August 5 at 8,520 feet (2,600 m) in Rocky Mountain National Park.

Food and Predators. Little information is available on northern leopard frog food habits in Colorado, but invertebrates undoubtedly dominate the diet of adults. Gehlbach (1965) reported tenebrionid beetles in the diet of individuals from northwestern New Mexico.

Known predators on larvae in Colorado include the pied-billed grebe *(Podilymbus podiceps)* (R. Ryder, pers. comm.) and tiger salamander (Corn 1981). Ballinger, Lynch, and Cole (1979) reported predation on larvae by the plains garter snake in western Nebraska. Reported predators on metamorphosed frogs in Colorado include the great blue heron *(Ardea herodias)* (D. and J. Ward, pers. comm.), burrowing owl *(Athene cunicularia)* (Hamilton 1941), northern water snake, and western terrestrial garter snake (Cockerell 1910; Livo, pers. comm.). Adults and larvae are vulnerable to predation by various game fishes (Bagdonas 1968). Experiments with *R. blairi* (Ehrlich 1979) indicate that the eggs and smallest larvae probably are vulnerable to predation by bullfrog larvae.

Remarks. Information on hybridization between the northern leopard frog and plains leopard frog is summarized in the account of the latter species.

Taxonomy and Variation. Dorsal color may be green or brown. In Larimer County, the frequency of the brown morph in natural populations ranges from 19–68 percent (Fogleman 1974; Corn 1981). Fogleman, Corn, and Pettus (1980) demonstrated that dorsal color is controlled by a two-allele, one-locus system, with the allele for green color dominant to the allele for brown. Corn (1981)

Plate 7.67. Larval, metamorphosing, and newly metamorphosed northern leopard frogs (Jackson County, Colorado).

found that the brown morph had a faster rate of larval development.

Other variable characters include size, shape, and number of dorsal spots; coloration of dorsolateral folds (may or may not contrast with background color); and roughness of the skin.

No subspecies are recognized.

Plate 7.68. Adult wood frog (Larimer County, Colorado).

Wood Frog
Rana sylvatica (LeConte, 1825)

Recognition. Dark "mask" on each side of face; dorsolateral folds present; hind toes webbed; usually a light mid-dorsal stripe; skin relatively smooth; maximum SVL about 83 mm. *Mature male:* base of innermost digit on forefeet swollen; averages slightly smaller and darker than adult female; expanded vocal sacs, one on each side, extend above forelimbs; breeding call a rapid series of 1–8 (usually 3–5) rough clacking notes (a chorus sounds somewhat like a group of softly quacking domestic ducks). *Larvae:* dorsum with blackish and olive-gray pigment; sides shiny bronze or pinkish; eyes dorsal; tail fin high, strongly arched dorsally, with dark spots and blotches; labial tooth rows 2/3 or 3/4; oral papillae encircle mouth, with wide gap above mandibles; papillae indented at angle of jaw, dense at sides of mouth; anus on right side at front end of ventral tail fin; maximum TL 52 mm (Stebbins 1951). *Eggs:* black above, whitish below, about 2.0–2.1 mm in diameter (Bagdonas 1968), each surrounded by two jelly envelopes, deposited in large globular masses about the size of a baseball or tennis ball and usually including several hundred eggs.

Distribution. Ranges farther north than any other North American amphibian, extending from Alaska to Newfoundland, and south to Virginia, Georgia, Alabama, and Arkansas in the east and to Montana, Wyoming, and northern Colorado in the Rocky Mountains. Occurs in Colorado in the mountains surrounding North Park, along the upper tributaries of the Colorado River in Grand County, and in the upper Laramie River drainage of Larimer County. There is a recent photo-documented occurrence in central North Park; pending verification

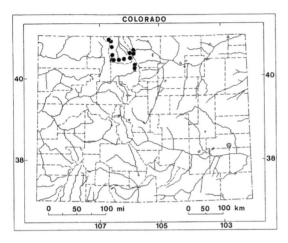

Map 7.19. Distribution of the wood frog in Colorado.

the distribution in the Park Range in Colorado north to the Big Creek Lakes area and confirmed Beardsley's earlier record from near Chambers Lake (UCM specimens). By 1959, the species was discovered in the upper Colorado River drainage (UCM specimens; McCoy 1962a). In 1961, David Pettus (unpublished, cited by Haynes and Aird 1981) observed wood frogs at the southern end of Shadow Mountain Reservoir (this population is believed to be extirpated). Bagdonas (1968, 1971) conducted the first intensive field study of Rocky Mountain wood frogs.

Bagdonas (1971) and Haynes and Aird (1981) described instances of human destruction/degradation of wood frog habitat that occurred in the late 1960s and early 1970s. Dredging of breeding ponds, clearing of shoreline vegetation, expansion of residential areas, and highway construction resulted in several population declines and extirpations in the vicinity of Rand, Chambers Lake, and Grand Lake. Largely as a result of these negative impacts and the limited distribution of the wood frog in Colorado, the Colorado Wildlife Commission classified the wood frog as "threatened" in December 1979.

Searches for wood frogs in Colorado in the late 1970s and early 1980s (Haynes and Aird 1981) revealed the persistence of the species throughout the major portions of its previously documented distribution. The overall known distribution did not change significantly as a result of these surveys (Hammerson 1981, 1982c). Recent surveys (Corn, Stoltzenburg, and Bury 1989; Corn, Jennings, and Muths 1997; Hammerson 1989a, 1992; Puttmann and Kehmeier 1994; Mourning 1997) indicate that wood frog populations in Colorado remain healthy

of a breeding population in that area, I did not include this site on the distribution map. Elevational range in Colorado is about 7,900–9,800 feet (2,400–3,000 m). The wood frog population in northern Colorado and adjacent southern Wyoming occupies a relatively small, disjunct area, presumably a remnant of a wider distribution that occurred during a formerly more mesic period after the last major episode of Pleistocene glaciation.

Conservation Status. The disjunct Southern Rockies population of wood frogs was discovered by Arthur E. Beardsley of the Colorado State Normal School (now the University of Northern Colorado) (Hammerson 1982a). Beardsley collected a specimen near Chambers Lake in Larimer County on August 16, 1898. Nearly half a century later, Vasco Tanner collected *Rana sylvatica* in the same area at Cameron Pass, Jackson County, on August 20, 1941 (BYU 12893), but this record evidently never was published. A specimen collected before World War II from the vicinity of the University of Wyoming science camp west of Laramie also went unreported at that time (George Baxter, pers. comm.). Several years later, Baxter (1946, 1947) and Maslin (1947c) provided the first published accounts of this species in the Southern Rockies, documenting populations in Wyoming and along the southern and western margins of North Park in Colorado (the Colorado collections were made in 1946). In 1950, Maslin extended

throughout the historic range and do not appear to be threatened. In response to this information, the Colorado Wildlife Commission removed the wood frog from state threatened status in 1998.

Haynes and Aird (1981) expressed concern that in the Southern Rockies, wood frog breeding habitats, most of which are glacial in origin, gradually are being eliminated through natural processes. However, pond basins that appear to be filling in (e.g., have a thick growth of sedges with little or no standing water) can brim with water in subsequent years (pers. obs.), due to normal climate fluctuations. Despite these variations, there seems to be no overall chronic shortage of, or major long-term decline in the number of, breeding sites. Protection of large natural wetland complexes with many pond basins of various sizes, some of which hold water even in the driest years, and minimization of logging and other erosion-causing activities in surrounding uplands should be enough to allow populations to persist through normal drought cycles and expand when wetter conditions prevail. Wide-scale alteration of natural wetlands and translocation of eggs or larvae (Haynes and Aird 1981; Puttmann and Kehmeier 1994) seem inadvisable at present, though hydrological management might be appropriate for particular breeding ponds being impacted by land development.

R. Bruce Bury (pers. comm.) reported finding a dead wood frog in Jackson County following treatment of a lake with rotenone. Larval die-offs associated with infections by the bacterium *Aeromonas hydrophila* and reduced breeding populations in subsequent years have been observed in wood frog populations in eastern North America.

Because wood frog populations typically undergo large fluctuations over periods of several years (Berven 1990), determination of long-term population trends in this species requires monitoring over decades. Recent surveys have provided baseline data for many populations in Colorado. Systematic monitoring of wood frog populations in the Southern Rockies should be continued.

Habitat. Wood frogs in Colorado inhabit subalpine marshes, bogs, pothole ponds, bea-ver ponds, lakes, stream borders, wet meadows, willow thickets, and forests bordering these mesic habitats. Willow–wet meadow mosaics and forested and willow-bordered stream courses are used primarily after frogs have dispersed from their breeding sites. In summer, wood frogs often can be found along the edges of marshy ponds and other wetlands. At midday, juveniles hide among vegetation or in muddy chambers under rocks (Bagdonas 1968). Winter hibernation occurs in holes under logs or rocks in forest areas (Bagdonas 1968) or perhaps in rodent burrows or similar underground sites.

Activity. Wood frogs are active in daytime during cooler periods in spring and may be active day or night during warmer summer months. Emergence from hibernation takes place primarily in May. Activity generally ends in September.

Wood frogs in the Rocky Mountains have relatively short hind legs and are poor leapers compared to leopard frogs. When disturbed, they may jump into the water, swim to the bottom, and sit motionless in full view or, on land, make several jumps and sit quietly beneath vegetation (Maslin 1947c).

Reproduction and Growth. Wood frogs usually breed in small, shallow, natural ponds that lack a permanent inlet and outlet. Less often, they breed in inactive beaver ponds. Wood frogs are somewhat adaptable and sometimes colonize and breed in human-created ponds. Lodgepole pine and aspen are found near most breeding sites. Breeding ponds typically have a shallow, sunny, north edge with an extensive growth of sedges in the water (Haynes and Aird 1981). Most breeding sites are ephemeral pools that dry in summer, and specific breeding locations change as hydrological conditions vary over the years. Such habitats have relatively small numbers of aquatic predators, enhancing the survival of frog larvae. The western chorus frog is the most common amphibian associate; northern leopard frog, mountain toad, and tiger salamander infrequently occur in wood frog breeding sites. Ponds inhabited by trout generally are not used for breeding by wood frogs. Studies in North Carolina indicate that wood frogs are able to detect

Plate 7.69. Egg masses of wood frog (Larimer County, Colorado). *Lauren Livo and Steve Wilcox.*

the presence of predatory fishes and avoid laying eggs in ponds these fishes inhabit (Hopey and Petranka 1994).

Males begin calling in May, before the last snowfall and when ice still forms at the pond surface at night. Calling males search actively for the secretive females and frequently change location. As in many other frogs, wood frog males attempt to clasp any frog that comes within reach, including males and other species. Amplexus lasts from 1–2 hours to as long as 2–3 days, during which time other males may attempt to displace the amplexing male. Amplexus does not necessarily occur at the site of eventual egg deposition.

The breeding season is short. The timing of breeding varies with temperature, persistence of snow, and spring storms, but in Colorado most eggs are laid at night from early May to early June (Bagdonas 1968), with the earliest breeding occurring at the lowest elevations. However, Maslin (1947c) reported that all but one adult female found near Rabbit Ears Peak on June 26 still retained her eggs. In a particular pond, breeding may last only a week or two, sometimes less. During this time, breeders apparently do not feed. Most adults leave the breeding ponds soon after the eggs are laid.

In Colorado, the number of egg masses found in a single pond generally ranges from 1–50 (Haynes and Aird 1981). Several females may deposit their eggs in a small area, often the same area in successive years. The number of eggs per mass is approximately 700–1,250, with an average near 900 (Bagdonas 1968; Porter 1969b; Corn and Livo 1989); each mass evidently represents a female's entire clutch (Corn and Livo 1989). Bagdonas (1968) stated that the eggs may be divided among 1–4 masses, but probably most females deposit the entire clutch as a single mass.

Eggs are laid mostly just below the water's surface or protrude slightly above it, often attached to sedges in water 10–15 cm deep at the north side of the pond, 1–3 m from shore, where maximal sun exposure (minimal shading by adjacent trees) results in warmer temperatures (Haynes and Aird 1981). However, water temperature surrounding developing eggs may vary from just above freezing to nearly 30°C. Sometimes, eggs are laid in warm water near underwater springs (Bagdonas 1968).

Daytime temperature within an egg mass generally exceeds surrounding water temperature, due primarily to absorption of solar energy and heat retention. Solar heating causes both water density changes and water movement through interstitial spaces in the egg mass and is an important mechanism by which eggs in the center of the mass are oxygenated (Seymour 1995). These centrally located eggs may be several degrees warmer than the surrounding water and may experience accelerated development, an advantage in ephemeral ponds (Waldman 1982; Waldman and Ryan 1983). Temperature also may affect sexual differentiation. Laboratory experiments with wood frog larvae from eastern North America by Witschi (1929) revealed that the sexes differentiate in the fourth week of larval development and that female larvae kept at high temperatures (32°C) become males. Whether temperature plays any role in sex determination under natural conditions in Colorado is unknown.

Some eggs perish due to desiccation or freezing if the water level drops too low and

Plate 7.70. Larval and metamorphosing wood frogs (Jackson County, Colorado).

the eggs are exposed to air, but clustering of egg masses reduces dehydration of eggs in the center of the aggregation. Some of these eggs may be able to survive several days of exposure (Forester and Lykens 1988). Reduced probability of mortality through desiccation may be another advantage of communal egg deposition.

Newly hatched larvae have been observed in Colorado from late May to late July, after 4–20 (often 4–7) days of embryonic development (Bagdonas 1968). Eggs in ponds at warmer, lower elevations hatch sooner than those at high elevations. Larvae metamorphose from mid-July to late August (Maslin 1947c; Stebbins 1951; McCoy 1962a; pers. obs.), usually 70–85 days after hatching (Bagdonas 1968). Newly metamorphosed frogs typically are 21–24 mm SVL, occasionally slightly smaller. Sometimes breeding ponds dry before the larvae metamorphose, resulting in total reproductive failure at that site. In ponds that retain water through summer, Bagdonas (1968) surmised that larvae sometimes overwinter and metamorphose the following spring, but no direct evidence of this was obtained. His "newly metamorphosed" frogs, found in June, may have been particularly small juveniles that metamorphosed late the previous year.

Immediately after metamorphosing, individuals spend several days feeding near the breeding ponds. Later they migrate at night to willow thickets and damp meadows, where they spend the remainder of the summer. Males are 34–40 mm SVL and females are 40–45 mm SVL by the end

of their second summer, and they reach 40–48 mm and 45–54 mm, respectively, by the third summer (Bagdonas 1968). Male wood frogs probably first breed in their second spring, females in their third (Bagdonas 1968).

A several-year study of wood frogs in Maryland (Berven 1990) yielded interesting results that probably apply to some extent to Rocky Mountain populations. The breeding population varied by a factor of 10 and the production of juveniles by a factor of 100. Fluctuation in the adult population was due largely to variation in juvenile recruitment, which was most affected by larval survival. Larvae constituted 92–99 percent of the wood frogs that died. Increased numbers of eggs deposited in a pond were associated with an increase in the duration of the larval period, reduced larval survival (possibly through competitive effects), and a decrease in the size at metamorphosis, which reduced survival during the juvenile stage and produced smaller adults that took longer to attain maturity. Large adult size is advantageous because it improves the probability that a male will mate and increases the number and size of eggs produced by a female. Adult survival improved with increasing seasonal precipitation. Less than 15 percent of the adults survived to breed the following year. Adults were 100 percent faithful to the ponds in which they first bred, but about 18 percent of juveniles bred in ponds other than their natal pond (Berven and Grudzien 1990). Ponds separated by more than 1,000 m were characterized by little or no genetic interchange.

Food and Predators. Bagdonas (1968) reported that the wood frog diet in Colorado includes small insects, worms, and spiders. I observed the forelimbs being used to subdue and ingest large prey. Foraging juveniles sometimes are covered with mud and resemble silt-covered pebbles (Bagdonas 1968). Wood frog larvae in eastern North America are effective predators on toad *(Bufo)* eggs and hatchlings (Petranka et al. 1994), but macrophagous predation by larvae has not been reported for Rocky Mountain wood frogs.

Known predators on larvae and metamorphosed individuals include diving beetle *(Dytiscus)* larvae, brook trout *(Salvelinus fontinalis),* rainbow trout *(Oncorhynchus mykiss),* brown trout *(Salmo trutta),* smallmouth bass *(Micropterus dolomieu),* and the western terrestrial garter snake (Bagdonas 1968). Captured wood frogs may feign death by going completely limp (Kreba 1977). This may reduce the chance of death or injury, because many predators are most vigorous in their attacks when the prey moves.

Remarks. Wood frogs tolerate partial freezing of their extracellular body fluids and, upon exposure to freezing conditions, enhance their resistance to freezing by breaking down liver glycogen and releasing glucose into the blood (Storey and Storey 1985; Layne and Lee 1987, 1995; Costanzo, Lee, and Loritz 1993). Glucose may serve as an antifreeze compound or may allow frozen cells to stay viable longer (Layne, Costanzo, and Lee 1998). Freeze tolerance allows wood frogs to hibernate close to the ground surface, which in turn facilitates quick detection of conditions suitable for breeding. It also expedites spring breeding activity at a time when temperatures often fall below 0°C. Breeding without delay is important because the shallow wetlands preferred as breeding sites often dry up in summer, killing all unmeta-morphosed larvae. Wood frogs also are remarkably tolerant of dehydration, surviving loss of up to 60 percent of their total body water, in contrast to the 38–50 percent documented for other ranid frogs (Churchill and Storey 1993, 1994). These characteristics are based on studies of wood frogs in eastern North America but probably apply also to wood frogs in the west.

Taxonomy and Variation. Wood frogs in the Southern Rockies morphologically closely resemble those in south-central Canada (Porter 1969a). Some average differences may reflect clinal variation (gradual changes over large distances). For example, in Colorado, the pale mid-dorsal stripe seems to be invariably present in metamorphosed wood frogs. Porter (1969a), however, found that the stripe was present in 67 of 72 wood frogs from southern Wyoming and in 23 of 50 individuals from Manitoba. Dunlap (1977) reported that wood frogs in the Big Horn Mountains of north-central Wyoming lack the dorsal stripe entirely. Among wood frogs in the Southern Rockies, tibiofibula length (relative to SVL) averages slightly shorter than that of wood frogs from Manitoba, though the range in the proportional length is the same (44–52 percent) for frogs from both areas (Porter 1969a).

Porter (1969b) recognized the disjunct population of wood frogs in the Southern Rocky Mountains as a distinct species, *Rana maslini,* based on his inability to successfully hybridize the frogs with *Rana sylvatica* from Canada. No major morphological differences between *"Rana maslini"* and *R. sylvatica* were identified. Breeding call differences between *"R. maslini"* and *R. sylvatica* amounted to only a small variation in the dominant frequency (Wyoming frogs were lower-pitched), but variation among *R. sylvatica* populations and responses of females to call variation was not investigated, so the significance of the variation cannot be determined. In contrast to Porter (1969b), Bagdonas and Pettus (1976) showed that wood frogs from Colorado and Canada are genetically compatible and can interbreed, despite being geographically separated for several thousand years. Thus, the primary basis for Porter's new species is not valid. Smith (1978) retained *maslini* as a subspecific name, but virtually all other herpetologists working with wood frogs in the Rocky Mountains have consistently referred to these frogs simply as *Rana sylvatica,* in accordance with the conclusion of Martof and Humphries (1959). Martof and Humphries summarized rangewide geographic patterns of morphological variation and identified five geographically discrete phenotypes, but they found little reason to assign formal names to these entities and recommended that subspecies not be recognized. Zeyl (1993) investigated genetic variation among several wood frog populations in North America but did not include any from the Rocky Mountains.

Chapter 8

Reptiles

The first fossils unquestionably representing the class Reptilia are found in early Pennsylvanian rocks approximately 315 million years old. Reptiles clearly evolved from amphibians, though there is disagreement over which amphibian group is ancestral to the reptiles. Reptiles flourished during the Mesozoic, occupying niches that later were filled by birds and mammals. The most famous of all reptiles, the dinosaurs, lumbered and sprinted across Colorado during this era but disappeared by the end of the Cretaceous, about 65 million years ago. As is true of amphibians, most groups of reptiles are extinct.

Reptiles that survive today are scaly animals comprising four major groups. The tuataras (order Rhynchocephalia) are lizardlike reptiles now found only on a few islands off the coast of New Zealand. The two living species are the only survivors of a formerly widespread group. The crocodilians (order Crocodylia) are the only extant members of the subclass Archosauria, which includes the dinosaurs and pterosaurs (flying reptiles). Today's crocodilians include 21 species of sprawling, amphibious reptiles that occur primarily in tropical and subtropical areas worldwide. Crocodiles inhabited the swamps of Colorado until at least the late Oligocene, some 25 million years ago. They disappeared as the formerly subtropical climate became cooler and drier. The turtles (order Testudines), with their distinctive protective shells, are familiar to almost everyone. The lizards, snakes, and amphisbaenians constitute the fourth major group, the order Squamata. Amphisbaenians comprise about 150 species of wormlike, burrowing animals

found in tropical, subtropical, and warm temperate regions of the world. All but a few species of amphisbaenians lack legs. The eyes are poorly developed. Turtles, lizards, and snakes are discussed in detail in sections preceding the species accounts for these groups.

Skin and Color. A characteristic that easily differentiates reptiles from amphibians is skin type. The outer layer of reptile skin usually is made up of epidermal scales, thick keratin plates separated by areas of thinner keratin. Scales may be overlapping, pointed, rounded, granular, smooth, or otherwise. Osteoderms (bony plates) are imbedded in the dermis of skinks, the Gila monster, and crocodilians.

In contrast to amphibians, reptile skin is mostly devoid of glands and performs a respiratory function in only a few species (the lungs are better developed than in amphibians). A superficial layer of dead cells (stratum corneum), the scale-forming deposits of keratin, and the virtual absence of secretory glands make the skin of a reptile drier and more impervious to water than that of an amphibian. Reptile skin also generally is more resistant to abrasion.

As in amphibians, reptile skin, mostly the upper dermis, has special color cells (chromatophores) that enable the animals to change color. Color changes often result from shifts in position of the pigment within certain chromatophores (melanophores). Color-change ability is greatest in lizards (it is limited or absent in snakes) and functions in background matching (avoiding detection by predators) and heat exchange (body temperature regulation).

Color changes occurring over a period of minutes or hours may be influenced by hormones and/or the autonomic nervous system, or chromatophores may change in direct response to light or temperature. Many lizards also undergo more gradual, seasonal color changes usually associated with breeding activities.

Reptiles periodically shed the skin, or more precisely, the dead outer (alpha and beta) layers of the stratum corneum, as new layers form beneath. Shedding occurs up to several times per year. Rapidly growing juveniles tend to shed most frequently. Turtles such as *Chrysemys* shed the shell scutes once a year. In other turtles, such as *Terrapene* box turtles, the scutes accumulate and are shed gradually. When snakes shed their skin, they also shed the spectacle covering the eye; it turns cloudy, then clears shortly before the process begins. The skin generally loosens about the lips, then around the rest of the head. A shedding snake crawls slowly along, rubbing against rocks, vegetation, or other objects and eventually slips out of the old skin, usually turning it inside out in the process. Snakes normally shed the skin in one piece, but other reptiles may shed it in many pieces.

Skeleton and Tail. Reptiles differ skeletally from amphibians in several major ways. Five digits typically are present on each foot (no more than four on the forefeet of amphibians). The skull and skeleton are bonier (less cartilaginous) than in amphibians. The ribs often are well-developed and may function in breathing (amphibians breathe via throat pumping). The vertebrae are better differentiated than in amphibians and include an atlas, axis, and usually two sacral (hip) vertebrae. A single occipital condyle connects the skull to the neck vertebrae.

A well-developed tail is present in most reptiles. Lizards usually have a fairly long tail, which in many species is rather easily detached. The tails of snakes and turtles generally break only when extreme force is applied, and significant regeneration does not occur.

Temperature, Metabolism, and Respiration. Most reptiles are ectothermic; that is, they derive their body heat from external sources. Their low metabolic rate generally produces insufficient heat to increase body temperature (insulation also is poor). Some reptiles, however, are able to generate and retain significant amounts of body heat. For example, a python brooding eggs may raise its body temperature several degrees above the ambient temperature through muscular contractions and increased metabolic rate. Monitors and sea turtles may generate and retain body heat during activity (the leatherback may be as much as 18°C above seawater of 7.5°C). Thus, large reptiles may be at least partially endothermic.

Contrary to popular belief, reptiles are not necessarily cold-blooded. By shuttling between sun and shade or between warm and cool surroundings, many species maintain fairly stable body temperatures that equal or exceed human body temperature, and some tolerate temperatures that would be lethal to humans. At night, however, their temperatures approximate that of the surrounding air or soil. Secretive reptiles, such as those usually found under rocks during daytime, obtain most of their body heat from the soil or from sun-warmed rocks. They generally maintain lower body temperatures than do those that bask in the sun. Lizards that bask maximize heat gain by lying low on the substrate; elevating the body generally reduces heat gain. At least some reptiles maintain the temperature of the head at a higher and/or more stable level during activity than that at the core of the trunk.

The typical level of body temperature during activity differs among groups of reptiles. For example, whiptail lizards generally average about 40°C during activity, whereas gopher snakes average about 25°C, with much greater variability. The characteristic body temperature may be influenced by several factors (e.g., presence of food in the stomach or eggs in the oviduct) and may fluctuate.

Despite their often thermophilic (heat-loving) habits, most reptiles cannot tolerate excessively high temperatures. For example, various diurnal lowland snakes exposed to the midday summer sun die of overheating within about 0.5–2 hours if prevented from escaping to shade. Reptiles active during daylight hours generally retreat to underground burrows or crevices during summer's midday heat. Most activity takes place in morning or late afternoon. Other reptiles, particularly snakes, confine their activity to twilight or nighttime hours. Some snakes shift their activity seasonally, becoming more nocturnal as the weather gets hotter.

The thermal preferences and tolerances of reptiles may prevent their exploitation of certain habitats and microhabitats and restrict their seasonal and daily activity. Reptiles in areas with cold winters may spend several months inactive underground at body temperatures a few degrees above freezing. If necessary, most temperate-zone reptiles can survive temperatures near freezing. Many species, including hatchlings that typically overwinter in shallow nests, escape the lethal effects of freezing by supercooling (without ice formation) to several degrees below 0°C. Aquatic turtles usually retreat to the unfrozen bottoms of lakes and ponds. They obtain oxygen from the water, mostly through the walls of the mouth cavity or the cloaca. The winter period of reptilian inactivity in Colorado generally extends from November to March. Although a few individuals may venture out during unseasonably warm weather, reptiles generally cannot be found during the cold season.

Compared to birds and mammals, reptiles have low rates of metabolism. For example, at 37°C a lizard may produce only one-seventh of the metabolic heat produced by a small rodent of similar size. This low energy expenditure during the warm season and the cold winter months allows reptiles to survive throughout the year on amazingly small amounts of food. They are exceptionally efficient at assimilating ingested calories. Reptiles are capable of bursts of activity but generally tire fairly rapidly. During vigorous activity, 50–90 percent of the energy is anaerobically derived; lactate builds up, eventually causing fatigue.

Rate of energy expenditure in reptiles is strongly influenced by temperature, as is capacity for activity, aerobic metabolic scope (i.e., the ability to increase metabolism), skeletal muscle performance, sensitivity of the inner ear to sound, rate of development and digestion, success in prey capture, and behavior. Metabolism and capacity for activity are minimal at low body temperatures and proceed optimally within the range of body temperatures at which most activity occurs.

Little energy is consumed during hibernation. Hibernating common garter snakes meet their minimal energy needs by metabolizing glycogen and proteins from liver and muscle tissues. Lipids stored in the abdominal fat bodies and elsewhere contribute little or nothing to overwinter energetics, but lipids may be important during activity in late fall and early spring and in species that hibernate at relatively high body temperatures or that are periodically active in winter.

Reptiles and Water. Organisms that inhabit dry environments, such as much of Colorado, potentially face severe water-balance problems. One way of conserving water is to reduce the amount lost through urine and feces. Typical dryland reptiles such as lizards, snakes, and terrestrial turtles eliminate nitrogen wastes mostly as uric acid and urates that precipitate out of the urine as a semisolid paste. Relatively little water is required to void uric acid; species that produce it have reduced water requirements and are better able to inhabit dry areas. In addition, water can be absorbed from the urine and feces in the cloaca. A urinary bladder, another potential site for water reabsorption, is present in all turtles, tuataras, and some lizards (including adults of some species, but neonates only in most or all Colorado species) but is absent in snakes, crocodilians, and other lizards.

In the highly aquatic crocodilians and the most aquatic turtles, nitrogenous waste from the digestion of protein is eliminated mostly as ammonia. Ammonia is relatively toxic and must be voided in large volumes of watery urine, but water availability is not a problem for these reptiles. Some turtles, such as the painted turtle, eliminate nitrogen wastes mostly as urea, plus some ammonia and uric acid.

Marine reptiles have glands (nasal in lizards, lachrymal in turtles, posterior sublingual or premaxillary in snakes, and lingual in crocodilians) that are effective in eliminating salts with minimal water loss, though these glands may serve other functions as well. The chuckwalla *(Sauromalus ater)*, a plant-eating desert lizard of southwestern North America, also has nasal salt-secreting glands.

Water loss through the skin is greatly reduced in reptiles, as compared to amphibians. Surprisingly, the water permeability of the scales is the same as that of the areas between the scales, where the keratin is reduced. This has been demonstrated in snakes by the similar water-loss rates of scaled and mutant scaleless individuals of the same species. Lipids in the skin of snakes are the main barrier to water loss. At high temperatures, water loss through respiration increases (and the evaporative water loss retards heat gain). Aquatic species lose water faster under dehydrating conditions than do terrestrial species of the same size.

In most reptiles there is no significant water intake through the skin. Food is an important source of water for many species, and most nonaquatic species drink water when it is available, such as after rainfall.

Senses. Many reptiles have good vision (consider the quick response of certain turtles and lizards to an approaching human). Visual detection of prey movement stimulates feeding behavior in many species. Vision is an important sense in foraging and avoiding predators in diurnal reptiles such as whipsnakes, racers, and many other snakes. Vision functions best at relatively close range. The aquatic snakes (garter snakes, water snakes) found in Colorado apparently see well in air but have relatively poor underwater vision.

Reptile vision is mostly monocular. Binocular vision usually is limited to 10–40 in front of the snout. Color vision apparently is good in turtles and some lizards. Many diurnal lizards and snakes have no rods in the retina and are virtually blind in darkness. Nocturnal species tend to be color-blind. At least one sea snake has light receptors in the skin of the tail.

Reptiles (except snakes) focus the eye by changing the shape of the lens and cornea. For close focusing, the ciliary muscle squeezes the lens, making it more spherical. The eyes of snakes, however, are fundamentally different. Most snakes focus the eye by moving the lens (iris muscles put pressure on the ocular fluid), as in amphibians, rather than by lens deformation, though in some species the iris squeezes the lens. The retina does not include the sensory structures needed to perceive color. Most reptiles have a round pupil, but a vertically elliptical pupil occurs in some nocturnal and crepuscular species. The elliptical pupil can be opened wide and closed more fully than a round pupil.

Some reptiles have a true nictitating membrane (third eyelid) that can sweep across the eye. Some species, such as certain skinks, have a transparent lower eyelid that protects the eye while permitting vision. Snakes, some geckos, and night lizards are unable to close their eyes because they lack movable eyelids. Each eye is protected by a clear, spectacle-like shield that is shed with the skin.

Ears and hearing are present in reptiles but are not well developed in most species. Most Colorado lizards have an externally visible eardrum and the usual structures of the middle ear to transmit sounds to the inner ear. Presumably, these lizards can hear reasonably well. The eardrums of the lesser earless lizard and some of the horned lizards are covered with scaly skin, which probably decreases their acoustic sensitivity. Burrowing reptiles generally have vestigial ear openings; alternatively, the ears may be covered with a flap of skin or totally absent. In snakes, the eardrum and middle-ear cavity are missing, but the inner ear is similar to that of other reptiles. The quadrate bone apparently functions in sound transmission. At least some snakes are moderately sensitive to sounds of 100–700 cycles per second (plus or minus one octave around middle C). The few species that have been studied hear better than a cat can at the low end of this range. Snakes are sensitive to ground vibrations in the same frequency range as those sounds perceived in the inner ear, and the snake brain makes no distinction between airborne sound and substrate vibration. The hearing ability of turtles evidently is about the same as that of snakes. Overall, field observations suggest that most reptiles are more or less unresponsive to airborne sounds. However, some geckos have a well-developed voice and hearing, and vocal communication is obviously important. The upper frequency range of hearing in reptiles is lower than in birds and mammals.

Some lizards that normally are silent produce audible sounds under duress. Certain snakes produce conspicuous sounds, generally in a defensive context. The hiss of a bullsnake is caused by air passing over a vertically oriented keel of cartilage in front of the glottis. Many snakes produce rattling sounds through tail vibrations in dry vegetation. And, of course, rattlesnakes have a specialized sound-producing rattle (see account of viper family).

Lizards and snakes have an excellent sense of smell, due primarily to their chemical-sensitive vomeronasal (Jacobson's) organs, paired pouches that open in the roof of the mouth cavity. The pouches are connected by nerves to the olfactory bulb of the brain. Airborne odors or chemical substances on the substrate or on other individuals are picked up on the tip of the protrusible tongue, which itself has no chemosensory structures, then transferred to the vomeronasal organs. Snakes frequently use their long, rapidly flicking, forked tongue in this way. They also exhibit peculiar slow-motion tongue flicks that seem to be most often (always?) associated with defensive behavior. Olfaction is important in snake reproductive and feeding behavior. For example, some snakes refuse to strike if the vomeronasal organs do not receive information. The importance of olfaction in reproduction is demonstrated by the elimination of courtship, mating, and fighting behavior in male snakes whose vomeronasal system has been anesthetized. Mate detection in snakes may involve the male following pheromone (odor) trails left by females. Using only chemical cues, garter snake males can distinguish among females of different garter snake species and preferentially select the trails of their own species. Newborn snakes may follow pheromone trails to locate den sites.

Recent studies indicate that chemoreception is also important in at least some lizards, even in species lacking a long, forked tongue. These lizards may frequently extrude the tongue and lick objects, and such licking may mediate tasting (taste buds are abundant in many lizards) or vomeronasal chemoreception, aiding in identifying potential food items, recognizing the chemical signature of other lizards, or gathering information in unfamiliar situations. Some lizards leave scent marks behind via waxy femoral pore secretions. Femoral pores are present in a single row along the underside of the hind limbs of most lizard species, and their secretions rub off onto rocks or other objects and may affect the behavior of other individuals. Generally, the glands are largest and most active in adult males. Fecal and excretory deposits also may function in chemical communication.

The vomeronasal organs are not well developed in turtles and are absent in adult crocodilians. Reptiles also have a "standard" odor-receptor system in the nasal passages.

The most notable odors associated with reptiles are those produced in the musk glands of certain turtles (see accounts of mud and musk turtle and snapping turtle families) and the cloacal sacs (scent glands) of snakes. Cloacal sacs, a pair of structures that open into the cloaca, are present in all snakes and produce a lipoidal secretion that varies chemically with species, sex, and age. The interspecies odor differences sometimes are distinct enough to be discerned by humans. Snakes of at least some species are able to spray the secretion. Possible functions of the scent glands include defense and intraspecific communication.

Certain snakes, include slender blind snakes, ground snakes, and black-headed snakes, have dense concentrations of touch receptors on the snout. Specialized thermal receptors are another prominent sensory mechanism in snakes. These are discussed in the account of the viper family.

The sensory systems of at least some reptiles endow them with well-developed homing abilities. For example, a blinded striped whipsnake successfully returned to its home den from a distance of more than 200 m. Box turtles have no problem in homing from distances of up to nearly 800 m, and some can return home from distances of as much as 3 km. The mechanisms of reptile homing and orientation are poorly known, but painted turtles, box turtles, and softshell turtles are able to use topographic features and celestial cues (e.g., the sun's position in the sky) to orient themselves within their home ranges. Airborne odors and large visual landmarks might aid individuals not too far displaced. Turtles of at least one species are able to locate aquatic habitats outside their familiar area; light cues may be used, as the turtles orient more accurately on sunny days than on cloudy ones. Available evidence suggests that they do not simply follow a "go downhill" rule. Garter snakes may be able to use solar cues, possibly polarized light, as an orientation guide.

Reproduction and Growth. In the temperate climate of Colorado, reptilian reproduction is distinctly seasonal. Breeding activities are at their height during spring and early summer. For most species, temperature evidently is the major factor influencing the timing of reproductive activity. Reproductive behavior in at least some snakes is induced by the increase in body temperature experienced upon emergence from hibernation. Other important factors for some species may include rainfall and food supply. In contrast to those of birds, photoperiod has no effect on the ovarian cycles of many reptiles.

In many reptiles, males begin to seek females soon after emerging from hibernation. Aquatic turtles and lizards seldom need to make any special effort to locate females because their relatively high population densities result in frequent male-female encounters. Population densities of snakes may be fairly low, and males may have to search actively for females, relying primarily on chemical cues.

Breeding often begins with a period of courtship in which males play the more active role. Male turtles may repeatedly bob the head or bite, bump, or stroke the female in an effort to entice her to mate. Lizard courtship often includes distinctive bobbing or "push-ups," during which brightly colored areas of the body are displayed. The presence or absence of some of these colored areas greatly affects social status. Males of some lizard species bite or nip at the female during courtship. Male snakes often court females by crawling over them and rubbing the chin and underside over the female's dorsum. Tongue-flicking and intertwining of tails often accompanies the body undulations. Males of some species (common kingsnake, bullsnake, black rat snake, racer) bite the head/neck of the female just prior to and during copulation.

Reptiles reveal their sex and species to one another by these distinctive behaviors and by their reactions to such behaviors. The sense of smell also may be critical in species recognition and sexual attractiveness, particularly in snakes. Outward appearance, in the absence of appropriate behavioral or chemical cues, often is not enough to allow recognition or stimulate reproductive behavior. The role of pheromones in the reproductive behavior of snakes is discussed in the accounts of the common and plains garter snakes.

Mating in reptiles in Colorado takes place mostly in spring, though also in summer or fall in some snake species (sperm is stored by the female until spring ovulation). Most temperate- and subtropical-zone snakes produce sperm in summer and store it in the vas deferens until spring, when mating occurs. Only one snake *(Rhamphotyphlops braminus)* is known to be completely parthenogenetic, but a few others may occasionally produce young without ever having mated.

Courtship usually leads to copulation. Fertilization is internal in all reptiles. Male lizards, snakes, and turtles release sperm into the cloaca of the female via a grooved copulatory organ. Male lizards and snakes have two copulatory organs, each of which is called a hemipenis (plural hemipenes). Copulation takes place as a hemipenis everts through the vent (cloacal opening) of the male and pushes into the gaping cloaca of the female. Initial evagination of the basal part of the hemipenis is under muscular control; engorgement with blood and lymph contributes to the turgidity of the fully expanded organ. Only one hemipenis is used during each mating. Mating may last minutes or hours, during which time the males of some species grasp in their jaws the head, neck, or shoulders of the female. When not in use, the hemipenes are withdrawn inside-out in the base of the tail.

Turtles have a single, erectile penis that is inserted after the male mounts the female from the rear. Mating is facilitated in most turtle species by the concave shape of the male's plastron (lower shell), which conforms with the convex rear portion of the female's carapace (upper shell). When not in use, the penis is withdrawn through the vent into the base of the tail.

Sperm may be stored in specialized structures (seminal receptacles) in the oviduct or in the posterior part of the oviduct. Sperm storage makes possible multiple paternity (i.e., different fathers for young in a single clutch or litter). Certain turtles and snakes are able to store viable sperm for up to several years.

Reptile eggs differ radically from amphibian eggs. Reptile embryos develop in a fluid-filled chamber that is enveloped by membranes produced by the embryo. In most reptiles, energy for development is derived from the egg's abundant yolk. There is little or no albumen present in the eggs of lizards and snakes.

The mass of the eggs may constitute 5–50 percent of the total mass of a female lizard, generally about 15–40 percent in phrynosomatids, 15–35 percent in crotaphytids, and 10–25 percent in teiids. In snakes, the clutch or litter mass is about 20–45 percent of total female mass, with the lowest values occurring in viviparous (live-bearing) species such as garter snakes and pit vipers. Clutch size generally increases with female body size.

All turtles, crocodilians, tuataras, and most lizards and snakes are oviparous and lay shelled elliptical or elongate eggs. The shell is secreted by glands in the oviduct.

The eggs of most lizards and apparently all snakes have thin extensible shells with little or no crystalline calcareous layer. Many turtles produce eggs with somewhat flexible shells with a well-defined calcareous layer. The shell is brittle in some turtle species (e.g., box turtles and, ironically, softshell turtles), parchmentlike in painted turtles, and intermediate in snapping turtles. Flexible-shelled eggs absorb water under favorable hydric conditions. The eggs of *Sceloporus* lizards may triple in mass due to absorption of water during incubation. The rigid shells of some geckos, certain turtles, crocodilians, and the tuatara allow little water exchange. In addition to its packaging function, the shell serves as a source of calcium for the developing embryo. The eggs of most egg-laying lizards and snakes reside in the oviduct for approximately half of the total period of embryonic development. Turtles may retain shelled eggs for up to several weeks.

Because the eggs are laid on land, many reptiles assume a completely terrestrial existence. Although reptiles lay eggs and reproduce successfully even in the driest of deserts, the eggs may fatally desiccate if not sheltered in a suitably humid micro-environment. Hence, reptiles bury their eggs in the soil or lay them under rocks or in burrows, though at least one turtle species in Australia lays its eggs in seasonally flooded substrates under shallow water (the eggs develop after the water recedes).

The reptilian life cycle does not include the free-living larval stage typical of amphibians. The newly born or hatched reptile begins life as a miniature, sexually immature version of the adult. Young reptiles cut through the shell with a pointed projection (egg tooth, or caruncle) that is shed soon after hatching in lizards and snakes but may persist for weeks in turtles.

Some lizards, water snakes, garter snakes, and most vipers are viviparous. Young of viviparous species are enclosed in a membranous sac and retained in the oviduct until birth. A placental connection with the mother occurs in some viviparous reptiles. Viviparous species are most prevalent at high elevations and high latitudes. Viviparity may enhance oxygen delivery to the embryo (via a placenta) and allows, through thermophilic behavior of the female, warmer temperatures during development.

Most reptiles abandon their eggs soon after oviposition. Females of some skinks *(Eumeces)* may attend their eggs and young until several days after hatching. Female boas and slender blind snakes may brood their eggs. Some snakes occasionally exhibit communal nesting behavior. Neonates are able to fend for themselves. Hatching or birth occurs in summer and early fall in Colorado reptiles.

Fat bodies in the abdominal cavity provide most of the nutrition for reptilian reproduction. Poor feeding conditions may reduce reproductive output due to inadequate fat storage. Periods of drought and food shortage may result in smaller clutch sizes in lizards. Female snakes may produce young annually when they have abundant food but may skip a year when their food intake has been low. Female snakes generally do not feed toward the end of gestation, probably as the result of the digestive system's being pushed aside by the growing bulk of the reproductive system.

Growth rates of reptiles typically are high in juveniles and very low in adults. Growth rate is directly related to food intake. Thus, age classes may overlap in size, depending on the feeding history of each individual. Large individual size in amphibians and reptiles seems to be more a result of rapid juvenile growth than of old age. Sexual maturity occurs in 1–2 years in most lizard species and 2–4 years in many snakes; most turtle species take several years to mature. Larger reptile species tend to mature at an older age than do smaller ones.

Feeding. Most reptiles eat other animals, but herbivory occurs in turtles and some lizards. All Colorado reptiles are predominantly or exclusively carnivorous. Most reptiles have small, relatively simple teeth, though some lizards and snakes have specialized teeth, and turtles have none at all. Reptile teeth are polyphyodont; that is, they may be replaced several times. Adjacent teeth generally are replaced at different times. Replacement teeth come in alongside or directly under older teeth. Land-dwelling reptiles usually have a well-developed tongue that helps move prey down the throat in turtles and lizards (but not in snakes). Additional information on feeding is included in the introductory sections for turtles, lizards, and snakes.

Predation and Mortality. As in amphibians, mortality is highest among the young, most of which do not survive their first year. Winter conditions kill many individuals. Predators (mainly carnivorous mammals, raptors, passerine birds such as ravens and other corvids, large snakes, and lizards), disease, and other factors also take their toll.

Turtles

Turtles (order Testudines) are among the most distinctive of animals. Turtle is a general term that can be applied to any species popularly known as a turtle, tortoise, or terrapin. The turtle shell is a bony structure formed by extensive dorsal and ventral dermal (skin) ossification and usually covered with horny plates, the sutures of which are offset from the bone sutures. The ribs are expanded and incorporated into the bony carapace.

The earliest known turtles had a full shell. The immediate ancestors of turtles are unknown. *Proganochelys,* a characteristic Triassic turtle, had teeth in the palate. All recent turtles have a horny beak without teeth (though there are teeth in softshell turtle embryos). Early turtles apparently could not retract the head. Some Cretaceous turtles exceeded 3 m in length and were larger than any living turtle species.

Two evolutionary lines became established early on; these are represented by the suborder Cryptodira (most turtles, all of those in the United States) and the suborder Pleurodira (about 45 species in the Southern Hemisphere). Members of the Cryptodira withdraw the head into the shell via a vertical, S-shaped flexing of the neck, whereas Pleurodira employ a lateral flexing of the neck.

Turtles occupy the tropical, subtropical, and warm temperate regions of the world, including various terrestrial, freshwater, and marine habitats. Of the world's 244 species,

about 56 occur in the United States, 5 in Colorado.

Turtles have developed a unique breathing mechanism—hardly surprising for an animal encased in a bony shell. Lizards and snakes breathe through muscular actions that move the ribs. In turtles, breathing is accomplished by muscles pulling or pushing the viscera against or away from the lungs. The skin and the lining of the pharynx serve as supplementary respiratory structures in softshell turtles. Other respiratory structures include the paired cloacal bursae of many aquatic turtles (bursae are chambers that can be filled and emptied of water for oxygen exchange). Sea turtles, tortoises, and softshell turtles lack these bursae. Fresh-water turtles may store large volumes of water in their cloacal bursae and copious urine in the bladder. These fluid reservoirs may be used to control buoyancy.

Turtles have impressive tolerance of anoxia. Breathing pure nitrogen at 22°C (a warm condition in which oxygen needs are relatively high), most lizards and snakes survive 0.5–1.5 hours, but many turtles survive 15 hours or more. Tolerance increases with decreasing temperature. At 10°C, a painted turtle can survive without access to oxygen for more than two weeks. At 3°C, a painted turtle can survive anoxic conditions for about five months (Ultsch, Hanley, and Bauman 1985). Submerged hibernating turtles at lower temperatures (0–4°C) may periodically pump water into and out of the mouth and/or cloacal bursae and extract some oxygen through these structures. Individuals buried in mud evidently experience and tolerate extended anaerobic conditions for several months each year. Prolonged tolerance to anoxia by painted turtles at low temperatures is due to a greatly reduced metabolic rate, slow accumulation of plasma lactate, modest hypercapnia, and compensatory ion changes that greatly retard the development of acidosis (death results if blood pH falls by about 1.0 pH units).

The sex of hatchlings is genetically determined at fertilization in most reptiles, but in turtle species other than softshells and perhaps some others, sex of the hatchlings is dictated by the temperature of the embryo during development. In general, low nest temperature (generally below 29–30°C) results in males, and high temperature yields females. At least in some turtles, the middle third of development is the sensitive period for sex determination. Temperature-dependent sex determination implies that the nest site chosen by the female could influence the sex of the hatchlings. A study of map turtles found that nests in the open yielded mainly females, whereas those shaded by vegetation part of the day yielded a greater percentage of males. A study of nest site selection in painted turtles revealed that females did not exhibit a consistent or alternating pattern of nest site selection from year to year. Also, nest temperature was more dependent on annual climatic fluctuation than on variation in the nest site. A complication in interpreting the effect of temperature on sexual differentiation in turtles is that sexual differentiation of the gonads of at least one sea turtle species is barely initiated at hatching, and sex reversal after hatching is a possibility. Temperature-induced gender in freshwater turtles appears to be permanent.

Some turtles (but not kinosternids) hatch with the remains of the yolk sac still protruding from the plastron. In painted turtles and snapping turtles, approximately half of the lipid present in the egg is still there at hatching. This is an important nutritional resource for the young turtle. Initially, hatchlings extract nutrients from whatever remains of the yolk. It usually takes 1–4 days for a hatchling to internalize the yolk sac, but the process may take as long as two weeks.

As a group, turtles are omnivorous, but animal matter, especially invertebrates, dominates the diet of each species in Colorado. Juveniles grow best on an animal diet. Food is detected by sight or, especially in aquatic species, smell. Turtles procure food by jutting the head forward and grasping the prey with a snap of the jaws. Small food items may be crushed in the jaws before being swallowed. Large prey generally are torn apart, sometimes with the aid of the forefeet.

Nests of freshwater turtles frequently are lost to predators such as raccoons, skunks, opossums, mink, and foxes (and sometimes certain snakes). This attrition results in part from the tendency of many turtles to nest along habitat edges where these predators are common. Clearly some of these mammals focus their attention on turtle nesting areas during the nesting season, but predators do not need to see a turtle or smell a turtle or egg scent to find a nest. They readily locate decoy nests containing ping-pong balls buried by humans but clean of human scent, possibly suggesting that predators detect potential food sources by cues associated with recent digging. Mammalian carnivores sometimes kill or maim adult turtles, and young turtles fall prey to various predators. Certain large predatory insects may kill and feed on hatchling turtles on occasion. Aquatic turtles are sometimes infested by leeches. Terrestrial species often host parasitic fly larvae.

SNAPPING TURTLES
Family Chelydridae

These turtles, including only two species, are characterized by their large size; massive head with hooked jaws; stout, heavily clawed limbs; small plastron; long tail; and skeletal peculiarities. The alligator snapper *(Macroclemys temminckii)* of the southeastern United States may weigh up to 114 kg. The other species, the snapping turtle, is smaller but no less impressive. These highly aquatic, bottom-dwelling turtles are restricted to the Americas. The alligator snapper is well known for using a small wormlike appendage on its tongue as a lure, something the snapping turtle lacks.

Plate 8.1. Adult snapping turtle (South Platte River, Logan County, Colorado).

Snapping Turtle
Chelydra serpentina (Linnaeus, 1758)

Recognition. Shell hard, often with attached mud or algae; rear edge of carapace saw-toothed; tail as long as or longer than carapace, with crest of large bony scales; head large, with hooked jaws; plastron relatively small, composed of nine shields; limbs strong, with webbed toes and powerful claws; maximum CL nearly 50 cm, usually less than 36 cm; average weight 16 kg, though fat captives may reach 39 kg. *Adult:* carapace relatively smooth, longitudinal ridges not very prominent. *Mature male:* anal opening farther from base of tail than in female, usually posterior to rear edge of carapace (under rear edge in female); grows larger than female. *Juvenile:* carapace with three longitudinal ridges. *Hatchling:* carapace rough, with conspicuous ridges, cryptically resembling a dead leaf. *Eggs:* shell moderately pliable, somewhat brittle, with visible pores; 23–35 mm x 22–31 mm (mean 28 mm x 27 mm), with egg size increasing with female size (Iverson et al. 1997); in one clutch that I measured in Logan County, average diameter was 24 mm (female was 26 cm CL).

Distribution. South-central and south-eastern Canada south through all of the eastern and central United States, and from eastern Mexico to northern South America. Introduced populations occur in several western states. Found in eastern Colorado at elevations below about 5,500 feet (1,680 m). The northern limit of distribution may be related to cooler conditions that inhibit effective/optimal egg incubation (Bobyn and Brooks 1994); perhaps this is true also for the upper elevational limit in Colorado.

Conservation Status. Small-game species in Colorado. The snapping turtle probably is more widespread and numerous in Colorado now than it was before the arrival of humans of European descent, due

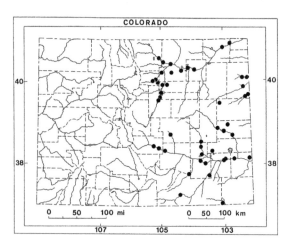

COLORADO

Map 8.1. Distribution of the snapping turtle in Colorado.

tle population at present. In terms of protection, the primary need is a limitation on harvest to prevent excessive exploitation.

Population density varies greatly and may reach several dozen individuals per hectare under favorable conditions (Tennessee, West Virginia), though more typical densities of 1.2 adults per hectare and 5 adults per hectare were recorded in South Dakota and Michigan, respectively (see Ernst, Lovich, and Barbour 1994). These lower densities seem to be characteristic of populations in Colorado.

to habitat augmentation through the creation of numerous ponds and reservoirs. Snapping turtles are fairly common in many areas along major river systems and do well in hydrologically altered and polluted aquatic habitats. However, populations are vulnerable and sensitive to excessive mortality and overharvesting of adults; populations in marginal areas of the range (such as Colorado) cannot be expected to sustain even minimal levels of exploitation without undergoing a population decline (Brooks et al. 1988; Brooks, Brown, and Galbraith 1991; Congdon, Dunham, and van Loben Sels 1994). Turtle harvesting and high mortality of adults do not stimulate greater reproduction or recruitment (Brooks, Brown, and Galbraith 1991), and in any event, nesting success is of less importance to population stability than is survival of adults and juveniles (Congdon, Dunham, and van Loben Sels 1994). In Colorado, some turtles are harvested for food, females moving to nesting sites often are killed by vehicles on roads, and individuals sometimes are inadvertently killed in water-control structures; these threats, however, are not significant for the state tur-

Habitat. The primary habitat in Colorado consists of permanent streams, lakes, reservoirs, and ponds, especially (but not exclusively) those with much submerged vegetation or woody debris. Temporary ponds and pools along intermittent streams also may be occupied. In Michigan, Congdon, Gotte, and McDiarmid (1992) found that hatchlings and juveniles inhabited shallower areas of a marsh than did larger individuals. The shallow-water preference of juveniles likely was related to enhanced food resources and avoidance of large predatory fishes and snapping turtles. In Colorado, large individuals commonly occur in shallow

Plate 8.2. Adult female snapping turtle with excavated eggs (Logan County, Colorado).

Plate 8.3. Juvenile snapping turtle
(Arapahoe County, Colorado).

water and undoubtedly also use
waters up to several meters deep.

Snapping turtles spend most of
their time underwater at the bottom, where they may sit quietly,
crawl slowly, or plow their way
through deep, soft mud. When
disturbed, they often dig down
into the mud and hang onto roots
with their front claws to ward off
capture. Not uncommonly in Colorado,
particularly when the water is cool (perhaps
most often in June), juveniles and adults
bask on protruding logs or float in warm
water at the surface.

Though highly aquatic, snapping turtles
of either sex may walk overland from one
water body to another, especially if their
pond or marsh dries. Terrestrial activity
also occurs in conjunction with nesting
(see "Reproduction and Growth"). Small
individuals dehydrate relatively quickly and
probably do not spend much time away from
wet or moist conditions.

Snapping turtles in Colorado spend the
winter in mud or among debris in shallow
water or perhaps in abandoned muskrat
(Ondatra zibethica) or beaver *(Castor
canadensis)* burrows. Small aggregations
may occur in these sites. Ellis and Henderson (1915) reported a snapping turtle found
in March that evidently had overwintered in
a straw pile on land.

In southeastern Canada, Brown and
Brooks (1994) found that snapping turtles
hibernated under logs, sticks, or overhanging banks in flowing streams; under wood
within 5 m of the shoreline in lakes; or in
deep mud in marshes or beneath floating
mats of vegetation, where water depth is
1 m or less. Temperatures of hibernating
individuals were 0–4°C. Aside from an
episode of river otter predation, overwinter
survival was good. Snapping turtles hibernated in sites either in or outside of their
summer home range and moved up to 4 km
(mean 1 km) between summer range and
hibernaculum. Most individuals chose sites
in which they had previously hibernated, but
some changed hibernacula each year. Small
changes in location sometimes occurred
during the hibernation period.

Activity. In Colorado, activity takes place
day or night, mainly from March or April
through October. Males are most active in
spring (peak in May), when they actively
search for females. Females are most active
in late May and June, when they seek nesting
sites (Brown and Brooks 1993). Activity
is reduced after feeding, and recently fed
individuals do not exhibit a heat-seeking
response (Knight, Layfield, and Brooks
1990; Brown and Brooks 1991).

Under laboratory conditions, snapping
turtles in thermal gradients maintain body
temperatures averaging 28–30°C, but under
field conditions they are active over a wide
range of temperatures. Active snappers may
be observed as long as the water temperature
is above about 5°C, but feeding seems to
occur only when the temperature is above
15°C (Ernst, Lovich, and Barbour 1994).
Temperatures exceeding 39–40°C are lethal
(Hutchison, Vinegar, and Kosh 1966). In
southeastern Canada, the mean body temperature of eight turtles in summer was about
23°C, much lower than the available maximum environmental temperature (Brown,
Brooks, and Layfield 1990), indicating that
selection of microhabitat is based on additional factors such as food supply. Snapping
turtles digest their food relatively quickly at
low temperatures, perhaps facilitating their
occupancy of relatively cool benthic habitats
(Parmenter 1981).

Snapping turtles defend themselves
by snapping vigorously with their sharp

Plate 8.4. Adult snapping turtle (Bent County, Colorado).

jaws, which are capable of lacerating human skin. Individuals approached on land or in shallow water often tile the shell, exposing more of the carapace to the predator (Dodd and Brodie 1975). The head is retracted, ready to make a quick, lunging, upward snap with the jaws. Hissing may accompany the postures and biting lunges. A nesting female emitted a short groaning "ahh" as I examined her freshly completed nest.

Small individuals can be handled safely by grasping the tail or rear portion of the shell. Large individuals, which can be injured if suspended by the tail, should be lifted by the hind limbs, keeping the carapace away from your legs (to avoid the snapping jaws).

When a snapping turtle is handled, pairs of glands along the shell margin at the base of each forelimb secrete an odorous fluid that can be seen (if the turtle is dry) and smelled. Presumably, the secretion functions in social interactions or self-defense.

Home ranges are extremely variable in size, ranging from less than 1 ha (Obbard and Brooks 1981; Galbraith, Chandler, and Brooks 1987) to (rarely) 28.4 ha (Pettit, Bishop, and Brooks 1995). Home ranges overlap between sexes and between individuals of the same sex, and no evidence of territoriality has been found, despite breeding-season aggressiveness in males (Ernst, Lovich, and Barbour 1994; pers. obs.). In South Dakota, the mean distance traveled within one year averaged 0.9 km (Hammer 1969).

Hatchlings put their relatively long tail to use in righting themselves if overturned, in maneuvering during terrestrial locomotion, and perhaps in counterbalancing the head during swimming (Finkler and Claussen 1997).

Reproduction and Growth. Mating reportedly may occur anytime during the warmer months (Ernst, Lovich, and Barbour

1994; Mahmoud and Licht 1997), but most often occurs from the end of hibernation to the end of the nesting season (Brown and Brooks 1993), probably April to early July in Colorado. Combat between adult males, which involves vigorous wrestling and biting, also is common during this time. Mating takes place in the water as the male clasps the shell of the female with claws of all four limbs. The male may bite the female's head or neck during copulation (Ernst, Lovich, and Barbour 1994). The sperm from a single mating may last several months or even years. Multiple paternity (eggs in a single clutch having more than one father) has been documented in southeastern Canada (Galbraith et al. 1993). Eggs are retained in the oviduct for about two weeks between ovulation and oviposition (Mahmoud and Licht 1997).

Eggs generally are laid in a burrow dug by the female with her hind feet in soft soil in open areas such as roadsides or plowed fields, or sometimes in a muskrat lodge. In the dry climate of Colorado, ground-softening rains stimulate nesting, much as they do in South Dakota (Hammer 1969). In a small area in Logan County in mid-June, I found four females nesting in the morning following a rainy thunderstorm the previous night.

Nests may be immediately adjacent to water or up to several hundred meters away (Packard et al. 1985; pers. obs.). In southeastern Canada, females may move to nesting sites up to several kilometers from their usual home range (Obbard and Brooks 1980). Some females nest in the same site in successive years. In Michigan, Congdon et al. (1987) found that completely shaded nests are too cold for the completion of development.

Snapping turtles in North America typically nest from late May to early July (mainly in June), rarely retaining eggs as late as early August (Galbraith, Graesser, and Brooks 1988). In Colorado, the seasonal occurrence of females found away from water suggests that most nesting takes place from late May to early July, with June being the norm. Packard, Packard, et al. (1981) observed snapping turtles constructing nests on June 7 and 16 in Logan County, and I observed several females nesting on June 12 in the same county. In Nebraska, nesting also occurs in June and lasts about 2.0–2.5 weeks (Iverson et al. 1997). The earliest nestings take place when spring temperatures are relatively warm.

In Nebraska, females begin digging nests in the morning (5:30–6:30 a.m.) or in the evening (9:30–10:30 p.m.) (Iverson et al. 1997). Nest excavation often takes nearly two hours (Congdon et al. 1987). In Logan County, a female that I found depositing eggs at 7:28 a.m. began burying the nest at 8:58 a.m. Five successive eggs were laid at intervals of 43–55 seconds. The female rose on her front limbs just before releasing an egg. She touched the eggs with one hind foot and lifted the foot from the hole as an egg dropped. In the same area, a 34-cm-CL female dug a nest hole 11 cm long, 6 cm wide, and 22 cm deep, with a keyhole-shaped opening and a larger diameter near the bottom than at the top. In Nebraska, egg depth in nests generally ranges from 17–26 cm (Iverson et al. 1997). Most, if not all, mature

females in Nebraska nest each year, but likely a minority of females skip nesting in some years (Iverson et al. 1997). Individual females produce a maximum of one clutch each year.

Clutches often are quite large. A 26-cm-CL female that I observed in Logan County deposited a clutch of 61 eggs. Sperger et al. (1995a) reported that a female laid about 50 eggs on June 17 in Arapahoe County. Iverson et al. (1997) found that clutch size in Nebraska ranges from 20–73 (mean 47) and increases with female size among the smaller females but not among the larger ones. A clutch of 109 eggs deposited by a female in Nebraska is the largest known clutch ever produced by a snapping turtle (Packard, Packard, and Miller 1990). Indeed, the snapping turtle can produce in one batch more young than any mammal, bird, or nonmarine reptile in North America.

Hatching and emergence from the nest typically occur about 2.0–3.5 months after oviposition, from late August to early October (most often in September), but sometimes the young do not leave the nest before winter. These probably die of freezing (Packard, Ruble, and Packard 1993). Hatchlings are about 24–31 mm CL. The sex of a hatchling is determined by the temperature of the embryo during development (Yntema 1976). In the field, eggs from the top of a nest are warmer and generally produce females, whereas those at the bottom are cooler and often yield exclusively males (Wilhoft, Hotaling, and Franks 1983). Rarely, twins hatch from a single egg (O'Connell 1997; Tucker and Janzen 1997). The rate of growth of young snappers depends on numerous factors, including the incubation environment, genetic makeup, and social interactions (Brooks et al. 1991; McKnight and Gutzke 1993; Miller 1993), as well as success in finding food. Eggs and young experience high mortality.

Sexual maturity is attained only after several years of growth.

Plate 8.5. Scent gland secretion of juvenile snapping turtle.

Four nesting females that I found in Logan County were 26, 29.5, 31.5, and 34 cm CL. In Nebraska, the smallest nesting females were 28–29 cm CL and 10–12 winters old (Iverson et al. 1997). In Iowa, females typically mature a few years younger than this (Christiansen and Burken 1979), and in southern Ontario, Canada, females may not mature until they are 17–19 years old (Galbraith, Brooks, and Obbard 1989). Some females reproduce well beyond the age of 30. In southeastern Canada, the mean age of nesting females was estimated at 33–40 years (Galbraith and Brooks 1989).

In Michigan, an average of 23 percent of the eggs laid produce a hatchling that emerges from a nest (Congdon et al. 1987; Congdon, Dunham, and van Loben Sels 1994). Under natural conditions, annual survivorship of adult females tends to be high, 88–97 percent in Michigan and southeastern Canada (Brooks, Brown, and Galbraith 1991; Congdon, Dunham, and van Loben Sels 1994). Some individuals may live up to five decades.

Food and Predators. Snapping turtles are not very particular about their diet. They eat plant material (duckweed and various rooted aquatic and wetland plants), decaying animal carcasses, waterfowl eggs (Thorp and Clark 1994), and nearly any kind of live animal that can be captured, including many invertebrates, amphibians, snakes, small mammals, and birds, especially young waterfowl and sometimes shorebirds (Pryor 1996). The extent of predation on waterfowl often is overrated—exotic predatory fishes and native egg-eating mammals surely do far more harm. Most feeding takes place in the water. Typically, a rapid gape-and-suck strike is employed.

The flesh of this turtle is quite edible and, as a result, humans are the chief predators of adults. However, before making turtle stew, be aware that snapping turtles in polluted areas may have high levels of toxic chemicals in their tissues (see Ernst, Lovich, and Barbour 1994). Coyotes *(Canis latrans)* occasionally kill and eat adults. Brooks,

Brown, and Galbraith (1991) described a multiyear episode of heavy predation by river otters on hibernating adult snapping turtles in southeastern Canada. Eggs are eaten by a wide variety of predators, mostly raccoons *(Procyon lotor)* and various other carnivorous mammals, but sometimes crows *(Corvus brachyrhynchos)* or hognose snakes (Ernst, Lovich, and Barbour 1994). In a local population, low reproductive success due to predation on eggs is not uncommon (Petokas and Alexander 1980; Congdon et al. 1987; Congdon, Dunham, and van Loben Sels 1994). Hatchlings are preyed on by a wide assortment of animals, including wading birds, raptors, bullfrogs, water snakes, and large fishes, in addition to the usual egg-eaters (Ernst, Lovich, and Barbour 1994).

Snapping turtles commonly are infested with up to hundreds of parasitic leeches (*Placobdella* spp.) per turtle (Herrmann 1970) and by a protozoan blood parasite *(Haemogregarina balli)* that is transmitted by the leeches. In southeastern Canada, these parasites had no negative impact on female reproductive output (Brown, Bishop, and Brooks 1994). Observations by Burke et al. (1993) in Michigan suggest the tantalizing possibility that nesting snapping turtles may sometimes dig into ant nests to have their leech parasites removed by the ants. Given the abundance of ant nests in eastern Colorado, this behavior should be watched for here.

Remarks. Though snapping turtles have been described as "ugly both in appearance and disposition" (Conant and Collins 1991:41), these turtles are beautifully equipped for survival, both physically and behaviorally.

Taxonomy and Variation. The subspecies in Colorado is *Chelydra serpentina serpentina*. Data from mtDNA suggest that the two subspecies occurring south of the United States may warrant recognition as distinct species (Phillips, Dimmick, and Carr 1996), though morphological and allozyme data do not indicate the existence of multiple species.

POND TURTLES AND BOX TURTLES
Family Emydidae

This family of nearly 100 species occurs in temperate and tropical latitudes of the Americas, Europe, and Africa. Most U.S. turtles are members of this family, which is rather diverse and difficult to characterize in brief, simple terms. Most species are semiaquatic and have a somewhat flattened shell, but a few are terrestrial, with a high, domed shell. The top of the head has no large scutes and is covered with skin that is more or less smooth. Ernst, Lovich, and Barbour (1994) described various skeletal characteristics. The pragmatic approach to ascertaining that a turtle is a member of Emydidae is to first determine that it is not a member of any of the more distinctive turtle families (this is easily accomplished in Colorado). Of the 31 species found in the United States and Canada, most occur in eastern and central North America, and 2 inhabit Colorado.

Plate 8.6. Adult painted turtle (Weld County, Colorado).

Painted Turtle
Chrysemys picta (Schneider, 1783)

Recognition. Shell hard, somewhat flattened; bright yellow lines on head and limbs; lower shell orange or reddish, with dark markings (most conspicuous in juveniles); carapace often with narrow yellow lines (less yellow in larger individuals), less often with dark reticulation (see "Taxonomy and Variation"); upper jaw notched at tip; maximum CL about 25 cm, though rarely more than 21 cm, in female, much smaller in male, which averages several centimeters shorter. *Mature male:* vent located beyond rear edge of carapace with tail extended; claws on forefeet very long; plastron flat. *Mature female:* vent at or inside rear edge of carapace with tail extended; claws on forefeet relatively short. *Juvenile:* deep crease across abdominal shields of plastron. *Hatchling:* carapace keeled; plastron vivid orange/red, with a central dark figure having a sinuous outer edge; 19–28 mm CL (average 23–24 mm) in western Nebraska (Rowe 1995). *Eggs:* elliptical, whitish, smooth surface with small pores; shell initially flexible, then becomes more rigid, 21–36 mm x 15–21 mm (mostly about 29–33 mm x 18–19 mm) in western Nebraska (Iverson and Smith 1993; Rowe 1994a, 1995).

Distribution: Southern Canada, from British Columbia to Nova Scotia, south through Oregon, northern Idaho, Colorado, and most of the central and eastern United States (but not Florida), disjunctly southwest to southwestern Colorado, New Mexico, Texas, and Chihuahua, Mexico; introduced in several locations in the western United States and western Canada. Occurs at elevations mostly below 6,000 feet (1,830 m) in the plains region of eastern Colorado and at about 6,000–8,500 feet (1,830–2,590 m), mostly below 7,500 feet (2,290 m), in southwestern Colorado. A clearly introduced population apparently is established along the valley of the North Fork of the Gunnison River in Delta County (Janos and Guadagno 1997). Adults have been observed in the Colorado River valley in Mesa County (Mourning 1997), but whether the species is established there is unknown. I suspect that introduced populations exist and may be established elsewhere in the state.

Conservation Status. The painted turtle is numerous in many locations in northeastern Colorado and occurs in lower numbers in scattered areas in the southern part of the plains region. It is fairly common in its disjunct range in southwestern Colorado.

Substantial numbers often inhabit single large ponds (up to hundreds of turtles per hectare), and it is not unusual to see dozens crowded together on favored basking logs. Historically, the distribution was concentrated in the larger rivers and associated floodplain ponds and pools. These have been greatly augmented by hundreds or thousands of human-created ponds and reservoirs that are readily used by painted turtles. Even highly unnatural wastewater lagoons may provide favorable habitat. On the other hand, various local populations have suffered from habitat alteration associated with residential, commercial, and agricultural development.

Aside from availability of quiet, permanent water, the primary habitat constraint on populations may be the number of suitable nesting sites, which perhaps are relatively scarce for a shallow-nesting, nonburrowing turtle in the dry climate of Colorado. However, little is known about nesting success in Colorado, so this notion remains speculative. In Washington, a local painted turtle population declined by about 70 percent after two years of drought, evidently due to mortality and movement out of the area (Lindeman and Rabe 1990).

Many populations seem to be dominated by adults, but small juveniles are difficult to detect and generally are more common than they seem. However, true scarcity can result from poor nesting success in consecutive years. This usually is counteracted by reproductive longevity of adults.

Females on nesting forays are very sensitive to disturbance (Iverson and Smith 1993); human activity (e.g., fishing) around ponds, even at a distance, can disrupt nesting activity. Artificially high populations of mammalian egg predators

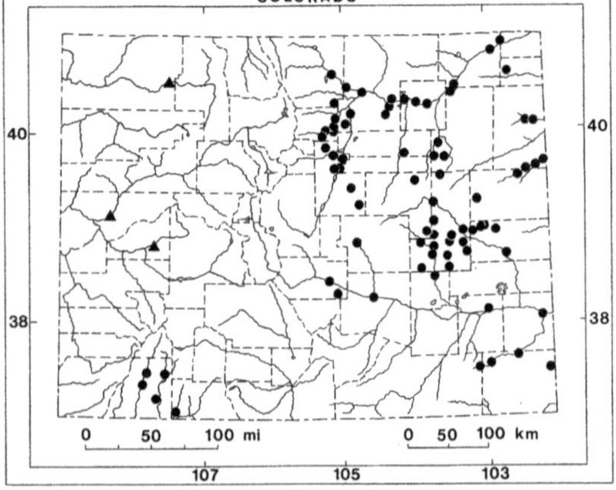

COLORADO

0   50   100 mi

0   50   100 km

107   105   103

Map 8.2. Distribution of the painted turtle in Colorado. Triangles indicate known introduced populations.

Plate 8.7. Typical and melanistic adult painted turtles (Weld County, Colorado).

(resulting from human-augmented food resources) probably depress abundance in some areas. Despite these factors, the regional population of painted turtles likely will be relatively stable and secure for the foreseeable future.

Habitat. Typical habitat includes permanent ponds, reservoirs, marshes, river backwaters, and the slow-moving portions of streams. The largest populations appear to occur in permanent bodies of water with a soft bottom, abundant aquatic plants, and partially submerged logs or other places for basking. In Michigan, hatchlings and juveniles inhabited shallower areas of a marsh than did larger individuals (Congdon, Gotte, and McDiarmid 1992). Probably, this was related to enhanced food resources for the young and avoidance of large predators such as snapping turtles. Painted turtles seldom move far from water but may leave permanent waters (where they hibernate) to colonize nearby temporary ponds and seasonally flooded areas, moving back when these dry up in summer (McAuliffe 1978) or prior to hibernation. I have seen such movements in April and October in Colorado. Painted turtles spend much time in sun-warmed shallows.

Winter generally is spent underwater. St. Clair and Gregory (1990) found that painted turtles in southeastern British Columbia hibernated in shallow (1 m) water on top of the bottom mud. In other areas, the turtles are reported to burrow into anoxic bottom mud, conditions they tolerate well (see introduction to accounts of turtles). However, hibernation underwater is not without its hazards in a drought-prone environment with cold winters. For example, in Iowa, 132 painted turtles that had hibernated underwater were found dead in a pond that froze to the bottom during drought conditions (Christiansen and Bickham 1989).

Activity. Painted turtles in Colorado typically emerge from hibernation in March or April. Activity may continue through at least mid-November if the weather remains mild. Basking may occur rarely during unusually warm weather in late fall and winter months. Activity takes place during daylight hours, generally at ambient temperatures above 9–10°C, though feeding requires warmer temperatures, usually above 15°C. In the morning, the turtles emerge from their nocturnal underwater resting sites and climb onto a log or rock to bask in the sun before feeding, especially in spring and September-October, when the water is relatively cool. Basking turtles often extend one foot into the water; this probably aids in regulation of body temperature. Periods of basking may interrupt other activities throughout the day. One probable function of basking is to increase body temperature and accelerate digestive processes (Parmenter 1981). Baskers sometimes exhibit aggressive interactions with one another (Bury, Wolfheim, and Luckenbach 1979). A turtle disturbed from its basking perch by a person soon sticks its head out of the water and looks at the source of disturbance. A few active individuals found on land in Colorado had body temperatures of 22–34°C.

Painted turtles generally are quite mobile. Individuals may move throughout the ponds they inhabit, and the home ranges of adults in rivers regularly encompass stream segments up to several kilometers long (MacCulloch and Secoy 1983). Juveniles appear to be more sedentary.

Plate 8.8. Plastron of painted turtle (Boulder County, Colorado).

Plate 8.9. Long claws of adult male painted turtle (Boulder County, Colorado).

In hand, painted turtles may withdraw into the shell or thrash vigorously with their limbs. Sometimes they release fluid from the vent and occasionally bite.

Reproduction and Growth. Courtship and mating usually occur in spring but may take place in summer and fall as well. A large male captured in late August in Weld County and held by the shell repeatedly everted its penis. A courting male faces the female and uses the long claws on his forefeet to stroke her head and neck in an effort to entice her to mate.

Nesting in Colorado probably occurs from mid-May to mid-July, as in western Nebraska (Iverson and Smith 1993) and southern New Mexico (Christiansen and Moll 1973). I have found nesting females in Colorado in June and early July. In Weld County, I was surprised when a large female, captured in late August in a drying pool of an irrigation canal and placed in a box, laid an egg about one hour after capture.

Probably most nesting takes place after rains have softened the soil. Adult females dig their nests, typically in late afternoon and early evening but sometimes in the morning, in soft soil in a sunny area, immediately adjacent to or within several hundred meters of the water's edge. The female generally releases fluid from her vent before digging. The nesting process may take up to four hours or more.

Clutch size in the painted turtle varies with latitude and in Colorado may be similar to or somewhat less than that in western Nebraska, where the average is about 14 eggs (range 6–21) in the Sandhills region but only 8 in southwestern Nebraska (Iverson and Smith 1993). Also in western Nebraska, Rowe (1994b) found an average clutch size of 12–14 eggs (range 5–22) in large sandhills ponds and only 8–9 eggs (range 3–14) in smaller floodplain ponds. Clutch size in southern New Mexico averages 9 eggs (range 5–15) (Christiansen and Moll 1973).

Plate 8.10. Adult male painted turtle showing penis (Weld County, Colorado).

Habitat conditions may influence the number of eggs per clutch. In northern Idaho/eastern Washington, Lindeman (1991, 1996) found that clutch size averaged 2–3 eggs larger in a wastewater lagoon population than in a natural lake. Shelled eggs may be retained for up to 2–3 weeks before being laid (Gibbons 1968). Clutch size and egg size increase with female body size. In western Nebraska, individual females usually produce two, sometimes three, and rarely four clutches per season, typically at intervals of 2–3 weeks (Iverson and Smith 1993), compared to 1–2 (occasionally 3) weeks in southern New Mexico (Christiansen and Moll 1973). Mature females sometimes skip a year between nestings.

Hatchling painted turtles in Colorado usually are first observed in spring. This conforms with the pattern of late summer hatching (after 2–3 months of incubation), overwintering in the nest, and spring (late March–June) emergence documented elsewhere (Christiansen and Gallaway 1984; Lindeman 1991). Emergence from a nest sometimes occurs over a period of 1–2 weeks. Young occasionally leave nests in late summer or early fall (Christiansen and Gallaway 1984).

Sex of hatchlings is determined by the incubation temperature; generally, temperatures above 30°C yield only females, and those at about 21–23°C yield only males, with a transitional zone at intermediate temperatures (Etchberger et al. 1992), though some researchers have reported a few females at 20–22°C. Eggs incubated at temperatures consistently below 20°C fail to hatch. Laboratory studies suggest that large egg size and moist nest conditions appear to be most favorable for embryo and hatchling survival (Packard, Packard, and Birchard 1989).

Hatchlings overwintering in typically shallow nests (only 8–12 cm deep at most) are exposed to subfreezing temperatures but often withstand this by supercooling to several degrees below 0°C without ice forming in the body. The heart keeps beating in supercooled turtles but at less than one beat per minute (Birchard and Packard 1997). Packard (1997) and Packard et al. (1997) monitored nests in Nebraska and found that nest temperature fell as low as -21°C. All hatchlings survived at temperatures as low as -7°C, and some survived -13°C, but all died in nests that experienced lower temperatures. Such tolerance of freezing temperatures has been observed elsewhere in the range of the painted turtle, which indeed is the only reptile known to survive body temperatures below -10°C. Under laboratory conditions, painted turtles survive freezing of extracellular body fluids at –2°C for several days, and at -4°C for not more than a few hours (Churchill and Storey 1992; Costanzo et al. 1995), but hatchlings under field conditions likely survive subfreezing temperatures by supercooling without freezing (Packard 1997; Packard et al. 1997). However, St. Clair and Gregory (1990) documented nearly complete overwinter mortality, presumably related to freezing, in nests in British Columbia. Snow cover in winter probably enhances hatchling survival by keeping nest temperatures from falling much below freezing.

The young grow quickly, but growth rate declines rapidly after the first few years (Iverson and Smith 1993). In western Nebraska, females typically mature at about 16.0–16.5 cm CL (sometimes as little as 14 cm CL in small floodplain habitats) after about 6–7 winters (Iverson and Smith 1993; Rowe 1994a, 1994b), compared to 14 cm CL and a year younger in New Mexico (Christiansen and Moll 1973) and a similar size of 16–17 cm CL (15–16 cm PL) in northern Idaho/eastern Washington (Lindeman 1996) and southern Saskatchewan (MacCulloch and Secoy 1983). Males mature at about 9 cm CL in their third year of growth in New Mexico (Christiansen and Moll 1973) and 9–10 cm PL in Idaho/Washington (Lindeman 1996). Lindeman found that painted turtles began to mature at a younger age in a nutrient-rich wastewater lagoon (2 years in males, 6–7 years in females) than in a natural lake (3 years in males, probably 8–10 years in females). Frazer, Greene, and Gibbons (1993) found that a warming trend in the 1980s in Michigan resulted in males maturing at least one year earlier during the warmer portion of the decade. In Colorado, the few nesting females that I found were 17–18 cm CL.

Annual adult survivorship in western Nebraska was at least 92 percent, and some females apparently lived beyond 30 years of age (Iverson and Smith 1993). Very few may live as long as 40 years.

Food and Predators. The painted turtle feeds in the water on a wide variety of living and dead plants and animals, including bryozoans; worms; leeches; insect larvae, pupae, and adults; water mites; spiders; crustaceans; snails; clams; and fishes. I observed scavenging on a dead bullhead in Boulder County. An adult seen in Yuma County was biting at an algal mass. Juveniles can feed effectively on crustacean zooplankton (Maurer 1995). Foraging turtles may seek prey anywhere in the water column and are most responsive to moving prey. The amount of plant material in the diet may increase as the turtle grows larger.

In western Nebraska, Iverson (1990a) frequently observed hognose snakes following the trails of painted turtles to the turtles' nest sites, pushing the snout through the soil plug, and eating the eggs. The snakes were efficient at finding the turtle nests even long

after nest construction, and they consumed virtually all of the eggs each year. Raccoons and skunks appear to be the most frequent egg predators in some areas. They destroy many nests, often within 24 hours of oviposition. Evidence of raccoon predation is a scooped-out nest site with soil strewn all around and no eggshells evident. Skunks generally leave the scattered shells after eating the contents.

Mammalian carnivores, members of the heron family, water snakes, racers, and bullfrogs are typical predators of small turtles. Largemouth bass *(Micropterus salmoides)* and possibly other predatory fishes rarely eat small painted turtles. Bass generally spit out (unharmed) turtles that they have ingested and eventually learn to avoid them, perhaps due to the damage that the clawing and/or biting of an ingested turtle might inflict (Britson and Gutzke 1993). Perhaps the bright orange, yellow, and blackish coloration of the plastron helps identify the turtles as an unpalatable meal. Giant water bugs (Hemiptera: Belostomatidae) are capable of killing hatchlings and small juveniles (Gotte 1992).

These turtles sometimes are infested with leeches (Herrmann 1970).

Remarks. Gelatt and Kelley (1995) observed painted turtles basking on a loon nest mound and even on the back of an incubating common loon *(Gavia immer)* in Minnesota. The loon generally was unresponsive to the turtles' presence, though once it pecked at but did not displace a turtle. On another occasion, the loon returned to its nest and kicked the turtles backward out of the nest before settling into place.

Moles *(Scalopus aquaticus)* may enter painted turtle nest chambers and scatter the hatchlings (Packard 1997).

Taxonomy and Variation. Some individuals, especially (perhaps only) males, exhibit well-developed dark pigmentation (reticulate melanism) on the head and carapace (Smith, Kritsky, and Holland 1969; Stuart 1998b). The subspecies in Colorado is *Chrysemys picta bellii* (Gray, 1831).

Plate 8.11. Adult female ornate box turtle (Baca County, Colorado).

Ornate Box Turtle

Terrapene ornata (Agassiz, 1857)

Recognition. Carapace hard, domed, dark with yellow streaks or spots; lower shell transversely hinged in adults, allowing the shell to be tightly closed (Bramble 1974); maximum CL about 14.6 cm. *Mature male:* innermost toe of hind foot thick and turned inward; iris and spots on forelimbs usually reddish; rear portion of lower shell slightly concave; vent located beyond rear edge of carapace with tail extended. *Mature female:* toe not turned inward; iris yellowish or brownish; spots on forelimbs yellowish; rear part of lower shell not concave; vent at or inside rear edge of carapace with tail extended. *Juvenile:* carapace with yellowish dots and a prominent mid-dorsal stripe; hinge on plastron not functional for the first few years of life. *Hatchling:* carapace round, average length generally 26–30 mm, with yellow spots and a yellow dorsal stripe; plastron yellowish or cream, with large dark blotch in middle. *Eggs:* relatively large, 31–41 mm x 20–26 mm (average 36 mm x 22 mm) in Kansas (Legler 1960b); average

width 27 mm in New Mexico (Nieuwolt-Dacanay 1997).

Distribution. Southeastern Wyoming, southern South Dakota, Iowa, southern Wisconsin, and western Indiana south to southeastern Arizona, northern Mexico, Texas, and Louisiana. Occurs throughout most of eastern Colorado, mainly at elevations below 5,500 feet (1,680 m). Box turtles are scarce or absent in the area north of the South Platte River, on the western crest of the Platte-Arkansas Divide, and west of Baca County south of the Arkansas River.

Escaped and released captives often are found near cities where box turtles do not naturally occur. This has made it difficult to determine the natural western margin of the range in Colorado. The very few specimens from Fort Collins, Boulder, Denver, Colorado Springs, and Pueblo likely represent introductions, based on the absence or paucity of evidence for occurrences in these areas in early accounts (Ellis and Henderson 1913). No established populations are known to exist in these areas at present. Any former populations would have been lost due to massive habitat destruction. If native populations formerly existed, I would expect to find more substantial evidence of

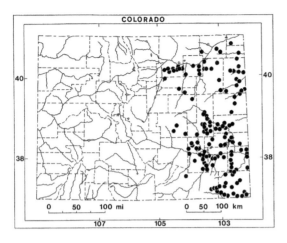

Map 8.3. Distribution of the ornate box turtle in Colorado.

or escape from captivity. Ornate box turtles, including healthy individuals in natural habitats, regularly are found in La Plata County near Durango and may become established in that area (Albert Spencer, pers. comm.). Livo, Hammerson, and Smith (1998) discussed a few other known or suspected box turtle tranlocations in Colorado.

this, considering the relatively high level of activity by scientific collectors in these areas and the ease with which this turtle can be detected, especially in areas with roads. A single specimen from Fremont County (Smith, Maslin, and Brown 1965) far up the Arkansas River valley also may reflect a translocated individual. I found an emaciated adult box turtle alive on a road in the Wet Mountain Valley, Custer County, at an elevation of 7,890 feet (2,405 m); the surrounding habitat (sandy grass-shrub) actually looked suitable, but the climate there is too cool for long-term persistence of box turtles, so translocation by humans is the most probable interpretation of the occurrence. I have excluded all of these questionable records from the map.

Rouse, Chiszar, and Smith (1995) speculated that a box turtle found in the vicinity of Rangely in Rio Blanco County, and others reported from that area, represent a natural population, and Smith and Chiszar (1996) accepted this interpretation; however, available evidence, including examples of other clearly translocated turtle species found in the same area, is consistent with the more likely explanation that these individuals are "imports." Other obvious translocations include records from Mesa County (Miller 1961), Mesa Verde National Park in Montezuma County (Douglas 1966), and elsewhere in western Colorado where box turtles regularly are introduced by travelers

Conservation Status. This turtle is listed in the Convention on International Trade in Endangered Species of Flora and Fauna (CITES) Appendix II, which includes species that are not now threatened with extinction but could become so unless trade is strictly controlled. No export is allowed without a permit from the country of origin.

The ornate box turtle is locally common within its range in Colorado, especially in the extensive sandhill regions south of the South Platte River, in Yuma County, along Big Sandy Creek, along the south side of the eastern part of the Arkansas River, and in Baca County. It appears that the range of this species has declined somewhat in the 1900s primarily as a result of agricultural development. Overall abundance undoubtedly has declined, but data are inadequate to quantify the extent. Long-term declines in ornate box turtle populations have been documented in Kansas and Wisconsin (U.S. Fish and Wildlife Service 1996).

Intensive cultivation tends to eliminate or severely reduce box turtle populations, presumably by destroying required microhabitats and food resources and by inadvertently killing animals in agricultural machinery. The most robust populations of box turtles in Colorado coincide with the remaining large areas of unplowed prairie (Map 2.12).

The greatest source of direct mortality for adults is vehicles on roads (Legler 1960b;

Anderson 1965; Blair 1976; Knight and Collins 1977; Ballinger, Lynch, and Cole 1979; Doroff and Keith 1990; Mackessy 1998; pers. obs.). The populations along major highways incur heavy mortality from vehicle traffic, undoubtedly amounting to thousands of kills per year. On long stretches of Interstate 76 in Weld County, I often have seen several smashed box turtles per mile. Much earlier, Rodeck (1949), too, found hundreds killed on roads after heavy rains in northeastern Colorado. Rodeck (1949) also found numerous medium-sized individuals dead along roads in the southeastern quarter of the state, where more recently Mackessy (1998) reported continued high mortality of box turtles on roads in Kiowa and Prowers counties. The large numbers of box turtles killed on certain sections of roads every summer certainly result in much-reduced population densities in those areas and make it difficult to imagine how those populations continue to exist. Probably, these roadside populations represent population "sinks," areas in which the death rate exceeds the recruitment rate but that persist due to an influx of individuals from adjacent healthy populations away from roads. Declines in box turtle populations attributable to excessive mortality from automobiles have been observed in Missouri, where Anderson (1965) found 90–156 live box turtles along a 160-km section of road in 1940 but only 5–35 live turtles under similar temperature and moisture conditions on the same stretch of road in 1959.

What can be done to alleviate the road mortality problem? Installation of roadside barriers and underroad passageways (Mackessy 1998) might be feasible in some situations but probably not on a regional scale. The use of barriers should be approached with caution because of possible detrimental impacts; these barriers might interfere with the movements of box turtles and other small animals between seasonally critical habitat areas. Further, barriers might result in the formation of artificial aggregations that could alter social behavior or promote disease transmission, or they might inhibit dispersal and negatively alter metapopulation dynamics. Alternatively, warning

signs in critical areas (e.g., "Caution—turtle crossing next 5 miles"), coupled with public education, might be useful low-cost methods for reducing the number of turtle deaths along the highways. Doroff and Keith (1990) recommended the establishment of roadless preserves of at least 100 ha as the most effective way to sustain viable box turtle populations. Unfortunately, the increasing human population and vehicle traffic in Colorado and the generally low priority given to reptile conservation are likely to impede attempts to protect this vulnerable species. However, the recent shortgrass prairie conservation initiative of The Nature Conservancy and its cooperators offers a mechanism for the protection of significant areas of high-quality habitat for the box turtle and its fellow prairie residents.

Box turtles are favorites in the pet trade, and some level of collecting undoubtedly occurs in Colorado, though most of it goes undetected. The low reproductive potential of box turtles (slow to mature, low fecundity) and the ease with which they can be collected in large numbers make them vulnerable to excessive, nonsustainable exploitation. Strict limitations on collecting and vigilant law enforcement are appropriate. In the early 1990s, tens of thousands of box turtles (*T. ornata* and *T. carolina*) were exported from the United States (U.S. Fish and Wildlife Service 1996). In response to concerns that a nonsustainable harvest was taking place, the Office of Scientific Authority of the U.S. Fish and Wildlife Service reduced the export quota to zero for 1996. Hopefully, exports will remain strictly limited.

In Kansas, Legler (1960b) found that favorable habitat may harbor about 6–16 box turtles per hectare. Density was about 0.5–0.9 adults per hectare in Texas (Blair 1976) and 2.9–5.0 adults per hectare in Wisconsin (Doroff and Keith 1990). Metcalf and Metcalf (1979) presented data that suggest possible multiyear cyclicity in mortality and abundance in a Kansas population over a 20-year period.

Populations appear to be dominated by adults, but the seemingly scarce juveniles

Plate 8.12. Adult male ornate box turtle (Baca County, Colorado).

Plate 8.13. Plastron of adult female ornate box turtle (Baca County, Colorado).

may be more cryptic than rare. The smallest individuals observed rarely are smaller than about 8–10 cm CL (Rodeck 1950).

Habitat. Sandhills and shortgrass prairie (often with scattered yucca and prickly pear cactus) are the primary habitat. Soft, sandy soils are ideal, because they enable the turtles to burrow easily to escape excessive heat or cold. In spring and summer, box turtles often burrow shallowly in the shade near a shrub or in mounds created by pocket gophers (Geomyidae), or they may use the burrows of kangaroo rats *(Dipodomys ordii)* or pocket gophers (Vaughan 1961). Winter is spent in deeper burrows dug by the turtle or by mammals. Hibernation occurs at depths of up to about 0.5 m in Kansas (Legler 1960b) and at 0.5–1.8 m in the colder climate of Wisconsin (Doroff and Keith 1990). Box turtles in Wisconsin often hibernate in the same site in successive years, a tendency noted also in Kansas by Metcalf and Metcalf (1976); several individuals may hibernate within 0.5 m of each other. Though terrestrial, this turtle

sometimes enters shallow, slow-flowing streams or quiet creek pools to drink or soak (Rodeck 1949; pers. obs.)

Activity. In Colorado, box turtles are active mainly from late April through October, with most records from May to September. Warm spring rains appear to prompt spring emergence and dispersal from hibernation sites (Legler 1960b; Grobman 1990). Rains in summer also stimulate activity. After spring emergence, box turtles in Nebraska may move up to 1 km to water to drink, then return to their usual home range (J. Iverson, cited by Degenhardt, Painter, and Price 1996). Activity occurs primarily during daylight hours. Midday activity is the norm in spring and fall; during hot summer weather, activity peaks in morning and late afternoon. As days lengthen near the summer solstice, activity in Colorado may begin as early as 7:00 a.m. and extend as until nearly 9:00 p.m. Even in mild weather in mid-May, these turtles may be abroad until at least 7:30 p.m. Rodeck (1949) found active box turtles at sunrise among sand dunes along the Cimarron River in Baca County. Night is spent burrowed in the ground.

Home range size and movements are quite variable. In Kansas, Legler (1960b) found that box turtles move an average of 60–90 m per day in summer over a home range of about 2 ha (mean maximum diameter about 170 m). In another area in eastern Kansas, Metcalf and Metcalf (1970) recorded a mean maximum home range diameter of 152 m for males and 267 m for females. Displaced individuals returned to their home area from distances of up to 3.2 km, but some turtles did not return home after displacements of 1 km (Metcalf and Metcalf 1978). In Wisconsin, annual home range size of adults varies greatly (0.2–58.1 ha, mean 8.7 ha); juveniles have much smaller ranges (Doroff and Keith 1990). Blair (1976) calculated an average maximum home range diameter of about 100 m in Texas. In central New Mexico, mean home range size is 1.6 ha (mean maximum diameter 276 m), with considerable overlap among individuals (Nieuwolt 1996).

Significant day-to-day differences in movement occur. Large pulses of activity take place after summer rains (when many turtles are killed as they cross roads). Rodeck (1949) reported that heavy July rains brought out thousands of box turtles in northeastern Colorado; similar observations have been made by numerous observers in subsequent years. Gravid females seeking nesting sites may move hundreds of meters in a single day (Legler 1960b).

Body temperatures during activity average 28–30°C (range 13–36°C); in Kansas, individuals in the open usually have a body temperature of 24°C or higher (Fitch 1956c; Legler 1960b). Temperatures above 40°C cannot be tolerated for long. In New Mexico, activity is most common when air temperature just above ground is 13–24°C (Nieuwolt 1996). Box turtles in Wisconsin are most active at ambient temperatures of 21–25°C (Doroff and Keith 1990) and have body temperatures that average several degrees lower than those in Kansas. This is not simply a passive result of the cooler environment in Wisconsin but rather a behavioral difference (Ellner and Karasov 1993). Rose, Scioli, and Moulton (1988) documented a pattern of substantial daily and seasonal changes in body temperatures in Texas.

The typical adult defensive response is to close the shell, which surrounds all of the fleshy areas of the body and creates a very difficult package for a predator to penetrate. When picked up by a human, some adults do not close the shell. Those that do may soon emerge, flail, and push off with their limbs. Juveniles have less effective shell protection and may release an odorous fluid when handled (Legler 1960b). Adults often release fluid from the vent, but I have not noticed that it is malodorous. The fluid may be released before the turtle has been touched. Sometimes box turtles open the mouth and feign biting.

Reproduction and Growth. Mating may occur in spring or late summer/early fall. In Baca County, I observed a pair mating on June 8, whereas Smith, Maslin, and Brown (1965) reported mating on August 17. Livo (pers. comm.) observed copulation on June 1 in Weld County. The male mounts the female from the rear and grips her shell with his hind feet during copulation. The specialized inner toe facilitates his grip. In turn, the hind legs of the male are grasped by those of the female. Reproductive males sometimes engage in antagonistic behavior. Nieuwolt (1996) observed an interaction between two males that involved shell bumping and attempted bites. However, Legler (1960b) found no evidence of territoriality or a social hierarchy.

Small clutches of eggs are laid in late spring and early summer. Nesting takes place in May, June, or July, peaking in mid-June in eastern Kansas (Legler 1960b). In New Mexico, females carrying shelled eggs can be found from May through August; most nesting evidently occurs in July, though some may nest as early as June and a few may not lay their eggs until August (Nieuwolt-Dacanay 1997). Gravid females generally dig a nest in soft, well-drained soil in the evening; nest completion usually occurs after dark (Legler 1960b).

Plate 8.14. Hatchling ornate box turtle (Weld County, Colorado).

Clutch size in Kansas usually is 2–8 eggs (average about 5) (Legler 1960b). Legler examined ovaries and concluded that all mature females ovulate each year, but whether all actually nest is unknown. Females that nest early may deposit a second clutch. In eastern Kansas, an estimated one-third of the adult females produce two clutches in a single season (Legler 1960b).

In New Mexico (Nieuwolt-Dacanay 1997), clutch size is smaller (1–4 eggs, average 2.7). A larger percentage of females produce eggs in years with wetter spring weather (e.g., 42 and 61 percent in wet years vs. 10 percent in a dry year). No females produce more than one clutch in a single season, and only a small proportion of females produce eggs in two consecutive years.

In Wisconsin (Doroff and Keith 1990), clutch size averages 3–4 eggs, 50–63 percent of adult females nest each year, no double clutching occurs, and hatchlings per female average 0.7.

Eggs hatch two months or more after being laid, usually in August or September. In Wisconsin, eggs hatch in about nine weeks (Doroff and Keith 1990). Under laboratory conditions at 29°C, eggs hatch in 7–8 weeks (Packard, Packard, and Gutzke 1985). Legler (1960b) found that hatchlings may emerge in late summer or, if the soil is too dry, wait until the following spring. In Wisconsin, hatchlings burrow beneath the nest, overwinter there, and surface the next spring (Doroff and Keith 1990). Hatchlings, which are more vulnerable to predation than are adults, apparently spend most of their time underground or under cover and rarely are observed. The caruncle (egg tooth) is lost before the spring after hatching. Sex is determined by the incubation temperature (Vogt and Bull 1982a; Packard, Packard, and Gutzke 1985).

In eastern Kansas (Legler 1960b), most males mature at 10–11 cm PL at an average age of 8–9 years, and most females mature at 11–12 cm PL and an average age of 10–11 years; some individuals attain maturity a few years earlier. Growth essentially stops shortly after puberty. In Texas, where the growing season is longer, maturity occurs earlier; a male was sexually mature at age seven, a female at age eight (Blair 1976). In New Mexico, gravid females are 10.7–12.8 cm CL (Nieuwolt-Dacanay 1997). Similarly, my limited data for Colorado indicate that most mature females are 11–13 cm CL and at least 10 years old (based on counts of plastral scute layers).

Box turtles that can avoid humans may live a long life. Mean annual survival of adults more than 10 years old is about 80 percent in Wisconsin, though this is not high enough to result in a stable population (Doroff and Keith 1990). Legler (1960b) estimated maximum longevity at about 50 years, but subsequent studies indicate that *T. ornata* does not live much beyond 30 years under natural conditions. Blair (1976) determined that the oldest individual in a Texas population was 32 years old. A population in Kansas studied by Metcalf and Metcalf (1985) included several individuals that lived at least 28 years.

Food and Predators. The diet throughout most of the active season consists primarily of insects, especially beetles, caterpillars, grasshoppers, and crickets (Rodeck 1949; Legler 1960b). Box turtles sometimes search for insects beneath cattle dung. On roads, I have seen box turtles biting dead Texas horned lizards, box turtles, and kangaroo rats *(Dipodomys ordii).*

In some cases, the turtles may have been attracted to insects on the carcasses, but insects were not always present. Mackessy (1998) also reported scavenging on carrion in Colorado. Plant material (e.g., prickly pear fruits and pads, as well as other fruits) may be eaten in quantity, and there are reports of box turtles consuming spadefoot toad tadpoles and the eggs and young of ground-nesting birds (Legler 1960b; Blair 1976; Ernst, Lovich, and Barbour 1994). A female I found in Weld County defecated the remains of small beetles and a clump of five 4-cm-long feathers. Small stones may be ingested, sometimes deliberately; these may aid in the breakdown of hard-bodied insects. Food items may be ingested whole or dismantled with the aid of the forefeet.

Although few instances of nonhuman predation on adult box turtles have been recorded (Legler 1960b; Doroff and Keith 1990), it is likely that a wide array of predatory animals, especially mammalian carnivores, attack box turtles on occasion, smaller individuals being more vulnerable than adults. In addition to species not present in Colorado, Legler (1960b) recorded the Chihuahuan raven *(Corvus cryptoleucus)* and the raccoon *(Procyon lotor)* as predators on hatchling box turtles (Legler 1960b). Various other birds and mammals, as well as racers, coachwhips, and hognose snakes, probably also prey on hatchlings occasionally as well. Legler (1960b) determined that box turtles can visually detect the presence of intruders, presumably including large predators, at distances of more than 100 m in open country.

Metcalf and Metcalf (1979) described an episode of increased mortality in box turtles hibernating in eastern Kansas. Many had been dug out of their hibernation sites and partially consumed (typically the head and forelimbs had been removed). From circumstantial evidence, the authors thought that the turtles had died from disease and were then located and exhumed by a coyote *(Canis latrans)* or other mammal attracted to the odor of decaying flesh. However, the incident may have represented predation on live turtles.

Naney and Bushnell (1986) found that some box turtles, especially females, examined in September in Yuma County were infested with larvae of the bot fly *Sarcophaga cistudinus.* The larvae occupied subcutaneous areas at the base of the neck, tail, and limbs. Rodeck (1949) reported parasitism by the same species in August near the Cimarron River in Oklahoma.

Remarks. The soiled shell of a live box turtle that I found in eastern Colorado suggested its untimely presence directly beneath the rear end of a cow.

Taxonomy and Variation. The subspecies in Colorado is *Terrapene ornata ornata* (Agassiz, 1857). The species also is widely known as the western box turtle. Minx (1996) examined phylogenetic relationships among turtles of the genus *Terrapene* based on morphological characters.

MUD AND MUSK TURTLES
Family Kinosternidae

This family includes about two dozen species, ranging from southern Canada to South America. Most occur in Central America, but nine species inhabit the United States. For the most part, these turtles are aquatic bottom-dwellers, though some (e.g., the stinkpot or common musk turtle, *Sternotherus odoratus,* of the eastern United States) are good climbers and may bask in trees that lean over water. Habitats typically are permanent waters, though the yellow mud turtle, the only representative of the family in Colorado, commonly occurs in temporary pools in the Great Plains and Southwest. Members of this family are distinctive in having musk glands, 10 or 11 scutes on the single- or double-hinged plastron, 23 marginal scutes, and various unique skeletal characteristics.

Plate 8.15. Adult yellow mud turtle (Yuma County, Colorado). *Lauren Livo and Steve Wilcox.*

Yellow Mud Turtle
Kinosternon flavescens (Agassiz, 1857)

Recognition. Shell hard, smooth, oval-shaped, sometimes with extensive attached algae; throat yellow, with several nipplelike barbels; ninth marginal scute distinctly higher than eighth in adults; plastron with 11 shields (shield under neck may be partially divided), with a transverse hinge anteriorly and posteriorly, allowing partial closing of the shell (Bramble, Hutchison, and Legler 1984); all toes webbed; maximum CL about 18 cm, usually less than 14 cm. *Mature male:* slightly concave plastron, two patches of conspicuous, rough scales on inner surface of each hind leg; tail thick, tipped with a horny nail, extends well beyond rear edge of carapace, usually curled to one side; grows to larger size than female and has relatively larger head and claws that are longer and more curved. *Mature female:* no tuberculate scale patches on hind limbs, tail very short, barely reaching rear edge of carapace. *Hatchling:* 18–24 mm CL in Nebraska in first spring

(Iverson 1991); 20–28 mm CL in Texas (Long 1986b); at hatching, plastron boldly black and yellow, black dot on rear border of carapace scutes. *Eggs:* hard-shelled, 22–31 mm x 14–18 mm in Nebraska (X-ray measurements) (Iverson 1991), 23–30 mm x 15–20 mm in northern Texas (Long 1986a); average in Colorado probably about 26–27 mm x 16–17 mm.

Distribution. Nebraska south to northern Mexico, west to southern Arizona (Iverson 1989); disjunct populations in Illinois, Iowa, and Missouri. Occurs in eastern Colorado in the Republican, Arkansas, and Cimarron River drainages at elevations below 5,000 feet (1,525 m).

Conservation Status. The yellow mud turtle is fairly common in localized areas along the eastern margin of Colorado and is perhaps easiest to find in the Republican River drainage. A recent observation of this turtle in Lincoln County (Bergman and colleagues, unpublished observations), if a natural occurrence, suggests that additional isolated populations may exist in the Arkansas River drainage north of the Arkansas River. Extensive general surveys in recent decades by Mackessy (1998), Lauren Livo,

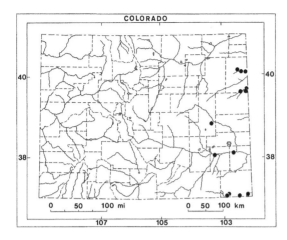

COLORADO

0   50   100 mi

0   50   100 km

107   105   103

Map 8.4. Distribution of the yellow mud turtle in Colorado.

sandy or muddy bottoms are frequented, and areas with aquatic vegetation (if available) are preferred (Mahmoud 1969; Webster 1986). In Yuma County, Maslin (1950) found mud turtles in sodden vegetation at the water's edge or in cattle tracks in marshy areas near water. Sometimes mud turtles bask in the sun at the edge of the

and me indicate that this turtle is localized in distribution and usually not particularly abundant throughout its historical range in Colorado. Little information is available to determine the population trend. Local pond populations appear to fluctuate with water availability, but there is no indication that a regional population decline has occurred. No major existing threats are known. Present populations should persist into the foreseeable future under current land use patterns. Pesticide applications and the plowing of sandhills can be regarded as potential threats.

Throughout the range of this species, population density is extremely variable. A single pond may harbor hundreds of individuals. Mahmoud (1969) estimated the density at 28 turtles per hectare of suitable habitat in a stream in Oklahoma. Quantitative measures of abundance in Colorado are not available.

Habitat. Typical habitat in Colorado includes permanent and intermittent streams, permanent ponds, isolated temporary ponds and rain pools far from permanent water, irrigation ditches, soggy fields, and the surrounding grasslands and sandhills. Terrestrial habitats, particularly sandhills, are used extensively in summer, especially by nesting females and during the midsummer period of dormancy. On an annual basis, more time is spent on land than in the water. Aquatic habitats with

water or on partially submerged logs, but extensive growths of algae on the shells of some individuals indicate that much time may be spent in the water. Yellow mud turtles appear to colonize small ponds and move to more permanent water if a pond dries up. Hence, not all overland movements are associated with nesting. During hot weather, movements on land are most common in the early morning and evening hours (Punzo 1974b).

Winter is spent burrowed in the soil, under debris, or, rarely, underwater in a stream or pond. In Iowa, hibernation usually occurs 300–500 m from water, sometimes closer (Christiansen et al. 1985). In Nebraska, individual mud turtles generally hibernate in the sandhill location used the previous year; turtles from different sand-hill hibernation sites may use the same aquatic habitat in summer (Iverson 1991).

Activity. In Colorado, most activity occurs from April through October. The actual duration of activity each year may vary with climatic conditions; dry conditions restrict activity. In Oklahoma, feeding generally does not begin until late April or May, when temperatures have warmed to above 15°C (Mahmoud 1969). In Iowa, mud turtles usually are active in their aquatic feeding habitat from late April to mid-July, sometimes for as little as 1.0–2.5 months. This is followed by a period of terrestrial estivation that generally takes place in midsummer (Christiansen, Cooper, and Bickham 1984; Christiansen et al. 1985). Yellow mud turtles have relatively large stores of fat that enable them to remain dormant through extended periods of drought (Long 1986a). Though some can survive dormancy of up to two years (Rose 1980), such a long interval of inactivity surely never occurs in Colorado. Field observations indicate that yellow mud turtles are most active between sunrise and sunset.

Available evidence indicates that individual yellow mud turtles exhibit strong fidelity to their home ranges and tend to occupy the same aquatic and terrestrial locations in successive years (Semmler 1979; Iverson 1991). In Oklahoma, Mahmoud (1969) found that home range size averages a little more than 0.1 ha.

When disturbed, these turtles expel a foul-smelling musk from glands near the junction of the carapace and plastron. Otherwise, they are mild-mannered and seldom attempt to bite.

Reproduction and Growth. Courtship and mating usually take place in the water. The male may initiate courtship by nudging and sometimes biting the female (Lardie 1975). Eventually, he mounts her and clasps her shell with all four feet and the end of his tail, while nuzzling or biting the top of her head. Then he shifts rearward, holds the edge of her carapace between the scaly patches on one rear leg, grasps her carapace with the toes and claws of his opposite foot, curls his tail under hers, and inserts his penis. Copulation may last just several minutes or up to 2.5 hours (Lardie 1975). Males sometimes engage in aggressive interactions with each other (Lardie 1983).

Iverson (1990a, 1991) studied the life history and unique nesting behavior of the yellow mud turtle in the sandhills of western Nebraska, and his observations, summarized in the following paragraphs, probably apply well to yellow mud turtles in Colorado. Females emerge from the water to nest during the first three weeks of June. In other states, nesting appears to peak in June but may extend into early or mid-July (Christiansen and Dunham 1972; Long 1986a). In Colorado, I have found

non-gravid, probably postnesting adult females moving from sandhills to wetlands in early to mid-June. About 75–95 percent of the mature females in Nebraska nest in a given year, but the proportion may fall to below 50 percent when particularly dry or cold spring conditions exist in either the current or previous year. Warm, wet springs seem optimal for nesting. Nesting migrations occur primarily in the early morning (8:00–10:00 a.m.) or late afternoon/early evening (5:00–8:00 p.m.), with midday activity on cool days. Nesting females move nonstop 21–191 m to generally south-facing slopes of sandhills and burrow into the soil. While completely buried at about 13 cm, females excavate their nests, apparently using only the hind limbs, and lay their eggs.

In the Nebraska sandhills, mean clutch size is 6.5 eggs (range 6–9, increasing with female body size), compared to a mean of 5.3 in southwestern Nebraska and 5.0 in several other areas south of Nebraska. As is typical elsewhere in the northern part of the range (e.g., Long 1985, 1986a), females produce only one clutch each year. Tuma (1993) found that each of two females in Illinois dug two nests 2–3 mm apart on consecutive days and divided her clutch between them.

In Nebraska, eggs are deposited 17–23 cm below the soil surface. The soil around the eggs evidently is moistened with fluid released from the female's vent. Females remain with their eggs for just a few hours or up to 38 days or more before emerging from the soil and returning to the water. Evidently, females are most likely to remain buried for extended periods in dry summers. Some females may remain buried over winter and return to water the following spring.

Iverson found that after hatching in "fall," the young burrow deeper (to 41–66 cm) and overwinter near the nest. They move to water the following spring in May and June (as elsewhere, Christiansen and Gallaway 1984; Long 1986b). In northern Texas, emergence of hatchlings appears to be stimulated by rainfall and warming soil temperatures (Long 1986b). Iverson found that overwinter survival in Nebraska apparently is very high, though some hatchlings never make it to water and presumably die or are killed. Survivorship during the first year of life ranged from 12–31 percent in different years.

Sex of hatchlings is determined by the incubation temperature, with cooler temperatures producing males and warmer ones yielding females (Vogt et al. 1982). Under laboratory conditions, eggs incubated at temperatures below 24°C do not hatch (Ewert and Iverson, unpublished data).

In Nebraska, females mature at about 9 cm CL (as they do in New Mexico [Christiansen and Dunham 1972]) at an average age of 11 years (range 10–16 years), later than the 6–7+ years estimated for New Mexico (again, Christiansen and Dunham 1972). In northern Texas, females attain sexual maturity at 9.5–10 cm CL and an estimated minimum age of 8–9 years (Long 1986a). Males are slightly younger when they mature, at about 8 cm CL. Evidently, maturity is size-related; environmental conditions may affect the growth rate and, therefore, age at maturity. Iverson found that survivorship in Nebraska is high (80–90 percent or greater) after individuals reach the age of three and that mud turtles commonly survive for 25 years or more.

Yellow mud turtles are unusual in having two sets of enlarged ovarian follicles each spring, representing the current year's clutch and that of the following year, plus a third set being readied for ovulation two years hence (Long 1986a; Iverson 1991a).

Food and Predators. These turtles eat annelid worms, leeches, flatworms, nematodes, insects, various crustaceans, centipedes, millipedes, spiders, a wide variety of insects, snails, amphibian larvae, fishes (usually dead or dying), animal carcasses, and plant material (which may be ingested incidental to feeding on animal prey) (Punzo 1974b; Ernst, Lovich, and Barbour 1994). They feed in the water and on land. Moll (1979) found that under experimental conditions, mud turtles buried in sand ate large nightcrawlers that happened to burrow nearby.

Eggs are highly vulnerable to predation by western hognose snakes, skunks (presumably both *Mephitis mephitis* and *Spilogale putorius*), raccoons *(Procyon lotor),* and rodents (Iverson 1990a). Hognose snakes have no trouble digging into the soil to reach the eggs. In Iowa, egg predation by raccoons appears to be a major factor reducing nesting success (Christiansen and Gallaway 1984).

Predatory fishes and water snakes probably prey on small mud turtles. Adults likely are attacked occasionally by the usual assortment of larger predatory animals. Iverson (pers. comm.) found mud turtles in Colorado that had been stepped on and killed by cattle. In summer, leeches are commonly attached to the skin.

Taxonomy and Variation. The subspecies in Colorado is *Kinosternon flavescens flavescens* (Agassiz, 1857). Recent taxonomic appraisals include Houseal, Bickham, and Springer (1982) and Berry and Berry (1984).

SOFTSHELL TURTLES
Family Trionychidae

Members of this family occur in North America, Asia, Africa, and Indonesia. Three of the 22 species are native to the United States; one of these occurs in Colorado. An Asian species grows to about 1.2 m long, but in the United States maximum size is about 0.5 m CL. Females grow larger than males.

These are distinctive, highly aquatic, fast-swimming turtles with a flattened rounded shell covered with soft skin (horny scutes are absent); a small, partially cartilaginous plastron; a tubular snout; and webbed feet each with three claw-bearing digits. Chromatophores in the skin allow color change.

Plate 8.16. Juvenile spiny softshell (Bent County, Colorado).

Spiny Softshell
Trionyx spiniferus (LeSueur, 1827)

Recognition. Shell flattened, with flexible edges and covered with leathery skin; small conical tubercles on front edge of carapace; snout tubular, with a ridge along inner margin of each nostril; forefoot with three claws; vent near tip of tail; maximum CL in central Great Plains region about 52 cm in females, much smaller in males, which average about 10 cm shorter; Rodeck (1950) reported an eastern Boulder County female that was 40 cm CL and 4.7 kg; in New Mexico, females average 22 cm CL, males 16 cm CL (Degenhardt, Painter, and Price 1996). Dorsal color pattern can change in response to surroundings and lighting (Ernst, Lovich, and Barbour 1994; pers. obs.). Painter (1993) reported a xanthic (yellow, no dark blotches, white irises) adult female found in the Rio Grande in New Mexico. *Mature male:* carapace sandpapery, with small dark spots or circles; tail thick and long, with vent well beyond rear edge of carapace; tubercles at front edge of carapace small and conical. *Mature female:* carapace not notably sandpapery, often blotched or mottled; tubercles at front edge of carapace conical or knoblike; tail relatively short. *Juvenile:* carapace not sandpapery; tail short; coloration of carapace as in adult male. *Hatchling:* carapace olive to tan, with small dark circles, spots, or dashes, and a yellowish margin bordered by a black line; snout upturned; 30–40 mm CL. *Eggs:* hard and thick-shelled, smooth with numerous minute pores, white, 24–32 mm in diameter (Ernst, Lovich, and Barbour 1994).

Distribution. Much of eastern and central United States from southeastern Canada to northern Florida, west to the Rocky Mountains and northeastern Mexico; introduced in New Jersey and the Gila–lower Colorado River system in California, Arizona, Nevada, Utah, and New Mexico. Occurs in eastern Colorado at elevations below about 5,500 feet (1,680 m).

Conservation Status. Data are inadequate for determining population trends, but this turtle appears to occupy essentially all of its historical range in Colorado. It is fairly common along portions of the South Platte, Arkansas, and Republican rivers, and it still occurs in the highly environmentally disturbed Denver area (Livo 1993; Engeman

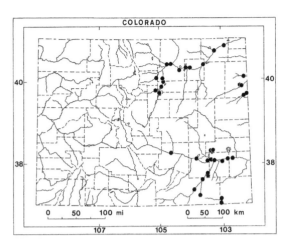

Map 8.5. Distribution of the spiny softshell in Colorado.

Habitat. The spiny softshell inhabits streams ranging from large rivers to intermittently flowing creeks with permanent pools. It also occurs in stream impoundments and ponds adjacent to permanent flowing streams. Major rivers seem to be the primary habitat. Sunny bodies of water with sand or mud banks or bars and soft bottoms are preferred, and softshells often are found where there is a great deal of submerged woody plant material. Most of the softshells I have seen in Colorado were basking (usually facing the water) at the water's edge on a sandy or muddy bank or bar or on a partially submerged log, or swimming slowly at the surface or in vegetated stream-edge shallows. Some were buried in muddy sand in warm shallows. A few were seen burying in deeper water. Burial is accomplished by plowing forward into the substrate, then wiggling vigorously to settle substrate on top of the shell (Graham and Graham 1991). Submerged turtles may rest quietly with the head withdrawn completely into the shell or with the head and neck partially extended (sometimes pumping water into and out of the pharynx by raising and lowering the throat). Occasionally, a submerged turtle extends the neck fully to reach the surface and take a breath of air. Winter is spent at the bottom of a permanent body of water. In Arkansas, Plummer and Burnley (1997) found hibernating softshells buried singly a few centimeters deep in stream-bottom sediments where water depth averaged 46 cm, within the turtles' summer home range. Spiny softshells studied in Vermont by Graham and Graham (1997) wintered in the deepest part of a river, evidently buried in deep, soft sand at water depths of 6–7 m, about 3 km from their lake/river-mouth nesting area; most individuals in the local population

1994). However, river habitat probably has been degraded by water pollutants deriving from urban and agricultural sources. Some turtles are killed in water diversion structures associated with agricultural irrigation, as Stebbins (1954:188) observed in Logan County. Dams and water diversion structures that have changed sediment transport and flooding patterns likely have reduced vegetation scouring and sandbar creation and hence the availability of suitable nesting habitat. Mining of sand and gravel, off-road vehicle use (Capron 1987), and other activities that disturb or remove river sandbars degrade or destroy nesting habitat. On the other hand, ponds created through streamside sand and gravel excavation have augmented the availability of foraging habitat in some areas. Nesting softshells are sensitive to disturbance and usually flee to the water if approached prior to depositing the first egg. Thus, frequent human recreational activity along rivers may be detrimental during the nesting season. Softshell turtles may be vulnerable to rotenone poisoning (which leads to oxygen deprivation) at concentrations typically used in fisheries management (Carr 1952; Dundee and Rossman 1989).

Capron (1987) estimated population density at 500–700 individuals per river mile along the Arkansas River in central Kansas. I doubt that softshells are that numerous in Colorado.

Plate 8.17. Same juvenile spiny softshell as in 8.16, showing color change
(Bent County, Colorado).

appeared to winter in the same
general area.

Compared to other freshwater
turtles, spiny softshells are not
especially tolerant of anoxic conditions, but physiological adjustments and low energy demands
at cold temperatures allow them
to survive the winter buried in
bottom substrates (probably aerobic sands).
At 10°C, somewhat warmer than wintering
conditions, softshells can survive more
than two weeks when submerged in water
of normal oxygen content (Ultsch, Herbert,
and Jackson 1984), a result of effective
extrapulmonary respiration (Stone, Dobie,
and Henry 1992a). During the active season,
the amount of time spent totally submerged
decreases with the oxygen content of the
water and rarely exceeds 20 minutes (Stone,
Dobie, and Henry 1992b).

When out of the water, softshells dehydrate relatively quickly (Robertson and
Smith 1982) and may die if kept in dry
conditions for more than a day or two.
Body temperatures of 40–42°C or higher
are lethal (Hutchison, Vinegar, and Kosh
1966). However, these turtles do sometimes
cross warm, dry land between bodies of
water when, for example, they are exposed
to falling water levels (Williams and Christiansen 1981).

Activity. In Colorado, the annual period
of activity usually extends from April to
October (mainly May to September). In
Vermont, softshells enter and emerge from
river-bottom hibernation sites when water
temperatures fall below and rise above about
12°C (Graham and Graham 1997). Softshells
are diurnal and rest buried in the bottom
substrate or among submerged branches at
night. Little documentation of daily patterns
of activity is available.

Home range and movement data are not
available for softshells in Colorado. Annual
home range size along a small stream in
Arkansas was 784–2,310 m (average 1,750

m) of stream length for males and 683–2,145
m (average 1,400 m) for females (Plummer,
Mills, and Allen 1997). During the activity
season, softshells were quite mobile and
moved on 85 percent of days.

Spiny softshells are very wary. When
disturbed while basking on land, they dash
into the water, which is always close by.
Turtles approached in the water generally
swim away quickly. In Louisiana, Platt and
Brantley (1991:57) "observed a female spiny
softshell (CL = 37.8 cm) squirt blood from
both eyes in response to handling." Presumably, the blood emerged from the eyelid or
other tissue bordering the orbit rather than
from the eyeball itself.

In hand, the spiny softshell may scratch
with its claws and strike vigorously with its
sharp jaws, extending its neck a surprising
distance. Despite its long neck, this turtle can
retract its head completely within the shell;
the vertebrae fold into a squashed S along the
midline within the shell, which displaces and
rotates the heart nearly 90 (Dalrymple 1979)
without ill effect.

Reproduction and Growth. Mating
occurs in spring (Ernst, Lovich, and Barbour
1994). Eggs generally are laid in open areas
within 15 m of water, though sometimes as
far as 100 m away (Vogt 1981). Most nests
are 10–25 cm deep. Packard, Taigen, et al.
(1979, 1981) reported that softshells along
the South Platte River in Logan County dig
nests in coarse sand or fine gravel on high
sandbars. The nesting process can take place
rather quickly. In Minnesota, a female dug a
nest cavity in 15 minutes, laid 17 eggs in 6
minutes, and filled and covered the nest in

Plate 8.18. Yearling spiny softshell (Baca County, Colorado).

5 minutes (Breckenridge 1960). In Vermont, nesting occurred between 10:30 a.m. and 4:30 p.m. (Graham and Graham 1997).

Along the South Platte River in Logan County, nests that had been constructed not more than a few days earlier were found on June 2 and June 22 in two successive years (Packard, Taigen, et al. 1979, 1981), suggesting that nesting peaks in June. Three nests in Logan County contained 15, 26, and 33 eggs (G. Packard, pers. comm.). On June 13 in the same area, Miller et al. (1989) found a nest that contained 39 eggs, apparently the largest clutch ever recorded for this species. Average clutch size in western Nebraska is 31–32 eggs, and nesting females average 37 cm CL (Iverson and Moler 1997). In Colorado, it is not known whether individual females ever produce more than one clutch per season, but Iverson and Moler (1997) indicated that at least some females in western Nebraska produce two clutches per season. Larger females in Tennessee may have produced two clutches in a single season (Robinson and Murphy 1978). E. O. Moll (1979) stated that females in Illinois may produce 4–5 clutches per season.

Under laboratory conditions at 29°C, eggs begin to hatch after 51–53 days of incubation (Packard, Taigen, et al. 1979, 1981). Neither hatching success nor size of hatchlings correlates with the wetness of the incubation substrate; embryos develop successfully without an external source of water (Packard, Taigen, et al. 1979). Compared to turtles with pliable-shelled eggs, the spiny softshell's eggs allow relatively little exchange of water (Packard, Taigen,

et al. 1981). Under natural conditions in Wisconsin, eggs hatch in 82–84 days (Ewert 1979). In Colorado, hatching probably takes place primarily in August and September. In Iowa, young typically emerge from nests in late summer or early fall (Christiansen and Gallaway 1984). I know of no firm evidence that young successfully overwinter in the nest, though Minton (1972:192) stated that some clutches do not hatch until spring, citing an Indiana study that found a nest with "well formed young with large yolk masses" in mid-November. Graham and Graham (1997) found that four caged nests left to overwinter in Vermont did not yield hatchlings the next spring. In contrast to other turtles in Colorado, sex of spiny softshell hatchlings is under genetic control and is not determined by the incubation temperature (Vogt and Bull 1982b).

A nest exposed by storm erosion on June 22 along a river in Oklahoma contained a clutch of 12 eggs (Carpenter 1981). A month later, one of the eggs contained live twin embryos apparently near hatching.

Little is known about growth rates in Colorado. A 47-mm-CL softshell that I found in mid-June in Baca County undoubtedly had hatched the previous summer. Generally, sexual maturity is attained at about 13–15 cm CL (and about 4–5 years old) in males and 25–28 cm CL (and 8–9 years old) in females (Webb 1962). Maximum lifespan is at least 25 years, but probably few live that long.

Food and Predators. Softshells forage in the water, often in vegetated shallows. Opportunistic generalists, they frequently feed on the bottom. Crayfish and various aquatic insects are major foods, but snails, small clams, worms, isopods, terrestrial insects that enter the water, fishes (alive and carrion), amphibians, and plant material are eaten, too (Williams and Christiansen 1981; Ernst, Lovich, and Barbour 1994). Prey may be actively chased, captured by ambush, or flushed from cover. The forefeet may be used to help push food items into the mouth or to hold prey as it is torn apart by the jaws.

Egg predators include skunks (*Mephitis mephitis, Spilogale* spp.), raccoons *(Procyon lotor),* and probably opossums *(Didelphis virginiana),* foxes (*Vulpes* spp.), and others; various predatory animals occasionally capture and eat the young (Webb 1962). Sometimes these turtles are hooked by anglers using live or dead animal bait. Unfortunately, this usually results in the turtles' intentionally being killed.

Taxonomy and Variation. Meylan's (1987) taxonomic revision of trionychid turtles subdivided the genus *Trionyx* into several genera, and native U.S. species were placed in the genus *Apalone.* In this arrangement, the spiny softshell is *Apalone spinifera* (LeSueur, 1827). Webb (1990) felt that this action was premature and retained the U.S. species in the genus *Trionyx.* Some authors have adopted Meylan's arrangement, whereas others have followed Webb. Without refuting the merits of Meylan's treatment, I choose to follow Webb (1990), Ernst, Lovich, and Barbour (1994), and Degenhardt, Painter, and Price (1996) in using *Trionyx* as the generic name for North American softshell turtles until further data clarify the situation. The subspecies in Colorado is *Trionyx spiniferus hartwegi* (Conant and Goin, 1948).

Lizards

Lizards occur throughout most of the world and are absent only from cold arctic and antarctic regions and some isolated islands. Many species inhabit desert regions. Arboreal, terrestrial, fossorial, semiaquatic, and semimarine lifestyles are represented, and there are even a few gliders. The smallest lizards are certain geckos less than 70 mm TL. The largest is the Komodo monitor, which grows to more than 3 m. Of the 3,700 extant species worldwide, about 105 occur in the United States, 18 of them in Colorado. Lizards (order Squamata) traditionally are placed in a single suborder (Lacertilia, formerly Sauria), but this is an artificial arrangement that ignores the phylogenetic relationships of the constituent groups.

Lizards generally can be recognized as such by their four legs and long tail, though several species (none in Colorado) lack legs and resemble snakes. Many of these legless lizards can be identified by their movable eyelids and/or external ear openings, which snakes never have, and unlike snakes, they usually have a pectoral girdle and sternum.

One of the notable characteristics of lizards is the easily detachable tail in many species. Among Colorado lizards, the skinks have notoriously fragile tails. A slight tug or bump is all that is necessary to break it. Bright tail coloration in certain species may attract a predator's attention to that expendable part of the body. A detached tail usually thrashes vigorously for a few minutes, so a captured lizard may escape if the predator is distracted by it. The importance of having a detachable tail is suggested by the sometimes high percentage of individuals with a regenerated tail. Tail loss may result from aggressive interactions among lizards as well as from predation attempts. Not all lizards lose their tails so readily. Notable among Colorado lizards is the collared lizard, whose sturdy tail is rarely detached.

For most lizards, a broken tail does no great physical harm. The tail bones have a predetermined fracture zone (septum of cartilage or connective tissue) that minimizes damage to the skeletal system. A clean break can happen within any of multiple tail vertebrae, though generally the break does not occur at the base of the tail, where the hemipenes are located. Regeneration does not take place if the tail breaks between vertebrae. Some snakes (e.g., *Coluber, Nerodia, Thamnophis*) have a moderately fragile tail that breaks between, rather than within, the vertebrae and does not regenerate to any significant extent.

Upon breakage, the tail muscles separate smoothly. The caudal (tail) artery of lizards that readily lose their tail has segmentally arranged sphincters that reduce blood loss. The regrown portion of the tail is generally shorter and duller than the original and is supported by a rod of cartilage rather than bone, which does not regenerate. The scaly covering on the new tail also differs from the original.

Tail loss does have a cost. Many tailless lizards are rather clumsy and slow and may be more vulnerable to predation. Other drawbacks include the loss of stored energy (e.g., in certain geckos) and slowed body growth.

Many lizards, including most of those occurring in Colorado, have a tiny structure called the parietal eye, or parapineal organ, on top of the head. The parietal eye originates as an evagination of the brain, next to the pineal organ (which is a light receptor in amphibians). It resembles an eye in fine structure (it has a lens and light-sensitive sensory layer) and has a nerve connection to the brain, but there are no eye muscles or focusing mechanisms. The parietal eye cannot form an image but probably can distinguish light from dark. It seems to function as a light meter, controlling in part the amount of time the lizard exposes itself to the sun. Removal or shielding of the parietal eye results in behavioral changes that lead to greater exposure to light on the part of the lizard. A time lag in the response to parietalectomy in short-horned lizards suggests that the parietal eye exerts its effect through hormones, which are slower acting than the nervous system. In the laboratory, short-horned lizards with inactivated parietal eyes had higher body temperatures than did controls, and panting was triggered at a higher body temperature for these altered individuals. Field studies of the effect of parietalectomy are less clear; no impact on energy expenditure or body temperature was found in fence lizards *(Sceloporus occidentalis).*

Arthropods dominate the diets of all Colorado lizards. Some of the larger lizard species eat small vertebrates, particularly small lizards, as well. In most lizards, food is detected by sight; movement of the prey alerts the lizard to a potential meal. Some lizards, especially whiptails, appear to use their sense of smell to detect small animals buried in the soil. Lizards of most species are equipped with small teeth usually attached in a single row along the edges of both the upper and lower jaws and in patches on the roof of the mouth. Food items are crushed in the jaws and swallowed, with little chewing. A few species (none in Colorado) that feed on snails have broad rear teeth that facilitate crushing the shells. Food items generally pass through the digestive tract in a day or two.

I have adopted the family-level taxonomy of Frost and Etheridge (1989), who divided the large family Iguanidae into several smaller families, two of which occur in Colorado. This taxonomy has been adopted in most herpetological publications in recent years, though Macey et al. (1997) recommended that the families recognized by Frost and Etheridge be maintained as subfamilies of the Iguanidae.

COLLARED AND LEOPARD LIZARDS
Family Crotaphytidae

This is a recently recognized family of 12 species of terrestrial or rock-perching lizards occurring in southwestern and south-central North America (Smith and Brodie 1982; Frost and Etheridge 1989; McGuire 1996). Though the group clearly seems to constitute a distinct evolutionary lineage, it nonetheless lacks any "descriptively unique morphological features" (Frost and Etheridge 1989:23). The body is covered with small scales, and the limbs and tail are relatively long and strong. These lizards may use only their hind limbs when running at high speed. When agitated, high-pitched sounds may be emitted (Wever, Hepp-Raymond, and Vernon 1966; Smith 1974; Crowley and Pietruszka 1983). Gravid females develop a pattern of vivid, hormone-induced red-orange coloration (Medica, Turner, and Smith 1973). Large size and reliance on comparatively large food items result in low population density relative to most other Coloradan lizards.

Two of the eight U.S. species occur in Colorado.

Formerly, the collared lizards and leopard lizards both were included in the genus *Crotaphytus,* but these two groups exhibit various fundamental differences that now place them in two genera. *Crotaphytus* lizards have a nonregenerative tail (no fracture zones are present in the vertebrae), poorly developed palatine teeth, and weakly subheterodont dentary teeth, whereas *Gambelia* is characterized by a regenerative tail, well-developed palatine teeth, and distinctly heterodont dentary teeth (Weiner and Smith 1965). *Crotaphytus* also has a broader head and more cylindrical tail.

Plate 8.19. Female *(left)* and male *(right)* collared lizards as I found them (Mesa County, Colorado).

Collared Lizard
Crotaphytus collaris (Say, 1823)

Recognition. Head large, sometimes bright yellow; tail long; two areas of coloration resembling incomplete black collars around narrow neck; dorsum with smooth, granular scales, turquoise to greenish to brown with numerous small light spots

in adult; toes of adults yellow in western Colorado; lining of pharynx usually black; maximum TL about 36 cm; maximum SVL about 13.1 cm in males, 10.6 cm in females. This is a lizard of stunning beauty. *Mature male:* bulge of hemipenes evident at base of tail; throat with dark spots or circles (pale reticulation) most evident in western Colorado, or throat yellow to orange in southeastern Colorado; head especially large; enlarged postanal scales and femoral pores. *Mature female:* orange-red bars or spots on sides of body and neck during breeding season; throat unmarked or faintly spotted. *Juvenile:* dorsum with wide dark bands or rows of large dark spots separated by narrow light lines, sometimes with red/orange spots on neck and sides of chest. *Hatchling:* 31–42 mm SVL, often about 40 mm SVL. *Eggs:* average about 19–21 mm x 11–13 mm (Webb 1970; Vitt 1977; Smith 1983); 28–29 mm x 21–22 mm in Texas after about two months of incubation (McAllister 1984).

Distribution. Western and south-central United States, from eastern Utah, Colorado, Kansas, and Missouri south through Arizona, New Mexico, Oklahoma, Arkansas, and Texas to northern Mexico (McGuire 1996). Occurs mainly south of the Arkansas River in southeastern Colorado and south of the Roan Plateau in western Colorado; reaches 7,000 feet (2,135 m) in the southeast and 8,000 feet (2,440 m) in the west but is most common below 6,000 feet (1,830 m). Recent reports of collared lizards from Dinosaur National Monument, Browns Park, and the vicinity of Craig in Moffat County, if valid, undoubtedly represent introduced individuals (J. Roth, in Livo, Hammerson, and Smith 1998); this easily detected lizard certainly would have been found in these areas long ago if it naturally occurred there.

Conservation Status. The collared lizard occurs primarily in areas not subject to extensive urbanization, agricultural development, or other major human impacts on habitat. Residential development has encroached into a small portion of the habitat in the vicinity of several cities, but most habitat remains intact. Grazing of livestock takes place in collared lizard habitat, but its impact on this species is not well known. The presence of thick stands of cheatgrass that cover the ground between scattered rocks appears to exclude collared lizards from otherwise suitable habitat. Grasshopper-control activities likely are detrimental through pesticide toxicity and impacts on lizard food resources. Axtell (1989) described circumstantial evidence that agricultural pesticides may have played a role in the disappearance of *Crotaphytus* from an area in Texas. A few populations in some easily accessible recreational areas in Colorado probably have been depleted by collectors, but most populations are in areas infrequently visited by humans and thus not subject to overexploitation. The overall distribution in Colorado apparently has remained stable, and this lizard continues to be fairly common in many areas. It should be secure for the foreseeable future.

Local collared lizard populations usually appear to be fairly stable over time, presumably due in part to the relatively long (several-year) lifespan of individuals, but Axtell (1989) anecdotally described a population in Texas that suddenly mushroomed, then became scarce the following year, then disappeared altogether. No explanation was offered, but the population was in a developing area of metropolitan El Paso.

Habitat. Typical habitat includes rocky canyons, slopes, and gullies; rocky ledges above cliffs; exposures of bedrock; and areas with scattered large rocks and sparse

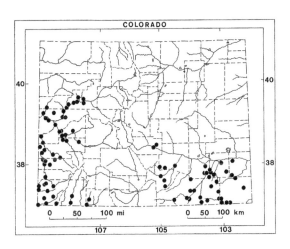

Map 8.6. Distribution of the collared lizard in Colorado.

Plate 8.20. Adult male collared lizard (Mesa County, Colorado).

vegetation. Collared lizards commonly venture away from their usual habitat into adjacent rockless gullies, flat canyon bottoms, and mesa tops where soils are firm. Typical vegetation in collared lizard habitat includes piñon pine, junipers, sagebrush, rabbitbrush, greasewood, scrub oak, other shrubs, and sparse herbaceous plants. Watson (1939) reported on three collared lizards that lived for at least 2–3 years confined in seminatural conditions on the museum patio at Mesa Verde National Park. Collared lizards often bask and watch for prey while perched atop large rocks.

At night and during active-season hot weather or cold spells, collared lizards hide under rocks or in crevices and burrows. Warmed-up individuals disturbed from resting areas beneath rocks soon return to their retreats. Hibernation takes place underground. In Oklahoma and Texas, hibernating collared lizards have been found in small burrows under rocks (McAllister 1983).

Activity. Collared lizards emerge from hibernation generally in late March or (more often) April and are active on sunny days in spring and summer. Earlier seasonal emergence occasionally may occur. McAllister (1987) found a young adult active on February 19 in north-central Texas, but such early activity is exceptional, even there. Some adults begin to hibernate in August, at about the time the young hatch; by September, most of the individuals still active are hatchlings, which may not hibernate until October.

Activity occurs throughout the warm part of the day, usually between 9:00 a.m. and 6:00 p.m., but sometimes earlier, or as late as about 7:30 p.m. Nine active adults that I sampled in Colorado had body temperatures of 36.6–41.7°C (average 38.7°C). Individuals active during the heat of the day may perch with limbs extended and body high off the substrate, reducing heat gain from the ground and facilitating cooling by the wind. Sometimes, collared lizards active at midday exhibit exceptionally pale body coloration, which presumably reduces heat gain from the sun.

Adult male collared lizards are intolerant of other adult males, especially in the vicinity of females during the breeding season (Yedlin and Ferguson 1973). Males patrol their territories, aggressively threaten intruders with bobbing displays (the body may be laterally compressed and the dewlap may be extended), and, if necessary, attack and chase trespassers. Younger males manage to occupy nondefended home ranges within adult male territories through subordinate behavior and by avoiding the adults as much as possible (Baird, Acree, and Sloan 1996). Females generally are tolerant of each other and exhibit little aggression. However, they may defend nesting sites from other females (Yedlin and Ferguson 1973). Their home ranges overlap with one another and with immature males but typically coincide with that of just a single adult male (sometimes two) (Baird, Acree, and Sloan 1996). In Kansas, males maintain home ranges averaging about 0.4 ha and spend most of their time in a small portion of this area (Yedlin and Ferguson 1973).

Collared lizards perched on rocks often allow humans to approach closely, if the humans move slowly. Once a lizard vacates its initial perch, getting close becomes more

Plate 8.21. Adult male collared lizard (Mesa County, Colorado). *Audrey DeLella Benedict.*

difficult. Startled individuals may dash off using only their hind legs (Snyder 1952) and often take refuge under a rock or beneath a juniper. Rarely, a lizard enters water to escape. Captured collared lizards should be carefully handled. Their powerful jaws are capable of lacerating human skin. A lizard with a good purchase on your finger may bite hard, with periodic increases in pressure, and often is reluctant to let go.

Reproduction and Growth. Courtship and mating in Colorado occur primarily in May and June. Ballinger and Hipp (1985) concluded that mating probably takes place from April to June in Texas, where warm spring weather arrives earlier. Courtship behavior includes push-ups, lateral compression of the body, body elevation, dewlap extension, and mounting by the male, as well as body contact and tandem circling by male-female pairs (Baird, Acree, and Sloan 1996). Males approach females with the head held low and usually nodding (Yedlin and Ferguson 1973). Females approached by males may extend the dewlap, raise the tail, and sometimes compress the body laterally while walking with a stiff gait (Baird, Acree, and Sloan 1996). Females raise their pelvic region by bowlegged extension of the hind limbs (pers. obs.). Sometimes, females approach males and nudge them with the snout, evoking courtship behavior in the male (Yedlin and Ferguson 1976). Males bite the neck skin of the female prior to copulation (pers. obs.). A female may resist by rolling onto her back after the male bites her neck (Yedlin and Ferguson 1973). A mated male and female may perch together on the same rock during the courtship period.

Orange spots/bars develop on the sides of reproductive females. A change from faint to bright orange takes place in less than 12 hours; maximum brightness occurs prior to ovulation and 10–13 days prior to oviposition (Ferguson 1976). In north-central Kansas, maximum brightness was observed from late May to mid-June (Ferguson 1976). Copulation happens probably within a day or two before development of bright orange coloration (Fitch 1956d).

In Colorado, the period of egg deposition is not known but probably falls somewhere between late May and late July. Egg-laying has been recorded as early as late April in Texas (Ballinger and Hipp 1985) and as late as the end of July in north-central Kansas (Ferguson 1976). Throughout the western part of the range, clutch size varies from 1–14 eggs, averaging about 9 in western Kansas (Werth 1972), 5–6 in northeastern Kansas (Fitch 1956d), 5 in New Mexico (Parker 1973), and 7–9 in Texas (Ballinger and Hipp 1985). Clutch size increases with female size. In much of the range, females lay 1–2 clutches per season, perhaps (rarely) 3 in Texas (Ballinger and Hipp 1985), with older females more likely to produce multiple clutches than are first-time breeders. Individuals in northern (Ferguson 1976) and high-elevation locations, such as Colorado, may produce only a single clutch.

Eggs hatch about 7–13 weeks after oviposition (Fitch 1956d; Trauth 1978; Smith 1983). In Colorado, hatchlings first appear in August, and hatching may extend into September. Growth is rapid. In northeastern Kansas, a male hatchling reported by Fitch and Tanner (1951) grew from a total length of 104 mm on August 20, 1949, to 273 mm on September 8, 1950. In Missouri, hatchlings grew quickly, and some reached

Plate 8.22. Juvenile collared lizard
(Otero County, Colorado).

78 mm SVL before their first
hibernation (Sexton, Andrews,
and Bramble 1992). By midsummer of the following year, these
individuals were indistinguishable
in size from older adults.

Throughout most of the range,
collared lizards may become
reproductively active at the end of
their first year of life (second calendar year), with females maturing at a size
of at least 7 cm SVL (Trauth 1978, 1979;
Ballinger and Hipp 1985; Sexton, Andrews,
and Bramble 1992; Baird, Acree and Sloan
1996). In northeastern Kansas, some first-
year females do not reproduce (Fitch 1970).
In Oklahoma, first-year females are 60–86
mm SVL in April; those that are at least 70
mm SVL in April become reproductively
active in their first year (Baird, Acree, and
Sloan 1996). First-year males in Oklahoma
are 60–90 mm SVL in April, become sexually mature in their first year, but have low
mating success (females often reject them),
whereas those males nearly two years old or
more and at least 100 mm SVL have high
mating success (Baird, Acree, and Sloan
1996). In New Mexico, gravid females are
82–96 mm SVL, females that are 62–74 mm
SVL during the reproductive season are not
gravid, and all males 83 mm SVL or more
are mature (Parker 1973). As in New Mexico (Gehlbach 1965), adult males in Missouri (Sexton, Andrews, and Bramble 1992)
average about 10 cm SVL, adult females
9 cm SVL. Males reach their maximum
size by the age of three, whereas females
appear to grow throughout life, though little
growth takes place after the first three years.
In the relatively short growing season of
Colorado, collared lizards do not reproduce
until they are nearly two years old (third
calendar year); nonreproductive yearlings
are smaller than 7 cm SVL and typically
have orange markings on the neck and sides
during the May-June breeding period (pers.
obs.). In Colorado, most breeding females
are about 84–95 mm SVL, and breeding

males typically are 84–118 mm SVL
(pers. obs.). Maximum longevity probably
exceeds 10 years (Degenhardt, Painter, and
Price 1996).

Food and Predators. The diet consists
mainly of arthropods and small lizards.
Throughout the range, beetles and grasshoppers often dominate the diet (Knowlton
1934; Fitch 1956d; Werth 1972; McAllister
1985; Best and Pfaffenberger 1987). Various other small animals and some plant
material occasionally are eaten. Watson
(1939) observed collared lizards eating
plateau lizards, sagebrush lizards, plateau
striped whiptails, insects, and flowers at
Mesa Verde; on one occasion, an adult
male stuffed himself with two adult whiptails within 3–4 hours, and another adult
commonly ate two *Sceloporus* in a single
day. Young individuals eat small insects
and spiders. Small stones sometimes are
ingested and perhaps aid in food breakdown.
Collared lizards are opportunistic feeders, so
the diet may change seasonally as different
prey becomes available.

Collared lizards typically sit quietly and
watch for potential prey. Prey movement
usually stimulates an attack. Prey may be
stalked with cautious advances or quick
open-mouth dashes; a chase of up to several
meters may ensue if the opening attack
fails (McAllister 1985). Victims may be
swallowed head- or tailfirst. The lizard
often returns to its initial perch to await
additional prey.

The powerful jaws of the collared lizard,
especially adult males, can easily kill small
lizard-sized vertebrates with a single bite.
I noticed that in canyons of west-central

Colorado, side-blotched lizards are scarce or absent within collared lizard territories but plentiful in nearby areas lacking collared lizards.

The full range of predators is not known but includes diurnal raptors and snakes *(Coluber, Masticophis)* (Fitch 1956d). Under a rock in Baca County, Lauren Livo and I found a female night snake that had eaten an adult collared lizard (see account of the night snake). Perched atop a rock, these lizards are very conspicuous and seem a likely target for a hungry hawk. However, their habit of perching out in the open and their general lack of wariness suggest that they are not particularly vulnerable to predation.

Patches of orange mites sometimes are found in the shoulder region.

Taxonomy and Variation. McGuire (1996) reasoned that the nominal subspecies of *C. collaris* represent pattern classes exhibiting extensive areas of intermediacy and thus are not independent lineages warranting taxonomic recognition. In addition, the reported characteristics of these subspecies do not correspond very well with the ranges they are supposed to occupy.

Hence, McGuire recognized no subspecies in *C. collaris* and concluded that the previously named subspecies do not represent useful pattern classes. Other discussions of variation in *Crotaphytus* relevant to Colorado include Burt (1928a) and Fitch and Tanner (1951).

Adults, especially males, from western Colorado often have a fluorescent yellow head and neck (except at low temperatures) and bright yellow feet as well. Collared lizards from southeastern Colorado also may have yellow head pigmentation, but it is never as bright as that of typical individuals from the western part of the state.

McCoy et al. (1997) found that sexual differences in coloration varied significantly among three populations in Oklahoma. The population appraised as most brightly colored was not the one with the greatest degree of color difference between males and females.

In a Texas population, Walker (1980) found several males and females that had a partial second row of femoral pores, but no such rows were found among 350 specimens from Colorado and a few other states.

Plate 8.23. Adult female longnose leopard lizard (Mesa County, Colorado).

Longnose Leopard Lizard

Gambelia wislizenii (Baird and Girard, 1852)

Recognition. Dorsum of adult light brownish-gray with numerous small, round brown spots (light lines across back fade with age); dorsal scales small and smooth; tail long, slender, and round; a big lizard, up to about 38 cm TL (14.5 cm SVL in females and 12 cm SVL in males). *Mature male:* row of several somewhat polygonal or rectangular enlarged postanal scales. *Mature female:* during breeding season, red-orange spots on sides (color fades to a darker red after eggs are laid, still evident in August), underside of tail vivid orange or red. *Hatchling:* dorsum with several distinct light crossbands and red spots (crossbands become less evident with age); alternating black and white bars on head; 42–47 mm SVL at hatching in Colorado (McCoy 1967), 38–48 mm SVL in Utah (Parker and Pianka 1976). *Eggs:* average about 20 mm x 14 mm in Colorado (McCoy 1967).

Distribution. Oregon (questionably Washington) and southern Idaho south through eastern and southern California, Nevada, Utah, western Colorado, Arizona, New Mexico, and western Texas to northern Mexico (McGuire 1996). Occurs in west-central Colorado and extreme southwestern Colorado at elevations below about 5,200 feet (1,585 m).

Conservation Status. The longnose leopard lizard probably declined in range and abundance in Colorado during the twentieth century. The current distribution in the Grand Valley of Mesa County suggests that this species formerly occurred throughout the valley in sagebrush and semidesert shrubland habitats that have been extensively replaced by intensive agriculture and residential and commercial development. Thick stands of exotic cheatgrass *(Bromus tectorum)* now carpet formerly sparsely vegetated ground in much of the remaining shrubland habitat in the Grand Valley. These thick growths interfere with leopard lizard locomotion and foraging behavior, though cheatgrass may be used for cover by lizards in areas having nearby open habitat (pers. obs.). Though McCoy (1967) found leopard lizards in areas with cheatgrass cover in Mesa County, it is now difficult to find this lizard in cheatgrass-invaded shrublands in the northern Grand Valley, even in sites where the lizards formerly occurred. I suspect that large, high-density cheatgrass stands have eliminated leopard lizards or depressed their populations in many sites in western Colorado and elsewhere in the range.

As of the late 1990s, leopard lizards were still present in the vicinity of Colorado National Monument and the lower Dolores River valley in Mesa County (Hammerson 1991f; Mourning 1997). I have not been able to verify that leopard lizards still occur in Bridge Canyon (Montezuma County), where they were reported in the 1970s (Bury 1977), and I am not aware of recent observations of this species elsewhere in Montezuma County. Probably, the dearth of recent records for southwestern Colorado reflects inadequate data rather than an absence of leopard lizards; large areas of suitable habitat remain but have not been well surveyed. I found this lizard in the 1990s in adjacent San Juan County, Utah, not far from the Colorado border. Leopard lizards seem to be rare in adjacent northwestern New Mexico (Degenhardt, Painter, and Price 1996). Better information on current distribution and abundance in Colorado and the Four Corners region is needed.

Leopard lizards have a relatively low reproductive rate and exhibit low population density (e.g., variable, but about 5 per hectare in one year in southern Nevada [Tanner and Krogh 1974a]). The activity season is short, and the lizards' sometimes unwary behavior makes them vulnerable to human exploitation. In Colorado, the range is limited, and the populations are localized. Persons observing this lizard in Colorado should thrill to their good luck, spend some time watching from a distance, and leave the lizards alone. Protection of low-valley stands of sagebrush and semidesert shrubland and their associated burrowing rodent populations, as well as land management that favors native grass and forbs, are needed to ensure the continued presence of this magnificent lizard in Colorado.

Habitat. Leopard lizards inhabit flat or gently sloping shrublands with a large percentage of open ground. On the south side of the Grand Valley in Colorado, they inhabit stands of greasewood and sagebrush on deep sandy soils and broad outwash plains in or near the mouths of canyons (McCoy 1967). On the north side of the valley, they occur on clay soils in saltbush-sagebrush shrublands and among fairly dense stands of saltbush, greasewood, rabbitbrush, and (not-too-thick) cheatgrass near arroyos and in the floodplains of semipermanent streams (McCoy 1967). Along the Dolores River, leopard lizards inhabit areas with sandy-rocky soils and scattered sagebrush *(Seriphidium tridentatum),* junipers, and skunk brush *(Rhus aromatica* ssp. *trilobata)* in canyon bottoms. Habitats in Montezuma County include mesa tops above canyons (Bury 1977). In San Juan County, Utah, I observed leopard lizards in plateau-top stands of blackbrush *(Coleogyne ramosissima)* with much bare ground.

Leopard lizards are most common where the ground surface between shrubs is bare or sparsely vegetated. These lizards seem to occur only where soil mounded at the base of shrubs is riddled with

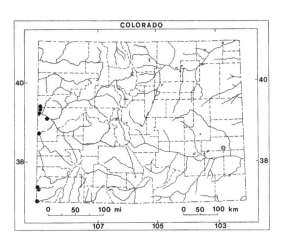

Map 8.7. Distribution of the longnose leopard lizard in Colorado.

Plate 8.24. Adult female longnose leopard lizard (Mesa County, Colorado).

rodent burrows, which are used as nighttime and winter refuges. A burrow may be used on several successive nights (McCoy 1967). Debris piles made by packrats *(Neotoma)* also are used for shelter in spring and summer. The surface of the ground is the usual microhabitat, but sometimes lizards bask on low rocks or climb into bushes. Individuals may use certain rocks near their burrow as favored basking sites (McCoy 1967).

Activity. In extreme southwestern Colorado, emergence from winter hibernation occurs by mid-May. In Mesa County, emergence takes place in the latter half of May, long after other lizard species have emerged (McCoy 1967). May emergence seems also to be typical of leopard lizards in Utah (Parker and Pianka 1976), northwestern Nevada (Snyder 1972), and western Texas (Tinkle 1959). Emergence in April (sometimes March) occurs in the warmer climate of southeastern Arizona (Mitchell 1984), southern New Mexico (Baltosser and Best 1990; Degenhardt, Painter, and Price 1996), and southern California (Miller and Stebbins 1964:372). Adults in Colorado are active through June and July, then disappear underground by early August. Hatchlings may remain active through early September. In southeastern Arizona, Mitchell (1984) found that hatchlings ceased activity in late August,

after the adults. Tanner and Krogh (1974a) observed activity into October in Nevada; males were more commonly observed early in the season, whereas females were more often seen in summer after oviposition. October activity also takes place in New Mexico (Baltosser and Best 1990; Degenhardt, Painter, and Price 1996).

Leopard lizards are strictly diurnal and are most active 2–6 hours after sunrise (Parker and Pianka 1976). In Mesa County (McCoy 1967), they emerge in the morning, sometimes as early as 7:30 a.m., and bask in the sun. After warming, they watch for prey or actively hunt for food until about 12:30 or 1:00 p.m., when air temperatures commonly approach 35°C and soil temperatures are 50°C. Activity generally peaks between 10:00 and 11:00 a.m. Typically, the hottest part of the day is spent underground or elsewhere in the shade, though activity may continue throughout the afternoon if the weather is not excessively hot. On hot days at about 4:30 or 5:00 p.m., leopard lizards may re-emerge for another period of basking or casual feeding, then retreat to a burrow until the next morning. Activity may take place in the shade as long as warm temperatures prevail. Bimodal morning and late afternoon activity also has been observed in southern New Mexico (Creusere and Whitford 1982). A tendency toward greater activity before early afternoon than afterward occurs throughout the range of the species (Parker and Pianka 1976).

Average air temperature during activity is about 26°C, and activity rarely occurs when the air temperature is less than 20°C (Parker and Pianka 1976). Body temperature during activity usually is 35–40°C (range 29–42°C, average 37–39°C) (Tanner and Krogh 1974; Parker and Pianka 1976). Body temperatures of three active individuals that I captured in Mesa County were 35.5, 38.5, and 40°C.

Individuals approached by humans may run to the base of a nearby shrub and remain

Plate 8.25. Copulating longnose leopard lizards (San Juan County, Utah). *Audrey DeLella Benedict.*

there motionless, freeze where they are, or, in areas where shrubs are short, flee dozens of meters in the opposite direction. High-speed running may be bipedal (Snyder 1952). These lizards can be caught easily by noosing. In hand, their strong jaws can inflict a painful bite.

Tanner and Krogh (1974a) recorded home range sizes of 0.67, 1.54, and 2.35 ha over periods of 2–3 years for three individuals in Nevada. There is some home range overlap, particularly between males and females. Territorial behavior apparently does not occur and, other than interactions associated with mating, adults seem rather oblivious to each other (McCoy 1967). Some individuals appear to be somewhat nomadic. In northern Utah, Parker and Pianka (1976) recorded long-distance movements by juvenile males (up to 806 m over two weeks; 1,186 m over 20 months), whereas adult males moved 0–450 m (average 125 m) over periods of about 2–4 weeks.

Reproduction and Growth. In Mesa County, mating has been observed in late May and early June (McCoy 1967). In Utah and Nevada, mating leopard lizards have been recorded from mid-May through June (see McCoy 1967; Tanner and Krogh 1974a). Egg-laying in Mesa County occurs in late June or early July (McCoy 1967), compared to mainly the second half of June in northern Utah, and mid-June to early July in southern Idaho (Parker and Pianka 1976). Shaw (1952) reported a clutch laid in late June in east-central Utah.

Clutch size in Colorado is about 6–10 eggs (average 7.3). This is the highest value reported from anywhere in the range. Average clutch size is 5–6 eggs in most areas but as low as 2.7–3.4 eggs in some sites in Nevada and Idaho (Parker and Pianka 1976). These variations may in part reflect female size in the samples (clutch size increases with female size and

age [Parker and Pianka 1976]). Individual females in Colorado produce one clutch per year (McCoy 1967), as is the case in most of the range (e.g., Tanner and Krogh 1974; Parker and Pianka 1976; Mitchell 1984), though Montanucci (1967) and Turner, Lannom, et al. (1969) found evidence that some females in southern California and southern Nevada may produce two clutches in a single year.

Eggs are laid underground. Parker and Pianka (1976) observed that females in northern Utah dug L-shaped nesting burrows in the sandy soil of an unused dirt road and returned to the same area to nest in successive years. Burrows were about 20 cm long and 7–8 cm deep while still under construction. Up to three gravid females were found in a single burrow.

Hatchlings first appear in Mesa County in early to mid-August (McCoy 1967). Hatching usually occurs in August in the northern part of the range but takes place in late June and early July in southern California and southern Arizona (Montanucci 1967; Parker and Pianka 1976). In Nevada, most hatchlings appear in August, but a few emerge at the very end of July (Tanner and Krogh 1974a).

As in other areas in the northern part of the range (Parker and Pianka 1976), young leopard lizards in Colorado grow rapidly and begin breeding during their second spring at an age of about 22 months (McCoy 1967). In the southern part of the range, age at maturity may vary from 1–2 years, depending on conditions (Turner, Lannom, et al. 1969; Tanner and Krogh 1974a; Parker and Pianka 1976).

In Colorado and other northern sites, males mature at just over 8 cm SVL, females usually at or slightly larger than 9 cm SVL (McCoy 1967; Parker and Pianka 1976; Mitchell 1984). Reproductive success may vary considerably in different years (Tanner and Krogh 1974a). Annual adult survivorship in northern Utah and southern Nevada is about 50 percent; juvenile survivorship is much lower (Turner, Lannom, et al. 1969; Parker and Pianka 1976). The oldest individual in a population in southern Nevada was nearly 10 years old (Medica and Turner 1984).

Food and Predators. The known diet in Colorado includes grasshoppers, beetles, spiders, wasps, ant lions, caterpillars, and lizards, including the western whiptail, side-blotched lizard, and plateau lizard (McCoy 1967). Caterpillars, robber flies, and other arthropods and lizards (e.g., other *Sceloporus* and *Cnemidophorus* species, *Holbrookia, Phrynosoma,* and smaller leopard lizards) may be eaten as well (Knowlton 1934; Gehlbach 1956; Montanucci 1967; Parker and Pianka 1976; McGuire 1996). Grasshoppers often dominate the diet. Leopard lizards sometimes attack and successfully ingest lizards nearly as large as themselves (Gracie and Murphy 1986). McCoy (1967) found a 10.2-cm-SVL leopard lizard that recently had swallowed a 7.1-cm-SVL western whiptail. He also found an 11.7-cm-SVL leopard lizard that apparently had choked to death while trying to swallow an 8.0-cm-SVL western whiptail. In southeastern Arizona, Mitchell (1984) found a 10.2-cm-SVL male leopard lizard that had eaten a 5.5-cm-SVL western whiptail. Hatchlings sometimes eat hatchling plateau lizards. Pietruszka, Wiens, and Pietruszka (1981) described a few instances of opportunistic predation on diurnally active pocket mice *(Perognathus longimembris)* in Nevada. Leopard lizards often intentionally ingest the fruits of *Lycium* (matrimonyvine).

Foraging behavior includes "sit and wait" hunting (short run used to nab prey) and active searching, including well-developed stalking behavior not present in collared lizards (Montanucci 1976; not observed by Tanner and Krogh 1974).

Predators are poorly known but, in addition to larger leopard lizards as noted earlier, probably include various raptors, carnivorous mammals, and large snakes.

Taxonomy and Variation. In the latest taxonomic revision of this species, McGuire (1996) noted that the nominal subspecies of *G. wislizenii* exhibit broad zones of intergradation (Tanner and Banta 1963, 1977) and that dorsal color pattern classes typical of these subspecies occur sporadically throughout the range of the species (Montanucci 1978). On these bases, McGuire did not recognize any subspecies of *G. wislizenii.* The leopard lizard formerly was included in the genus *Crotaphytus.*

PHRYNOSOMATIDS
Family Phrynosomatidae

The approximately 120 species in this family (Reeder and Wiens 1996; Wiens and Reeder 1997) occur primarily in the southwestern United States and Mexico. Members of this family formerly were included in the family Iguanidae, but the phrynosomatids represent a distinct evolutionary lineage (Frost and Etheridge 1989). Generally, these lizards are small, insectivorous, active, conspicuous, abundant, and diurnal, and they may be terrestrial, rock-dwelling, sand-dwelling, or arboreal (Reeder and Wiens 1996). Most species lay eggs, but a few give birth to fully formed young. Many species are cryptically colored dorsally but have bright ventral or lateral coloration that functions in visual communication and social behavior. Of the 37 species inhabiting the United States, 9 species representing five genera occur in Colorado.

Plate 8.26. Adult lesser earless lizard (Weld County, Colorado).

Lesser Earless Lizard
Holbrookia maculata (Girard, 1851)

Recognition. Dorsum striped or speckled, with smooth granular scales; external ear openings absent; two black marks on each side of belly; maximum size about 13 cm TL and about 6 cm SVL (adults average about 5 cm SVL). *Mature male:* enlarged postanal scales; black, blue-edged bars on belly; may have yellowish wash on sides. *Mature female:* black bars on belly lack blue edge; reproductive females during the breeding season have yellow-orange on throat and on sides of head and neck and orange on sides of body. *Hatchling:* in western Nebraska, 24–25 mm SVL, reaching an average of 33 mm SVL after two months of growth (Jones and Ballinger 1987); 19–23 mm SVL in eastern New Mexico (Gennaro 1974); 32–38 mm SVL in late August to mid-September in northeastern Colorado (Bauerle 1971; pers. obs.). *Eggs:* average about 10–12 mm x 7 mm (Walker 1965; Vitt 1977; Droge, Jones, and Ballinger 1982).

Distribution. Southeastern Utah, southwestern Colorado, southern South Dakota, and eastern

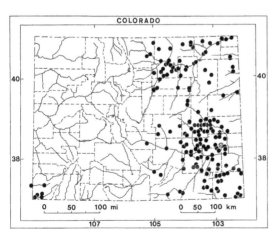

Map 8.8. Distribution of the lesser earless lizard in Colorado.

Plate 8.27. Adult lesser earless lizard (Montezuma County, Colorado).

Wyoming south though Nebraska, Kansas, Oklahoma, Arizona, New Mexico, and Texas to central Mexico. Occurs throughout eastern Colorado and in the southwestern corner of the state in Montezuma County; reaches 5,300 feet (1,615 m) in northeastern Colorado and 6,000 feet (1,830 m) in the southern part of the state. Douglas (1965) and others have been unable to confirm an old record for Mesa Verde National Park (Barry 1933a); evidently, it no longer occurs there, if indeed it ever did. Yarrow's (1875) record of *H. maculata* from Twin Lakes, Lake County, is obviously in error; the elevation there (9,200 feet [2,805 m]) is much too high for this lowland species. The single specimen (UCM 216, a large adult female collected in September 1907) from Boulder is a questionably valid record; certainly additional specimens would have been collected had the species naturally occurred there. I have not included this record on the map. A specimen recorded as having been collected in Chaffee County (UCM 32285) on March 30, 1965, clearly reflects inaccurate data (specimen later was destroyed by museum personnel).

Conservation Status. The lesser earless lizard is common in many areas of eastern Colorado and appears to be fairly common in its small range in Montezuma County, though data for the latter area are scant. It appears to be tolerant of—even partially dependent upon—disturbances (e.g., fires, or cattle and bison grazing) that create areas of bare ground. Thick grass cover that develops after the cessation of cattle grazing reduces habitat suitability and results in population declines (Ballinger and Jones 1985; Ballinger and Watts 1995). Though this species does not require pristine habitat, it does not occur or is greatly reduced in the many areas in eastern Colorado now subject to large-scale intensive cultivation. However, a large

extent of suitable habitat remains, and this lizard should remain a common element of the fauna of Colorado for the foreseeable future.

In a section of prairie in El Paso County, the lesser earless lizard was second in abundance only to the many-lined skink in pitfall trap samples (Banta and Torbit 1965). In western Nebraska, Jones and Ballinger (1987) recorded population densities (not counting hatchlings) of 8–34 per hectare (average 20 per hectare) in late May–early June and 8–28 per hectare (average 18 per hectare) in late July–early August (Jones and Ballinger 1987).

Habitat. Lesser earless lizards inhabit sandhills, sandy or gravelly areas along streams, plains grassland having a sparse cover of grass and low shrubs, prairie-dog towns, and other relatively flat areas with expanses of open ground. These lizards occur regularly along dirt roads in the rangelands of eastern Colorado. The largest populations typically are in areas dominated by sandy soils. Similarly, in western Nebraska, the major habitat is open sparse grassland (Jones and Droge 1980). Periods of cold and excessively hot weather are spent underground. Vaughan (1961) reported that these lizards sometimes hide in pocket gopher (Geomyidae) burrows but seem to prefer the smaller burrows of pocket mice *(Perognathus)*. The burrows of kangaroo rats *(Dipodomys ordii)* (Gehlbach 1965) and other mammals also are used. Sometimes earless lizards bury themselves by plunging headfirst into the soil and wriggling the body until hidden.

Plate 8.28. Gravid female lesser earless lizard (Bent County, Colorado).

Home range size averages about 0.4–0.5 ha in males and about 0.2–0.4 ha in females, with both intersexual and intrasexual overlap, especially at high population densities (Nebraska [Jones and Droge 1980], Arizona [Hulse 1985]). Lesser earless lizards exhibit no evidence of well-developed territorial behavior.

Activity. The annual period of activity in Colorado usually extends from late March or April through October, with November activity possible if warm weather prevails. Individuals active in fall are primarily juveniles. Spring emergence generally occurs in early to mid-April in western Nebraska, and activity continues through mid-October, with a few records as early as mid-March and as late as mid-November (Jones and Ballinger 1987). Activity from late March or early April to early November is the norm in eastern New Mexico (Gennaro 1974).

Activity generally is diurnal, though rarely individuals are found on roads at night (Degenhardt, Painter, and Price 1996). In summer, activity tends to peak in the morning and late afternoon; the hottest part of the day is spent inactive in the shade. Individuals sometimes avoid the heat by climbing into vegetation. On typical summer days in western Kansas, peaks in activity occur between 11:00 a.m. and noon and between 4:00 p.m. and 5:00 p.m. (Werth 1972). In Lincoln County, Livo (pers. comm.) observed 19 of these lizards basking on an 8.4-mile stretch of rural highway between 1:30–2:00 p.m. at an air temperature of 24°C. Activity tends not to occur where air or soil temperature exceeds 39–40°C (Dixon 1967; Sena 1978). In Nebraska, body temperatures of active individuals averaged 36°C (Jones and Ballinger 1987). In Colorado, three active adults that I captured had body temperatures of 32.6, 34.8, and 37.0°C. Individuals active during hot weather may stand high on extended limbs.

Reproduction and Growth. Courtship interactions include bobbing displays by the males; unreceptive females perform sidling hopping movements. Based on studies of a related species, the unique coloration of adult females probably identifies them as such to courting males and also may convey information about the female's reproductive status (Cooper 1986).

Breeding in Colorado may begin in late April or early May. In Weld County, Cuellar and Fawcett (1971) found that the sex organs of males were near maximum size and filled with sperm by early May.

Oviposition occurs primarily in June and July. Females containing 3–6 large eggs have been found in Colorado from early June through mid-July. A female (54 mm SVL) collected in late June in Arapahoe County laid four eggs in early July. A female from Otero County laid six eggs on July 11. In Nebraska, yearlings produced a single clutch in mid- to late July; older females produced two clutches per year from late May or early June through late July (Jones, Ballinger, and Porter 1987; Jones and Ballinger 1987). In eastern New Mexico, a female deposited a clutch in mid-June and another in July (Gennaro 1974).

Clutch size in this species increases from north to south, averaging 3–4 eggs in Nebraska (Droge, Jones, and Ballinger 1982), 5 in Kansas (Fitch 1970), 6 in Texas (Walker 1965), and 7 in New Mexico (Gennaro 1974). In Nebraska, yearlings averaging 47–52 mm SVL produced clutches averaging 3 eggs; older females averaging 51–60 mm SVL produced clutches averaging 4–6 eggs (Jones, Ballinger, and Porter 1987). In New Mexico, a 60-mm-SVL female contained an exceptionally large clutch of 9 oviductal eggs on July 4 (Parker 1973).

Hatchlings have been observed in Colorado as early as July 8, but most seem to appear in August. Bauerle (1971) found hatchlings from late August to mid-September in northeastern Colorado. In Nebraska, hatchlings emerge in late July or early August, and hatching continues through mid-September (Jones and Ballinger 1987). Hatchlings are first evident from early July to late August in eastern New Mexico; they grow quickly and double their SVL prior to hibernation (Gennaro 1974).

In western Nebraska, survivorship up to the age of one year is very low (4–33 percent, average 16 percent), but an average of more than 50 percent of the yearlings survive until at least their third calendar year (Jones and Ballinger 1987). Females in Nebraska initiate reproduction at an age of 10.5–11.0 months, after reaching 41–43 mm SVL (Droge, Jones, and Ballinger 1982; Jones and Ballinger 1987). The age of maturity is one year in Kansas, Texas, and New Mexico; size at maturity is 45 mm in Texas and New Mexico (Walker 1965; Fitch 1970; Gennaro 1974). Males in Nebraska have enlarged testes by the age of seven months (at an average length of 34 mm SVL).

The population turnover rate is high. In Nebraska and New Mexico, the majority of breeders are yearlings (Gennaro 1974; Jones and Ballinger 1987). Females in Nebraska live a maximum of four years, and some males live five years. Mortality appears to be greatest during the overwintering period.

Food. Earless lizards feed opportunistically on various small invertebrates. Grasshoppers, bugs, ants, Lepidoptera, beetles, and spiders often compose a significant portion of the diet in Kansas and New Mexico, and adults occasionally eat hatchling lizards *(e.g., Sceloporus, Cnemidophorus)* (Burt 1928b; Dixon and Medica 1966; Werth 1972). In western Nebraska, food generally does not appear to be a limiting resource (Jones and Ballinger 1987).

Known predators in Colorado include the burrowing owl *(Athene cunicularia)* and loggerhead shrike *(Lanius ludovicianus)* (R. Ryder, pers. comm.). In western Nebraska, Jones and Ballinger (1987) found a hatchling in the stomach of a six-lined racerunner but in general found that predation on this species is low. The longnose leopard lizard is a known predator in New Mexico (Degenhardt, Painter, and Price 1996). Other potential predators include western hognose snake, racer, bullsnake, milk snake, western rattlesnake, and various hawks and carnivorous mammals, including the northern grasshopper mouse *(Onychomys leucogaster)* (Jones and Ballinger 1987).

Taxonomy and Variation. According to the traditional classification, *Holbrookia maculata maculata* Girard, 1851, is the subspecies in eastern Colorado and *H. m. approximans* Baird, 1858, is represented in southwestern Colorado. The former tends to have pale stripes on the dorsum, whereas in the latter the dorsum may be strongly speckled. However, many *maculata* in Colorado are just as spotted along the sides as *approximans,* and some of the latter have only a few spots. Single localities throughout the range of the species commonly exhibit a wide range of variation in coloration, and many individuals do not conform with the characteristics of the subspecies to which they are assigned or are identical to individuals of other subspecies that occur elsewhere in the range (Gehlbach 1965; Taylor 1982). Thus, the named subspecies of *Holbrookia maculata* do not appear to represent distinct evolutionary lineages and probably should not be given taxonomic recognition.

Plate 8.29. Adult Texas horned lizard (Otero County, Colorado).

Texas Horned Lizard
Phrynosoma cornutum (Harlan, 1825)

Recognition. Body wide and flattened; spines at back of head much longer than width at base; two rows of enlarged scales fringing each side of body; dark bars radiate from eye; adults may have yellow suffusion on chest and sides, in front of vent, and on dorsum; in Colorado, most adults are less than 80 mm SVL, but a few females reach 85–95 mm SVL (pers. obs.); dorsal coloration typically cryptic against prevailing soil color. *Mature male:* underside of base of tail with two hemipenial swellings; sometimes with enlarged postanal scales; tail length averages longer than that of female. *Hatchling:* usually around 26–32

mm SVL, 35–45 mm TL (Montgomery and Mackessy, in Mackessy 1998); head spines initially absent but grow quickly. *Eggs:* average about 14 mm x 9 mm (Vitt 1977); oviductal eggs 11–14 mm x 6–9 mm in Texas (Ballinger 1974).

Distribution. Colorado, Kansas, and southwestern Missouri south through southeastern Arizona, New Mexico, Oklahoma, Arkansas, and Texas to northern Mexico; introduced and apparently established in several areas in the southeastern United

Map 8.9. Distribution of the Texas horned lizard in Colorado.

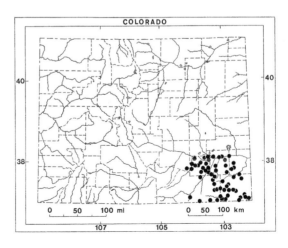

States (Price 1990). Occurs chiefly south of the Arkansas River at elevations below about 6,000 feet (1,830 m) in southeastern Colorado. Cope's (1900) records of *P. cornutum* from Archuleta and El Paso counties are based on *P. hernandesi* (see Chapter 1; also, Hammerson 1984). This species periodically is picked up by travelers and released in areas outside the natural range. I regard records from the cities of Fort Collins, Boulder, and Denver (Ellis and Henderson 1913; Maslin 1959; Smith, Maslin, and Brown 1965), far from other known populations, invalid due to the likelihood that the specimens were translocated (Maslin 1959; Hammerson 1984; Livo, Hammerson, and Smith 1998).

The Texas horned lizard and short-horned lizard have essentially complementary ranges in Colorado; the ranges meet but do not overlap to any large degree (Hammerson 1982c). Recent surveys confirm this pattern (Mackessy 1998; Montgomery 1998). Both species are represented by records from Trinidad, Las Animas County, but the Texas horned lizard apparently has not been found there subsequent to Ellis and Henderson's (1913) original record. The specimens probably came from two different locations in the general vicinity of Trinidad, and the Texas horned lizard likely was collected some distance away in eastern Las Animas County.

Conservation Status. This species has virtually disappeared from areas in eastern Texas where it formerly was widespread and abundant. Population declines and/or local extirpations also have occurred in other areas of Texas and in parts of Oklahoma. Intensive agriculture, habitat alterations, collecting for the pet and curio trades, and indiscriminate use of insecticides to combat introduced fire ants have been suggested as possible explanations for the lizard declines (Price 1990; Donaldson, Price, and Morse 1994). In Colorado, recent intensive surveys by personnel from the University of Northern Colorado (Mackessy 1998; Montgomery 1998), the Colorado Natural Heritage Program, and me indicate that Texas horned lizards remain widespread and fairly common in their historic range. They

still occur in many sites in the Oklahoma panhandle (Mark Lomolino, pers. comm., 1997).

Humans seem to find horned lizards irresistibly attractive and often bring them home as pets. The magnitude and impact of such collecting (now illegal without a proper license) probably is severe in heavily used recreation areas but insignificant in most parts of the range. Horned lizards are relatively difficult to maintain in good health in captivity, and many adopted as pets die of starvation. They should not be removed from the wild.

Vehicular traffic is a serious threat to some local populations, resulting in many deaths (Mackessy 1998; pers. obs.); fortunately, however, most of the habitat in Colorado is not traversed by busy roads. The major potential threat appears to be large-scale intensive cultivation, which is incompatible with viable horned lizard populations. The Texas horned lizard tolerates, and even thrives on, the usual levels of livestock grazing on native grasslands. The species should remain secure in Colorado if ranching remains the primary land use in the existing prairie habitats in southeastern Colorado.

Desert populations fluctuate in abundance, perhaps following cycles in availability of their primary prey, harvester ants (Price 1990). In southern New Mexico and Texas, density of adults generally is about 1–3 per hectare (Worthington 1972; Whiting, Dixon, and Murray 1993) but may reach nearly 30 per hectare in some years (Whitford and Creusere 1977). Henke and Montemayor (1998) captured 692 individuals over four years during systematic sampling along a 19.5-km road transect in southern Texas; only 43 individuals were recaptured.

Small juveniles are relatively scarce (or at least difficult to detect) nearly everywhere. For example, out of 689 individuals captured over four years in southern Texas, none was less than 61 mm SVL (Henke and Montemayor 1997). In Colorado, Montgomery and Mackessy found 17 hatchlings among a total of 298 individuals (in Mackessy 1998).

Fair and Henke (1997a) discussed capture methods used for a low-density population in Texas.

Habitat. The Texas horned lizard is a ground-dwelling species that inhabits plains grassland in Colorado, especially where there are large patches of bare ground. The soil may be sandy, gravelly, or loamy. This lizard often is observed on paved and dirt roads within such areas. Ample bare ground, such as results from livestock grazing, is a characteristic feature of the habitat throughout the range (Whiting, Dixon, and Murray 1993; Fair and Henke 1997b), though these lizards generally are absent from areas that are barren due to extensive plowing. In Colorado, the lower limit of juniper growth often marks the upper limit of the habitat in canyons and at the foot of mesas. Nighttime is spent buried in the soil or in rodent burrows. Rarely, south of Colorado, Texas horned lizards have been found 1–2 m aboveground on tree trunks at night and/or after heavy rainfall (Sheffield and Carter 1994). Winter is spent underground.

Activity. In Colorado, emergence from hibernation occurs by mid-April if conditions are warm enough, compared to usually the third week in March in southern Texas (Henke and Montemayor 1998). Activity continues during suitably warm weather through spring and summer. In southern Texas, Henke and Montemayor (1998) recorded the largest number of captures in May, followed by June and July. The annual period of activity in Colorado generally ends by late September but may extend into warm periods in October. Activity usually ceases in early to mid-October in southern Texas (Henke and Montemayor 1998).

Daily activity in Colorado typically begins from 8:00–8:30 a.m., though it may start as early as 7:30 a.m. (pers. obs.). Whitford and Bryant (1979) found no activity before 8:00 a.m. (about two hours after sunrise) in southern New Mexico, but activity sometimes takes place as early as 6:30 a.m. in southern Texas (Henke and Montemayor 1998). In Colorado, as in Texas (Henke and Montemayor 1998),

midday activity is characteristic of the cooler months. In summer, activity is most intense in mid- to late morning or early afternoon, and basking occurs in the morning and late afternoon. A midafternoon lull in activity is typical of the warmest months, though individuals sometimes can be found on asphalt roads even on hot summer afternoons. In May in southern Texas, Henke and Montemayor (1998) encountered Texas horned lizards most frequently in the afternoon and early evening; in June and July, they encountered them most often in the morning.

These lizards seek shade under vegetation or climb into plants to escape hot ground temperatures (Whitford and Bryant 1979). In Colorado, body temperatures of 16 active individuals ranged from 22.7–44.7°C (average 34–35°C) (pers. obs.); the unusually low temperature of 22.7°C was from an individual found on a road at 8:20 p.m. Pianka and Parker (1975) reported an average body temperature of 37–38°C for active individuals.

Activity generally ceases in early evening, but on a few occasions, I have found Texas horned lizards crouched on warm pavement in Colorado at dusk or after dark; the lizards ran quickly off the road when I approached on foot. Henke and Montemayor (1998) found these lizards on roads in southern Texas as late as 8:46 p.m. in June. Williams (1959) reported that nocturnal activity results from disturbance or other abnormal conditions, but I regard activity at dusk as natural, though atypical, behavior. In general, lizard activity coincides with the activity period of the prey, harvester ants.

Horned lizards are well camouflaged and in the natural habitat difficult to spot until they move. They tend to freeze until nearly stepped on, then bolt for cover. They can run rather quickly, considering their relatively short legs, but generally are not difficult to capture by hand. Individuals that I have caught have responded by raising the head and jabbing the spines into my hand, by biting (rarely), or by spurting blood onto my shirt. This blood originates from the lower eyelid. Blood-squirting apparently most often occurs during tactile stimulation

Plate 8.30. Adult Texas horned lizard (Las Animas County, Colorado).

by a coyote *(Canis latrans)* or fox *(Vulpes)*; attacks by roadrunners and grasshopper mice do not elicit this behavior (Middendorf and Sherbrooke 1992). Presumably, it protects horned lizards from canid predation because the blood is distasteful (Cowles and Bakker 1977:161–162). Time of day and lizard body temperature have no impact on blood-squirting behavior. In Texas, 4 of 56 males and 3 of 41 females ejected blood when handled by researchers (Lambert and Ferguson 1985).

Combative interactions sometimes occur between adult males and may include head bobbing, push-up displays, mutual retreat, chasing, climbing atop the other individual, scratching, licking, and jabbing with the horns, which may result in bleeding puncture wounds (Whitford and Whitford 1973; Whitford and Bryant 1979). Peslak (1986) observed a larger male atop a smaller male, with the former holding one of the latter's horns in its jaws, but no struggle or horn stabbing was evident.

During daytime or nighttime rainfall, Texas horned lizards sometimes adopt a head-down, arched-back posture with lateral spreading of the body. This results in water running over the skin and toward the mouth, where it is taken in as the jaws open and close (Sherbrooke 1990b).

Home range size and movements seem quite variable. Munger (1984a) found that single-season home range size in southern Arizona averaged 1.3 ha in females and 2.4 ha in males. Home range length often was 100–300 m and sometimes extended up to 400 m. Some individuals that were observed

more than 30 times moved over an area less than 55 m across, but not all lizards remained in a limited area. Overlap of home ranges occurred but was not extensive. In southern New Mexico, home range size was about 1 ha or less (Worthington 1972). Whitford and Bryant (1979) recorded movements of 9–91 m per day (average 47 m) in New Mexico. Individuals followed a zigzagging course and rarely crossed their own path. In Colorado, Montgomery and Mackessy (in Mackessy 1998) reported that a juvenile moved approximately 100 m in two days. Another juvenile was recaptured 480 m from its original capture location after 47 days.

Reproduction and Growth. Mating occurs probably in May or June. Montgomery and Mackessy (in Mackessy 1998) observed adult male-female pairs on June 21 in Colorado, though courtship behavior was not evident. Degenhardt, Painter, and Price (1996) observed a copulating pair in late May in southern New Mexico. During copulation, the male holds the temporal horn of the female in his jaws (Milne 1938).

Evidence from Texas and New Mexico (Ballinger 1974; Howard 1974; Pianka and Parker 1975; Degenhardt, Painter, and Price 1996) suggests that most oviposition occurs in late May, June, and July. Montgomery and Mackessy (in Mackessy 1998) reported that a female found in Colorado in late May contained shelled eggs, suggesting possible nesting in late May or early June. I found a Colorado female that contained small yolking follicles on June 10, suggesting egg deposition in late June or July. In Texas, individuals apparently produced only one clutch per year, but this was not conclusively demonstrated (Ballinger 1974). In the relatively short activity season of Colorado, individual females have time to produce only a single clutch per year. Eggs are laid in nests dug in tunnels about 15–20 cm below the ground surface (Ramsey 1956).

Texas horned lizards appear to be prolific breeders in the southern part of their range. In Arizona, New Mexico, and Texas, clutch size averages 24–29 eggs (range up to 49) (Ballinger 1974; Pianka and Parker 1975). Clutches are smaller in Colorado. Montgomery and Mackessy (in Mackessy 1998) found a dead-on-the-road, 75-cm-SVL female containing six shelled eggs (other eggs may have been lost), and I observed an 85-mm-SVL female that contained 14 yolking follicles.

Montgomery and Mackessy (in Mackessy 1998) found newly emerged hatchlings in Colorado from mid-August to mid-September. Hatching in New Mexico also occurs in August-September (Degenhardt, Painter, and Price 1996).

In areas south of Colorado, females and males generally attain sexual maturity at an age of just under two years (third calendar year) at about 7 cm SVL (Ballinger 1974; Howard 1974; Pianka and Parker 1975). In Colorado, where this lizard is relatively small, size at maturity likely is closer to 6 cm SVL. First reproduction probably occurs in the third calendar year (possibly the fourth in some individuals), based on the presence of individuals less than 6 cm SVL throughout the summer, including some not much larger than hatchling size as late as June, and some just reaching 5 cm SVL in mid-August (pers. obs.; Mackessy 1998). Maximum longevity is at least nine years in captivity (Baur 1986).

Food and Predators. Harvester ants (*Pogonomyrmex* spp.) generally are the primary prey (Pianka and Parker 1975; Whitford and Bryant 1979; Munger 1984b; Montgomery 1998), but other small arthropods also may be eaten and sometimes constitute the more significant portion of the diet (Milstead and Tinkle 1969). The stomachs of road-killed individuals that I found in southeastern Colorado contained primarily harvester ants but also a few bugs and beetles. In New Mexico, Cohen and Cohen (1990) observed an adult eat without ill effect 11 large blister beetles (Meloidae), which contain a terpenoid compound that is generally regarded as toxic to vertebrates.

Ants are ingested quickly without chewing. Foraging on ants may occur at colony entrances, along ant columns, or opportunistically elsewhere, and a lizard may visit more than one colony in a single day (Whitford and Bryant 1979; Munger 1984b). Individual horned lizards generally do not decimate single ant colonies; doing so not only would reduce aboveground ant activity but would be imprudent if the colonies are to be used as a long-term resource (Whitford and Bryant 1979; Munger 1984c). In Arizona, most lizards spend less than 30 minutes at any given colony and generally eat up to several dozen ants during a single feeding, though one female ate 171 ants in 26 minutes (Munger 1984b). In New Mexico, Whitford and Bryant (1979) found that on a daily basis, individual lizards ingest an average of 71 ants of up to four different species (Whitford and Bryant 1979). Hatchlings eat just a few ants, then retreat to vegetative shelter for 20–30 minutes before feeding again (Whitford and Bryant 1979). One might wonder how horned lizards cope with the potent sting of harvester ants. Schmidt, Sherbrooke, and Schmidt (1989) discovered that the blood of horned lizards contains a factor not common among reptiles in general that makes them resistant to the sting venom.

These lizards appear to be sensitive to climate-associated variations in food supply. For example, drought may reduce food availability and result in lizard weight losses (Whitford and Bryant 1979).

Little information exists on predation on Texas horned lizards. Montgomery and Mackessy (in Mackessy 1998) recorded predation by the loggerhead shrike *(Lanius ludovicianus)* and Swainson's hawk *(Buteo swainsoni)* in Colorado. The former species also has been documented as a predator in extreme northern Chihuahua, Mexico (Lemos Espinal et al. 1998). Swainson's hawks eviscerate the lizards and leave the spiny head behind (Pilz 1983). Grasshopper mice *(Onychomys* spp.) are capable of killing juveniles during predatory attacks (Sherbrooke 1991). Roadrunners *(Geococcyx californianus)* can kill and eat adults (Sherbrooke 1990a). Responses of the horned lizards to attack included fleeing, inflating the lungs, hissing, opening the mouth, charging, biting, flattening and tilting the body, and displaying or thrusting the horns. In the grasp of a predator, the horns may be raised and the back arched, which may inhibit ingestion by the predator (Sherbrooke 1987). Munger (1986) recorded two instances of predation by coyote *(Canis latrans)* or fox *(Vulpes)* in Arizona. Degen-hardt, Painter, and Price (1996) listed the Harris hawk *(Parabuteo unicinctus)*, road-runner, and coachwhip as known predators in New Mexico.

Remarks. Horned lizards may look fero-cious, but they are harmless to humans.

Taxonomy and Variation. No subspecies have been described. Montgomery (1998) described rangewide patterns of clinal variation.

Plate 8.31. Short-horned lizard (Weld County, Colorado).

Short-horned Lizard
Phrynosoma hernandesi (Girard, 1858)

Recognition. Body wide and flattened; spines at back of head approximately same length as width at base; one row of enlarged scales fringing each side of body; dorsal coloration usually blends cryptically with soil; maximum size about 15 cm TL. *Mature male:* underside of base of tail with two hemipenial swellings; sometimes with enlarged postanal scales; tail proportionally longer than that of female. *Newborn young:* usually 20–26 mm SVL in Colorado and northwestern New Mexico (Burt 1933a;

Gehlbach 1965; pers. obs.); average 24 mm SVL for one litter from southwestern Wyoming (Ashton and Ashton 1998); in Boulder County, up to about 38 mm SVL prior to first hibernation; 30–33 mm TL in Utah (Tanner 1953); coloration pink or gray in southwestern Wyoming (Ashton and Ashton 1998).

Distribution. Extreme southern Alberta and Saskatchewan south through Montana, Wyoming, the western Dakotas, eastern Nevada, Utah, Colorado, western Nebraska, Arizona, New Mexico, and western Texas to south-central Mexico (Zamudio, Jones, and Ward 1997). Occurs throughout most of western, southern, and eastern Colorado; absent from the high mountains in the central part of the state and from all or most of extreme eastern Colorado. Range meets that of the Texas horned lizard in southeastern Colorado. Occurs at elevations below 5,700 feet (1,740 m) in northeastern Colorado but in mountainous areas elsewhere in the state, it ranges to at least 8,500 feet (2,575 m). Reaches 11,000 feet (3,355 m) in La Plata County (A. Spencer, pers. comm.). Gehlbach (1965) found this species at an elevation of 11,300 feet (3,445 m) in northwestern New Mexico. Barry's (1932a) Baca County record of a short-horned lizard has not been confirmed by additional observations and is not included on the map. A published record of *P. hernandesi* from Bent County (Secoy and Brown 1968) is based on a misidentified *P. cornutum* (Hammerson 1982b).

Conservation Status. Scanty evidence suggests that short-horned lizards still occur throughout most of their broad historic range in Colorado. They are locally fairly common in some areas, but in most of the range they are seldom encountered. Finding more than one adult in a single day is unusual in most areas. This apparent scarcity may be due to their cryptic coloration and behavior, naturally low population density, and highly localized distribution. The relatively few records I have for the 1970s–1990s are greatly outnumbered by earlier records. This is due at least partly to the decrease in collecting for museums that has taken place

in recent decades. Adequate survey effort in the historic range usually reveals that the lizards are still present. For example, intensive surveys in southeastern Colorado during 1995–1997 yielded dozens of sightings in areas where there were relatively few historical collections (Mackessy 1998). Nevertheless, all recent observations of this species should be brought to my attention or that of the Colorado Division of Wildlife to better determine the present statewide conservation status.

Localized extirpation has occurred in areas of intensive cultivation and in urban areas such as most of the Denver metropolitan region. Habitat degradation and increased vehicular traffic due to oil and gas exploration and development probably have reduced populations in some areas. Rangeland "improvements" such as clearing sagebrush and replacing it with grass communities can result in population declines of short-horned lizards (Reynolds 1979). Despite these various local threats, large areas of apparently suitable habitat remain throughout the range in Colorado. The preferred habitat in lowland areas and many upland regions generally corresponds with areas used for livestock grazing, which appears to be compatible with the persistence of short-horned lizard populations. The use of pesticides for grasshopper control on rangelands is a potential threat, due to direct toxic effects on the lizards and impacts on their food resources.

Humans generally find horned lizards irresistibly attractive and often bring them home as pets (Douglas 1966). The magnitude and impact of such collecting (now illegal without a proper license) probably is severe in heavily used recreation areas but insignificant in most

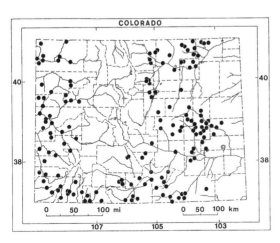

Map 8.10. Distribution of the short-horned lizard in Colorado.

Plate 8.32. Short-horned lizard (San Juan County, Utah).

parts of the range. Horned lizards are relatively difficult to maintain in good health in captivity, and many that are adopted as pets die of starvation.

Habitat. Short-horned lizards occur in diverse habitats over their broad geographic range in Colorado. Habitats include short-grass prairie, sagebrush, semidesert shrubland, shale barrens, piñon-juniper woodland, pine-oak woodland, oak-grass associations, and open conifer forests in the mountains (Harris 1963; Douglas 1966; pers. obs.). Sparse vegetation at ground level and easy access to sunlight are among the most important habitat features. Soil texture may vary from sandy to rocky, though rocky habitats generally have at least some patches of soft soil or underground access via rodent burrows. Clark et al. (1982) found this species common at Gunnison's prairie-dog towns. Periods of inactivity are spent underground (in rodent burrows or similar sites) or buried in the soil.

Activity. In Colorado, short-horned lizards are active during warm daylight hours usually from about mid-April into September, and at lower elevations into mid-October. Most individuals still active in fall are juveniles. A similar seasonal activity pattern occurs in southeastern Idaho (Guyer and Linder 1985). In summer, these lizards seek shelter at midday if conditions are hot. In La Plata County, Albert Spencer (pers. comm.) observed one lizard active on warm ground during a heavy snow squall in mid-September.

This lizard often closely matches the color of the soil and is highly cryptic until it moves (except where conspicuous on roads). Defensive behavior includes open-mouth hissing and enlargement of the body through inflation of the lungs. When handled, some individuals may squirt blood from tissue at the margin of the eye (Mackessy 1998). Blood squirting is discussed further in the account of the Texas horned lizard.

Average body temperature of active short-horned lizards from various parts of the range is 32–35°C (Pianka and Parker 1975; Guyer and Linder 1985; Powell and Russell 1985b). Phillips and Harlow (1981) found that under experimental conditions, short-horned lizards from Colorado consistently retreat from hot substrates when body temperature reaches 37–39°C.

Movement patterns are poorly known. In Utah, a juvenile displaced 400 m from its capture location returned to that site after 280 days (Pianka and Parker 1975).

Reproduction and Growth. Courtship behavior has been observed in Colorado in mid-April (D. Woelfel, pers. comm.) and in early May in southeastern Idaho (Guyer and Linder 1985). Montanucci and Baur (1982) described courtship behavior of this species. Courtship involves head bobbing by both sexes, and the male may lick the female's head and neck. The male typically grasps the neck skin of the female in his mouth before curling his tail under the female's tail and thrusting a hemipenis into her cloaca. The whole process lasts about five minutes. Females may become unreceptive to males shortly after mating, though some females may mate more than once within a period of a few days. An unreceptive female may run away, seek shelter, bury into the soil, roll onto her back, or stand with the tail elevated (sometimes wagging). Males sometimes elevate the tail if approached by a larger male or female.

Plate 8.33. Short-horned lizard (Rio
Blanco County, Colorado).

Unlike other lizards in Colorado, the short-horned lizard does not lay eggs—it gives birth to live young. The eggs develop inside the female during spring and early summer, and in Colorado the young are born in late July or, more commonly, in August after a gestation period of about three months. August births seem to be the norm throughout much of the range (Burt 1933a; V. Tanner 1942; W. Tanner 1953, 1954; Harris 1963; Douglas 1966; Goldberg 1973; Pianka and Parker 1975; Guyer and Linder 1985; Ashton and Ashton 1998), but births peak around the end of July in southern Alberta (Powell and Russell 1991). Gehlbach (1965) reported an amazingly early parturition date of June 25 for a female from northwestern New Mexico.

For 12 Colorado females I examined, litter sizes, based primarily on large-yolked follicles or oviductal embryos, ranged from 13–24 (average 17); five litters of live neonates ranged from 14–18. These numbers are consistent with average litter sizes of 16–17 reported by Goldberg (1973) and Pianka and Parker (1975). In Utah, four litters included 7, 8, 13, and 13 young (Tanner 1942, 1953, 1954). In northwestern New Mexico, Gehlbach (1965) found that six females produced litters of 6–21 young (average 12). A 70-mm-SVL female from southwestern Wyoming produced a litter of 13 young (four stillborn) (Ashton and Ashton 1998). In Alberta, females produced relatively small litters of 6–11 live neonates (average 8.5) (Powell and Russell 1991). At the other end of the scale, litter sizes of up to 48 newborns (average 23–24) were reported by Howard (1974) for females from the southwestern United States and Mexico.

Neonates quickly shed their surrounding membranes and yolk sac and make feeding attempts within 1–2 hours of birth (Powell and Russell 1991). Gehlbach (1965) observed a female give birth to 10 young in a period of 10 minutes; all of the young dug down into the soil as soon as they were free of the membranes.

The following examples illustrate the growth rate of marked individuals in natural habitat in Utah (Pianka and Parker 1975). A neonate male grew from 30 mm SVL in early September to 42 mm SVL in mid-June of the next year. A female grew from 56 mm SVL in late June to 73 mm SVL in early August of the same year.

The size structure of the population and the presence of small nonreproductive individuals throughout the summer months indicate that lizards in Boulder County and probably most of Colorado begin breeding just before the age of two (their third calendar year). In Colorado, gravid females generally are at least 63 mm SVL, except in the San Luis Valley, where females as small as 49 mm SVL are reproductive and probably at least two years old (smaller nonreproductive individuals are present throughout the summer). Elsewhere in the range, the minimum size of pregnant females is about 64–66 mm SVL, and the minimum age at maturity is about two years (Goldberg 1971; Pianka and Parker 1975; Powell and Russell 1991). The minimum size of reproductive males is reported as 59–62 mm SVL (Howard 1974; Pianka and Parker 1975).

Food and Predators. Ants generally dominate the diet of this lizard, with miscellaneous other insects and spiders consumed in lesser amounts (Knowlton 1934; Pianka and Parker 1975), though individuals may gorge themselves on a single food that happens to be easily available. The stomach of a short-horned lizard found dead at Mesa Verde, Montezuma County, contained ants (Douglas 1966). In northeastern Colorado, Evans and O'Neill (1986) observed several short-horned lizards feeding on swarming male *Bembecinus* wasps. The diet at opposite ends of the range in southern Alberta and northern Mexico is dominated by ants, beetles, and small grasshoppers (Montanucci 1981; Powell and Russell 1984).

Few records of predation are available. Douglas (1966) found a young short-horned lizard in the stomach of a striped whipsnake at Mesa Verde. Marti (1974) found that the burrowing owl *(Athene cunicularia)* sometimes preys on short-horned lizards in Colorado.

Taxonomy and Variation. Zamudio, Jones, and Ward (1997) examined mtDNA variation in short-horned lizards throughout western North America and concluded that the Pacific Northwest segment of the population should be recognized as a distinct species *(P. douglasii)*. In addition, there was no genetic support for the recognition of any of the nominal subspecies. I found (1981) that the formerly recognized subspecies of short-horned lizards in Colorado could not be distinguished adequately using the morphological criteria of Reeve (1952). Dorsal coloration and relative spine length (see following paragraph) correlate more closely with local soil characteristics and body size than with partic-

ular geographic regions. Similarly, Eaton (1935), Gehlbach (1965), and Hahn (1968) found that two of the nominal subspecies (*hernandesi* and *ornatissimum*) were not clearly distinguishable. Degenhardt, Painter, and Price (1996) reviewed some of the confusion surrounding these two subspecies. The genetic data of Zamudio et al. (1997), in combination with doubtful morphological distinctions, demonstrate that the traditionally recognized subspecies of short-horned lizards do not warrant taxonomic recognition.

The most striking geographically coherent pattern of variation in *P. hernandesi* in Colorado involves the exceptionally small body size of the San Luis Valley population (first noted by Hahn [1968]). The dwarfed condition of these individuals is especially noteworthy when compared to populations as little as 50–115 km to the east, where short-horned lizards grow as large as they do anywhere in North America (Table 8.1). The small size of short-horned lizards in the San Luis Valley is not an artifact of including only juveniles in the sample; several of the females in the sample were pregnant. Zamudio et al. (1997) did not examine the genetic characteristics of the San Luis Valley population, so the taxonomic status of this possibly unique population remains unknown.

Still unresolved are suitable English names for *P. douglasii* and *P. hernandesi*. The widely used name for the former subspecies *douglasii* ("pygmy short-horned

	Mean SVL	Maximum SVL
Northeastern Colorado		
Males (23)	55	64
Females (29)	58	86
Southeastern Colorado		
Males (6)	58	73
Females (13)	74	94*
San Luis Valley		
Males (16)	43	51
Females (16)	54	66
Western Colorado		
Males (18)	52	70
Females (22)	64	100

* Near Raton Pass in Las Animas County, Colorado, Kerfoot (1962) found a female that was 104 mm SVL.

Table 8.1. Body size of short-horned lizards in Colorado (Hammerson 1981). Data are for preserved museum specimens exceeding 30 mm SVL (sample sizes in parentheses).

lizard") probably should be used for *P. douglasii* (the spelling "pygmy" is preferred). Because of the wide distribution, broad habitat tolerance, and variable body size of *P. hernandesi,* I feel that the English names for other former subspecies of short-horned lizards (e.g., mountain, eastern, Salt Lake) are inappropriate for *P. hernandesi.* So, for now, I prefer to call this species simply "short-horned lizard."

Plate 8.34. Adult roundtail horned lizard (Otero County, Colorado). *David Schmidt and Cindy Ramotnik.*

Roundtail Horned Lizard

Phrynosoma modestum (Girard, in Baird and Girard, 1852)

Recognition. Back of head with four enlarged spines of about equal length; tail cylindrical and banded; sides of body between forelimbs and hind limbs lack a fringe of enlarged scales; dorsum grayish, brownish, yellowish, reddish, or bluish (hue often matches soil color), with dark blotch on each side of neck and on body just in front of each hind limb (patterning may change with temperature); maximum SVL about 6.6 cm in males, 7.1 cm in females (Fitch 1981). This lizard's unusual color pattern and behavior, including a humpbacked posture when immobile, cause it to strongly resemble a small stone (Stebbins 1985; Sherbrooke and Montanucci 1988). *Mature male:* two bulges of hemipenes evident at base of tail; enlarged postanal scales may be present. *Hatchling:* 21–30 mm SVL (Degenhardt, Painter, and Price 1996).

Distribution. Southeastern Arizona, New Mexico, and western and central Texas south into central northern Mexico; apparently disjunct populations occur in the westernmost portion of the Oklahoma panhandle and in southeastern Colorado. Known distribution in Colorado is restricted to a small area several kilometers south-southeast of Fowler in extreme northwestern Otero County at an elevation of about 4,500 feet (1,370 m) (Ramotnik 1998). There may be other undetected populations, but if so, they must be few and localized, given the extensive field surveys that have been conducted in southeastern Colorado by me, Lauren Livo, Hobart Smith, personnel from the University of Northern Colorado (Mackessy 1998), and others.

A record from the "Wet Mountain country" of Custer County (Ellis and Henderson 1913) is based on a specimen, now lost, collected by T.D.A. Cockerell and identified by an unknown individual. Maslin (1959) regarded this record as doubtful. If the collection site was in the mountains or in the high Wet Mountain Valley, then the lizard certainly must have been *P. hernandesi*, which occurs in those areas, and not the lowland species *P. modestum*. However, given the recently confirmed occurrence of *P. modestum* in Otero Country, an occurrence in the lowlands of extreme northeastern Custer County, where elevations are about 6,000 feet (1,830 m), seems remotely possible.

P. modestum, along with other warm-climate species, occurred in southwestern Kansas during the Pleistocene, prior to the last major period of glaciation (Hibbard and Taylor 1960; Hibbard 1970). At that time, it also may have occurred in southeastern Colorado. The existing population in Colorado may be a relic of that formerly more northern distribution, but more likely the species was extirpated from Colorado during the last glaciation and re-expanded its range there during a postglacial warm period, surviving later general cooling in the relatively warm environment of the Arkansas River valley.

Conservation Status. Two specimens (BS/FC 5676–5677, formerly at Colorado State University, now at the University of New Mexico) collected in extreme northwestern Otero County by Tom Fedde on April 14, 1963, represent the first documented occurrence of this species in Colorado. This record went unpublished and unnoticed (Smith, Maslin, and Brown 1965) or was regarded as a possible data error or translocation (Hammerson 1982c) until Cindy Ramotnik and David Schmidt investigated it and, amazingly, found that the roundtail horned lizard does indeed occur in northwestern Otero County (the confirmation was based on an adult female that they collected on August 25, 1997 [BS/FC 7771]). The collection site is about 177 km northwest of the closest previously known occurrence of this species, in the vicinity of Black Mesa State Park in the western part of the Oklahoma panhandle (Webb 1962; Ramotnik 1998). Whiting and Dixon (1996) did not map the two known Oklahoma panhandle records, but this was an oversight rather than a rejection of the records (Ramotnik 1998).

Known from only one site in Colorado, this species may be especially vulnerable to extirpation. And as the northernmost population of this species, apparently separated from the rest of the range by a wide gap (Whiting and Dixon 1996; Ramotnik 1998), the Otero County population is of ecological and biogeographic interest. Hence, exceptional efforts should be made to ensure its protection. Presumably, the population will persist if existing land use and management are maintained. Specific activities that should be avoided include cultivation, pesticide spraying, excessive use of vehicles within the habitat, and collecting by humans. Additional field surveys are needed

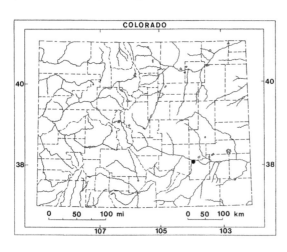

Map 8.11. Distribution of the roundtail horned lizard in Colorado.

Plate 8.35. Adult and hatchling round-tail horned lizard (Arizona).

to determine whether the known population in Colorado is truly isolated and unique.

Little information is available on population density anywhere in the range. Shaffer and Whitford (1981) estimated the density in one area in New Mexico at 2 per hectare (Shaffer and Whitford 1981).

Habitat. The specimen collected in 1997 was found along the pebble-strewn edge of a dirt road in an area with scattered sunflowers, adjacent to plains grassland dominated by patches of grama grass (*Bouteloua* sp.), Russian thistle *(Salsola iberica)*, and yucca (*Yucca* sp.) (Ramotnik 1998). Other lizards found at the site included the lesser earless lizard and Texas horned lizard. In New Mexico, this species inhabits dry grassland and shrubland habitats, especially on lowland slopes and along the margins of arroyos on gravelly to rocky soils (Degenhardt, Painter, and Price 1996). Winter is spent in a rodent burrow or other underground site.

Activity. Activity occurs during daylight hours from April to probably September or early October in Colorado. Known records of activity in Colorado include two individuals found in mid-April and an adult female active at 8:30 a.m. in late August (Ramotnik 1998). Activity in February-March and October-November has been observed in the warmer climate of southern New Mexico (Degenhardt, Painter, and Price 1996). In southern New Mexico, feeding activity peaks in late morning and early afternoon (Shaffer and Whitford 1981). Pianka and Parker (1975) reported an average body temperature of 36–37°C for active individuals. These lizards generally move into shade or burrow into the soil when the surface temperature exceeds this level.

Research in southern Arizona indicates that single-season home range size is quite variable and averages a little more than 0.1

ha in females and about 0.4 ha in males (Munger 1984). Home range length extends up to about 205 m but generally is less than 100 m. Overlap of home ranges occurs but is not extensive.

Apparently, this species does not exhibit the defensive blood squirting characteristic of other horned lizards in Colorado (Sherbrooke and Montanucci 1988; see account of Texas horned lizard).

Reproduction and Growth. Mating probably occurs in late spring. Minton (1959) observed copulation in mid-May in western Texas. Oviposition extends from May to July in various parts of the range (Howard 1974; Pianka and Parker 1975) and probably takes place in June-July in Colorado. Clutch size generally is 6–19 eggs, with an average of about 11–13 eggs in different areas (Howard 1974; Pianka and Parker 1975; Vitt 1977). Hatchlings have been observed as early as early July in the warmer parts of the range (Minton 1959; Howard 1974; Degenhardt, Painter, and Price 1996), but hatching probably does not occur before late July or early August in Colorado. The minimum SVL at sexual maturity has been reported as 41 mm in males and 42 mm in females (Howard 1974), but Pianka and Parker (1975) found that females are not mature until they reach 50 mm SVL.

Food and Predators. Ants dominate the diet, but various other arthropods, including termites, caterpillars, and bugs, also commonly are eaten (Pianka and Parker 1975; Barbault and Maury 1981; Shaffer and Whitford 1981). In Arizona, six individuals spent 15 minutes to two hours at a given colony and ate 8–53 ants during a single feeding (Munger 1984b). However, roundtail horned lizards tend to harvest ants away from colony entrances (Munger 1984b). Shaffer and Whitford (1981) observed that feeding usually occurs under bushes in southern New Mexico.

Grasshopper mice (*Onychomys* spp.) are capable of killing adults and juveniles (Sherbrooke 1991). Horned lizards respond to attack by inflating the lungs, hissing, opening the mouth, charging, biting, flattening and tilting the body, and kicking. In the grasp of a predator, the horns may be raised and the back arched, which may inhibit ingestion (Sherbrooke 1987). Munger (1986) observed

several instances of apparent predation by grasshopper mice in Arizona. Loggerhead shrikes *(Lanius ludovicianus)* also commonly prey on roundtail horned lizards (Reid and Fulbright 1981; Munger 1986); roadrunners *(Geococcyx californianus)* also easily kill and eat them (Sherbrooke 1990). Degenhardt, Painter, and Price (1996) added the collared lizard to the list of known predators.

Stone mimicry by this lizard probably helps it avoid detection by predators that locate prey visually (Sherbrooke and Montanucci 1988).

Taxonomy and Variation. No subspecies have been described. Local populations may exhibit color polymorphism (Sherbrooke 1981).

Plate 8.36. Adult sagebrush lizard (Mesa County, Colorado).

Sagebrush Lizard

Sceloporus graciosus (Baird and Girard, 1852)

Recognition. Dorsum with small spiny scales, usually with a pale dorsolateral stripe on each side; scales on rear of thigh very small, some often granular and unkeeled; no distinct blue patches on sides of throat (throat may be blue-mottled); supraocular scales (supraoculars) separated from median head scales by complete row of small scales; maximum size 15 cm TL; usually less than 6.5 cm SVL in Colorado; adults in Colorado average about 56 mm SVL (Deslippe and M'Closkey 1991). *Mature male:* enlarged postanal scales; underside of base of tail with two hemipenial swellings, blue patch (may be black-edged) on each side of belly; throat mottled or streaked with blue. *Mature female:* blue areas faint or absent (or pale yellowish-green when inactive under rocks); gravid females may develop red/orange color along sides (e.g., rusty spot in axilla). *Hatchling:* usually 23–28 mm SVL in Colorado and Utah (Douglas 1966; Turner 1974; Ferguson and Brockman 1980; Tinkle, Dunham, and Congdon 1993; pers. obs.). *Eggs:* 14 mm x 8 mm in Montezuma County (Douglas 1966); average of 12 mm x 6 mm to 13.5 mm x 8 mm in different females in New Mexico (Gehlbach 1965).

Distribution. Washington, Idaho, Montana, and western North Dakota south to northern Baja California, central Arizona, and northwestern New Mexico (Censky 1986). A disjunct population in southeastern New Mexico and western Texas lately has come to be regarded as a distinct species, *S. arenicolus* (Degenhardt, Painter, and Price 1996). Occurs throughout much of western Colorado at elevations primarily below 7,000 feet (2,285 m) but up to at least 8,500 feet (2,590 m) in the southwestern part of the state.

Conservation Status. The sagebrush lizard is common throughout most of its historical range in Colorado. Localized instances of habitat destruction have occurred, but vast areas of suitable habitat boast healthy populations. Rangeland "improvements"

such as clearing of sagebrush and replacing it with grass communities have resulted in population declines of sagebrush lizards in Idaho (Reynolds 1979), and this probably has occurred in some areas of Colorado as well.

The sagebrush lizard is the most abundant lizard in some parts of its range. In Mesa County, Deslippe and M'Closkey (1991) found that early-season density at one site was 69–75 individuals per hectare over two years. In southern Utah, Tinkle (1973) recorded densities slightly exceeding 200 individuals per hectare. In northern Utah, Parker (1976) found a minimum density of 74 individuals per hectare for adults and subadults.

Habitat. Habitats include piñon-juniper woodland, semidesert shrubland (including saltbush-sagebrush associations), shale hills with sparse grasses and low shrubs, oak-grass associations, mountain shrubland, and montane woodland (e.g., mountainous areas and canyons with ponderosa pine or Douglas-fir) (Cary 1911; Maslin 1950; Stock 1962; Harris 1963; Gehlbach 1965; Douglas 1966; Ferguson 1973; pers. obs.). This species ranges to higher elevations in montane woodland than does *Sceloporus undulatus*. The sagebrush lizard can be found at the base of rocky ledges or on gently sloping exposures of bedrock, but more often it occurs on the ground on shrubby expanses of fine-grained soils. It often coexists with *S. undulatus* but is less inclined to perch on rocks. Sagebrush lizards in Colorado and Utah often perch on junipers and other plants, usually near the ground but sometimes at heights of 1–2 m (Knowlton 1934; Deslippe 1989). Winter, night, and hot midday periods are spent under rocks or in rodent burrows (e.g., those of prairie dogs) or in similar underground or sheltered sites.

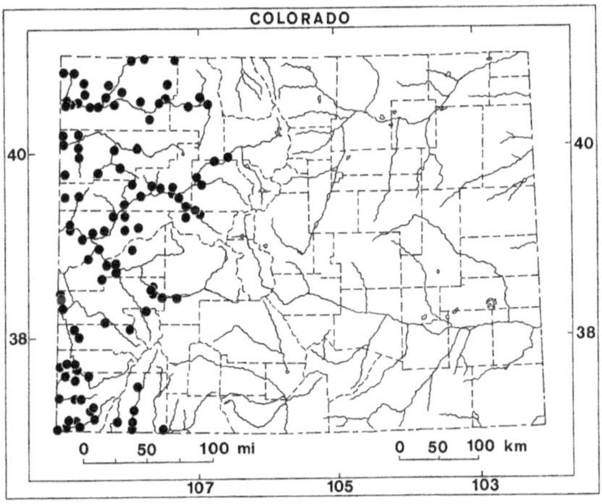

Map 8.12. Distribution of the sagebrush lizard in Colorado.

Plate 8.37. Adult male sagebrush lizard (Moffat County, Colorado).

Activity. In Colorado, emergence from hibernation takes place primarily in April. Most of the early-emerging individuals are adult males (Turner 1974). Adults are active throughout the spring and summer but become scarce in September (Turner 1974). By the end of September, most individuals still active are hatchlings. A similar pattern of seasonal activity occurs in southern Idaho (Guyer and Linder 1985) and Utah (Burkholder and Tanner 1974; Tinkle, Dunham, and Congdon 1993). Some activity (hatchlings, a few adults) takes place during warm weather in March and October.

Activity occurs during daylight hours, in summer from just after sunrise to shortly after sunset, with peaks in the warmer summer months at about 10:00 a.m. and 4:30–5:30 p.m. (Turner 1974). Midday activity is typical during cooler weather at low elevations and in the cooler climate of higher elevations. Midday activity in summer also takes place in the northern part of the range in Idaho (Guyer and Linder 1985). Body temperatures of active individuals usually are 28–37°C and average 33–35°C (Turner 1974; Burkholder and Tanner 1974; Congdon and Tinkle 1982).

Male sagebrush lizards are territorial and exclude other males from their home areas with bobbing (push-up) displays and, if necessary, chasing, fighting, and biting. Male territories are larger than, and overlap with, the home ranges of adult females (and sometimes juvenile females) (Deslippe and M'Closkey 1991). The bobbing territorial display of males consists of up to two initial double head-bobs, up to five single head-bobs, and up to seven terminal double head-bobs (Ferguson 1971a, 1973; Carpenter 1978; Martins 1991); the bobbing includes alternating quick bobs and slow ones. These bobs may be accompanied by lateral flattening of the body and lowering of the throat area (exhibiting the blue colors), especially when another adult male is nearby. During the push-ups, only the front legs, or both the front and hind legs, may be extended. Small males lacking blue ventral coloration nevertheless may perform the push-up displays. Another male display, similar to a female display, includes rapid up-and-down body vibrations with the back arched upward.

Home range size is relatively small, averaging about 400–600 m^2 in Utah (Burkholder and Tanner 1974). In Mesa County, M'Closkey et al. (1997) found that areas experimentally depopulated of this species are quickly recolonized from surrounding areas.

Reproduction and Growth. Courtship and mating generally begin in May. Males approach females with rapid nodding of the head. Females may respond with arched-back rapid bobbing (apparently a rejection behavior).

In Colorado (Turner 1974; Deslippe 1989) and in southern Utah (Tinkle, Dunham, and Congdon 1993), most adult females produce two clutches of eggs per year. In Garfield County, the first clutch, laid in early June, averages about five eggs; the second clutch, averaging about four eggs, is laid in early July (Turner 1974). At Mesa Verde, eggs are laid evidently in early to mid-July, and clutch size usually is 3–7 eggs (Douglas 1966). Deslippe (1989) reported that gravid females were still present in Mesa County in August. Clutches averaging four eggs are laid in June and July in southern Utah (Ferguson and Brockman 1980; Tinkle, Dunham, and Congdon 1993). Other studies in Utah yielded a larger average clutch size of 5–6 eggs (Woodbury and Woodbury 1945; Parker 1973; Burkholder and Tanner 1974). Females begin searching for a suitable egg deposition site about a week before the eggs are laid (Deslippe 1989). At 26°C, eggs in Utah hatch after an average of 55 days (Ferguson and Brockman 1980).

In west-central Colorado, eggs in the first clutch hatch in early to mid-August, and occasionally in late July (Deslippe 1989), whereas those in the second clutch hatch in mid-September (Turner 1974). Douglas (1966) observed the earliest hatchlings in early August at Mesa Verde. The first hatchlings usually appear in early to mid-August in southern Utah (Tinkle, Dunham, and Congdon 1993) and at Yellowstone National Park, Wyoming (Mueller and Moore 1969).

In Mesa County, late spring populations consist of distinct size classes of juveniles (usually 34–45 mm SVL) and adults (greater than 50 mm SVL) (Deslippe 1989; pers. obs.). In southern Utah (Tinkle, Dunham, and Congdon 1993), individuals in their second calendar year grow from an average of about 35–36 mm SVL in May to an average of 49–51 mm SVL in August. Most females in that area produce their first clutch at an age of 22–24 months at a minimum SVL of about 50 mm; yearlings rarely reproduce. Gehlbach (1965) found a similar size at maturity in northwestern New Mexico, and Burkholder and Tanner (1974) found a slightly larger minimum in Utah. The sizes of breeding males indicate that they first participate in breeding when just under two years old (Parker 1973; Burkholder and Tanner 1974).

The survival rate of the young is quite variable, but roughly half of the older lizards survive from one year to the next. For example, over several years, annual survival rate in Utah was 12–66 percent for the egg-to-yearling stage, about 40–50 percent for yearlings, and about 40–70 percent for adults;

mean annual survival rate for yearlings and older individuals combined was 45 percent (Tinkle, Dunham, and Congdon 1993). Other studies in Utah indicate that about three-fourths of the hatchlings do not survive their first year (Tinkle 1973; Burkholder and Tanner 1974). In Mesa County, minimum annual survival of yearlings and adults was 56 percent (Deslippe 1989). A very few individuals live as long as 6–7 years (Tinkle, Dunham, and Congdon 1993). Resource limitation appears to affect survival rate, growth rate, and age at first reproduction (Tinkle, Dunham, and Congdon 1993).

Food and Predators. Ants appear to be the most important food; other typical prey includes termites, grasshoppers, leaf bugs, leafhoppers, beetles, lepidopterans, flies, spiders, mites, and pseudoscorpions (Knowlton 1934; Knowlton and Nye 1946; Douglas 1966; Turner 1974; Burkholder and Tanner 1974; pers. obs.). A neonate captured and ate a tachynid fly in Mesa County (pers. obs.). Adults likely eat hatchling lizards on occasion. Turner (1974) described this lizard as widely foraging in Garfield County.

The sagebrush lizard is food for probably a wide assortment of mammals, birds, and reptiles. Douglas (1966) found a sagebrush lizard in the stomach of a striped whipsnake that had been hit by a car at Mesa Verde, Montezuma County. Turner (1974) reported that a plateau lizard ate a hatchling sagebrush lizard in Garfield County. In Moffat County, I saw American kestrels (Falco sparverius) carrying *Sceloporus,* possibly this species, to nests in cottonwood trees. Degenhardt, Painter, and Price (1996) reported the collared lizard as a known predator in New Mexico. Predation by the ash-throated flycatcher *(Myiarchus cinerascens)* has been observed in Arizona–New Mexico (Johnson 1982).

Taxonomy and Variation. Thompson and Sites (1986a) found that this species normally is diploid throughout its range (including sampled sites in Colorado and eastern Utah), but they reported one sterile triploid individual from California and a chromosomally aberrant individual from southern Utah.

Thompson and Sites (1986b) examined allelic variation in the eastern portion of the range and found that a major dichotomy separates populations in the eastern part of the Colorado River basin (Abajo Mountains, Utah; Flaming Gorge, Utah; and Parachute, Colorado) from the rest of the populations, with a second minor distinctive cluster in Yellowstone National Park, Wyoming, and Butte County, Idaho. Surprisingly, samples from Dead Horse Point and the Henry Mountains in Utah clustered with samples from farther west rather than with the geographically more contiguous samples just mentioned.

Morphology exhibits a large degree of geographic variation, much of it clinal (Kerfoot 1968) and thus not of taxonomic significance. Within Colorado, a notable pattern in dorsal scale count is evident, with individuals from the plains of southwestern Montezuma County having relatively large scales (low dorsal scale count). In this region, the dorsal blotches tend to be reduced in size and distinctness. These lizards are rather strikingly different in appearance from those at nearby Mesa Verde.

Plate 8.38. Adult male desert spiny lizard (Montezuma County, Colorado).

Desert Spiny Lizard
Sceloporus magister (Hallowell, 1854)

Recognition. Dorsum with large spiny scales; sides often with scattered yellowish or gold scales; supraoculars large, usually in a single row of five, the posterior one or two in contact with median head scales; head yellowish or orange in adult; maximum TL 33 cm; in Utah, maximum SVL about 10 cm in females, slightly more than 10 cm in males (Tinkle 1976). *Mature male:* a beautifully impressive lizard with enlarged postanal scales; underside of base of tail with two hemipenial swellings; blue patch at center of throat; vivid black-edged blue or blue-green patch on each side of belly; large black mark on each side of neck. *Mature female:* blue areas faint or absent. *Juvenile:* head not yellowish or orange; dorsum with conspicuous crossbands; hatchlings usually 30–35 mm SVL (Tanner and Krogh 1973; Vitt and Ohmart 1974; Tinkle 1976). *Eggs:* average about 15–17 mm x 9–11 mm (Tanner and Krogh 1973; Vitt and Ohmart 1974; Vitt 1977).

Distribution. Central California, Nevada, southern Utah, and southwestern Colorado south through Arizona, New Mexico, and western Texas to northeastern Baja California and northwestern and north-central mainland Mexico (Stebbins 1985; Grismer and McGuire 1996; Taylor, Holland, et al. 1996). Occurs in extreme southwestern Colorado at elevations below about 5,100 feet (1,555 m).

Conservation Status. The desert spiny lizard still exists throughout most, if not all, of its small historic range in Colorado. Adequate data are not available to evaluate the trend in abundance, but this lizard is fairly common in some areas. Overall, the population appears to be stable and there are no known significant threats. Livestock grazing is the primary land use in its otherwise relatively undisturbed range. The habitat in some areas has been altered by the growth of thick stands of salt-cedar *(Tamarix)*, but desert spiny lizards commonly occur in these areas and make use of these exotic plants as cover.

Studies in southern Utah and Nevada indicate that population density varies among habitats from as low as a few lizards per hectare to as many as 50 per hectare (Tanner and Krogh 1973; Tinkle 1976). In southern New Mexico, Whitford and Creusere (1977) found that territorial behavior and stable availability of habitat and food resources resulted in populations that were relatively constant over a five-year study.

Habitat. The habitat in Colorado includes shrub-covered dirt banks and sparsely vegetated rocky areas near flowing streams or arroyos. These lizards prefer soft soils beneath greasewood, rabbitbrush, salt-cedar, and other shrubs and also frequently perch on large rocks or in large shrubs or trees (e.g., cottonwood). In southern Utah, Tinkle (1976) found that hatchlings occurred most often on the ground. Periods of inactivity are spent in burrows made by mammals, in spaces under rocks, under dense vegetation, or in similar sites.

Activity. The primary period of activity in Colorado extends from May to September, but activity in April and October is likely during intervals of warm weather. This species is active March-November in the warmer climate of southern New Mexico (Degenhardt, Painter, and Price 1996) and along the lower Colorado River in Arizona (Vitt and Ohmart 1974).

Activity takes place during daylight hours, usually from 8:30 a.m. to as late as just after sunset, with a midafternoon lull in summer when the lizards seek shade during excessive heat. Tanner and Krogh (1973) found a few gravid females along roads at night in Nevada; these females may have been moving to areas suitable for egg-laying. Body temperatures during activity usually are 29–39°C (average 33–35°C) (McGinnis and Falkenstein 1971; Parker and Pianka 1973; Tanner and Krogh 1973). Body temperature may drop a few degrees during the hot midday period when the lizards seek shade.

Adult males are strongly territorial and defend their home areas against other adult males

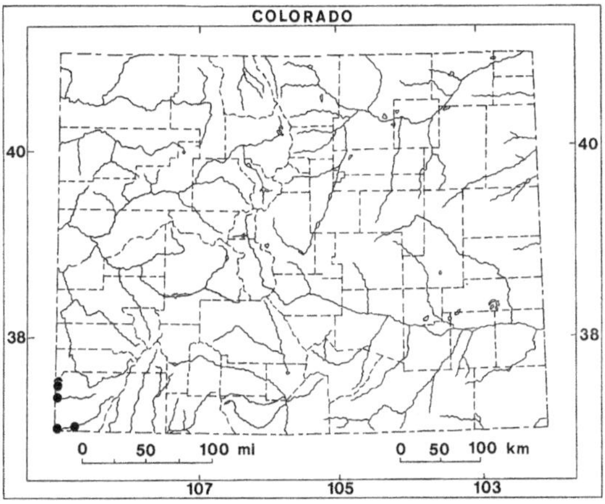

Map 8.13. Distribution of the desert spiny lizard in Colorado.

with conspicuous bobbing displays, chasing, butting, fighting, and biting. Males not uncommonly incur injuries during these encounters (Vitt et al. 1974). In territorial and aggressive displays, males typically adopt a broadside stance toward the intruder, with the body laterally compressed and the throat area lowered (presenting the bright colors), and usually perform a series of single, slow push-ups that may become more rapid and of lesser amplitude at the end of the display (Vitt et al. 1974; Carpenter 1978; pers. obs.). Despite the intolerance of adult males toward other conspecific adult males, they may share perches with smaller male *S. magister* lizards and lizards of other species. In Montezuma County, I saw an adult male northern plateau lizard *(S. undulatus)* perched partially atop an adult male *S. magister* on a large boulder. Evidently, the smaller *S. undulatus* was too big to eat and therefore ignored.

Adults generally remain in a relatively small home range that does not change much from year to year, whereas juveniles may move several hundred meters before establishing a small territory or home range (Tanner and Krogh 1973). Individuals sometimes spend hours on a single perch without engaging in much activity.

Desert spiny lizards generally respond to the approach of a human by fleeing for cover (dense vegetation, rodent burrow) or, in the case of some adult males, by holding their ground and performing an apparently assertive push-up display. Individuals encountered in trees either hide in the woody debris usually present at the base of the trees or climb up the trunk or onto higher branches. Taylor, Holland, et al. (1996)

reported unusual behavior of individuals along the Green River in eastern Utah, where the lizards were described as exceptionally abundant and easily caught by hand (generally, but not always, this is quite difficult).

Reproduction and Growth. Courtship and mating take place primarily in May and possibly early June. Females (probably gravid ones) may respond to courting males (or approaching humans) with an arched-back bobbing display, which might signify "stay away." Adult males and females sometimes perch together in spring. In different parts of the range, oviposition occurs from late May through approximately mid-July (mainly June) (e.g., Tanner and Krough 1973). The egg-deposition period may be somewhat longer in Colorado; a female that I obtained in mid-July in Montezuma County laid six eggs later that month, but this egg-laying incident may have been delayed due to the conditions of captivity. Females may leave their home range to oviposit (Tanner and Krogh 1973).

Clutch size is 2–9 eggs (average about 6) in southern Utah (Tinkle 1976), 4–10 eggs (average 7) in Nevada (Tanner and Krogh 1973), and 10–18 eggs (average about 12) in southern Arizona, based on a small sample of large individuals (Vitt and Ohmart 1974); clutch size averages 8–9 eggs in the southwestern portion of the range (Parker and Pianka 1973). Individuals produce only one clutch per year in Nevada (Tanner and Krogh 1973). Tinkle (1976) believed that most females in southern Utah produce two clutches, but no direct evidence was obtained and postreproductive females were seen no earlier than late June. Colorado females probably produce only one clutch each year, but this needs to be confirmed.

Hatchlings first appear in early August in Colorado, in early August (possibly late July) in southern Utah (Tinkle 1976), and in late July and August in southern Nevada (Tanner and Krogh 1973).

Plate 8.39. Adult male desert spiny lizard (San Juan County, Utah).

Plate 8.40. Juvenile desert spiny lizard (Montezuma County, Colorado).

Hatchlings appear earlier in the warmer southern parts of the range.

Growth rates are moderate. In southern Utah, juveniles grow to 51–75 mm SVL by June-July of their second calendar year (Tinkle 1976). In southern Nevada, the young reach adult size just before their second hibernation (Tanner and Krough 1973).

Males and females do not breed until after their second hibernation. Sexually mature females are at least 8 cm SVL, though few females in Nevada reproduce until they are at least 9 cm SVL; males mature at about 83 mm SVL in Nevada and at about 95 mm SVL in other areas (Parker and Pianka 1973; Tanner and Krogh 1973; Tinkle 1976). In Nevada, Tanner and Krogh (1973) found that an adult population consisted primarily of individuals 3–5 years old, though several were older (Tanner and Krogh 1973). In southern Utah, about 17 percent of the hatchlings, 23 percent of the yearlings, and 42 percent of the adults survived from one year to the next (Tinkle 1976).

Food and Predators. Desert spiny lizards feed opportunistically on available arthropods, occasional small lizards, and some plant material. Food items may be located by visual searching as the lizards perch or move. Some insects are obtained by digging in the ground (Vitt and Ohmart 1974), suggesting that odor detection plays a role in locating prey. When abundant prey is found, it is not unusual for individuals to eat hundreds of that species to the exclusion of all others. Johnson (1966) found that ants and beetles are major food items in Montezuma County; others include bugs, grasshoppers, termites, lepidopterans (probably mainly caterpillars [Knowlton

1934]), spiders, and centipedes, plus significant quantities of plant material in spring. Small fruits also are eaten (Knowlton 1934). Tanner and Krogh (1973) found *Lycium* berries in the diet in Nevada. Small lizards, including young western whiptails and conspecifics, sometimes are attacked and eaten (Knowlton 1934; Knowlton and Thomas 1934; Tanner and Krogh 1973; Vitt and Ohmart 1974).

Predators are not well known. In Utah, Tinkle (1976) found a collared lizard that had partly swallowed a juvenile desert spiny lizard. Degenhardt, Painter, and Price (1996) listed the longnose leopard lizard and coachwhip as known predators in New Mexico. It would be surprising if predatory birds did not occasionally pluck these lizards from their conspicuous perches.

Taxonomy and Variation. Grismer and McGuire (1996) determined that populations in most of Baja California formerly included in *S. magister* represent a distinct species, *S. zosteromus*. They also recognized the Mexican insular endemic *S. lineatulus* as a distinct species. Citing a lack of significant genetic differences among populations throughout the range of *S. magister* (Hunsicker 1987), and adopting a lineage-based species concept (Frost and Hillis 1990), Grismer and McGuire regarded *S. magister* as monotypic. Previously, Stebbins (1985) included Colorado populations in the subspecies *S. m. cephaloflavus* Tanner, 1955. Tanner (1955) did not specifically allocate populations in San Juan County, Utah, or Montezuma County, Colorado, to subspecies *cephaloflavus*, but the lizards in this area appear to fit Tanner's description. Prior to Tanner's revision, desert spiny lizards from the Four Corners region were included in *S. m. bimaculosus* Phelan and Brattstrom, 1955. Phelan and Brattstrom, like Tanner, apparently did not actually examine any specimens from the Four Corners region. Regardless, the recognition of subspecies does not appear to be warranted.

Plate 8.41. Adult *Sceloporus undulatus* (Weld County, Colorado).

Prairie and Plateau Lizards

Sceloporus undulatus (Bosc and Daudin, 1801)

Recognition. Dorsum with spiny scales; scales on rear of thigh keeled and overlapping; supraoculars separated from median head scales by complete row of small scales; coloration extremely variable (see "Taxonomy and Variation"); maximum TL about 19 cm. *Mature male:* enlarged postanal scales; underside of base of tail with two hemipenial swellings. See "Taxonomy and Variation" for other sexual differences. *Hatchling:* usually 22–28 (average 24–25) mm SVL (Gehlbach 1965; Ferner 1976; Ferguson and Brockman 1980; Jones and Ballinger 1987; Smith, Rand, et al. 1991). *Eggs:* 11.5–15.0 mm in length in Elbert County (Smith, Rand, et al. 1991); 16 mm x 8 mm in Montezuma County (Douglas 1966); average about 13 mm x 7–8 mm (Vitt 1977).

Distribution. Utah, southern Wyoming, southern South Dakota, Missouri, southern Illinois, southern Indiana, Ohio, Pennsylvania, and southern New York south to northern Mexico, the Gulf Coast, and central Florida. Occurs throughout most of Colorado; absent from the high mountains in the central part of the state; ranges from below 3,500 feet (1,070 m) in eastern Colorado to about 7,000 feet (2,135 m) in northwestern Colorado, about 7,500 feet (2,285 m) in north-central Colorado, and 9,200 feet (2,805 m) in the southern part of the state. Secoy and Brown (1968) erroneously reported *S. undulatus* from Pitkin County (Hammerson 1982b). See "Taxonomy and Variation" for information on the distributions of the four Colorado subspecies and explanations of map symbols.

Conservation Status. *Sceloporus undulatus* is common and often abundant throughout most of its historic range in western, southern, and central Colorado. Some herpetologists believe that prairie populations (subspecies *garmani*) have declined in abundance in recent years, though good comparative data for a quantitative evaluation of the trend are not available. Subspecies *garmani* remains locally abundant in at least Yuma County (pers. obs.), but a status review based on new field surveys of all historic sites in the state for this subspecies is needed.

Prairie populations of this species may thrive on disturbances that maintain areas of open ground, such as fire, or cattle and bison grazing. Thick grass cover that develops after the cessation of cattle grazing reduces habitat suitability and results in population declines (Ballinger and Jones 1985; Ballinger and Watts 1995).

Tinkle and Ballinger (1972) estimated the population density of adults and yearlings at about 14 per hectare at a site in Mesa County. Ferner (1976) found that the number of juveniles in the foothills of Boulder County varies from year to year, whereas the number of adults remains fairly constant at about 25–35 per hectare. Tinkle (1982) recorded spring densities of 45–65 individuals per hectare in riparian habitats in Arizona. In western Nebraska, density generally is 15–24 individuals per hectare (average 19) in spring and 12–21 per hectare in summer (average 16–17), not including hatchlings (Jones and Ballinger 1987). A large increase in population density occurs in late summer as hatchlings emerge. For example, Ferguson, Brown, and DeMarco (1982) found that late summer densities in south-central Kansas increased from 113 individuals per hectare in early August to 865 per hectare in early September.

Habitat. Throughout most of Colorado, *S. undulatus* inhabits sunny, rocky habitats including cliffs, talus, old lava flows and cones, canyons, hogbacks, and various outcroppings. Vegetation adjacent to and among the rocks is variable and may include coniferous montane forest (e.g., ponderosa pine, Douglas-fir), piñon-juniper woodland, mountain shrubland, semidesert shrubland, or various grasses and forbs. Within these habitats, perch sites often are on rocks but also include trees (especially junipers [Deslippe 1989]), logs, piles of debris, buildings, and dirt banks, though the lizards also may spend a considerable amount of time on the ground. In southern Colorado, common habitat includes montane woodland with downed logs.

The typical habitat and habits of *S. undulatus* in northeastern, east-central, and extreme southeastern Colorado are strikingly different—this lizard (northern prairie lizard, subspecies *garmani*) is a ground-dweller in these regions, occurring in areas with soft sandy soil. Sand sagebrush (*Artemisia filifolia*) generally is an indicator of suitable conditions. In the western Nebraska sandhills, Jones and Droge (1980) found *garmani* most often associated with barren wind-eroded areas and patches of yucca. In some areas, *S. u. garmani* is associated with rocky scarp woodlands and sandstone- or limestone-capped bluffs and buttes (Maslin 1947b; Baxter and Stone 1985; Collins 1993; pers. obs.), and in prairie habitats, *garmani* commonly occurs in association with isolated rocks, debris, or other cover. Burrows, spaces under rocks, and various crevices are used as shelter during extended periods of inactivity or as refuges from danger.

Activity. Emergence from winter hibernation generally occurs in March and April, and activity continues through spring and summer. Most adults

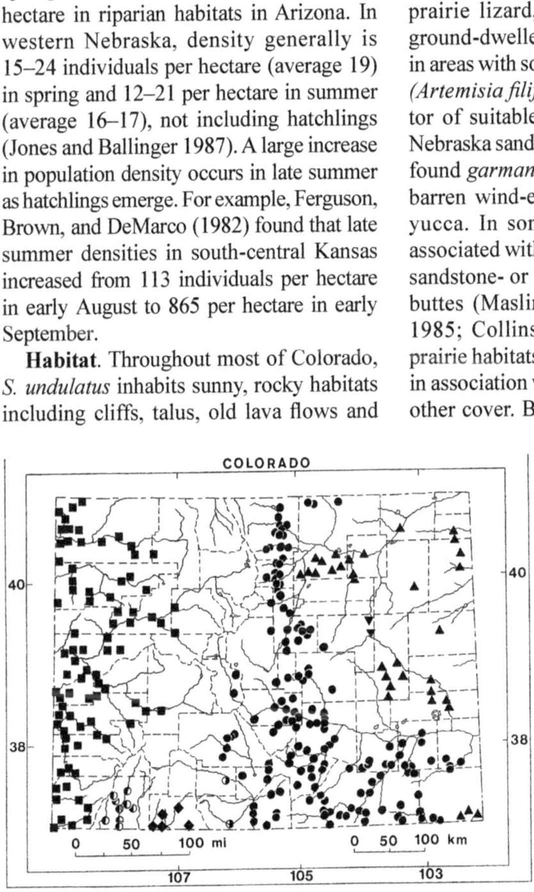

COLORADO

40

40

38

38

| 0 | 50 | 100 mi | | 0 | 50 | 100 km |

107   105   103

Map 8.14. Distribution of the plateau and prairie lizards in Colorado. For explanation of symbols, see "Taxonomy and Variation."

Plate 8.42. Adult male *Sceloporus undulatus* (Montezuma County, Colorado).

Plate 8.43. Adult male *Sceloporus undulatus* (Montezuma County, Colorado).

begin to disappear underground in September and October. Hatchlings commonly are active through October and sometimes into early November. Some basking may take place during warm mid-November days in western Colorado. This pattern varies somewhat statewide. In Boulder County (Rand 1991), adult males emerge in mid-March (rarely in late February). Activity is minimal through the end of March, but by early April many males have moved 70–120 m from their original location. Home ranges are established by mid-April. Adult females emerge from early to mid-April. Ferner (1976) found that activity in Boulder County usually begins in April and that juveniles emerge prior to adults. Female emergence in Huerfano County occurs in late April or early May (Gillis and Ballinger 1992). Along the Rio Grande in the southern San Luis Valley, activity begins in late April and ends by early October (Crowley 1985b). Douglas (1966) found that activity at Mesa Verde begins in April (rarely in late March),

extending into mid-September and, for some individuals, through mid- to late October. Spring emergence generally takes place in early to mid-April in western Nebraska, and activity continues through mid-October, with a few records as early as mid-March and as late as mid-November (Jones and Ballinger 1987).

Most activity in late spring and early summer occurs from soon after sunrise to shortly after sunset, usually between 7:00 a.m. and 8:30 p.m. In summer, these lizards sun themselves in the morning and late afternoon but generally prefer shade at midday. The warmer the air temperature, the more likely it is for lizards to seek shade (Waldschmidt 1980). Upon initial morning emergence, lizards generally orient themselves perpendicular to the sun's rays or sprawl on sun-warmed rocks. Activity peaks at midday during the cooler weather of spring and late summer/ early fall.

In both lowland and montane habitats, body temperature during activity ranges

Plate 8.44. Adult female *Sceloporus undulatus* (Moffat County, Colorado).

consist of an initial double push-up followed by a single push-up and then a series of double push-ups (Carpenter 1978; pers. obs.). These may be accompanied by lowering of the throat and lateral compression of the body, which exposes the blue colors on the lizard's sides. The displays vary somewhat in different parts of the range (Ferguson 1973). In Boulder County, Rand (1991) found that if displays do not intimidate an intruder into retreat, then the displaying male may give chase. Afterward, the male in pursuit perches atop a rock and does a push-up display, whereas the chased male rarely performs push-ups or perches on rocks. In contrast, females do not behave aggressively toward other females.

from 29–37°C and averages about 33–35°C (Gehlbach 1965; Turner 1974; Jones and Ballinger 1987; Gillis 1991; Grover 1996; pers. obs.). Some seasonal changes are evident. Crowley (1985b) found that body temperature in Conejos County averages 28°C in May, 33°C in June, 35°C in July and August, 34°C in September, and 32°C in October. These variations reflect constraints imposed by the cooler environmental conditions in spring and fall; given a gradient of temperatures under laboratory conditions, the lizards maintain an average body temperature of 35°C. Activity sometimes occurs at unusually low body temperatures. Crowley (1985b) found that during and after thunderstorms in June, some individuals may forage while perched on wet rocks at body temperatures as low as 21.5°C. In Utah, Grover (1996) found that daytime regulation of body temperature was accomplished primarily by moving between sun-exposed and shaded portions of large rocks.

Adult males are intolerant of each other during the breeding season and defend territories. Their territorial displays typically

Home range size of *Sceloporus undulatus* in various locations in Colorado and adjacent states averages about 300–900 m² (Ferner 1974; Waldschmidt 1978; Jones and Droge 1980). Home range size may exhibit large annual variations (Ferner 1974) that probably reflect changing food resources, habitat conditions, and social structure. Ferner (1974) found that the home range size of males in the foothills of Boulder County (subspecies *erythrocheilus*) averages more than twice that of a typical female and shrinks greatly after the breeding season. He also found that the home ranges of different males often overlap. Deslippe (1989) discovered a similar pattern in Mesa County. Surviving individuals tend to

Plate 8.45. Adult male (top) and female (bottom) *Sceloporus undulatus* (Archuleta County, Colorado).

occupy the same home range in successive years (Ferner 1974). Adult males may shift the location of their home ranges as necessary to include nearby adult females (Rand 1991).

In Mesa County, M'Closkey et al. (1997) found that areas experimentally depopulated of this species were quickly recolonized from surrounding areas.

Reproduction and Growth. Reproductive characteristics of *S. undulatus* vary with location and subspecies.

Ferner (1974, 1976) and Rand (1991) provided information on breeding of subspecies *erythrocheilus* in the foothills of Boulder County. Bobbing courtship displays occur from May through early July, with most copulations in early June. Females do not tolerate rapid advances by courting males and reject male advances just prior to ovulation. Rejection behavior of the females (hunched back, lowered head, jerky two-step lateral walk) was observed by these authors in late May and early June (I observed this behavior

through mid-June in Las Animas County). An individual male may mate with up to several females occupying his territory. The male grasps the female's shoulder area in his jaws during attempted copulation (pers. obs.). Ferner (1974, 1976) concluded that females lay one clutch of about 8–12 eggs (average 9–10), usually in late June or early July, but the presence of oviductal eggs as early as late May suggests that some females may produce two clutches. Individuals first breed in their third calendar year at an age of about 21 months. Average SVL is 62 mm (range 54–71 mm) in adult males, 67 mm (59–75 mm) in adult females, 50 mm (33–62 mm) in subadult (second-calendar-year) males, and 52 mm (39–65 mm) in subadult females. Hatchlings first appear in early August in some years and in late August in other years. Annual turnover rate in the resident adult population is about 35 percent. Few individuals live longer than four years.

In Huerfano County (Gillis and Ballinger 1992), territorial and aggressive behav-

Plate 8.46. Adult male *(right)* and female *(left)* *Sceloporus undulatus* (Archuleta County, Colorado).

Plate 8.47. Juvenile *Sceloporus undulatus* (Douglas County, Colorado).

Plate 8.48. Adult male *Sceloporus undulatus* (Las Animas County, Colorado).

ior in adult *erythrocheilus* males occurs commonly from mid-May to mid-July. Adult females produce a clutch averaging 10–12 eggs in late May or early June and another in early to mid-July, sometimes in late July. Hatchlings first appear in August. Reproductive females are 64–82 mm SVL and at least 20–21 months of age. Yearlings apparently do not reproduce. Some of my own observations of reproduction in *erythrocheilus* include the following: four females collected in Conejos County in mid-July contained 7–9 oviductal eggs; a gravid female that I found in early June in Bent County was only 57 mm SVL.

In western Colorado, I observed that male displays in subspecies *elongatus* include a few deep push-ups followed by a sequence of alternating shallow and deep bobs. The third push-up has a distinct pause at the summit. Sometimes two fast push-ups are followed by two slow ones and then two fast ones. I observed mating in late May in Moffat County. Females reject courting males through arched-back bobs or lurches and sometimes by biting; this occurs frequently in late May and June. In southwestern Wyoming, Ashton (1998a) saw a female roll onto her back and dislodge a mounting male that had the side of her neck in his jaws.

In Mesa County (Tinkle and Ballinger 1972), most females of subspecies *elongatus* lay two clutches, one in May and one in June, though some females may be egg-laden as late as July or early August. Each clutch averages about 8 eggs (range 5–12). Newly hatched individuals appear aboveground from mid-July through at least early September. The young average 5 cm SVL 9 months after hatching, 6 cm SVL 12 months after hatching, and 7 cm SVL at 24 months. About 30 percent of the yearlings and 35 percent of adults survive through their next year. Females breeding for the first time are at least 58 mm SVL and almost two years old. Two-year-olds contribute the most (about 70 percent) to the reproductive output of the population.

Maximum observed longevity is four years, and only a small percentage live as long as three years. Also in Mesa County, Deslippe (1989) found two distinct size classes corresponding with yearlings and adults, with the size difference most pronounced in spring. He determined that at least 10 of 22 individuals (adults and yearlings) survived from July to May of the next year. I observed that neonates in Mesa County reach 34–35 mm SVL by early October, at which time males have small, blue throat and belly patches.

At Mesa Verde in southwestern Colorado, Douglas (1966) collected gravid females (subspecies *elongatus*) containing 5–8 eggs in June and early July. Young of the year were not seen until late September. Adult males at Mesa Verde average 63 mm SVL, females 67 mm SVL. Fitch (1978) recorded an average SVL of 63 mm (range 55–71 mm) in adult males and 72 mm (65–83 mm) in adult females from southwestern Colorado. Burnett (1926) reported that two specimens collected in May in the same county contained 7 and 11 eggs. Smith (1991) collected a female with eggs nearly ready for oviposition in early July in Ouray County. Throughout the westernmost counties of Colorado, I found females (66–77 mm SVL) carrying large eggs from late May through mid-July.

Plate 8.49. Gravid adult female *Sceloporus undulatus* (Elbert County, Colorado).

Ballinger, Droge, and Jones (1981) and Jones and Ballinger (1987) found that adult females in sandhill populations in western Nebraska (subspecies *garmani*) produce 1–3 clutches between mid-May and mid-July; clutches average about 4–5 eggs in yearlings and 7–8 eggs in older females. The number of clutches per female varies from year to year. Hatchlings first appear in late July or early August, and hatching continues through mid-September. (In sandhill populations in eastern Colorado, newly hatched individuals appear as soon as early July in some years.) In Nebraska, females begin breeding at an age of 9–10 months, at 44–45 mm SVL. Survival varies from year to year but averages about 10 percent for the egg-to-yearling stage, about 50 percent for yearlings, and about 20–25 percent for older individuals. Yearlings contribute the most to a population's reproductive output. Few or none live more than four years. Mortality appears to be greatest during the overwintering period.

In south-central Kansas, clutch size for subspecies *garmani* averages 7 eggs; females produce two clutches per year and mature the year after hatching, at 47 mm SVL (Ferguson, Bohlen, and Wooley 1980). Juveniles reach an average length of 4 cm SVL before their first hibernation (Ferguson and Brockman 1980). Eggs incubated at 26°C hatch in 72 days (Ferguson and Brockman 1980). Only about one-fourth of the adults survive from one year to the next. Under laboratory conditions, Ferguson and Snell (1986) were able to induce reproduction in *garmani* after a 35-day hibernation period; females produced 1–2 clutches averaging about seven eggs for the first clutch and six eggs for the second. In north-central Oklahoma, five females deposited clutches of 5–9 eggs (Heger and Fox 1992). Heger and Fox (1992) stated that *garmani* in Oklahoma rarely survives

longer than one year. These authors found that *garmani* eggs, which may be laid in floodplain soils along streams, readily survived simulated flooding for at least several hours.

In Elbert County, gravid females collected in late June deposited 2–4 eggs (average 3.8) in early to mid-July (Smith et al. 1991). Incubated at about 23–25°C, the eggs hatched in late August. Sexual maturity at about 22 months was indicated for this population.

My observations of subspecies *tristichus* in Archuleta County indicate that clutch size usually is 5–9 eggs (average 7); females containing large eggs can be found from at least late May through late July. In nearby northwestern New Mexico, Gehlbach (1965) found that most females more than 4 cm SVL collected before mid-July are gravid, whereas those collected in August generally do not contain eggs. Large eggs taken from females frequently hold well-developed embryos, indicating a significant period of egg retention. Gehlbach found 10 eggs in a small depression under a sandstone slab in late July. The first appearance of hatchlings in northwestern New Mexico varies from late July to mid-August in different years (Gehlbach 1965).

Food and Predators. In rocky areas, *S. undulatus* usually waits on a perch until it sees potential prey, then dashes after it. The same sit-and-wait approach also is typical of ground-dwelling populations. I have seen individuals leap upward several centimeters to catch low-flying insects.

Sceloporus undulatus eats whatever small arthropods are readily available. Common

Plate 8.50. Adult *Sceloporus undulatus* impaled by loggerhead shrike (Weld County, Colorado).

food items in Boulder County include flies, grasshoppers, beetles, insect larvae, spiders, and ticks (Ferner 1976). Douglas (1966) reported that leafhoppers, beetles, lepidopterans, flies, wasps, and ants are eaten at Mesa Verde in Montezuma County. Ladybird beetles, snout beetles, and ants are dominant foods at a lower elevation in Montezuma County (Johnson 1966). Turner (1974) reported that *S. undulatus* ate a hatchling sagebrush lizard in Garfield County. An adult male that I observed in Mesa County caught a large grasshopper (three times as long as the lizard's head) and battered it against a rock before swallowing it whole. Ants are the most significant food in western Kansas (Werth 1972) and south-central Kansas, where adults also eat beetles, bugs, flies, grasshoppers, and neuropterans (DeMarco, Drenner, and Ferguson 1985). Similarly, ants are prominent in the wide variety of arthropods consumed in eastern Utah (Knowlton 1934, 1937). Termites, beetles, lepidopteran caterpillars, ants, and grasshoppers dominate the diet in central Arizona (Toliver and Jennings 1975). In Dinosaur National Monument, Utah, Engeman and Hannes (1988) found an individual whose stomach was bulging hugely with what was probably a Mormon cricket *(Anabrus simplex)*. Crowley (1987) observed lizards drinking from the Rio Grande and adjacent small pools and puddles in Conejos County.

A wide assortment of predators attacks these lizards. Douglas (1966) found a striped whipsnake that had eaten *S. undulatus* at Mesa Verde in Montezuma County. Chiszar, Smith, and Defusco (1993) documented predation of an adult *S. undulatus* by a juvenile western rattlesnake in Elbert County. Ferner (1976) saw a racer make an unsuccessful attempt to capture one of these lizards in Boulder County. Ferguson, Brown, and DeMarco (1982) recorded successful predation on *S. undulatus* by juvenile racers in Kansas. In Weld County I saw several individuals hanging impaled on thornlike projections of plants, indicating predation by the loggerhead shrike *(Lanius ludovicianus)*. In Moffat County, I saw American kestrels carrying *Sceloporus,* possibly this species, to nests in cottonwood trees. Among the species present in Colorado, Degenhardt, Painter, and Price (1996) listed the collared lizard, leopard lizard, lesser earless lizard, and striped whipsnake as known predators in New Mexico. In western Nebraska, Jones and Ballinger (1987) found that mortality due to predation is low.

Remarks. Rand (1990, 1991, 1992) and Morrison, Rand, and Frost-Mason (1995) studied the biology of facial coloration in populations in Boulder County. Chin color of adults is either orange or yellow and is most intense in spring. (A rare hyper-melanized morph lacks this coloration.) Chin coloration first appears in most subadults by late June at an age of 11 months. Color change from yellow to orange apparently does not occur. Adult females have yellow or orange coloration, not as intense as in males, from about the time of ovulation in late May through early summer. The yellow morph was absent at one study site in the Lyons area. Orange males usually are dominant over yellow males and evoke a flight response from the latter. In an aggressive encounter, even a small orange lizard may win when matched with a larger yellow individual.

Yellow males perch motionless or flatten in response to perched orange males. Females do not behave differently toward orange and yellow males.

Taxonomy and Variation. *Sceloporus undulatus* is known also as the eastern fence lizard, a name I choose to discard in favor of more appropriate designations for the western populations. This species comprises geographically distinctive populations with strikingly different characteristics. I suggest that these populations (subspecies) be referred to by the common names suggested by Stebbins (1985), as in the key that follows, with the exception of *S. u. erythrocheilus,* the so-called red-lipped plateau lizard, which I amend to orange-lipped plateau lizard because the facial color is actually orange or yellow (Rand 1990).

In most cases, subspecies identification can be made simply by referring to the distribution map. In questionable cases, adults of the four subspecies in Colorado can be distinguished using the following key.

1A. Usually 45 or more scales along middle of back between interparietal scale and rear edge of thigh; light stripes along sides of back crossed by dark wavy bands, or stripes absent — 2.
1B. Usually 44 or fewer scales between interparietal scale and rear edge of thigh; light stripes along sides of back usually distinct and not crossed by dark bands — 3.
2A. Blue patches on throat meet at midline in adult male; lips, chin, and/or face of adults usually orange or yellow during breeding season (peak coloration in May), though some adult males may lack this coloration and have extensive black ventral coloration instead (Rand 1990, 1991); dorsum with dark wavy crossbands — *S. u. erythrocheilus* Maslin, 1956 (orange-lipped plateau lizard).
2B. Blue patches on sides of throat usually do not meet at midline; lips and chin never orange or yellow; dark crossbands on back often faint, discontinuous, or absent (large individuals may show tendency toward uniformity in dorsal coloration [Legler

1960a]); dark lateral stripe usually present on adult male — *S. u. elongatus* Stejneger, 1890 (northern plateau lizard).
3A. Blue patches on sides of throat and belly, with wide black margin in adult males; Archuleta County — *S. u. tristichus* Cope, 1875 (southern plateau lizard).
3B. Usually no blue patches on sides of throat; eastern Colorado — *S. u. garmani* Boulenger, 1882 (northern prairie lizard).

In our region, subspecies *elongatus* (squares on map) usually occurs in rocky areas throughout eastern Utah, western Colorado, southwestern and south-central Wyoming (Hammerson and Lapin 1980c), and south into northern Arizona and northwestern New Mexico. Subspecies *tristichus* (diamonds on map) occurs mainly in Arizona and New Mexico, but its range extends north to Archuleta County, Colorado, where it inhabits mountainous areas with rocks and logs. Subspecies *erythrocheilus* (solid circles on map) is a rock-dweller, occurring along the eastern edge of the Rockies in Colorado and southern Wyoming, in canyons and areas with volcanic rocks in southeastern Colorado, throughout most of the San Luis Valley, and south into northeastern New Mexico and the panhandle of Oklahoma. Gillis (1989) found that populations of *erythrocheilus* vary in dorsal coloration and generally match the rocks in their habitat. Subspecies *garmani* (flat-bottomed triangles on map) generally inhabits sandy prairie areas and the vicinity of rocky bluffs and buttes from South Dakota south through Nebraska, Kansas, southeastern Wyoming, and northeastern and extreme southeastern Colorado to Oklahoma and northern Texas.

Smith (1938:14) stated that specimens of both *garmani* and *elongatus* (which included *erythrocheilus* at the time) were available from Milton Reservoir, Weld County. However, the pertinent specimen of *erythrocheilus* bears no locality data other than "Weld County" (William Duellman, pers. comm.). The specimen probably was collected in northern Weld County, where *erythrocheilus* is known to occur, not at Milton Reservoir, where only *garmani* occurs.

Sample area	Dorsals[1]	Snout-vent length[2]		Gular patches[3]		Stripes[4]
		Males	Females	Males	Females	
M	49.0 (35)	64.8 (17)	66.6 (19)	0 (17)	0 (19)	0 (36)
L	45.4 (17)	58.0 (6)	66.1 (12)	0 (6)	0 (12)	33 (18)
A	44.5 (30)	53.4 (13)	60.7 (17)	0 (13)	0 (17)	70 (30)
W	44.4 (22)	54.5 (11)	61.5 (9)	36 (11)	0 (9)	24 (22)
E	48.2 (52)	59.4 (34)	61.7 (18)	97 (35)	63 (16)	4 (52)

[1] Number of mid-dorsal scales (mean, sample size) between interparietal and rear edge of thigh.
[2] Snout-vent length in millimeters (mean, sample size).
[3] Specimens with blue gular patches in contact midventrally (%, sample size).
[4] Specimens with distinct, continuous, light dorsolateral stripes (%, sample size).

Table 8.2. Characteristics of *Sceloporus undulatus* in southern Colorado. Data are for preserved specimens exceeding 50 mm SVL. Sample areas are Montezuma County (M), La Plata County (L), Archuleta County (A), western San Luis Valley (W), and central and eastern San Luis Valley (E). Samples from M to E represent a 300-km west-to-east transect from southwestern to south-central Colorado.

I have examined specimens of *erythrocheilus* supposedly collected just east of Kit Carson along Big Sandy Creek, Cheyenne County, an area from which all other *S. undulatus* have been *garmani*. Maslin (1959) reported these *erythrocheilus* specimens under both *garmani* and *erythrocheilus*. Until verification is available, I must regard this *erythrocheilus* record as erroneous.

As far as I know, subspecies *garmani* and *erythrocheilus* inhabit mutually exclusive areas and do not come into contact. They are separated by no less than 20 miles (32 km) anywhere in Colorado. The ranges are adjacent but do not overlap in Oklahoma (McCoy 1961, 1975). Maps in Baxter and Stone (1985) indicate that these two subspecies may occur much closer to each other in Wyoming, but they do not overlap.

In northeastern Elbert County, Smith et al. (1991) discovered a population (flat-topped triangles on map) that most closely resembled *garmani* in size, dorsal coloration, and dorsal scale count but exhibited some weakly developed *erythrocheilus* characteristics, particularly greater development of the ventral semeions (blue patches) as compared with *garmani*. The population is not near any existing populations of *erythrocheilus* or *garmani*. It is associated with shrubby sandstone-capped bluffs bordered by sandy soils, which is suitable habitat for *garmani* in Colorado (Maslin 1947b), Wyoming (Baxter

and Stone 1985), and south-central Kansas (Collins 1993). Smith et al. (1991) suggested that this population is a relict of past intergradation. Further consideration of the situation, however, indicates that intergradation between these two taxa is very unlikely (Smith et al. 1993). Instead, the Elbert County population more likely represents relictual intermediates between *S. u. garmani* and *S. u. consobrinus,* a peripheral variant of *garmani,* or "an isolated remnant of an ancestral population, with modest semeion development, that elsewhere continued the reductional trend in semeions, becoming the current *S. u. garmani* " (Smith et al. 1993: 33).

Intergradation between subspecies *elongatus* and *tristichus* (left-half-black circles) and between *tristichus* and *erythrocheilus* (right-half-black circles) occurs in southwestern Colorado (Table 8.2). Specimens from Archuleta County are relatively small (though living males and females are up to at least 67 and 71 mm SVL, respectively), have low dorsal scale counts, generally have distinct and continuous dorsolateral stripes, and have gular patches that do not meet; I believe these represent subspecies *tristichus*. They strongly resemble specimens of *tristichus* from Lakeside, Arizona, illustrated by Smith (1946). Specimens from Montezuma County are typical *elongatus* (high dorsal scale count, large size, gular patches that do not meet, no light dorsolateral stripes). Specimens from the intervening area in La Plata County exhibit a mixture of *elongatus* and *tristichus* characteristics or are intermediate. Gehlbach (1965) documented intergradation between *elongatus* and *tristichus* in northwestern New Mexico. Smith and Chiszar (1989) determined that these two taxa also intergrade in southwestern Utah.

Specimens from the central and eastern parts of the San Luis Valley are typical examples of *erythrocheilus* (high dorsal scale count, relatively large size, gular patches typically in contact, and usually lacking distinct striping). Populations from the southwestern corner of the valley show a mixture of *erythrocheilus* and *tristichus* characteristics or are intermediate (Hahn 1968; pers. obs.). Sexual differences in body size appear to be greater in *tristichus* and in the two areas of intergradation than in the samples of *elongatus* and *erythrocheilus*. The zone of intergradation between *erythrocheilus* and *tristichus* in Colorado appears to be narrow, as Applegarth (1969) found in northern New Mexico.

Maslin (1956) included specimens from Santa Fe County, New Mexico, in the material assigned to *erythrocheilus* in his original description of that subspecies. By doing so, he apparently included the type locality of *tristichus* (Taos, New Mexico) in the range of *erythrocheilus* (Hahn 1968). I have examined the Santa Fe County specimens, and they appear to more closely resemble *tristichus* (Smith 1938, 1946) than *erythrocheilus*. Applegarth (1969) identified an apparent zone of intergradation between *erythrocheilus* and *tristichus* northeast of Taos in the vicinity of the Vermejo River at Dawson, Colfax County, New Mexico. Hence, the range of *erythrocheilus* probably does not extend as far south as Maslin indicated.

This species is badly in need of a thorough taxonomic revision. Genetic and morphological evidence presented by Wiens and Reeder (1997) suggest that most or all of the subspecies in Colorado could be regarded as distinct species under the phylogenetic species concept. In particular, *S. u. erythrocheilus* might warrant recognition as a distinct species under the PSC, though intergradation with *S. u. tristichus* argues against species status under the biological species concept. Experimentation by Niewiarowski (1995) and Niewiarowski and Roosenburg (1993) indicates that genetic differences account for a significant part of the phenotypic variation among populations of *S. undulatus* in different environments. This supports the use of morphology in making taxonomic allocations.

Plate 8.51. Adult tree lizard (Mesa County, Colorado).

Tree Lizard

Urosaurus ornatus (Baird and Girard, 1852)

Recognition. Dorsum with dark cross-bars; scales of at least two distinct sizes along middle of back; fold of skin across throat; at least one scale on top of head and behind eyes obviously larger than scales on middle of back; maximum SVL at least 55 mm in Colorado, with no sexual size dimorphism evident (Deslippe 1989; pers. obs.); average SVL 48–51 mm in adult females in four populations south of Colorado (Dunham 1982). *Mature male:* enlarged postanal scales; two hemipenial swellings on underside of base of tail; amber, light green, blue, or blue-green patch on each side of belly (usually blue-green in Colorado); color of belly patches may change with temperature (Morrison, Sherbrooke, and Frost-Mason 1996); throat orange, orange-green, orange-blue, green, blue-green, or blue, rarely yellow (Carpenter 1995; pers. obs.). *Mature female:* blue belly patches faint or absent; throat yellow-green, yellowish, or ochre. *Hatchling:* 24–27 mm SVL in Colorado and New Mexico (Gehlbach 1965; Douglas

1966; Michel 1976); 20–21 mm SVL in Texas and Arizona (Martin 1973; Dunham 1982). *Eggs:* in New Mexico, largest average about 13 mm x 7 mm (Gehlbach 1965); average about 9–10 mm x 6 mm (Vitt 1977).

Distribution. Utah, extreme southwestern Wyoming, and western Colorado south through southeastern California, southern Nevada, Arizona, New Mexico, and western and central Texas to northern and northwestern Mexico. Occurs throughout much of western Colorado at elevations up to at least 6,500 feet (1,080 m) in the north and 8,000 feet (2,440 m) in the south. Harris (1963) was unable to confirm and doubted the validity of Cary's (1911) record of *U. ornatus* from southwestern Archuleta County. However, habitat in that area looks suitable, and I believe this record may be valid. Perhaps there is an isolated and currently unknown population, or the population no longer exists. Yarrow's (1875) record of *U. ornatus* from Twin Lakes, Lake County, is highly dubious; the elevation there is much too high (9,200 feet [2,805 m]) and the area is on the eastern side of the Continental Divide.

Conservation Status. The tree lizard is locally common in its suitable habitat

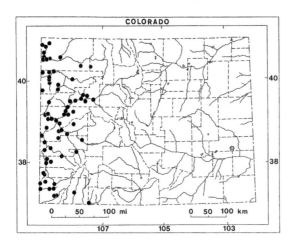

Map 8.15. Distribution of the tree lizard in Colorado.

of bedrock, talus slopes with large boulders, and other areas strewn with huge rocks. Piñon pine, juniper, and various shrubs generally are present. Despite their common name, in Colorado these lizards most often perch on steeply sloped expanses of rock. In some areas, usually in canyons or riparian zones, tree lizards do frequently perch on the trunks of trees, often junipers (e.g., Smith 1991) or cottonwoods. Sometimes they frequent piles of flood-deposited logs along rivers. These agile lizards easily run up or down vertical rock or wood surfaces. In southeastern Arizona, Smith (1996) found that individuals of varying sizes prefer different habitats; those favoring wooded habitat tend to be larger than those favoring rock-slide habitat.

throughout its historical range in Colorado. There is no evidence of a decline in distribution or abundance, and no significant threats currently exist, mainly because the lizard's habitat is largely incompatible with human uses. In localized areas, some habitat may have been eliminated as a result of juniper eradication to improve livestock grazing conditions.

Abundance of this lizard varies greatly from location to location and year to year, the latter due at least in part to climatic fluctuation. In various areas in Texas, New Mexico, and Arizona, adult population density may be as low as 40–60 individuals per hectare or as high as 290–720 per hectare (Dunham 1982). Density may decline substantially during periods of drought (Ballinger 1977, 1984), evidently due to reduced food resources (Dunham 1980).

In Mesa County, M'Closkey et al. (1997) found that areas experimentally depopulated of this species gradually are recolonized from surrounding areas, and in southern Arizona, M'Closkey and Baia (1990) found that depopulated areas are quickly recolonized from adjacent areas the next year. In contrast, in central Arizona, populations in areas subjected to density reduction remain moderately to greatly depressed in following years (Tinkle and Dunham 1983).

Habitat. Typical habitat in Colorado includes cliffs, canyon walls, steep exposures

In Colorado, winter presumably is spent underground. In the warmer climate of Arizona and Texas, winter may be spent under tree bark, in stumps, or in rock crevices (Vitt 1974; Worthington and Sabath 1966). Wintering lizards may aggregate (Tinkle and Dunham 1983; Boykin and Zucker 1993). Vitt (1974) found 155 tree lizards under the bark of two stumps in Arizona. In New Mexico, many wintered in abandoned burrows of digger bees (Anthophoridae) in a vertical, south-facing sediment bank along a stream (Seely, Zegers, and Asquith 1989).

Activity. Activity in Colorado takes place primarily from April through October. In the warmer parts of the range, minimal activity may occur in fall and winter (Worthington and Sabath 1966; Parker 1973; Vitt 1974; Tinkle and Dunham 1983; Degenhardt, Painter, and Price 1996). In late spring and summer, most activity takes place between 8:00 a.m. and 7:30 p.m., often with peaks in mid- to late morning and in late afternoon and early evening (before sunset). Tree lizards bask in the sun in the morning, late afternoon, and, during cool weather, midday. In summer, shaded perches often are used during the hottest part of the day. Smith and Ballinger (1994a, 1995a) determined that desert and lower montane populations in Arizona and New Mexico do not differ in average body temperature during activity (35°C) or in heat tolerance. Because desert populations experience warmer conditions, this consistency in body temperature suggests that the lizards adjust their use of the sun-shade environment and time of activity depending on conditions. In Colorado, I found that four active adults had body temperatures of 35.8–38.0°C (average 36.8°C).

Most adult males are territorial and actively defend their home areas against other adult males. Male displays include bobbing with the body compressed. Usually, 2–3 deliberate whole-body lifts, involving all four limbs, precede a series of lesser, more rapid bobs. Females also sometimes perform bobbing displays not associated with rejection of male courtship. In Mesa County, Deslippe (1989) found that the territories of adult males are disjunct and are not significantly larger than the home ranges of adult females. Females have been reported as unaggressive and nonterritorial (M'Closkey, Baia, and Russell 1987; Deslippe et al. 1990a, 1990b), territorial only after the breeding season (Dunham 1980), or territorial throughout the activity season, with no overlap of territories during gravidity (Mahrt 1998). M'Closkey and Baia (1987) found that males tend to abandon territories if the females are removed.

Tree lizards generally have relatively small home ranges. In western Colorado, home range size averages 154 m² in males and 109 m² in females (Christian and Waldschmidt 1984). In New Mexico, Zucker (1989) found that home range size is highly variable among individuals and averages 70 m² in males and 39 m² in females (Zucker 1989). Some individuals may remain within areas just a few meters in diameter; others

range over much larger territories (Zucker 1989). Additional studies have found large annual variations in home range size (see Zucker 1989).

In one study area in southern New Mexico, Zucker (1989) found that some males assume a very dark, almost black dorsal coloration, whereas others resemble the cryptic gray-brown of females. Dark males occupy areas separate from other dark males, and these areas usually are inhabited by multiple females. Light males overlap somewhat with dark males and are behaviorally subordinate. Light males sometimes become dark and dominant after taking over a vacant territory or supplanting other males.

Tree lizards approached by humans may remain relatively motionless or run away out of view. In hand, these small lizards may struggle, but they cannot bite very hard. In New Mexico, Mahrt (1996) observed two small adult male tree lizards ooze blood from the orbital region in response to handling.

Reproduction and Growth. A male may mate with one or more females within his territory. In Mesa County, mating is mostly monogamous and involves isolated pairs (Deslippe 1989). Nonterritorial adult males may attempt to mate using a "satellite" or "sneaker" strategy (see "Remarks").

At Mesa Verde, Douglas (1966) found females containing 3–5 large eggs each in mid-May, late June, and early July. Females

Plate 8.52. Adult male tree lizard (Montezuma County, Colorado).

examined in late May and early June contained only small eggs. These observations suggest that each female produces two clutches per year or that some females oviposit earlier and others later. Perhaps older females produce two clutches (or only an early one), and females breeding for the first time lay a single clutch in June or July. In Mesa and lowland Montezuma counties, I observed females (43–55 mm SVL) containing large eggs in late May. Throughout western Colorado, mature males are 45–54 mm SVL; a male that was 35 mm SVL in early June apparently was an immature yearling. Douglas (1966) observed the earliest hatchlings at Mesa Verde in late August. Earlier hatching is expected in areas at lower elevations.

The age at sexual maturity in Colorado has not been determined but apparently is older than in areas to the south where the growing season is longer. First breeding probably occurs in the second spring. Accordingly, in Mesa County, Deslippe (1989) concluded that both juvenile and adult size classes are present in summer before the appearance of young of the year, though these classes were difficult to distinguish. He found that three of four individuals survived from July until May of the following year.

In the Zuni Mountains of northwestern New Mexico, Gehlbach (1965) found gravid females containing 2–5 eggs from mid-June to mid-July, but females with large eggs were observed only in mid-July (Gehlbach 1965). By late July, females were postreproductive. It seems likely that an earlier (May) clutch in the Zuni Mountains may have gone undetected. Gehlbach observed newly hatched young in mid- to late August.

Most information on tree lizard reproduction and growth is based on studies in areas substantially south of Colorado in Arizona, New Mexico, and Texas or at lower elevations where the growing season and reproductive season are longer (Martin 1973b, 1977; Parker 1973; Ballinger 1977, 1984; Vitt 1977; Dunham 1980, 1981, 1982; Tinkle and Dunham 1983; van Loben Sels and Vitt 1984; Smith and Ballinger 1994b,

1995b). Reproductive characteristics of tree lizards in these areas were quite variable. Oviposition in some areas occurs as early as early May and extends as late as early September. Clutch size averages 5–9 eggs in different areas. In contrast to the small clutch sizes in Colorado and northwestern New Mexico, a female from the Organ Mountains in southern New Mexico contained an amazing 17 oviductal eggs (Zucker and Guillette 1985). Clutch size is largest in the largest females and tends to decline through the reproductive season. Number of clutches per adult female per year ranges from one to possibly six (though two or three is typical). Drought conditions tend to decrease reproductive output, probably by reducing food resources. The first appearance of hatchlings occurs as early as June in some areas but not until late August or September in others. Reproductive females are at least 39–45 mm SVL, and breeding males are at least 45–47 mm SVL; all individuals are sexually mature at an age of one year or less. In central Arizona, females that lay early clutches appear to be at least two years old. Annual survival rate of adults is variable (11–50 percent). In an Arizona study site, survival was high in late summer and through winter but low during the breeding season (Tinkle and Dunham 1983). Most individuals live long enough to participate in only one breeding season; relatively few participate in two. In at least some areas, survival of juveniles, growth rate, and body condition are reduced during drought. Overall, the tree lizard can be categorized as early-maturing and short-lived.

M'Closkey, Baia, and Russell (1987) found that females in an arboreal population in Arizona lay eggs in litter and sandy soil at the bases of occupied trees. Captive females may begin digging nesting chambers as much as a week before oviposition but dig most intensively two days before laying their eggs (Deslippe et al. 1990a). Rest periods frequently interrupt the digging. One female spent 91 minutes in the completed nest chamber before emerging devoid of her eggs. After basking, she then completely filled the nesting chamber with sand.

Food and Predators. Tree lizards feed opportunistically on small arthropods; diet varies with prey availability. At Mesa Verde, the diet includes various small invertebrates such as thrips, aphids and other bugs, beetles, caddisflies, lepidopterans, flies, wasps, ants, and spiders (Douglas 1966). Knowlton (1934) recorded a similar ant-and-fly-dominated diet in Utah. Various reptiles, birds, and mammals probably prey on these lizards, but few instances of predation actually have been documented (e.g., see Tinkle and Dunham 1983) and none are known for Colorado.

Remarks. Tree lizards exhibit interesting variation in throat color. In southern New Mexico (Carpenter 1995a, 1995b), initial throat color in both sexes is pale orange and develops at an age of about three weeks (25–27 mm SVL). In females, the throat remains orange or becomes yellow. As males grow, throat color changes to green, orange-green, blue-green, blue, or yellow, or remains orange; yellow sometimes appears before the development of green, blue-green, or blue coloration, and green occurs before a change to blue-green or blue. Color change continues for up to several months but then becomes more or less fixed in adults, though some yellowish females turn orange just prior to ovulation (Zucker and Boecklen 1990). Blue throats fade to blue-green or green seasonally or in response to social interactions. Orange coloration may inhibit aggression from adult males. Adult males with blue or green throats generally are dominant over orange-throated males. However, the range of coloration varies among different populations. In populations lacking significant variation in adult male throat color, experience is a better predictor of dominance status than is throat color. Male size also plays an important role in dominance relations.

In central Arizona, throat color of males is solid blue, solid yellow, solid orange, or blue rimmed with orange or yellow (Thompson and Moore 1991a). Different populations exhibit up to all five color morphs. Males with orange-blue throats are aggressively territorial and dominant over orange-throated males (fighting ability increases with size of blue area); orange-throated males are less aggressive and adopt a "sneaker" or "satellite" strategy for securing mating opportunities (i.e., skulking near a dominant male and attempting to mate with nearby females) (Thompson 1991b; Thompson, Moore, and Moore 1993). Carpenter (1995a, 1995b) provided additional references to the substantial literature on this topic.

Taxonomy and Variation. Under a classification recognizing subspecies (e.g., Mittleman 1942), the subspecies in Colorado is *U. o. wrighti* (Schmidt, 1921). Several authors have described problems with Mittleman's (1942) diagnoses of *U. ornatus* subspecies (see Gehlbach 1965). In recent guides and checklists, Stebbins (1985) and Collins (1997) did not recognize any subspecies of *U. ornatus*. Wiens (1993) analyzed phylogenetic relationships within the genus *Urosaurus* based largely on morphological characteristics and concluded that none of the nominal subspecies of *U. ornatus* merit recognition as species, and none of the subspecies were recognized as an evolutionary entity in Wiens's phylogenetic classification.

Haenel (1997) examined mtDNA variation among populations in east-central New Mexico, southwestern and south-central New Mexico, and south-central Texas. Each population had unique mtDNA restriction-site haplotypes. The two most geographically separated populations had the most similar haplotypes. These results probably reflect the isolation of populations in disjunct habitats with restricted gene flow among populations. Evolutionary mechanisms may be responsible for some of the observed variation in ecology and life history (Haenel 1997).

Plate 8.53. Adult side-blotched lizard (Mesa County, Colorado).

Side-blotched Lizard
Uta stansburiana (Baird and Girard, 1852)

Recognition. Dorsum of uniform color or with numerous small light and dark dots; scales along middle of back of uniform size; dark blotch on each side of chest (a large blue-black streak is present in some males); throat often with blue with orange rim (colors less intense in late summer); at least one scale on top of head and behind eyes obviously larger than scales on middle of back; in Colorado, SVL usually 4.5–5.2 cm in males and up to about 4.7 cm in females; over the species' range, average size of adults and degree of sexual dimorphism (males larger than females) increases from north to south (Parker and Pianka 1975); a large percentage of adults have broken or regenerated tails. *Mature male:* two hemipenial swellings on underside of base of tail; enlarged postanal scales; dorsum with light spots and turquoise or blue dots. *Mature female:* dorsum with dark spots. *Hatchling:* 21–22 mm SVL (Tinkle 1967; Bakewell, Chopek, and Burkholder 1983). *Eggs:* average about 11 mm x 6–7 mm (Douglas 1966; Vitt 1977).

Distribution. South-central Washington, southeastern Idaho, Utah, western Colorado, and southwestern Oklahoma south through Oregon, California, Nevada, Arizona, New Mexico, and Texas to southern Baja California and northwestern and north-central mainland Mexico. Related species are found on islands in the Gulf of California (Grismer 1994). Occurs throughout much of lowland western Colorado at elevations generally below 6,000 feet (1,830 m) but up to 6,500 feet (1,980 m) or more in Montezuma County. Cary (1911) reported this lizard at 7,000 feet (2,135 m) at Spruce Tree House at Mesa Verde, but recent records from that area are restricted to lower elevations farther south, at the southern end of Chapin Mesa (Douglas 1966). Most occurrences are in Mesa and Garfield counties in west-central Colorado. Mourning (1997) found this lizard as far east as western Eagle County. Gehlbach (1965) recorded this species as a rarity at elevations as high as 6,900 and 7,100 feet (2,100 and 2,165 m) in northwestern New Mexico.

Conservation Status. The side-blotched lizard is locally common to abundant in suitable habitat throughout its historical range in Colorado. Local instances of habitat destruction have occurred, but no known factors significantly threaten the regional population. The overall population trend cannot be quantified but appears to be stable.

Where it is most common, the side-blotched lizard is the most abundant reptile in its habitat. Density of adults in Mesa County generally is 25–42 per hectare, with males and females about equally abundant, but density varies with year and habitat (Tinkle 1967). In Garfield County, Bound (1977) found that different methods of density estimation yielded values of 43 per hectare and 122 per hectare. In southern New Mexico, density may be as high as 25 adults per hectare and up to 60 subadults and juveniles per hectare (Whitford and Creusere 1977). Abundance of this lizard tends to increase with the amount of precipitation the previous year, presumably reflecting enhanced food resources and better survival (Parker and Pianka 1975). In Mesa County, M'Closkey et al. (1997) found that areas experimentally depopulated of this species were quickly recolonized from surrounding areas.

Habitat. Typical habitat in Colorado consists of washes, arroyos, boulder-strewn ravines, rocky canyon slopes, bedrock exposures, rimrock outcroppings, rocky cliff bases, and flat, shrubby areas in canyon bottoms where soils are soft and deep. Most occurrences are in the bottoms or mouths of canyons in areas of open piñon-juniper woodland, semidesert shrubland, or patchy streamside vegetation. Usually, these lizards are found where there is plenty of bare ground. When disturbed, they generally seek cover in crevices or under plants or rocks. Wintering sites include burrows, deep crevices, or other underground cavities. Sometimes several or dozens of individuals hibernate in close proximity to one another (Tinkle 1967; Degenhardt, Painter, and Price 1996; pers. obs.).

Activity. The primary period of activity in Colorado extends from April through October. Limited activity may take place during warm weather in March and November. Larry Valentine observed a few side-blotched lizards basking and doing push-up displays in early December in Delta County. In warmer areas south of Colorado, some activity may occur during warm weather throughout the winter (Alexander and Whitford 1968; Baltosser and Best 1990).

Side-blotched lizards are active during daylight hours. In Colorado, I have found them out from 7:00 a.m. until 8:00 p.m. In Mesa County, morning emergence from nighttime retreats generally takes place between 8:00 and 9:00 a.m. in May and June (Tinkle 1967) and earlier during warmer summer weather.

In summer, side-blotched lizards expose themselves to the sun in the morning and late afternoon and generally prefer shade at midday. The probability of being in the shade increases with rising air temperature (Waldschmidt 1980). Females are more likely than males to bask at midday. Lizards usually orient themselves perpendicular to the sun's rays upon initial emergence in the morning. Under a wide range of climate conditions throughout the range of this species, body temperature during

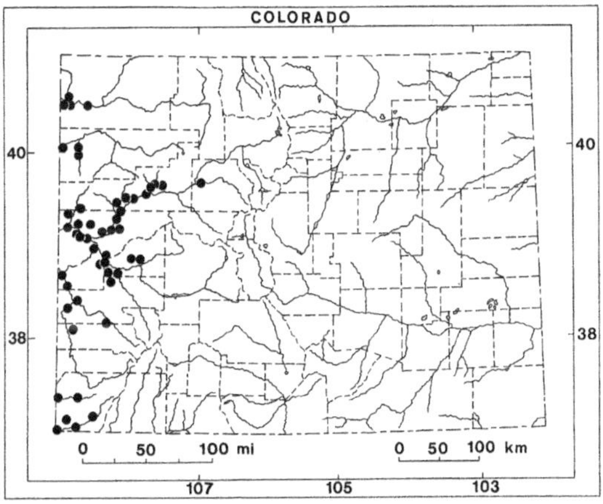

Map 8.16. Distribution of the side-blotched lizard in Colorado.

Plate 8.54. Adult side-blotched lizard (Montezuma County, Colorado).

activity averages about 35–36°C (Ferguson 1970, 1971b; Parker and Pianka 1975), though seasonal variations occur. Body temperatures of several active individuals in Colorado were 33.5–35.7°C in spring and summer and 29.4–31.5°C in fall (pers. obs.).

Side-blotched lizards are only weakly territorial, and their home ranges usually overlap (Tinkle 1967; Bound 1977; Waldschmidt 1979; Waldschmidt and Tracy 1983). Interactions among males are best characterized in terms of a dominance hierarchy (Bound 1977). Compared to individuals in Texas, side-blotched lizards in Colorado are noticeably less aggressive toward each other, though occasional chases and fights do happen (Tinkle 1967; Ferguson 1970). Male displays of aggression consist of a series of bobs (push-ups) done with the back arched, the body compressed, and the throat lowered. A series of low-amplitude vibrations occurs at the summit of each push-up. Neonates and adult females also perform push-up displays, at least when confronted by a human.

In Mesa County, Tinkle (1967) and Tinkle and Woodward (1967) found that home range size is no more than a few hundred square meters, but individuals, especially males, sometimes make long-distance movements of up to several hundred meters. Distance from the hatching site to the center of the home range was about 6 m for one female and 20–42 m (average 33 m) for four males.

Home range size in western Colorado averages about 440–610 m² in males and about 190–225 m² in females (Tinkle 1967; Waldschmidt 1979; Christian and Waldschmidt 1984). Waldschmidt and Tracy (1983) observed a large reduction in average home range size of males from more than 500 m² to about 100 m² between June and July and suggested that this resulted from decreased breeding activity and from seasonal heating that reduced the amount of space in which a suitable body temperature could be maintained.

Reproduction and Growth. Courtship begins in spring soon after emergence from hibernation. Ferguson (1970) described courtship and mating behavior of *U. stansburiana* in Mesa County. Courtship may begin with an initial push-up display by the male, followed by an approach toward the female, usually accompanied by a quick nodding of the head. Sometimes the male circles the female. The male then usually licks the female, does more push-ups and/or nodding, grasps her neck/shoulder in his jaws, does more push-ups, swings the female back and forth, strokes her with his hind leg (which results in her raising her pelvic region and tail), and eventually inserts a hemipenis into her cloaca. Copulation lasts about 0.5–4.0 (average about 1.0) minutes and may involve a dozen or more pelvic thrusts. Unreceptive females reject approaching males with a shuddering bob that resembles the male's courtship nod. Females may store and use sperm for up to several months after mating (Cuellar 1966).

In Mesa County (Tinkle 1967), females that are at least two years old may lay up to three clutches (some definitely lay two) averaging about three eggs each, with the earliest clutches deposited in mid-April and the latest in July. Early clutches average four eggs. Females breeding for the first time may produce only two clutches. All adult females appear to be reproductive during the breeding season. Hatching begins as early as late July and continues through August. Individuals attain sexual maturity during the middle of the breeding season in the year after hatching. Females become reproductive at 36–38 mm SVL, males evidently at about 42 mm SVL. The usual lifespan is short. Only about 20 percent of the hatchlings survive as long as one year (most die during winter). Similarly, only about 22 percent of the adults survive until the next year. Only about one-third of the adult population consists of individuals two or more years old. Similarly, Whitford and Creusere (1977) documented a high turnover rate in the adult population in southern New Mexico. Compared to a population Tinkle studied in Texas, side-blotched lizards in Colorado mature at a smaller size (but similar age), produce fewer eggs, have a shorter breeding season, and live longer. Tinkle (1967) did not find any nest sites of side-blotched lizards, despite much effort. In California, Mautz (1982) found three clutches under a single firmly embedded rock.

Limited information is available from elsewhere in Colorado. Douglas (1966) found a female containing two small ova and two females carrying four large eggs each in mid-May in small samples from Mesa Verde. I found egg-laden females in late May in the same county. Bound (1977) saw hatchlings in early August in Garfield County. Hatchlings grow quickly, and males exhibit blue-orange throat coloration by the end of their first season, at 30–34 mm SVL (pers. obs.)

In northern Utah (Parker and Pianka 1975), females with oviductal eggs may be found from late May through mid-July; average clutch size (3–5 eggs) varies in different areas and from year to year. Most females apparently produce only one clutch per season. Hatchlings emerge in August.

Comparative reproductive data for side-blotched lizards from throughout other parts of the range (Dixon 1967; Turner et al. 1970; Tanner 1972; Parker and Pianka 1975; Medica and Turner 1976; Bakewell, Chopek, and Burkholder 1983) are as follows: smallest mature male 40–50 mm SVL, larger in south than in north; smallest mature female usually 40–44 mm SVL; average clutch size 3–5 eggs, smallest later in the season, largest in the largest females; number of clutches per female per year usually 1–2 in the north, 2 or more in the south; first appearance of hatchlings in late June (Texas, Nevada, Idaho) or late July (Nevada at higher elevations, Oregon). The Oregon population occurs in an area with a short growing season, and approximately half of the females fail to breed in the year after hatching (Nussbaum and Diller 1976). In southern New Mexico, (Worthington 1982) found that drought may result in a one-egg reduction in the average clutch size.

Food and Predators. Side-blotched lizards are opportunistic foragers (Parker and Pianka 1975). Generally, they wait on a slightly elevated perch and make short dashes for arthropods that move or land nearby. Sometimes, they stalk prey before making a quick short-range attack. Prey may be beaten against the ground before being swallowed. Food items in Utah, and probably in Colorado, commonly include grasshoppers, beetles, leafhoppers and other bugs, ants, various insect larvae, and spiders; in addition, termites may be eaten in large numbers in the southern parts of the range (Knowlton and Janes 1933; Knowlton 1934; Knowlton and Thomas 1936; Pianka and Parker 1975; Barbault and Maury 1981; Best and Gennaro 1984). As in many lizard species, cannibalism sometimes occurs. Wilson (1990) found adult males (46–49 mm SVL) that had eaten juvenile *U. stansburiana*.

Most predation on this lizard undoubtedly goes undetected. Known predators in Colorado include the striped whipsnake and leopard lizard (McCoy 1967; Tinkle 1967). In Nevada, Turner et al. (1982) found that leopard lizards have a profound effect on the survival rates of adult side-blotched lizards. Predation by the western whiptail and coachwhip has been observed in New Mexico (Degenhardt, Painter, and Price 1996). Wilson (1991) presented a long list of potential reptile, bird, mammal, and invertebrate (spider, scorpion, solpugid) predators of *U. stansburiana*.

Remarks. In Mesa County, tails that I accidentally detached wiggled vigorously for about 20–60 seconds and ceased moving after 5–7 minutes. A 15-mm piece of detached tail from a hatchling did not twitch at all. Niewiarowski et al. (1997) found that tail loss in hatchlings slows growth but generally does not reduce survival.

Taxonomy and Variation. The subspecies in Colorado is *Uta stansburiana uniformis* Pack and Tanner, 1970.

WHIPTAILS
Family Teiidae

About 225 species occur in the Americas, from the United States south through South America and the West Indies. Most members of this family have elongate bodies, large head scales, granular dorsal scales, rectangular ventral scales, and a long tail. Some (none in the United States) are fossorial, with reduced limbs; others are arboreal. Five of the approximately 20 species in the United States occur in Colorado.

All U.S. species (*Cnemidophorus* whiptails) are diurnal, terrestrial, thermophilic invertivores. Individuals of most species can tolerate body temperatures of up to 45°C or more. The tongue is long, forked, frequently extruded, and covered by scalelike papillae, except at the tip. Tongue extrusion probably mediates vomeronasal chemoreception. The posterior teeth are bi- or tricuspid. All *Cnemidophorus* species appear to be primarily generalized opportunistic feeders on arthropods.

All species are oviparous. Several species in the United States, including three in Colorado, are all-female and reproduce by parthenogenesis (egg develops without fertilization; chromosome complement doubles prior to normal meiotic divisions). These species originated through hybridization between two bisexual species or, in some instances, through hybridization of one these hybrids with another bisexual species, resulting in the production of a triploid species. Some or all of these parthenogens occasionally produce male progeny, apparently as a result of hybridization with a bisexual species.

Courtship and copulation behavior in the genus *Cnemidophorus* is stereotyped as follows: male approaches female, investigates her with his tongue; male grasps female's neck skin or foreleg in his jaws, mounts female, scratches her sides with his legs, presses her down; male curls his tail beneath the female, places his cloaca next to hers, inserts a hemipenis, and shifts his jaw grip to the female's abdominal region, assuming a contorted posture; male dismounts and leaves after several minutes (Crews and Moore 1993). Surprisingly, this same behavior commonly occurs between mature females of the parthenogenetic species (at least in captivity), although, of course, no hemipenial intromission occurs. Malelike behavior is seen most often in gravid females, whereas femalelike behavior is nearly restricted to females in which vitellogenesis (yolking of ovarian follicles) is taking place (Crews and Moore 1993). Individual females may assume either role at different times. This pseudocopulatory behavior appears to stimulate increased reproductive output. Pseudocopulation has been observed in the field in at least one parthenogenetic *Cnemidophorus* species, but its frequency under natural conditions is unknown.

Plate 8.55. Triploid checkered whiptail (Las Animas County, Colorado). *Lauren Livo and Steve Wilcox.*

Triploid Checkered Whiptail

Cnemidophorus neotesselatus (Walker, Cordes, and Taylor, 1997)

Recognition. Body and tail long and slender; dorsum with small granular scales; belly with larger rectangular scales; scales along front edge of fold of skin across throat conspicuously enlarged; paravertebral pale stripes gray, uninterrupted, straight, often fused with spots; mid-dorsal (vertebral) stripe gray and, if present on the neck, relatively straight, or stripe on neck followed by spots; lateral stripe (lowermost stripe on side of body) gray, relatively straight, frequently interrupted by narrow areas of black ground color, usually fused with some spots and/or bars; area between the two uppermost pale stripes (not counting the vertebral line) on each side of the dorsum with linear series of pale spots, some fused with stripes; dorsal surface of thighs with numerous pale spots often fused into a reticulum; allotriploid chromosome number = 69; maximum SVL about 10.7 cm (Walker, Cordes, and Taylor

1997). *Hatchling:* in Pueblo County, 39–48 mm SVL (Knopf 1966). Eggs: in Pueblo County, 19–21 mm x 10–12 mm (Knopf 1966).

Distribution. This species occurs only in southeastern Colorado. Its distribution is spotty, ranging from the foothills of the Rocky Mountains in Fremont County (at elevations up to 6,900 feet [2,105 m] [Banta and Kimmel 1965]) eastward to Pueblo and Stone City in Pueblo County. It also is found in several sites in southern Pueblo County, Otero County, and Las Animas County. It is sympatric with *C. tesselatus* in a few areas within several miles of the Purgatoire River near Higbee, Otero County (Walker, Cordes, and Taylor 1997; Walker et al. 1997). This is the only area where coexistence between diploid and triploid speciation stages in any complex of parthenogenetic *Cnemidophorus* is known to occur (Walker and Cordes 1998). Walker et al. (1997) described the distributional relationships and community assemblages of *C. neotesselatus, C. tesselatus,* and *C. sexlineatus* in this area of Otero County.

Conservation Status. This species evidently was extirpated from the Pueblo area east of Interstate 25 around 1973, apparently as a result of habitat destruction, alteration, and/or fragmentation associated with urbanization (Walker, Cordes, and Taylor 1996). Yet this lizard is tolerant of a good deal of habitat disturbance and commonly dwells in rural landfill sites. It remains present and locally common west of I–25 in areas such as the Pueblo Nature Center and Pueblo State Recreation Area (Walker, Cordes, and Taylor 1997). Populations in shrub–grass or weed habitats in the Ninemile Valley at Higbee, Otero County, have declined greatly in recent decades and may face extirpation as a result of conversion of habitat to agricultural uses; nearby juniper-grassland escarpment populations are not threatened by human activity (Walker et al. 1997).

Habitat. Habitat of this ground-dwelling lizard includes hillsides, arroyos, and canyons associated with the Arkansas River valley; the canyon-grassland transition along the Huerfano River; grassland-surrounded rocky arroyo habitat along tributaries of the Apishapa River; and roadsides, shrubby areas, and juniper-grass associations in valleys, arroyos, and canyons associated with the Purgatoire River and some of its tributaries (Walker, Cordes, and Taylor 1997; Walker et al. 1997). Knopf (1966) described the habitat of a locally abundant population on bluffs above the Huerfano River as follows:

The area is heavily overgrazed, supports decidedly scanty vegetation (rabbitbrush, sparse grasses, prickly-pear cactus, Russian thistle, and yucca) and contains several man-made changes in topography. . . . A large ditch, sand bank and gravel pit . . . have provided optimum habitat. . . . The importance of these features are [sic] reflected not only in high lizard density, but certain physical phenomena associated with these changes (slope, exposure, drainage, soil type) make them preferred sites for burrows, nests and hibernacula. A broad area of unfavorable habitat encircles the population site.

Knopf found that the whiptails dig burrows in which they spend the night. These burrows may be used day after day and are defended against other conspecific individuals. All of the hibernation sites that he observed were on southeast-facing slopes devoid of vegetation. Leuck (1982) observed that captives often construct burrows in open sand and that multiple lizards may hide together under single objects.

Activity. In Pueblo County (Knopf 1966), emergence from hibernation usually occurs in mid- to late April but varies with spring weather conditions. Smaller individuals emerge first. Large adults generally end their activity in late August, but the young are active through mid-October. Activity takes place during warm, sunny weather. Daily activity in summer typically begins between 8:00 and 10:00 a.m. (sometimes as early as 7:15 a.m.) and peaks between 10:00 a.m. and 1:00 p.m. Individuals spend about 70 percent of the daily active period searching for food. Usually, they are not active after 6:30 p.m. Only part of the population is active on any given day. Body temperatures during

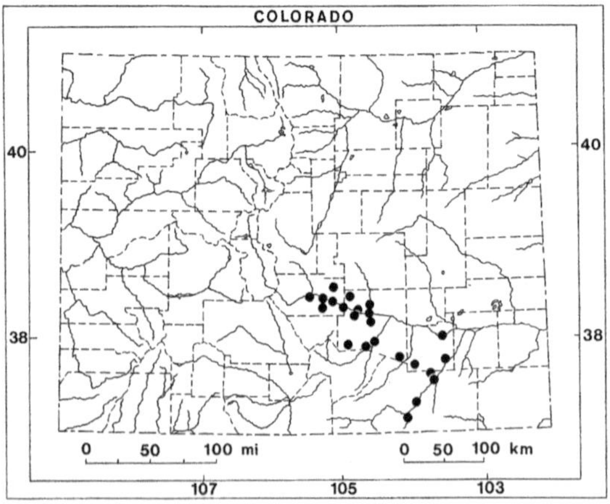

Map 8.17. Distribution of the triploid checkered whip-tail in Colorado.

activity range from 34–43°C (average 39°C). Home ranges of adults generally overlap, are not defended, and occupy about 650–1,010 m².

Leuck (1985) found that captives from Fremont County are less aggressive than captive six-lined racerunners. Leuck (1993) found that *C. tesselatus* and *C. neotessela-tus* from Otero County exhibit more social tolerance and less aggressiveness toward conspecifics than toward the other species.

This lizard is not particularly wary and often allows close approach by humans.

Reproduction and Growth. This is an all-female species. Maslin (1966, 1971) demonstrated unequivocally that males are not required for reproduction. Individuals kept in total isolation from the egg stage through sexual maturity produce eggs that yield fertile female offspring.

In Pueblo County (Knopf 1966), individuals carrying oviductal eggs can be found between mid-June and late July. Eggs are retained for 3–7 days or more before being laid. Apparently, a single clutch of 1–4 eggs (average approximately 3) is laid in some years and two clutches in other years. Oviposition is not highly synchronized; older individuals often lay their eggs before younger ones do. Eggs are laid about 18–23 cm below the ground surface in burrows dug with the lizard's forefeet in soft, well-drained soil. About two hours are required to dig the nest, which typically is sited in a sunny area devoid of vegetation. On occasion, several lizards may dig their nests in a small area. Nesters plug the burrow entrance behind them and spend 1–2 days underground while depositing their eggs. Eventually, they dig out of the burrow by another route. Nest sites are defended during and immediately after oviposition. Incubation lasts 60–74 days. Nests may exhibit a wide range of temperatures (at least 12–34°C). Eggs from early clutches hatch from late August to mid-September. Hatching in later clutches continues through early October. Hatchlings dig their way out of the nest burrow and sometimes return to it at night. Some return to the nest burrow to overwinter. The youngest reproductive individuals are in their third calendar year and are at least 70 mm SVL. Walker, Taylor, and Cordes (unpublished data) found that gravid females are 73–101 mm SVL (average 87–88 mm). The July population studied by Knopf consisted of about 20 percent juveniles, 20 percent subadults, 35 percent young adults, and 25 percent old adults; about 60 percent of the population reproduced. Annual turnover rate of the population was about 20 percent. Some individuals lived five or more years.

This species sometimes hybridizes with male *C. sexlineatus,* resulting in male tetraploid offspring (presumably sterile) and possibly of new parthenogenetic female lineages as well, though this has not been documented (Taylor, Currie, and Baker 1989; Walker et al. 1990; Walker, Taylor, and Cordes 1994).

Food and Predators. These whiptails feed opportunistically on available invertebrates. Paulissen et al. (1993) found that the diet of adults includes various arthropods, particularly grasshoppers, termites, adult and larval beetles, and caterpillars; hatchlings commonly eat leafhoppers, spiders, and moths.

In Pueblo County, Knopf (1966) documented predation by adult and hatchling coachwhips.

Taxonomy and Variation. This species formerly was included in *C. tesselatus* but was recognized as a distinct species, *C. neotesselatus,* by Walker, Cordes, and Taylor (1997). Wright (1993) maintained this species as *C. tesselatus* and referred to the diploid populations I call *C. tesselatus* as *C. grahamii.* Walker, Cordes, and Taylor (1997) discussed the problems in Wright's proposal. These include applying the name *C. tesselatus* to triploid populations, disregarding the fact that the name *tesselatus* was based on a diploid population, and disruption of nomenclatural stability by substituting the name *C. grahamii* for populations that long have been known as *C. tesselatus.* Zweifel (1965); Wright (1993); Walker, Taylor, and Cordes (1994, 1995); Walker, Cordes, and Taylor (1997); and Taylor, Walker, and Cordes (1996) discussed the complicated systematic history of this species and provided citations of relevant earlier literature.

This species originated through hybridization between a female *C. tigris marmoratus* (= *C. marmoratus*) and a male *C. septemvittatus* (= *C. gularis septemvittatus*), followed by hybridization between one of these hybrids with a male *C. sexlineatus* (Wright 1993;

Walker, Taylor, and Cordes 1995). *Cnemidophorus neotesselatus* includes three dorsal color pattern classes that Zweifel (1965) referred to as A, B, and C, but these may be arbitrary subdivisions of a single historical group (Maslin 1967; Frost and Wright 1988).

Plate 8.56. Adult six-lined racerunner (Bent County, Colorado).

Six-lined Racerunner
Cnemidophorus sexlineatus
(Linnaeus, 1766)

Recognition. Body long and slender; dorsum with small granular scales; belly with larger rectangular scales; three pale stripes along each side of back, plus a mid-dorsal stripe sometimes divided into two stripes; no light spots or bars in dark fields between stripes; neck and shoulders of adults often with bright-greenish wash; stripes may not contrast sharply with dark areas on shoulders; scales on undersurface of base of forelimb not enlarged; maximum size about 27 cm TL and 8.8 cm SVL. *Mature male:* belly pale blue. *Mature female:* belly whitish. *Hatchling:* 31–35 mm SVL; tail bright blue; light stripes contrast sharply

with dark areas on shoulders (Hardy 1962; Paulissen 1987b).

Distribution. Southeastern Wyoming, southern South Dakota, southeastern Minnesota, southwestern Wisconsin, northern Indiana, and Maryland south to the Gulf Coast from southern Texas to southern Florida, and west to the eastern edge of the Southern Rocky Mountains (Trauth and McAllister 1996). Occurs throughout eastern Colorado at elevations below 6,500 feet (1,980 m) in the north and 7,500 feet (2,285 m) in the south (Wet Mountains [Banta 1964]). Hahn (1968) mentioned a possible record of this species from near Saguache in the San Luis Valley, but this has not been confirmed, and occurrence of this species there seems unlikely.

Conservation Status. Six-lined racerunners are locally common in many areas of eastern Colorado. There is no evidence

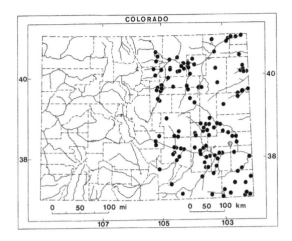

COLORADO

0   50   100 mi   0   50   100 km

107   105   103

Map 8.18. Distribution of the six-lined racerunner in Colorado.

In Oklahoma, Paulissen (1988b) found that the microhabitats of juveniles are less vegetated than are those of adults during most of the active season. Apparently, adults are more at risk of overheating.

Activity. Most activity in Colorado occurs during daylight hours from May to September, though some takes place in late April and October. Adults become progressively less active after July and have a short annual activity season. Most individuals still active in September and October are hatchlings. A similar pattern is found in Kansas (Hardy 1962).

These lizards favor warm conditions but may rest inactive in the shade during the hottest midday periods in summer. In eastern Kansas, morning emergence generally occurs between 8:00 and 10:00 a.m. in summer (Hardy 1962). Werth (1972) found that racerunners in western Kansas emerge from their burrows each summer morning when soil temperatures reach about 29–31°C. A peak in activity occurs between 1:00 p.m. and 4:00 p.m. In Oklahoma, spring and late summertime activity is greatest in the afternoon and generally commences earlier in the summer (Paulissen 1988a). In Colorado, I observed active racerunners between 9:00 a.m. and 6:00 p.m. (most often in mid- to late morning and early afternoon) at air temperatures of 19–34°C and soil surface temperatures of 29°C to more than 50°C. Body temperature during activity generally is 30–45°C, with an average of 38–40°C (Fitch 1956c, 1958; Hardy 1962; Paulissen 1988c). As might be expected from these data, activity usually occurs when the sun is shining, though Hardy (1962) found racerunners with low

of a significant decline in distribution or abundance, and no major widespread threats currently exist, though presumably the lizards are negatively affected by grasshopper-control activities. These lizards tolerate moderate to heavy habitat alteration as long as some semiwild habitat persists.

This species can be locally abundant. In Kansas, population density at one 0.23-hectare site extrapolated to about 100–175 per hectare, excluding hatchlings (Fitch 1958).

Habitat. Habitat in Colorado includes plains grassland (including rocky outcroppings and roadsides), sandhills, sandy or gravelly banks and floodplains of streams, grassy openings among ponderosa pines in the foothills, and open areas among rocks at the base of the mountains. In all habitats, unvegetated or sparsely vegetated openings are required; the lizards spend nearly all of their active time moving about on the ground. During periods of inactivity, racerunners hide beneath rocks, logs, and various debris, or underground. Vaughan (1961) reported that abandoned pocket gopher burrows are the favored retreat in sandhill areas. Where ready-made burrows are scarce, or where soils are soft, racerunners commonly dig their own burrows under objects or in sandy soil. Specific burrows may occupied once or twice, or day after day for many weeks (Hardy 1962).

body temperatures excavating tunnels in late afternoon.

Racerunners are almost always on the move when outside their burrows. They walk in a rather jerky manner, often flicking the tongue. When approached, they may head for cover at speeds of up to 29 km per hour (Hoyt 1941). Escaping adults may climb tree trunks to a height of two meters (Paulissen and Harvey 1985). In Colorado, I have seen individuals skitter across shallow pools of water while fleeing. In Arkansas, Trauth et al. (1996) saw a juvenile dive into a shallow pool of water and stay submerged for 1.5–2.0 minutes, and there are a few other reports of racerunners taking refuge underwater (see Hardy 1962 and Trauth et al. 1996). Racerunners do not always avoid humans—individuals that I watched on a sandy beach at a lake in Bent County foraged among several prostrate sunbathers. In hand, racerunners usually struggle vigorously and attempt to bite.

In Kansas, home range size averages about 800–1,000 m², but individuals some-times roam outside their normal range and occasionally move to new areas hundreds of meters away (Fitch 1958). Home ranges overlap, with no evidence of lizard territo-riality, though Hardy (1962) found that in May and early June, aggressive interactions are common among adult males in patches of favorable habitat, and adults frequently chase yearlings. Threat displays of males include body compression and exposure of the blue venter, downward tilting of the head with the jaws open, tail vibration, circling movements, and sometimes head bobbing (Hardy 1962).

Reproduction and Growth. Breeding occurs in late spring and early summer. Large aggressive males dominate (chase, fight) smaller males during the breeding season and may do most of the mating (Carpenter 1960a; Hardy 1962; Brackin 1978, 1979). In central Oklahoma, sexual behavior extends from mid-May through July, with a peak in June and early July (Brackin 1979). Before copulation, which lasts up to half an hour or so, the male may twitch his tail and rub his vent and femoral pores on the substrate; during copulation,

he grasps the female in his jaws (Hardy 1962).

Most of the following information is based on studies in Kansas by Fitch (1958) and Hardy (1962). Oviposition occurs from the beginning of June through the beginning of August. Early clutches are deposited by the oldest females and late clutches by the youngest and by older females laying a second clutch. Eggs are buried shallowly in sandy soil. Clutch size averages 3 eggs (range 1–6) and increases with female size. Hatchlings first appear in early August, before they typically appear in Colorado in mid-August (pers. obs.), after an incubation period of about 7–9 weeks. Peak emergence of hatchlings in Kansas takes place in the latter half of September. Breeding first takes place after the second hibernation. Egg-laying females are just under 7 cm SVL or larger (see also Vitt and Breitenbach 1993). Walker, Taylor, and Cordes (unpublished data) found that gravid females in Otero County, Colorado, are 63–76 mm SVL (average 69 mm). In Kansas, individuals emerging from their second hibernation average 73 mm SVL. It takes 4–5 years for average SVL to exceed 8 cm. Maximum longevity is at least six years, but few live more than four years. More than half of the breeding population consists of individuals that are almost two years old. Racerunners in Oklahoma and Texas depart only slightly from this pattern (Carpenter 1959, 1960b; Hoddenbach 1966; Clark 1976).

Food and Predators. The diet includes various small arthropods; adults generally eat larger prey, whereas juveniles take smaller, more numerous prey items (Paulissen 1987a). Prey may be obtained from the ground surface, in low vegetation, or by digging in the soil or vegetative debris (Fitch 1958; Hardy 1962). In Oklahoma, foraging young commonly climbed bushes to a height of nearly 1 m (Paulissen and Harvey 1985).

The diet varies with prey availability; in our region, it typically includes grass-hoppers, crickets, adult and larval lepi-dopterans, beetles, bugs, ants, spiders, and snails (Hardy 1962; Werth 1972; Ballinger, Lynch, and Cole 1979; Paulissen 1987b).

Protruding prey parts, such as grasshopper legs, moth wings, and caterpillar fuzz, usually are shaken or rubbed off. In western Nebraska, Jones and Ballinger (1987) found a hatchling lesser earless lizard in the stomach of a six-lined racerunner. Adults rarely eat conspecific juveniles (Etheridge and Wit 1982). The stomach of a racerunner from Boulder County was filled with grasshoppers (pers. obs.).

In Kansas and western Nebraska, typical predators include snakes (e.g., racer, coachwhip), hawks, and various carnivorous mammals (Fitch 1958; Hardy 1962; Ballinger, Lynch, and Cole 1979). Hardy (1962) found that hatchling racers were important predators on hatchling race-runners in eastern Kansas.

Taxonomy and Variation. The subspecies in Colorado is *Cnemidophorus sexlineatus viridis* Lowe, 1966.

Plate 8.57. Adult diploid checkered whiptail (Baca County, Colorado).

Diploid Checkered Whiptail

Cnemidophorus tesselatus (Say, 1823)

Recognition. Body and tail long and slender; dorsum with small granular scales; belly with larger rectangular scales; scales along front edge of fold of skin across throat conspicuously enlarged; paravertebral pale stripes gray-tan to tan or gold, irregular in outline, interrupted, and/or fused with bars; mid-dorsal (vertebral) stripe gray-tan to tan (or absent), single and irregular, or doubled or partly doubled; lowermost lateral stripe gray, irregular, and/or interrupted and fused with spots and/or bars (these stripes may be partly or entirely lost in older individuals); area between two uppermost pale stripes (not counting the vertebral line) on each side of dorsum with pale spots, either longitudinally fused into supernumerary line or transversely expanded into bars; dorsal surface of thighs with profuse pale spotting and some spots fused; maximum SVL about 10.6 cm (Walker, Cordes, and Taylor 1997). *Hatchling:* 38 mm SVL (Taylor, Walker, and Cordes 1997).

Distribution. Discontinuous from southeastern Colorado (extending north to the vicinity of the Ninemile Valley of the Purgatoire River at Higbee, Otero County) south through extreme western and southwestern Oklahoma, New Mexico, possibly extreme southeastern Arizona, western Texas, and well into Chihuahua, Mexico, along the Río Conchos (Walker, Cordes, and Taylor 1997). The different pattern classes occur syntopically in limited areas (Taylor, Walker, and Cordes 1997; Walker et al. 1997). Records for Pueblo, Pueblo County (triangle on map), consist of the material upon which the original description (Say, in James 1823) was based, clearly indicating a diploid *C. tesselatus*, and a single specimen collected near the Colorado State Hospital in 1962 (Taylor, Walker, and Cordes 1996; Walker, Cordes, and Taylor 1997). Recent surveys indicate that *C. tesselatus* no longer occurs in the vicinity of Pueblo (Walker, Cordes, and Taylor 1997). It is known from a few areas in Baca, Otero, and Las Animas counties, and there is an unconfirmed record from Bent County (Smith, Maslin, and Brown 1965). This species is sympatric with *C. neotesselatus* in a few areas within several miles of the Purgatoire River near Higbee, Otero County (Walker, Cordes, and Taylor 1997; Walker et al. 1997; Walker and Cordes 1998). Walker et al. (1997) described the distributional relationships and community assemblages of *C. neotesselatus, C. tesselatus,* and *C. sexlineatus* in this area of Otero County.

Conservation Status. This whiptail occurs in most of its relatively limited historic range in Colorado. Abundance trends are difficult to evaluate, but collection

records and recent surveys suggest that this lizard may be less common now in some sites than it was in former years (Walker, Cordes, and Taylor 1997; Walker et al. 1997). Most of the range in Colorado is not subject to extensive human development of an incompatible nature. The lizards tolerate a good deal of habitat disturbance (though they do not depend on it). However, as noted previously, populations in the vicinity of Pueblo have disappeared, and populations in shrub–grass and weed habitats in the Ninemile Valley at Higbee, Otero County, have declined greatly in recent decades and may face extirpation as a result of conversion of habitat to agricultural uses (nearby juniper-grassland escarpment populations are not threatened by human activity) (Walker et al. 1997).

Habitat. Typical habitat in Colorado for this ground-dwelling species consists of the bottoms, slopes, and escarpments of rocky canyons, often where grassland or grassy-weedy associations meet open juniper woodland. Hiding places include burrows and spaces under rocks. Winter is spent underground. Leuck (1982) observed that captives often construct burrows in open sand, and multiple individuals commonly hide together under single objects.

Activity. Most activity in Colorado occurs from the latter half of April into October; lizards active late in the season are mainly juveniles. Activity takes place during sunny hours and peaks during the warm midday period. In Texas, most activity occurs 2.5–8.5 hours after sunrise (Schall 1993). In Texas, body temperature of active individuals averages 40°C (Schall 1977).

Price (1992) found that this species in New Mexico is relatively unwary of humans. Leuck (1993) found that *C. tesselatus*

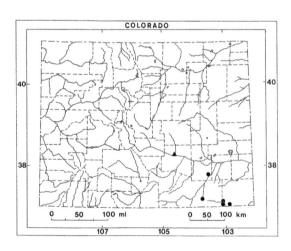

Map 8.19. Distribution of the diploid checkered whiptail in Colorado.

Plate 8.58. Adult diploid checkered whiptail (Baca County, Colorado).

may have resulted from hybridization between a diploid of pattern class C and a male *C. sexlineatus*. If this interpretation is correct, it supports the hypothesis that the creation of parthenogenetic lineages (such as *C. neotesselatus*) is an ongoing process (Walker, Taylor, and Cordes 1994). Taylor, Currie, and Baker (1989) reported the occurrence of rare hybrid (*C. tesselatus* x *C. sexlineatus*) males.

Food and Predators. These lizards feed opportunistically on available invertebrates. In southeastern Colorado, the adult diet includes various arthropods, particularly grasshoppers, beetles, caterpillars, ants, termites, and bugs; hatchlings eat mainly mites, spiders, termites, and leafhoppers (Paulissen et al. 1993). In Texas, the most important food item is termites excavated from dead plant material (Schall 1993).

Predators are poorly known. In southern New Mexico, nesting Swainson's hawks *(Buteo swainsoni)* occasionally prey on this species (Pilz 1983).

Taxonomy and Variation. This species originated as a result of hybridization between a female *C. tigris marmoratus* (= *C. marmoratus*) and a male *C. septemvittatus* (= *C. gularis septemvittatus*) (Wright 1993). This species includes Zweifel's (1965) pattern classes C, D, and E. These represent subtly different dorsal color patterns that are recognizable with practice. Pattern class D may have originated as a mutation from pattern class C (Taylor, Walker, and Cordes 1996). Walker et al. (1997:77) noted ecological differences between pattern classes C and D in Otero County and suggested that the Colorado variant of pattern class D "should be evaluated as a diagnosable entity with its own evolutionary trajectory" (i.e., as a possibly distinct species). Taylor, Walker, and Cordes (1997) documented some fundamental biological differences between syntopic populations of pattern classes C and E

and *C. neotesselatus* from Otero County exhibited more social tolerance and less aggressiveness toward conspecifics than toward the other species.

Reproduction and Growth. This essentially all-female species reproduces by parthenogenesis (see account of *C. neotesselatus*). In Colorado, the pattern of reproduction probably closely resembles that described for *C. neotesselatus*.

In New Mexico and in Texas, individuals carrying oviductal eggs can be found from late May to mid-July, and clutch size is 1–6 eggs (average 3–4) (Parker 1973; Schall 1978). Large females probably produce more than one clutch per season (Parker 1973). Parker (1973) observed that gravid females are 82–110 mm SVL, whereas Schall (1978) found that the minimum size of reproductive individuals is 66 mm SVL. This discrepancy may in part reflect differences in the reproductive characteristics of the different pattern classes (see "Taxonomy and Variation"). For example, at one site in east-central New Mexico, Taylor, Walker, and Cordes (1997) found that the minimum size of individuals with enlarged yolking follicles was 88 mm SVL in pattern class C (several individuals 70–74 mm SVL were examined but were not gravid) and 70 mm SVL in pattern class E. Sexual maturity apparently was attained in the third year of life in C and in the second year of life for some individuals in E. Clutch size averaged 4 eggs (range 2–5) in C and 3 eggs (range 1–4) in E. Hatching occurred in August.

Walker, Taylor, and Cordes (1994) described a triploid Otero County female that

in New Mexico (see "Reproduction and Growth"), raising the possibility that they might warrant separate taxonomic status. Additional information on the taxonomy of lizards of this complex is included in the account of *C. neotesselatus*.

The type locality for this species is in Pueblo County, Colorado (Maslin 1950, 1959).

Plate 8.59. Adult male western whiptail (Montezuma County, Colorado).

Western Whiptail

Cnemidophorus tigris (Baird and Girard, 1852)

Recognition. Body long and slender; dorsum with small granular scales; belly with larger rectangular scales, unmarked or with black marks on the front edge of some; dorsum with light stripes; dark fields between light stripes interrupted by light areas, or dark fields broken into separate bars or spots; large individuals gray around the shoulders and tan near the hind limbs; scales along front edge of fold of skin across throat not conspicuously enlarged; throat may be pinkish or orangish in adults; maximum size about 31 cm TL and 10.4 cm SVL (9.6 cm in west-central Colorado [McCoy 1965]). *Hatchling:* usually 35–39 mm SVL in Colorado (McCoy 1965; Taylor et al. 1992); skin dark brown-black, with four sharply defined dorsal stripes (there also may be one or two stripes on the sides); tail bright blue; dorsal color pattern more sharply defined than in adults (Taylor 1983). *Eggs:* average 17–19 mm x 9–10 mm (McCoy and Hoddenbach 1966; Vitt 1977).

Distribution. Eastern Oregon and southern Idaho south through California, Nevada, Utah, western Colorado, Arizona, New Mexico, and western Texas to southern Baja California and northwestern and north-central Mexico (see "Taxonomy and Variation"). Occurs throughout most of western Colorado at elevations below 6,000 feet (1,830 m).

Conservation Status. The western whiptail is locally common throughout its historic range in Colorado. There is no evidence of a significant decline in distribution or abundance, and no significant widespread threats are known to exist.

At a site in Mesa County studied by McCoy (1965), density was relatively low,

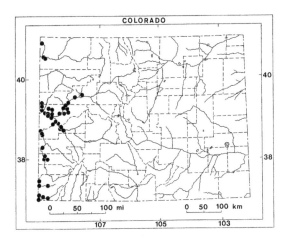

COLORADO

Map 8.20. Distribution of the western whiptail in Colorado.

individuals hibernate in the same burrow (McCoy 1974).

Activity. In Colorado, emergence from hibernation occurs in late April or early May. Activity steadily diminishes after May. Adults, especially males, become scarce in late summer, and by mid-September all adults have gone underground (McCoy 1965). Hatchlings may be active through mid-October. Pianka (1970), too, found that activity of adults diminished after May-June in northern populations of this species. Hendricks and Dixon (1984), among others, documented the earlier seasonal activity that takes place in warmer, longer growing seasons south of Colorado. However, the activity season for most individuals ends at about the same time (September-October) in Colorado, New Mexico, Texas, and Mexico.

In Colorado, I observed active individuals between 8:00 a.m. and 7:20 p.m., with a definite peak from midmorning to early afternoon. Activity occurs at air temperatures as low as 19°C (perhaps even lower) if sunshine is available. In Mesa County, McCoy (1965) found that daily activity in summer begins at about 8:00 a.m., when the soil surface temperature in the sun is about 35°C, similar to the 8:30 a.m. emergence at 36–38°C observed south of Colorado by Kay, Anderson, and McKinney (1973). Activity peaks between 10:30 and 11:00 a.m. When the soil temperature reaches 52°C in early afternoon, the lizards retreat underground. A few emerge again in late afternoon (as late as 5:30–6:00 p.m.), but in general, little activity takes place then. Midday activity with late morning emergence may be the norm at the beginning of the activity season, when conditions are cooler (Pianka 1970). In western Texas, most activ-

only 17 per hectare, including individuals of all ages. Similarly, Turner, Medica, et al. (1969) recorded 8–20 individuals per hectare in southern Nevada. Population densities of up to 185 per hectare have been recorded in southwestern Texas (Milstead 1965). Temperature and moisture fluctuations impact population densities. In southern New Mexico, populations vary with hatchling overwinter survival rates (Whitford and Creusere 1977). In California, populations tend to increase with arthropod abundance associated with periods of higher precipitation (Anderson 1994). Similarly, density varies with drought conditions in southwestern Texas (Milstead 1965).

Habitat. This lizard occupies nearly all lowland habitats in the river valleys of western Colorado. It ranges from canyon bottoms to adjacent low mesa tops. Openly spaced stands of shrubs (e.g., greasewood, sagebrush, rabbitbrush) or piñon pine and juniper on friable soils seem to be ideal. Areas along rivers with patchy shrubs and scattered cottonwood trees also are inhabited. Most activity takes place on the ground, but in Mesa County I saw individuals climb the trunks of cottonwood trees to a height of about 2 m. One lizard jumped several inches from rock to rock over a flowing rivulet. Periods of inactivity are spent in rodent burrows (especially in winter) or self-dug burrows. The burrows are plugged when occupied (McCoy 1965). Sometimes, multiple

ity occurs 2.5–9.0 hours after sunrise, but on hot evenings, activity sometimes extends to 14 hours after sunrise, well after dark (Schall 1993). Vitt and Ohmart (1977) found that whiptails in the hot climate along the lower Colorado River (Arizona-California) sometimes are active as much as 30 minutes before sunrise in late June and July. McCoy (1965) found that the body temperature of active individuals in Colorado averages about 40°C. In northern populations of this species, body temperature during activity averages around 39°C at air temperatures averaging 25°C (Pianka 1970). Larger individuals of this species tend to spend more time in the shade than do juveniles, despite similar thermal preferences and tolerances (Asplund 1974).

Home range size in Mesa County averages 1,335 m² in males and 1,010 m² in females (McCoy 1965). Home ranges overlap and are not defended. In general, other lizards of the same or other species are ignored. Much larger home ranges occur in California (e.g., about 10,000 m² in adult males and about 3,200 m² in adult females [Anderson 1993]). Jorgensen and Tanner (1963) found intermediate home range sizes of 2,900 m² in males, 5,200 m² in females, and 2,200 m² in juveniles in Nevada. Some of his variation results from methodological differences and may not reflect biological differences.

Garland (1993) reviewed information on activity and metabolism in this species. The western whiptail has a high rate of energy expenditure, a result of its high level of activity. In California, these lizards may move as much as 900 m per day (Anderson 1993), though more modest movement has been recorded by other researchers. When forced to run, the western whiptail exhibits high endurance and high aerobic capacity and is capable of running at speeds of up to 23 km per hour, perhaps more.

In hand, these lizards often twist strongly and attempt to bite. In Mesa County, a 61-mm-SVL juvenile (body tem-

Plate 8.60. Vent region of adult male western whiptail (Montezuma County, Colorado).

Plate 8.61. Death feigning by juvenile western whiptail (Mesa County, Colorado).

perature at capture was 40.3°C) feigned death for 1.5 minutes after I handled it for about 2 minutes. First the eyes closed, then it went totally limp. Later it gulped air and revived completely, struggling against my hold.

Reproduction and Growth. In Colorado and adjacent Utah, courtship and mating occur from late May to mid-June (Lombard 1949; McCoy 1965). During this time, adult males often closely trail adult females (pers. obs.) and form temporary monogamous pairs that last through several copulations (McCoy 1965). During copulation, the male grasps the female's neck area in his jaws. Females with large developing eggs appear to burrow and spend considerable time underground prior to egg deposition (Schall 1978; Hendricks and Dixon 1988). After oviposition, they emerge and feed to build up their energy reserves.

In Mesa County, McCoy (1965) found that eggs are laid in mid- to late June. Females breeding for the first time lay usually three eggs; older females lay four. Each adult female lays only one clutch per year. Eggs hatch in early August, about 50 days after being laid. First-time breeders are about 22 months old. Taylor et al. (1992, 1994) found that gravid females of the subspecies in Colorado are at least 76 mm SVL. McCoy's data indicate that about 80 percent of the adults survive from one year to the next. Few live more than six years, but Medica and Turner (1984) observed that on rare occasions, an individual in Nevada may live as long as eight years.

In Utah, females carrying 2–6 (average 4) oviductal eggs can be found from mid-June through early July (Parker 1973). Gravid females are 77–100 mm SVL (average 88 mm), mature males 76–98 mm SVL (average 90 mm). Hatchlings generally first appear in early September.

In southern California, Goldberg (1976) found that a montane population at elevations similar to those in Colorado (1,585–1,830 m) was characterized by exceptionally big adults (smallest mature female was 83 mm SVL; maximum SVL 118 mm) and large clutch size (up to 7 eggs, average 4). Despite an activity season of similar length

in montane California and Colorado, about half of the mature females in California produce two clutches per year (versus one in Colorado). Hatchlings in montane California first appear in mid-August, later than in Colorado.

At the northern end of the range of this species in southwestern Idaho, mating takes place in the first half of June, and oviposition occurs in late June and July (Burkholder and Walker 1973). Clutch size averages 2–3 eggs, and individual females produce one clutch per year. Hatchlings appear by mid-August. Reproductive individuals are at least 67–70 mm SVL and 20–23 months old.

South of Colorado, where the growing season is longer, western whiptails may produce two clutches per year and mature within one year (McCoy and Hoddenbach 1966; Pianka 1970; Parker 1972; Hendricks and Dixon 1984; Vitt and Breitenbach 1993), but size of reproductive females and average clutch size (independent of female size) are both larger in Colorado (Taylor et al. 1992). Egg-laying occurs as early as the beginning of May, and hatchlings first appear as early as mid-June at the southern end of the range in Mexico (Hendricks and Dixon 1984).

Growth and reproduction vary with environmental conditions. Clutch size and growth rates tend to increase with arthropod abundance associated with higher levels of precipitation (Pianka 1970; Anderson 1994).

Food and Predators. Western whiptails feed opportunistically on available arthropods, focusing on those obtainable in plant litter at the base of perennial plants (Pianka 1970; Vitt and Ohmart 1977; Anderson 1993). They forage widely and intensively (Anderson 1993), probing into leaf litter, digging out buried prey, and sometimes climbing into plants to obtain prey. Much flicking of the tongue suggests that odors help reveal potential prey. Taste buds on the tongue of this species are rare (Schwenk 1985), indicating that tongue flicking simply transfers molecules to the sensitive vomeronasal organs in the roof of the mouth. Taste buds are abundant, however, in the oral epithelium of the western whiptail and on the tongue of various crotaphytid and phrynosomatid lizards that extrude the tongue less often than does the whiptail (Schwenk 1985). Though western whiptails infrequently obtain prey by pursuit, McCoy (1965) observed that they have good vision and are able to detect prey movement at distances up to at least 5–6 m.

Important foods in Mesa County include lepidopteran caterpillars and pupae, carabid and curculionid beetles, grasshoppers, and spiders; scorpions and side-blotched lizards also sometimes are eaten (McCoy 1965). Johnson (1966) reported a similar diet in Montezuma County, as did Knowlton (1934) in Utah. Throughout the northern part of the range, grasshoppers, beetles, and insect larvae are the most important foods. Generally, these foods plus termites and ant lions dominate the diet in the south (Pianka 1970; Best and Gennaro 1985; Schall 1993). Lombard (1949) reported predation on small *Sceloporus* lizards in northeastern Utah.

Roadrunners *(Geococcyx californianus),* hawks, collared lizards, leopard lizards, whipsnakes, and racers probably are the most important predators. Known predators in Colorado include the longnose leopard lizard (McCoy 1965). In southern New Mexico, *C. tigris* is an important component in the diet of nestling Swainson's hawks *(Buteo swainsoni)* (Pilz 1983). Pianka (1970) found that about one-third of the individuals in northern populations of this species have broken or regenerated tails, largely the result of unsuccessful predation attempts. McCoy (1965) found that 15 percent of individuals in western Colorado have broken tails.

Taxonomy and Variation. Hendricks and Dixon (1986) regarded populations encompassing north-central Mexico, western Texas, and most of southern New Mexico as a distinct species, *C. marmoratus,* based on morphological and genetic distinctions. Dessauer and Cole (1991) examined genetic variation and concluded that *marmoratus* freely interbreeds with *C. tigris gracilis* (now *C. tigris punctilinealis* [Taylor and Walker 1996]) along a narrow zone of contact, with no loss of fertility or selection against hybrids, and that the speciation process is not complete; they retained *marmoratus* as a subspecies of *C. tigris*. The taxonomic status of *marmoratus* is largely a philosophical issue, reflecting one's preferred species concept.

The subspecies in Colorado is *Cnemidophorus tigris septentrionalis* Burger, 1950. The type specimen of *septentrionalis* was collected by E. V. Prostov at the Roan Cliffs, opposite Una, Garfield County, on June 25, 1941 (FMNH 38217) (Burger 1950). This subspecies intergrades with subspecies *tigris* in extreme southwestern Utah and northwestern Arizona (Taylor 1983, 1988). Taylor and Buschman (1993) summarized geographic variation in *septentrionalis* morphology and found a pattern suggesting that this subspecies as presently construed does not represent a unique evolutionary lineage and thus does not warrant recognition as a distinct taxon. An analysis of variation in the subspecies *tigris* would help clarify the evolutionary relationships among populations of this species in much of the western United States (Taylor and Buschman 1993).

Plate 8.62. Adult plateau striped whiptail (Mesa County, Colorado).

Plateau Striped Whiptail

Cnemidophorus velox (Springer, 1928)

Recognition. Body long and slender; dorsum with small granular scales; belly with larger rectangular scales; dorsum and sides with six or seven light stripes (the mid-dorsal stripe, if present, is less distinct than the other stripes and may exist as an intermittent line); dark fields between stripes uninterrupted by light areas; venter white or pale blue-green; tail blue (pale in adult, bright in juvenile); scales on underside of base of forelimbs not greatly enlarged; maximum size about 28 cm TL and 8.7 cm SVL (Maslin 1950; Stuart 1998a). *Hatchling:* 33–37 mm SVL

(Gehlbach 1965; Douglas 1966). *Eggs:* average about 15–16 mm x 6–11 mm in different females (Gehlbach 1965).

Distribution. Southern Utah, western Colorado, northern and central Arizona, and northern and central New Mexico. An introduced population is established at Cove Palisades State Park, Jefferson County, Oregon (Brown et al. 1995), and another has been reported for Phoenix, Arizona (L. J. Vitt, cited by Degenhardt, Painter, and Price 1996). Occurs south of the Roan Plateau in

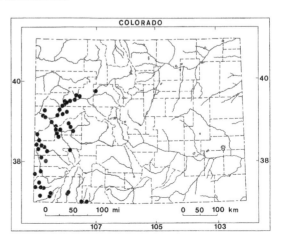

COLORADO

Map 8.21. Distribution of the plateau striped whiptail in Colorado.

western Colorado at elevations below 7,500 feet (2,290 m). Mourning (1997) found this lizard as far east as western Eagle County.

Conservation Status. The plateau striped whiptail occurs throughout its historic range in Colorado, with no evidence of a significant decline in distribution or abundance. The habitat in Colorado is largely intact and unthreatened.

Habitat. Habitats in Colorado include piñon-juniper woodland, sagebrush, semidesert and mountain shrublands, and lowland riparian zones, encompassing rocky slopes and, in flat areas, deep sandy soils. This ground-dwelling lizard often occurs in areas inhabited by the western whiptail, but it also ranges into higher elevations where the latter species is absent. At Mesa Verde, Douglas (1966) found the plateau striped whiptail mostly at lower elevations along the southern halves of the mesas. In New Mexico, Bowker (1993) found this whiptail in upland areas of relatively dense vegetation (piñon pine, juniper, Gambel oak).

Activity takes place almost exclusively on the ground. Periods of inactivity are spent in burrows or other underground sites. A captive observed by Douglas (1966) exhibited a strong tendency to dig beneath objects, perhaps suggesting that these lizards in the wild may burrow under rocks. The front limbs were used to dig and to push excavated soil. One chamber constructed by the captive had two access tunnels that the lizard plugged before it curled up in the small chamber.

Activity. In Colorado, most activity takes place from May to September but may occur during warm weather in late April. Hatchlings may be active through at least mid-October. Larry Valentine reported seeing active juveniles in mid-November in Delta County. Observation of cold individuals under rocks on warm days in spring suggests that plateau striped whiptails may not be active every day.

Daily activity occurs during sunny warm weather, mostly from midmorning to early afternoon. In Colorado, I observed active individuals as early as 8:00 a.m. (air temperature 23°C, soil temperature 44°C). In October, I observed juveniles active in

Mesa County at an air temperature of 19°C and a soil surface temperature of 41°C in the sun. When the air is cool and foraging has occurred in the shade, active individuals often pause and lie down on sun-warmed soil. The lizards occupy shaded sites during the hottest midday periods in summer.

Similarly, in New Mexico (Bowker 1993), foraging activity in June occurs during a relatively brief period between 9:30 a.m. and 12:40 p.m. Body temperature of active individuals averages 38–39°C. Ground temperature during activity averages 40–41°C in the sun and 25°C in the shade, and air temperature averages 23–24°C. Experimentation suggests that conservation of water is an important factor determining the length of daily activity.

When pursued, these whiptails may skitter through small pools or rivulets. In southern Utah, Woodbury (1928) saw one take refuge in a pool of muddy water. When extracted it went limp, as if feigning death (see account of western whiptail). In hand, they typically squirm vigorously and attempt to bite.

Reproduction and Growth. This species consists only of females and reproduces by parthenogenesis (Maslin 1962, 1966; Duellman and Zweifel 1962) (see account of *C. neotesselatus*). Pseudocopulatory behavior (Crews and Moore 1993) is described in the account of the family Teiidae. My observations and those of Maslin (1950) and Douglas (1966) suggest that in Colorado, clutches of 3–5 eggs are laid in late June or early July. In northwestern New Mexico, Gehlbach (1965) found individuals (73–80 mm SVL) containing large eggs from late May through June, but none in July. I observed newly emerged hatchlings in early to mid-August in Mesa County. Douglas (1966) first observed hatchlings in late August at a higher elevation in Montezuma County. Hatchlings first appear in mid- to late August in northwestern New Mexico (Gehlbach 1965). Colorado populations include nonreproductive yearlings (second calendar year); first reproduction evidently occurs in the second spring (third calendar year).

Food and Predators. This lizard appears to feed opportunistically on arthropods found on the ground or shallowly buried, including spiders, caterpillars, grasshoppers, crickets, adult and larval beetles, aphids, leafhoppers, and other insects (Woodbury 1928; Knowlton 1934, 1937); infrequently, ants may be eaten (Knowlton and Nye 1946). In Mesa County, I watched an adult bite, shake, and swallow a dead scarab beetle; between the initial biting and swallowing, the lizard flicked its tongue and yawned widely. Later, I saw this individual digging to a depth of 2–3 cm with both forelimbs and the snout, apparently seeking buried prey. One actively foraging adult investigated but did not bite a circus beetle (darkling beetle, *Eleodes*), which is known to emit noxious chemicals when disturbed. Predators likely include various birds, reptiles, and mammals.

Taxonomy and Variation. Lowe (1955a) sorted out previous taxonomic confusion in recognizing this species as distinct. *Cnemidophorus velox* is a triploid species that originated through hybridization between a female *C. costatus barrancorum* or *C. burti stictogrammus* (or an unidentified taxon closely related to them) and a male *C. inornatus*, followed by hybridization between this probably parthenogenetic hybrid (likely now extinct) and a male *C. inornatus* (Moritz, Wright, and Brown 1989; Wright 1993). Histocompatibility data and other evidence suggest that this species consists of multiple historical groups of independent origin (Cuellar 1977; Dessauer and Cole 1989; Moritz, Wright, and Brown 1989). Some authors (e.g., Maslin 1966, Dessauer and Cole 1989) have regarded *C. velox* and *C. uniparens* as conspecific, but Wright (1993) and most other recent treatments separate them as distinct species. Diploid populations in the vicinity of Kanab, Kane County, Utah, that were described as *Cnemidophorus sackii innotatus* by Burger (1950) and that have been included in *C. velox* by some authors were regarded as a distinct species *(C. innotatus)* by Wright (1993). Additional diploid forms currently included in *C. velox* may occur in New Mexico (Cuellar and Wright 1992) and eventually could be recognized as distinct species.

Taylor, Walker, and Medica (1967) and Taylor, Currie, and Baker (1989) described a rare (possibly tetraploid) male, which may have originated through hybridization between *C. velox* and a male *C. tigris*.

SKINKS
Family Scincidae

Skinks occur throughout the tropical, subtropical, and temperate regions of the world. Many species have colonized oceanic islands. Most of the more than 1,030 species inhabit the Old World. Most skinks are terrestrial/fossorial and secretive, spending most of their time under cover. Some are good climbers.

Skinks tend to be fairly small (most species are under 40 cm TL), elongate, and have a long, easily detached tail (often brightly colored, at least in juveniles). Some skinks have vestigial legs; others lack legs entirely (though limb girdles are always present).

Most species have smooth cycloid scales underlain with osteoderms, which make the animal feel hard-bodied. Femoral pores are absent. Some skinks have a spectacle over each eye, and others have a transparent window in the lower eyelid, but North American skinks have unspecialized movable eyelids.

The tongue is moderately long, nicked at the tip, and covered with scalelike papillae. Taste buds are abundant, and licking may mediate gustation. Chemical reception plays an important role in skink biology. For example, when applied to the skin of a postreproductive female, secretions of the cloacal glands of a reproductive female *Eumeces* elicit courtship behavior by males, which normally ignore post-reproductive females. Some male *Eumeces* are known to follow the scent trails of females by engaging in substrate licking. Sexual differences in coloration also play a role in skink communication.

Skinks are either oviparous (all U.S. species) or viviparous. Female *Eumeces* skinks stay with the eggs until hatching and may eat addled eggs. Behavior in which the male grasps the female's neck in his jaws may be essential for successful copulation.

Three of the 16 skink species inhabiting the United States occur in Colorado.

Plate 8.63. Adult variable skink (La Plata County, Colorado). *Lauren Livo and Steve Wilcox.*

Variable Skink

Eumeces gaigeae (Taylor, 1935)
(or *Eumeces multivirgatus gaigeae*)

Recognition. Dorsum of adults light to dark olive brown with two dark-edged white dorsolateral stripes; dorsal scales smooth, shiny, tightly overlapping, with rounded rear edge; scales on sides of body (midway between limbs) in horizontal rows; tail (if never broken) 1.5–2.0 times as long as head and body; maximum size about 19 cm TL and 7.3 cm SVL. See "Taxonomy and Variation." *Mature male:* lips orange or reddish during breeding season. *Hatchling:* tail bright blue; dorsum dark with three bold light stripes; 22–29 mm SVL in New Mexico and Texas (Gehlbach 1965, Mecham 1967, Doles, Painter, and Gorum 1996). *Eggs:* 11 mm x 6 mm in Archuleta County (Maslin 1957); 14–15 mm x 8–10 mm in New Mexico (Gehlbach 1965); average 11 mm x

7 mm and 14 mm x 10 mm for two sets of brooded eggs in Mexico (Van Devender and Van Devender 1975).

Distribution. Southern Colorado and southeastern Utah south to northern and central Arizona, New Mexico, and western Texas; reported also from locations in Chihuahua, Mexico, but the taxonomic status of most of these populations is uncertain (Mecham 1980). Occurs in montane areas of south-central and southwestern Colorado at elevations up to 8,500 feet (2,590 m).

Conservation Status. This lizard is secretive and somewhat difficult to detect without labor-intensive pitfall trapping, which has not been widely used in Colorado. Evaluation of its status must be based primarily on serendipitous observations. These indicate that this skink occurs throughout nearly all of its historical range in the state. Nothing definitive can be said about trends in abundance. The species is locally common in some areas and evidently scarce, or at least much harder to detect, in many others.

Intensive cultivation may have eliminated some habitat in the San Luis Valley, but the majority of the Colorado habitat is intact and appears capable of supporting viable populations. The species is not significantly threatened in this state.

Habitat. The variable skink occurs mostly in rocky, mountainous areas. Maslin (1957:90) reported that this skink was found "under partially buried, rounded boulders on a steep, open, grassy slope in a forested area above a stream-watered valley" in Archuleta County. Hahn (1968) usually found it at the edges of rocky canyons in the San Luis Valley. Hahn observed variable skinks in piñon-juniper woodland and under a log along a stream in the mountains surrounding the valley. Justin Hobert (pers. comm.) found this species along a southeast-facing rocky outcrop in piñon-juniper woodland in Las Animas County. Douglas (1966) saw a variable skink at the edge of an oak thicket at Mesa Verde. In northwestern New Mexico, most of Gehlbach's (1965) observations were in oak–mountain mahogany associations and riparian zones with abundant leaf litter; a few were in piñon-juniper and ponderosa pine associations. Near Taos, New Mexico, skinks were found burrowing under small, flat rocks on a steep hillside in barren hills along a stream (Taylor 1935). In southeastern Utah, Maslin (1957) found variable skinks under rocks in rocky-grassy clearings surrounded by ponderosa pine

and scrub oaks on the slopes and floor of a narrow canyon. Variable skinks also occur in flat, sandy tracts with scattered shrubs (e.g., greasewood-rabbitbrush) on the floor of the San Luis Valley (Hahn 1968; pers. obs.).

These skinks seldom are seen away from cover. Usually, they are found under objects such as rocks, logs, or trash. They go underground (e.g., into abandoned rodent burrows) and are difficult to find when surface conditions are hot and dry. Hibernation takes place underground. In northern New Mexico, Stuart and Painter (1993b) found variable skinks in February hibernating with smooth green snakes and western terrestrial garter snakes under slabs of granite.

Activity. Activity in Colorado extends primarily from April to September or October. Daily patterns of activity are poorly known. In northwestern New Mexico, Gehlbach (1965) found variable skinks throughout the day, with most observed in early morning.

Reproduction and Growth. Courtship and mating take place in spring or early summer. Male sexual behavior includes tongue flicking, tail waving, anteriorly progressing biting of the female, wiggling atop the female, insertion of a hemipenis, and brief copulation (five minutes) accompanied by a persistent bite and periodic pelvic thrusting (Everett 1971). Females attend their clutches until after hatching.

Information on reproduction in this skink is limited to a smattering of observations as follows. At an elevation of 8,000 feet (2,440 m) in Archuleta County, four of six adult females were gravid with five, five, five, and seven oviductal eggs in late June (Maslin 1957). At 8,300 feet (2,530 m) in southeastern Utah, four females with four, four, four, and three developing ovarian eggs

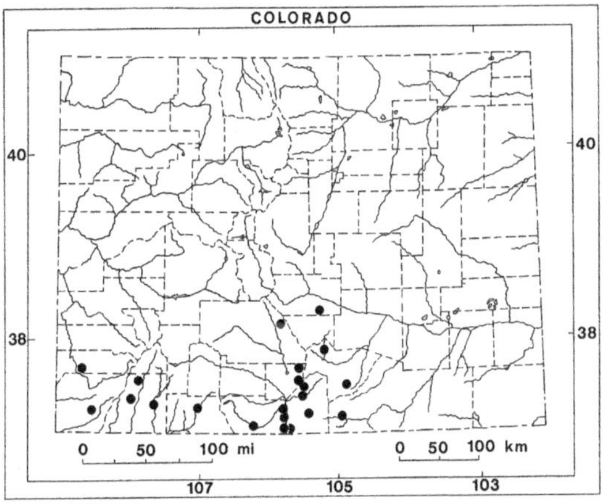

Map 8.22. Distribution of the variable skink in Colorado.

were found in early June (Maslin 1957). In northwestern New Mexico, Gehlbach (1965) found a female brooding three eggs in late June under a rock in a creek bed at 7,200 feet (2,195 m). Another female with five eggs was found in early August. A female with four hatchlings was observed in mid-August, and another hatchling was seen in late July. In mid-June in Eddy County, New Mexico, Doles, Painter, and Gorum (1996) found an adult female (66 mm SVL, 36 mm tail) with nine hatchlings in a nest chamber that extended about 15 cm below a rock. Curiously, no eggshells were found in the nest, suggesting that the female had eaten them. This record of nine young exceeds the previous known maximum of seven (see Doles, Painter, and Gorum 1996). A female from the high plains of Texas deposited four eggs in late May (Mecham 1967). Van Devender and Van Devender (1975) found two females (65–71 mm SVL) attending clutches in moist soil under rocks in mid-June in northern Mexico. Evidently, females in Colorado-Utah deposit 3–7 eggs as early as late June or early July, with earlier oviposition taking place farther south. Hatching in Colorado probably begins in early August.

Food and Predators. The diet is little known but presumably includes various small invertebrates.

Taxonomy and Variation. In recent decades, this skink has been regarded as a subspecies of *E. multivirgatus*. Here I review patterns of variation in *E. multivirgatus* and *E. gaigeae* and set forth my reasons for recognizing them as distinct species.

In the Great Plains region north of the Arkansas River, adults of the *multivirgatus-gaigeae* group have many dark stripes and intervening pale gray stripes; the dorsolateral pale stripes are barely (if at all) lighter than the other pale dorsal and lateral stripes. Juveniles are dark with tiny light spots that form basically three stripes along the back; the dorsolateral stripes are brightest, and the mid-dorsal stripe (involving scale row 1 on each side) may be faint. These populations represent the taxon usually recognized as subspecies *E. m. multivirgatus* (Mecham 1957, 1980). Habitat consists of sandy-shrubby low-elevation plains; this skink is absent from adjacent montane habitats to the west.

In mountainous regions of southern Colorado and southeastern Utah (south and west of the Arkansas River) and in states to the south, adults are more variable than in northeastern Colorado. Typically, they are olive brown with two dark-edged, highly prominent white dorsolateral stripes. Additional dark stripes may be present, but all of them may be greatly reduced in large adults (Maslin 1957; Mecham 1957; Tanner 1957a; Gehlbach 1965). However, a very large adult (UCM 6128) from Catron County, New Mexico, has bold dark dorsal and dorsolateral stripes. Juveniles are dark with three bold, light dorsal stripes. These populations represent the taxon generally known as subspecies *E. m. gaigeae* Taylor, 1935 (Mecham 1957, 1980). Habitat varies but mainly encompasses rocky semiwooded areas in the mountains. The Arkansas River valley completely separates the ranges of *multivirgatus* and *gaigeae* by a gap of about 70 km, and there is no evidence of intergradation between these taxa in that region.

Gehlbach (1965) thought that *multivirgatus* and *gaigeae* intergrade in the Zuni Mountains of northwestern New Mexico. However, he incorrectly categorized *multivirgatus* young as possessing

Plate 8.64. Adult variable skink (Costilla County, Colorado).

a pronounced light mid-dorsal stripe, and he assumed that adults of *gaigeae* lack dark dorsal stripes, which is not always the case. In addition, he did not take into account the relative brightness of the stripe on scale row 3 or the dorsal ground color per se, both important characters in separating *multivirgatus* from *gaigeae* (Mecham 1957). Gehlbach's data indicate primarily that *gaigeae* in that region tends to lose its dark stripes and blue tail as it grows. Variation in a labial scale character mentioned by Gehlbach (after Maslin 1957) has not been adequately studied in *multivirgatus* or *gaigeae*. That character may be taxonomically insignificant. Mecham (1957) found that color and pattern are the only characters in *E. multivirgatus/E. gaigeae* displaying concordant geographic variation.

Hahn (1968) doubted that intergradation between *multivirgatus* and *gaigeae* could occur in the Zuni Mountains area, but he thought that intergradation does occur in the San Luis Valley of Colorado, where he observed what he believed to be the *gaigeae* juvenile color pattern and the adult *multivirgatus* pattern. My observations confirm that San Luis Valley juveniles have the strongly three-striped pattern typical of *gaigeae*, but adults from the valley differ from *multivirgatus* in ground color (brown versus pale gray) and in the character of the dorsal dark stripes (series of melded dark spots versus solid, straight-edged stripes). Skinks from the San Luis Valley do bear the closest similarity to the *multivirgatus* coloration that I have seen in specimens from south and west of the Arkansas River, but all are readily distinguishable from *multivirgatus*. Also, geographic considerations make the San Luis Valley an unlikely location for intergradation because skinks there are separated from typical *multivirgatus* by populations of *gaigeae* in south-central Colorado southwest of the Arkansas River. It is perhaps significant that skink habitat in the San Luis Valleys includes flat, shrubby plains of pale, sandy soil quite similar to that favored by *multivirgatus* in northeastern Colorado.

Dixon (1971), Dixon and Medica (1965), and Mecham (1967) described specimens from the plains and limestone-capped mesas of southeastern New Mexico and adjacent western Texas, far south of the range of *multivirgatus*, as partially resembling *multivirgatus* in their pale ground color, but none of the specimens had distinctive *multivirgatus* striping but rather included the zigzag lines characteristic of *gaigeae*. These specimens, plus those from the San Luis Valley, suggest that dorsal coloration in *E. gaigeae* reflects selection for background matching, with pale ground color favored in plains habitats and darker brown ground color favored on darker montane substrates. Thus, partial resemblance of *multivirgatus* by *gaigeae* in some areas appears to reflect convergent evolution in similar environments rather than genetic affinity. This possibility was raised but discounted by Mecham (1967), who believed that the similarity of southeastern New Mexico and adjacent Texas plains populations to northern *multivirgatus* was due to former genetic contact with *multivirgatus* of the northern plains, with subsequent extermination of intervening populations by agricultural development. Given the existence of intact plains habitat between eastern Colorado and the New Mexico–Texas plains populations, I find this explanation doubtful.

In conclusion, all many-lined skinks from north of the Arkansas River *(multivirgatus)* are readily distinguishable from those to the south and west *(gaigeae)*. I have examined no specimens that I would call intergrades. Reported possible intergrades in the San Luis Valley and the plains of eastern New Mexico and adjacent Texas may represent convergent evolution toward a pale adult phenotype in sandy plains habitats (hence they are ecomorphs rather than taxonomic entities). The pattern of variation in the Zuni Mountains region of northwestern New Mexico is typical of *gaigeae* and does not represent intergradation. Because all adults and juveniles of *gaigeae* are readily distinguishable from *multivirgatus* on the basis of well-defined differences in coloration, with no evidence of intergradation in the area where the ranges of the two taxa are in closest proximity (vicinity of the Arkansas River in southeastern Colorado), and because they exhibit dramatic ecological differences, I disagree with previous interpretations and conclude that the two are distinct species. Genetic data would allow a more definitive assessment of the situation.

A patternless morph of *E. gaigeae* has been observed in New Mexico, Texas, and Arizona (Lowe 1955b, Mecham 1957), but to my knowledge it has not been recorded in Colorado or Utah. Mecham (1957) demonstrated that this morph is simply a variant color phase of the more typical pattern, as opposed to a distinct taxonomic entity.

The name *Eumeces epipleurotus* Cope, 1880, used in place of *gaigeae* by some authors (after Axtell [1961]), is a nomen oblitum (Smith and Williams 1962) that has lost nomenclatural priority through disuse. Prior to Axtell (1961), the name *epipleurotus* had not been used for this lizard for several decades and, under the provisions of the International Code of Zoological Nomenclature, the name *gaigeae* should have been maintained. Technicalities aside, Axtell's revival and promotion of the long-forgotten name *epipleurotus* did not serve the interests of nomenclatural stability. The original spelling of *gaigeae* was *gaigei*, but because the taxon was named in honor of Helen Gaige, the spelling should be rendered in the feminine form (Maslin 1957).

Plate 8.65. Adult many-lined skink (Weld County, Colorado).

Many-lined Skink

Eumeces multivirgatus (Hallowell, 1857 [1858])

Recognition. Dorsum of adults pale gray with bold, dark, and more or less straight-edged uppermost stripes; dorsal scales smooth, shiny, tightly overlapping, with rounded rear edge; scales on sides of body (midway between limbs) in horizontal rows; tail (if never broken) 1.5–2.0 times as long as head and body (in El Paso County, Banta [1966] found that most adults have a regenerated tail); maximum size about 19 cm TL and 7.3 cm SVL. *Mature male:* lips reddish during breeding season. *Hatchling:* tail bright blue; dorsum dark with light stripes consisting of rows of minute spots, with the dorsolateral stripes brighter than the mid-dorsal stripe; 22–29 mm SVL; 31–41 mm SVL in late August-September in Weld County (Bauerle 1971; pers. obs.). *Eggs:* length 9–12 mm for oviductal eggs in northeastern Colorado (pers. obs.); 13 mm x 8 mm in Nebraska (Taylor 1935).

Distribution. Southern South Dakota, Nebraska, and southeastern Wyoming south to eastern Colorado north of the Arkansas River. Occurs in northeastern and east-central Colorado at elevations principally below 5,500 feet (1,675 m).

Conservation Status. This lizard is secretive and somewhat difficult to detect without labor-intensive pitfall trapping, which has not been widely used in Colorado. Evaluation of its status must be based primarily on serendipitous observations. These indicate that this skink occurs throughout nearly all of its historical range in the state. Nothing definitive can be said about trends in abundance. The species is locally common in some areas and evidently scarce, or at least much harder to detect, in many others. In prairie habitat in El Paso County, this skink was more abundant in pitfall trap samples (more than 300 specimens) than all other reptiles and amphibian species combined (Banta and Torbit 1965).

Urbanization probably has extirpated or reduced some populations along the eastern base of the Front Range, and intensive cultivation may have done the same locally in northeastern Colorado, but the majority of the habitat is intact and appears capable of supporting viable populations. The species is not significantly threatened in Colorado, though pesticide use on rangelands is a potential danger.

Habitat. The many-lined skink inhabits areas of loose sandy soil and prairie-dog towns in eastern Colorado. Many-lined skinks sometimes inhabit vacant lots in cities and residential areas (e.g., Denver, at least formerly [Taylor 1935:351]).

These skinks seldom are seen away from cover. Usually, they are found under objects such as rocks, logs, trash, or cattle dung (Taylor 1935; Hudson 1942). They go underground and are difficult to find when surface conditions are hot and dry. Hibernation takes place underground. Burnett (1932) reported that two specimens were found 12 inches (30 cm) underground in November in Larimer County.

Activity. Activity in Colorado extends primarily from April (sometimes late March) to September or October. Daily patterns of activity are poorly known. Captives from Nebraska were most active during early to midmorning and in late afternoon and were inactive at night (Heyl and Smith 1957). They burrowed in the sandy substrate that was provided and emerged when grasshoppers (readily eaten) moved on the surface or when water was sprinkled on the sand.

In hand, many-lined skinks vigorously twist and squirm, and the tail may become detached during these struggles.

Reproduction and Growth. Courtship and mating, described by Everett (1971), evidently take place in spring or early summer. Females attend their clutches until after hatching.

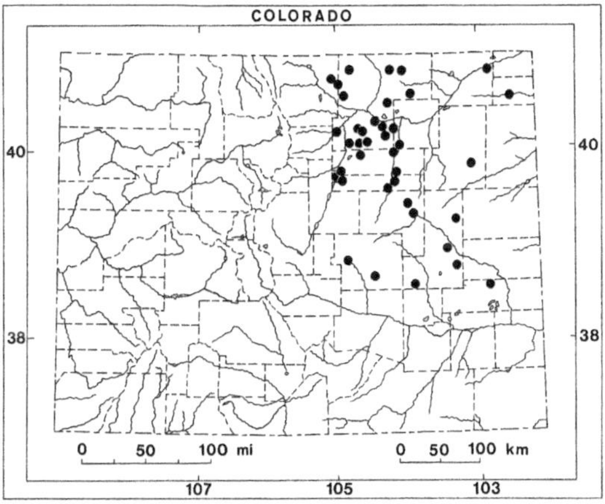

Map 8.23. Distribution of the many-lined skink in Colorado.

Plate 8.66. Hatchling many-lined skink (Weld County, Colorado).

Of the seven adult females (61–70 mm SVL) I examined that were collected in May in northeastern Colorado, one had five oviductal eggs in mid-May, one had six oviductal eggs in late May, and five collected over the course of the month had small ovarian follicles 1–4 mm in diameter. A female collected in late March contained seven follicles 2–3 mm in diameter. This evidence indicates that clutches may be laid in mid- to late May and early June and that individual adults may not produce eggs every year.

I observed hatchlings as early as mid-July at about 5,000 feet (1,525 m) in Weld County. Mecham (1967) reported that *E. gaigae* eggs laid on May 23 and incubated apparently at room temperature in Texas hatched on June 24 or 25. In the cooler climate of Colorado, one might expect that development to hatching would take longer, so the mid-July hatchling observed in northeastern Colorado corresponds well with oviposition in late May or early June.

In Nebraska, Gehlbach and Collette (1959) found a male with red head coloration in late June, at which time two adult females had only slightly enlarged (less than 1.9 mm) ovarian follicles. Fitch (1970) stated that this indicates a late breeding season, but given the occurrence of oviductal eggs in May in Colorado, these females may already have laid their eggs or perhaps were nonreproductive during that year. Individual females probably produce only one clutch per year. Better information on reproduction is needed.

Food and Predators. The diet is little known but presumably includes various small invertebrates. Barry (in Taylor 1935:349) found this skink "under cow dung in a prairie dog town, feeding on ant larvae."

The only record of predation on this skink in Colorado was reported by Barry (in Taylor 1935), who stated that an American kestrel that was shot held one of these skinks in its claws.

Taxonomy and Variation. See account of variable skink, *Eumeces gaigeae*.

A patternless morph has been observed in Nebraska (Heyl and Smith 1957; Ballinger, Lynch, and Cole 1979), but to my knowledge it has not been recorded in Colorado. Mecham (1957) demonstrated that this morph is simply a variant color phase of the more typical pattern, as opposed to a distinct taxonomic entity.

Plate 8.67. Adult Great Plains skink (Baca County, Colorado).

Great Plains Skink
Eumeces obsoletus (Baird and Girard, 1852)

Recognition. Dorsal scales smooth, shiny, tightly overlapping, with rounded rear edge; scales along sides of body in oblique (diagonal) rows; tail no more than 1.5 times as long as head and body; most adults with relatively short, regenerated tails; maximum size about 35 cm TL and 14.2 cm SVL. *Adult:* dorsal scales pale with dark edges forming stripes or irregular pattern; males and females difficult to distinguish; sides of head of adult males slightly enlarged during breeding season; reddish marks on lips of some adults (probably males) during breeding season. *Juvenile:* dorsal scales with dark edges forming a regular netlike pattern; tail blue. *Hatchling:* dorsum solid black; whitish and orange spots on head; tail blue; 33–43 mm SVL (Fitch 1955; Degenhardt, Painter, and Price 1996). *Eggs:* 18–19 mm x 11–12 mm (Fitch 1955).

Distribution. Nebraska and southwestern Iowa south through eastern Colorado, Kansas, western Missouri, western Arkansas, Oklahoma, Texas, New Mexico, and central and southwestern Arizona to north-central and northeastern Mexico. Occurs mainly south of the Arkansas River and along the south portion of Big Sandy Creek at elevations below 7,200 feet (1,890 m) in southeastern Colorado and in the Republican River drainage in northeastern Colorado at elevations below 4,500 feet (1,370 m). Reports of this species from Larimer and Weld counties (Ellis and Henderson 1913; Maslin 1959; Smith, Maslin, and Brown 1965) are based on misidentified specimens of the many-lined skink (Hammerson 1984).

Conservation Status. The Great Plains skink is locally fairly common throughout its historic range in Colorado, though its secretive habits prohibit any quantitative assessments of abundance. It occurs in many areas not subject to intensive development and is tolerant of a good deal of periodic habitat disturbance. In Kansas, Fitch (1955) found that heavy livestock grazing and fires in early spring create conditions favorable for this species, unless the vegetation is almost totally eliminated. In Kansas, local populations have been depleted by commercial collectors (Fitch 1955), but this does not seem to be a problem in Colorado, where

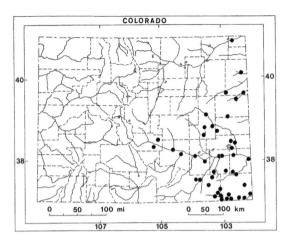

Map 8.24. Distribution of the Great Plains skink in Colorado.

Fitch (1955) indicate that rainfall may stimulate emergence from cover to drink.

Individuals disturbed by humans may dash for cover or even into water (Livo 1989). In hand, they vigorously struggle and twist, defecate, and often bite hard and persistently. Individuals captured in the open by Fitch (1955) had body temperatures of 23–36°C (usually at least 28°C). In general, body temperatures of about 30–36°C are maintained when conditions are suitable.

Fitch (1955) found that these skinks are somewhat sedentary; most live in home ranges not more than 30 m in diameter. Adult males are more mobile than females and juveniles. Sometimes individuals make longer movements of 100 m or more. Home range location is rather fluid. Individuals often live in one area for a while, then shift to another. Hall (1971) reported a maximum home range size of about 800 m².

Reproduction and Growth. Most of the following information is from Fitch (1955, 1970), Hall (1971), and Hall and Fitch (1972). Sexual behavior of the male toward the female includes approach or pursuit, touching with the tongue, nipping or nudging, and grasping of her shoulder area in his jaws. Copulation usually lasts several minutes. Male-female pairs often are found together in spring. In Kansas, the height of the breeding season occurs in mid-May (Fitch 1955). Copulations in captivity have been reported from late April through mid-June (see Fitch 1955). Eggs are laid in damp soil in spaces excavated under rocks in June or early July. Known clutch size based on oviductal eggs or eggs actually deposited is 8–15. Larger reported clutch sizes are based on counts of enlarged ovarian follicles, some of which may not yield fully developed eggs.

this skink is relatively more difficult to find. No widespread threats of major significance are known. The species can be regarded as secure in Colorado for the foreseeable future.

Habitat. Habitat in southeastern Colorado includes rocky slopes and outcrops, canyon bottoms, floodplains of streams, and areas along irrigation ditches in prairie and semiwooded regions, usually in sites near water. This skink has been found in sandhill habitats in northeastern Colorado. It is a secretive lizard that usually is found beneath rocks, logs, wood, and other items on the ground. Sun-warmed objects seem to be favored. Logs and rocks along streams or debris around old, abandoned ranch buildings provide favorable habitat. Winter is spent underground. Well-developed burrowing behavior is facilitated by the long claws and, perhaps, by the protruding scales on the underside of the forefeet (Fitch 1955).

Activity. This skink is most active during warm weather from May through September and, to a lesser degree, in April and October. In Kansas, Fitch (1955) captured many more individuals in July and August than in other months. Activity takes place during daylight hours, but patterns are difficult to characterize due to the skink's secretive behavior. These skinks are active in the open only when the weather is warm; on such occasions, they are highly alert and generally close to cover. Observations by

The female remains with the eggs for about seven weeks, until after they hatch. This probably enhances their chances of survival. She may assist the young in escaping from the shell (Evan 1959). Individuals produce only one clutch annually, and a large percentage of adult females skip at least a year between clutches. Reproductive success seems to vary greatly from year to year.

In Colorado, hatchlings begin appearing in late July or early August. In Las Animas County, Minette Church found an adult and 17 hatchlings in a nest cavity several centimeters deep on August 9. If the young were from one clutch, this observation would represent the largest clutch ever recorded. Hatchling emergence in early to late July has been observed in New Mexico (Degenhardt, Painter, and Price 1996).

Based on research in Kansas (Fitch 1955), males mature after their third hibernation, at about 32 months old. Females do not mature until they are 3–4 years old. Apparently mature males in Kansas are at least 10 cm SVL, and reproductive females are at least 10.5 cm SVL. Maximum longevity is eight years, perhaps longer.

Food and Predators. This lizard feeds opportunistically on various invertebrates (e.g., beetles, bugs, roaches, grasshoppers, crickets, flies, lepidopteran caterpillars and adults, ants, snails, slugs, spiders) and occasionally lizards; noxious or venomous animals such as millipedes, centipedes, scorpions, and wasps are avoided (Fitch 1955; Hall 1972). A juvenile that I found in Bent County defecated the remains of ants and spiders. Food items may be detected by sight or odor (Fitch 1955).

In Kansas, Fitch (1955) observed predation by an adult racer on an adult skink and found a hatchling skink in the stomach of a juvenile racer. Skinks grasped by a snake usually turn and bite their attacker. Various snakes, hawks, carnivorous mammals, other predators occasionally capture and eat these lizards (Fitch 1955; Hall 1971). Degenhardt, Painter, and Price (1996) reported that domestic cats may be serious predators in some urbanized areas of New Mexico.

Plate 8.68. Juvenile Great Plains skink (Baca County, Colorado).

Plate 8.69. Hatchling Great Plains skink (Las Animas County, Colorado). *Lauren Livo and Steve Wilcox.*

Taxonomy and Variation. From the mid–1800s through the 1920s, the adults and young of this skink were classified as separate species. In fact, the original descriptions of these two "species" were published in the same year in the same journal, and the two "species" were placed in different genera. No subspecies have been described.

Snakes

Take him up tenderly,
Lift him with care.
Fashioned so slenderly,
Scaly and bare.

—Dartt 1879

Snakes (order Squamata, suborder Serpentes) may have evolved from anguimorph lizards. The earliest known snake fossils are boalike and date from the early Cretaceous. Most extant snake species occur in the warmer regions of the world, especially the tropics and subtropics. A few species range north of the Arctic Circle in the Old World. Of the world's 2,700 species, about 135 occur in the United States, 26 of them in Colorado.

Snakes are elongate, legless reptiles with unblinking eyes, a short to very long tail, and numerous vertebrae (up to more than 400). Some snakes have vestiges of the pelvic girdle and hind limbs, but no snake has a pectoral girdle or sternum. Snake limblessness probably resulted from a fossorial or nearly fossorial lifestyle in snake ancestors. Many skull bones present in other reptiles are absent. Osteoderms are never present in the skin. Most snakes have an odd number of rows of overlapping scales on the dorsum and sides, and wide straplike scales with a free rear edge on the belly. The ventral scales occur in a 1:1 ratio with the vertebrae in most snakes (though not in sea snakes). Sexual differences in color and pattern tend to be subtle if present. In most species, females grow to a greater length than males, but this pattern is reversed in other species. Males generally have a proportionally longer, more gradually tapering tail than females. In contrast to many lizard species, temperate-zone snakes under natural conditions are not known to produce more than one clutch or litter per year.

To move forward, snakes undulate laterally, applying force against whatever is touching the sides of the body. Small movements of the belly scales and ribs, accordion-like movements, or, on slippery substrates, side-winding (accomplished through thrusting the body forward in a series of flat, S-shaped curves) also produce forward motion.

In conformity with the narrow torso, most snakes have only one lung. The left lung is reduced to 30–80 percent of the size of the right one in boas and pythons. The slenderness of the body also affects the reproductive system. The right ovary of many snake species is larger than the left one, and the right testis is farther forward. These organs generally are symmetrical in reptiles with wider bodies.

The elongate body of snakes poses certain potential problems, especially for those that climb. Arboreal species avoid blood pressure difficulties and pulmonary edema through adjustments and adaptations in the cardio-vascular system, including vasoconstriction and accelerated pumping of the heart when the head is elevated. In climbers, the heart is far forward, so the weight of the blood column above it is less of a problem. The pulmonary vessels, which may swell when the snake is vertical, extend over only a short length of the lung in arboreal species. And the taut body wall of climbers resists the accumulation of fluids in the lower part of the body when the snake is vertically oriented.

All snakes are carnivorous and swallow food whole, but species differ greatly in the kinds of food eaten and the method by which it is dispatched. In general, snakes are more specialized in their diets than lizards. In Colorado, the smallest snakes eat invertebrates, simply grasping them in the jaws and swallowing them. Larger snakes eat small vertebrates and large invertebrates. Some of these snakes catch their prey with a quick, open-mouth strike and swallow it alive (if it has not been killed by the bite). Other snakes, called constrictors, grasp prey in the jaws and immediately coil the body around it. As the coils tighten, the prey's heart and lungs cease their rhythms and the victim dies. The snake then loosens its coils and swallows its meal, most often headfirst. Details of constriction behavior vary from species to species. For example, all boids constrict with their venter facing their head, whereas rat snakes *(Elaphe)* constrict with their dorsum toward their head; other species may not be as predictable. Some constrictors, including kingsnakes *(Lampropeltis)* and gopher snakes *(Pituophis)* simultaneously can constrict multiple prey. Some snakes not regarded as constrictors (e.g., garter snakes) may wrap loops of the body around the prey (especially mammals), but such behavior simply immobilizes prey and facilitates ingestion. Rattlesnakes have highly specialized feeding behavior described in the account of the viper family (Viperidae). Some snakes use movements of the tail to lure prey; in some species the tail may be brightly colored.

Snakes have an instinctive response to their usual prey. For example, naive newborn snakes often respond most strongly to species-typical prey. Garter snakes respond to extracts of fishes and worms, for example, but not to insect extracts. Smooth green snakes respond to insect extracts but not to foods preferred by garter snakes. Rat snakes respond to extracts of their favored mouse and bird prey but not to insect extracts.

However, the response can be modified through exposure to different food items. Snakes of most species detect potential prey through visual or chemical cues. Though there is also evidence to the contrary, taste buds appear to be rare or absent in snakes. Snakes digest bones, but the fur of mammals passes through the stomach and intestines and appears in the feces.

The jaws of many snake species are well structured for manipulating and swallowing large prey. In most species, the upper jaw has on each side two rows of teeth that can move independently. The lower jaw typically contains a single row of teeth on each side. The two sides of the lower jaw are independently movable, articulating with the quadrate bones that swing downward and outward to increase size of the swallowing passageway. The lower jaw is also expandable at the front via an extensible ligamentous connection. Food items are positioned and pulled into the throat by coordinated forward-backward movements of the jaws. The curved teeth facilitate snaring and moving prey into the mouth and resist slippage as swallowing proceeds. The neck skin is very elastic between the scales, and there is no pectoral girdle or sternum, allowing large prey to pass. Ingestion of food items is usually headfirst, except for small items that may be swallowed in either direction. The mode of feeding and the elongate body form of snakes sometimes combine to a startling effect: on occasion, captive snakes have died as a result of inadvertently swallowing themselves!

After eating, snakes typically reduce activity and often rest in sites where they can maintain the warm body temperature needed for efficient digestion. Species such as whipsnakes digest a lizard or mouse within 2–3 days, but it may take a large rattlesnake two weeks to process a packrat *(Neotoma* spp.). Active digestion in the stomach occurs mainly at the posterior end. In at least some snakes, digestion is accompanied by a large increase in the bulk of the intestinal wall. Females with large developing eggs or young typically and individuals that are about to shed feed little, if at all.

SLENDER BLIND SNAKES
Family Leptotyphlopidae

The approximately 80 species in this family occur mainly in tropical and subtropical areas of Africa, southwestern Asia, and the Americas, with 2 species ranging into the southern United States, 1 of them in Colorado. These are wormlike burrowing snakes that have a cylindrical body, short tail, and vestigial eyes and pelvic girdle. In this family, the upper jaw is fused to the skull, teeth are present only at the front of the lower jaw, and the left oviduct is absent.

Plate 8.70. Adult Texas blind snake (Baca County, Colorado).

Texas Blind Snake
Leptotyphlops dulcis (Baird and Girard, 1853)

Recognition. Body slender, wormlike; scales smooth (unkeeled) and shiny, with those on belly same size as dorsal scales; eyes evident only as dark spots; short spine at tip of tail; maximum TL 29 cm (Hahn 1979). *Hatchling:* as small as 6.5 cm TL (Conant and Collins 1991). *Eggs:* probably similar to the 15 mm x 4.5 mm eggs of *L. humilis* reported by Klauber (1940b).

Distribution. Southeastern Arizona, central and southern New Mexico, south-eastern Colorado, and southern Kansas south through Oklahoma and Texas to north-central and northeastern Mexico. Known from elevations of about 4,300–5,000 feet (1,315–1,530 m) in southeastern Colorado (Lapin and Hammerson 1982; Jaggi et al. 1983; Hammerson et al. 1991a; Mackessy 1998); an unconfirmed sighting exists for the area south of the Mesa de Maya in Las Animas County (W. Louden, pers. comm.).

Conservation Status. This snake is known in Colorado from just a few locations. I found a recently shed skin under a rock in Baca County on May 31, 1982 (Lapin and Hammerson 1982). At another location in Baca County, Jaggi et al. (1983) found three individuals under rocks on June

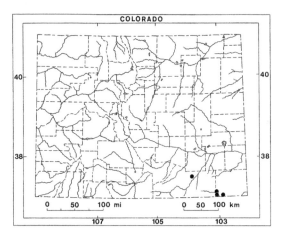

Map 8.25. Distribution of the Texas blind snake in Colorado.

southwest-facing slopes below canyon cliffs (Jaggi et al. 1983).

This snake spends most of its time in damp, loose soil among and under rocks. Apparently, it moves deeper underground when the surface soil becomes dry in summer. Jackson and Reno (1975) found that scales of this species have an exceptionally long semitransparent posterior edge (free margin) that may keep debris out of the hinge region between scales and/or serve as a traction agent in burrowing (see "Food and Predators" for a third potential function of the expanded free margin). Vanzolini (1970) reported that blind snakes readily climb trees that harbor ants.

Activity. Little is known about the activity patterns of this species, other than that it is found mostly frequently under rocks in late spring when the soil surface is moist and that it is most likely to crawl in the open on warm summer nights, particularly during and after rainfall. Surface activity in Colorado likely occurs primarily from April–May to September. A specimen from the prairie of Las Animas County was found crawling in the parking area in front of a ranch house as fireworks were being set off on July 4, 1987, at 10:30 p.m. (T. Laurion, pers. comm.). In a canyon bottom in Baca County, one crawled into camp at night on September 1, 1995 (Mackessy 1998).

This species is known to form bisexual and unisexual aggregations of up to two dozen or more individuals (Watkins, Gehlbach, and Kroll 1969; Rundquist et al. 1978). Perhaps clustering together retards water loss, but it likely has a social function as well.

In hand, blind snakes may defecate, release odorous cloacal sac secretions, and exhibit silvery coloration and "vigorous,

11, 1983. A specimen from Las Animas County was found on July 4, 1987 (T. Laurion, pers. comm.). Mackessy (1998) reported another single individual observed on September 1, 1995. This is a small, secretive, burrowing species that is relatively difficult to detect, so additional occurrences will likely be reported. Certainly, there is plenty of suitable habitat in southeastern Colorado that has not been adequately surveyed by appropriate methods. It probably does not range north of the Arkansas River and may be restricted to Baca and Las Animas counties. Judging by the few occurrences and individuals that have been found in areas searched with some regularity and intensity, the species appears to be relatively scarce in Colorado, though I suspect that there are pockets where the snake is locally numerous. Habitat conditions in southeastern Colorado are relatively stable, and no threats of widespread significance have been identified.

Habitat. In Baca County, I found a recently shed skin of this snake under a rock at the base of a rocky, south-facing slope of a flat-bottomed canyon (Lapin and Hammerson 1982). Piñon pine, junipers, and various shrubs were scattered over the slope, and grasses, yucca, and cane cactus covered the canyon floor. In the same county, another individual was found in a canyon bottom (Mackessy 1998), and three more were found under sandstone rocks on steep

Plate 8.71. Adult Texas blind snake (Baca County, Colorado).

semirigid, serpentine locomotion," or even go limp and feign death when captured (Gehlbach 1970).

Reproduction and Growth. Tightly entwined clusters of up to a dozen individuals were reported by Webb (1970) and Tennant (1984). Tennant stated that these were mating aggregations in which males outnumbered the females. Evidence from other states indicates that this snake lays clutches of 2–7 eggs in underground cavities in late June or July. Females often remain with, and coiled around, the eggs after oviposition. Several females may nest in a small area. In early July in southwestern Kansas, Hibbard (1964) found four gravid females within 1 m of each other about 45 cm below the surface and 60 cm back from the edge of a cut bank. Old dried eggshells suggested that the nest site had been used in previous years. The next year in a nearby area, also in early July, he found 42 eggs, apparently representing six clutches, attended by females in a bank beneath a layer of sandstone at a depth of about 75 cm. Force (1936) reported that two gravid females from Oklahoma were 19.3 and 19.5 cm TL.

Food and Predators. The diet is dominated by termites and ants, including the egg, larval, pupal, and adult stages of both, and especially the larvae, pupae, and soft parts of termite workers (Smith 1957; Reid and Lott 1963; Watkins, Gehlbach, and Baldridge 1967). Other soft-bodied invertebrates commonly are ingested as well (Punzo 1974a). The snakes find ant nests by following ant scent trails (Watkins, Gehlbach, and Baldridge 1967). When raiding ant nests, blind snakes protect themselves against particularly vigorous defensive attacks of ants by coiling up and smearing themselves with feces and cloacal sac secretions released from the vent (Gehlbach, Watkins, and Reno 1968; Watkins, Gehlbach, and Kroll 1969). Outward tilting of the free margins of the snake's body scales allows the fluid to enter the hinge regions between the scales, where it is stored as a deterrent against further attacks (Watkins, Gehlbach, and Plsek 1972). The secretions also to some degree repel snakes of different species but attract other blind snakes (Watkins, Gehlbach, and Kroll 1969). Nearly all of the odorous material in the cloacal sac secretion consists of free fatty acids (Blum et al. 1971).

Gehlbach and Baldridge (1987) described an intriguing relationship between blind snakes and eastern screech owls. The owls bring live blind snakes to their nestlings. Normally, the owls deliver dead prey to their nests. Some of the snakes are eaten, but others escape and take up residence in the nest material, where they feed on the larvae of insects, some of which are parasitic on the owls, or consume prey the owls have stockpiled. Amazingly, owl nestlings with blind-snake nestmates grow faster and experience less mortality than do owl broods without them. Webb (1970) reported predation on this snake by a night snake in Oklahoma.

Taxonomy and Variation. The subspecies in Colorado in *Leptotyphlops dulcis dissectus* (Cope, 1896). Klauber (1940b), Smith and Sanders (1952), Webb (1970), Hahn (1979), Smith and Chiszar (1993), and Schaefer, Chiszar, and Smith (1995) discussed the systematics of *Leptotyphlops dulcis,* which includes three subspecies. One of these *(L. d. myopicus)* formerly was regarded by some as a distinct species.

COLUBRIDS
Family Colubridae

Approximately 1,750 species are included in this "catch-all" family of essentially worldwide distribution (mainly tropical, subtropical, and warm temperate zones, though only a few species in Australia). Some divide colubrids into several families, but the relationships among the snakes in this group are as yet too poorly understood to allow a definitive multifamily classification. Colubrids typically have large scales on the top of the head, well-developed eyes, unspecialized teeth, and wide belly scales. They lack a functional left lung and have no pelvic girdle elements. The largest U.S. colubrid is the indigo snake *(Drymarchon corais),* which reaches a length of 2.6 meters in the United States and 3 meters farther south. Of the 110 species in the United States and Canada, 23 inhabit Colorado.

A few members of this family (none in Colorado) have saliva that is more toxic than the venoms of vipers; human fatalities have occurred as a result of the bite of certain colubrids. The herpetologist Karl P. Schmidt died after being bitten by a boomslang *(Dispholidus typus).* The source of the saliva toxins is Duvernoy's gland, which may be homologous with the venom glands of vipers and cobras. Duvernoy's gland usually is located on each side of the head, above the angle of the mouth, beneath the upper labial scales. Its single duct opens near the posterior maxillary teeth of the upper jaw.

Several U.S. colubrids have enlarged and/or grooved teeth at the back of the upper jaw. The Duvernoy's gland secretions of these snakes apparently are toxic enough to immobilize small prey, and they also facilitate swallowing. Examples of species with grooved teeth include the ground snake *(Sonora semiannulata),* shovelnose snakes *(Chionactis),* hooknose snakes *(Gyalopion* and *Ficimia),* black-headed snakes *(Tantilla),* lyre snake *(Trimorphodon),* black-striped snake *(Coniophanes),* and cat-eyed snake *(Leptodeira).* The night snake *(Hypsiglena torquata),* pine woods snake *(Rhadinaea),* and hognose snakes *(Heterodon)* have enlarged ungrooved teeth in the back of the upper jaw. The rear maxillary teeth of garter snakes are somewhat bladelike.

None of the colubrids in the United States have a bite that is dangerous to humans, but some persons have exhibited mild to moderate symptoms of envenomation from the bites of various "harmless" colubrid snakes, including garter snakes; in most cases, it is difficult to determine whether the symptoms were caused by the snake's saliva, by food residues or microorganisms in the snake's mouth, or by other factors. In any event, the toxicity of the secretion is low in garter snakes and other U.S. colubrids capable of biting a human, and many persons do not react at all to a typical colubrid bite. I have been bitten hundreds of times by a wide variety of colubrid snakes; some of these bites bled profusely for a short time, but none resulted in swelling, unusual pain, or even infection, despite no use of disinfectants. The secretions of Duvernoy's gland in these harmless colubrid snakes may aid in the initiation of digestion and/or may have significant antibacterial action.

Plate 8.72. Adult glossy snake (Otero County, Colorado).

Glossy Snake
Arizona elegans (Kennicott, 1859)

Recognition. Dorsum with smooth (unkeeled) scales and numerous blotches on pale background; belly whitish, immaculate; single anal scale; lower jaw inset; two prefrontal scales; pupil of eye subcircular; maximum TL about 142 cm but usually less than 117 cm in Colorado (Klauber 1946). *Hatchling:* 21–26 cm SVL in New Mexico (Aldridge 1979). *Eggs:* length about 32–33 mm (Aldridge 1979).

Distribution. Central California, southern Nevada, southern Utah, Colorado, and western Nebraska south through Arizona, New Mexico, Kansas, Oklahoma, and Texas to southern Baja California and central Mexico. Occurs in southwestern Colorado (Hammerson et al. 1991g) and eastern Colorado at elevations below 5,000 feet (1,525 m).

Conservation Status. The overall distribution of this snake in Colorado is not yet fully known. Over the decades, new distributional records have slowly continued to accumulate (the first occurrences in western Colorado were not found until 1988

[Hammerson et al. 1991g]). Populations distant from known locations probably remain undiscovered in the large sandhill tracts along the South Platte River, in El Paso County, and perhaps elsewhere in areas with suitable sandhills or soft alluvial soils. Gubanyi (1990) recently reported the first record of this species from the sandhills region (Thomas County) of Nebraska. The only known record for the South Platte River drainage in Colorado is from Logan County on June 11, 1973 (Cohen 1974), but additional occurrences in that region likely will be found along the band of sandhills south of the South Platte River west to Weld County.

The distribution and abundance of this snake in Colorado undoubtedly have declined with the advent and spread of intensive cultivation in large areas of eastern Colorado. Habitat and land use considerations suggest that the population trend now may be relatively stable in most areas. However, this is speculation, as nearly all occurrences of this species in Colorado are based on single or several specimens found dead or alive on roads. The glossy snake's highly secretive behavior makes it difficult to assess distribution and abundance. My

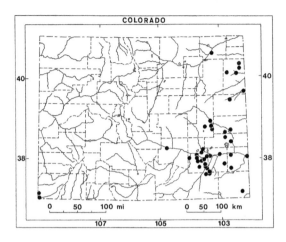

Map 8.26. Distribution of the glossy snake in Colorado.

(average 24–25°C, n = 12); snake body temperatures were 20.4–28.3°C (average 24–25°C, n = 9). Cowles and Bogert (1944) reported a comparable lower temperature limit for activity in desert regions. In central New Mexico, the body temperatures of nine active individuals were a similar 22–26°C (average 23°C) (Aldridge 1979). Though

field observations indicate that the species is fairly common at least in Otero County and adjacent areas and in the southwestern corner of Montezuma County in southwestern Colorado.

Habitat. The glossy snake inhabits sandhills and plains grassland, including riparian zones and areas with soft alluvial soils, as well as canyon bottoms and plains with firm soils. When inactive, it burrows underground or occupies rodent burrows or similar sites. It is rarely found under objects on the ground.

Activity. The limited available records indicate that most activity in Colorado takes place from late May through September, with hatchlings and some adults active into mid-October. In the warmer climate and longer growing season of New Mexico, records extend from February to November (Degenhardt, Painter, and Price 1996), but most activity occurs from May through August, with May records by far the most common (Aldridge 1979a).

I have had good luck finding active glossy snakes at dusk and during the first few hours of darkness, under both dry and rainy conditions. Smith, Maslin, and Brown (1965) reported specimens found active as late as 2:00 a.m. in southeastern Colorado under both dry conditions and shortly after a heavy rain. In Colorado, I found active glossy snakes at air temperatures 21–28°C

surface activity in this species is seen most often during periods of twilight or darkness, diurnal activity does sometimes occur (Taylor 1929; Klauber 1946; Mackessy 1998).

When confronted in daylight (as in captivity), some individuals repeatedly strike with audible exhalations; sometimes they bite. In hand, glossy snakes generally release odorous cloacal sac secretions and may extend the body straight forward, hook the head and neck around objects, wrap tightly around your hand, or undulate the anterior portion of the body from side to side.

Reproduction and Growth. A 60-cm female from central New Mexico contained eight shelled eggs on June 13 (Degenhardt, Painter, and Price 1996). Published dates of oviposition range from late June in California to early July in central New Mexico (Aldridge 1979b). Clutch size ranges from 3–12 eggs (with one extraordinary clutch of 23) and averages 8–9 eggs (Fitch 1970, 1985; Aldridge 1979b). Based on laboratory studies, the incubation period is about 10 weeks. In central New Mexico, newly emerged hatchlings appear from late August to mid-September (Aldridge 1979b). In Colorado, hatchling emergence may be most common in September. Aldridge (1979b) found that mature females (50–90 cm SVL) apparently sometimes skip a year between clutches. In Colorado, I found juveniles (28–37 cm

SVL and clearly in their second calendar year) in mid-June and individuals as small as 36 cm SVL in late July. Eleven adults or near-adults that I found in June were 48–80 cm SVL (average 63 cm). This suggests that individuals first breed no sooner than their second spring and some (most?) probably not until their third spring.

Food and Predators. Lizards and small rodents are the primary food; other small vertebrates are occasionally eaten as well. A 56-cm-SVL male that I found in Otero County had eaten an adult lesser earless lizard. Small prey tends to be grasped in the jaws and swallowed without delay, whereas larger prey may be killed by constriction before being swallowed. Glossy snakes exhibit versatile constricting behavior that may be related to their apparent habit of attacking prey in narrow burrow systems (Willard 1977). An individual that I fed in captivity usually constricted and quickly killed mice *(Peromyscus)* with venter-forward coils (i.e., the snake's belly faces its head) but some-times used coils that were more difficult to characterize.

Taxonomy and Variation. Major systematic analyses include Klauber (1946), Dixon (1959), and Fleet and Dixon (1971). The subspecies in eastern Colorado is *Arizona elegans elegans* Kennicott, 1859. *Arizona e. blanchardi* Klauber, 1946, formerly regarded as the subspecies in eastern Colorado, was synonymized with *elegans* by Fleet and Dixon (1971). The subspecies in western Colorado is *Arizona e. philipi* Klauber, 1946. Subspecies *elegans* and *philipi* differ in average dorsal and ventral scale counts and number of dorsal blotches.

Collins (1991) proposed that glossy snakes in California, southern Nevada, southwestern Utah, western and most of southern Arizona, Baja California, and northwestern Mexico should be recognized as a distinct species, but an adequate analysis of morphological and genetic variation supporting such an arrangement has not been published.

Plate 8.73. Adult glossy snake (Montezuma County, Colorado).

Plate 8.74. Adult racer (Douglas County, Colorado).

Racer
Coluber constrictor (Linnaeus, 1758)

Recognition. Dorsal scales smooth (unkeeled), plain brown or olive in adults; venter plain yellow or cream; eyes large; anal scale divided; nostril bordered by two separate scales; usually 15 dorsal scale rows just anterior to the vent; lower preocular scale wedged between upper lip scales; adults often 56–82 cm SVL; females grow larger than males; average SVL for males 64 cm in western Colorado–northeastern Utah and 63 cm in Larimer County, and for females, 70 cm and 74 cm, respectively (based on individuals larger than 39 cm SVL) (Corn and Bury 1986). *Hatchling:* dorsum with numerous brown blotches (blotched pattern disappears at approximately 50 cm SVL); eyes relatively large; SVL in Colorado 22–28 cm (average 27 cm) (Swain and Smith 1978; pers. obs.); SVL in Utah 20–24 cm (Brown and Parker 1984). *Eggs:* surface granular; size varies greatly within a clutch, averaging 26–38 mm x 16–22 mm (Carpenter 1958; Fitch 1963; Swain and Smith 1978; Brown and Parker 1984; Iverson et al. 1995).

Distribution. Southern British Columbia, extreme southern Saskatchewan, North Dakota, the southern Great Lakes region, New York, and New England south through most of the United States to northeastern Mexico (Smith 1971), the Gulf Coast, and southern Florida; absent from most of the desert Southwest and Rocky Mountains. Occurs at elevations generally below 6,000 feet (1,830 m) in eastern Colorado and usually below about 5,500 feet (1,680 m) in western Colorado. In Boulder County, I found one of these snakes on a canyon slope at 8,250 feet (2,515 m). Corn and Bury (1986) reported one found at 7,350 feet (2,240 m) in Larimer County.

Conservation Status. This snake is widespread and appears to occupy the vast majority of its historical range in eastern Colorado. Recent fieldwork has demonstrated that it is more widespread in western Colorado than previous records indicated (e.g., Hammerson et al. 1991h; Roth and Chiszar 1992). Abundance is difficult to assess, but the species is locally common in many areas. The racer is ecologically versatile and tolerant of a fair amount of human impact on the habitat, but extensive/intensive agricultural development has

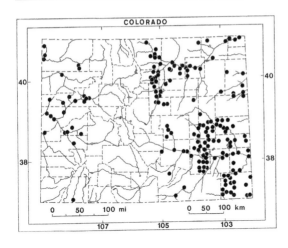

Map 8.27. Distribution of the racer in Colorado.

eliminated or reduced habitat in some areas. Capron (cited by Collins 1993) reported that dozens of racers were killed by mowing machines in late spring and early summer in agricultural areas in southern Kansas. Heinrich and Kaufman (1985) reported that 12 racers were killed by a prescribed prairie fire in late April in eastern Kansas. Populations near human habitation may be depleted when needlessly fearful people intentionally kill juveniles. Many die on roads. Nevertheless, populations in most areas of Colorado appear to be stable and not significantly threatened.

Parker and Brown (1973) observed a den in northern Utah over two decades and documented a swelling population that may have been related to increasing precipitation and more abundant herbivorous prey (crickets, grasshoppers). Overall density of the population after dispersal from the den was estimated at 0.8 individuals per hectare (Brown and Parker 1984), much less than the densities of up to 15 per hectare (2–7 adults per hectare in early summer) reported for eastern Kansas (Fitch 1963, 1982).

Habitat. Habitats in eastern Colorado include prairie grasslands, sandhills, open riparian woodlands, and shrubby foothills and canyons. In western Colorado, this snake inhabits semidesert shrublands and lowland riparian habitats and adjacent areas in valleys and canyon bottoms, in some areas ranging into rocky piñon-juniper woodlands

bordering valley bottoms. In both regions, it can be found in agricultural areas where farming and ranching operations are mixed with patches of undisturbed habitat. The racer is primarily terrestrial but also commonly climbs into shrubs and small trees. Daily retreats in spring and summer include rodent burrows and spaces under rocks or plants. Brown and Parker (1982) found that racers in northern Utah spend a great deal of time underground.

Winter is spent below ground, often in aggregations that may include other species. At the western edge of the Great Plains, hibernating sites include deep rock crevices in the Dakota Hogback and other sedimentary outcrops. Brown and Parker (1976) found natural communal den sites in sagebrush shrubland in northern Utah in outwash deposits of rocks averaging 30 cm in diameter; a single den harbored 192 racers, 42 gopher snakes, 40 striped whipsnakes, and 12 western rattlesnakes (the whipsnake and rattlesnake populations had been decimated by humans). In the same area, the highest number of racers at one den was 271 (Brown and Parker 1984). Dens sometimes are beneath buildings or in structures. Brown, Parker, and Elder (1974) described a winter den in an old filled well at a depth of 1.0–1.6 m used by 17 racers and 9 western terrestrial garter snakes in northern Utah; body temperatures of hibernating snakes were 4–7°C. A den in an old well in Kansas harbored 122 racers, plus two gopher snakes and two common kingsnakes (Collins 1993). A group of 27 racers and six Great Plains rat snakes was found hibernating in the concrete foundation of a house in Oklahoma (Webb 1970).

Activity. In Colorado, emergence from hibernation typically occurs in April, but some individuals are active during episodes of warm weather in late March. Activity continues through spring and summer until the weather turns cold in early fall. Many individuals still active in September and October are hatchlings, but some adults also are active well into October.

These warmth-loving snakes are active only during daylight hours. Racers begin each day by protruding the head several centimeters outside the overnight burrow. Within a half hour or so, they emerge completely, still with a low body temperature but with the head warmed, and bask for up to another half hour before beginning activity (Hammerson 1987). In Colorado, activity may begin as early as 8:30 a.m. (but usually not before 9:00–9:30 a.m.).

Throughout the large range of this species, body temperature during daily activity averages about 32–33°C (Fitch 1963; Hirth et al. 1969; Brown 1973; Hammerson 1987; Plummer and Congdon 1996). Ten active racers in Colorado had body temperatures of 26.5–38.6°C (average 32°C) (pers. obs.). During hot weather in summer, they are most active in midmorning and late afternoon. Racers usually cease daily surface activity when conditions no longer allow them to maintain a body temperature near 32°C, though activity at lower temperatures sometimes occurs in late afternoon and early evening. On long days around the summer solstice and during subsequent warm summer weather, activity and lingering on warm roads may extend into early evening, sometimes as late as 7:30–8:30 p.m.

After a meal, racers typically reduce locomotion and digest their food in secluded sites (Hammerson 1987). Inactivity also occurs just prior to shedding of the skin (Plummer and Congdon 1994). Over the course of the summer, racers tend to be active on 70–80 percent of the days (Fitch 1963; Plummer and Congdon 1994).

Active racers can move quickly over the ground and are adept climbers as well. Males may be more likely to climb than females (Fitch and Shirer 1971). Among snakes, racers and their whipsnake relatives have a very high capacity for activity and are able to increase their aerobic and anaerobic energy production tremendously (Ruben 1976), which may help during bouts of intense activity associated with foraging, avoiding predation, or sexual behavior.

In Utah, males and females disperse an average of several hundred meters (up to 1.8 km) from the winter den to their summer ranges (Brown and Parker 1976). In Utah, four migrating females traveled 100 m per day on days that they moved. Less frequent, shorter movements occur once the snakes arrive on their summer ranges. Nearly all survivors hibernate in the dens they used the previous winter. One female followed the same migration route and occupied the same home range in successive years. Young racers arrive at the den later than adults and many spend their first hibernation away from it. Migrations averaging about 400 m also take place in Kansas, but racers there do not always use the same winter den in successive years (Fitch 1963).

In Kansas and Utah, nonmigrating racers move an average of 33–37 m on days they are active, but average summer home range size is much larger in Kansas (about 10 ha) than in Utah (around 1 ha) (Fitch 1963; Fitch and Shirer 1971; Brown and Parker 1976; Plummer and Congdon 1994). Large home ranges averaging 12 ha were recorded in South Carolina by Plummer and Congdon (1994). Home ranges in Utah exhibit little overlap (Brown and Parker 1976).

Adult racers generally flee when approached by humans, but juveniles often pugnaciously hold their ground, vibrate the tail, and defend themselves by striking, a trait that sometimes causes them to be mistaken for rattlesnakes and killed by humans. In hand, adults generally thrash back and forth and attempt to bite; the teeth can lacerate human skin. They also may release feces and odorous fluid from the cloacal sacs. Snakes held gently typically flinch in response to nearby abrupt motion, reflecting their visual alertness. Some handled individuals coil and attempt to hide the head.

In early June in a small canyon in Dinosaur National Monument, Utah, Engeman, Scrips, and Bonzer (1984) found two individuals (55 and 60 cm long) struggling, each with the other's head or jaw in its mouth.

Plate 8.75. Juvenile racer (Otero County, Colorado).

southwest-facing hillside, returned on June 15 to a marsh beside the lake, and that same day captured and ate a 55-cm-TL plains garter snake and buried herself in soft sand in front of a kangaroo rat *(Dipodomys ordii)* burrow complex 62 m from the lake (Iverson et al. 1995). Egg-laying sites in Kansas usually are 13–20 cm deep in tunnels made by burrowing mammals (Fitch 1963). In Douglas County, I found a nest in a crevice beneath a concrete walkway.

Unfortunately, the snakes were separated by the observers and the sexes were not determined, so interpretation of this intriguing event was not possible.

Reproduction and Growth. Courtship and mating take place on the ground or aboveground in vegetation in spring. Males apparently find receptive females by following their scent trails (Lillywhite 1985). In Kansas, mating may occur chiefly in May (Fitch 1963), though Lillywhite (1985) observed copulation in late June in eastern Kansas. Courtship and close association of males and females was observed in mid- to late May in northern Utah (Brown and Parker 1976). In southeastern Utah, copulation was observed on June 10 (Tanner and Hayward 1934; Cottam 1937).

In Colorado, egg-laden females often can be found in mid-June. The eggs probably are laid mainly from late June to mid-July (see following paragraph). Fitch (1963) reported that oviposition in Kansas usually extends from mid-June to mid-July, but some clutches may be laid as late as early August. In Nebraska, Iverson et al. (1995) found gravid females in June and documented egg deposition in mid-June. In northern Utah, oviposition occurs in late June and early July (Brown and Parker 1984); a gravid female traveled 374 m on June 19 and laid her eggs on June 21 (Brown and Parker 1976). In the Nebraska sandhills, a gravid 93-cm-SVL female found on June 11 in a meadow near a lake traveled more than 600 m up into the sandhills over 2.5 days, laid her eggs on June 13 or 14 in an abandoned rodent burrow 14–18 cm underground on a

Clutch sizes are relatively large in the Great Plains region. Corn and Bury (1986) reported clutch sizes of 9–14 eggs (average 12) in six females from Larimer County. An 86-cm-SVL racer that I captured in Sedgwick County in mid-June laid 16 eggs on July 11. In Kansas, Fitch (1963, 1970, 1985) recorded clutch sizes of 5–22 eggs (average 11–12), with two-year-olds averaging 9 eggs per clutch and the oldest, largest females averaging 16 eggs per clutch. In Nebraska, four females measuring 78–101 cm SVL laid clutches of 16–31 eggs (Iverson et al. 1995). A 88-cm-SVL female from Oklahoma laid 11 eggs over five hours in mid-July (Carpenter 1958). In contrast, racers in western Colorado and Utah produce small clutches. Corn and Bury (1986) reported clutch sizes of 4–10 eggs (average 7–8) in five females from northwestern Colorado and northeastern Utah. A 68-cm-SVL female that I found in Dinosaur National Monument in mid-June contained six large eggs. At one site in northern Utah, clutch size was 4–8 eggs, with a mode of 5 and an average of 6; clutch size ranged up to 11 eggs in another area in northern Utah (Brown and Parker 1984).

Swain and Smith (1979) described a communal nest found 45 cm below the ground surface under a large rock at the lower montane–plains grassland ecotone in Boulder County. The nest contained 89 eggs and 29 empty shells from eggs laid in previous years. Obviously, several females

Plate 8.76. Racer hatching (Sedgwick County, Colorado).

had laid their eggs at the same site. The eggs began hatching immediately after the nest was discovered in mid-August. All eggs that hatched (82) had done so by August 24. Hatchlings are commonly observed in Colorado in late August and September.

In Utah, eggs hatch in mid- to late August after an incubation period of 45–50 days (Brown and Parker 1984). In Kansas, incubation generally lasts 43–63 days, and hatching occurs in the latter half of August and early September (Fitch 1963). In Nebraska, eggs incubated at 27°C reach the pipping stage after an average of 47 days; variation in substrate moisture does not affect embryonic survival or growth (Packard and Packard 1987).

In Utah (Brown and Parker 1984), juveniles are 23–30 cm SVL upon emergence from their first hibernation. Growth is best in years with relatively high rainfall. The smallest sexually mature males are about 39 cm SVL. The age of maturity is about one year, with first breeding occurring in the second spring. Gravid females are 54–75 cm SVL. A small percentage mature as two-year-olds; 77 percent mature by the age of three. Most produce their first clutch at an age of about four. In any given year, about 88 percent of adult females are reproductive. Reproductive success varies annually.

In Kansas (Fitch 1963), a few females mate in their second spring and lay their first eggs at an age of two years, but most clutch-producing females are older. Gravid females are as small as 59 cm SVL. The percentage of reproductive females increases with age, though in any single year, only about 80 percent of the oldest females lay eggs (Fitch 1963). Racers in Kansas grow faster than those in Utah and mature at a larger size. About 60 percent of adult racers in Kansas are less than 5 years old, but a few percent are 10 years old or older.

In different years in Utah (Brown and Parker 1984), 62–76 percent of the popu-

lation consists of individuals less than six years old. Overwinter survival is high (average 93 percent). Annual survivorship is 23 percent in juveniles and about 60 to nearly 80 percent in adults, with decreased survival during drought conditions. Compared to the Kansas population studied by Fitch (1963), racers in Utah have a lower population density, smaller body size, slower growth rate, smaller clutch size, larger egg and hatchling size, older age distribution, and higher adult female survivorship. Data for Utah and Kansas probably apply in large part to western and eastern Colorado, respectively.

Food and Predators. The racer is a wide-ranging predator that searches for small animals and sometimes employs quick bursts of speed to capture them. Prey may be crushed and killed in the jaws or swallowed alive. Despite its scientific name, this snake is not a constrictor (though it may pin the prey under a loop of the body). Most feeding occurs aboveground, on the soil surface or higher, where warm temperatures allow the snakes to maintain maximum speed and agility.

Racers feed opportunistically on small mammals, birds (including those obtained from nests in trees or shrubs), snakes, lizards, hatchling turtles, amphibians, and large insects (Hardy 1962; Fitch 1963; Webb 1970; Ballinger, Lynch, and Cole 1979; Iverson et al. 1995). Many studies have documented the importance of grasshoppers and crickets in the diet, and these insects constitute nearly all of the diet in northern Utah (Brown and Parker 1982, 1984). Ballinger, Lynch, and Cole (1979) noted predation on abundant sphinx moths (larvae?) on Russian olive trees in western Nebraska. Hardy (1962) found that hatchling racers are important predators on hatchling racerunners in eastern Kansas.

The few known prey items in Colorado include the plateau lizard (Ferner 1976), six-lined racerunner (L. Livo, pers. comm.), gopher snake, garter snake, newborn western rattlesnake, and various insects. Juveniles (41 and 47 cm SVL) that I found in Otero County had eaten grasshoppers, as had an adult in Bent County. An adult that I observed in Dinosaur National Monument regurgitated a 5-cm-long noctuid moth caterpillar, and another adult (73 cm SVL) I found in the same area had eaten an adult Mormon cricket *(Anabrus simplex)* and two smaller grasshoppers. A 75-cm-SVL adult male that I found dead on a road in Garfield County contained a juvenile western terrestrial garter snake (24.5 cm SVL, 32 cm TL). An 80-cm-SVL racer retrieved from a road in Yuma County had eaten a plains garter snake (48 cm SVL, 64 cm TL). The observational records of Dinosaur National Monument include an account of a 110-cm racer that ate a 45-cm gopher snake at Jones Hole, just west of the Colorado border. A 117-cm-TL female found dead at the Lodore boat ramp along the Green River in Dinosaur National Monument had partially ingested a 90-cm-TL female gopher snake (Steve Corn, pers. comm.).

Predators of racers probably include the usual array of carnivorous mammals, birds, and reptiles. A red-tailed hawk *(Buteo jamaicensis)* was seen carrying a racer in Lincoln County (Mackessy 1998), and in Oklahoma, the remains of a juvenile were found in the nest of the same species (Webb 1970). In Kansas, a 98-cm individual, covered with bites apparently inflicted by prairie dogs *(Cynomys ludovicianus),* was found dead at the entrance to a prairie-dog burrow (Halpin 1983). In western Nebraska, Ballinger, Lynch, and Cole (1979) found a western hognose snake eating racer eggs.

Taxonomy and Variation. Racer populations in Utah and western Colorado usually have been assigned to subspecies *Coluber constrictor mormon* Baird and Girard, 1852, whereas those in eastern Colorado and Wyoming represent the subspecies *C. c. flaviventris* Say, 1823. Fitch, Brown, and Parker (1981) pointed out morphological, reproductive, and ecological differences between populations of *mormon* in Utah and *flaviventris* in Kansas and concluded that *mormon* should be elevated to species status. However, Fitch, Brown, and Parker did not study any populations from the area where intergradation between these two taxa might be expected to occur; hence their conclusions are dubious. The one specimen from a possible intergrade zone for which they presented data conforms closely with *mormon* but was collected within the presumed range of *flaviventris*.

Corn and Bury (1986) demonstrated clearly that subspecies *mormon* and *flaviventris* intergrade over a broad area in northern Colorado and northern Utah; intergradation undoubtedly occurs in southern Wyoming as well. Specimens from this region tend to be intermediate between the two subspecies. Most individuals have seven upper labial scales (upper labials) on each side of the head, but the percentage with eight upper labials increases slightly from east to west. The average number of pairs of scales on the underside of the tail increases slightly from east to west, as does the average number of teeth in the lower jaw. The tail constitutes a slightly greater proportion of the total length in the west. SVL of the largest individuals decreases somewhat from east to west. The demonstration by Corn and Bury (1986) of clinal variation in *Coluber constrictor* over a broad area in the Rocky Mountain region casts doubt not only on the proposal by Fitch, Brown, and Parker (1981) but also on the validity of recognizing *mormon* and *flaviventris* as separate subspecies. In addition, Greene (1984) presented data indicating that the nominal subspecies *mormon, flaviventris,* and *oaxaca* may form a continuum in the Chihuahuan Desert region.

Plate 8.77. Adult ringneck snake (Baca County, Colorado).

Ringneck Snake
Diadophis punctatus (Linnaeus, 1766)

Recognition. Dorsal scales smooth (un-keeled), gray to olive; usually an orange ring or partial collar around neck; belly orange with black spots; underside of tail red; maximum TL about 42 cm; maximum SVL about 32 cm in males, 39 cm in females in Kansas (Fitch 1975); mixed-sex spring samples in Colorado typically are 16–28 cm SVL. *Hatchling:* in Kansas, males 10 cm SVL, females 11–12 cm SVL (Fitch 1975). *Eggs:* surface rough; white with thin translucent areas; variable size, 17–43 mm x 5–10 mm, average 25 mm x 7 mm, in Kansas (Fitch 1975); several eggs that I examined from Coloradan ringneck snakes fell within this size range.

Distribution. Washington, Idaho, Utah, Colorado, southeastern South Dakota, the Great Lakes region, and southeastern Canada south to northern Baja California, much of northern and central Mexico, the U.S. Gulf Coast, and southern Florida. Occurs below 6,000 feet (1,830 m) in southeastern Colorado. The mapped record for Trinidad,

Las Animas County, is based on a reliable (A. E. Beardsley) collection made in the 1800s. I have a secondhand report of an occurrence (not mapped) from Fountain, El Paso County, and I would not be surprised if this snake occurs there along Fountain Creek. Cope's (1900:746) record of Diadophis from the "mouth of Cache Creek, Colorado—?" (later repeated and restricted to Cache Creek, Chaffee County, Colorado, by Maslin [1959:55]) is based on a specimen from Oklahoma (McCoy, in Smith, Maslin, and Brown 1965).

Conservation Status. The distribution and abundance of this secretive snake in Colorado are not well known. Most occurrences are represented by small samples, though the snake is locally abundant in the Carrizo Creek drainage in Baca County, where diligent searching under appropriate conditions may yield a dozen or more in a day. Additional occurrences likely will be found in southeastern Colorado. The ringneck snake is tolerant of a moderate amount of habitat alteration, such as occurs with typical rural human communities, and it is found primarily in areas not presently subject to intensive development. The population in Colorado likely is stable and

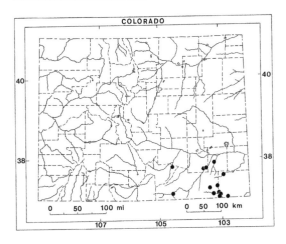

Map 8.28. Distribution of the ringneck snake in Colorado.

surface activity seems to occur when the weather is mild and damp. Daily patterns of activity in Colorado are poorly known, but observations in other parts of the range indicate that individuals may be active day or night. In Kansas, ringneck snakes are active over a wide range of air temperatures and generally maintain body temperatures of 25–30°C by selecting appropriately warmed shelter (Fitch 1975). Basking occasionally occurs when the air is cool.

Movements of ringneck snakes in Kansas vary widely (Fitch 1975). Some ringnecks may move distances of up to 1,700 m between capture points, but usually they do not move very far. Typically, maximum home range length is less than 140 m.

When disturbed, ringneck snakes coil the tail and display the bright red underside (Smith 1976). This may warn of the malodorous fluid ready to be discharged from the vent (Greene 1973) or the apparently toxic bite (see "Food and Predators"). Ringneck snakes in most of the eastern United States lack the bright red undertail coloration and generally do not display the tail. In some areas, handled snakes may squirm, cock or hide the head, shift their gaze angle, and/or feign death (Gehlbach 1970). A 22-cm-SVL individual that I found in Baca County coiled the tail, attempted to hide the head, then lay immobile for about a minute after I placed it on the ground, belly-side up. A 28-cm-SVL ringneck snake found under a rock in Baca County thrashed vigorously, coiled the tail, and released odorous fluid from the vent when grasped. It held its head/neck bent sharply to one side while maintaining many tight S-shaped curves along the body.

Reproduction and Growth. Females with enlarged ovarian follicles have been

not significantly threatened. Lauren Livo (pers. comm.) suggested that replacement of native cottonwood stands by salt-cedar *(Tamarix)* may pose a potential threat to this snake. Downed, decaying cottonwood logs surely are better refuges and egg deposition sites than are the skimpy fallen branches of salt-cedar.

In eastern Kansas, where this species is more abundant than in Colorado, Fitch (1975) documented population densities of about 720–1,850 individuals per hectare (average 1,270 per hectare) over several years.

Habitat. In Colorado this snake inhabits plains grassland, especially where abundant surface cover is present, and, more often, canyon bottoms or riparian areas. It is infrequently seen in the open. I found ringneck snakes under flat rocks beneath cottonwood trees, under rocks in grassy-shrubby areas, under boards in an open grassy area, and in and under damp rotting wood, usually in canyon bottoms bordered by rocky, juniper- or shrub-covered slopes. Sometimes several individuals of various ages and either sex aggregate under a single rock or log, especially in spring. Winter is spent in various underground sites, including old wells and cracked foundations.

Activity. Active individuals have been found in Colorado from April through September. Activity undoubtedly extends into October when conditions are suitable. Most

Plate 8.78. Ringneck snake hatching (Baca County, Colorado).

found in Colorado in late May. In Baca County, I found a single ringneck snake egg under a heavy log in a field near a stream in mid-July; close by was the dry, empty shell of an egg probably laid the previous year. Five eggs laid in mid-July by a 28-cm-SVL female captured in Baca County in late May hatched in early September (incubated at room temperature). Captivity may have delayed oviposition and hatching.

In eastern Kansas (Fitch 1975) courtship has been observed in late September and copulation in early May. Time of egg deposition varies from mid-June to late July (mainly late June and early July). One female had oviductal eggs with well-developed embryos in early August. Eggs are laid, often communally, in damp soil under large rocks or similar sites. Clutch size is 1–10 eggs (average about 4). Hatching generally occurs at the end of August or in September. Males are reproductive after their second hibernation at a minimum size of 16–17 cm SVL. Females first breed after their third hibernation, typically at 23–24 cm SVL (but as small as 21 cm). Annual mortality rate in adults is about 25 percent, and a few individuals live 15 years or more. Reproductive characteristics observed in most other parts of the range are similar and confirm that this species is long-lived, somewhat slow to mature, and has low reproductive capacity (Blanchard, Gilreath, and Blanchard 1979; Fitch 1985a; Clark, Bunck, and Hall 1997). Favorable moisture levels and resulting augmented food resources may increase reproductive output in some years.

Limited data are available for ringneck snakes in other states adjacent to Colorado. A 60-cm-SVL female collected in Arizona in mid-April laid three eggs in late July; they hatched after 52 days (Vitt 1975).

Food and Predators. Ringneck snakes in Kansas eat a diet limited almost exclusively to earthworms (Fitch 1975) and small

frogs (Henderson 1970). In other areas, salamanders, frogs, lizards, small snakes, insects, and other small animals may be consumed. Vertebrates are important in the dry southwestern part of the range. Predators in Kansas that also occur in Colorado include the racer, milk snake, red-tailed hawk *(Buteo jamaicensis),* great horned owl *(Bubo virginianus),* moles *(Scalopus),* mice, bullfrog, and no doubt various other species, but these probably have little impact on the population (Fitch 1975).

Rossi and Rossi (1994) made an intriguing observation of a ringneck snake that avoided predation by a longnose snake nearly twice as large by allowing itself to be ingested, then biting and holding onto the floor of the longnose's mouth just before total engulfment. This behavior not only prevented successful predation but resulted in the death of the longnose snake after 16 hours. The ringneck snake eventually let go and crawled out of its dead attacker. Gehlbach (1974) observed that ringneck snakes from Texas attempt to hold onto the original bite site when they attack small snakes and that such prey may be immobilized or killed within 40–375 minutes. The ringneck snake has enlarged teeth at the back of the upper jaw (Fitch 1975:11). Apparently, they function in conjunction with possibly toxic saliva to immobilize prey or thwart certain predators.

Taxonomy and Variation. The subspecies in Colorado is *Diadophis punctatus arnyi* Kennicott, 1859. Blanchard (1942) regarded *Diadophis* as comprising multiple species, but in recent decades it has been regarded as a variable single-species genus. Ringneck snakes in Arizona, western New Mexico, and adjacent northern Mexico (subspecies *regalis*) grow to relatively large body size (adults average twice the length of those in Colorado); smaller *arnyi-regalis* intergrades occur in western and central Texas (Gehlbach 1974). Patterns

of serum albumin variation indicate that this species may in fact comprise at least two genetically distinct species, one of them western-midwestern, one of them eastern (Pinou, Hass, and Maxson 1995). Further study is needed to determine the phylogenetic relationships among the various ringneck snake populations.

Plate 8.79. Adult Great Plains rat snake (Otero County, Colorado).

Great Plains Rat Snake
Elaphe guttata (Linnaeus, 1766)

Recognition. Dorsum gray (light gray in eastern Colorado, often dark gray in adults in western Colorado, or at least there is less contrast between the background color and the dorsal blotches in western Colorado) with numerous dark-edged blotches; dorsal scales weakly keeled along middle of back, unkeeled on sides; numerous square-cornered dark marks on belly; anal scale divided; dark stripes usually on underside of tail; maximum TL in Great Plains region about 180 cm but generally less than 125 cm; smaller in western Colorado, usually up to 60–80 cm TL, rarely up to 110–120 cm

TL (Weir 1993; Schulz 1996). *Hatchling:* 30–35 cm TL (subspecies *emoryi*) (Schulz 1996), probably sometimes smaller. *Eggs:* sometimes adherent, with or without crystalline surface deposits (Clark 1953); 51–61 mm x 20–22 mm in Kansas (Clark 1953); 40–50 mm x 27–31 mm in Texas (Werler 1951).

Distribution. Southeastern Colorado, southern Nebraska, Missouri, and southwestern Illinois south to northeastern Mexico, coastal Texas, and Louisiana (Vaughan, Dixon, and Thomas 1996); disjunct population in eastern Utah–western Colorado. Occurs below 6,000 feet (1,830 m) in southeastern and west-central Colorado. A July 27, 1982, record from 3.2 km north of the Jones Hole campground just west of the Colorado border along the Green River

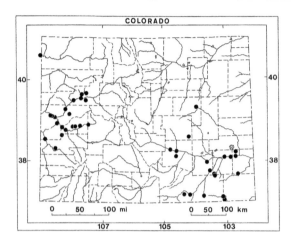

Map 8.29. Distribution of the Great Plains rat snake in Colorado.

these areas, it commonly dwells in semiagricultural and rural residential areas, especially rodent-infested outbuildings. The rat snake is active on the ground and also is a good climber in shrubs, trees, rocky crevices, and buildings. Caves may be occupied where available. Periods of inactivity are spent in burrows and other secluded locations, including the foundations of old buildings and similar sites. A group of 27 racers and six rat snakes was found hibernating in the concrete foundation of a house in Oklahoma (Webb 1970). Sometimes individuals can be found under objects on the ground during daylight hours.

Activity. Most activity takes place during dry or wet weather at dusk and on warm nights from May to September, though some activity probably occurs during warm periods in April and October. In Colorado, 11 individuals, mostly juveniles, that I found between 9:15 and 11:30 p.m. in May and June were active at air temperatures of 17–27°C. Daytime activity also sometimes occurs. Woodbury and Woodbury (1942) mentioned an individual found in late afternoon crawling among cottonwood trees on the bank of the Green River in Utah.

Defensive behavior includes tail vibration, defecation, release of odorous cloacal sac fluid, and sometimes biting. Stebbins (1954) described the odor of the cloacal sac fluid as disagreeable, but in Mesa County a juvenile's cloacal sac secretion had a pleasant smell that reminded me of corn tortillas.

Reproduction and Growth. A courting male mounts the female, moves his chin over her dorsum, writhes his body atop hers, flicks his tongue, and twitches his tail just before curling it under her tail and attempting

in extreme northeastern Utah (Bury 1983) suggests that this snake occurs in western Moffat County, Colorado.

Conservation Status. The general pattern of distribution in Colorado is well known, but the relatively sparse records leave room for new observations within the range. Recent discoveries of shed skins (Chiszar, Drew, and Smith 1993; H. Smith, unpublished record) have extended the range northward in the Arkansas River drainage. Several occurrences are based on single specimens, but this snake is locally common in at least some areas. It tolerates a good deal of habitat alteration such as that typical of rural human communities but probably has declined locally in extensively altered landscapes associated with intensive agricultural development and in urbanized areas with networks of heavily traveled roads. Overall, much suitable habitat remains occupied, and the state population probably is relatively stable and unthreatened.

Heinrich and Kaufman (1985) reported that 11 rat snakes were killed in a late April controlled burn in prairie habitat in Kansas.

Habitat. In Colorado, the Great Plains rat snake is closely associated with river valleys, stream courses, and canyon bottoms. It inhabits grassland, weedy areas, shrubland, plains shelterbelts, open conifer woodlands, and lowland riparian zones but usually does not venture far from a permanent or intermittent stream or arroyo. Near

intromission (Gillingham 1979). Copulation is accompanied by slow movements of the tail region and lasts 15–30 minutes. Biting does not occur during courtship or copulation. Based on studies of *E. guttata* from the eastern part of the range, courtship and copulation may not occur until 3–4 weeks after emergence from hibernation (Ford and Cobb 1992).

A female found in Otero County in early July was laden with nine large eggs nearly ready for oviposition. Clutch size in western Colorado generally is 5–8 eggs (Schulz 1996). Two females captured in mid-May in Kansas laid clutches of four and five eggs in early July (Clark 1953). At 27–29°C, the incubation period is 55–58 days for eggs from western Colorado (Weir 1994). The smallest reproductive female *E. guttata* from the southeastern United States recorded by Bechtel and Bechtel (1958) was 55 cm TL, and under favorable captive conditions with no hibernation, sexual maturity was attained in 1.5 years, suggesting that it takes at least

three years to mature under natural conditions. In captivity, this snake may live more than 20 years.

Food and Predators. The diet consists mainly of rodents and sometimes other vertebrates such as birds and lizards. A 26-cm-SVL juvenile found in Delta County had eaten a neonate mouse. Snakes are rarely eaten, but in captivity, an 85-cm-SVL female *E. guttata emoryi* ate a 60-cm-SVL garter snake (McCrystal 1982). Large prey are killed by constriction.

Taxonomy and Variation. Rat snakes in eastern Utah and western Colorado formerly were regarded as a distinct subspecies, *Elaphe guttata intermontana,* originally described as *Elaphe laeta intermontanus* Woodbury and Woodbury, 1942. More recently (Dowling 1952), these snakes have been regarded as consubspecific with the Great Plains subspecies *E. guttata emoryi* (Baird and Girard, 1853).

Weir (1993), basically reiterating the characteristics mentioned by Woodbury

Plate 8.80. Juvenile Great Plains rat snake (Delta County, Colorado).

Plate 8.81. Adult Great Plains rat snake (Otero County, Colorado).

and Woodbury (1942), concluded that *E. g. intermontana* warrants subspecific status, and Schulz (1996) regarded the western Colorado–Utah population as the most differentiated geographical form of *E. guttata*. However, neither Weir nor Schulz conducted an extensive study of geographic variation throughout the western range of *E. guttata*. In contrast, Smith et al. (1994) examined specimens from throughout the range west of the Mississippi River and found that the western Colorado–Utah population is distinctive only in its relatively small size and usually darker background coloration but not sufficiently so to warrant recognition as a distinct subspecies.

Smith et al. (1994) and Vaughan, Dixon, and Thomas (1996) identified areas of intergradation between the western subspecies *emoryi* and *meahllmorum* (circumscribed differently in the two papers) but did not detect intergradation between the subspecies *guttata* and the western subspecies, suggesting that the two western subspecies together could be regarded as a distinct species *(Elaphe emoryi)*. Smith et al. (1994) discussed this possibility and concluded

that the three taxa should continue to be regarded as conspecific. Given the uncertain taxonomic identity of snakes of this group in critical areas in the region of Louisiana (Raymond and Hardy 1983; Dundee and Rossman 1989), I agree that *guttata* and *emoryi* should be treated as conspecific, at least until further data clearly demonstrate otherwise.

Walls (1997) argued that New World rat snakes should be removed from the genus *Elaphe* and placed in a separate genus (*Pantherophis* Fitzinger, 1843), based largely on the finding by Keogh (1996) that Old World *Elaphe* differ from New World Elaphe in one internal anatomical characteristic (presence of an intra-pulmonary bronchus), but no additional support for this proposal was presented. Keogh stated that a split of the genus *Elaphe* would be premature without a complete revision of the genus.

This species also is known as the corn snake, but I prefer to use the more appropriate name, rat snake, that has been associated with the western populations, especially in view of the possibility that the western and eastern populations are distinct species.

Plate 8.82. Adult western hognose snake (Lincoln County, Colorado).

Western Hognose Snake

Heterodon nasicus (Baird and Girard, 1852)

Recognition. Snout upturned, spadelike; dorsal scales keeled; 23 or fewer rows of dorsal scales at midbody; prefrontal scales separated by small scales; underside of tail mostly black; in Kansas, maximum TL about 90 cm, but few males exceed 55 cm and females rarely grow longer than 65 cm (Platt 1969); in Colorado, relatively few exceed 50 cm TL. *Male:* usually 35 or more blotches along mid-dorsal line between head and vent. *Female:* usually 40 or more mid-dorsal blotches. *Hatchling:* in Nebraska, average 14–15 cm SVL (Iverson 1995); in Kansas, 17–20 cm TL, average 18 cm TL (Platt 1969). *Eggs:* smooth, typically not adherent, usually 26–38 mm x 14–23 mm (Platt 1969; Iverson 1995).

Distribution. Southern Alberta, southern Saskatchewan, and southern Manitoba south through the Great Plains to central Mexico, west to southeastern Arizona, disjunctly east to Illinois and eastern Missouri. Occurs in eastern Colorado at elevations below 6,000 feet (1,830 m); known from a small area in the vicinity of Maybell in Moffat County in northwestern Colorado at an elevation of about 6,000 feet (1,830 m) (Roth, Johnson, and Smith 1989).

Conservation Status. The western hognose snake occurs throughout essentially all of its historic range in eastern Colorado, where it is locally fairly common. It is tolerant of the kind of habitat alterations typical of rural ranching and semiagricultural landscapes. It probably has been eliminated or greatly reduced in abundance in areas of extensive agricultural cultivation. Local declines undoubtedly have occurred due to habitat destruction and heavy road traffic in the urbanized corridor along the eastern base of the Front Range.

Discovery of a population of this snake in Moffat County was one of the most astonishing recent herpetological events in the region. Never before had this species been found on the west side of the Continental Divide north of New Mexico, and the location in northwestern Colorado is far from the nearest known populations in eastern Colorado and central and eastern Wyoming (Censky and McCoy 1985a; Conant and Collins 1991). The population was first documented by two specimens collected in late May 1989 (Roth, Johnson, and Smith 1989). Both were alive on roads when found; one, a 43-cm-SVL female with six large yolking follicles, had just been trampled and mortally injured by sheep. A third specimen (UCM 56075) not mentioned by Roth, Johnson, and Smith (1989) was collected in the same area in mid-September 1989. Roth, Johnson, and Smith (1989) reported that a western hognose snake had been photographed a few years earlier and that local residents told of seeing this snake in the 1960s. Roth, Johnson, and Smith (1989) pointed out a patchy distribution of sand-dune habitat present in low-elevation areas in southern Wyoming through which this species may have dispersed to

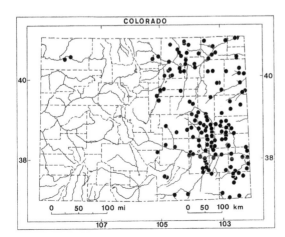

Map 8.30. Distribution of the western hognose snake in Colorado.

Plate 8.83. Adult western hognose snake (Yuma County, Colorado).

Plate 8.84. Adult western hognose snake (Yuma County, Colorado).

northwestern Colorado during the early Holocene climatic optimum several thousand years ago. The present distribution and abundance of the hognose snake in northwestern Colorado are uncertain but apparently limited. Habitat conditions are relatively stable.

In Kansas, population density, not including hatchlings, was estimated at about 3.7–6.2 per hectare in pasture habitat and less than half that in an ungrazed area (Platt 1969).

Habitat. Typical habitat includes sandhills, plains grassland, and sandy floodplains, often in the vicinity of, or along the margins of, streams, irrigation ditches, and ponds. Hognose snakes are terrestrial and fossorial. Periods of inactivity are spent burrowed in the soil, in mammal burrows, or, less commonly, under rocks or debris.

Activity. Activity in Colorado occurs primarily from late April to about mid-October. Most individuals found active early in the season are males (Platt 1969). Morning

and early evening are the primary activity periods, with an apparent lull in early and midafternoon. My records of active individuals in Colorado fall mainly between 7:20 a.m. and 1:30 p.m. and between 5:30 and 9:00 p.m., with a few snakes active as late as about 10:00 p.m. Platt (1969) found these snakes active at a wide range of body temperatures (21–36°C, mode 31–33°C). The few body temperatures that I measured in Colorado were 25.0–35.1°C (average 31°C, n = 5).

Home range size apparently has not been studied in detail using adequate methods (i.e., radiotelemetry). In Kansas, Platt (1969) usually found marked individuals within a few hundred meters of their previous capture sites. Occasionally, capture locations in different years were separated by 1 km or more.

Hognose snakes exhibit elaborate defensive behavior. When disturbed, they may spread, flatten, and raise the head and neck and may vigorously strike with the snout (typically with the mouth closed), emitting a hiss or snort with each strike; this behavior appears to represent mimicry of rattlesnakes. The hognose snake rarely actually bites during these strikes. Some individuals hide the head beneath the coiled body and strike with the tail when touched. If these ploys fail to put off an attacker, the snake may writhe and roll onto its back, regurgitate, evert the cloacal lining, defecate, release the odorous contents of the cloacal sacs, hang the tongue out of the open mouth, and lie immobile, feigning death. Opening of the mouth and extrusion of the tongue does not always accompany this behavior. The illusion of death is reinforced by the cloacal sac secretion odor and the black-and-yellowish ventral coloration (decomposing snakes may turn dark ventrally and do smell bad). If turned right side up, the snake immediately twists onto its back again. Individuals sometimes stop "playing dead" then reinitiate the activity multiple times during a single defensive episode. Kroll (1977) observed that death-feigning individuals, if handled, sometimes bite themselves (one of seven that did this died as a result). If left alone for a few minutes, the snake turns over and crawls away. Burghardt and Greene (1988) found that eastern hognose snakes *(Heterodon platirhinos)* end their death simulation sooner if the observer is not visible to the snake. The hognose snake's defensive behavior presumably improves its chances of survival during encounters with predators, but few relevant field observations have been made. Many predators attack only when the prey is mobile, so the hognose snake's death-feigning behavior might stop an attack. Perhaps a bird or mammal, thinking the snake dead, might cease its attack and take the snake home to feed its young, only to have the snake escape from the nest later (Greene 1997).

Reproduction and Growth. Based on studies of the eastern hognose snake, male *H. nasicus* likely find females by following their scent trails (Plummer and Mills 1996). In south-central Kansas, mating occurs mainly

Plate 8.85. Death feigning by western hognose snake (Yuma County, Colorado).

Plate 8.86. Defensive posture of western hognose snake (Lincoln County, Colorado).

in May, and eggs are laid in July (Platt 1969). In Nebraska, six gravid females captured in late May or June laid eggs in late June and, in a colder year, in mid-July (Iverson 1995). One nest site in Kansas was a few inches below the surface in sandy soil.

Clutch size exhibits intriguing variation. In Kansas, small adults average about 5 eggs per clutch, and the largest adults average about 14 (Platt 1969). In Nebraska, Iverson (1995) documented clutch sizes of 3, 4, 9, 12, 12, and 15 eggs, despite little variation in the size of the females (48–54 cm SVL). Jones (in Roth, Johnson, and Smith 1989) hypothesized that the unusual pattern of variation in clutch size in this species may result from differences in the activity of the ovaries (one active versus two active).

Eggs hatch after about two months (Platt 1969). Incubated at 25–30°C, Nebraska clutches laid in June hatched in mid-August, whereas the July clutches hatched in early September (Iverson 1995). In Colorado, hatchling emergence probably peaks in late August and early September.

Females in Kansas mature at 21–33 months old, at 35–40 cm TL; males mature in their second spring at an average size of about 31 cm TL (Platt 1969). Fewer than half of the adult females in Kansas are reproductive in any one breeding season. My limited data for Colorado are consistent with Platt's conclusions for Kansas. In Colorado, I found small juveniles (13–23 cm SVL, 15–25 cm TL) in mid-June, indicating little growth in fall and early spring in some individuals and first breeding no sooner than the third or fourth calendar year (an individual of 15 cm TL in mid-June of its second calendar year is unlikely to attain mature size [> 30 cm TL] before the next breeding season). In Colorado, a female that was 34 cm SVL (38.4 cm TL) in mid-June contained five developing eggs.

Platt (1969) determined that young individuals constitute the bulk of the population—only about 30 percent of a Kansas population was in its fourth year or older. Maximum longevity under natural conditions is about eight years (Platt 1969). In captivity, this snake may live two decades.

Food and Predators. Toads, lizards, and reptile eggs seem to be the primary foods (Platt 1969; Ballinger, Lynch, and Cole 1979), but mice, small birds, bird eggs, other reptiles and amphibians, and insects also may be eaten. Evans and O'Neill (1986) implied that short-horned lizards are among the prey eaten in northeastern Colorado. Swenson and Rodeck (1948) reported that a 23-cm hognose snake ate a plains garter snake nearly 25 percent longer than itself. Prey encountered in the open may be grasped with an open-mouthed attack. Secretions of the enlarged adrenal glands may neutralize the toxins absorbed from ingested toads (Smith and White 1955).

Hognose snakes use their spadelike snout to dig out buried prey detected by odor. For example, in western Nebraska, Iverson (1990) frequently observed that hognose snakes follow scent trails of painted turtles to the turtles' nest sites, push the snout through the soil plug, and eat the eggs. The snakes are efficient at finding the turtle nests even long after nest construction, and they may consume virtually all of the eggs produced by a local population. In addition, the snakes commonly find and eat yellow mud turtle eggs. Also in western Nebraska, Ballinger, Lynch, and Cole (1979) found a western hognose snake eating racer eggs. Toads and lizards buried in the soil may be obtained in the same way. An adjustable flap in the nostril keeps sand out when the snake is burrowing.

Hognose snakes have a pair of enlarged, ungrooved teeth on each side of the rear of the upper jaw. These teeth may function in introducing toxic saliva into prey items or may facilitate the manipulation and deflation of toads that fill their lungs with air when captured (a deflated toad is, of course, much easier to swallow). Humans inadvertently bitten while feeding captive hognose snakes sometimes have developed moderate symptoms of envenomation (swelling, pain). This topic was discussed by Bragg (1940), Smith and White (1955), Edgren (1955), McAlister (1963), Platt (1969), Grogan (1974), Kroll (1976, 1977), Minton (1978), and Morris (1985).

The few definitely known predators

include hawks (*Buteo* spp.), crows *(Corvus brachyrhynchos),* and coyotes *(Canis latrans)* (Platt 1969).

Taxonomy and Variation. The subspecies in Colorado is *Heterodon nasicus nasicus* Baird and Girard, 1852.

Plate 8.87. Adult night snake (Bent County, Colorado).

Night Snake
Hypsiglena torquata (Günther, 1860)

Recognition. Dorsum with smooth (unkeeled) scales and numerous dark blotches, the largest and most conspicuous ones on neck; 19–21 dorsal scale rows at midbody; pupil vertically elongate, may close to a narrow slit or two pinpoint openings in bright light; anal scale divided; maximum size about 53 cm SVL, 61.5 cm TL (Yancy 1997). *Hatchling:* 13–19 cm TL (Werler 1951; Clark and Lieb 1973), perhaps as small as 10 cm TL (Wright and Wright 1957). *Eggs:* smooth, surface nongranular, quite variable in size—for example, average about 45 mm x 12 mm (Vitt 1975) versus 28 mm x 10 mm (Clark and Lieb 1973).

Distribution. Extreme southern British Columbia, Idaho, Utah, Colorado, and southern Kansas south through the western

United States from the Pacific Coast to Texas and into southern Mexico. Occurs in southeastern Colorado at elevations below 6,000 feet (1,830 m). Known to occur in west-central Colorado at about 4,500–6,600 feet (1,370–2,010 m) and at Mesa Verde in southwestern Colorado at about 7,900 feet (2,410 m).

Conservation Status. This is a small, secretive snake that often occurs in rugged terrain. Its presence and abundance are relatively difficult to determine without the use of special devices such as drift fences or pitfall traps. Most records are based on single specimens found on paved roads (the snake is difficult to see on dirt roads) or occasionally under rocks. Available information indicates that it is widespread in southeastern Colorado, chiefly south of the Arkansas River. Additional occurrences are to be expected in the many areas with suitable habitat in that region. The distribution in western Colorado certainly is more extensive than is now known. Most specimens have been found

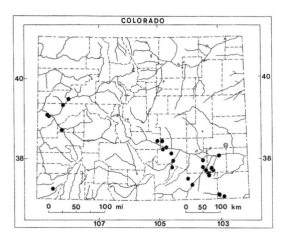

Map 8.31. Distribution of the night snake in Colorado.

under rocks or in crevices.

In Idaho (Diller and Wallace 1986), night snakes are most abundant in canyon rim habitat and rocky slopes, though they also occur in nonrocky shadscale *(Atriplex)* and greasewood *(Sarcobatus)* shrubland. They can be found under rocks in spring but usually not in summer. In Colorado, they are found beneath rocks mainly during the mild weather of spring, late summer, and fall. In nonrocky habitats in Idaho, they take shelter in the burrows of white-tailed antelope squirrels *(Ammospermophilus leucurus)* and kangaroo rats *(Dipodomys ordii)*.

in frequently visited Colorado National Monument and Mesa Verde National Park, but much additional suitable habitat exists in the intervening area, where paved roads are scarce and few adequate surveys have been made. Eventually, I expect that populations will be discovered in most counties along the state's western border. The night snake inhabits landscapes that generally are not suitable for extensive development, and the habitat of this snake in Colorado is largely intact and not threatened. Habitat alteration and associated road traffic in urbanizing areas probably have caused local declines in a few areas, but no other significant threats are known.

Little information exists on population density, but these snakes can be locally common in some areas. In Idaho, three workers looking under rocks for eight hours in spring found 21 individuals (Diller and Wallace 1986). Ten were found by turning over rocks in a 100 m x 10 m area. In drift-fence samples, this species was outnumbered only by the gopher snake and striped whipsnake. Similar efforts at searching under rocks in Colorado are much less productive (pers. obs.).

Habitat. Typical habitat includes rocky slopes and canyons sparsely vegetated with piñon-juniper woodland and/or various shrubs and grasses. Occasionally, this snake has been found in flat plains grassland far from rocky slopes. It is a ground-dwelling species that seems to spend most of the time

Activity. Night snakes have been observed in Colorado from May to October. Usually, they are found under rocks during the day or on roads at night. In Idaho, Diller and Wallace (1986) found that night snakes first appear on the surface (beneath rocks) in late April. The first major annual movement (detected in drift-fence samples) occurs in mid-May and consists almost exclusively of males. A major peak in activity happens in early June. Surface activity ends in early September. Activity appears to take place solely at night. The presence of night snakes in the nests of day-active hawks in Idaho suggests occasional daytime activity by night snakes but more likely indicates scavenging of snakes found dead on roads.

Night snakes exhibit interesting defensive behavior that warrants further study. A 37-cm-SVL night snake that I found in Bent County repeatedly attempted to hide its head under its body as I tried to position it for a photograph. Disturbance sometimes causes a night snake to flatten its head and body, with the body coiled and the head on the top; occasional hissing may accompany this posture (Webb 1970). Individuals removed from pitfall traps in New Mexico usually attempted to crawl away, but some coiled tightly and maintained this posture for at least several minutes, even if further disturbed (Price 1987). When startled, a 29-cm-SVL male from New Mexico assumed a stiff sigmoidal posture with parts of the body slightly elevated (Stuart 1988). When touched, this snake violently flexed its body, reversing the orientation of the body curves; often this was accompanied by a brief hiss and sometimes cloacal discharge. In Arizona, an exposed male flattened its head and attempted to flee (Mitchell 1985). When held by the posterior end of the body, it coiled, exhibited rhythmic writhing and exaggerated lateral tail movements, and attempted to hide its head under its coils. When picked up, it released fluid from the vent. Left alone, it uncoiled and crawled away. A night snake placed in a cage with a larger racer (a snake predator) exhibited a slow, stiff crawl with the lateral curves of the body elevated, followed by a raising of the tail and discharge from the cloaca; rapid breathing occurred throughout the episode (Hayes 1985). Later on, when being swallowed tailfirst by a captive kingsnake, the same individual attempted to burrow into the substrate but soon ceased struggling and was engulfed while virtually motionless.

Reproduction and Growth. Relatively little information is available on reproduction. In spring, pairs may be found under rocks, but these often are male-male associations rather than male-female couples interacting sexually (Diller and Wallace 1986). Lauren Livo and I observed copulating night snakes in Baca County in late May. The snakes were under a flat rock on a hillside in midmorning. The female was 32 cm SVL, and the male was 30 cm SVL. I found a gravid female (36 cm SVL) in early June in Bent

County. A female found in southwestern Kansas in mid-June contained four eggs (Hibbard 1937). A night snake collected in eastern Utah in mid-June produced three eggs and a folded cluster of nine shells on the day of collection (Tanner 1944). A female from Oklahoma laid six eggs on July 7 (Stebbins 1954). In southern Idaho, Diller and Wallace (1986) found that three females of 38, 42, and 52 cm SVL contained three, four, and seven large ovarian eggs, respectively. Of the immature females also found, the two largest were about 41 cm SVL. Males apparently attained sexual maturity within one year; the smallest males with sperm in the ductus deferens were 29 cm SVL. Egg-laying in Idaho evidently takes place in June or early July. Clark and Lieb (1973) reported that females 31–35 cm SVL from Texas and Arizona produced clutches of 2–6 eggs. Together these observations indicate that (1) night snakes in Colorado and other northern parts of the geographic range produce small clutches of usually 2–7 eggs (clutch size increases with female size), (2) females become mature at about 30–40 cm SVL, and (3) at Colorado's latitude, most clutches are laid between mid-June and mid-July.

In areas farther south, clutches may be of similar number (and positively correlated with female size), and oviposition may occur both earlier and later. A female captured in Texas on March 10 laid four eggs on April 25; two of these hatched on June 18 (Stebbins 1954). Clark and Lieb (1973)

Plate 8.88. Copulating night snakes (Baca County, Colorado). Female contains a partially digested adult collared lizard.

reported that females from Texas and Arizona laid clutches from late April to mid-July. Specimens collected in early to mid-June in Arizona contained enlarged yolked follicles (Vitt 1975). A 39-cm-SVL female collected in Arizona in mid-August laid three eggs on September 1 (Vitt 1975). A 57-cm specimen from Sonora, Mexico, captured on August 12 laid eight eggs on August 28 and one egg a week later (Tanner and Ottley 1981). The eggs hatched after about two months. The wide range of egg-laying dates in the southern part of the range may reflect an extended breeding season, with different females breeding at different times, or perhaps the production of multiple clutches by some females. Night snakes have a potential longevity of at least nine years (T. Brown, in Degenhardt, Painter, and Price 1996).

Food and Predators. Small lizards, especially *Sceloporus* and *Uta,* dominate the diet (H. Greene, pers. comm.). Barry (1933b) reported that a night snake found dead on a road at Mesa Verde had eaten

a sagebrush lizard. Tanner (1929) found a canyon treefrog in the stomach of a night snake in southern Utah. In Idaho, Diller and Wallace (1986) recorded the following food items: side-blotched lizard, western whiptail, the eggs of these species, Great Basin spadefoot, grasshoppers, and probably a cicada; the lizard eggs and insects apparently were eaten independently of the lizards. Blind snakes *(Leptotyphlops)* have been found in the stomachs of night snakes in Oklahoma (Webb 1970) and New Mexico (T. Brown, in Degenhardt, Painter, and Price 1996).

I suspect that most lizards are captured beneath rocks or in crevices during the lizards' nocturnal period of inactivity, when temperatures are low and lizard muscular performance is suboptimal. When a night snake encounters a lizard, it bites and holds on. One or two enlarged ungrooved teeth at the rear of each side of the upper jaw pierce the lizard, allowing the saliva, which is toxic to the lizard, to seep in and subdue the struggling victim. The toxic saliva and

Plate 8.89. Night snake found dead on a road (Mesa County, Colorado).

Plate 8.90. Night snake (Baca County, Colorado).

the snake's habit of hunting when lizards are most lethargic allow the little night snake to prey occasionally on relatively large lizards. For example, the female of one copulating pair contained a partially digested adult collared lizard. This instance of predation is impressive because the powerful jaws of a fully warmed adult collared lizard are capable of inflicting severe damage on (or even killing) an attacking night snake (the snake in this case was uninjured). Circumstances made it unlikely that the lizard had been scavenged from a road.

Instances of predation on this snake rarely are observed. The remains of night snakes have been found in the nests of the red-tailed hawk *(Buteo jamaicensis)* in Idaho (see Diller and Wallace 1986), but as previously mentioned, this may reflect scavenging rather than predation. In Texas, Hibbitts (1992) observed a dead night snake (30 cm TL) being eaten by a large scorpion. There was no evidence that the scorpion had not killed it.

Taxonomy and Variation. Dixon and Dean (1986) examined morphological variation and determined that all samples of *Hypsiglena* from the central and eastern parts of the range, including southeastern Colorado, represent *Hypsiglena torquata jani* (Dugès, 1865); these night snakes have one loreal scale on each side of the head. Night snakes from eastern Utah and western Colorado, *Hypsiglena torquata loreala* Tanner, 1944, usually have two large loreals on each side. Subspecies *loreala* and *jani* may intergrade in northwestern New Mexico (Gehlbach 1965).

Over the years, there has been disagreement about the number of species that should be recognized in this genus. Some have favored a taxonomy that would change the name of the species in Colorado to *Hypsiglena ochrorhynchus* (see Frost and Collins 1988 for a discussion of the spelling of the specific name), but recent classifications place all night snakes in *H. torquata*.

Plate 8.91. Adult common kingsnake (Montezuma County, Colorado).

Common Kingsnake
Lampropeltis getula (Linnaeus, 1766)

Recognition. Dorsal scales smooth (un-keeled), black or dark brown, with either yellowish speckling or broad whitish or yellowish bands; single anal scale; usually two rows of scales on underside of tail; maximum TL about 183 cm (usually less than 100 cm);

two adult males from Montezuma County, Colorado, and San Juan County, Utah, were 77–88 cm SVL (pers. obs.). *Hatchling:* 24–25 cm SVL, 27–29 cm TL in Otero County (pers. obs.); 20–24 cm SVL, 23–28 cm TL in Oklahoma (Grimpe and Benefield 1981; Secor 1983). *Eggs:* adherent; 28–37 mm x 19–21 mm in Oklahoma (Carpenter 1958; Grimpe and Benefield 1981; Secor 1983).

Distribution. Oregon, Nevada, Utah, Colorado, Nebraska, Iowa, Illinois, Indiana, Ohio, West Virginia, Maryland, Pennsylvania, and New Jersey south through the southern United States to southern Baja California, central mainland Mexico, the U.S. Gulf Coast, and southern Florida. Known to occur in southwestern Colorado in western Montezuma County (and

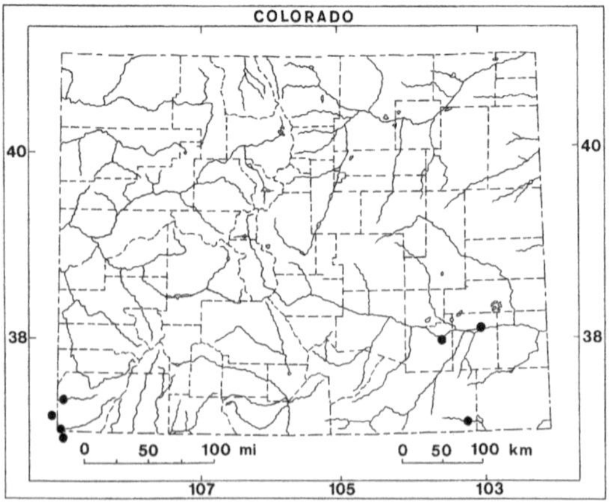

COLORADO

40

38

0   50   100 mi

0   50   100 km

107   105   103

Map 8.32. Distribution of the common kingsnake in Colorado.

Plate 8.92. Hatchling common kingsnake (Otero County, Colorado).

adjacent San Juan County, New
Mexico [Davenport, Stuart, and
Sias 1998] and San Juan County, Utah [pers. obs.]) at elevations of about 4,600–5,200 feet
(1,400–1,585 m) (Spencer 1974;
Hammerson et al. 1991o) and in
southeastern Colorado at about
3,800–5,000 feet (1,160–1,525 m)
(Kappel 1977a, 1977b; Boback,
Link, Bergman, et al. 1996; Bergman, Montgomery, et al. 1998a).

Conservation Status. The first record
of the common kingsnake in southwestern
Colorado was reported by Spencer (1974),
who found an individual run over by a car
in McElmo Canyon, Montezuma County,
on September 12, 1966. The next records
from the southwest part of the state were
of two adults found in June 1988 and June
1990 near the San Juan River (Hammerson
et al. 1991o). I found another adult just
west of the Colorado border, 17 km north
of the Four Corners monument in 1997. The
first reported observations of this species
in southeastern Colorado were made in
the vicinity of La Junta, Otero County, in
July and September 1976 (Kappel 1977a,
1977b). Since then, several additional
kingsnake sightings have been recorded in
that area and in Bent and Las Animas counties. It is likely that the common kingsnake
will be discovered in additional locations
in both southwestern and southeastern
Colorado.

Usually, this snake is found on roads,
but roads are relatively scarce in most of
the Colorado range, and, due to difficulty
of access, adequate surveys have not been
made in most areas of the state where this
species might be expected to occur. Occurrences along the Arkansas River in extreme
western Kansas (Taggart 1992a), in the
Cimarron National Grasslands in extreme
southwestern Kansas (Ball 1992), and at
the extreme western end of the Oklahoma
panhandle (Webb 1970; pers. obs.) suggest
the presence of this snake in Prowers and

Baca counties in Colorado. Surely the range
in southwestern Colorado is continuous with
that in southern and south-central Utah (Cox
and Tanner 1995). The infrequent observations of this snake in Colorado suggest that
it exists at low densities and/or is highly
localized.

This species inhabits not only natural landscapes but also areas altered by
low-intensity farming, ranching, and rural
residential development. Populations of
this snake in Colorado probably are not
significantly threatened by existing or
foreseeable land use patterns. Increased
road traffic associated with casino visita-
tion in southwestern Colorado and with
population growth and road improvements
in southeastern Colorado may be causing
declines in nearby local populations, but the
density of paved roads is low in the areas
occupied by this species.

Habitat. In Montezuma County, Spencer
(1974) found this snake in the broad bottom
of a canyon through which a permanent
stream flows. Much of the area, formerly
covered by semidesert shrubland, has been
converted to hayfields. Residents of the
canyon reported that this snake is seen most
frequently near human habitations. In the
same region, I found kingsnakes in areas of
low, hilly semidesert shrubland. In adjacent
San Juan County, New Mexico, Davenport,
Stuart, and Sias (1998) found a kingsnake
in a cottonwood–Russian olive grove 30 m
from the San Juan River. In southeastern
Colorado, this snake has been found near
irrigated fields on the floodplain of the
Arkansas River, in rural residential areas

in plains grassland, near stream courses, and in other areas dominated by shortgrass prairie. Most activity occurs on the ground or in rodent burrows. Periods of inactivity are spent in burrows and logs, in or under old buildings, in other underground spaces, or beneath various types of cover.

Activity. The few available records indicate an activity period extending from May through September, though activity probably occurs during warm weather in late April and October. In southern New Mexico, Price and LaPointe (1990) found kingsnakes active much more frequently in July than in any other month, coinciding with the beginning of the summer rainy season. Activity may take place day or night. Diurnal activity may be most common during the cool weather of spring and fall. During the warmer weather of late spring and summer, activity becomes mainly nocturnal. Two kingsnakes that I found in the Four Corners region in May and June were active at 9:30 p.m. and 11:05 p.m. at air temperatures of 24–25°C; body temperature of one was 26.8°C.

When disturbed, these snakes commonly vibrate the tail, strike, bite, void or spray cloacal sac secretions, and hiss. Some are relatively docile when handled and simply release odorous fluid and hide the head beneath the coiled body.

Reproduction and Growth. Courtship and mating in our area occur primarily in late spring. Male courtship behavior includes chasing and mounting of the female, forward body jerks, rubbing of his chin on her dorsum, writhing and entwining of the bodies, grasping of her neck or trunk in his jaws, and curling of his tail under her tail just prior to insertion of a hemipenis (Lewke 1979; Secor 1987). These snakes generally alternate between the two hemipenes with each successive mating if mating occurs within a few days of the previous copulation (Zweifel 1997). Males approach and court the female from the side opposite that of the hemipenis used in the last copulation. Secor's (1987) data are consistent with the pattern reported by Zweifel (1997). Copulation may last up to several hours. Alternation of hemipenes may allow more efficient renewal of seminal fluid and assure maximal sperm supply for the hemipenis being used (Zweifel 1997). Possibly this pattern exists in other (all?) squamate reptiles. Males of this species engage in combative interactions that may result in one individual becoming dominant over the other (Carpenter and Gillingham 1977).

Scant data are available on reproduction in Colorado. A 94-cm-TL female that I obtained in mid-June in Otero County laid eight eggs on July 27. Incubated under relatively cool conditions at room temperature, the eggs hatched on the unusually late date of November 5. Under natural conditions, the eggs probably would have been laid earlier and hatched sooner, based on the 60-to-80-day incubation period reported by others (Fitch 1970). The eggs were tightly adherent, as has been observed in other individuals of this species. Adherence probably enhances the survival of the eggs by making it more difficult for egg-eating snakes to swallow them.

Reproductive data for kingsnakes in areas adjacent to Colorado include the following. A 94-cm-SVL female found in Oklahoma on June 1 laid 18 adherent eggs on June 24 (Secor 1983). Incubated at 28–33°C, they hatched in mid-August. A 94-cm-SVL female from Okla-

Plate 8.93. Adherent eggs of common kingsnake (Otero County, Colorado).

homa laid 16 eggs on June 28 (Carpenter 1958). A 63-cm-SVL female found in Oklahoma on May 15 laid nine eggs on June 20. Incubated at 24–32°C, these eggs hatched on August 9–10. A female from Oklahoma laid 12 eggs on June 15 that hatched on August 17 (Webb 1970). Two additional clutch sizes for kingsnakes, presumably from Oklahoma, were 8 and 11 eggs (Secor 1983). Eggs from a clutch of 10 laid on June 22 by a female from Kansas began hatching on August 24 (Gloyd 1928). Collins (1993) reported that two females from Kansas laid clutches of 11 and 12 eggs in mid-June and mid-July. Two kingsnakes from central and southern New Mexico laid clutches of 5–7 eggs in early July; hatching occurred in mid-September (T. Brown, in Degenhardt, Painter, and Price 1996). A female from southern Arizona laid six eggs in mid-June that hatched in mid-August (Humphrey 1956). Thus, oviposition in the region takes place most often from mid-June to early July; hatching typically occurs in mid- to late August, or as late as mid-September. In general, clutch size (average 4–6 eggs) in common kingsnakes from the southwestern United States is notably smaller than in populations from Kansas and Oklahoma eastward (Fitch 1985a). Incubation periods for this species range from as short as 49–54 days to as long as 60–80 days (Fitch 1970; Zweifel 1980; Grimpe and Benefield 1981; Secor 1983), largely reflecting differences in incubation temperature. Production of two clutches in a single year has been observed (Lewke 1979), but undoubtedly this was an artifact of captivity. Based on studies of captive individuals, sexual maturity may be attained in 3–4 years, and potential longevity exceeds three decades.

Food and Predators. Common kingsnakes feed on a wide range of vertebrate prey typically including rodents, birds, bird eggs, lizards, snakes (including rattlesnakes), reptile eggs, and amphibians. Foraging may occur in burrows, on the surface of the ground, or even in trees (Eichholz and Koenig 1992). The blood serum of this snake is effective at neutralizing the venom of rattlesnakes, whereas the blood of the bullsnake (which does not prey on rattle-

snakes) is not (Weinstein, DeWitt, and Smith 1992). Webb (1970) recorded predation on a northern water snake in Oklahoma.

These powerful constrictors can kill large prey, including other constrictors larger than themselves, such as gopher snakes *(Pituophis)*. In California, I observed a 206-g common kingsnake attacking a 355-g gopher snake. The gopher snake struggled to pull away from the kingsnake as the kingsnake held the gopher snake's head in its jaws and wrapped two coils of its body tightly around the gopher snake's neck. After 35 minutes, the gopher snake was dead and the kingsnake attempted to swallow it. Ninety minutes later, with its prey three-fourths ingested, the kingsnake regurgitated the dead gopher snake, which clearly was too large to consume.

The cloacal sac secretions of the common kingsnake appear to be effective in defensive behavior but not in intersexual communication (Price and LaPointe 1981). When grasped, kingsnakes often spray the secretion. Mammalian carnivores appear to find the secretion distasteful.

Remarks. Two-headed individuals have been found (Shaw and Campbell 1974; Belfit and Nienaber 1983). Under good care in captivity, they may live several years. One head may or may not become dominant. In one of these snakes, the two heads sometimes attempted to crawl in different directions, and one head usually attempted to take away the food that the other head was attempting to swallow.

Taxonomy and Variation. Kingsnakes in southwestern Colorado, *Lampropeltis getula californiae* (Blainville, 1835), have alternating black and white bands encircling the body. The striped and banded-striped intermediate morphs that occur in California and Baja California (Zweifel 1981) and certain other areas have not been observed in Colorado.

In southeastern Colorado, kingsnakes conform well with the characteristics expected in the area of intergradation between *Lampropeltis getula holbrooki* Stejneger, 1902, and *L. g. splendida* (Baird and Girard, 1853) in adjacent regions of neighboring states (Blaney 1977). The sides are dotted with yellow, the middle of the back is black with yellowish crossbars (accentuated in juveniles), and the cream-colored belly is sparsely or heavily marked with black. The large area of intergradation between *holbrooki* and *splendida* suggests that these nominal subspecies do not warrant recognition as distinct taxa.

The specific name of this snake formerly was *getulus,* but Frost and Collins (1988) reasoned that the feminine form *getula* should be used.

Plate 8.94. Juvenile milk snake (Delta County, Colorado).

Milk Snake
Lampropeltis triangulum (Lacepède, 1788)

Recognition. Black, whitish, and red or orange bands around body; dorsal scales smooth (unkeeled); belly with much dark banding; anal scale single; two rows of scales on underside of tail; generally less than 85 cm TL in the western Great Plains region and less than 72 cm TL in western Colorado (Tanner and Loomis 1957; Williams 1988; Painter and Hibbitts 1997). *Hatchling:* 16–29 cm TL in Colorado, Utah, New Mexico, Wyoming, and Kansas (Tanner 1941; Fitch and Fleet 1970; Smith 1977; Williams 1988; Schuett 1994; Degenhardt, Painter, and Price 1996). *Eggs:* slightly granular, adherent; 37–44 mm x 13–14 mm in New Mexico (T. Brown, in Degenhardt, Painter, and Price

1996); 29–35 mm x 13–16 mm in Kansas (Fitch and Fleet 1970).

Distribution. Montana, South Dakota, the Great Lakes region, New England, and southeastern Canada south to southern Florida, the U.S. Gulf Coast, Mexico, and Central America to northern South America, possibly the widest distribution of any snake species worldwide. Occurs throughout most of eastern, southern, and western Colorado at elevations primarily below 8,000 feet (2,440 m). A record from "Irish Canyon, abt. 10,000 feet," supposedly in Jackson County, Colorado (UCM 7646), is confusing. There is an Irish Canyon in Moffat County, where the species likely occurs, but the elevation is nowhere near 10,000 feet, which is much higher than this species typically occurs. No known occurrences exist in the vicinity of Jackson County.

Conservation Status. The known distribution of this snake in Colorado reflects, in part, the distribution of humans—records are concentrated along the eastern edge of the Front Range, where large human populations exist and people are likely to encounter and report this colorful snake, and in the sandhills of Weld and Morgan counties, where snake hobbyists from urban areas traditionally go to obtain specimens of this species. Milk snakes probably are equally common in many other areas of the state that are less often visited by persons likely to report or collect snakes. The recent discovery of this species in Moffat County (Roth and Smith 1990b) suggests a wider range in western Colorado than existing records indicate. The present paucity of records from the Dolores and White River drainages may be an artifact of inadequate survey efforts and this snake's secretive behavior.

Populations of this species undoubtedly have been eliminated and reduced in areas of intensive urbanization along the Front Range, but moderate habitat alteration typical of rural human communities seems to be well tolerated by milk snakes. Overall, most of the habitat remains suitable and not significantly threatened. Collecting for the pet trade has reduced the abundance of milk snakes in some local, well-known populations in southern Weld County, but most areas inhabited by milk snakes are not significantly impacted.

Taggart (1992b) found that the milk snake was the most abundant snake species in an area in central Kansas. In Colorado, it can be locally common in some sandhill areas, but abundance in most of the state is uncertain. The species surely is outnumbered by each of several other snake species (e.g., bullsnake, western rattlesnake, coachwhip, various garter snakes) throughout the majority of its range in Colorado. In most areas, it is infrequently encountered, even during intensive surveys (Mourning 1997; Mackessy 1998; pers. obs.).

Habitat. The milk snake occurs in a wide variety of habitats in Colorado, including shortgrass prairie, sandhills, shrubby hillsides, canyons and open stands of ponderosa pine in the foothills, piñon-juniper woodlands, and arid river valleys. Except at night, this snake generally stays hidden. Harris (1963) found this species under a rotting log near the mouth of a canyon wooded with pine and Gambel oak in Archuleta County. Hahn (1968) found a milk snake under debris on the floor of an abandoned mine in the San Luis Valley. Many milk snakes have been found under discarded railroad ties in sandhill regions. Various underground sites are occupied in winter (Tanner 1941; Woodbury and Hansen 1950; Wright and Wright 1957; Hahn 1968). A hibernaculum in the San Luis Valley was shared with gopher snakes, western terrestrial garter snakes, and western rattlesnakes (Hahn 1968). Near the mouth of a canyon in Jefferson County, Livo (pers. comm.) observed a juvenile milk snake (hatched the previous summer) in a hibernaculum with western terrestrial garter snakes.

Activity. Emergence from hibernation generally occurs in April in eastern Colorado. In the high elevation and cool climate of the San Luis Valley, Hahn (1968)

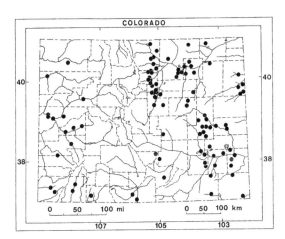

Map 8.33. Distribution of the milk snake in Colorado.

and may void feces and cloacal sac secretions. Like many snakes, they often become docile if gently handled.

Movement data are few. Based on recaptures, Fitch and Fleet (1970) estimated average home range size in Kansas at about 20 ha.

Reproduction and Growth. Courtship and mating occur in spring. Sexual behavior of the male includes biting the neck region of the female.

observed milk snakes emerging from a den in a rock crevice along the Rio Grande in early June. Activity generally extends into October. Woodbury and Hansen (1950) reported milk snakes entering hibernacula in mid-October in Utah. Burnett (1926) reported a young specimen taken on November 15 near Montrose, but the weather and collection circumstances were not mentioned.

Most activity appears to take place at dusk or at night, but sometimes these snakes are found abroad in daylight. They may be encountered during moist surface conditions, such as after rainfall, or, less often, when conditions are dry. In Colorado, 12 individuals (26–61 cm SVL) that I found crossing roads in June and July were active between 9:30 p.m. and 10:30 p.m. at air temperatures of 18–26°C; two body temperatures were 23.5°C and 26.2°C. Similarly, Mackessy (1998) recorded six occurrences of milk snakes found alive on roads in southeastern Colorado between 8:30 p.m. and 10:00 p.m. A 19-cm neonate was active at 9:07 p.m. in late August in Delta County (Larry Valentine, pers. comm.). A milk snake active near dawn in Yuma County had several cactus spines embedded in its facial scales (L. Livo, pers. comm.). In Wyoming, a live adult female was found on a road at 10:36 a.m. during a light rain at a temperature of 25–27°C in early May, and a neonate was active on the ground surface at 6:25 p.m. in late September (Schuett 1994).

When first disturbed, milk snakes commonly rear up and strike, vibrate the tail,

In Colorado and adjacent areas, adult females generally lay a clutch of about 4–6 eggs between mid-June and mid-July, as the following observations demonstrate. A female found in Delta County on June 11 contained six large eggs (Larry Valentine, pers. comm.). Williams (1988) listed four clutches (of four, four, and six eggs), one of which was laid in mid-June and three of which were laid in early July by females from Weld County. Clutch sizes of eight females from Colorado and Nebraska averaged 5–6 eggs (Fitch 1985a). A 65-cm female found on July 4 along a stream in a foothill canyon in Boulder County laid four eggs on July 15 (Smith 1977). Two of the eggs hatched, on August 29 and September 1, consistent with the usual incubation period of about 6–9 weeks, depending on the temperature. Several females from Kansas laid clutches between mid-June and early July (Fitch and Fleet 1970; Collins 1993). Early July clutches that hatched in late August have been observed in New Mexico (Degenhardt, Painter, and Price 1996). Hatchlings generally first appear in Colorado in late August, though probably most appear in September.

In Kansas, some females attain sexual maturity in their third or fourth year at about 45–50 cm SVL (Fitch and Fleet 1970). Small, nonreproductive individuals (26–37 cm SVL) are present in western Colorado in July and August, suggesting that first breeding takes place no sooner than the third or fourth calendar year. Maximum longevity in captivity exceeds 20 years.

Food and Predators. This constrictor feeds opportunistically on a wide variety of small vertebrates, including mammals, birds, lizards, and snakes. It also consumes bird and reptile eggs. A milk snake found in the San Luis Valley by Hahn (1968) disgorged seven reptile eggs of undetermined species. Prey items in extreme western Kansas include the prairie lizard and six-lined racerunner (Collins 1993). Tanner (1941) reported that two individuals collected in Utah had eaten adult sagebrush lizards.

Taxonomy and Variation. My observations (Hammerson 1981), together with those of Williams (1988), indicate the following variation in Colorado. Northeastern Colorado: snout black-and-white-mottled, or pale orange with black spots; 26–34 (average 29, n = 27) red body rings (excluding those on tail). Front Range foothills: snout black-and-white-mottled; 21–31 (average 26, n = 40) red body rings; among various geographic areas in Colorado, snakes from this region have by far the lowest percentage of red rings interrupted mid-dorsally by black (less than 10 percent, versus an average of 25–55 percent in other areas). Southeastern Colorado: snout black-and-white-mottled; 21–25 (average 23, n = 6) red body rings; up to at least 81 cm TL; a specimen (AMNH 50833) supposedly collected at Beulah, Pueblo County, has unusually wide red rings and may be a mislabeled specimen.

Southwestern and south-central Colorado: snout black-and-white-mottled, or mainly black with white spots; 26–27 red body rings (n = 2). West-central Colorado and eastern Utah: snout all black, or light with black along midline; average of 28 (range 22–41, n = 14) red body rings; usually less than 72 cm TL.

According to Williams (1988), *Lampropeltis triangulum taylori* Tanner and Loomis, 1957, occurs in west-central Colorado. Intergrades between *L. t. taylori* and *L. t. celaenops* Stejneger, 1903, occur in southwestern and south-central Colorado. Intergrades between *L. t. gentilis* (Baird and Girard, 1853) and *L. t. multistriata* Kennicott, 1860 (see Frost and Collins 1988 for a discussion of the spelling of the subspecific name) occur in northeastern Colorado. *Lampropeltis t. gentilis* occurs in the remainder of eastern Colorado. Roth and Smith (1990b) concluded that intergradation between *L. t. taylori* and *L. t. multistriata* occurs in northwestern Colorado.

This snake exhibits a great deal of geographic variation over its wide range, and at least some of this warrants taxonomic recognition. However, in the western and central United States, variation is largely clinal, and the nominal subspecies are joined by extensive areas of intergradation, suggesting that these subspecies are arbitrary subdivisions rather than evolutionarily meaningful lineages.

Plate 8.96. Adult smooth green snake (Montrose County, Colorado).

Smooth Green Snake
Liochlorophis vernalis (Harlan, 1827)

Recognition. Dorsum with smooth (unkeeled) scales, typically a uniform grass green (bluish after death, including in preservative); venter immaculate white; anal scale divided; nostril centered in single scale; maximum size in our region at least 62 cm TL (44 cm SVL) (pers. obs.). *Juvenile:* dorsum olive gray. *Hatchling:* dorsum gray or brown; 10–15 cm TL (Smith 1963; Radaj 1981; Lawson 1983; T. Brown, in Degenhardt, Painter, and Price 1996). *Eggs:* thin-shelled; 20–27 mm x 9 mm in Moffat County (Smith et al. 1991); 19–34 mm x 8–18 mm in Michigan (Blanchard 1933).

Distribution. Southern Saskatchewan east through the Great Lakes region to the Maritime Provinces of Canada and Virginia, disjunctly southwest to Utah (including the mountain ranges of eastern Utah), New Mexico, Texas, and Chihuahua, Mexico. Occurs in Colorado at 5,500–9,000 feet (1,675–2,745 m) on both sides of the Continental Divide.

Conservation Status. The known range of this

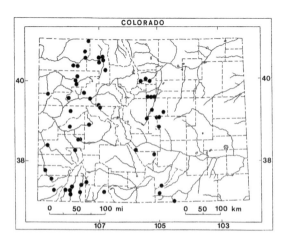

Map 8.34. Distribution of the smooth green snake in Colorado.

snake in Colorado has steadily expanded over the past several decades as new occurrences are discovered in suitable habitat throughout the lower mountainous regions of the state. Most occurrences, however, are documented by few specimens or observations, which may indicate relatively low abundance, secretive green snake behavior, or inadequate survey efforts or methods (these snakes are small and tend to stay well hidden, even when active). The species is known to be locally abundant in at least some areas. Suitable habitat in Colorado remains plentiful and generally not threatened. Human activities that eliminate shrubby/grassy riparian vegetation are likely detrimental. Impoundments have flooded some areas of suitable habitat and pose a potential threat in several others. Paved and dirt roads traverse green snake habitat; local populations of this snake therefore may be reduced through mortality caused by automobiles. However, ample roadless habitat also is present in numerous locations. The statewide population can be regarded as secure for the foreseeable future.

Habitat. Typical habitat in Colorado includes lush growths of herbaceous and shrubby vegetation along mountain and foothill streams and meadow habitats adjacent to riparian vegetation. In western Colorado, this snake may be common in mountain shrublands far from water, as along the rim of the Black Canyon of the Gunnison. Most activity occurs on the ground, but sometimes these snakes climb into low vegetation. Periods of inactivity are spent underground, beneath rocks or wood, or in rotting logs. Communal hibernation with other reptile species has been reported in New Mexico (Stuart and Painter 1993; Degenhardt, Painter, and Price 1996) and in eastern North America. In Manitoba and Minnesota, as many as 100–150 smooth green snakes have been found hibernating, sometimes partially submerged in water, in inactive ant nests (Criddle 1937; Lang 1969). Use of such sites has not been documented in Colorado.

Activity. In Colorado, most activity takes place from May to September, with some activity likely during warm periods in April and October. Activity appears to be largely diurnal, but in Montrose County I found one individual active on a warm asphalt road at 8:30 p.m. (dusk) during warm, dry weather in mid-August. This snake is rather gregarious, and multiple individuals can be found under a single rock or log. When grasped by hand, the snakes may squirm and emit pungent cloacal sac secretions. Otherwise, these small snakes are rather mild-mannered.

Reproduction and Growth. Courtship and mating behavior are poorly known. Copulation has been observed in mid- to late August in Ontario (Fitch 1970) but might also occur in late spring.

In Colorado and adjacent regions, oviposition apparently takes place primarily in July, and clutches usually contain 4–8 eggs (average 7) (Peterson 1974; Grobman 1989; Smith, Hammerson, et al. 1991; T. Brown, in Degenhardt, Painter, and Price 1996; pers. obs.). Egg-laying sites in Colorado are unknown but likely include spaces under rocks, wood, or other objects; burrows; or cavities within rotting wood (Gregory 1975). Cook (1964), Fowler (1966), Gregory (1975), and Lawson (1983) observed communal nesting in Ontario, Michigan, Manitoba, and Maine, but this has not yet been reported for Colorado.

Hatching occurs in late August or September. In the Black Hills (Wyoming and South Dakota), eggs laid on July 21 hatched within 30 days (Peterson 1974). In the same area, clutches found under stones in late August hatched in early to mid-September (Smith 1963). Smooth green snakes may retain shelled eggs and deposit them in an advanced state of embryonic development. In Michigan, eggs hatched as soon as four days after oviposition (Blanchard 1933). Hatching commonly takes place only 3–4 weeks after the eggs are laid (Blanchard 1933; Radaj 1981).

East of Colorado, reproductive phenology seems to vary quite a bit. Egg-laying may take place as early as late June in northern Illinois (Stille 1954) and Manitoba (Gregory 1975) or as late as mid-August in Michigan (Blanchard 1933). Hatching in eastern North America usually occurs between early August and mid-September (Blanchard 1933; Stille 1954; Wright and Wright 1957; Lawson 1983).

The smallest reproductive females recorded by Grobman (1989) were 24–25 cm SVL, but in Jefferson County, I found a gravid female that was only 22 cm SVL. In early July in Moffat County, a 26-cm-SVL female was gravid, and a 31-cm-SVL female was not (Smith, Hammerson, et al. 1991), suggesting that individual adult females may not lay eggs every year. Small individuals measuring 14 cm SVL and 19 cm TL in May suggest that first reproduction occurs no sooner than the third calendar year.

Food and Predators. Insects, spiders, and other invertebrates are the primary foods. In Custer County, I found an adult (34 cm SVL) that had eaten two moths and a 2.5-cm-long crayfish, suggesting that this snake occasionally may enter water when foraging, though the crayfish probably was obtained at the water's edge. The stomach of a 22-cm-SVL individual that I found dead on a road in Rio Blanco County contained a spider and a 4-mm-diameter planorbid snail. Baxter and Simon (1985) reported attempted predation on a moth in Wyoming.

Albert Spencer (pers. comm.) observed two instances of predation by the western terrestrial garter snake in La Plata County. Individuals that I examined in Jefferson County in July were infested with red mites between the ventral scales.

Taxonomy and Variation. Smooth green snakes in Colorado are regarded by some as representatives of the western subspecies *Opheodrys vernalis blanchardi* Grobman, 1941 (Grobman 1941, 1992; Smith 1963; Smith, Hammerson, et al. 1991), based on patterns of variation in the number of ventral scales. Other authors regard the species as monotypic, citing clinal variation or effects of environmental gradients on morphological variation (Peterson 1974; Collins 1990). The type specimens of subspecies *blanchardi* were collected by Helen T. Gaige on July 25, 1925, at 8,000 feet at the Spanish Peaks, Colorado (county not specified) (Grobman 1941).

This species formerly was included in the genus *Opheodrys,* but Oldham and Smith (1991) pointed out several categorical differences between *O. aestivus* and *O. vernalis* and established the new genus *Liochlorophis* for the latter species.

Plate 8.97. Adult coachwhip (Bent County, Colorado).

Coachwhip

Masticophis flagellum (Shaw, 1802)

Recognition. Dorsum brown, pink, or red, often with dark crossbars, especially on anterior end of body in juveniles; dorsal scales smooth (unkeeled); lower preocular scale small, wedged between upper lip scales; 13 or fewer rows of dorsal scales immediately anterior to vent; coloration of rear portion of body results in resemblance to braided whip; anal scale divided; maximum TL about 203 cm; many adults in Colorado reach more than 150 cm TL. *Hatchling:* 29–33 cm SVL, 38–44 cm TL for two individuals captured in early September in Colorado (Livo, pers. comm.); 29–37 cm TL (Wilson 1970; Degenhardt, Painter, and Price 1996). *Eggs:* surface granular; up to 57 mm long (Stebbins 1954); usually about 34–44 mm x 22–27 mm (Carpenter 1958; T. Brown, in Degenhardt, Painter, and Price 1996).

Distribution. California, Nevada, Utah, Colorado, Nebraska, Missouri, southern Illinois, Kentucky, and North Carolina south to southern Baja California, central mainland Mexico, the U.S. Gulf Coast, and southern Florida. Occurs in southeastern Colorado usually below 6,000 feet (1,830 m) but has been found at elevations up to 7,700 feet (2,345 m) on the slopes of the Wet Mountains in Custer County (Banta

and Brechbuhler 1965; Banta 1968). Also occurs in the Republican River drainage in northeastern Colorado at elevations of about 3,400–4,500 feet (1,035–1,370 m). Records of the coachwhip from Boulder County (Ellis and Henderson 1913) are based on misidentified juvenile specimens of *Coluber constrictor* (Hammerson 1984). A record of an individual within a crawl space at the Colorado Grange Museum in the Denver metropolitan area in western Arapahoe County (Blanchard et al. 1997) is questionable as a natural occurrence; pending confirmation of a population in that area, I have omitted this record from the map.

None of the reports of the possible occurrence of *M. flagellum* from southwestern Colorado (Jones-Burdick 1939; Maslin 1959; R. Smith 1980) are documented by specimens. Maslin (1959) reported a possible sighting in western Montezuma County but obtained no documentation. A report by R. Smith (1980:41) that "red racers are found only around Colorado's Mesa Verde National Park" is accompanied by a photograph of *M. flagellum*. However, the photographer (not Smith) informed me that the photograph was taken in Phantom Canyon, Fremont County, not at Mesa Verde, as Smith's statement implied. The reference to Mesa Verde probably was based on an unsupported statement by Jones-Burdick (1949). There is no tangible evidence that this species occurs in southwestern Colorado, and it does not encroach on the Colorado border in southeastern Utah (Cox and Tanner 1995) and northwestern New Mexico (Degenhardt, Painter, and Price 1996).

Conservation Status. Extensive/intensive agricultural development has eliminated habitat in some areas, but the coachwhip persists throughout most

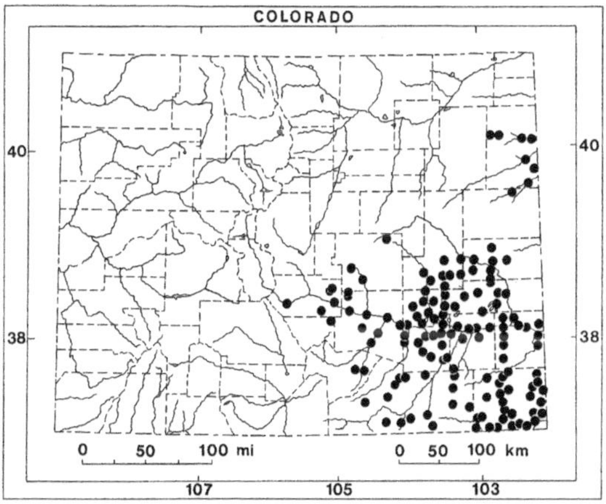

Map 8.35. Distribution of the coachwhip in Colorado.

of its historical range in Colorado and is fairly common in many areas (Mackessy 1998; pers. obs.). It tolerates moderate habitat alterations typical of rural plains communities and persists in undeveloped patches in semiagricultural areas. These warmth-loving snakes have an unfortunate habit of basking on warm roads and often become roadkill. Surely hundreds die annually in this manner. However, most of the habitat in Colorado has a low density of heavily traveled roads. It remains suitable and unthreatened by incompatible development. In rural areas, some coachwhips are killed by humans who (erroneously) view them as a threat to their chickens.

Habitat. Habitat in Colorado includes flat or hilly shortgrass prairie, including rocky bluffs and outcrops within these areas; sandhills; canyon slopes with scattered piñon pine and juniper; open riparian woodlands; and mosaics of prairie and agricultural land. The coachwhip is a ground-dwelling snake that commonly climbs into shrubs or small trees to bask or search for prey. When inactive in summer, it occupies burrows, crevices, spaces under rocks or wood, and other secluded sites. Some coachwhips may occasionally spend the night in vegetation aboveground, if conditions are warm enough. In the desert near Lake Mead on the lower Colorado River, Cowles and Bogert (1936) found a juvenile entwined in the branches of a shrub at 10:00 p.m. In southern California, and likely in Colorado as well, natural hibernation sites include abandoned rodent burrows (Secor 1995). Sometimes these snakes hibernate in spaces under old buildings.

Activity. In Colorado, emergence from hibernation generally begins with the onset of warm weather around mid-April. Activity, which may continue into mid-October, usually occurs only during warm daylight hours. In Colorado, I have encountered fully active coachwhips throughout the day, generally

Plate 8.98. Adult coachwhip (Pueblo County, Colorado). *Charles Loeffler.*

Plate 8.99. Juvenile coachwhip (Otero County, Colorado).

Plate 8.100. Death feigning by adult coachwhip (Bent County, Colorado).

from 8:20 a.m. until 5:15 p.m., but basking on roads in summer may, on rare occasions, extend until about 7:30 p.m.

For the coachwhip, a typical summer day begins with approximately 30 minutes of morning head basking that raises head temperature several degrees above overall body temperature (Hammerson 1977). Emergence from the nighttime retreat takes place at soil surface temperatures (in the sun) averaging about 33°C. Full-body basking then raises the body temperature to about 28–35°C, at which point activity begins (Hammerson 1977, 1989b; Jones and Whitford 1989). Throughout the remainder of the day, active foraging and locomotion occur at body temperatures of 30–35°C (Hammerson 1989b; Secor 1995). By adjustments in microhabitat use and exposure to the sun, coachwhips maintain a body temperature averaging 32–33°C during activity in summer, regardless of transient weather conditions, as long as sunshine and the opportunity to thermoregulate prevail (Hammerson 1989b; Secor 1995). Coachwhips shift from a relatively short midday activity period during mild spring weather to a longer but bimodal (peaking in midmorning and late afternoon) activity period during the hottest weather (Hammerson 1989b; Jones and Whitford 1989; Secor 1995). Activity generally ends in late afternoon when soil surface temperatures fall through the mid-30s°C. At night, they remain immobile in a secluded retreats at body temperatures close to the ambient temperature.

Individual coachwhips spend a great deal of time moving and are active over large areas. They often pause with the head held high, as if searching for potential prey or sources of danger. In desert habitat in southern California, adult home ranges are quite large (average 58 ha), and movements average 186 m per day (Secor 1995). In southern New Mexico, movements are

extensive in spring but restricted in summer (Jones and Whitford 1989), perhaps due in part to unfavorably hot conditions that prevail throughout much of the day.

Coachwhips are among the fastest snakes and when fully warmed and moving are rather difficult to capture. Their speed is associated with unusually long major axial muscle units (Ruben 1977). Among snakes, whipsnakes have a very high capacity for activity and are able to increase their aerobic and anaerobic energy production tremendously (Ruben 1976), perhaps for use while actively foraging, avoiding predation, or engaging in sexual behavior.

Escape behavior includes climbing into trees or shrubs or fleeing rapidly into thick cover or a burrow. When pursued and cornered, coachwhips may turn toward the attacker, vibrate the tail, and strike repeatedly. Large individuals may rear up and strike, seemingly directing the strike toward the onlooker's face. Lauren Livo caught one that, when released, rapidly crawled away, then assumed a posture with the head held very high as it continued to retreat. When hand-captured, coachwhips usually twist and struggle vigorously, defecate and/or release cloacal sac secretions, and bite hard. The bite may lacerate human skin but generally poses no more danger than any other small cut. Sometimes these snakes attempt to hide the head. An individual that I encountered in the open on a cool, cloudy day coiled and hid its head as I approached it.

A small percentage of individuals feign death when hand-captured. Death-feigning behavior may include downward or sideward cocking of the head, salivation, downward rotation of the eyes, extrusion of the tongue, and relaxed immobility (Gehlbach 1970; Tucker 1989). A large (111-cm-SVL) coachwhip that was crawling across a dirt road in Bent County at 5:12 p.m. coiled when I quickly approached it. As I picked it up, I noticed foamy saliva around the mouth, and the snake voided fluid from its vent as I measured its cloacal (33.2°C) and esophageal (34.7°C) temperatures. The snake was unusually calm as I held it for a few minutes. When placed on the ground, it remained immobile and crooked the neck downward, with the snout pressed into the soil. When I tried to place the snake on its back, it righted itself forcefully but then resumed the immobile, deathlike, bent-neck posture for several more minutes. I picked it up and laid it out full length, whereupon the snake adopted an alert, head-up posture, then crawled away shortly after I retreated to a distance of several meters.

Reproduction and Growth. Courtship and mating in our area presumably take place in late spring. Copulation has been observed from late April to late May in Texas and New Mexico (Minton 1958; Degenhardt, Painter, and Price 1996).

In Colorado and nearby areas, coachwhips lay clutches of about 4–18 eggs between late June and mid-July, with some clutches deposited as early as mid-June in New Mexico (Brennan 1936; Marr 1944; Degenhardt, Painter, and Price 1996; pers. obs.). Four gravid females in Colorado and Oklahoma were 114–124 cm SVL (Carpenter 1958; Webb 1970; pers. obs.). A 114-cm-SVL female that I found dead on a road in Crowley County on June 24 was laden with 15 large eggs. Lauren Livo (pers. comm.) found recently hatched individuals in Baca County on September 7 and 8. Based on the sizes of nonreproductive juveniles and gravid females, it appears that females first breed no sooner than their third spring, though this needs to be confirmed (as does the minimum size of reproductive individuals). Maximum longevity, based on observation of captives, is probably at least 20 years.

Food and Predators. The coachwhip feeds opportunistically on small mammals,

birds and their eggs, lizards (often), snakes (including rattlesnakes), small turtles, frogs, and large insects (Stebbins 1954; Whiting et al. 1992). The diet of hatchling and adult coachwhips in Pueblo County includes triploid checkered whiptails (Knopf 1966). An adult that I found in Baca County had eaten large grasshoppers. Known prey in Oklahoma that also occur in Colorado includes the lesser earless lizard, prairie lizard, six-lined racerunner, lizard eggs, racer, nestling cowbird *(Molothrus ater)*, grasshoppers, and cicada nymphs; a juvenile coachwhip ate two racerunner hatchlings (Carpenter 1958; Webb 1970). In Texas, coachwhips sometimes eat bats captured at cave entrances (Herreid 1961). Carrion occasionally may be eaten. Cowles (1946) found a coachwhip ingesting the odorous front end of a dead poorwill *(Phalaenoptilus nuttallii)* in southern California. Small, Tabor, and Fazzari (1994) observed a coachwhip retrieve and carry off a road-killed glossy snake.

Much foraging involves active searching, but in New Mexico, Jones and Whitford (1989) observed coachwhips that were coiled at the base of woody plants ambush prey, and snakes that had their tails wrapped around plant stems caught lizards. Prey is sought from ground level to high in the trees, where warm temperatures and exposure to sun allow the coachwhip to maintain maximum speed, strength, and agility. Hunting coachwhips also make brief sojourns into burrows. Prey items are grasped in the jaws and swallowed. This snake is quick enough to capture fleeing lizards and may pursue them into burrows. Coachwhips sometimes use odor cues to locate prey hidden in burrows or buried in sandy soil (Whiting et al. 1992; Secor 1995; pers. obs).

Hawks may be the most common predator. Chuck Loeffler (pers. comm.) observed a red-tailed hawk *(Buteo jamaicensis)* carrying an adult coachwhip in its talons in Pueblo County. Lauren Livo (pers. comm.) saw one of these snakes carried by a hawk in Las Animas County. In Oklahoma, a dead coachwhip was found in the nest of a red-tailed hawk (Webb 1970).

Taxonomy and Variation. Coachwhips from the western Arkansas River drainage, especially in Fremont, Pueblo, and El Paso counties, are distinctly pink or reddish in overall body coloration. Maslin (1953) argued that the red phase in southeastern Colorado should be considered a different subspecies than the populations in northeastern Colorado and surrounding states where this phase was thought to be absent. However, Wilson (1970) pointed out that populations including reddish individuals also occur in Texas and New Mexico. Because reddish individuals and populations are scattered within the general distribution

of the tan southern Great Plains variety of *M. flagellum*, Wilson (1970, 1973) concluded that the red populations are simply a color phase of *M. f. testaceus*, to which all Colorado populations should be assigned.

The type locality of *M. f. testaceus* (Say, 1823) was restricted by Maslin (1953:193) to the "junction of Turkey Creek with Arkansas River, 12 mi. W Pueblo, Pueblo Co., Colorado," the probable collection site of the specimen upon which Say based the original description of the subspecies (see also Dundee 1996).

Plate 8.101. Adult striped whipsnake (Uintah County, Utah).

Striped Whipsnake
Masticophis taeniatus (Hallowell, 1852)

Recognition. Dark stripe centered on each of first four dorsal scale rows on each side of body; underside of tail pink in adults; dorsal scales smooth (unkeeled), in 15 rows at midbody; eyes large; head scales with pale borders; lower preocular scale small, wedged between upper lip scales; anal scale divided; eyes large, with a prominent ridge above each; maximum TL about 183 cm

(135 cm SVL). *Hatchling:* 24–31 cm SVL in Utah (Parker and Brown 1980). *Eggs:* one egg from Moffat County was 63 mm x 14 mm (Maslin 1947a); a New Mexican clutch similarly averaged 62 mm x 15 mm, but another from New Mexico had shorter eggs (36–52 mm x 15–18 mm) (T. Brown, in Degenhardt, Painter, and Price 1996).

Distribution. Southern Washington and southern Idaho south through eastern California, Nevada, Utah, western Colorado, Arizona, New Mexico, and western and central Texas into central northern Mexico (Camper 1996); ranges to an elevation of

10,100 feet (3,080 m) in southern California (Stumpel 1995). Occurs throughout western Colorado at elevations up to about 7,000 feet (2,135 m) in the north and 8,100 feet (2,470 m) in the south.

Conservation Status. The striped whipsnake occurs throughout its historical range in Colorado. Significant numbers are killed on roads in some areas (e.g., Mesa Verde [Douglas 1966]), which may deplete local populations. The vast majority of the occupied habitat is intact, with few heavily traveled roads, and unthreatened by detrimental alterations.

In northern Utah, Parker and Brown (1973) found that a den population of this species decreased from 185 individuals in 1950 to 82 in 1966 and 40 in 1972, evidently due to collection and killing by humans. In 1974, a fire destroyed the vegetation in a large area surrounding the den (Brown and Parker 1982). Subsequently, wind-blown sand filled in the den area, eliminating a major communal hibernaculum not only for whipsnakes but also for formerly large populations of the western rattlesnake, gopher snake, and racer that had been studied over several decades by Brown, Parker, and their predecessors (Woodbury et al. 1951; Hirth et al. 1969).

Parker (1976) calculated that a three-den complex in northern Utah was inhabited by 442–543 whipsnakes and that postdispersal density was 0.15–0.22 individuals per hectare, not including juveniles less than a year old. In another area in northern Utah, equivalent postdispersal density was 0.11–0.33 individuals per hectare, with 0.33 per hectare representing conditions at a previously undisturbed site (Parker and Brown 1980).

Habitat. Habitats in Colorado include semidesert shrublands in broad basins, piñon-juniper woodlands and shrublands on mesa tops and rocky slopes, and intermittent stream courses and arroyos in the bottoms of canyons. Most activity takes place on the ground surface, but these snakes easily and readily climb into vegetation in some areas. When inactive, whipsnakes hide in burrows underground or beneath rocks or other cover.

In northern Utah, winter den sites include south- or east-facing crevices in rock outcroppings (Parker 1976). In some cases, dens are shared with western rattlesnakes, gopher snakes, and/or other snakes. Most juveniles in northern Utah do not use communal den sites; those that do arrive at the dens later than the adults (Hirth et al. 1969; Brown and Parker 1982). Large communal denning aggregations have not been reported for Colorado.

Activity. Most activity in Colorado occurs from April to early October. In northern Utah (Parker and Brown 1980), emergence from hibernation takes place from late March to late May (mainly in April and early May), depending on weather conditions. Among those that emerge early, males outnumber females. Arrival at hibernating dens extends from early September through mid-October. Whipsnakes are active in the vicinity of dens for several days or weeks after emergence and

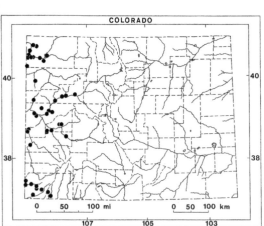

Map 8.36. Distribution of the striped whipsnake in Colorado.

before hibernation (Hirth et al. 1969; Parker and Brown 1980).

Activity takes place during warm daylight hours, with a midday lull during the hottest summer weather. In northern Utah, morning emergence and basking begins between 8:00 and 10:00 a.m. in early spring and as early as 6:00–7:30 a.m. in summer (Parker and Brown 1980). Like the racer and coachwhip, this snake often depends on its great speed to escape predation and capture prey. Body temperatures in northern Utah average 32–33°C in actively moving individuals (Parker and Brown 1980). In hand, these snakes often twist the body and may attempt to bite.

In northern Utah, whipsnakes disperse up to 3.6 km from their winter dens (Hirth et al. 1969). One adult male emerged from a den in mid-April and was found at another den 16.8 air kilometers away on the other side of a mountain range in late September of the same year, but such a long move is highly unusual. Most individuals use the same den in successive years. Parker and Brown (1980) found that dispersal distances from the den were 0.4–1.7 km (average 1 km) in six males and 0.8–2.8 km (average 1.5 km) in four females.

Reproduction and Growth. Breeding activities may begin in late April or in May. At that time, males defend small mating territories around adult females and may wrestle with and bite intruding males (Bennion and Parker 1976). Male courtship behavior includes mounting the female and writhing his body over hers, rubbing his chin on her dorsum, and moving his head from side to side while flicking his tongue (Bennion and Parker 1976). A male may stay with a female for several days prior to copulation (Parker 1974). Hirth et al. (1969) observed copulation in late April and early May in northern Utah.

In Colorado, egg deposition evidently occurs mainly in late June and early July, and clutch size usually is 4–5 eggs. On June 20 in Moffat County, Maslin (1947a) found two females, each carrying four large eggs about ready for oviposition. A 130-cm-TL female that I captured on May 29 in Montezuma County laid five eggs in early July. Another female found on the same date in Dinosaur National Monument contained five palpable eggs. An 86-cm-SVL female from the same area was noticeably gravid on June 15. Newly hatched whipsnakes begin appearing in Colorado by late August.

In northern Utah, eggs are laid from mid-June to early July in abandoned mammal burrows at a depth of 36–41 cm on south-facing slopes lacking perennial vegetation (Parker and Brown 1972). Some oviposition burrows are used for the same purpose by the racer or gopher snake. Clutch size usually is 3–10 eggs (average 6). One clutch that was studied in the field hatched after 44–58 days (Parker and Brown 1972). Similarly, two striped whipsnakes from New Mexico produced clutches of five and six eggs in late June and mid-July (T. Brown, in Degenhardt, Painter, and Price 1996).

The young grow rapidly, but growth slows significantly after the first 2–3 years. Males may attain sexual maturity within one year, in time for mating in their third calendar year, but they may be prevented from accessing adult females by larger dominant males (Parker 1974). In northern Utah (Parker and Brown 1980), most females lay their first clutches in the early summer of their fourth calendar year. The smallest reproductive females are 71–77 cm SVL. Adult females appear to lay eggs every year. Nearly all adults survive winter, but most juveniles do not. Annual survival rate in northern Utah is low (about 8 percent) in juveniles but high (86 percent) in adults. Some individuals may live well into their second decade.

Food and Predators. These snakes feed opportunistically on various small vertebrates and insects such as grasshoppers and beetles; lizards are a mainstay of the diet. The stomachs of three whipsnakes run over by cars at Mesa Verde contained an adult sagebrush lizard, a young short-horned lizard, and mouse *(Peromyscus)* fur (Douglas 1966). In northern Utah, the sagebrush lizard and side-blotched lizard are major prey items, and other typical food includes the western whiptail, horned lizards, sagebrush lizard, racer, striped whipsnake, pocket mouse (*Perognathus* sp.), deer mouse *(Per-*

omyscus maniculatus), and montane vole *(Microtus montanus)* (Parker 1976; Parker and Brown 1980).

Predators in northern Utah and probably Colorado, too, include larger whipsnakes and racers, the common raven *(Corvus corax),* red-tailed hawk *(Buteo jamaicensis),* and long-tailed weasel *(Mustela frenata)* (Smith and Murphy 1973; Parker and Brown 1980).

Remarks. In northern Utah, most individuals shed the skin twice a year, in June-July and September-October (Parker and Brown 1980). Juveniles shed 1–2 weeks after hatching.

Taxonomy and Variation. Camper and Dixon (1994) examined geographic variation in the *M. taeniatus* complex and determined that populations in southern Texas and eastern Mexico represent a distinct species, *M. schotti* Baird and Girard, 1853. Populations in Colorado were retained in the subspecies *Masticophis taeniatus taeniatus* (Hallowell, 1852) (Camper 1996).

Plate 8.102. Adult northern water snake (Boulder County, Colorado).

Northern Water Snake

Nerodia sipedon (Linnaeus, 1758)

Recognition. Anterior portion of body crossbanded, posterior portion crossbanded or blotched; pattern sometimes obscure, especially in large individuals; belly often with red or orange blotches; dorsal scales keeled, with a pair of apical pits near the tip of each scale; anal scale divided; more than two scales between eye and nostril; maximum TL about 150 cm, but very few in Colorado exceed 100 cm; males usually less than 62 cm SVL, females usually less than 82 cm SVL; end of tail often missing. *Mature male:* knobbed keels on dorsal scales near vent. *Newborn:* average SVL 16–19 cm.

Distribution. Minnesota to southern Quebec and New England south to the central U.S. Gulf Coast and North Carolina, west to Nebraska, eastern Colorado, Oklahoma, and extreme northern Texas. Occurs along major streams in the Great Plains region of eastern Colorado at elevations below about 5,500 feet (1,675 m). Ellis and Henderson (1913) listed specimens collected in Baca and Las Animas counties by A. E. Beardsley, but to date no specific localities in those counties have been documented.

Conservation Status. The northern water snake is present throughout its historic range in Colorado. The trend in abundance is unknown, but the species is locally common in some areas. The historical stream habitat in Colorado has been augmented by numerous adjacent bodies of permanent water created through sand and gravel excavation. These ponds now harbor abundant water snake food resources, including large populations of small, mostly introduced fishes. In addition, irrigation canals have expanded the habitat in many areas. As a result of this increased area of favorable habitat, I suspect that this species is more abundant in Colorado today than it was before the arrival of humans of European descent. No threats of major significance have been identified, and the status in Colorado seems secure for the foreseeable future.

This snake is wary and usually avoids humans (e.g., anglers) who, mistaking it for a venomous cottonmouth (absent from Colorado), might be inclined to kill it. However, northern water snakes frequenting fishing areas do face hazards. In Georgia, Herrington (1985) found an individual that had died after its head became caught in a discarded beer can.

Limited information is available on population densities in our region. Data from Kansas (Beatson 1976) indicated a density of about 35–40 juveniles and adults per km of stream.

Habitat. Typical habitat includes creeks, rivers, reservoirs, ponds, marshes, flooded meadows, and canals along major drainage systems. Rarely are these snakes found away from the immediate vicinity of water. They often can be seen swimming along marsh edges or basking in semisecluded onshore sites, on log jams in streams, on mats of algae, on clumps of dead cattails, or up to 2 m high in woody streamside vegetation. Sometimes they can be found under rocks or wood at the water's edge. Wintering sites include various burrows and crevices belowground; submerged sites have been reported for some parts of the range.

Activity. Most activity in Colorado occurs between late March and early October. Limited basking may take place during warm periods earlier in March and in November. Activity may occur day or night, with nighttime activity most common in water shortly after dark in late spring and summer (Tiebout and Cary 1987; pers. obs.). Basking peaks in the morning and in late afternoon. In Ontario, Canada, Robertson and Weatherhead (1992) observed that the body temperature of basking individuals averages about 26°C; by adjusting their sun exposure, the snakes prevented their internal temperature from exceeding 33°C. Tiebout and Cary (1987) found that water snakes in Wisconsin do not have a home range in the usual sense; instead they shift their activity over areas encompassing several hectares.

Water snakes disturbed onshore generally flee rapidly into the water, whereas those perched

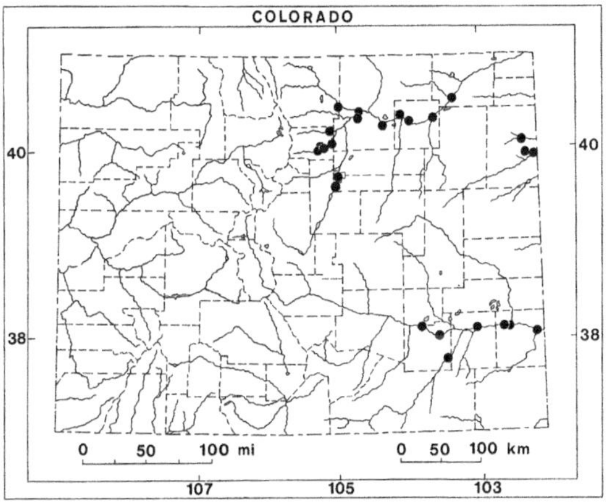

Map 8.37. Distribution of the northern water snake in Colorado.

Plate 8.103. Adult northern water snake (Boulder County, Colorado).

high in vegetation often allow close approach by humans (Weatherhead and Robertson 1992; pers. obs.). If captured by hand, they may release copious fluid from the vent, including malodorous secretions from the cloacal sacs, and they usually bite, often drawing blood with sharp teeth. Adults have high endurance and expend considerable energy in fleeing or defending themselves (Pough 1978). In contrast, juveniles flee a short distance, then freeze; they rapidly become exhausted during brief bouts of activity and may hide the head under the body rather than mount an active defense (Pough 1978). The cryptic nature of the strongly banded pattern in juveniles seems to be enhanced with abrupt cessation of forward movement (Pough 1976). In Kansas, Beatson (1976) found that the banded young tend to inhabit small rocky stream courses where they are camouflaged among debris. In contrast, older, plainly colored individuals more often are seen in larger bodies of water, where a banded pattern would render them more conspicuous and therefore more vulnerable to predation.

Reproduction and Growth. Courtship and mating occur mainly in the morning from late April to early June (see Mushinsky 1979). Male courtship behavior involves rubbing the chin on the female and writhing atop her body. Sometimes multiple males court a single female simultaneously. On June 1 in Boulder County,

a basking pregnant female that was approached to within 0.5 m by another adult (sex unknown) lashed her tail back and forth several times while the rest of her body remained immobile. The approaching snake stopped, flicked its tongue, and froze with its head facing the female. After a minute, the approaching snake moved slightly, whereupon the female immediately lashed her tail again a few times, causing the other snake to remain motionless again for several minutes. Eventually, the approaching snake swam away. Perhaps this behavior represented that of a sexually non-receptive female toward an adult male, but this could not be verified.

The northern water snake is viviparous. Baby water snakes are enclosed in a membranous sac from which they emerge during or shortly after delivery. This snake is a prolific breeder, with litter sizes in some parts of the range reaching several dozen young in the largest females, though 15–30 young (average 18–25) is more typical for females of average size (Webb 1970;

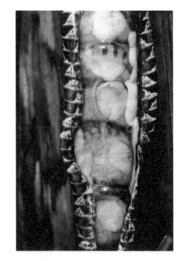

Plate 8.104. Developing young in a northern water snake (killed by a person in a wildlife refuge).

Beatson 1976; Bauman and Metter 1977; Aldridge 1982; Fitch 1985a). Very large litters may be most common in habitats that provide abundant food resources (e.g., fish hatcheries). A female collected in early September in Boulder County produced a litter of 14 young (UCM). A consistent rangewide pattern suggests that most births in Colorado probably occur between mid-August and mid-September; later births are fairly typical of captive individuals. Several studies have found that the percentage of adult females producing young increases with SVL.

In Missouri, males begin breeding at about 21 months old; reproductive females are generally 60 cm SVL or larger and at least 33 months old (though some two-year-olds do breed) (Bauman and Metter 1977; Aldridge 1982). Maximum lifespan is at least 10 years. Females that produce young tend to be emaciated in late summer and may exhibit reduced overwinter survival (Brown and Weatherhead 1997).

Food and Predators. Northern water snakes forage actively, primarily in shallow water. Fishes and adult and larval amphibians dominate the diet, but crayfish and other small animals occasionally are eaten. Known prey in Colorado includes small cyprinid fishes (minnows), sunfish *(Lepomis)*, yellow perch *(Perca flavescens)*, and northern leopard frog (pers. obs.). Predators are not well known. Webb (1970) reported an instance of predation by the common kingsnake in Oklahoma.

Remarks. Water snakes of the genus *Nerodia* appear to have no specialized physiological adaptations for diving (Baeyens, Patterson, and McAllister 1980), in accordance with their shallow-water habitat and tendency to swim at the surface.

Taxonomy and Variation. This snake formerly was included in the genus *Natrix*. That name is now restricted to water snakes in Eurasia and North Africa. All North American water snakes are now included in the genus *Nerodia* (Rossman and Eberle 1977). Some herpetologists regard *Nerodia sipedon* as conspecific with *Nerodia fasciata* of the southeastern United States. The subspecies in Colorado is *Nerodia sipedon sipedon* (Linnaeus, 1758).

Plate 8.105. Defensive posture of adult bullsnake (Otero County, Colorado).

Bullsnake/Gopher Snake

Pituophis catenifer (Blainville, 1835)

Recognition. Dorsum yellowish or cream with numerous dark blotches; central dorsal scales keeled; anal scale single; four prefrontal scales; vertical plate (preglottal keel) at opening of windpipe; maximum TL about 254 cm, rarely more than 180 cm. *Hatchling:* average generally 28–37 cm SVL for a clutch (Parker and Brown 1980; Platt 1984; Gutzke and Packard 1987) (range was 26–30 cm SVL for one clutch I observed in Logan County); usually 36–43 cm TL (Imler 1945). *Eggs:* adherent, usually about 5–7 cm long.

Distribution. Southern British Columbia, southern Alberta, southern Saskatchewan, Minnesota, and Indiana south to southern Baja California, southern Mexico, and southern Texas. Occurs at elevations below about 8,500 feet (2,590 m) throughout most of Colorado; most common below about 7,000 feet (2,135 m). Smith (1991) reported an unconfirmed sight record for Ouray County.

Conservation Status. The bullsnake, also known as the gopher snake, is one of the most widespread snakes in Colorado and is common

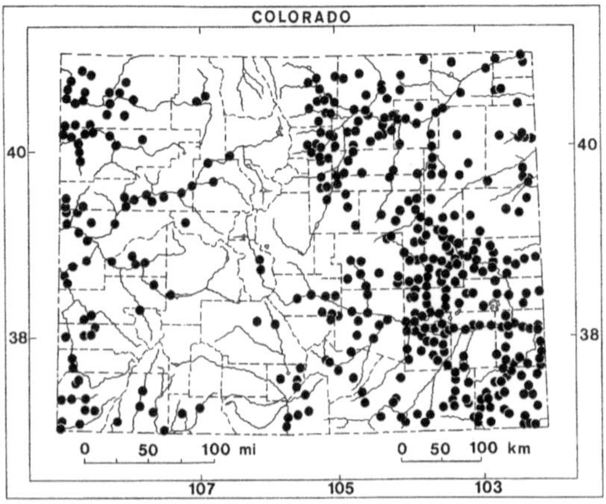

Map 8.38. Distribution of the bullsnake/gopher snake in Colorado.

Plate 8.106. Defensive posture of adult bullsnake (Otero County, Colorado).

Plate 8.107. Juvenile gopher snake (Montezuma County, Colorado).

in many areas throughout the state. Urbanization and large-scale intensive agriculture have eliminated significant areas of habitat, but great expanses of natural habitat remain. This snake tolerates a great deal of habitat alteration and does well in semiagricultural landscapes and around the margins of towns. An appalling number (thousands) of these beneficial snakes are killed on roads in Colorado each year. Most such deaths occur in agricultural areas where these rodent-eaters should be ardently protected. Certainly, populations along major roadways have been depleted as a result. People who fear snakes and are ignorant of their beneficial qualities intentionally kill perhaps hundreds of bullsnakes in Colorado every year. In several parks and wildlife refuges, I found bullsnakes that had been beheaded or chopped to pieces by visitors; others were the targets of rock-throwing campers. Public education could do much to enhance conservation of these interesting and valuable elements of our wildlife fauna. Chuck Loeffler (pers.

comm.) reported that it was common for snakes, particularly bullsnakes, to be found dead in mesh erosion blankets used for habitat rehabilitation. Capron (cited by Collins 1993) reported that dozens of bullsnakes were killed by mowing machines in late spring and early summer in agricultural areas in southern Kansas. Bauerle, Spencer, and Wheeler (1975) found that bullsnakes from the Pawnee National Grassland in northeastern Colorado had low levels of chlorinated hydrocarbons in their tissues.

The bullsnake has been subject to control measures implemented to maximize duck reproduction in some areas. Over a period of five years, 2,105 bullsnakes were trapped and intentionally killed at the so-called Crescent Lake National Wildlife Refuge in Nebraska (Imler 1945). Gutzke, Paukstis, and McDaniel (1985) indicated that a similar predator-control program was in operation at the Valentine National Wildlife Refuge in Nebraska in the early 1980s. Maintenance of high-quality habitats to benefit populations of ducks and other wetland wildlife is commendable, but the slaughter of native bullsnakes simply to reduce the incidence of predation on duck eggs is no less ecologically deplorable than was the narrow-minded extermination of wolves, grizzlies, and other predators that took place in North America in the early 1900s.

A few studies have examined population density and dynamics. In Idaho, density in various habitats was 0.1–1.9 individuals per hectare (Diller and Johnson 1988). Density at one site in Utah was calculated at 0.32 per hectare (Parker and Brown 1980). Over two decades at a den in northern Utah, Parker and Brown (1973) documented an increasing population that may have been related to elevated precipitation levels and more abundant prey.

Habitat. The bullsnake occurs in a wide variety of habitats in Colorado, including plains grassland, sandhills, riparian areas, marshes, pond and lake edges, stream-margin logjams, rocky canyons, semidesert and mountain shrublands, piñon-juniper woodlands, ponderosa pine and other montane woodlands, rural and outlying suburban residential areas, and agricultural areas. Most activity takes place on the ground or in burrows. This snake is an accomplished burrower; the snout is used to dig, and the head and neck region are used to scoop soil out of the excavation area (Carpenter 1982). In Utah, Parker and Brown (1980) found that *Pituophis* spends a great deal of time underground or beneath rocks. Vaughan (1961) observed that bullsnakes he pursued in eastern Colorado usually crawled into abandoned pocket gopher burrows. Bull-

snakes commonly crawl in marsh waters and are capable climbers that sometimes ascend high into trees.

Winter is spent in various underground crevices (Parker and Brown 1980) and burrows, including those excavated by the snakes themselves in sandy substrates (Burger et al. 1988). Hahn (1968) reported that bullsnakes hibernate deep in volcanic rock crevices along the Rio Grande in the San Luis Valley, sharing dens with western rattlesnakes, western terrestrial garter snakes, and milk snakes. Yarrow (1875) saw hundreds of bullsnakes occupying dens in lime concretions formed by springwaters at Pagosa Springs in Archuleta County. Communal dens used by gopher snakes, striped whipsnakes, racers, western rattlesnakes, and other snake species exist in Utah (Parker and Brown 1980). Individuals generally use the same den site year after year, but switching sometimes occurs, usually within a local den complex (Brown and Parker 1980).

Activity. Emergence from hibernation occurs primarily in April and May. Bauerle (1972) reported that emergence from hibernation took place in mid- to late May at a site in Weld County, but I have records of activity in April in that county. Individuals encountered in April and May tend to be males (Imler 1945; Iverson 1990b), probably because males are especially active then as they search for sexually receptive females. Activity continues throughout the spring and summer and generally winds down by the end of October, though later activity sometimes occurs. Ellis and Henderson (1915) stated that large individuals often were seen near hot springs in late November in the upper Arkansas River valley. The majority of active individuals encountered after August are juveniles.

Plate 8.108. Adult gopher snake with triangular head (Garfield County, Colorado).

Plate 8.109. Adult bullsnake showing preglottal keel (Otero County, Colorado).

Plate 8.110. Hemipenes of adult male bullsnake found dead on a road (Weld County, Colorado).

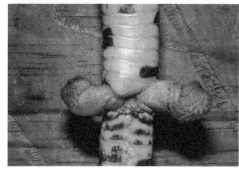

In southern New Mexico, Price and LaPointe (1990) found a higher number of gopher snakes active in September than in any other month, presumably reflecting the appearance of the young of the year. In Utah (Parker and Brown 1980), gopher snakes emerge from dens mainly in early April (rarely in late March) in most years but not until early May in colder years. They usually return to dens between mid-September and late October, with juveniles arriving at the dens later than adults. In southern Idaho, gopher snakes sometimes are seen in warm weather in late March, but frequent sightings do not begin until mid-April in most years (Diller and Wallace 1996). Sightings peak in late May and early June. Activity generally ends by late October.

Bullsnakes seem to be most active from early morning through the first few hours of darkness. These snakes often linger on paved roads in the morning and early evening. Nocturnal activity occurs mainly during warm weather in late spring and summer. My data

for Colorado indicate that activity may take place anytime from about 7:00 a.m. until 11:00 p.m., peaking at about 8:00–11:00 a.m. and (in spring) 4:00–7:00 p.m. or (in summer) 8:00–9:00 p.m. Midday activity occurs mainly during the cooler, shorter days of early spring and late summer/early fall and during cool spells in summer. Air temperatures during activity generally are 15–30°C. Body temperatures of 22 active individuals were 18.0–38.0°C (average = 27.0°C, mode 27–28°C [pers. obs.]).

Activity patterns in Colorado are consistent with those in nearby states. In Utah, Parker and Brown (1980) found that surface movements in summer are observed most often from 7:00–10:00 a.m. and 3:00–8:00 p.m. In southern Idaho, activity takes place primarily during daylight hours, with a peak between 10:00 a.m. and 2:00 p.m. in April and May, and from about 8:00–11:00 a.m. and about 6:00–10:00 p.m. in June and July, with captures typically occurring at air temperatures of approximately 22°C and body temperatures averaging 28.6°C (Diller and Wallace 1996). Webb (1970) reported that in Oklahoma, adults are diurnal, whereas juveniles often are nocturnal.

Relatively little is known about movement patterns. In Utah, gopher snakes move about 500 m (average) from the winter den to the summer home range, which averaged about 1 ha in two males and 2 ha in four females (Parker and Brown 1980).

Maximum aerobic physiological performance and predatory efficiency occur at body temperatures of around 27–30°C (Greenwald 1971, 1974), which is the usual body temperature of individuals found active in the wild (Brattstrom 1965; see also preceding paragraphs). Gopher snakes are less thermophilic than are racers and whipsnakes (Parker and Brown 1980; Hammerson 1987, 1989b), which enables them to exploit relatively cool microhabitats during activity, perhaps explaining in part why nestlings of burrowing mammals are common in the diet of *Pituophis* (pers. obs.) but not in those of racers and whipsnakes.

This snake is remarkably variable in its behavior. Some individuals lie motionless when approached, remaining passive even when handled. Others respond to approach by coiling and striking (often lunging forward and grunting with each strike), hissing loudly, and vibrating the tail. Strikes frequently are directed toward the intruder's face, even if another object is extended toward the snake. The jaws may be spread, giving the head the triangular shape typical of rattlesnakes. In dry vegetation, the vibrating tail may produce a sound like a rattlesnake's rattle. Some individuals produce a rattling hiss that closely resembles the sound of a rattlesnake. My observations in Colorado indicate that among adults at typical body temperatures, males are most likely to exhibit vigorous defensive behavior, whereas females are more likely to be relatively passive when approached and handled.

Unfortunately, many of these harmless snakes are killed because they "mimic" rattlesnakes so effectively. Sweet (1985) found that gopher snakes and western rattlesnakes in shortgrass plains in California resembled each other in color and pattern, evidently due primarily to convergence of cryptic coloration in a similar environment. In this open habitat, adults of both species exhibited a greater tendency to mount overt defensive displays (hissing, tail vibration) than they did in other environments with greater cover (and where the species were less similar in appearance). Thus, the morphological and behavioral resemblance of gopher snakes to rattlesnakes may result from factors other than true mimicry. Regardless, the visual and auditory similarity of bullsnakes to rattlesnakes can be uncanny.

The loud hiss of this snake is produced by air moving through the windpipe past a vertical, cartilaginous preglottal keel as the snake expands and contracts its lungs (Saiff 1975). In hand, bullsnakes often wrap the body very tightly around the captor's hand or arm, leaving the head and neck free to strike. Careful handling sometimes precludes release of odorous cloacal sac secretions.

Reproduction and Growth. Males evidently find receptive females by following their scent trails (Smith and Iverson 1993). A courting male rubs his body over the female's dorsum and may grasp her with his jaws during copulation. Bauerle (1972) found copulating bullsnakes on May 27 in Weld County. Combat between males, mainly involving pushing and climbing atop the opponent, may occur during the breeding period.

Information on reproduction in Colorado is sketchy but suggests that eggs are laid between late June and mid-July, similar to the pattern in Kansas (Collins 1993), Nebraska (Imler 1945), Utah (Parker and Brown 1980), and southern Idaho (Diller and Wallace 1996). A 120-cm-SVL female killed by a car on May 26 in Mesa County contained nine 4-cm-long follicles. A road-killed 75-cm-SVL female found in Moffat County on June 4 contained six enlarged follicles (15, 25, and 35–40 mm); this individual was near the minimum size for reproductive females. A female found on June 12 in Boulder County contained 16 eggs large enough to be palpated through the belly. A female captured on July 8 at

7,100 feet (2,165 m) in Boulder County laid an unknown number of eggs a week later. A bullsnake that I captured on June 13 in Logan County laid 13 eggs on July 16. Swenson and Rodeck (1948) reported that a female found at 6,700 feet (2,065 m) in Boulder County laid 20 eggs. These clutch-size data for eastern Colorado are similar to those for western Nebraska and elsewhere in the Great Plains region, where clutches of 5–23 eggs (average 13) have been recorded (Imler 1945; Fitch 1985). The smaller clutches in western Colorado conform with the clutches typical of Utah and Idaho, which contain 3–15 eggs (average 7–8) (Parker and Brown 1980; Diller and Wallace 1996). Adult females that have fed infrequently may have low fat reserves and may not produce eggs. However, in Idaho, nearly all adult females were gravid in the year of capture, suggesting an annual reproductive cycle (Diller and Wallace 1996).

Pituophis females lay their eggs in abandoned rodent burrows and other underground cavities, including shallow burrows excavated by the snakes themselves, usually in open, sunny sites (Parker and Brown 1980; Burger and Zappalorti 1991). Human-disturbed areas may be used, as long as a relatively warm, moist, soft substrate is present. Communal and multispecies oviposition sometimes occurs at the same site (Brodie, Nussbaum, and Storm 1969; Parker and Brown 1980). In the eastern United States, *Pituophis* females commonly use the same nesting site in successive years (Burger and Zappalorti 1992). In Utah, eggs are deposited at depths of about 34–42 cm (Parker and Brown 1980).

At an incubation temperature of 27°C, eggs hatch in 8 weeks; at 22°C, incubation lasts 13.5 weeks (Gutzke and Packard 1987). Under laboratory conditions, Parker and Brown (1980) found that eggs hatch after about 7.0–8.5 weeks. As in Kansas (Platt 1984; Collins 1993) and Nebraska (Imler 1945), newly hatched bullsnakes first appear in Colorado in late August and September. In southern Idaho, hatching reportedly does not occur until October (Diller and Wallace 1996). Gehlbach (1965:310) reported that a 38.5-cm-TL juvenile found in late July at

7,100 feet (2,165 m) in northwestern New Mexico was "undoubtedly a hatchling as it had a fresh yolk-sac scar," but rather than an exceptionally early hatchling, this individual may have been an unusually small young of the previous year.

In Nebraska, one-year-old juveniles are about 70–80 cm TL; individuals of 125 cm TL may be about 5–6 years old (Imler 1945). In southern Kansas, Platt (1984) found that young bullsnakes reach 79 cm SVL at one year of age. Growth rate may be reduced when prey populations and feeding rates are low. Platt's growth data indicate that bullsnakes reach about 95 cm SVL at 2 years of age, 103 cm at 3 years, and 120 cm at 7–8 years.

Parker and Brown (1980) found that growth rate in Utah is much slower than in Kansas. One-year-olds average about 61–62 cm SVL. It takes 4–5 years to reach 90 cm SVL, and an estimated 18–20 years to reach 120 cm SVL. Males in Utah first mate in their second spring, whereas females lay their first clutches at an age of 3–5 years, at a minimum SVL of 78 cm. Similarly, in southern Idaho, minimum SVL of sexually mature individuals is 72 cm in males (they are probably three-year-olds) and 81 cm in females (Diller and Wallace 1996).

My observations in western Colorado indicate that late spring populations include 2–3 age classes of immatures ranging from 39–80+ cm SVL. Females usually breed no sooner than their third spring, based on (1) the average annual growth rates recorded by Parker and Brown (1980) (initially about 28 cm the first year, 14 cm the second, then 7–8 cm per year for two years), (2) my observed minimum size of 75 cm SVL for reproductive females in western Colorado, and (3) the occurrence of some nonreproductive females larger than 80 cm SVL. Some grow more slowly; for these, first reproduction probably is delayed at least another year.

In Utah, most adults survive the winter, but most juveniles do not (Parker and Brown 1980). Annual survival rate is around 75 percent in adults and 20 percent in juveniles. Some individuals may survive more than 15 years. In Nebraska, young generally did not feed prior to hibernation, and their overwinter survival rate was low (Imler 1945). Records of captives indicate that this snake has a potential longevity of more than 30 years.

Food and Predators. The diet consists primarily of rodents and other small mammals, which should make these snakes welcome in agricultural areas, on ranchlands, and near human habitation. Small mammals may be dug out of plugged burrows, and the frequency with which neonate mammals are ingested (Diller and Wallace 1996; pers. obs.) reflects this snake's habit of raiding underground rodent nests. Bullsnakes also eat birds and their eggs and may be especially attracted to nests containing nestlings (Eichholz and Koenig 1992). Juveniles commonly eat lizards (e.g., plateau and prairie lizards [Gehlbach 1965]). Individuals that have recently eaten a relatively large prey item may preferentially sun the stomach region, perhaps enhancing digestion (Ashton 1998c).

The following examples illustrate the bullsnake's dietary versatility. A bullsnake found by Douglas (1966) at Mesa Verde regurgitated a juvenile white-throated woodrat *(Neotoma albigula)* when captured. In Moffat County, I found an adult bullsnake that had eaten an adult female sagebrush vole *(Lemmiscus curtatus)* and three sparsely furred young; the adult had been swallowed first. In the same area, I found a 157-cm male that had eaten two adult golden-mantled ground squirrels *(Spermophilus lateralis).* In Weld County, a large adult had clumps of rabbit fur projecting from its mouth, though its stomach was empty, perhaps indicating an unsuccessful strike. Vaughan (1961) twice found bullsnakes swallowing pocket gophers caught in traps in eastern Colorado; Gehlbach (1965) found one with a freshly caught pocket gopher in a burrow in New Mexico. Dartt (1879) reported that a bullsnake found 3 m up in a cottonwood tree along the South Platte River disgorged five young flickers *(Colaptes auratus),* a species of woodpecker. In Pitkin County, M. Bosch (pers. comm.) found a gopher snake preying on nestling American robins *(Turdus migra-*

torius); one bird was in the snake's mouth, another in its coils, and a third under its body in the nest. Other known foods in Colorado include the thirteen-lined ground squirrel *(Spermophilus tridecemlineatus,* Streubel 1975; recorded also in Oklahoma by Webb 1970), probably the spotted ground squirrel *(Spermophilus spilosoma,* Streubel 1975), northern rough-winged swallow *(Stelgidopteryx serripennis)* (young taken in nest tunnel [D. Alles, pers. comm.]), mountain bluebird *(Sialia currucoides)* eggs (taken in tree hole [D. and J. Ward, pers. comm.]), mallard *(Anas platyrhynchos)* and pintail duck *(Anas acuta)* eggs (Rockwell 1911; Ellis and Henderson 1913; Ryder 1951; Grieb 1952; pers. obs.), and long-billed curlew *(Numenius americanus)* eggs (Kingery 1998). Kuzarn (1995) presented photos showing a bullsnake scaling a cottonwood tree north of Sheridan, Wyoming; the snake apparently preyed on nestling grackles *(Quiscalus quiscula).*

In Nebraska, bullsnakes are significant predators on duck eggs, which are swallowed whole and usually broken in the throat by projections from the vertebrae (Imler 1945). Other foods in Nebraska include eggs and nestlings of various water and land birds, plus a wide assortment of small mammals, particularly voles *(Microtus),* pocket gophers (probably *Geomys*), kangaroo rats *(Dipodomys ordii),* and young rabbits (Imler 1945; Ballinger, Lynch, and Cole 1979). Juveniles generally eat pocket mice or young voles. In Utah, food items include voles *(Microtus),* pocket mice *(Perognathus),* other mice *(Peromyscus),* side-blotched lizard, Orthoptera, cottontail *(Sylvilagus),* white-tailed antelope squirrel *(Ammospermophilus leucurus),* and nestling barn swallows *(Hirundo rustica)* (Parker and Brown 1980). In Idaho, deer mice *(Peromyscus maniculatus)* are the most frequent prey item, though juvenile ground squirrels *(Spermophilus townsendii)* and juvenile cottontails *(Sylvilagus nuttallii)* dominate the diet in terms of biomass (Diller and Wallace 1996). Gopher snakes in Idaho consumed an estimated 22–43 percent of the juvenile cottontail population (Diller and Johnson 1988).

The bullsnake is a powerful constrictor that generally kills large prey in its coils before swallowing. Constricting methods vary, depending on the situation and the size and type of prey (Willard 1977; de Queiroz 1984). Small animals such as lizards may be swallowed without being constricted. Bullsnakes kill rodents in their narrow burrows by pinning them to the burrow wall with a loop of the body. According to Greenwald (1978), a predatory strike takes 0.05–0.26 seconds to reach the prey and involves 12–50 percent of the snake's body length; striking the prey and encircling it with coils takes 0.8–3.1 seconds and involves 40 percent of the body length.

Some potential prey may harass or even attack bullsnakes (Loughry 1989). In Kansas, a female prairie dog buried a bullsnake in a burrow, and a group of prairie dogs attacked a 150-cm bullsnake, inflicting bites and causing the snake to flee into a burrow (Halpin 1983). In Dinosaur National Monument near the Colorado-Utah border, a golden-mantled ground squirrel periodically charged and attacked the head of a large gopher snake, drawing blood (Engeman and Delutes 1994). The snake recently had eaten, which may explain why it did not attempt to capture the ground squirrel.

Among the various birds and mammals that prey on this snake, hawks are probably the most significant threat. In Colorado, known predators include only the red-tailed hawk *(Buteo jamaicensis)* (pers. obs.) and Swainson's hawk *(Buteo swainsoni)* (W. Ervin, pers. comm.). In Utah, Parker and Brown (1980) observed predation by a red-tailed hawk that captured a gopher snake, apparently on a road, at about 5:00 p.m. Racers and common kingsnakes (see accounts of those species) also prey on the bullsnake.

Taxonomy and Variation. Klauber (1947) provided the most widely followed classification of the western subspecies of *Pituophis catenifer*. In the Great Plains subspecies *sayi,* the snout is somewhat pointed when viewed from above, and the rostral scale at the tip of the snout is narrow, much higher than wide, and usually raised

conspicuously above the adjacent scales. In the Great Basin subspecies *deserticola,* the snout is rather blunt when viewed from above, the rostral scale is not much higher than wide and is flush with or raised only slightly above adjacent scales, and there is often a dark band along each side of the neck. The number of scale rows at midbody is usually 31 or 33 in *sayi* and typically 29, 31, or 33 in *deserticola.*

I examined several hundred specimens of *P. catenifer* from throughout Colorado. According to Klauber's (1947) criteria, specimens from the western border counties of Colorado are readily identified as *deserticola.* Those from the plains of eastern Colorado generally conform with *sayi* characteristics but exhibit wide variation in coloration. Specimens from the San Luis Valley fall well within the range of variation in *sayi* from eastern Colorado but exhibit a slight tendency toward *deserticola* size and shape of the rostral scale. South-central and southwestern Colorado (San Luis Valley west to La Plata County) appears to be an area of intergradation between *sayi* and *deserticola,* and possibly *affinis* as well (Hahn 1968; Hammerson 1981). Subspecies *affinis* resembles *deserticola* but is characterized by anterior dorsal blotches that are usually brown and well separated rather than black and confluent (Klauber 1947). Maslin (1959) assigned specimens from Archuleta County to *affinis,* whereas Klauber (1947) identified specimens from this region as *deserticola.* Maslin did not examine any specimens from Archuleta County, basing his allocation instead on habitat similarities between Archuleta County and the New Mexico range of *affinis.* Klauber (1947) and Gehlbach (1965) indicated intergradation between *affinis* and *deserticola* in northeastern Arizona and northwestern New Mexico. Several specimens that I examined from La Plata and Archuleta counties most closely resembled *deserticola,* but one of them had a moderately raised rostral scale, a characteristic of *sayi.* Individual variation, clinal shifts in characteristics, and the rather subjective differences among these taxa render subspecies determination rather inconclusive.

The taxonomy of North American *Pituophis* has become unstable in recent years, largely reflecting differences in taxonomic perspective and opinion rather than newly available data. Over the past few decades, *P. catenifer* generally has been treated under the name *Pituophis melanoleucus* (Daudin, 1803). Sweet, in an unpublished abstract cited by Sweet and Parker (1990), recognized four groups within *P. melanoleucus* based on differences in cranial morphology and evidence of distributional contacts with little or no intergradation: *melanoleucus* (eastern races), *sayi* and *affinis, catenifer* (six western races), and *vertebralis.* These were retained as subspecies of *P. melanoleucus* by Sweet and Parker (1990). Knight (1986) demonstrated that with respect to snout morphology, *P. m. sayi* clearly is more similar to the eastern subspecies (pine snakes) than to the western gopher snakes. Reichling (1995) concluded the same thing, based on morphological data. Nevertheless, *sayi* and the pine snakes each are distinctive, and there is no evidence that *sayi* intergrades with any populations of the pine snake group. Auffenberg (1963:183) pointed out a difference between *melanoleucus* and the western groups (including *sayi*) in the relative size of the neural spine of the vertebrae, but the difference may have been a result of comparing individuals of different ages.

As I see it, *sayi* and *affinis,* and *affinis* and *deserticola,* clearly intergrade over broad areas (Gehlbach 1965; Hahn 1968; Hammerson 1981) and thus are conspecific. They appear to be conspecific with all other western subspecies as well. Auffenberg's observations and the absence of *sayi*–pine snake intergradation suggest that *sayi* is specifically distinct from the pine snakes of the eastern United States. Hence, a treatment recognizing *P. catenifer* as a species distinct from the pine snakes appears to be warranted and is adopted in this book. However, genetic data are needed to clarify the relationships among the nominal taxa in this complex. Such information might reveal whether the morphological similarities between *sayi* and the pine snakes reflect genetic affinities or simply analogous morphology related to similar fossorial behavior.

Plate 8.111. Adult female longnose snake (Bent County, Colorado).

Longnose Snake

Rhinocheilus lecontei (Baird and Girard, 1853)

Recognition. Small white spots on sides of black "saddles" across back of adults; spaces between black saddles pink or red; dorsal scales smooth (unkeeled); belly whitish or yellowish, with few dark spots; snout long, with slightly raised rostral scale; anal scale single; scales on underside of tail mostly in single row; maximum TL about 104 cm, though rarely more than 75 cm. *Hatchling:* white speckling on sides may be reduced or absent, red pigmentation reduced; 19–24 cm TL (subspecies *tessellatus* [Klauber 1941]). *Eggs:* average 53 mm x 41 mm in Arizona (Vitt 1975); 36 mm x 16 mm (Conant and Downs 1940).

Distribution. California, Nevada, southern Idaho, Utah, Colorado, and southwestern Kansas south through the southwestern and south-central United States to central Baja California and central mainland Mexico. Occurs in southeastern Colorado at elevations below 5,000 feet (1,525 m). Records from southeastern and east-central Utah (Tanner and Heinrichs 1964; Grogan and Tanner 1974; Cox and Tanner 1995) suggest that this snake may occur in southwestern Colorado.

Conservation Status. This secretive snake probably is more widespread in southeastern Colorado than present records indicate, but it likely does not occur north of the Arkansas River drainage. Multiple observations of this species in the eastern part of the Arkansas River valley suggest that it may be fairly common there. Elsewhere, it is known from single specimens and seems to be genuinely scarce. Most of the range in Colorado is not now subject to large-scale habitat alterations that would threaten this snake. The population in Colorado probably can be considered small but secure.

Habitat. The longnose snake in Colorado inhabits plains grassland and, more often, sandhill habitat, plus weedy areas in river valleys. Periods of inactivity are spent under rocks or in burrows. Tanner (1941) reported that one of these snakes was found in southwestern Utah by a sexton digging a grave.

Activity. Records of activity in Colorado extend from mid-May to early September, but limited activity may also occur during warm weather in late April and possibly October. This snake has been found under rocks in late April in southwestern Kansas (Smith, Pflanz, and Powell 1993). Activity takes place primarily at night, but occasionally the longnose snake may be seen abroad in daylight. Individuals commonly are found crossing roads during the first few hours of darkness in late spring (Klauber 1941). Longnose snakes may be active under cool, windy conditions, generally at temperatures above 15°C (Klauber 1941; Shaw and Campbell 1974).

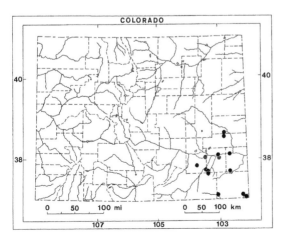

Map 8.39. Distribution of the longnose snake in Colorado.

When alarmed, longnose snakes may vibrate the tail. Some individuals coil and hide the head; others, especially if handled or harassed, squirm and emit a bloody fluid mixed with cloacal sac secretions and/or fecal material from the gaping vent (McCoy and Gehlbach 1967; Smith, Pflanz, and Powell 1993). Some individuals may bleed from the nose or mouth. Such hemorrhaging has been observed only in females and may be a physiological side effect of defensive activity. Or perhaps the bloody fluid is distasteful and deters mammalian predators. Juveniles tend to be more actively defensive than the relatively passive adults.

Osborne (1984) observed two males that were completely intertwined and crawling rapidly at 11:00 p.m. in early July in northwestern Mexico. Perhaps this represented male combat behavior.

Reproduction and Growth. Reproductive behavior of this snake is poorly known. A female captured in Bent County on June 19 laid eight eggs on July 6. Incubated at room temperature, most succumbed to fungal attack. Two unhatched but molding eggs that I opened in early November contained dead, nearly fully developed young. A female collected in mid-June in Arizona laid three eggs in mid-July (Vitt 1975). Rangewide, clutch size averages 6–7 eggs (Fitch 1970). Klauber (1941) reported gravid females as small as 61 cm TL.

Food and Predators. The diet of this snake typically includes lizards and their eggs, rodents, small snakes, and sometimes insects. Known prey in Kansas includes the six-lined racerunner (see Collins 1993). Large prey items are killed by constriction before being swallowed. Like gopher snakes and glossy snakes, the longnose snake exhibits versatility in its constricting behavior that may be related to its apparent habit of attacking prey in narrow burrow systems (Willard 1977).

Taxonomy and Variation. The subspecies in Colorado is *Rhinocheilus lecontei tessellatus* Garman, 1883. *Rhinocheilus l. lecontei* Baird and Girard, 1853, which has a blunter and less up-tilted snout than *tessellatus* (Klauber 1941), may occur in southwestern Colorado. Medica (1975) provided the latest taxonomic synopsis of this species.

Plate 8.112. Adult ground snake (Otero County, Colorado).

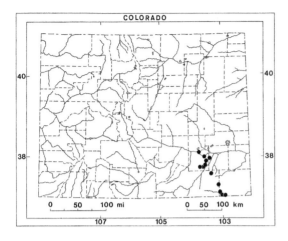

Map 8.40. Distribution of the ground snake in Colorado.

this region have not been adequately surveyed for this species, and it is likely that additional populations will be discovered. Intensive general herpetological surveys have yielded few observations but suggest that the ground snake is locally fairly common, at least in some easily accessible areas with abundant surface rocks that facilitate successful searches (Mackessy 1998; pers. obs.). Habitat in southeastern Colorado is largely intact and not significantly impacted by activities that would threaten this species.

Ground Snake
Sonora semiannulata (Baird and Girard, 1853)

Recognition. Dorsum with smooth (unkeeled) scales in 15 rows; coloration light brown, gray, or orange, usually with dark crossbands; anal scale divided; loreal scale present; maximum TL about 48 cm, rarely more than 35 cm; a sample of five live adults from Baca and Otero counties was 23–25 cm SVL (28–30 cm TL). *Hatchling:* 7–13 cm TL in Oklahoma, Texas, and New Mexico (Kassing 1961; Degenhardt, Painter, and Price 1996). *Eggs:* surface smooth, 13–28 mm x 4–8 mm in Oklahoma and Texas (Kassing 1961).

Distribution. Eastern Oregon, southern Idaho, Utah, Colorado, Kansas, and southwestern Missouri south through the southwestern and south-central United States to southern Baja California and northern mainland Mexico. Occurs in southeastern Colorado at elevations below 5,500 feet (1,675 m). Records from northeastern and east-central Utah suggest the possible occurrence of this species in western Colorado.

Conservation Status. The status of this small, secretive snake in Colorado is poorly known, but it appears to be restricted to southeastern Colorado, ranging north to the Arkansas River valley. Many areas in

Habitat. In Colorado, ground snakes typically occur in fractured shale outcroppings with numerous platelike rocks, on hillsides with many scattered flat rocks partially imbedded in the soil, in canyon bottoms, and in sand blows, all in areas dominated by shortgrass prairie. These snakes usually are found under rocks and other objects on the ground during daylight hours, and they also occupy abandoned mammal burrows. Sometimes a single rock shelters multiple individuals. These rocks typically have small burrows or holes beneath them, allowing the snakes access to cooler, moister conditions should the surface soil become too dry or warm. Exposed ground snakes often attempt to escape by quickly crawling down these holes.

Activity. Available information indicates that surface activity in Colorado extends from late April through at least September. Ground snakes are easiest to find in late spring and at other times when soil surface conditions are mild and moist. Activity in the open occurs mainly at dusk and night, and occasionally in the morning, before it gets too warm. In Otero County, I observed two individuals, 235 and 245 mm SVL, as they emerged into the open from a burrow under a rock outcrop at 6:50 p.m. (before dusk) in early June (cloudy, air temperature 25°C).

Reproduction and Growth. Mating in this snake has been observed in April through June and in September in Oklahoma, Texas, and Missouri (Kassing 1961; Anderson 1965; Kroll 1971). Sexual behavior of males includes rubbing the chin on the female's dorsum and sometimes biting. Males may wrestle with and bite each other during the breeding season (Kroll 1971).

Known clutch sizes in this species range from 3–6 eggs (Kassing 1961; Anderson 1965). A female found in Otero County in late May contained five large ova (15 mm x 5 mm) (Mackessy 1998). In Oklahoma, eggs are laid from mid-June to early July, maturity is attained in 1.5 years at 23–24 cm TL, and hatching takes place about two months after oviposition (Kassing 1961). Anderson (1965) reported late June clutches in Missouri. An early June clutch was reported for New Mexico, and in Texas, clutch deposition takes place from at least early June to early July (Kassing 1961; Degenhardt, Painter, and Price 1996). In the cooler climate and shorter growing season of Colorado, clutches probably are laid sometime between mid-June and mid-July. Hatchlings have been found in Colorado on September 1, indicating hatching in late August (Mackessy 1998).

Food and Predators. A 24-cm-SVL individual that I found in Otero County had eaten two spiders (15–20 mm head-body length).

Food items documented elsewhere in the range include mainly spiders, centipedes, and scorpions, plus crickets, grasshoppers, beetles, Hymenoptera, Lepidoptera, and insect larvae (Kassing 1961; Stebbins 1985). The rear teeth of the upper jaw are shallowly grooved, suggesting that the saliva may be toxic to small animals. Degenhardt, Painter, and Price (1996) found a ground snake attempting to eat a dead lizard.

Webb (1970) mentioned predation by a collared lizard in Oklahoma. Veer, Chiszar, and Smith (1997) described antipredation behavior of a 30-cm individual from Arizona. Held in the jaws of a predatory snake, the ground snake gripped itself with its jaws, forming a small, complete loop that interfered somewhat with the predator's attempts to engulf it.

Taxonomy and Variation. Ground snakes in Colorado formerly were known as *Sonora episcopa,* following Stickel (1938), but now the genus is regarded as comprising only the monotypic species *S. semiannulata* (Frost and Van Devender 1979; Frost 1983b).

Most specimens from southeastern Colorado have prominent black crossbands along the length of the body. Occasionally, individuals lack crossbands and have only an orange dorsal stripe. Others have prominent dark bands across the head and neck but only faint dorsolateral dark marks where the full crossbands typically are found. Melanistic and albinistic individuals have been found in other parts of the range.

Plate 8.113. Adult southwestern black-headed snake (Delta County, Colorado).

Southwestern Black-headed Snake

Tantilla hobartsmithi (Taylor, 1936 [1937])

Recognition. Dorsum with smooth (unkeeled) scales, uniformly brownish, with dark cap on head usually extending three or fewer dorsal scale lengths beyond the rearmost large scales on top of the head; rear edge of dark cap typically straight or rounded; belly orangish; anal scale divided; maximum TL 31 cm. Painter, Tomberlin, and Gee (1997) reported partial albinos from New Mexico. *Hatchling:* as small as 9.3 cm TL (Cole and Hardy 1981); in Delta County, a young of the previous year was 13 cm TL in May. *Eggs:* 23–28 mm x 6–7 mm in Texas (Easterla 1975); 17 mm x 4 mm in California (Stebbins 1954).

Distribution. Southern California, southern Nevada, Utah, Arizona, western Colorado, southern New Mexico, western Texas, and northern Mexico (Cole and Hardy 1981). Occurs in west-central Colorado at elevations of about 4,500–6,500 feet (1,370–1,980 m). The presence of this snake in Desolation

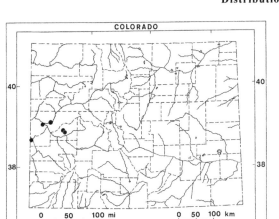

Map 8.41. Distribution of the southwestern black-headed snake in Colorado.

Plate 8.114. Adult southwestern black-headed snake (Delta County, Colorado).

Canyon, Carbon County, Utah (Hammerson and Benedict 1998), suggests its potential occurrence in northwestern Colorado, and there is no apparent reason why this species should not occur in southwestern Colorado as well. I have an unverified sight record from Dry Mesa, possibly in Montrose County (L. Valentine, pers. comm.).

Conservation Status. This snake was first discovered in Colorado on May 10, 1963, when two were found alive on roads in and near Colorado National Monument in Mesa County (McCoy, Knopf, and Walker 1964). A third specimen was discovered in the summer of that year in the same area. Putnam et al. (1964) reported an individual found near Palisade, also in Mesa County; two juveniles (UCM 42259–42260) were collected in that area in November 1964. For the next 20 years, this snake was regarded as very rare in Colorado. In 1986, one was sighted at the junction of the Colorado and Gunnison rivers in Mesa County (Bruce Bauerle, pers. comm.). In the mid–1980s, Larry Valentine found one of these snakes in Delta County, and his subsequent surveys through the 1990s revealed that an apparently large population is present in the area and not confined to the original discovery site. I extended the range to the Dolores River drainage in 1990 (Hammerson et al. 1991m). Additional populations of this secretive snake likely remain undiscovered. The known populations do not appear to be threatened by incompatible habitat alterations or other harmful factors; however, those populations along roads probably incur increased mortality as a result of vehicular

traffic. Tanner (1954) reported these snakes to be relatively abundant in spring in southern Utah.

Habitat. In Mesa County, Mc-Coy, Knopf, and Walker (1964) found this species in the mouths of large canyons in areas dominated by sandy, rock-laden soils and xerophytic shrubs (greasewood, sagebrush, saltbush). In the same county, I observed a specimen in the narrow bottom of a deep, rocky canyon between a streamside band of cottonwood trees and a steep slope with piñon-juniper woodland. Over several years in Delta County, Larry Valentine (pers. comm.) found numerous individuals active on roads through rocky, shrubby slopes above a creek; others were found beneath rocks in piñon-juniper woodland and under trash in a dump area. Tanner (1954) found these snakes in rocky patches in piñon-juniper woodland in southern Utah.

Activity. Active *T. hobartsmithi* have been observed in Colorado from early May through at least late August, most often in May and June. Activity at the end of April and in late summer/early fall is likely. The circumstances surrounding the November collections mentioned earlier are unknown. Activity in the open generally occurs only at dusk and at night and seems to peak shortly after dark (often from 9:00–10:00 p.m. in late spring/early summer); in crossing roads, these snakes tend to move quickly (L. Valentine, pers. comm.). In New Mexico, these snakes were found alive on roads at air temperatures of 15–25°C (Degenhardt, Painter, and Price 1996).

Reproduction and Growth. Limited data indicate that egg-laying occurs from early June to early August in western Texas (Minton 1958; Easterla 1975; Tennant 1984) and in early June in California (Stebbins 1954). Typical clutches appear to consist of a single egg (Stebbins 1954; Minton 1958; Easterla 1975; Tennant 1984), but a clutch of three was laid in mid-

June by a female from Texas (Degenhardt, Painter, and Price 1996). The occurrence of small, immature individuals in late spring indicates that first reproduction occurs no sooner than the second spring (third calendar year).

Food and Predators. Known food items include centipedes, millipedes, beetle larvae, and caterpillars (see Cole and Hardy 1981). Tanner (1954) reported that a large individual found in southern Utah had eaten a 44-mm centipede. The two (rarely three) grooved fangs at the rear of each side of the upper jaw may be used in conjunction with toxic saliva to subdue prey.

A large captive adult from Delta County took notice when I placed two centipedes in its cage. It trailed one of them and after five minutes bit the centipede at midbody, immediately wrapped two loose coils around it, then released the prey after about four seconds. The snake then lay immobile, opened and closed its mouth, and seemed to take no further interest in the centipede.

Several hours later, the snake had eaten the centipede. I found another of my captives dead in a contorted posture soon after it ate a 3-cm centipede, suggesting that there may be some risk involved in attacking such prey (centipedes have strong jaws and associated venom glands).

These snakes may be subject to predatory attacks, from which they sometimes escape. In a sample of 13 adults I examined, 4 had an incomplete (stubbed) tail. However, factors other than attempted predation could be responsible for the tail loss.

Taxonomy and Variation. This snake formerly was known in Colorado as *Tantilla utahensis* Blanchard, 1938, or *Tantilla planiceps* (Blainville, 1835). Cole and Hardy (1981) reviewed the systematics of snakes related to *Tantilla planiceps* and determined that populations in Colorado belong to the widespread species *Tantilla hobartsmithi.* Previously, variation in this snake had been discussed by Blanchard (1938), Tanner and Banta (1962), McCoy, Knopf, and Walker (1964), and Tanner (1966).

Plate 8.115. Adult plains black-headed snake (Baca County, Colorado).

Plains Black-headed Snake

Tantilla nigriceps (Kennicott, 1860)

Recognition. Dorsum with smooth (unkeeled) scales, uniformly light brown; belly pink or orange; dark cap extends 3–5 dorsal scale lengths beyond rearmost large scales on top of head; rear edge of dark cap usually somewhat pointed; anal scale divided; maximum TL about 39 cm (33 cm SVL) (Perry and Hauer 1996). Painter, Tomberlin, and Gee (1997) reported a partial albino from New Mexico. *Hatchling:* 9–10 cm SVL, 12–13 cm TL in Colorado (pers. obs.) and New Mexico (T. Brown, in Degenhardt, Painter, and Price 1996); possibly as small as 6.25 cm (Tennant 1984). *Eggs:* 22–25 mm x 7 mm in New Mexico (T. Brown, in Degenhardt, Painter, and Price 1996).

Distribution. Eastern Wyoming (Censky and McCoy 1985b; Hayes et al. 1990), eastern Colorado, and southwestern Nebraska south through New Mexico, Kansas, western Oklahoma, and Texas to northern Mexico, west into south-central Arizona. Occurs throughout southeastern Colorado, in the Republican River drainage of northeastern Colorado, and along the eastern base of the mountains, where it ranges to at least 6,120 feet (1,865 m) (Banta and Kimmel 1965). I have an undocumented report of an occurrence at about 7,500 feet (2,285 m) in Clear Creek Canyon, Clear Creek County.

Conservation Status. This small, secretive snake easily escapes detection even in areas where it is common, and many areas have not been adequately searched. Probably, it is more widespread in eastern Colorado than present records indicate. Intensive agriculture and urbanization likely have eliminated some populations, but most of the known range in Colorado encompasses large expanses of suitable habitat that currently are not significantly threatened. The plains black-headed snake can be regarded as secure in Colorado.

Though many occurrences are represented by single or several specimens, this snake can be locally abundant. Under mild, moist circumstances in May in Oklahoma, two persons searching under rocks found 10 individuals in less than 30 minutes (Webb 1970).

Plate 8.116. Belly of plains black-headed snake (Las Animas County, Colorado).

Habitat. Known habitats in Colorado include flat plains grassland, sandhills, mountain foothills, and rocky canyons. Sometimes the snake can be found in old rubbish dumps. It is a terrestrial and fossorial species that during daylight hours can be found beneath rocks, wood, dried cow dung, or other debris; in yucca plants; and in rotting logs near streams. Hibernation occurs underground. One snake was found in Boulder as a trench was being dug in December. In western Kansas, two individuals were found 2.4 m underground in January (Tihen 1937).

Activity. Records of surface-active individuals in Colorado extend from mid-April through September, with most observations occurring in late spring and early summer. Presumably some activity also takes place in early October. Most of my records of this snake are of individuals found under cover in moist microhabitats from late April through July. In southern New Mexico, Price and LaPointe (1990) found plains black-headed snakes active much more frequently during warm moist periods in July than in any other month. Black-headed snakes crawl in the open primarily at night or under cloudy skies. Several that I found alive on roads at night were active shortly after dark at air temperatures of 20–22°C. Mackessy (1998) recorded a few instances of these snakes crossing roads in daytime in southeastern Colorado. Individuals on roads tend to keep moving and not linger. In hand, they often probe between and wrap around the captor's fingers (L. Livo, pers. comm.; pers. obs.).

Reproduction and Growth. Reproduction in this species is poorly known. Mating presumably occurs in spring, followed by oviposition probably in late June or July and hatching in August and September. Clutch size likely ranges from 1–3 eggs. Juveniles as small as 10–11 cm SVL (preserved size almost a centimeter shorter) have been collected in Colorado in mid- to late July, indicating little growth since hatching the previous year. A 10-cm-SVL individual found in Baca County in mid-August probably was a recent hatchling. A 35-cm-TL female from New Mexico laid three eggs in late June; hatching occurred in late August (T. Brown, in Degenhardt, Painter, and Price 1996).

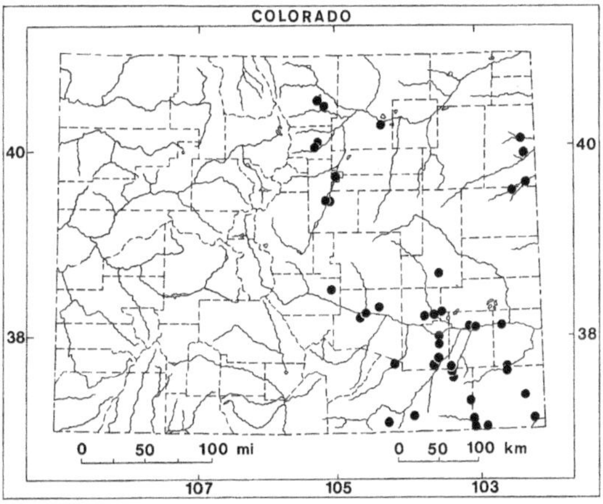

COLORADO

40
40

38
38

0 50 100 mi

0 50 100 km

107 105 103

Map 8.42. Distribution of the plains black-headed snake in Colorado.

Food and Predators. Reported food items include spiders, millipedes, centipedes, and insect larvae, pupae, and adults (Stebbins 1954, 1985; Webb 1970). The grooved fangs at the rear of the upper jaw may be used in conjunction with toxic saliva to subdue prey. A female observed by Ted Brown held centipedes in the jaws for several minutes before swallowing (Degenhardt, Painter, and Price 1996).

Taxonomy and Variation. Cole and Hardy (1981) regarded this species as monotypic.

Plate 8.117. Blackneck garter snake (Las Animas County, Colorado).

Blackneck Garter Snake

Thamnophis cyrtopsis (Kennicott, 1860)

Recognition. Top of head gray; white stripes on sides on second and third scale rows above lateral edges of belly scales; yellowish stripe along middle of back; two large black blotches on neck; heavy black marks on vertical sutures between upper labial scales; dorsal scales keeled; anal scale single; maximum TL about 114 cm (Rossman, Ford, and Seigel 1996) but seldom more than 75 cm TL. The western terrestrial garter snake often is mistaken for this species. *Newborn young:* about 18–23 cm TL.

Distribution. Southeastern Utah and Colorado south through Arizona, New Mexico, and western and central Texas to southern New Mexico (Rossman, Ford, and Seigel 1996). Known to occur as far north as the Arkansas River valley in southeastern Colorado, in John Brown Canyon in Mesa County in west-central Colorado, and in southern La Plata and Archuleta counties in southwestern Colorado; occurs below 6,000 feet (1,830 m) in the southeast and below 6,500 feet (1980 m) in the southwest. Maslin's (1959) record of *T. cyrtopsis* from "Rio Grande, Colorado," is based on a specimen of *T. elegans,* originally reported erroneously as *Eutaenia sirtalis* (= *Thamnophis sirtalis*) by Yarrow (1875) (see account of *T. sirtalis*).

Conservation Status. This snake appears to be uncommon in most of its spotty range in Colorado. It can be found most readily in the Carrizo Creek drainage of Las

Animas and Baca counties. I am aware of only a few observations of this species in western Colorado since the 1960s, which may reflect scarcity, inadequate survey effort, and/or a declining population. My fieldwork, and recent surveys in southeastern and western Colorado by Mourning (1997), Mackessy (1998), and Livo (pers. comm.), yielded few observations, indicating that the species truly is rare. This scarcity in Colorado does not appear to be associated with habitat loss or degradation or other identifiable factors.

Habitat. In Colorado, blackneck garter snakes generally live in the vicinity of permanent and intermittent streams, often in canyon bottoms with rocky slopes covered in oak and/or juniper. These snakes frequently wander away from streams and sometimes are observed in open grassland, especially near dry washes or at temporary pools used by breeding toads. In Archuleta County, Harris (1963) found this snake on a road between riparian and oak/juniper/pine habitat several hundred feet from the Piedra River. Gehlbach (1965) found one at a breeding aggregation of New Mexico spadefoots and red-spotted toads miles from the nearest stream of appreciable size in northwestern New Mexico. In spring, Jones (1990) found a few of these snakes as far as 0.5 km from aquatic habitats in western Arizona. Periods of inactivity are spent under rocks or wood, in crevices or burrows, or among exposed streamside tree roots (Jones 1990).

Activity. In Colorado, these snakes are active primarily from mid-April through September, with earlier and later activity expected during warm weather. Activity takes place over a wide range of temperatures, usually in daytime but also at night during periods of hot, dry weather. In New Mexico and Arizona, active individuals generally have body temperatures of 22–35°C (average 26–28°C) (Fleharty 1967; Rosen 1991).

When approached, these snakes flee into cover or swim away. In hand, they generally writhe and release excrement and the contents of the cloacal sacs. Sometimes they bite. Disturbed individuals may flatten and broaden the head and body (Stebbins 1954) or hide the head under body coils (L. Livo, pers. comm.).

Reproduction and Growth. Male sexual behavior in garter snakes generally involves mounting the female, rubbing the chin on the female's dorsum, and writhing the body during springtime copulation, which lasts only several minutes (Rossman, Ford, and Seigel 1996). Reproduction in Colorado is not well known. Neonates have been found in Pueblo County on August 11 (UCM 17202–17204). Maslin (1950) reported a specimen of 29 cm TL collected in late August in southeastern Colorado; this may have been a neonate born earlier that year. In Baca County, young of the year may attain a length of about 24–28 cm SVL (30–37 cm TL) by early September (L. Livo, pers. comm.).

Births may occur much earlier in areas to the south, where the growing season is longer. Two females (46 cm and 53 cm SVL) collected in early April in Arizona contained

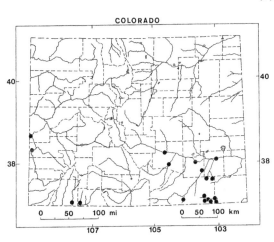

COLORADO

40

40

38

38

0   50   100 mi

0   50   100 km

107   105   103

Map 8.43. Distribution of the blackneck garter snake in Colorado.

6 and 10 enlarged yolked follicles, plus additional smaller follicles; a third female gave birth to eight young and an "apparently infertile ovum" in early July (Vitt 1975:84). In Arizona, Jones (1990) observed four broods of 14–22 young (average 19) from late June to mid-July; the females gave birth while partially submerged in landlocked pools. Young of the year have been found as early as late July in New Mexico (Degenhardt, Painter, and Price 1996). Minton (1958) found newborn young in late June in western Texas. Sabath and Worthington (1959) reported that a 39.5-cm-TL female from Texas gave birth to seven young in mid-August; her size may be near the lower limit for reproductive females, which likely require 2–3 years to attain maturity. Males mature at a smaller size, probably a year sooner than females.

Food and Predators. The blackneck garter snake feeds opportunistically on land and in shallow water on available larval and adult amphibians (especially anurans), small fishes, and tadpole shrimp (Fouquette 1954; Fleharty 1967; Stebbins 1985; Jones 1990). Dead and dying fishes and tadpoles in drying pools are also eaten (Mosauer 1932; Jones 1990). A 38-cm-SVL individual that I found along a creek in Las Animas County had eaten a juvenile (2.5-cm-SVL) Woodhouse's toad. In the same area, another individual captured an adult plains leopard frog.

Taxonomy and Variation. Over the years, Colorado populations of this snake have been referred to under the names *T. eques, T. megalops,* and *T. dorsalis.* Rossman, Ford, and Seigel (1996) summarized the taxonomic history of this species. The subspecies in Colorado is *Thamnophis cyrtopsis cyrtopsis* (Kennicott, 1860).

Plate 8.118. Adult western terrestrial garter snake (Larimer County, Colorado).

Western Terrestrial Garter Snake
Thamnophis elegans (Baird and Girard, 1953)

Recognition. Pale (but not white) stripes on sides of body on second and third scale rows above lateral edges of belly scales; mid-dorsal stripe bright and runs the length of the body in some localities, stripe dull and fades at midbody in other areas; often two large black marks on neck; irregular black marks frequently on belly; usually eight upper labial scales on each side of head; narrow dark marks (if any) on upper lips confined to front edge of vertical suture between labial scales; dorsal scales keeled; anal scale usually single (but see Tanner 1950); typically 21 scale rows at midbody; in Colorado, few individuals exceed 60 cm SVL or 76 cm TL. Albino and albinistic specimens have been found in Colorado (Banta and Hahn 1966; Smith, Somers, and Chiszar 1975; UCM 15296). This variable snake often is mistaken for the blackneck garter snake, common garter snake, and checkered garter snake (*Thamnophis marcianus,* not known to inhabit Colorado). *Newborn young:* usually 10–19 cm SVL, 17–24 cm TL in Colorado, Utah, and New Mexico (V. Tanner 1949a; Gehlbach 1965; Degenhardt, Painter, and Price 1996; Kasper and Kasper 1997; pers. obs.).

Distribution. Central British Columbia, central Alberta, and southwestern Saskatchewan south through the western United States to northern Baja California, southern Arizona, and southern New Mexico, west to the Pacific coast, and east to the extreme western portions of South Dakota, Nebraska, and Oklahoma. Present throughout most of Colorado, excluding most of the plains region in the northeastern quarter of the state; usually occurs below 11,000 feet (3,355 m) but has been found at 13,100 feet (3,992 m) in San Miguel County (MCZ 62473–62474).

Conservation Status. This garter snake is present throughout its historic range in Colorado. Declines in certain amphibian prey species have not adversely impacted this snake significantly, doubtless due to its ability to exploit a variety of food resources, including alternate amphibian species and invertebrates where amphibians are scarce. Blair (1951) reported that in Gunnison County, small glacial ponds each supported a half dozen or more individuals. It is not unusual to find this number within a few hours in the vicinity of many mountain wetlands. The population trend is uncertain (data are inadequate), but overall the state population appears to be stable and not threatened by habitat loss or other negative factors.

Habitat. This garter snake can be found in almost any terrestrial or wetland habitat in the vicinity of virtually any flowing or nonflowing body of water within its broad geographic and elevational range in Colorado. In the Sierra Nevada of California, this species is strongly associated with aquatic habitats in which amphibians are present (Jennings, Bradford, and Johnson 1992), but in Colorado it is not restricted to riparian-aquatic environments and frequently occupies terrestrial habitats far from water (Cary 1911; Stock 1962; Douglas 1966; pers. obs.). Occasionally, this species can be found in alpine tundra, but such occurrences are rare. Similarly, Hendricks (1996) found only one individual in alpine habitat over several years of extensive searching in northern Wyoming. Activity takes place on the ground, in water, or in low vegetation.

Hibernation occurs in various situations. Scott (1978) found that *T. elegans* winters in abandoned ground-squirrel burrows

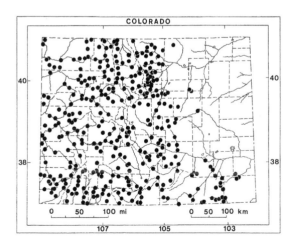

Map 8.44. Distribution of the western terrestrial garter snake in Colorado.

Plate 8.119. Adult western terrestrial garter snake (Las Animas County, Colorado).

beneath rocks near ponds in the mountains of Larimer County. Hahn (1968) found a population in the San Luis Valley wintering in communal dens with bull-snakes, milk snakes, and western rattlesnakes in fissures in volcanic rocks along the Rio Grande. In a canyon mouth in Jefferson County, small groups of these snakes hibernate in rock-crevice dens shared with the racer, milk snake, bullsnake, plains garter snake, and western rattlesnake. In northern Utah, Brown, Parker, and Elder (1974) described a communal winter den shared with racers at a depth of 1.0–1.6 m in an old filled well; snake body temperatures during hibernation were 4–7°C. Tanner (1950) reported that an aggregation of 76 individuals hibernated in loose sandy soil at the base of an willow stump in northern Utah. In central New Mexico, Stuart and Painter (1993) found these snakes hibernating with smooth green snakes and variable skinks under rocks imbedded in soil on a steep, west-facing canyon slope.

Activity. In lowland areas, emergence from hibernation regularly occurs as early as March; activity may continue through October and rarely into early November. Occasionally, individuals emerge during mild weather in winter. The annual period of activity is more restricted in the mountains. Scott (1978) found that this species is most active from early June to mid-September at 8,530 feet (2,600 m) in Larimer County, with limited activity extending into mid-May and early October. In southern Wyoming, spring emergence from hibernation occurs from late March to mid-May, with the peak in mid- to late April; males emerge earlier than females (Graves and Duvall 1990).

Activity takes place primarily during daylight hours. Throughout Colorado, I found active individuals between 8:30 a.m. and 9:30 p.m. (mainly between 10:00 a.m. and 6:00 p.m., with a peak between 10:00

a.m. and noon) during weather conditions ranging from cool and rainy to sunny, dry, and warm. Body temperatures of 21 active individuals were 17–32°C (average 25°C).

In the mountains of Larimer County, Scott (1978) found that morning emergence from the nighttime retreat occurs from 7:30–11:15 a.m., and individuals occasionally are active as late as 6:30–10:00 p.m. Body temperatures during activity usually are 13–35°C (average 27°C). Cool weather in May and September often prevents the snakes from attaining their typical summer body temperature of 26–32°C (average 29°C) (Scott, Tracy, and Pettus 1982). Warmed rocks serve as heat sources late in the day. Snakes avoid the sun during the hottest part of the day in summer and rarely occur on open ground when the surface temperature exceeds 30°C. A similar pattern of behavior was recorded in Washington by Peterson (1987) and in New Mexico by Fleharty (1967). Body temperatures of 25–35°C are best for efficient locomotion and digestion (Stevenson, Peterson, and Tsuji 1985).

Defensive behavior includes fleeing for cover on land or in water; repeated striking, or hiding the head under the body with the tail up when cornered; and release of excrement and cloacal sac secretions and biting when captured. Snakes that are grasped frequently wrap the tail and rear portion of the body around vegetation or other objects. This behavior, common in many snakes, presumably makes it more difficult for a predator to capture and ingest the snake.

Reproduction and Growth. Courtship and mating occur primarily in spring, soon after emergence from hibernation, though late summer sexual activity has been observed in some parts of the range. In Moffat County, Kyle Ashton (pers. comm.) observed two copulations on May 10 at 2:00 and 4:00 p.m., within 10 m of a den. Large, sexually receptive females sometimes attract multiple males. Ashton (pers. comm.) observed two males intertwined with a single female. In Larimer County, a large female was accompanied by 10 males in mid-April (Duane Baxter, pers. comm.).

Available data for Colorado indicate relatively small broods of 6–11 young. In the mountains, neonates are most often seen in August and early September; at lower elevations, they sometimes are seen as early as mid-July. A female found dead on a road in Bent County on June 9 contained seven developing young. A 54-cm-SVL female from Baca County contained 10 developing young on June 16. A 51-cm-SVL female from Las Animas County contained nine developing young in early July. A 64-cm (probably TL) female collected in Montezuma County on June 27 gave birth to 10 young shortly after her capture (Ellis and Henderson 1913). In lowland Delta County, newborn young were found on July 27 in two consecutive years, and a female containing six fully formed young was found on July 26 (L. Valentine, pers. comm.). A female from Mesa County gave birth to 11 young. A 53-m-SVL female found at 7,500 feet (2,285 m) in Boulder County on August 22 contained 11 well-developed young. Females first breed no sooner than their second spring, probably in the third spring in most high-elevation populations. Fitch (1940) found that most sexually mature females of subspecies *vagrans* were larger than 50 cm SVL, but some were as small as 38 cm SVL in Arizona and New Mexico (based on preserved specimens subject to shrinkage).

In neighboring states, broods are born at about the same time as they are in Colorado, but known brood sizes often are larger, perhaps an artifact of a lack of data for large fecund females from Colorado. Vasco Tanner (1949a) recorded newborn broods in early August in northern Utah; one female contained 16 live young, plus six embryos not fully developed. At 7,200 feet (2,195 m) in northwestern New Mexico, females of 75, 98, and 105 cm TL produced broods of 13, 15, and 20 young in mid-July, early July, and late August, respectively (Gehlbach 1965). Kasper and Kasper (1997) reported that a female captured in New Mexico on August 3 gave birth to three young on August 20. Additional New Mexican females of 64–85 cm TL produced litters of 10, 12, 20, 26, and 27 in late July and early August (Degenhardt, Painter, and Price 1996). In some areas, pregnant females form aggregations.

Food and Predators. This species feeds opportunistically on a wide range of vertebrates and invertebrates obtained on land or in water. Some foraging occurs while swimming along pond bottoms. Known food items in Colorado include leeches, earthworms, snails, slugs, various fishes (minnows, small trout, entrails of fishes gutted by anglers), larval and metamorphosed tiger salamanders, larval and metamorphosed frogs (leopard frogs, chorus frogs) and toads (spadefoot toads, Woodhouse's toad), plateau lizards, newborn conspecifics, smooth green snakes, small birds (such as ground-nesting songbirds), voles *(Microtus)*, chipmunks *(Tamias)*, mice *(Peromyscus)*, and other rodents (Ruthven 1908; Cockerell 1910; Ellis and Henderson 1913; Blair 1951; Pennock 1960; Harris 1963; Hahn 1968; Scott 1978; Albert Spencer, pers. comm.; pers. obs.). Metamorphosing and newly metamorphosed frogs and toads seem to be the primary food in late summer. Frogs and toads may be swallowed headfirst or hindquarters-first. Some specific examples of prey in Colorado are included in Table 8.3.

In Utah and New Mexico, Tanner (1949) and Gehlbach (1965) recorded similar diets, also including grasshoppers, the sagebrush lizard, the short-horned lizard, and pocket mice *(Perognathus flavus)*, plus two lizards not found in Colorado. Fleharty (1967) determined that the diet in New Mexico comprises mostly amphibians. In southwestern Colorado and adjacent New Mexico, several

Prey	Garter snake SVL (cm)	County	Source
Three 10-to 14-mm slugs, four 4-mm slugs, eight snails 3-6 mm in diameter	24	Garfield	Pers. obs.
One 25-mm slug, four 5- to 10-mm slugs, one snail 3 mm in diameter	26	Chaffee	Pers. obs.
Three leeches 5-6 cm long	26	Boulder	Pers. obs.
15 small slugs	29	Jackson	Pers. obs.
One mostly digested fish	32	Dolores	Pers. obs.
One mostly digested fish	32	Costilla	Pers. obs.
Two 1-cm slugs	38	Delta	Pers. obs.
One adult chorus frog	40	Conejos	Pers. obs.
One metamorphosed tiger salamander	43	Jackson	Pers. obs.
Two 7- to 10-cm earthworms, four snails	43	Saguache	Pers. obs.
One unidentified vole	50	Conejos	Pers. obs.
One 5-cm fathead minnow (*Pimephales promelas*)	50	Costilla	Pers. obs.
One adult red-spotted toad	50	San Miguel	Pers. obs.
One mostly digested 5-cm fish	57	Hinsdale	Pers. obs.
One adult montane vole (*Microtus montanus*)	58	Archuleta	Pers. obs.
Two mostly digested 5-cm fishes	59	Hinsdale	Pers. obs.
One juvenile deer mouse (*Peromyscus maniculatus*)	60	Conejos	Pers. obs.
One 9.2- cm sucker (*Catostomus*), additional unidentified prey	62	Boulder	L. Livo, pers. comm.
Three spadefoot (*Spea*) larvae	Adult	Las Animas	Pers. obs.
17 newly metamorphosed Woodhouse's toads	Adult	Dolores	Pers. obs.
Smooth green snake (2 instances)	Unknown	La Plata	A. Spencer, pers. comm.

Table 8.3. Examples of prey of the western terrestrial garter snake in Colorado. Listed prey were regurgitated by individual snakes.

western terrestrial garter snakes were caught in snap traps set in rodent runways through riparian or marsh vegetation (Harris 1963).

Shine (1991) demonstrated that Colorado females have a larger head than do males of the same SVL; whether this correlates with differences in foraging and diet is unknown. The posterior maxillary (upper jaw) teeth, which are the first teeth to contact the prey, are long and bladelike and apparently function in impaling, holding, and manipulating prey (Wright, Kardong, and Bentley 1979). Secretions of Duvernoy's gland (the duct opens near these teeth) have a myonecrotic effect on mammal muscle tissue (Jansen 1987).

In subduing mammals, these snakes may wrap loops of the body around the prey (Gregory, Macartney, and Rivard 1980).

However, this is a variable method of prey immobilization that differs from the killing technique used by bullsnakes and other constrictors.

Predators in Colorado are poorly known but include the pied-billed grebe (*Podilymbus podiceps*) (R. Ryder, pers. comm.). In Eagle County, a red-tailed hawk (*Buteo jamaicensis*) carried a dead adult to a perch in a tree, where the snake became entangled in branches and was dropped as I approached.

Taxonomy and Variation. Populations in Colorado generally have been assigned to the subspecies *Thamnophis elegans vagrans* (Baird and Girard, 1853). Tanner and Lowe (1989) described populations in the upper Colorado River basin of eastern Utah (and presumably western Colorado) as a new subspecies, *T. e. vascotanneri,* and populations in portions of eastern Arizona and western New Mexico as another new subspecies, *T. e. arizonae,* based primarily on the distinctness of the mid-dorsal stripe (broad and bright in *arizonae,* much reduced or absent in *vascotanneri,* and intermediate in *vagrans*). However, a broad, bright dorsal stripe occurs in populations in southeastern Colorado and the San Luis Valley and in occasional specimens in northwestern Colorado, with intervening populations exhibiting a variably reduced stripe. Fitch (1940:22) noted the "sporadic occurrence of populations having unusually distinct dorsal yellow stripes" and reported that distinctness of dorsal stripe is a character that shows great variation, "but this is mainly individual rather than geographic" (Fitch 1940:20). Furthermore, Fitch found that populations with a reduced dorsal stripe are not restricted to the upper Colorado River basin. Gehlbach (1965:298) observed that in the Zuni Mountains of northwestern New Mexico, some individuals have "only a trace of the middorsal light stripe," whereas others have a "brilliant lemon-yellow stripe." These observations suggest *"vascotanneri"* and *"arizonae"* are pattern classes rather than distinct, geographically coherent evolutionary lineages.

Basic difficulties with the taxonomy proposed by Tanner and Lowe are that geographic variation throughout the range was not considered, and the complete geographic scope of the new subspecies and areas of intergradation were not described. In addition, the proposed taxonomic rearrangement places three subspecies (*vagrans, vascotanneri,* and *arizonae*) in the San Juan River drainage, which appears to conflict with the scenario of evolution through isolation as a result of postpluvial desiccation described by Tanner and Lowe. *Thamnophis elegans* from throughout the range of subspecies *vagrans* as defined by Fitch (1940) appears to be genetically uniform (Lawson and Dessauer 1979; R. Lawson, pers. comm. to H. M. Smith). These circumstances suggest that *vascotanneri* and *arizonae* are not valid taxa and should be regarded as junior synonyms of *T. e. vagrans.*

Plate 8.120. Adult western ribbon snake (Louisiana).

Western Ribbon Snake
Thamnophis proximus (Say, 1823)

Recognition. Light stripes on sides of body on third and fourth scale rows above lateral edges of belly scales; mid-dorsal stripe orange; upper lips whitish, dark marks absent; dorsal scales keeled, in 19 rows at midbody; anal scale single; tail long (25–34 percent of TL); maximum TL about 123 cm but usually much smaller. *Newborn young:* 15–23 cm SVL in Oklahoma (Carpenter 1958) and New Mexico (T. Brown, in Degenhardt, Painter, and Price 1996); up to 30 cm TL in Missouri (Powell 1983).

Distribution. Eastern Nebraska, Iowa, Wisconsin, and Indiana south to eastern New Mexico, Costa Rica, and the Gulf Coast of Texas, Louisiana, and Mississippi (Rossman, Ford, and Seigel 1996). Known in Colorado only from Furnish Canyon, southwestern Baca County. The nearest populations in adjacent states occur in southwestern Kansas (Collins 1993), the Oklahoma panhandle (Webb 1970), and northeastern New Mexico (Degen-hardt, Painter, and Price 1996).

COLORADO

40 — 40

38 — 38

0   50   100 mi

0 50 100 km

107   105   103

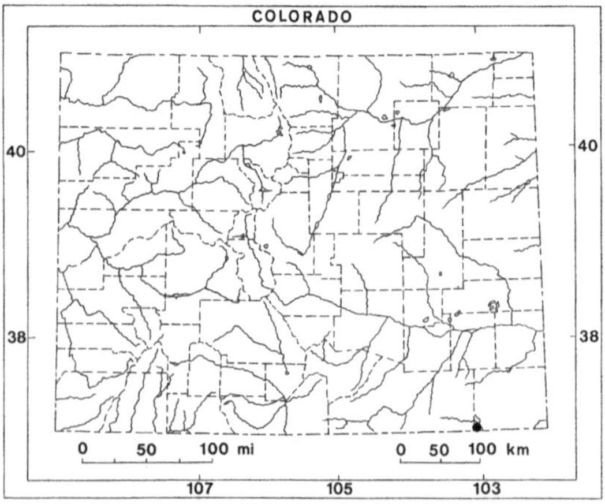

Map 8.45. Distribution of the western ribbon snake in Colorado.

Conservation Status. Fourteen ribbon snakes were collected from a small stream at the former Singer Boys' Ranch in Furnish Canyon in 1931 (Barry 1932); five of these are in the University of Colorado Museum (11669–11673). These specimens, which are correctly identified, document the only known occurrence of the ribbon snake in Colorado. I and others have searched for this snake in Furnish Canyon and adjacent areas several times but have found only other *Thamnophis* species. No obvious reason for the disappearance of ribbon snakes is evident. Perhaps temporary habitat changes associated with drought in the 1930s, competitive interactions with other garter snakes, predation by an increasing bullfrog population, and/or excessive collecting from a small remnant population resulted in the elimination of this snake from Colorado. Though this species has not been found in Colorado for more than 65 years, the recent rediscovery of the canyon treefrog in southeastern Colorado after an interval of more than 100 years suggests that additional surveys should be made before the ribbon snake is definitively regarded as extirpated from the state.

The 1931 collection in Colorado suggests that this snake may have been locally abundant. In Texas, Clark (1974) calculated that population density, not including young of the year, was 16–61 individuals per hectare over three years.

Habitat. In arid regions such as southeastern Colorado, this species generally occurs in close proximity to permanent water. The stream in Furnish Canyon flows intermittently but has permanent pools in some areas and many bullfrogs. In Oklahoma, this snake usually is found in brush very near ponds or pools, into which it dives when approached (Rossman, Ford, and Seigel 1996). Habitats in New Mexico include dense vegetation at the edge of streams (including intermittent creeks with large, deep pools containing abundant frogs and fishes), irrigation canals, and stock tanks (Degenhardt, Painter, and Price 1996). In Kansas, it occurs along the edges of aquatic and wetland habitats (Collins 1993). Activity takes place on the ground, in water, and

in low vegetation; these snakes commonly climb into vegetation beside or above water to bask.

Activity. In Kansas, activity occurs from March to October (Collins 1993). Western ribbon snakes appear to be mainly diurnal but may forage in ponds at night.

Reproduction and Growth. Spring is the primary mating season. In Oklahoma and Missouri, females may be gravid as early as April (Carpenter 1958; Powell 1982). In Kansas, Oklahoma, and New Mexico, broods of 4–12 young are born from late July to mid-September; reproductive females are as small as 44–46 cm SVL (Gloyd 1928; Carpenter 1958; Collins 1993; Degenhardt, Painter, and Price 1996), compared to 48–52 cm SVL for the smallest gravid females in Louisiana and Texas, where most births occur in July and August (Tinkle 1957; Clark 1974). Fitch (1985) recorded an average of 12 young per brood (range 4–28) in samples from the central and south-central United States. Births may occur as early as late June and early July in the warmer parts of the U.S. range (Wright and Wright 1957; Clark 1974; Powell 1982).

Most adult females appear to be gravid each year (Rossman, Ford, and Seigel 1996). Clark (1974) concluded that most females in Texas begin mating in their second spring, and most males start breeding in their first. In the shorter growing season of Colorado, at least an additional year likely is needed to attain maturity.

Food and Predators. The diet in Colorado is unknown but elsewhere is dominated by fishes and adult and larval frogs and salamanders, including newly metamorphosed toads but usually not adult toads (Rossman 1963; Clark 1974). Webb (1970) found several individuals in Oklahoma by locating the distress calls of ranid frogs being eaten. In Texas, Wendelken (1978) observed this snake lunging across a streambed and chasing cricket frogs that were flushed by its movements. Scavenging of road-killed *Bufo* was observed on a rainy summer night in Missouri (Resetarits 1983).

Taxonomy and Variation. The subspecies in Colorado is *Thamnophis proximus* *diabolicus* Rossman, 1963. Rossman (1962, 1963) and Gartside, Rogers, and Dessauer (1977) discussed taxonomy and variation in this species. Rossman (1963) noted that the populations in Colorado, northeastern New Mexico, and Hartley County, Texas, show more affinity to populations in the Pecos River drainage to the south than to populations in the Cimarron and Canadian River drainages to the east. Rossman (1963:37) speculated that these isolated populations are "relicts of an older population that was continuously distributed when conditions were more mesic."

Plate 8.121. Adult plains garter snake (Baca County, Colorado).

Plains Garter Snake
Thamnophis radix (Baird and Girard, 1853)

Recognition. Pale stripes on sides of body on third and fourth scale rows above lateral edges of belly scales; black vertical bars on upper lips; bold yellow or orange stripe along middle of back; dorsal scales keeled, in 19–21 rows at midbody; anal scale single; tongue red or orange at base; maximum TL about 109 cm, rarely this big in Colorado, usually not more than 85 cm TL in the state. Albino specimens have been found in Colorado; the Morrison Museum had one on display in 1998 (L. Livo, pers. comm.). *Newborn young:* average 14 cm SVL in Boulder County (Rossman, Ford, and Seigel 1996); 17–24 cm TL (Ernst and Barbour 1989; T. Brown,

in Degenhardt, Painter, and Price 1996 [New Mexico]).

Distribution. Southern Alberta, southern Saskatchewan, and southern Manitoba south through the Great Plains region to northeastern New Mexico, northern Texas, and northern Oklahoma, east to Ohio. Occurs throughout the Great Plains region of Colorado, primarily at elevations below 6,000 feet (1,830 m), but individuals sometimes range to 7,000–7,500 feet (2,135–2,285 m) in foothill canyons. A record of *T. radix* from Minnie Lake at 8,700 feet (2,650 m) in Boulder County (UCM 10740) probably represents an introduction and is not included on the map.

Conservation Status. The plains garter snake appears to be locally common throughout the vast majority of its historical range in Colorado. It is tolerant of moderate habitat alteration and in most areas does not appear to be threatened by natural processes or human activities. However, many are killed on roads. I found one that had been chopped to pieces in a state wildlife area in Otero County. In Ohio, mowing of fields is also a significant cause of mortality (Dalrymple and Reichenbach 1984).

Dozens of these snakes sometimes aggregate in terrestrial sites with good cover and abundant food (e.g., earthworms), and many may congregate at ponds with abundant food resources (e.g., amphibian larvae). Ballinger, Lynch, and Cole (1979) observed 30–40 individuals feeding on salamander larvae in a pond in western Nebraska. Bauerle (1971) indicated that 63 were found in a single day at a single pond in late June in Weld County; a total of 140 individuals were found at the pond between May 24 and September 1. Bauerle (1972) estimated population density at 800–1,200 individuals per hectare in this area of Weld County, as compared to 52–123 per hectare in Ohio (Reichenbach and Dalrymple 1986) and 845 per hectare in Illinois (Seibert 1950).

Habitat. This amphibious snake can be found in the vicinity of virtually any permanent or semipermanent flowing or nonflowing body of water in the plains of eastern Colorado. Typically, it inhabits the shores and shallows of marshy areas but often strays far from water, showing up in residential areas, dry grasslands, and sandhills. Ellis

and Henderson (1915) mentioned several killed along a half mile of railroad tracks after a train passed. Periods of inactivity are spent underground or beneath rocks, logs, or similar cover.

Activity. Emergence from hibernation takes place mainly in April, but usually a few individuals can be observed as early as mid-March. Bauerle (1972) reported that these snakes hibernate until May at the Pawnee National Grassland in Weld County, but I have several records of individuals active in late April in that county. Activity commonly extends through mid-October, and rarely into November (mainly neonates rather than adults). Bauerle (1972) reported that plains garter snakes in Weld County ended activity nearly a month earlier than sympatric bullsnakes and rattlesnakes. Anomalous emergence in winter occasionally occurs (Smith and Chiszar 1981).

Activity takes place primarily during daylight hours but may occur at night if temperatures are not too cold. In Colorado, I found active individuals mainly between 7:30 a.m. and 10:30 p.m.; later activity sometimes is seen in summer but seems to be relatively rare (this may, however, be due to the fact that few nocturnal studies of pond and wetland habitats have been done). Midday activity takes place in the cooler months, and sometimes in summer under favorable conditions, but bimodal activity in morning and late afternoon/evening, with midday retreat to cover, is typical of the hottest days of midsummer (Gerrard 1973; Hart 1979; Reichenbach and Dal-rymple 1986). Body temperatures of 11 active individuals in Colorado were 22.0–32.4°C (average 26.5°C), conforming in general with the pattern observed in Manitoba (Hart 1979) and Ohio (Reichenbach and

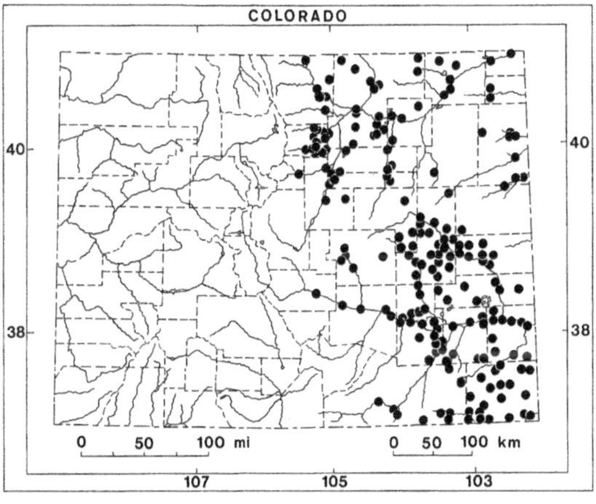

Map 8.46. Distribution of the plains garter snake in Colorado.

Dalrymple 1986). In Illinois, air temperatures of 21–29°C are most favorable for observing this snake (Seibert and Hagen 1947). Limited data suggest that these snakes may have relatively small home ranges (Seibert and Hagen 1947).

Escape behavior includes fleeing into cover or diving underwater and remaining submerged for a long time. When cornered, these snakes may coil and hide the head, wave the tail (perhaps drawing attention away from the head), and/or strike repeatedly, usually without biting (Arnold and Bennett 1984). In hand, plains garter snakes often attempt to bite and typically expel foul-smelling fluid from the vent.

Reproduction and Growth. Males find mates by following female scent trails and are able to distinguish trails of their own species from those of other garter snakes (Ford and Schofield 1984). Courtship and mating behavior are similar to that of the blackneck garter snake. Sometimes, multiple males simultaneously attempt to court a single female. I observed courtship on May 21 in Otero County; the snakes were wrapped around a clump of cattails a few inches above water. Bauerle (1972) observed mating in late May and early June in Weld County. Courtship and mating also may occur earlier than this, probably soon after emergence from hibernation, or even late the previous summer, based on observations of obviously pregnant females in mid-May. As part of the mating process, the male deposits a gelatinous, pheromone-containing "mating plug" in the female's cloaca, which may render the female at least temporarily unattractive to other sexually active males (Ross and Crews 1978). The plug is produced by secretions of the male's renal sex segment. Expulsion of the plug renews the female's sexual attractiveness but fails to restore her sexual receptivity.

Brood sizes of nine females from Colorado (based on dissections of preserved specimens) ranged from 9–21 young (average 16). Ford (in Rossman, Ford, and Seigel 1996) found that litter size was 5–20 young (average 11–12) in a sample of eight females from Boulder County. Fitch (1985) reported an average of 21 young in 16 females from Nebraska, Kansas, and Colorado. A female from Baca County had 20 eggs about 10 mm long in mid-May. A 60-cm-SVL female from Boulder County contained 21 large eggs in early July, and Ellis and Henderson (1913) reported that another female collected at the same time in the same county contained 20 well-developed embryos. A 51-cm-SVL female from Boulder County contained 14 developing young in mid-July. A 61-cm-SVL female that I found in Bent County contained nine small developing young (with large yolk masses) in late July. A female in Douglas County was heavily pregnant on July 31. A dead-on-the-road female found in eastern Colorado on August 19 contained seven nearly fully developed young (L. Livo, pers. comm.). Gerrard (1973) reported that pregnant females in burrows emerged partially and exposed the midsection of the body to the sun, probably raising the temperature of the developing young.

In Colorado, young of the year usually first appear in late July or early August, though some females may give birth earlier, or perhaps as late as September. Further study is needed. Degenhardt, Painter, and Price (1996) recorded births from mid-August to early September in New Mexico.

Two Colorado specimens that were 16 and 23 cm SVL (preserved size) in late April were obviously young of the previous year; others that were 35–36 cm SVL in mid-April were probably in their second spring. In some parts of the range, females likely begin breeding in their second spring (Seibert and Hagen 1947; Gregory 1977), but the age of maturity in Colorado is uncertain. Based on the size distributions of mature and immature individuals, I suspect that most females breed no earlier than their third spring. Adult females do not necessarily produce young every year.

Food and Predators. Plains garter snakes feed opportunistically, so the diet may shift with the seasons. Known prey in Colorado includes earthworms, grasshoppers, New Mexico spadefoot, western chorus frog (adults and larvae), adult plains leopard frog, and larval and metamorphosing bullfrogs (Mackessy 1998; Livo, Hammerson,

Smith, et al. 1998; pers. obs.). Specific examples of prey in Colorado follow (listings include SVL, prey, and county): 81 cm, four large bullfrog larvae, Baca; 35 cm, earthworm, Baca; 48 cm, plains leopard frog, Las Animas; adult (size unknown), seven plains spadefoot larvae, Weld; adult (size unknown), juvenile spadefoot *(Spea)*, Las Animas. In western Nebraska, prey included larvae of the tiger salamander, plains spadefoot, western chorus frog, and northern leopard frog (Ballinger, Lynch, and Cole 1979); tiger salamanders were eaten after being carried to shore. In other areas, small fishes, other amphibians (including larvae), small mammals, leeches, gastropods, other insects, and carrion are eaten as well (Hart 1979; Stebbins 1985; Collins 1993). Shine (1991) demonstrated that Colorado females have a larger head than do males of the same SVL; whether this is correlated with differences in foraging and diet is unknown.

Predators are not well known. In Yuma County, I found a 80-cm-SVL racer that had eaten a 48-cm-SVL plains garter snake. Swenson and Rodeck (1948) reported that a plains garter snake was consumed by a smaller western hognose snake. Mackessy (1998) reported predation by a bullfrog in Prowers County. Marti (1974) found that three garter snakes (probably of this species) were eaten by a burrowing owl *(Athene cunicularia)*. Another known but infrequent predator in Colorado includes the broad-winged hawk *(Buteo platypterus)* (D. and J. Ward, pers. comm.). American crows occasionally kill this species at dens in Manitoba (Gregory 1977). These snakes sometimes are missing the end of the tail, suggesting unsuccessful predation attempts.

Taxonomy and Variation. Formerly, Colorado populations were assigned to the subspecies *Thamnophis radix haydenii* (Kennicott, 1860) per A. G. Smith (1949). Rossman, Ford, and Seigel (1996) pointed out problems with Smith's diagnoses and recommended that this species be regarded as monotypic.

Plate 8.122. Adult common garter snake (Boulder County, Colorado).

Common Garter Snake
Thamnophis sirtalis (Linnaeus, 1758)

Recognition. Pale stripes on sides of body on second and third scale rows above lateral edges of belly scales; belly pale and unmarked; red blotches between stripes on back (red may be confined to skin between scales); usually seven upper labials (lacking heavy black markings) on each side of head; dorsal scales keeled, in 19 rows at midbody;

anal scale single; tongue red at base; maximum TL about 124 cm, but usually much smaller in Colorado. The tail sometimes is incomplete due to breakage. *Mature male:* knobbed keels on dorsal scales near vent. *Newborn young:* average about 17 cm SVL in Kansas (Fitch 1965); 17–25 cm TL in Utah (V. Tanner 1949a) and New Mexico (Degenhardt, Painter, and Price 1996).

Distribution. Northern British Columbia, southern Northwest Territories, central Manitoba, central Ontario, southern Quebec, and the Maritime Provinces of Canada south to southern California, western Nevada, northern Utah, northeastern Colorado, the U.S. Gulf Coast, and southern Florida; disjunctly south to New Mexico and northwestern Chihuahua, Mexico (Rossman, Ford, and Seigel 1996). This snake ranges farther north

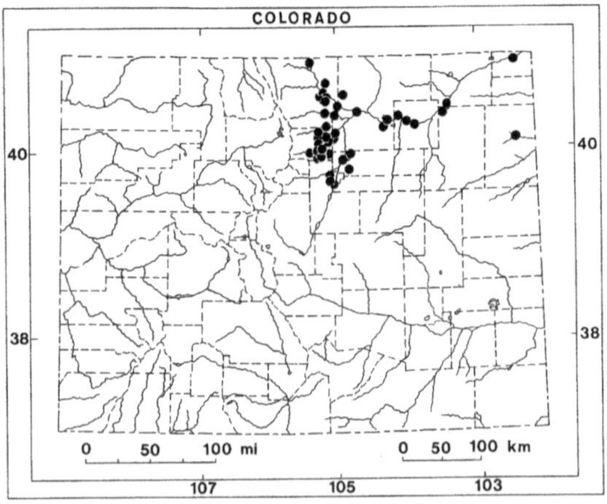

Map 8.47. Distribution of the common garter snake in Colorado.

Plate 8.123. Adult common garter snake (Yuma County, Colorado).

(to 60° north latitude) than any other North American reptile. Occurs in northeastern Colorado along the South Platte River and its tributaries at elevations below 6,000 feet (1,830 m) and in the North Fork Republican River drainage in Yuma County at about 3,500–3,600 feet (1,065–1,100 m) (Hammerson and Smith 1993b); widely distributed along the eastern base of the Front Range. Records of *T. sirtalis* from outside the South Platte and Republican River drainages in eastern Colorado (Maslin 1959; Secoy and Brown 1968), from northwestern Colorado (Cockerell 1910), and from the Rio Grande in the San Luis Valley of Colorado (Yarrow 1875; Fitch 1980) all are based on misidentified *Thamnophis elegans* (Ruthven 1908; Fitch and Maslin 1961; Hahn 1968; Hammerson 1981, 1982b, 1984), as is, in all likelihood, a record (UMMZ 70108, not examined) from near Pinecliffe, Gilpin County. A record from near the Colorado border in northern New Mexico (Fitch and Maslin 1961) also appears to be erroneous (Degenhardt, Painter, and Price 1996).

Conservation Status. Better information is needed on the current range and abundance of this snake in Colorado. It is known primarily from tributaries of the South Platte River along the eastern base of the Front Range, an area where this snake at least formerly was common. The area currently is undergoing rapid and extensive residential and commercial development. The snake remains common in parts of this area, but recent survey data are not available for much of the historical range. In the vicinity of Riverside Reservoir in Weld County, this garter snake may have become extirpated at about the same time that the northern leopard frog disappeared from that area; neither species has been observed there in recent years (L. Livo, pers. comm.). There are old records but apparently no recent observations of the common garter snake in the Denver metropolitan area.

Capron (cited by Collins 1993) reported that in southern Kansas, many of these snakes were killed during agricultural mowing operations in spring and early summer. In Colorado, the snake is restricted mainly to riparian areas and generally is directly unaffected by nonriparian agricultural operations. However, drift and runoff of pesticides used on agricultural fields may have harmful impacts on the adjacent riparian and riverine ecosystems upon which this snake depends.

Typical population density in Colorado is unknown. In eastern Kansas, Fitch (1965) recorded densities of up to about 20 individuals per hectare in early summer and up to 45 per hectare in late summer after birth of the young.

Habitat. In Colorado, the common garter snake inhabits marshes, ponds, and the edges of streams. For the most part, it is restricted to aquatic, wetland, and riparian habitats along the floodplains of streams. Unlike the plains garter snake, and common garter snakes in the eastern United States, this species in Colorado seldom is found away from water or at isolated ponds. Activity occurs in shallow water and on land adjacent to water.

Winter is spent in various underground sites. In Boulder County, one winter den that I have observed for more than two decades is within or beneath a mostly buried automobile body at the edge of a marshy pond. In some parts of the range, underwater sites may be chosen, or even preferred, for hibernation (Costanzo 1985). Submerged snakes retain more body water and conserve more energy than do snakes in dry sites, and at the low temperatures of hibernation, the snake's oxygen needs can be met even while it is underwater (Costanzo 1989a, 1989b). If necessary, the snakes can survive temporary entombment in ice (Costanzo 1988). Locally, this species sometimes hibernates in small groups, but the spectacular denning aggregations of several thousand individuals known to occur in southern Manitoba do not occur in Colorado.

Activity. It is always exciting to see the season's first reptiles, and these snakes generally are among the earliest to emerge from hibernation, often in mid- to late March. Activity continues through September, with small numbers sometimes active in October. These snakes seem to be most active on sunny days, but they avoid exposure to the sun during the hottest part of the day in summer. Nocturnal aquatic foraging may occur when temperatures are not too cold. Body temperatures of six individuals that I captured near hibernacula in Colorado in early spring were 19.9–26.5°C (average 22.9°C); these snakes were basking. Two active in late spring/early summer had body temperatures of 29.4–31.4°C. In Manitoba, Canada, sexually active males in spring had body temperatures of 25–29°C (Garstka, Camazine, and Crews 1982).

In Kansas, Fitch (1965) found that activity ranges average about 14 ha in males and 9 ha in females. Average dispersal distance from the winter den to the summer range is about 350 m in males and 530 m in females. In southern Canada, common garter snakes may make long migrations (up to 18 km one-way [Gregory and Stewart 1975]) from dens to summer ranges (Larsen 1987; Lawson 1989). In Colorado, hibernation appears to occur very close to or within the summer range.

When approached, these snakes generally attempt to flee into thick vegetation or water, where they may swim rapidly on or below the surface. Sometimes they respond to harassment by flattening the head and body, or by coiling and striking.

If grasped, they may squirm vigorously, release excrement and cloacal sac secretions, open the mouth, and attempt to bite. Two that I captured in Boulder County exhibited cloacal hemorrhaging. In Kansas, Fitch (1965) found that snakes grasped by the tail sometimes twisted violently enough to the detach the tail, which wiggles much like a broken lizard tail.

Reproduction and Growth. Males find females by following their scent trails (Ford 1982). Mating takes place primarily just after emergence from hibernation, though it may also occur to a limited extent in late summer. One study demonstrated that males are attracted to a pheromone in the female's skin. The pheromone is vitellogenin, a blood-borne precursor of yolk. Males prefer larger females (which have more vitellogenin). Males also court males that have had vitellogenin rubbed on the back. Bona-Gallo and Licht (1983) found that females may be attractive in the absence of vitellogenesis (yolking of the follicles) and that mating is a prerequisite for vitellogenesis. In Canada, Garstka, Camazine, and Crews (1982) determined that two males simultaneously can copulate with a single female, though females usually mate only once per season. A pheromone-laced copulatory plug deposited by the male in the female's cloaca may inhibit further courtship by other males; the plug usually is expelled within a few days (Devine 1975, 1977). Copulation lasts an average of 15–20 minutes (Garstka, Camazine, and Crews 1982). Males may mate with multiple females and generally seem to forego feeding until after the mating season is over. Aleksiuk and Gregory (1974), Hawley and Aleksiuk (1975, 1976), Garstka and Crews (1981), Crews and Garstka (1982), Garstka, Camazine, and Crews (1982), Bona-Gallo and Licht (1983), and Krohmer and Crews (1989) discussed the factors that affect mating activity.

Few reproductive data are available for Colorado. In Boulder County, I observed that a 78-cm-SVL female contained 19 enlarged yolked follicles in early June, a 67-cm-SVL female contained 20 large embryos in early July, and a 62-cm-SVL

Plate 8.124. Common garter snake swallowing fish (Boulder County, Colorado).

female contained 24 well-developed young (each about 185 mm TL) in late July. In Yuma County, I found a 66-cm-SVL female that contained approximately 16 developing young (determined through palpation) in mid-June. Probably most young are born in late July and August, but better information on birth dates in Colorado is needed. Spring populations include individuals only slightly larger than neonates, and others around 33 cm SVL (including non-reproductive females), suggesting that first reproduction occurs no sooner than the third spring.

Fitch (1965, 1985) and Seigel and Fitch (1985) provided information for Kansas. Average litter size is 19–20 young (up to 42) but varies from year to year, probably reflecting changes in food resources that are related to fluctuating weather conditions. About 65 percent of adult females are reproductive; this percentage increases with female size (essentially all of the largest females are reproductive), as does average litter size. Births occur in late July and early August. Sexual maturity is attained at about 50 cm SVL in females and 39 cm SVL in males. Females first mate generally in their second or third spring. Annual survival rate of adults is about 50 percent.

Degenhardt, Painter, and Price (1996) reported litters of 3, 21, 24, and 47 young born from late July to late August in New Mexico; the largest litter, produced by a 112-cm-TL female, was born over a period of two weeks. Vasco Tanner (1949a) recorded broods of 5 (plus two "unhatched eggs"), 10, and 16 born in early August in northern Utah. In some parts of the range, gravid females sometimes form aggregations in sites with favorable thermal characteristics and cover.

Food and Predators. Common garter snakes feed opportunistically on frogs, toads, fishes, and earthworms. In Colorado, the known diet of adults includes various fishes, small metamorphosed bullfrogs, northern leopard frogs, other larval and adult amphibians, and earthworms. Other small vertebrates likely are eaten on occasion. Specific examples follow: (listings include size or age class, prey, and county): 56 cm SVL, 78-mm-TL green sunfish *(Lepomis cyanellus)*, Boulder; 46 cm TL, small metamorphosed bullfrog, Boulder; large adult, 10-cm-TL centrarchid fish, Morgan; adult, two 8- to 10-cm-TL pumpkinseeds *(Lepomis gibbosus)*, Boulder. In Kansas, adults eat mostly ranid frogs, and sometimes voles and mice, and juveniles prey mostly on earthworms (Fitch 1965, 1982). Jones, Ballinger, and Nietfeldt (1981) observed predation on a Woodhouse's toad in Nebraska.

On numerous occasions, I have observed adults capturing and devouring fishes that had been carried through a culvert draining into the shallow edge of a marsh in Boulder County. The snakes waited at the outflow of the culvert and caught the disoriented fishes as they floundered in a shallow pool.

A common garter snake that was hunting frogs in a marsh in Boulder County quickly moved toward a small bullfrog and struck at it. The frog took two quick leaps and stopped motionless. The snake searched for the frog for several minutes, crawling back and forth through the area where the frog had fled. It did not flick its tongue during the search. After the snake had been immobile for several minutes, I decided to see if it was attracted to splashes such as the frog might make. I tossed a small stone into the water in front of the snake. It quickly swam forward to the location of the splash and appeared to search the site visually. This behavior was duplicated several more times in response to repeated stone-caused splashes.

No doubt the usual array of predators occasionally take this snake, but I know of no specific instances of predation in Colorado (other than some snakes killed intentionally by humans).

Taxonomy and Variation. The subspecies in Colorado is *Thamnophis sirtalis parietalis* (Say, 1823). Rossman, Ford, and Seigel (1996) provided a brief overview of the taxonomy of this species.

Plate 8.125. Adult lined snake (Denver County, Colorado).

Lined Snake
Tropidoclonion lineatum (Hallowell, 1856)

Recognition. Belly whitish, typically with double row of black semicircular marks along middle; five or six upper labials on each side of head; dorsal scales keeled, in 17–19 rows at midbody; anal scale single; maximum TL about 57 cm, but usually less than 40 cm. Knobs are present on the dorsal scales in the region of the vent in maturing and mature males and in large mature females (Force 1935). *Newborn young:* usually 10–13 cm TL in Colorado (Maslin 1950; Smith, Pague, and Chiszar 1996).

Distribution. Nebraska, southeastern South Dakota, southwestern Minnesota, and Illinois south through Colorado, Kansas, Missouri, New Mexico, and Oklahoma to southern Texas. Occurs probably throughout most of eastern Colorado below 6,000 feet (1,830 m) but definitely most abundant in southeastern Colorado. A record from Gunnison County (WTSU 14523) undoubtedly reflects a data transposition during specimen processing (H. M. Smith, pers. comm.; Livo, Hammerson, and Smith 1998).

Conservation Status. The distribution in Colorado is not well known, due to the small size and secretive behavior of this species. Most early records were from the Denver-Boulder area, but accumulating information indicates that populations occur in scattered locations throughout much of eastern Colorado, and future surveys are likely to reveal additional populations within this region. Lined snakes are locally abundant in both natural and urban habitats. Small aggregations can be found in canyon-bottom

Plate 8.126. Belly of lined snake (Denver County, Colorado).

are unknown. In early June, I found several lined snakes crawling in the open at 9:45–10:15 p.m. at air temperatures of 22–23°C.

When disturbed, lined snakes may flatten the body and often hide the head beneath the body. When grasped, they usually thrash vigorously while voiding muddy excrement and odorous secretions from the vent.

grasslands. Livo (1985) recorded a minimum of 78 individuals in a 0.6-ha site in Denver. Development probably has eliminated or reduced some formerly more widespread populations in the Denver and Boulder areas. Known populations elsewhere do not appear to be significantly threatened. This species may persist in areas with a great deal of habitat alteration.

Habitat. Habitats include damp sites in flat plains grasslands, canyon bottom grasslands, riparian areas, and grassy vacant lots and gullies in cities. During daylight hours, these secretive ground-dwelling and burrowing snakes hide in loose soil or under rocks, wood, dried cattle dung, or debris.

Activity. In Colorado, lined snakes generally emerge from hibernation in late March and April and remain active into October, prowling at dusk and at night and sometimes basking in the morning (Ramsey 1953). They are most active after spring and summer rains, which stimulate activity of their prey. Individuals active early or late in the year tend to be juveniles (Livo, unpublished data). Lined snakes found under cover by Livo (1985) had body temperatures of 14–32°C (average 25°C), but temperatures characteristic of foraging and reproductive activity

Reproduction and Growth. In Colorado, births occur in August and September, and litter sizes of 11 females ranged from 5–10 (average 7) (Livo 1985; Smith, Pague, and Chiszar 1996; pers. obs.). Museum records indicate that Maslin's (1950) report of a litter of three is in error (it was actually six). Five reproductive females in Colorado were 24–29 cm SVL (Maslin 1950; pers. obs.). A 17-cm-SVL female found in Baca County appeared to be pregnant, but this was not confirmed. Mating apparently occurs primarily or exclusively in late summer, immediately after birth of the young (Ramsey 1953; Krohmer and Aldridge 1985a, 1985b; Livo 1985). Sperm are stored in the female's body over the winter, and ovulation and fertilization occur the following spring (Fox 1956). However, in early spring, I found several male-female

Map 8.48. Distribution of the lined snake in Colorado.

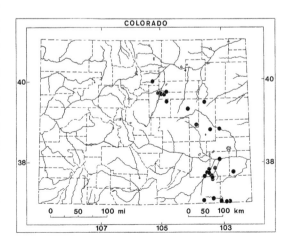

pairs coiled together, suggesting possible mating activity at that time.

Elsewhere in the range, litter size averages 6–8 young (range 2–17), births occur in August or September, growth is rapid during the first year of life, males are capable of mating at one year of age, females produce their first brood at two years of age (the smallest reproductive females are 21–22 cm SVL), and essentially all adult females are reproductive (Fitch 1970, 1985; Funk and Tucker 1978; Kromer and Aldridge 1985a, 1985b; Degenhardt, Painter, and Price 1996).

Food and Predators. Observations throughout the range indicate that the diet consists almost exclusively of earthworms.

Taxonomy and Variation. Based on the three-subspecies arrangement of Ramsey (1953) and Smith and Chiszar (1994a), the subspecies in Colorado is *Tropidoclonion lineatum lineatum* (Hallowell, 1856). Some authors (Conant and Collins 1991; Degenhardt, Painter, and Price 1996), however, regard this species as monotypic.

VIPERS
Family Viperidae

Vipers are well known as dangerously venomous animals. About 230 species occur worldwide, excluding Australia. *Vipera berus* occurs north of 68° north latitude in Scandinavia. The rattlesnakes are restricted to the New World. North American representatives are heavy-bodied, with a slender neck and a broad head. The dorsal scales of vipers are keeled, with few exceptions. Usually, at least several ventral scales at the base of the tail form a single row. The pupils are vertically elliptical. The largest member of the family is the bushmaster *(Lachesis muta)*, a Central and South American species that reaches 3.5 m in length. Vipers first appear in the fossil record in the Miocene in Europe and North America; the group probably originated in Eurasia.

Pit vipers (subfamily Crotalinae), represented in the United States by the rattlesnakes, cottonmouth, and copperhead, have a specialized infrared-sensing organ in a

pit on each side of the face. The pit organs are energy receptors sensitive to radiation that generally is not detectable by humans. Their primary function may be the detection and location of prey items differing in temperature from their surroundings. Using only information received through the pit organs, blind individuals and those in total darkness can accurately direct strikes (Kardong and Mackessy 1991). Strikes may occur in the absence of chemical cues from the prey (Hayes and Duvall 1991). The pits also may feature prominently in the detection and identification of mammalian predators.

Rattlesnakes exhibit a specialized noise-making structure of horny, loosely interlocking segments on the end of the tail. A new segment is added to this rattle each time the snake sheds its skin, which may occur a few times each year in a well-fed young snake. Vibration of the rattle produces a broad-spectrum sound (Fenton and Licht 1990) that is employed in a defensive context. The rattle probably evolved as an aposematic sound directed at threatening vertebrates (Greene 1992), but some have suggested that it evolved in association with use of the tail as a lure (Schuett, Clark, and Kraus 1984). Sisk and Jackson (1997) mentioned other pertinent literature on the evolutionary origin of the rattle.

When confronted by snake-eating predators such as kingsnakes, whipsnakes, and skunks, rattlesnakes may inflate the lungs and elevate and thrust the midsection of the body toward the advancing predator (Carpenter and Gillingham 1975; Weldon and Burghardt 1979). Sudden body flips and jerks may occur if the predator contacts the rattlesnake's body. Chemical cues from predators are enough to elicit this response. Presumably, the behavior reduces the probability that the attack will be successful.

Stille (1987) and McCranie (1988) presented morphological evidence suggesting that *Crotalus* and *Sistrurus* should be regarded as congeneric. Knight et al. (1993) concluded from mtDNA data that *Sistrurus* is monophyletic. Hence, I follow the usual practice of treating these two groups as distinct genera.

Plate 8.127. Western rattlesnake (Moffat County, Colorado).

Western Rattlesnake
Crotalus viridis (Rafinesque, 1818)

Recognition. Horny rattle or button on end of tail; numerous small scales on top of head; head much broader than neck; pit on each side of face between (but lower than) eye and nostril; dorsum usually blotched; dorsal scales keeled; pupil vertically elongate in bright light; rarely greater than 100 cm TL in Colorado; in eastern Colorado, adults average around 70 cm TL, with males averaging a few centimeters longer than females; in west-central and southwestern Colorado, adults rarely exceed 65 cm TL (see "Taxonomy and Variation"). *Newborn young:* as small as about 18 cm TL (subspecies *nuntius*) in Arizona (Klauber 1972), as small as 24 cm TL in northeastern Colorado (Klauber 1937); average 19 cm SVL in southwestern Wyoming (K. G. Ashton and T. M. Patton, unpublished data).

Distribution. Southern British Columbia, southern Alberta, and southern Saskatchewan south through all of the

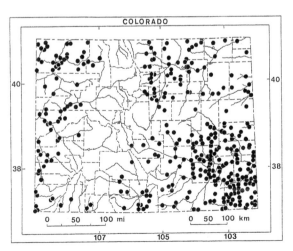

Map 8.49. Distribution of the western rattlesnake in Colorado.

Plate 8.128. Western rattlesnake (Mesa County, Colorado).

Plate 8.129. Western rattlesnake (Montezuma County, Colorado).

western United States and Great Plains region to central Baja California and north-central mainland Mexico. Occurs through-out most of Colorado, except the high mountains, reaching an upper elevational limit of 7,500–9,500 feet (2,285–2,895 m) in different areas of the state.

Conservation Status. The western rattlesnake occupies the vast majority of its historical range in Colorado (excluding some highly urbanized areas and land-scapes highly altered by agriculture) and remains numerous enough in most areas to be encountered frequently by humans. However, in many areas, long-term per-secution of these snakes undoubtedly has greatly reduced their numbers. C. B. Perkins removed more than 850 rattlesnakes from prairie-dog towns in a limited area in Weld County (Klauber 1972), including 99 in a single day near Milton Reservoir (Barry 1932b). Widmer (1967) also reported hun-dreds that were killed or collected at dens in active or abandoned prairie-dog towns

in Weld County. Hundreds were removed from the Ken-Caryl Ranch development in Jefferson County, beginning in the 1970s (Ludlow 1981). The *Rocky Mountain News* reported that in October 1937 at least 1,500 were killed by automobiles on the highway between Roggen and Wiggens in Weld and Morgan counties as the snakes moved north to denning areas (Klauber 1972:589). Even apart from such mass mortalities, thousands die each year on roads throughout the state, and on many occasions I found dead-on-the-road individuals that had been mutilated by humans (usually the head and rattle were cut off). Dynamite has been used to destroy some dens. Although a few rattlesnakes are killed out of legitimate concern for human safety, most of those slain by humans pose no significant threat; many are slaughtered by sadistic individuals in the name of "fun." In northern Utah, Parker and Brown (1973, 1974) found that a den population of this species decreased from more than 300 individuals in the 1940s to 232 in 1950 to

55 in 1966 to 12 in 1972, evidently due to predation by humans.

Some denning populations are relatively small. In southwestern Wyoming, Kyle Ashton (pers. comm.) found that three dens harbored only up to 35 individuals, including 2–10 adult females. One den population near a much-used fishing hole evidently had been decimated by human predation. He found that some former den sites visited by collectors were devoid of snakes.

Rattlesnakes are an interesting and significant component of Colorado's natural ecosystems, and they warrant the protection and careful management afforded other wildlife. They pose very little risk to humans (much less than riding in an automobile, playing most sports, or smoking). Public education is needed to reduce the number that are needlessly killed.

Habitat. The western rattlesnake occurs in virtually every terrestrial habitat within its broad geographic and elevational range in Colorado. Typical habitats include plains grassland, sandhills, semidesert shrubland, mountain shrubland, riparian zones, piñon-juniper woodland, and montane woodland. Soils vary from sandy to rocky. Only perennially wet areas and high mountains seem to be avoided. This snake is basically terrestrial, though it sometimes climbs into vegetation or onto rocks or logs.

Crevices, woodpiles, brushy vegetation, and the burrows of small mammals such as prairie dogs *(Cynomys),* pocket gophers *(Thomomys, Geomys)* (Vaughan 1961), and kangaroo rats *(Dipodomys ordii)* (Smith, Maslin, and Brown 1965) are used for cover during the active season. After eating a large meal, individuals in southern Wyoming secluded themselves in abandoned rodent burrows under greasewood shrubs (Brown and Duvall 1993). Dean and Stock (1961) found rattlesnakes among driftwood piles near a river in Archuleta County.

Hibernation generally occurs in rodent burrows or in crevices in rock outcrops. Along the junction of the Great Plains and Front Range, winter dens often are found in the characteristic tilted layers of sedimentary rocks. Hill (1943) stated that winter dens in northwestern Colorado were in rocky, south- or east-facing ridges. Finley (1958) described a den in talus at the base of the igneous dike in sagebrush-rabbitbrush habitat at Fortification Rocks in Moffat County. One rattler was found in a crevice five feet aboveground. In the San Luis Valley, Hammarstrom (in Klauber 1972:589) observed that rattlers wintered in dens in well-weathered volcanic rocks and migrated to summer foraging areas on the valley floor. In eastern Colorado, prairie-dog burrows are the major denning sites. Adults generally use the same den site year after year. Dens may be shared with any of several other snake species.

In late November 1974, a communal den of some 300 snakes was discovered in an open cellar in Kiowa County (Kiowa County Press, November 27, 1974). About half of the snakes reportedly were rattlesnakes; others included racers, coachwhips, "side winders" (?), and "pink sand snakes" (?).

Activity. Rattlesnakes usually emerge from their winter dens in eastern Colorado between mid-April and mid-May (varies from year to year) (Klauber 1937; Costello 1969; Bauerle 1972; Ludlow 1981; pers. obs.). Emergence as early as late March occurs in some years. Snakes begin to return to the dens in mid- to late September, though activity may extend through late summer and early fall until continuous cold weather arrives in October or (in some years) early to mid-November (Costello 1969; Bauerle 1972; Ludlow 1981; pers. obs.). Basking at den entrances is not uncommon during mild weather in early November (pers. obs.). Large numbers of rattlesnakes sometimes can be seen at the dens in spring, and especially fall. At prairie-dog towns in Weld County, Perkins found the largest concentrations in mid-October and mid-April.

In northwestern Colorado, dispersal from dens sites takes place in early May, return migrations commence in August, and hibernation begins in October or November (Hill 1943). The annual activity period is more restricted in cooler climates at higher elevations. At 7,500–8,300 feet (2,285–2,530 m) in the San Luis Valley, rattlesnakes do not depart from their rocky crevice dens until

Plate 8.130. Western rattlesnake (Otero County, Colorado).

early June and return by early September (Hahn 1968).

In south-central Wyoming, emergence from hibernation occurs from late April to late June, with a peak in late May (Graves and Duvall 1990). Snakes soon undertake long migrations of up to several kilometers in search of prey such as deer mice *(Peromyscus maniculatus)*. The snakes stop migrating or pause for some time when they arrive in areas with substantial mouse populations (Duvall et al. 1985, 1990, 1992). Both sexes return to the wintering dens in late summer and early fall. Males tend to follow relatively straight migration paths. In contrast, in southwestern Wyoming, Kyle Ashton (pers. comm.) found that where food resources were abundant, rattlesnakes did not migrate but rather stayed within about 500 m of the den. In northern Utah, emergence occurs throughout May and prehibernation arrivals take place from early September to early October (Hirth et al. 1969; Parker and Brown 1974). Hirth et al. found that in summer, some individuals move up to about 1.5 km from the winter den.

Jacob and Painter (1980) found that in New Mexico, basking outside winter dens occurs in fall and early spring on sunny days when the body temperatures of snakes in the den rises above 10°C. Snakes basking in March and October in New Mexico had body temperatures of 12–31°C (average 25°C) at air temperatures usually less than 17°C (Aldridge 1979a). In southern Idaho, activity extends from mid/late April to early October; observations peaked in late May

and early June (Diller and Wallace 1996).

I found that activity in Colorado takes place primarily in the afternoon and early evening (especially around 6:00–9:00 p.m.) during the mild weather of early spring (April-May) and fall (September-October). At this time, the air and ground may be cool, especially at night and in the morning, and during the day, the snakes bask in the sun or use sun-heated substrates to attain body temperatures warm enough for activity. From June through August, rattlesnakes usually prowl at dusk and at night, mostly in the early hours of darkness but sometimes throughout the night. From June through August, some can be found basking or on roads in the morning and early afternoon; others occasionally are active even in mid-afternoon on hot days. The vast majority of my observations of active rattlesnakes (e.g., those found crossing roads) in Colorado occurred at air temperatures of 19–30°C (most often 22–29°C), though coiled, basking individuals near cover were found at lower temperatures. Body temperatures of a few snakes basking near dens in spring were 15–19°C, whereas those of individuals found on roads most often were 27–36°C. Snakes found on warm roads on cool nights often had flattened their bodies significantly, evidently to maximize heat gain from the road surface.

Studies of captive snakes from Weld County under simulated moonlight indicates that bright moonlight reduces activity of adults, especially in open areas, but not that of juveniles (Clarke, Chopko, and Mackessy 1996). By avoiding moonlight and being active primarily under dark conditions, adults may reduce detection by visually searching predators and synchronize their activity with that of their nocturnally active, moonlight-shy rodent prey. Juveniles, which are small and less detectable to predators, prey on diurnally active lizards and neonatal rodents and may not benefit from avoiding moonlight (Clarke, Chopko, and Mackessy 1996).

In areas where nights are cool (northern latitudes or higher elevations), little or no nocturnal activity occurs, even in summer (Gannon and Secoy 1985; Diller and Wallace 1996). In southern Idaho, observable activity peaks between about 10:00 a.m. and 3:00 p.m. in April and May; in June and July, it is bimodal, peaking between 9:00 a.m. and 1:00 p.m. and again (to a lesser extent) at around 8:00 p.m. Probability of observation is highest at air temperatures around 22°C. Body temperature of active individuals averages 28–29°C. Most active *C. viridis* have body temperatures of 20–35°C (Ernst 1992). A change from lighter to darker coloration may occur as body temperature decreases (Rahn 1942a). Presumably, this affects heat exchange.

Western rattlesnakes are not aggressive but can be vigorously defensive. When encountered in the field, they often do not rattle but remain motionless or crawl away quietly. If a human rapidly approaches, however, they are likely to rattle and assume a coiled, ready-to-strike defensive posture, perhaps sensing that they may be stepped on or attacked. Rattlers in a striking posture commonly withdraw slowly from a looming human, though if the person moves, the snake will often strike. A few

individuals that I have captured tried to hide the head beneath the body. A rattler that I encountered in Douglas County attempted to rattle, but the sound was barely audible because the rattle was wet (the snake evidently had just crossed a small creek). Carefully approaching an immobile, coiled individual may elicit slow and fast tongue flicks but no other movement. If left alone, rattlesnakes encountered in the open may remain in place or crawl away in search of cover. If cornered or harassed, rattlesnakes defend themselves by striking. When grasped, they generally attempt to bite. Females that are pregnant tend to remain quiet and immobile when approached, but after giving birth and before the offspring have dispersed, they, too, rattle and assume a striking posture (Graves 1989b). Goode and Duvall (1989) found that gravid females exhibit a temperature-dependent shift in defensive behavior, with striking most common at low body temperatures and attempted escape more typical of higher body temperatures.

Costello (1969) reported that while killing 63 rattlesnakes at a site in Weld County, the odor of the cloacal sac secretions released by the dying snakes apparently caused nearby snakes to rattle, though, of course, other factors could have been involved. Costello likened the odor to that of green apples. Graves and Duvall (1988) confirmed that cloacal sac secretions may serve as an alarm pheromone.

Reproduction and Growth. Courtship and mating in our region appear to take place primarily in summer. In southern Wyoming, snakes disperse after emergence from hibernation and do not exhibit vernal courtship behavior in the denning area (Graves and Duvall 1990). Mating occurs in early to midsummer at sites 1–6 km from winter dens (Duvall, King, and Gutzwiller 1985; King and Duvall 1990; Schuett, Buttenhoff, and Duvall 1993). Males seek out females and spend several days courting them before

Plate 8.131. Top of head of western rattlesnake (Otero County, Colorado).

mating. Male courtship behavior includes pressing the chin along the female's body (Duvall, King, and Gutzwiller 1985). In Wyoming, copulation typically lasts about 90 minutes. The mating season usually ends by late August (Duvall, King, and Gutzwiller 1985; Duvall et al. 1990; Duvall, Arnold, and Schuett 1992). Consistent with this pattern, Smith, Maslin, and Brown (1965) reported that during the summer months, rattlesnakes found under cover are often in male-female pairs. In Nebraska, Holycross (1991) recorded five instances of males accompanying females, all during the period from midsummer to early fall; one instance of spring (early April) courtship was observed (Holycross 1995). Female sexual receptivity and attractiveness seem to peak soon after the skin is shed. The number of copulations an adult may participate in during a single season under natural conditions is unknown. Crabtree and Murphy (1984) found no conclusive evidence of multiple paternity in a small sample of three litters from Montana.

Male-male combat occurs during the mating season and may be associated with competition for reproductive females (and/or resources such as good foraging sites or shelter). During combat, the two males typically raise the front end of the body vertically and attempt to overtop the other (Hersek, Owings, and Hennessy 1992). Holycross (1995) observed combat once on August 1 in Nebraska.

Reproductive females emerge from hibernation with enlarged follicles that began growing the previous year. Ovulation takes place in late spring. Pregnant females in southern Wyoming generally form aggregations 30–600 m from the winter den and do not disperse widely (Duvall, King, and Gutzwiller 1985; Graves and Duvall 1993). These females often shelter together beneath the same rocks. Such close aggregation reduces heat loss for several hours at night or during cool cloudy weather (Graves and Duvall 1987). As a result, pregnant females maintain higher body temperatures than do nonpregnant females (averaging about 29–30°C versus 25–28°C in the afternoon, and remaining a few degrees higher on average

even at night). The higher body temperatures may increase the rate of embryonic development and allow births to occur well before the onset of cold fall weather. Aggregations of pregnant females also have been observed in other areas (Klauber 1972; Baxter and Stone 1985; Gannon and Secoy 1985). In southwestern Wyoming, pregnant females may occur alone or in groups, not far from their winter dens (K. G. Ashton and T. M. Patton, unpublished data). Usually, they remain in the vicinity of adjacent rocks. In South Dakota, one adult with young was in a prairie-dog burrow, and another was within a bed of cactus *(Opuntia)* (Cunningham, Hickey, and Gowan 1996). An adult (presumably the same one) had been observed in the cactus bed for a month prior to the appearance of its young, and both parent and brood remained at the same site for at least another week.

Rattlesnakes give birth in late summer or early fall. In Weld County, young adult females produce an average of about 6 newborns per brood, whereas older females average 15–16 (Klauber 1936). Overall, females produce a single litter of 4–21 young (average 12) in late August, September, or early October. Hahn (1968) observed a female giving birth on September 3 in the San Luis Valley. Fitch (1985b) found that litters in southwestern Kansas average 10 young, including stillbirths and abortive eggs (8.8 live births per litter). Births are concentrated in August and September. In southwestern Wyoming, litters of 2–7 (average 5) young are born between August 20 and September 18 (K. G. Ashton and T. M. Patton, unpublished data). In New Mexico, litter size usually is 5–16 young and varies greatly among snakes of approximately the same size (Aldridge 1979b). Fitch (1985b) indicated average litter sizes of 5–6 and 7–8 for two areas in Utah. In southern Idaho, 5–15 (average 8) young are born between early September and mid-October (Diller and Wallace 1996). In northern Idaho (Diller and Wallace 1984), young are born from early September to early October. Litter size typically is 3–4 in the smallest females and 8–10 in large females. Hill (1943) reported that rattlesnakes in northwestern

Plate 8.132. Complete rattle of western rattlesnake (Moffat County, Colorado).

Plate 8.133. Unusual partially striped western rattlesnake (Baca County, Colorado).

Colorado and southern Wyoming give birth to an average of 15 young in late August or September; exceptionally large individuals reportedly contained 27 and 35 young. However, these data depart significantly from all other evidence for this species and evidently include counts of small follicles rather than live births.

Neonates generally do not feed prior to their first hibernation. Some researchers have observed that neonates do not over-winter with adults (Jackley, in Klauber 1972), but in southern Wyoming (Graves and Duvall 1993) and southern Saskatchewan (Gannon and Secoy 1985), at least some neonates do. They may locate these winter dens by following the odor trails of adults. Winter survival appears to be good. In northern Utah, winter mortality in a declining population averaged only 3.6 percent over four winters (Parker and Brown 1974). In British Columbia, a minimum of 55 percent of neonates survived the winter (Charland 1989). However, in colder areas at the northern limit of the range in Saskatchewan, winter mortality may be much greater (Gannon and Secoy 1984); perhaps this applies to higher elevations as well. Growth rate of juveniles in northern Utah varies from 9.5–16.0 cm per year, compared to less than 3.5 cm per year in adults (Parker and Brown 1974).

Klauber (1936) found that the smallest reproductive female in a population in Weld County was 58–59 cm (apparently TL), but a large proportion of females smaller than 70 cm TL were not reproductive. At the time they gave birth, the smallest pregnant females were about 70 cm TL. In a collection of 841 individuals, 229 were juveniles, 85 were "adolescents," and 527 were adults. In New Mexico, the smallest reproductive female was 55 cm SVL (Aldridge 1979b).

In southwestern Kansas, most individuals with 7–8 rattle segments are probably in their third year and newly mature (Fitch 1985b). Adult males are 81–104 cm SVL, and adult females are 78–95 cm SVL. Estimated survival through the fifth year is only 2.5 percent.

In northern Utah, a female first captured at an age of one year reached sexual maturity at the age of four (66 cm SVL) and produced her first litter at the age of five (Parker and Brown 1974). Previous studies of this population found that some females mature at smaller sizes. Glissmeyer (1951) reported that northern Utah females mature in 3–4 years at 56–69 cm TL. Similarly, Klauber (1972:176) found that the smallest pregnant female of the Great Basin subspecies *lutosus* was 56 cm TL. Kyle Ashton (pers. comm.) found that females in southwestern Wyoming (subspecies *concolor*) reach maturity at about 40 cm SVL.

Minimum size of sexually mature individuals in southern Idaho is 56 cm SVL in males and 70 cm SVL in females (Diller and Wallace 1996). In northern Idaho, all males are mature at 50 cm SVL (2–3 years old, with 3–5 rattle segments) (Diller and Wallace 1984). The smallest reproductive females are 55 cm SVL, and nearly all females are mature at 59 cm SVL (4–6 years old, with 4–7 rattle segments). One 63-cm-SVL female with nine rattle segments was not mature. In British Columbia, males mature at 53–54 cm SVL (3–4 years old), females at 65 cm SVL (5–7 years old) (Charland 1989); many females do not produce litters until they are 70–76 cm SVL (Macartney, Gregory, and Charland 1990).

These data suggest that in Colorado, females probably produce their first litter at an age no younger than 4–5 years. Gannon and Secoy (1984) examined size frequency distributions in Saskatchewan and concluded that *C. viridis* there mature as young as two years old. However, the presumed age groupings were based on very small sample sizes and were not confirmed by measurements of recaptured individuals of known age; the age of maturity for females was likely underestimated.

In most years in Colorado and adjacent regions, about 50–75 percent of adult females produce young (Klauber 1936; Rahn 1942b; Aldridge 1979b; Gannon and Secoy 1984; Fitch 1985b; Diller and Wallace 1996). The frequency of reproduction among adult females sometimes is much lower (e.g., as low as 13 percent in Utah [Glissmeyer 1951]) and probably varies with resource availability and female nutritional status (Diller and Wallace 1996). Most adult females produce young at intervals of 2–3 years; pregnancy in successive years seems to be rare (Gannon and Secoy 1984; King and Duvall 1990; K. G. Aston and T. M. Patton, unpublished data).

Potential longevity, based on observation of captives, is about 30 years, but the oldest individuals in natural populations generally are much younger.

Food and Predators. Known prey in Colorado includes the plains spadefoot, side-blotched lizard, lesser earless lizard, short-horned lizard, prairie and plateau lizard, plateau striped whiptail, ringneck pheasant *(Phasianus colchicus)* (juvenile), nestling songbirds, pocket mouse *(Perognathus* sp.), prairie dog *(Cynomys* sp.), ground squirrel *(Spermophilus* sp.), chipmunk *(Tamias* sp.), Ord's kangaroo rat *(Dipodomys ordii)*, vole *(Microtus* sp.), deer mouse *(Peromyscus maniculatus* and other *Peromyscus*), western harvest mouse *(Reithrodontomys megalotis)*, and cottontail *(Sylvilagus* sp.) (Klauber 1937, 1972; Hill 1943; Stabler 1943; Smith, Maslin, and Brown 1965; Ludlow 1981; Chiszar, Smith, and Defusco 1993; Kyle Ashton, pers. comm.; pers. obs.). A 47.5-cm male that I found alive but mortally injured on a road in San Juan County, Utah, contained the tail of a whiptail lizard and a mostly undigested desert spiny lizard (80 mm SVL). Lizards are common in the diet of the young, whereas adults most often prey on small mammals. However, Graves (1991) reported that a neonate ate an adult deer mouse *(Peromyscus maniculatus)* that weighed three-fourths as much as the snake did.

In southern Wyoming, the most important prey species for adults is the deer mouse *(Peromyscus maniculatus)* (Duvall, King, and Gutzwiller 1985). In Idaho, it is juvenile ground squirrels and deer mice; in addition to other small mammals, the diet includes

Plate 8.134. Unusual nearly patternless western rattlesnake (Baca County, Colorado). *Fred Woeffle.*

western whiptails, horned lizards, and Great Basin spadefoot toads (Diller and Johnson 1988, 1996). Cannibalism is rare (Klauber 1972), but an 84-cm female *C. viridis* found in Montana had eaten a 26-cm *C. viridis,* along with four montane voles *(Microtus montanus)* (Genter 1984). Scavenging of carrion sometimes occurs (Diller 1990; Ernst 1992).

Adults of at least some ground squirrel species commonly approach rattlesnakes and kick dirt at them; sometimes they even attack and bite the snakes (Coss and Owings 1989). The blood proteins of ground squirrels exhibit strong natural resistance to rattlesnake venom (Coss and Owings 1989).

Western rattlesnakes are essentially ambush predators that wait for potential prey to come within striking distance, though hunger or scarcity of prey may result in active foraging (Chiszar et al. 1981; Duvall, King, and Gutzwiller 1985). Visual and thermal cues are important in stimulating a successful strike (Haverly and Kardong 1996). The typical strike consists of a sudden forward movement of the head as curves of the neck and anterior body are straightened, a biting or stabbing action with the open jaws, release of venom, and, often, a rapid recoil (Kardong 1986). Van Riper (1955) determined that the forward velocity of the strike averages 246 cm per second, with a maximum speed of 277 cm per second (6.2 miles per hour). After envenomation, rattlesnakes release rodent prey, which ensures that the rodent will not bite and injure the snake. Lizards, which pose relatively little threat to the snake, generally are not released by adults of subspecies *viridis* but usually are released by the smaller subspecies *concolor* (Hayes 1990). This behavior may be size-related; in Elbert County, Chiszar, Smith, and Defusco (1993) observed a juvenile *viridis* (less than one year old) bite, release, retrieve, and swallow an adult prairie lizard *(Sceloporus*

undulatus). Small birds, which might fly a short distance and escape retrieval, also are more likely to be held after envenomation (Hayes 1992).

When the snake strikes, two hollow fangs on the short rotatable maxillary bones at the front of the upper jaw swing downward and forward to deliver the venom. Fang length increases with the size of the snake. Several replacement fangs are located behind the functional fangs. The amount of venom injected increases with prey size (Hayes, Lavín-Murcio, and Kardong 1995). Nearly one-third of available venom is released when a mouse is bitten (Hayes 1990). The venom glands are positioned at the sides of the upper jaw. Venom not only kills prey but also aids in digestion (Thomas and Pough 1979). Venoms of juveniles and adults may differ in their relative toxicity and digestion-facilitating capacity. A bitten and envenomated rodent usually staggers away and quickly dies. The snake, flicking its tongue, eventually finds the rodent by following its scent trail. Using chemical cues derived from the venom, individual mouse odors, and fang puncture, the snake can differentiate the trail of the struck mouse from the trails of other mice and of the same mouse before it was envenomated (Chiszar et al. 1990, 1991; Furry, Swain, and Chiszar 1991; Lavín-Murcio, Robinson, and Kardong 1993; Lavín-Murcio and Kardong 1995). Eventually, the snake swallows its prey headfirst, using chemical and other cues to find the head.

Western rattlesnakes may drink water when the opportunity arises. Aird and Aird

(1990) reported that a *C. v. lutosus* drank from a small pool of water that had collected between its coils during a rainstorm. In southwestern Wyoming, Ashton and Johnson (1998) observed a *C. v. concolor* drink rainwater that had accumulated in a small depression in a rock and on the snake's own skin.

Humans are the most important "predators" on rattlesnakes in Colorado. Other primary predators probably include eagles, hawks, and occasional mammalian carnivores. Klauber (1972:1,081) reported the golden eagle *(Aquila chrysaetos)* as a predator in Colorado. Mackessy (1998) reported predation on an adult by a northern harrier *(Circus cyaneus)* in Baca County. Plumpton and Lutz (1993) found a western rattlesnake among prey remains at a burrowing owl *(Athene cunicularia)* burrow in Adams County and suspected that the snake may have been scavenged from a road. I have a report of a racer eating a juvenile rattlesnake; large coachwhips probably also prey on rattlesnakes in Colorado. Graves (1989a) reported several instances of dead, and living but lethargic, juveniles being attacked by ants in southern Wyoming and suggested that ant predation on small rattlesnakes may not be uncommon. However, all of the snakes had been implanted with radio transmitters that were quite large in relation to the size of the snake, and it is possible that the surgery/transmitter contributed significantly to the snakes' demise.

Remarks. This is a dangerously venomous snake. Envenomation in humans may result in tissue destruction, hemorrhaging, cardiovascular and respiratory degeneration, paralysis, and other debilitating effects. However, people are not often bitten in Colorado, and those that are rarely die as a result. Some bites inject little or no venom. Most result from careless handling by humans. Nevertheless, persons living in areas inhabited by rattlesnakes (including some suburban areas) should use appropriate caution. Gardeners, for example, should avoid reaching under bushes without looking first. Hikers should watch their step (and their handholds when scrambling up a rocky slope). Parents should exercise vigilance on behalf of their children—smaller humans are at higher risk of serious problems if envenomated. If you are bitten by a rattlesnake, call the Poison Control Center at (303) 629–1123 or dial 911 and follow instructions.

Venom toxicity decreases with the age and size of the snake. Venom of juveniles of the subspecies *viridis* is more toxic to mice than is an equal dose of adult venom (Fiero et al. 1972). Mackessy (1988) found that the venom of adult *Crotalus viridis* from California is less toxic but has higher protease activity (digestive function) than that of juveniles. The higher toxicity in juveniles may be due to greater neurotoxic action (Mackessy 1988). The higher protease activity of adult venom may be related to the fact that adults feed on relatively large, bulky prey that is more difficult to digest than the slender-bodied prey (often lizards) consumed by smaller individuals. Despite relatively low venom toxicity as compared to juveniles, large rattlesnakes are potentially more dangerous because they contain much more venom. In growing from 40 to 80 cm TL, the volume of venom that the snake is capable of injecting increases five times (Klauber 1972:812). Hayes (1990) reported that the quantity of venom injected increases exponentially with snake size.

Significant differences in toxicity also exist in the venoms of the two subspecies in Colorado. Glenn and Straight (1977) found that drop for drop, the venom of *concolor* is 10–30 times more toxic than that of any other *C. viridis* subspecies, perhaps due to its potent neurotoxic effect (Aird and Kaiser 1985; Mackessy 1988). Aird, Seebart, and Kaiser (1988) found that the composition of the venoms of subspecies *viridis* and *concolor* differs greatly from that of subspecies *lutosus* of Idaho and Utah.

The venom-conducting fangs of rattlesnakes are not as large as one might imagine. Klauber (1939) measured the fangs of hundreds of individuals from Weld County and found that they varied in length from 2.0–8.4 mm, with larger snakes having longer fangs. The fangs of small rattlesnakes in west-central Colorado and east-central Utah are usually about 4–5 mm long (Klauber 1939).

The rattle of a rattlesnake grows by one segment each time the snake sheds its skin, which may occur 1–4 times each year. Captives often develop long rattles (up to at least 38 segments [Chiszar and Smith 1994]), but under natural conditions the rattle is kept relatively short as a result of breakage. Klauber (1940a) found that most adults in Weld County possess 4–6 rattle segments; only one of 621 individuals had as many as 10. Rattlesnakes usually enter their second hibernation with five rattle segments (Klauber 1972:333). Fitch (1985b) found that in spring in southwestern Kansas, the modal number of rattle segments is 1 at age 0–1 years, 5 at 1–2 years, and 7–8 at 2–3 years (evidently, the basal segment was not counted). About 45 percent of his sample had 7–10 rattle segments. I observed complete rattles with four segments on 36-cm-SVL individuals (probably in their third calendar year) in late May in Montezuma County.

The sound emitted from a vibrating rattle is fairly loud and may continue uninterrupted for several minutes in an aroused snake. Chadwick and Rahn (1954) found that rattle speed of adult *C. viridis* from Wyoming increases from 21 cycles per second at 10°C to 99 cycles per second at 40°C. The burrowing owl and bullsnake, which share prairie-dog burrows with rattlesnakes, each produce a hissing vocalization that sounds very much like a rattlesnake's rattle.

Taxonomy and Variation. Klauber (1972) used scale counts, body size, and coloration to distinguish among the subspecies of *C. viridis*. Subspecies *viridis* typically has 27 or 25 dorsal scale rows at midbody, 13 or more scale rows at midtail, green or brown dorsal coloration, and an adult size commonly exceeding 85 cm TL. Subspecies *concolor* has 23 or 25 scale rows at midbody; 12 or fewer scale rows at midtail; straw, cream, or yellow coloration (pinkish in some areas); and rarely exceeds 65 cm TL. Subspecies *nuntius* resembles *concolor* in scalation and body size, but the coloration is pink, red, or red-brown. By Klauber's criteria, rattlesnakes from most of Wyoming,

eastern Colorado, and the San Luis Valley are readily identified as subspecies *viridis*. Those from Mesa, Delta, and Garfield counties (Table 8.4) and from east-central Utah fit well with Klauber's description of *concolor*. In southwestern Wyoming, rattlesnakes conforming with subspecies *viridis* occur in eastern Sweetwater County (Ashton, Smith, and Chiszar 1997), whereas those in the western part of the same county, along the Green River and its direct tributaries, reportedly are subspecies *concolor* (Baxter and Stone 1985). However, rattlesnakes from along the Green River in Colorado and from elsewhere in the northwestern portion of the state conform most closely with *viridis* in scalation but in coloration may resemble *viridis* or *concolor*, or exhibit intermediate coloration. Specimens resembling *viridis* in coloration are from northern Moffat and Rio Blanco counties. Specimens whose coloration resembles that of *concolor* are from the western and southern parts of the area. Individuals with intermediate coloration are scattered throughout the two-county area. Specimens from Moffat and Routt counties may exceed 90 cm SVL, yet some resemble *concolor* in coloration. Moffat, Routt, and Rio Blanco counties apparently constitute an area of intergradation between *concolor* and *viridis*.

Despite apparent intergradation, *C. v. viridis* and *C. v. concolor* appear to be well differentiated over most of their ranges. Foote and Macmahon (1977) found that allozyme samples of subspecies *viridis* from Colorado are not as close to subspecies *concolor* from Utah as other pairs of *Crotalus* species are to each other. Similarly, in an unpublished dissertation, Aird (1984a) found that *C. v. viridis, C. v. concolor*, and *C. v. lutosus* (Great Basin rattlesnake) are morphologically and genetically well differentiated, and he went so far as to conclude that these three taxa are "legitimate biological species." However, these studies did not adequately assess variation in the zones of apparent intergradation, so the status of these taxa must be regarded as unresolved.

McCoy (1962a) examined three specimens of *C. viridis* from Montezuma County

County (sample size)	Midbody	Midtail
Moffat (18)	25 (23-27)	13 (11-16)
Rio Blanco (7)	25 (25-27)	14 (12-14)
Mesa, Delta, Garfield (22)	23 (21-25)	12 (11-14)
Montrose (4)	25 (25)	13 (13)
San Miguel (1)	25	13
Montezuma (20)	25 (25)	13 (11-13)
La Plata (1)	23	13

Table 8.4. Variation (mode-range) in the number of dorsal scale rows in Crotalus viridis in western Colorado. The sample areas, from top to bottom, represent a north-to-south transect of about 440 km.

in southwestern Colorado and assigned them to the subspecies *nuntius* because they possessed 25 scale rows at midbody, 12 scale rows at midtail, and had tan or light brown dorsal ground color. However, these characteristics do not unequivocally identify the specimens as *nuntius*, according to Klauber's criteria. In his original description of *C. v. nuntius*, Klauber (1935) assigned a specimen from the Four Corners area to the subspecies *confluentus* (= *viridis*). More recently, Klauber (in Douglas 1966) examined six specimens from Mesa Verde, Montezuma County, and concluded that they were "stunted offshoots" of *viridis* that were more like *concolor* than *nuntius* in coloration and markings (Douglas 1966:738). The largest specimen from Mesa Verde examined by Douglas (1966) was 85 cm long and was thought to be a rather typical example of subspecies *viridis*. Thus, Montezuma County rattlesnakes do not appear to represent subspecies *nuntius*.

Additional material from Montezuma County has clarified the situation somewhat. In a sample of 20 specimens that I examined, all had 25 scale rows at midbody, a characteristic typical of local populations of *viridis*. About half of the specimens had 13 scale rows at midtail (a *viridis* characteristic); the others had 11 or 12 scale rows (typical of *concolor* and *nuntius*). Coloration in this area generally

is like that of viridis, or similar to *concolor*, or unlike typical *viridis, concolor*, or *nuntius*. The few specimens that I examined from elsewhere in southwestern Colorado also exhibited a mixture of *viridis* and *concolor* characteristics, with scalation tending toward intermediacy. The small number of specimens that I examined from extreme southeastern Utah also appeared to be unlike typical members of any of the three subspecies. One individual from San Juan County, Utah, was tan and lacked the *viridis* pattern of pale edging on the dorsal blotches and pale stripes on the sides of the head, but it was much larger (83 cm SVL) than typical *concolor* and *nuntius*. I therefore suggest that western rattlesnakes from southwestern Colorado (north to Montrose County and east to La Plata County, or perhaps Archuleta County) should be regarded as *viridis-concolor* intergrades or (better) simply as *Crotalus viridis*.

Western rattlesnakes in Colorado sometimes exhibit unusual coloration. Some individuals show extensive fusion of the dorsal blotches (pers. obs.), which also has been observed in southwestern Wyoming (Schuett and Kraus 1982). Others, in Baca and Yuma counties, are nearly patternless and lack the usual mid-dorsal and lateral blotches (Aird 1984b; pers. obs.). Patternless individuals are known from Montana as well (Slowinski and Rasmussen 1985).

Plate 8.135. Massasauga (Crowley County, Colorado).

Massasauga

Sistrurus catenatus (Rafinesque, 1818)

Recognition. Horny rattle or button on end of tail; usually nine large, symmetrically arranged scales on top of head (sometimes with several small scales interspersed); head broader than neck; pit on each side of face between (but lower than) eye and nostril; dorsum blotched; dorsal scales keeled; pupil vertically elongate in bright light; usually less than 50 cm SVL in Colorado, averaging around 38–40 cm TL (Hobert 1997); tail length 10–16 (average 12) percent of SVL in males, 8–13 (average 9) percent in females (Hobert 1997). *Newborn young:* 14–25 cm TL (Gloyd 1955; Greene and Oliver 1965;

Ernst 1992); average 14.8 cm SVL, 16.4 cm TL for one litter in Colorado (S. P. Mackessy, pers. comm.); in Colorado, 14–22 cm SVL before first hibernation (Hobert 1997); tail yellow.

Distribution. Great Lakes region of southern Ontario and western New York southwest through the Midwest and central and southern Great Plains to southeastern Arizona, northern Mexico, and southern Texas. Occurs in southeastern Colorado at

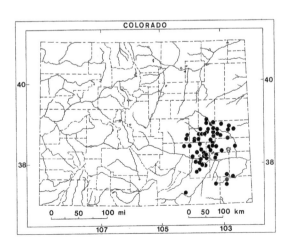

Map 8.50. Distribution of the massasauga in Colorado.

Plate 8.136. Massasauga with incomplete rattle (Lincoln County, Colorado). *Lauren Livo and Steve Wilcox.*

elevations below about 5,500 feet (1,675 m). Early distributional records were summarized by Maslin (1959), Smith, Maslin, and Brown (1965), Brown, Haberman, and Kappel (1970), and Hammerson (1982c). Recent surveys (Hammerson et al. 1991p; Pegler, Chiszar, and Smith 1995; Mackessy, Hobert, et al. 1996; Hobert 1997; Mackessy 1998; Montgomery et al. 1998c) expanded the known range in Colorado somewhat, particularly south into Las Animas, Baca, and the southern portions of Otero, Bent, and Prowers counties, and west into El Paso County. Previously (1882), the reliable biologist A. E. Beardsley collected a specimen in Baca County, but no specific location was recorded, so the record was not mapped (Hammerson 1982c). The heart of the range and maximum abundance in Colorado appear to be in southern Lincoln County (Hobert 1997; Mackessy 1998). There still remains a significant hiatus between the known distribution in Colorado and that in the adjacent states of Oklahoma (Webb 1970; Conant and Collins 1991), New Mexico (Degenhardt, Painter, and Price 1996), and, to a lesser degree, Kansas (Collins 1993). In Kansas, massasaugas range westward almost to the Colorado border (KU 221506). Possibly, additional fieldwork will document the presence of massasaugas in some of the intervening areas, but the hiatus may be real and perhaps attributable to natural habitat changes (basalt mesas and canyons along the southern edge of the range in Colorado) and habitat alterations resulting from human activity. Satellite imagery reveals an extensive agricultural landscape along the eastern and southeastern margins of the massasauga's range in Colorado.

Conservation Status. Within its restricted range in Colorado, the massasauga occurs in a large number of sites and is locally fairly common in some areas (Hobert 1997, Mackessy 1998). Some prairie habitat has been lost as a result of conversion to incompatible agricultural uses, and many massasaugas die on roads, but this snake should remain secure and unthreatened within most of its current range in Colorado as long as present land use (mainly livestock grazing) is maintained. Cattle ranchers sympathetic to, or at least tolerant of, the presence of massasaugas on their land do exist in southeastern Colorado, and some of them maintain large tracts of high-quality prairie rangeland that support the state's largest massasauga populations (Hobert 1997). Studies of massasaugas in eastern North America indicate that populations separated by only a few kilometers may exhibit significant genetic differentiation (Gibbs et al. 1997), implying that protection of many local populations will be necessary for effective conservation of the full range of genetic variation in this species.

Habitat. Habitat in Colorado consists of dry plains grassland and sandhill areas. Massasaugas may be attracted to sandy soils supporting abundant rodent populations (Hobert 1997). These soils also provide favorable habitat for other prey, such as lizards. The snakes hibernate singly in rodent burrows, often in firm, loamy soils adjacent to sandy areas used for feeding (Mackessy 1998). Seasonal movements between different habitats have been observed in eastern North America (Reinert and Kodrich 1982).

Activity. Emergence from hibernation in Colorado usually takes place in mid-April,

Plate 8.137. Massasauga showing large scales on top of head (Crowley County, Colorado).

and activity generally ends in late October, with a few individuals still active in early November in some years (Hobert 1997; Mackessy 1998). Hobert (1997) found massasaugas in Colorado most frequently in September and October.

In Colorado, this snake sometimes is active during daylight hours, especially in the afternoon in spring and fall. During hot summer weather, however, it prowls mainly in the early evening and at night (mostly during the first few hours of darkness), with some activity in the morning and before sunset. A similar pattern has been observed in Missouri (Seigel 1986). Hobert (1997) found that activity occurs at air temperatures of 14–30°C (mainly 20–26°C); I found one active at 6:30 p.m. in June at an air temperature of 31°C. Mackessy (1998) reported that radio-tagged massasaugas are most likely to be on the ground surface at air temperatures of 25–30°C.

Hobert (1997) found evidence of seasonally changing directional movements of dozens of massasaugas in an area in Lincoln County. Evidently, this reflects migrations between winter and summer habitats. Two snakes that were radio-tracked for a substantial period of time (94–100 days) during one activity season in Lincoln County had activity ranges of 0.9–1.2 km² (2.4–3.4 km maximum diameter) (Mackessy 1998), much larger than those of massasaugas in eastern North America (Reinert and Kodrich 1982; Weatherhead and Prior 1992).

Massasaugas encountered in the field may remain immobile and quiet, flee into a rodent burrow, or exhibit vigorous defensive behavior (striking, rattling).

Reproduction and Growth. The seasonal occurrence of courtship and mating are poorly known, as are most aspects of reproduction in Colorado. In captivity, Chiszar et al. (1976) observed courtship behavior in late June. Male courtship

behavior includes rubbing the chin on the female's head and neck and stroking the female's tail with a loop of his tail. A male and female possibly engaged in courtship were found on September 3 in southeastern Colorado (Mackessy 1996). A 38-cm-SVL female found dead in Colorado in late May contained five "eggs" (Hobert 1997). A 38.5-cm-SVL female collected on July 20 in Lincoln County gave birth to seven young on August 24 (S. P. Mackessy, pers. comm.). Field evidence indicates that the earliest births in Colorado occur in late August and early September (Hobert 1997). Litter size of massasaugas in the western part of the range averages around 6 young (range 3–11) (Gloyd 1955; Greene and Oliver 1965; Klauber 1972; Fitch 1985b).

Hobert (1997) found that the smallest reproductive female was 32.5 cm SVL (average 37 cm SVL), and he estimated from size-class structure that a massasauga of that size is in its third calendar year. The smallest pregnant females in the eastern part of the range generally are about 45–55 cm SVL (Wright 1941; Reinert 1981; Seigel 1986). In captivity, this snake may live at least 20 years.

Food and Predators. In the western part of the range, massasaugas feed opportunistically on various frogs, lizards, small snakes (such as the ground snake and lined snake), shrews, and mice, and they sometimes eat centipedes and scavenge road kills (Greene and Oliver 1965; Klauber 1972; Lowe, Schwalbe, and Johnson 1986; Greene 1990; Degenhardt, Painter, and Price 1996). In Colorado, young massasaugas generally eat lizards and add rodents to the diet as they grow larger. Known prey in Colorado includes the lesser earless lizard, prairie lizard, Great Plains skink, six-lined racerunner, western harvest mouse *(Reithrodontomys megalotis)*, plains pocket mouse *(Perognathus flavescens)*, deer mouse *(Peromyscus maniculatus)*, centipedes, and plains spadefoot (Hobert 1997). Schwammer (1983, cited by Ernst 1992) reported a massasauga feeding on carrion in Colorado. Webb (1970) recorded the collared lizard as a prey item in Oklahoma. Known prey in Kansas includes the Texas horned lizard (Greene and Oliver 1965) and eggs of the lark sparrow *(Chondestes grammacus)* (Brush and Ferguson 1986). Neonate massasaugas may wiggle the tail to lure insect-eating prey (Schuett, Clark, and Kraus 1984). Lizards or toads may mistake the yellow tail for an insect larva.

Probable predators in Colorado include various carnivorous mammals, hawks, racers, and coachwhips. Predation by the loggerhead shrike *(Lanius ludovicianus)* was observed in New Mexico (Chapman and Castro 1972).

Remarks. The massasauga is venomous, and its bite is dangerous to humans. However, this little snake is not aggressive (though it may be highly defensive when disturbed), and the bite rarely is fatal. Klauber (1939) found that the fangs are relatively short (4.5–5.5 mm). The sound of the rattle is much quieter than that of the western rattlesnake.

Taxonomy and Variation. With limited material, Maslin (1965) concluded that massasaugas in Colorado are intergrades between subspecies *S. c. edwardsii* (Baird and Girard, 1953) of the extreme southwestern part of the range and *S. c. tergemimus* (Say, 1823) of the central Great Plains region. Hobert's (1997) more comprehensive study using much larger samples demonstrated that massasaugas in Colorado are most similar to *edwardsii in coloration, scalation, size, and habitat and should be included in that subspecies.*

Appendix A

Species of Possible
Occurence in Colorado

Amphisbaenid (*Bipes* sp.). James's (1823) account of the Long Expedition that traveled through Colorado in 1820 mentions a two-legged amphisbaenid (worm lizard) reportedly found between Crook and Sterling in Logan County (Dundee 1996) in northeastern Colorado. Most herpetologists have dismissed this record as erroneous for two main reasons. First, James claimed that the individual was difficult to capture because it was too swift, impossible behavior for a slow-moving fossorial amphisbaenid. At the very least, this suggests that there was some confusion about field observations. The specimen was reported as missing, and the expedition lost its written description of the animal when certain members of the party deserted the group, so no evidence exists to confirm this dubious identification. Second, the nearest known occurrences of amphisbaenids are far away in Florida and Mexico. Nevertheless, several persons (not experienced herpetologists) claim to have seen animals resembling *Bipes* in Colorado and Nebraska, and the validity of James's record has been debated (Maslin 1959; Campbell 1980; Dundee 1980, 1996; Gans and Papenfuss 1980; Smith and Holland 1981). Certainly, there is plenty of suitable sandy soil in the area, but the climate seems much too cold. Because amphisbaenids can be locally abundant where they occur, it is likely that additional specimens would have been found in subsequent years if these reptiles actually occurred in Great Plains region.

Rubber boa *(Charina bottae).* Bernard and Brown (1978) and Simon (1979) indicated that the rubber boa occurs in Colorado, but these publications contain only generalized information, and the authors simply may have predicted that the boa occurs in the state, inasmuch as the species inhabits the Uinta Mountains of northeastern Utah. However, the observational records of Dinosaur National Monument contain a description of a juvenile rubber boa (about 38 cm long, with pinkish-maroon coloration) that reportedly emerged from a meadow, crossed a trail, and disappeared beneath a log by a rock escarpment on a warm, sunny day at noon on August 22, 1979, in the canyon bottom at Echo Park in Moffat County (observed by Lisa Green), but no evidence exists to confirm the identification. If rubber boas do occur in the region, one might expect to find them in montane riparian habitats at higher elevations rather than in a relatively dry and warm canyon bottom such as that at Echo Park. Yet the wooded canyon-bottom riparian zone at Echo Park may indeed be suitable—the high canyon walls shade the canyon bottom for much of the day, and streamside trees provide ample cover and shade in some areas. Nevertheless, until firm documentation is obtained, the status of this snake in Colorado remains uncertain. *Recognition:* Dorsal scales small and smooth (unkeeled); large scales on top of head; tail blunt, shaped almost like head; pupil vertically elongate; elongate throat scales absent; maximum size about 83 cm TL. Male: usually a spur near each side of vent (spur smaller, or absent, in female). Juvenile: dorsum pinkish to tan (olive green or brown in adult).

Eastern Hognose snake *(Heterodon platirhinos).* A large individual (UCM 1006) was collected along the Arkansas River nine miles west of Lamar in Bent County on May 3, 1943. The collector is listed as Gene Main. Maslin (1950:92), in discussing another species, stated that "Mr. Main entertains a clientele of truck-driving friends by identifying reptiles picked up by them on the highway," which perhaps casts some doubt on the accuracy of the collection data. Although no other *H. platirhinos* have been found in Colorado, this specimen and others from the southwestern margin of Kansas (Collins 1993) suggest the possible natural occurrence of this species in the Arkansas River valley or along the Cimarron River of southeastern Colorado. *Recognition:* The eastern hognose snake resembles the western hognose snake, but the eastern species has 25 (versus 23) dorsal scale rows at midbody, the prefrontal scales are in contact (versus separated by small scales), and the underside of the tail is not black; the eastern hognose also grows larger (to 116 cm TL).

Brown snake *(Storeria dekayi).* Ellis and Henderson (1913) listed a specimen (apparently no longer in existence) collected in Las Animas County by Arthur E. Beardsley in 1883 (Hammerson 1982a). The nearest occurrence of this species is in southwestern Kansas (Collins 1993). Because several other of Beardsley's questionable records have proven reliable (Hammerson 1981, 1982a), I believe that it was indeed this snake that Beardsley found and that the brown snake at least formerly inhabited Colorado. Considering that it took more than 100 years for Beardsley's record of the canyon treefrog in Las Animas County to be confirmed and that several other disjunct populations exist in southeastern Colorado, it would not be surprising if further field surveys yielded evidence of this snake.

Plethodontidae. Plethodontid salamanders of the genera *Plethodon* and *Aneides* were widespread in central North America during the early Tertiary (e.g., lower Miocene of southeastern Montana) (Tihen and Wake 1981). These genera are represented today in the mountains of New Mexico. I wonder whether a plethodontid might yet exist undetected in the mountains of Colorado. Cockerell (1927:112) also mentioned this possibility. I suspect that severe conditions in Colorado during the Pleistocene probably eliminated any that may have existed until then, but there is a remote possibility that an unglaciated area of the San Juan Mountains might harbor a population of one of these salamanders.

Amphibians and Reptiles in National Parks, National Monuments, and River Canyons of Colorado and Eastern Utah

Table B.1 indicates the species of amphibians and reptiles occurring in several of the frequently visited national parks and monuments in Colorado and eastern Utah, as well as some additional areas in eastern Utah popular with river rafters. Though this book focuses on Colorado, I include these eastern Utah locations because the composition of the herpetofauna and the natural history of the amphibians and reptiles in eastern Utah and western Colorado are very similar and because a detailed regional natural history guide to the herpetofauna of eastern Utah currently does not exist.

The following list of species that do not occur in Colorado but do inhabit eastern Utah west to the Colorado and Green rivers should be useful to the many travelers who visit both Colorado and eastern Utah each year. I did not include areas farther west in Utah because the composition of the herpetofauna changes significantly west of the Green and Colorado rivers.

Desert Horned Lizard *(Phrynosoma platyrhinos)*. A disjunct population occurs in the Ouray-Jensen area of Uintah County, Utah. This species differs from other horned lizards in the region by having large spines on the back of its head and one row of enlarged scales fringing each side of its body.

Chuckwalla *(Sauromalus ater)*. This large, robust, rock-dwelling lizard occurs around the Colorado River in eastern Utah from the vicinity of Glen Canyon Dam to near Hite and the Henry Mountains of southeastern Utah (Tanner and Avery 1964). It grows to about 42 cm TL and has a thick tail with a blunt tip. When the lungs are not greatly inflated, it has loose folds of skin along the sides of the body. Unlike other reptiles in the region, it is primarily a vegetarian.

Desert Night Lizard *(Xantusia vigilis)*. This secretive lizard occurs under and among rocks or fallen plant material (e.g., yucca) from the Henry Mountains and Natural Bridges National Monument (east of the Colorado River) south to the San Juan River (Tanner 1957b, 1958a). It is the only lizard in the region with lidless eyes and vertical pupils. It grows to about 6 cm SVL.

	Pawnee National Grassland (CO)	Comanche National Grassland (CO)	Rocky Mountain National Park (CO)	Black Canyon of the Gunnison (CO)	Great Sand Dunes Natl. Monument (CO)	Colorado National Monument (CO)	Mesa Verde National Park (CO)	Hovenweep National Monument (CO-UT)	Dinosaur National Monument (CO-UT)	Gray/Desolation Canyons (UT)	Arches National Park (UT)	Canyonlands National Park (UT)	San Juan River Canyon (UT)
Tiger Salamander	x	x	x	x	x	x	x	x	x	x	x	x	x
Couch's Spadefoot		x											
Plains Spadefoot	x	x			x			?					x
Great Basin Spadefoot						x			x	x	x	x	
New Mexico Spadefoot		x							x		x	x	x
Mountain Toad			x										
Great Plains Toad	x	x			x						x	x	x
Green Toad		x											
Red-spotted Toad		x				x	x	x			x	x	x
Woodhouse's Toad	x	x			x	x	x	x	x	x	x	x	x
Northern Cricket Frog	?												
Canyon Treefrog		?				x						x	x
Western Chorus Frog	x		x	x	x		x	x	x			?	
Narrowmouth Toad		x											
Plains Leopard Frog		x											
Bullfrog	?	x										x	?
Northern Leopard Frog	x		(x)	x		x			x	x	x	x	x
Wood Frog			x										
Snapping Turtle	x	x											
Painted Turtle		x											
Ornate Box Turtle		x											
Yellow Mud Turtle		x											
Spiny Softshell		x											
Collared Lizard		x		x		x	x	x			x	x	x
Longnose Leopard Lizard						x		x			x	x	x
Lesser Earless Lizard	x	x											?
Texas Horned Lizard		x											
Short-horned Lizard	x	x		x	x	x	x	x	x	x	x	x	x
Roundtail Horned Lizard		?											
Sagebrush Lizard				x		x	x	x	x	x	x	x	x
Desert Spiny Lizard								x				x	x
Plateau and Prairie Lizards	x	x		x	x	x	x	x	x	x	x	x	x
Tree Lizard				x		x	x	x	x	x	x	x	x
Side-blotched Lizard						x		x	x	x	x	x	x
Triploid Checkered Whiptail		x											
Six-lined Racerunner	?	x											
Diploid Checkered Whiptail		x											
Western Whiptail						x		x	x	x	x	x	x
Plateau Striped Whiptail						x	x	x			x	x	x
Variable Skink					x		x						
Many-lined Skink	x												
Great Plains Skink		x											
Texas Blind Snake		x											
Glossy Snake		x						x					x
Racer	x	x						x	x	x	x	x	
Ringneck Snake		x											
Great Plains Rat Snake		x				x			x	x	x	x	
Western Hognose Snake	x	x											
Night Snake		x				x	x				x	x	x
Common Kingsnake		x						x					x
Milk Snake	x	x		x	x	x	x	x	?		x	x	?	?
Smooth Green Snake		?		x			x	x	?				
Coachwhip		x											
Striped Whipsnake						x	x	x	x	x	x	x	x
Northern Water Snake	?	x											
Bullsnake/Gopher Snake	x	x		x	x	x	x	x	x	x	x	x	x
Longnose Snake		x											?
Ground Snake		x											
SW. Black-headed Snake						x					x	x	x	x
Plains Black-headed Snake	?	x											
Blackneck Garter Snake		x									x	x	x
W. Terrestrial Garter Snake	?	x	x	x	x	x	x	x	x	x	x	x	x
Western Ribbon Snake		?											
Plains Garter Snake	x	x											
Common Garter Snake	?												
Lined Snake		x											
Western Rattlesnake	x	x		x	x	x	x	x	x	x	x	x	x
Massasauga		x											

Table B.1. Amphibians and reptiles of the national parks and monuments and the river canyons of Colorado and selected areas in eastern Utah. Parentheses indicate former occurrence.

Key to Amphibians and Reptiles of Colorado

The following keys consist of a numbered sequence of paired alternative statements. Begin at number 1 and decide which of the two statements (1A or 1B) best describes the specimen in question (in a few cases, three alternative statements, A, B, and C, are listed). Each statement is followed either by the name of a species or by the number of the next pair of statements that should be consulted. Continue until the statement that best describes the specimen leads to a species name. The recognition section, photographs, and distribution maps in the species accounts can be used to verify doubtful identifications.

I have attempted to facilitate identification by using (whenever possible) easily observable, objective criteria and by including corroborative characteristics for the more difficult identifications. However, an aberrant or deformed specimen, or an escaped or released pet of a species that normally does not inhabit our area, may be difficult to identify or may "key out" to the wrong species.

1A. Skin scaly or digits (if present) clawed — "Key to Reptile Groups."

1B. Skin often smooth and slick, sometimes rough and warty, not scaly or leathery; digits (if present) unclawed; large tail fin sometimes present — 2.

2A. Limbs present — 3.

2B. Limbs absent — "Key to Amphibian Larvae."

3A. Tail fin large and membranous; no eyelids; strictly aquatic — "Key to Amphibian Larvae."

3B. Tail absent or, if present, lacking large membranous fin; eyelids present; aquatic or terrestrial — "Key to Metamorphosed Amphibians."

KEY TO AMPHIBIAN LARVAE

This key can be used to identify amphibian larvae in the later stages of development but prior to appearance of the front legs (Fig. C.1). Hatchlings are difficult to identify, so try to obtain large specimens for identification purposes. A hand lens or low-power microscope will be needed to examine mouth parts, which provide useful clues to tadpole identity. The labial tooth row formulas specified in the keys (e.g., 2/3) are translated as follows: number of tooth rows on upper (anterior) lip/number of tooth rows on lower (posterior) lip. A labial tooth row that has a gap in the middle is counted as a single row. Because the mouth parts (Fig. C.2) of anuran larvae are quite variable within species, and mouth parts are easily damaged during transport of specimens or through inadequate preservation, it is best to obtain and examine multiple specimens to maximize your chances of correctly identifying them. Fortunately, with practice, you can readily identify most species without having to examine mouth parts. Additional identification clues include habitat and time of year when found, so be sure to consult the "Reproduction and Growth" section of the species accounts when making your determinations. The following key is based in part on Stebbins (1951, 1985), Smith (1956), Altig (1970, 1987), Korky (1978), and Scott and Jennings (1985).

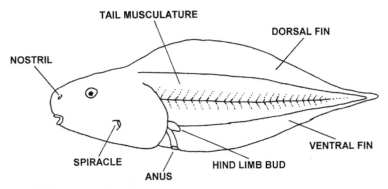

Fig. C.1. Anatomy of a larval frog.

1A. Three pairs of bushy gills or gill stubs on neck — Tiger salamander *(Ambystoma tigrinum)*.

1B. Gills not visible (except on newly hatched individuals) — 2.

2A. Horny mandibles, labial tooth rows, and oral papillae absent; spiracle on ventral midline, immediately ventral to anus; eyes lateral (Fig. C.3) — Great Plains narrowmouth toad *(Gastrophryne olivacea)*.

2B. Horny mandibles present; labial teeth present; spiracle on left side of body — 3.

3A. Oral papillae encircling mouth entirely or with only a small gap at mid-dorsal border; usually at least four tooth rows on lower lip — 4.

3B. Oral papillae confined to sides of mouth, wide gaps above and below mandibles; usually no more than three tooth rows on lower lip — 7.

3C. Oral papillae surround sides and lower margin of mouth, wide gap above mandibles — 11.

4A. Dorsum dark; upper mandible never cusped; lower mandible striated; body usually wider posteriorly than anteriorly; usually 35 mm TL or less; labial tooth rows usually 4/5 or 5/5, sometimes 4/4; no keratinized patch on roof of mouth cavity — Couch's spadefoot *(Scaphiopus couchii)*.

4B. Dorsum generally light to medium brown or gray; upper mandible sometimes cusped; lower mandible not striated; body sometimes wider anteriorly than posteriorly; often greater than 35 mm TL; keratinized patch on roof of mouth cavity — 5 (the species in 5 and 6 are difficult to distinguish from each other).

5A. Tail length/tail height = 1.9 or less; tail height/tail muscle height = 3.1 or more; tail fin arises abruptly from body; widespread in eastern Colorado and the San Luis Valley, possibly occurs in extreme southwestern Colorado — Plains spadefoot *(Spea bombifrons)*.

5B. Tail length/tail height = 2.0 or more; tail height/tail muscle height 2.9 or less; tail fin does not arise abruptly from body — 6.

6A. Found from Colorado River valley north in western Colorado — Great Basin spadefoot *(Spea intermontana)*.

6B. Found south of Colorado River valley or in southeastern Colorado — New Mexico spadefoot *(Spea multiplicata)*.

7A. Usually two tooth rows on lower lip; found in southeastern Colorado — Green toad *(Bufo debilis)*.

7B. Usually three tooth rows on lower lip; more widespread — 8.

8A. Tooth row farthest from mandibles on lower lip nearly equal in length to tooth row closest to mandibles on lower lip; throat unpigmented — Red-spotted toad *(Bufo punctatus)*.

8B. Tooth row farthest from mandibles on lower lip much shorter than tooth row closest to mandibles on lower lip — 9.

9A. Dorsal fin strongly arched; tooth row closest to mandibles on lower lip more than twice length of tooth row farthest from mandibles on lower lip; upper mandible strongly arched; wide gap in tooth row closest to mandibles on upper lip; dorsal color pattern of paired blotches appears prior to metamorphosis — Great Plains toad *(Bufo cognatus).*

9B. Dorsal fin not strongly arched; tooth row closest to mandibles on lower lip less than twice length of tooth row farthest from mandibles on lower lip; upper mandible not strongly arched; narrow gap in tooth row closest to mandibles on upper lip — 10.

10A. Fins heavily pigmented; muscles of tail not bicolored when viewed from side; found in high mountains — Mountain toad (*Bufo boreas* complex).

10B. Fins unpigmented or with only scattered dark spots; lower part of tail muscles light-colored when viewed from side; found in low mountains, plains, and low valleys — Woodhouse's toad *(Bufo woodhousii).*

11A. Oral papillae indented at corners of mouth; eyes dorsal; may exceed 5.5 cm TL — 14.

11B. Oral papillae not strongly indented at corners of mouth; eyes dorsal or lateral; less than 5.5 cm TL — 12.

12A. Usually two tooth rows on lower lip; wide gap in tooth row closest to mandibles on upper lip; tail tip often black; found in northeastern Colorado only — Northern cricket frog *(Acris crepitans).*

12B. Usually three tooth rows on lower lip — 13.

13A. Eyes lateral (Fig. C.3); upper edge of tail fin strongly arched; widespread — Western chorus frog *(Pseudacris triseriata).*

13B. Eyes not distinctly lateral; found in canyons of southwestern Colorado and Mesa de Maya in southeastern Colorado — Canyon treefrog *(Hyla arenicolor).*

14A. Four tooth rows on lower lip; tail fin strongly arched dorsally; found in mountains of north-central Colorado only — Wood frog *(Rana sylvatica).*

14B. Two or three tooth rows on lower lip — 15.

15A. Body and tail olive-green, large specimens with small, sharp-edged black dots on dorsum and tail; may exceed 9 cm TL — Bullfrog *(Rana catesbeiana).*

15B. Body and tail greenish or not, seldom with black dots; maximum TL about 9 cm — 16.

16A. Lower mandible heavily keratinized for one-half or less of anterior-posterior width of mandible — Wood frog *(Rana sylvatica).*

16B. Lower mandible heavily keratinized for nearly entire width of mandible — 17.

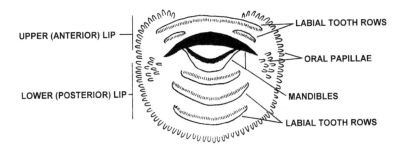

Fig C.2. Mouth parts of a larval frog.

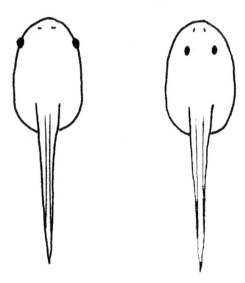

Fig. C.3. Dorsal view of frog larvae showing lateral *(left)* and dorsal *(right)* location of eyes.

17A. Body robust at posterior end; snout pointed in dorsal view; oral disc located at tip of snout in side view; iris has dorsal, ventral, and lateral dark spots; widespread in lowlands and mountains — Northern leopard frog *(Rana pipiens)*.

17B. Body more cylindrical; snout more rounded in dorsal view; oral disc located slightly below and posterior to tip of snout in side view; iris gold, lacks dorsal and ventral dark spots; found below 6,000 feet (1,830 m) in southeastern Colorado — Plains leopard frog *(Rana blairi)*.

KEY TO METAMORPHOSED AMPHIBIANS

1A. Tail present; hind limbs not greatly longer than forelimbs; eyes small; vertical grooves along sides of body; color pattern spotted, blotched, mottled, or unicolor — Tiger salamander *(Ambystoma tigrinum)*.

1B. Tail generally absent (a short stub may be present); hind limbs much longer than forelimbs; eyes usually large and protruding; no vertical grooves along sides of body (frogs and toads) — 2.

2A. Parotoid glands (Fig. C.4) well developed; skin warty; teeth absent from both upper and lower jaws (toads) — 3.

2B. Parotoid glands absent or indistinct; skin relatively smooth; teeth may be present in upper jaw — 7.

3A. Cranial crests (Fig. C.4) absent or indistinct; parotoid glands oval; numerous dark spots on chest; usually a light mid-dorsal stripe (absent or inconspicuous in juveniles, which may have reddish warts); tubercles on underside of foot lack a sharp edge; throat never extensively dark; found in high mountains only — Mountain toad *(Bufo boreas* complex).

3B. Cranial crests prominent or weak; parotoid glands round or elongate; tarsal fold weak or absent; chest spotted or unspotted; light mid-dorsal stripe present or absent; dark, sharp-edged tubercle sometimes present on underside of foot (Fig. C.5); breeding males with dark throat; widespread but not in high mountains — 4.

CRANIAL CREST

PAROTOID GLANDS

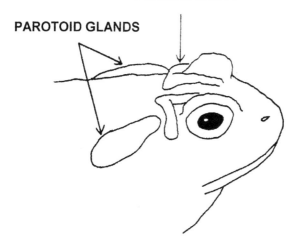

Fig. C.4. Anatomy of the head and neck of a toad *(Bufo)*.

4A. Parotoid glands round or transversely oval; head flattened; no light mid-dorsal stripe; dorsum gray or brown with numerous reddish warts; cranial crests weakly developed — Red-spotted toad *(Bufo punctatus)*.

4B. Parotoid glands distinctly longer than wide — 5.

5A. Parotoid glands large and broad, positioned low on shoulders; cranial crests weak or absent; head and body distinctly flattened; dorsum green with numerous small black spots and irregular lines — Green toad *(Bufo debilis)*.

5B. Parotoid glands elongate, not low on shoulders; cranial crests prominent; head and body not especially flattened — 6.

6A. Dorsum with large, dark, usually light-edged blotches in roughly symmetrical pairs (Fig. C.6), each blotch containing several warts (reddish in juveniles); cranial crests diverge posteriorly from a hard lump on top of snout; often a sharp-edged tubercle on underside of foot — Great Plains toad *(Bufo cognatus)*.

6B. Dorsum yellowish-brown, grayish, or olive, with asymmetrical pattern of small dark spots that typically contain 1–2 warts; generally a prominent light mid-dorsal stripe (absent or inconspicuous in juveniles, which usually have reddish warts); hard lump on snout usually absent; cranial crests parallel between eyes; dark, sharp-edged tubercle on underside of foot in large specimens — Woodhouse's toad *(Bufo woodhousii)*.

7A. Hard black spade (tubercle) on underside of foot (Fig. C.5); pupil vertically elongate in bright light — 8.

7B. Black spade absent; pupil round or horizontally elongate in bright light — 11.

8A. Spade sickle-shaped (Fig. C.5); parotoid glands present but indistinct; frontoparietal fontanelle absent (dissection required); dorsum greenish yellow — Couch's spadefoot *(Scaphiopus couchii)*.

8B. Spade wedge-shaped (Fig. C.5); parotoid glands absent; frontoparietal fontanelle usually present (may be

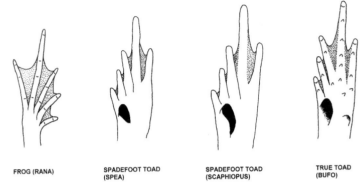

FROG (RANA)   SPADEFOOT TOAD (SPEA)   SPADEFOOT TOAD (SCAPHIOPUS)   TRUE TOAD (BUFO)

Fig. C.5. Underside of the hind foot of a frog (right foot is depicted) and three toads (left foot is depicted). Toad feet have dark tubercles.

small, sometimes absent); dorsum not greenish yellow — 9.

9A. Lump between eyes; frontoparietal bones arched (dissection required) — 10.

9B. No lump between eyes; frontoparietal bones flat, separated by large fontanelle — New Mexico spadefoot *(Spea multiplicata)*.

10A. Lump between eyes hard and bony, slightly forward of eyes; anterior ends of frontoparietal bones elevated and rough — Plains spadefoot *(Spea bombifrons)*.

10B. Lump between eyes glandular, directly between the eyes; middle portion of frontoparietal bones elevated, fontanelle relatively small — Great Basin spadefoot *(Spea intermontana)*.

11A. Extensive webbing between toes (Fig. C.5) — 12.

11B. Little or no webbing between toes — 17.

12A. Tips of digits distinctly enlarged, paddlelike — Canyon treefrog *(Hyla arenicolor)*.

12B. Tips of digits not paddlelike — 13.

13A. Ridge (dorsolateral fold) along each side of dorsum between eye and rump (Fig. C.7) — 14.

13B. Dorsolateral folds absent — 16.

14A. Light line on upper jaw; dark mask across eyes; light mid-dorsal stripe usually present — Wood frog *(Rana sylvatica)*.

14B. Light mid-dorsal stripe absent — 15.

15A. Posterior part of dorsolateral folds inset toward midline and often discontinuous (Fig. C.7); eardrum often with distinct light spot; dorsal background color brown; oviducts absent in male — Plains leopard frog *(Rana blairi)*.

15B. Posterior part of dorsolateral folds not inset toward midline; eardrum usually without distinct light spot; dorsal background color green or brown; vestigial oviducts usually present in male — Northern leopard frog *(Rana pipiens)*.

16A. Eardrum large, with fold of skin curving around top and rear edges; dorsum green or brown, usually with dark spots or mottling — Bullfrog *(Rana catesbeiana)*.

16B. Eardrum small and indistinct; dorsum grayish; whitish marks on upper jaw; dark triangle between eyes; dark stripe on rear of thigh; maximum SVL about 38 mm — Northern cricket frog *(Acris crepitans)*.

17A. Transverse fold of skin across back of head between eyes; snout pointed; eardrum not evident; dorsum gray or

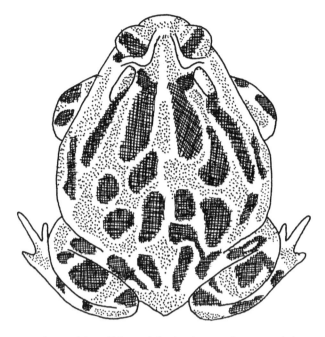

Fig. C.6. Dorsal view of Great Plains toad showing the somewhat symmetrical arrangement of dorsal blotches.

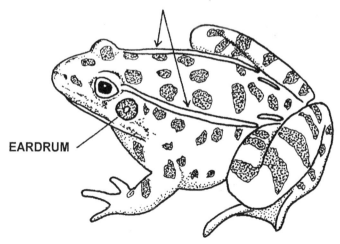

DORSOLATERAL FOLDS (DISCONTINUOUS AND INSET AT POSTERIOR END)

EARDRUM

Fig. C.7. Anatomy of a plains leopard frog.

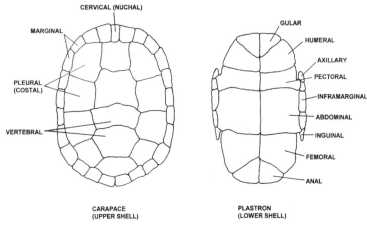

CERVICAL (NUCHAL)

MARGINAL

PLEURAL
(COSTAL)

VERTEBRAL

CARAPACE
(UPPER SHELL)

GULAR

HUMERAL

AXILLARY

PECTORAL

INFRAMARGINAL

ABDOMINAL

INGUINAL

FEMORAL

ANAL

PLASTRON
(LOWER SHELL)

Fig. C.8. Scutes of the shell of a turtle.

brown, with or without scattered dark spots — Great Plains narrowmouth toad *(Gastrophryne olivacea)*.

17B. Transverse fold of skin across back of head between eyes absent; eardrum conspicuous; dorsum green, brown, or reddish, with green or brown stripes or spots — Western chorus frog *(Pseudacris triseriata)*.

KEY TO REPTILE GROUPS

1A. Body enclosed in a shell — "Key to Turtles."

1B. Body not enclosed in a shell — 2.

2A. Limbs present — "Key to Lizards."

2B. Limbs absent — "Key to Snakes."

KEY TO TURTLES

1A. Shell flattened, with flexible edges and covered with leathery skin; snout tubular; three claws on each forefoot — Spiny softshell *(Trionyx spiniferus)*.

1B. Shell hard, covered by rigid, horny plates; snout not tubular; five claws on each forefoot — 2.

2A. Plastron (Fig. C.8) relatively small, cross-shaped; tail as long as or longer than carapace; tail with crest of large bony scales; rear edge of carapace serrated — Snapping turtle *(Chelydra serpentina)*.

2B. Plastron large; tail less than one-half carapace length, without crest of bony scales — 3.

3A. Plastron with 11 scutes (single scute under neck may be partially divided); throat yellow with several nipplelike projections (barbels) — Yellow mud turtle *(Kinosternon flavescens)*.

3B. Plastron with 12 scutes; barbels absent — 4.

4A. Bright yellow lines on head and limbs; plastron orange or reddish with dark markings (most conspicuous in juveniles); carapace somewhat flattened, often with irregular narrow yellow lines (reduced in larger individuals), less often with dark reticulation; plastron not hinged — Painted turtle *(Chrysemys picta)*.

4B. Yellowish or reddish spots on forelimbs; domed carapace dark with yellow streaks or spots; plastron transversely hinged; legs stout — Ornate box turtle *(Terrapene ornata)*.

KEY TO LIZARDS

1A. Dorsal scales smooth, shiny, tightly overlapping, and with rounded rear edge — 2.

1B. Dorsal scales pointed and overlapping,

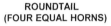

| ROUNDTAIL
(FOUR EQUAL HORNS) | SHORT-HORNED
(STUBBY HORNS) | TEXAS
(TWO LONG HORNS) |

Fig. C.9. Arrangement of the head spines of horned lizards.

or rounded and granular, or pointed and not especially shiny — 4.

2A. Scales on sides of body in diagonal rows; tail no more than 1.5 times as long as head and body — Great Plains skink *(Eumeces obsoletus).*

2B. Scales on sides of body (midway between limbs) in horizontal rows; tail (if never broken) 1.5–2.0 times as long as head and body — 3.

3A. Dorsum pale gray with many straight-edged dark stripes, or dorsum dark brown with two bold light dorsolateral stripes and a weaker mid-dorsal stripe — Many-lined skink *(Eumeces multivirgatus).*

3B. Dorsum light to dark brown with two dark-edged white dorsolateral stripes, or dorsum dark brown with two bold light dorsolateral stripes and a bold light mid-dorsal stripe — Variable skink *(Eumeces gaigeae).*

4A. Hard spines at back of head (Fig. C.9);

body wide and flattened; tail relatively short, not much more than half the length of head and body; snout blunt — 5.

4B. No hard spines at back of head; body not especially wide and flat; tail (if never broken) longer than head and body; snout not especially blunt — 6.

5A. Two rows of enlarged scales fringing each side of body (Fig. C.10); dark bars radiating from eyes; spines at back of head much longer than basal width (Fig. C.9) — Texas horned lizard *(Phrynosoma cornutum).*

5B. One row of enlarged scales fringing each side of body (Fig. C.10); no dark bars radiating from eye; spines at back of head short (Fig. C.9) — Short-horned lizard *(Phrynosoma hernandesi).*

5C. No enlarged scales fringing sides of body; four spines of about equal length at back of head (Fig. C.9); tail round

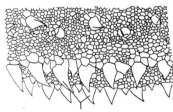
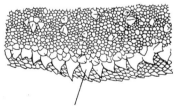

| TWO ROWS OF FRINGE SCALES | ONE ROW OF FRINGE SCALES |

Fig. C.10. Fringe scales along the side of the body of a Texas horned lizard *(left)* and short-horned lizard *(right).* From Maslin (1947b).

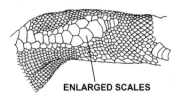 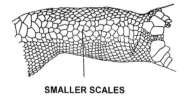

ENLARGED SCALES   **SMALLER SCALES**

Fig. C.11. Rear view of the forearm of a plateau striped whiptail *(left)* and six-lined racerunner *(right)*. From Maslin (1947b).

and slender; dark blotch on side near hind legs — Roundtail horned lizard *(Phrynosoma modestum)*.

6A. Head, body, and tail long and slender; dorsum with minute, rounded, non-overlapping, granular scales; venter with large rectangular scales — 7.

6B. Not as in 6A — 11.

7A. Dorsum with 6–7 light stripes; no light spots or bars in dark areas between stripes — 8.

7B. Dorsum with light stripes; dark fields interrupted by light areas, or dark fields broken into separate bars or spots — 9.

8A. Tail light blue (bright blue in juveniles); venter white or pale blue-green; enlarged scales on basal undersurface of forearm (Fig. C.11); found in western Colorado — Plateau striped whiptail *(Cnemidophorus velox)*.

8B. Tail not blue in adult; neck and shoulders sometimes greenish; scales on basal undersurface of forearm not enlarged; found in eastern Colorado — Six-lined racerunner *(Cnemidophorus sexlineatus)*.

9A. Scales anterior to fold of skin across throat (gular fold) conspicuously enlarged (Fig. C.12); found in southeastern Colorado — 10.

9B. Scales anterior to gular fold not conspicuously enlarged; western Colorado — Western whiptail *(Cnemidophorus tigris)*.

10A. Paravertebral pale stripes gray-tan to tan or gold, irregular in outline, interrupted, and/or fused with bars; mid-dorsal (vertebral) stripe gray-tan to tan (or absent), single irregular or doubled or partly doubled; lateral stripe (lowermost stripe on side of body) gray, irregular and/or interrupted and fused with spots and/or bars (these stripes may be partly or entirely lost in older individuals); area between two uppermost pale stripes (not counting the vertebral line) on each side of dorsum with pale spots either longitudinally fused into supernumerary line or transversely expanded into bars; dorsal surface of thighs with profuse pale spotting and some spots fused — Diploid checkered whiptail *(Cnemidophorus tesselatus)*.

10B. Paravertebral pale stripes gray, uninterrupted, straight, often fused with spots; mid-dorsal (vertebral) stripe gray and, if present on the neck, relatively straight, or stripe on neck followed by spots; lateral stripe (lowermost stripe on side of body) gray, relatively straight, frequently interrupted by narrow areas of black ground color, usually fused with some spots and/or bars; area between the two uppermost pale stripes (not counting the vertebral line) on each side of the dorsum with linear series of pale spots, some fused with stripes; dorsal surface of thighs with numerous pale spots often fused into a reticulum — Triploid checkered whiptail *(Cnemidophorus neotesselatus)*.

11A. Ear openings absent; dorsum with smooth, granular scales; two black bars on each side of belly — Lesser earless lizard *(Holbrookia maculata)*.

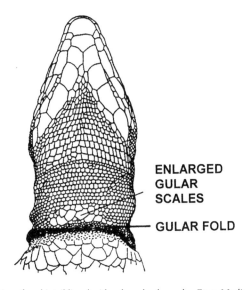

ENLARGED
GULAR
SCALES

— GULAR FOLD

Fig. C.12. Throat region of a whiptail lizard with enlarged gular scales. From Maslin (1947b).

11B. Ear openings present — 12.

12A. Scales on mid-dorsum pointed, overlapping, and strongly keeled; fold of skin on throat (gular fold) incomplete — 13.

12B. Scales on mid-dorsum granular, rounded, and nonoverlapping (or if some scales overlapping, few, if any, are strongly keeled or pointed; gular fold complete — 15.

13A. Dorsal scales very large and spiny; often scattered yellowish or gold scales on sides; scales on upper eyelids (supraoculars) large, in single row of five (usually), the posterior one or two in contact with parietal and frontoparietal scales (Fig. C.13); found in southwestern Colorado — Desert spiny lizard *(Sceloporus magister)*.

13B. Dorsal scales neither especially large nor spiny; yellowish or gold scales absent; supraoculars relatively small, separated from parietal and frontoparietal scales by complete row of small scales — 14.

14A. Dorsal scales relatively small; scales on rear surface of thigh very small, some often granular and unkeeled

(Fig. C.14); no distinct blue patches on sides of throat (may be blue-mottled); light stripe usually present along each side of dorsum — Sagebrush lizard *(Sceloporus graciosus)*.

14B. Dorsal scales of moderate size; scales on rear surface of thigh overlapping (Fig. C.14); dorsolateral stripes present or absent; blue patches on sides of throat present or absent — Plateau and prairie lizards *(Sceloporus undulatus)*.

15A. On top of head, at least one scale behind eyes much larger than scales on middle of back; always less than 14 cm TL — 16.

15B. On top of head, scales behind eyes not much larger than those on middle of back; usually greater than 14 cm TL — 17.

16A. Dark blotch on each side of chest; mid-dorsal scales of uniform size (Fig. C.15) — Side-blotched lizard *(Uta stansburiana)*.

16B. Dark chest blotch absent; mid-dorsal scales of at least two distinct sizes (Fig. C.15) — Tree lizard *(Urosaurus ornatus)*.

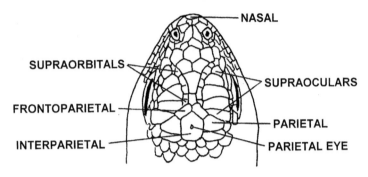

Fig. C.13. Top of head of a *Sceloporus* lizard with large supraocular scales partially in contact with the parietal and frontoparietal scales.

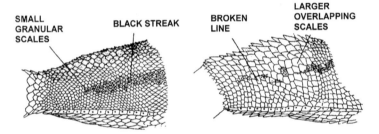

Fig. C.14. Rear view of the thigh of a sagebrush lizard *(left)* and plateau lizard *(right)*. From Maslin (1947b).

17A. Two distinct black collars around neck — Collared lizard *(Crotaphytus collaris)*.

17B. Black collars absent — Longnose leopard lizard *(Gambelia wislizenii)*.

KEY TO SNAKES

1A. Belly scales same size as dorsal scales; eyes evident only as dark spots — Texas blind snake *(Leptotyphlops dulcis)*.

1B. Belly scales obviously wider than dorsal scales; eyes well developed — 2.

2A. Rattle or horny button present on end of tail; head much broader than neck; pit present on each side of head between eye and nostril — 3.

2B. Rattle or horny button absent; head not much broader than neck; facial pit absent — 4.

3A. Usually nine large scales on top of head — Massasauga *(Sistrurus catenatus)*.

3B. Numerous small scales on top of head — Western rattlesnake *(Crotalus viridis)*.

4A. Elongate scales on throat; tail (if unbroken) tapers to a point — 5.

4B. Elongate throat scales absent; tail blunt, shaped almost like head; pupil vertically elongate in bright light — Rubber boa *(Charina bottae)*.

5A. Some or all of dorsal scales with longitudinal ridge (keeled) (Fig. C.17) — 6.

5B. All dorsal scales unkeeled — 16.

6A. Snout upturned or spadelike — 7.

6B. Snout not upturned or spadelike — 8.

7A. Underside of tail mostly black; 23 or fewer dorsal scale rows at midbody — Western hognose snake *(Heterodon nasicus)*.

7B. Underside of tail not black; 25 dorsal scale rows at midbody — Eastern hognose snake *(Heterodon platirhinos)*.

8A. Dorsal scales weakly keeled along mid-dorsum, unkeeled on sides; numerous square-cornered black marks on belly — Great Plains rat snake *(Elaphe guttata)*.

8B. Dorsal scales strongly keeled — 9.

9A. Two prefrontal scales (Fig. C.18); vertical plate at opening of windpipe inconspicuous or absent — 10.

9B. Usually four prefrontals; numerous brown or black blotches on dorsum; conspicuous vertical plate at opening of windpipe — Bullsnake *(Pituophis catenifer)*.

10A. Anal scale usually divided (Fig. C.19) — Northern water snake *(Nerodia sipedon)*.

10B. Anal scale usually undivided (Fig. C.18) — 11.

11A. Light stripe on second and third dorsal scale rows (Fig. C.17) above lateral edges of belly scales — 12.

11B. Light stripe on third and fourth dorsal scale rows — 15.

12A. Red marks on sides of body between stripes (red may be confined to skin between scales); usually seven upper labial scales — Common garter snake *(Thamnophis sirtalis)*.

12B. Red marks absent; usually more or less than seven upper labials — 13.

13A. Five or six upper labials; two rows of black, semicircular spots on white belly — Lined snake *(Tropidoclonion lineatum)*.

13B. More than six upper labials; black marks (if any) on belly not in two distinct rows — 14.

14A. Stripes on sides of body white; two black blotches at back of head; heavy black marks on sutures between upper labials — Blackneck garter snake *(Thamnophis cyrtopsis)*.

14B. Stripes pale but not white; often irregular black marks on belly; frequently two dark blotches at back of head;

ENLARGED SCALES   NO ENLARGED SCALES

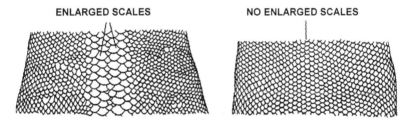

Fig. C.15. Dorsal view of the torso of a tree lizard *(left)* and side-blotched lizard *(right)*. From Maslin (1947b).

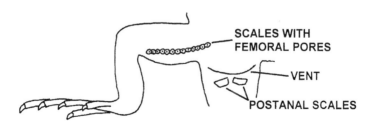

SCALES WITH FEMORAL PORES

VENT

POSTANAL SCALES

Fig. C.16. Vent region of a phrynosomatid lizard.

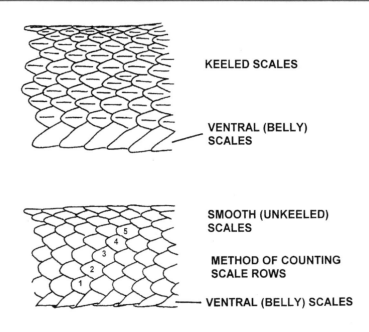

KEELED SCALES

VENTRAL (BELLY) SCALES

SMOOTH (UNKEELED) SCALES

METHOD OF COUNTING SCALE ROWS

VENTRAL (BELLY) SCALES

DORSAL SCALE ROWS OF SNAKE
(SIDE VIEW)

Fig. C.17. Keeled and unkeeled dorsal scales of snakes.

narrow dark marks (if any) on upper lips confined to anterior edge of vertical sutures between scales — Western terrestrial garter snake *(Thamnophis elegans)*.

15A. Black marks present on upper lips — Plains garter snake *(Thamnophis radix)*.

15B. Black marks absent on upper lips — Western ribbon snake *(Thamnophis proximus)*.

16A. Anal scale divided — 20.

16B. Anal scale undivided (may be creased) — 17.

17A. Scales on underside of tail (caudal scales) mostly in a single row (Fig. C.19) — Longnose snake *(Rhinocheilus lecontei)*.

17B. Caudals mostly in two rows (Fig. C.19) — 18.

18A. No markings on whitish venter; dorsum with numerous brown blotches on pale background — Glossy snake *(Arizona elegans)*.

18B. Venter not completely whitish; dorsum without brown blotches on pale background — 19.

19A. Black, whitish, and red or orange bands around body — Milk snake *(Lampropeltis triangulum)*.

19B. Red or orange bands absent — Common kingsnake *(Lampropeltis getula)*.

20A. Top of head dark; dorsum light brown; belly pink or orange — 21.

20B. Coloration not as in 20A — 22.

21A. Dark cap on head extends 3–5 dorsal-scale lengths beyond parietal scales (Fig. C.18); rear edge of head cap usually pointed — Plains black-headed snake *(Tantilla nigriceps)*.

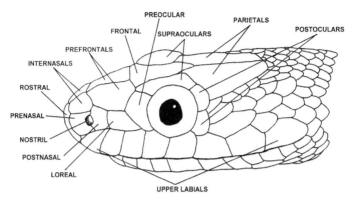

Fig. C.18. Head scales of a colubrid snake.

21B. Dark cap usually extends three or fewer dorsal-scale lengths beyond parietals; rear edge of head cap usually straight or rounded — Southwestern black-headed snake *(Tantilla hobartsmithi)*.

22A. Lower preocular scale very small, wedged between upper labials; often greater than 66 cm TL; eyes large; head noticeably broader than neck — 23.

22B. Lower preocular not wedged between upper labials; less than 66 cm TL; eyes not especially large; head not noticeably broad — 25.

23A. Light and dark stripes or lines on sides of body — Striped whipsnake *(Masticophis taeniatus)*.

23B. Stripes absent from sides of body — 24.

24A. Usually 15 dorsal scale rows just anterior to vent; dorsum olive or brown, and belly often yellow (adult), or dorsum with numerous brown blotches (juvenile) — Racer *(Coluber constrictor)*.

24B. Thirteen or fewer dorsal scale rows

just anterior to vent; dorsum brown or pink, often with dark crossbands, especially on anterior part of body in juveniles; belly never yellow — Coachwhip *(Masticophis flagellum)*.

25A. Dorsum uniformly dark, except for orange collar (rarely absent); belly orange with black spots; underside of tail red — Ringneck snake *(Diadophis punctatus)*.

25B. Coloration not as in 25A — 26.

26A. Dorsum uniformly green (bluish after death); nostril centered in single scale — Smooth green snake *(Liochlorophis vernalis)*.

26B. Coloration not as in 26A — 27.

27A. Pupil vertically elongate in bright light; dark blotches on rear of head and neck more elongate than other dorsal blotches — Night snake *(Hypsiglena torquata)*.

27B. Pupil not vertically elongate in bright light; dorsum usually with widely separated dark crossbands (some individuals lack crossbands or have only a dark collar band) — Ground snake *(Sonora semiannulata)*.

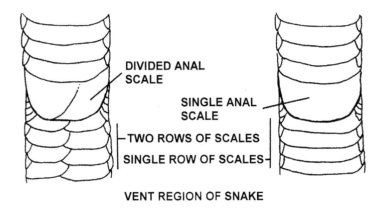

VENT REGION OF SNAKE

Fig. C.19. Vent region of snakes, showing caudal scales in one and two rows. Vent is hidden by the anal scale.

Appendix D

About Scientific Names

Most people will prefer using common (English) names rather than scientific names. However, confusion may result when a species is known by more than one common name. For this reason, biologists often use the scientific name, which is unique for each species (except where controversy exists) and usually eliminates uncertainty about which amphibian or reptile is being discussed.

The scientific name consists of two or three words that are generally underlined or italicized—for example, *Thamnophis elegans* or *Thamnophis elegans vagrans.* The first word, *Thamnophis,* is the genus, or generic, name and always begins with a capital letter. Several different but closely related animals may have the same generic name, or there may be only a single member of the genus (in which case, the genus is referred to as monotypic). The second word, *elegans,* is the species, or specific, name and always begins with a lowercase letter. The generic and specific names together denote a particular animal distinct from all others. Different species generally do not interbreed; if they do, such behavior occurs at a low level in a very restricted zone where the ranges of the species meet. Sometimes a third italicized word, the subspecific name (also uncapitalized), is included as well. Subspecies are discussed in Chapter 7.

Scientific names may be accompanied by the surname of a person and a year—for example, *Bufo cognatus* Say, 1823, or *Masticophis taeniatus* (Hallowell, 1852). The surname is that of the person or persons who wrote the original taxonomic description,

and the year is the year of publication. The name and year are included in parentheses if the species or subspecies originally was named as a member of a genus other than the one in which it is now included. Sometimes the specific name changes slightly for grammatical reasons when a species is reassigned to a different genus (e.g., *Scaphiopus intermontanus* vs. *Spea intermontana*).

Scientific names usually are derived from Greek or Latin words but sometimes commemorate significant naturalists or denote geographic areas. The formal rules of zoological nomenclature require that all scientific names be latinized, regardless of their derivation. Thus, a name honoring Hobart Smith becomes *hobartsmithi,* and a species restricted to Utah might be called *utahensis.* Usually, the names indicate morphological or behavioral characteristics of the taxon (e.g., *punctatus, spiniferus, pipiens*). Early taxonomists sometimes assigned inappropriate names to newly discovered species. For example, Linnaeus gave the racer the specific name *constrictor,* but this snake is not a constrictor. However, a scientific name cannot be changed simply because it is inappropriate.

For many people, scientific names are nothing more than a difficult-to-pronounce mouthful of words. The following list of translations and derivations will make these names more meaningful. However, as you consider how these names relate to the species that bear them, keep in mind that the older taxonomic literature did not explain these derivations, and in many cases, what the author had in mind when assigning a name is uncertain. Because the pronunciation of many of these names varies among herpetologists, I decline to make any recommendations. Most name derivations are taken from Jaeger (1955); Adler (1979, 1989) provided information on many of the persons included. See also the various accounts in the *Catalogue of American Amphibians and Reptiles,* published by the Society for the Study of Amphibians and Reptiles.

Scientific Names

Acris: locust.

affinis: related.

Ambystoma: amby-, rounded; *-stoma,* mouth.

Apalone: apalo-, soft; *-ne,* swimmer.

approximans: proximate to, similar; with regard to lizard subspecies *Holbrookia maculata approximans,* may refer to a similarity to subspecies *H. m. maculata.*

arenicolor: areni-, sand; *-color,* colored.

Arizona: pertaining to Arizona, from a Papago word meaning "place of little springs."

arnyi: for S. Arny, who collected the type specimen of *Diadophis punctatus arnyi* in Kansas in the mid–1800s.

auriceps: auri-, golden; *-ceps,* head.

australis: southern.

bellii: for Thomas Bell (1792–1880), English student of turtles.

Bipes: bi-, two; *-pes,* foot.

blairi: for W. Frank Blair (1912–1984), herpetologist at the University of Texas.

blanchardi: for Frank N. Blanchard (1888–1937), herpetologist at the University of Michigan.

bombifrons: bombi-, lump; *-frons,* forehead.

boreas: northern.

bottae: for Paolo Emilio Botta (1802–1870), explorer-diplomat who collected the type specimen of *Charina bottae* in California in 1827–1828.

Bufo: toad.

californiae: pertaining to California, where the type specimen of *Lampropeltis getula californiae* was collected.

catenatus: chained, probably refers to the dorsal color pattern of *Sistrurus catenatus.*

catenifer: cateni-, chain; *-fer,* bearing, refers to the appearance of the dorsal pattern of *Pituophis catenifer.*

catesbeiana: for Mark Catesby (1683–1749), English naturalist in what is now the southeastern United States.

celaenops: celaen-, dark; *-ops,* eye.

cephaloflavus: cephalo-, head; *-flavus,* yellow.

Charina: graceful.

Chelydra: water serpent, turtle.

Chrysemys: chrys-, golden; *-emys,* freshwater turtle.

Cnemidophorus: cnemido-, leg armor; *-phorus,* bearer.

cognatus: related.

collaris: having a collar.

Coluber: serpent.

concolor: con-, uniform; *-color,* color.

constrictor: constrictor.

cornutum: horned.

couchii: for Darius Nash Couch (1822–1897), U.S. Army officer who collected the type specimen of *Scaphiopus couchii* in Mexico in the mid–1800s.

crepitans: rattling.

Crotalus: pertaining to a rattle.

Crotaphytus: pertaining to the side of the head or the head of a hammer, probably refers to the relatively large head of *Crotaphytus* lizards.

cyrtopsis: cyrt-, curved; *-opsis,* appearance.

debilis: disabled, feeble; probably refers to the relatively unrobust body of *Bufo debilis.*

dekayi: for James E. De Kay (1792–1851), herpetologist in New York.

deserticola: desert-, desert; *-icola,* inhabitant.

Diadophis: diad-, crown; *-ophis,* snake.

dissectus: divided; refers to the labial scale of *Leptotyphlops dulcis dissectus.*

douglasii: for David Douglas (1799–1834), who collected the type specimen of *Phrynosoma douglasii* near the Columbia River in 1825 or 1826.

dulcis: sweet.

edwardsii: for L. A. Edwards, U.S. Army surgeon who collected the type specimen of *Sistrurus catenatus edwardsii* in Mexico in the mid–1800s.

Elaphe: deer or stag; probably refers to the antlerlike color pattern on the head of *Elaphe* snakes.

elegans: elegant.

elongatus: elongate.

emoryi: for William H. Emory (1811–1887), director of the U.S. and Mexican Boundary Survey.

epipleurotus: epi-, upon or over; *-pleurotis,* side or rib; possibly refers to the dorsolateral stripes of *Eumeces epipleurotus.*

episcopa: epi-, upon or over; *-scopa,* twig; may refer to the presumed habitat of *Sonora* snakes.

erythrocheilus: erythro-, red; *-cheilus,* lip.

Eumeces: eu-, good; *-meces,* length.

flagellum: whip.

flavescens: yellow.

flaviventris: flavi-, yellow; *-ventris,* underside.

gaigeae: for Helen T. Gaige (1890–1976), herpetologist at the University of Michigan.

Gambelia: for William Gambel (1819–1849), California ornithologist.

garmani: for Samuel Garman (1843–1927), herpetologist at Harvard University.

Gastrophryne: gastro-, belly; *-phryne,* toad.

gentilis: belonging to the same race or stock.

getula: a barbarism, or of unknown derivation.

graciosus: prone to slenderness, graceful.

guttata: spotted.

hammondii: for John F. Hammond, U.S. Army surgeon who collected the type specimen of *Spea hammondii* in California in the early 1800s.

hartwegi: for Norman E. Hartweg (1904–1964), herpetologist at the University of Michigan.

haydenii: for Ferdinand V. Hayden (1829–1887), explorer of the geology of the American West.

hernandesi: for Francisco Hernandez (1517?–1587), Spanish physician-naturalist who wrote the first review of the plants and animals of Mexico.

Heterodon: hetero-, different; *-don,* tooth.

hobartsmithi: for Hobart M. Smith (1912–), herpetologist at the University of Colorado.

holbrooki or holbrookia: for John E. Holbrook (1794–1887), author of *North American Herpetology.*

Hyla: a wood or forest.

Hypsiglena: hypsi-, high; *-glena,* eye.

insidior: seated, or cunning.

intermontana: inter-, between; *-montana,* pertaining to mountains.

janii: for Giorgio Jan (1791–1866), herpetologist in Italy.

Kinosternon: kino-, movable; *-sternon,* chest.

Lampropeltis: lampro-, shining; *-peltis,* a small shield (scale).

lecontei: for John L. LeConte (1825–1883), who collected the type specimen of *Rhinocheilus lecontei* in California in the mid–1800s.

Leptotyphlops: lepto-, slender; *-typhlops,* blind.

lineatum: lined.

Liochlorophis: lio-, smooth; *-chlor-,* green; *-ophis,* snake.

loreala: pertaining to the loreal scale.

maculata: spotted.

magister: chief.

maslini: for T. Paul Maslin (1909–1984), herpetologist at the University of Colorado.

Masticophis: mastic-, whip; *-ophis,* snake.

mavortium: warlike; may refer to the color pattern of *Ambystoma tigrinum mavortium.*

melanoleucus: melano-, black; *-leucus,* white.

melanostictum: melano-, black; *-stictum,* dotted.

modestum: modest, unassuming.

mormon: pertaining to the religious sect inhabiting the area where the type specimen of *Coluber constrictor mormon* was collected.

multiplicata: multi-, many; *-plicata,* folded.

multistriata: multi-, many; *-striata,* striped.

multivirgatus: multi-, many; *-virgatus,* lined.

nasicus: with a pointed nose.

Natrix: water snake.

nebulosum: clouded, dark.

neotesselatus: neo-, new; *-tesselatus,* checkered; refers to the newly recognized species related to *C. tesselatus.*

Nerodia: fluid swimmer.

nigriceps: nigri-, black; *-ceps,* head.

nuntius: messenger; in Hopi Snake Ceremonial, these snakes *(Crotalus viridis nuntius)* are used as messengers to the gods of the underworld (Klauber 1972).

obsoletus: without clear markings; refers to the absence of dorsal stripes in *Eumeces obsoletus.*

olivacea: olive-colored.

Opheodrys: opheo-, snake; *-drys,* tree.

ornata, ornatus: ornate, decorated.

parietalis: pertaining to the side of the body.

Phrynosoma: phryno-, toad; *-soma,* body.

picta: painted.

pipiens: peeping.

Pituophis: pitu-, pine; *-ophis,* snake; refers to the habitat of the first-known populations of *Pituophis* snakes.

planiceps: plani-, flat; *-ceps,* head.

Platirhinos: plati-, flat; *-rhinos,* nose.

Pseudacris: pseud-, false; *-acris,* locust.

punctatus: spotted.

radix: root.

Rana: frog.

Rhinocheilus: rhino-, nose; *-cheilus,* lip.

sayi: for Thomas Say (1787–1834), entomologist and the first biologist to record observations of Coloradan amphibians and reptiles.

Scaphiopus: scaphio-, shovel; *-pus,* foot.

Sceloporus: scelo-, leg; *-porus,* pore.

semiannulata: semi-, half; *annulata,* ringed.

septentrionalis: northern.

serpentina: like a snake.

sipedon: a siren, decoy.

sirtalis: like a garter.

Sistrurus: rattling.

Sonora: pertaining to the Mexican state of Sonora.

Spea: cave, tunnel; probably refers to the burrowing habits of *Spea* toads.

spinifera, spiniferus: spiny.

splendida: splendid.

stansburiana: for Howard Stansbury (1806–1863), U.S. Army captain who collected the type specimen of *Uta stansburiana* in Utah in 1849 or 1850.

Storeria: for David H. Storer (1804–1891), physician-herpetologist in Massachusetts.

sylvatica: living in the woods.

taeniatus: striped.

Tantilla: small.

taylori: for Edward H. Taylor (1889–1978), herpetologist at the University of Kansas.

tergeminus: ter-, thrice; *-geminus,* twin; refers to the number of rows of blotches on the back and belly, respectively.

Terrapene: terrapin.

tesselatus, tessellatus: checkered.

texana: pertaining to Texas.

Thamnophis: thamn-, bush; *-ophis,* snake.

tigrinum: tigerlike.

tigris: tiger.

torquata: adorned with a necklace, collared.

triangulum: tri-, three; *-angulum,* cornered; refers to the front edge of the first blotch of *Lampropeltis triangulum* (Williams 1994).

Trionyx: tri-, three; *-onyx,* claw.

triseriata: tri-, three; *-seriata,* in rows; refers to the (typically) three dorsal stripes.

tristichus: tri-, three; *-stichus,* in rows; refers to the striped dorsal pattern of *Sceloporus undulatus tristichus.*

Tropidoclonion: tropido-, keel; *-clonion,* twig.

undulatus: undulating, wavy.

uniformis: uniform.

Urosaurus: uro-, tail; *-saurus,* lizard.

Uta: pertaining to Utah (and thus to the home of the Ute people), where the type specimen of *Uta stansburiana* was collected in 1849.

utahensis: from Utah.

velox: swift.

vernalis: of spring.

viridis: green.

wislizenii: for Frederick Adolphus Wislizenus (1810–1889), U.S. Army surgeon who collected the type specimen of *Gambelia wislizenii* in Utah in 1849.

woodhousii: for Samuel W. Woodhouse (1821–1904), surgeon-naturalist who traveled in the western United States.

wrighti: for Albert H. Wright (1879–1970), herpetologist at Cornell University.

Glossary

Alluvium. Sedimentary material deposited by flowing water.

Amphibious. Inhabiting both land and water.

Amplexus. The sexual embrace of frogs and toads; the male clasps the female from above with his forelimbs.

Anal scale. In snakes, the large scale covering the vent; immediately anterior to the base of the tail on the underside of the body.

Anterior. In front of, or toward the front.

Anuran. A frog or toad.

Aquatic. Water-dwelling.

Arroyo. Dry gulch.

Arthropod. A joint-legged animal lacking a backbone, especially insects, spiders, and crustaceans.

Average. As used here, the arithmetic mean.

Basalt. A hard, dark volcanic rock.

Branchial slit. An opening on the side of the neck of a larval amphibian.

Breccia. Volcanic rock consisting of coarse fragments imbedded in finer material such as ash.

Boss. A glandular or bony lump between the eyes of certain toads.

Carapace. The upper portion of the shell of a turtle.

Carnivorous. Feeding on animals.

Cenozoic. The era including the Tertiary and Quaternary periods, from about 65 million years ago to the present.

CL. Carapace length.

Cloaca. The chamber into which the intestinal, excretory, and reproductive tracts discharge; empties to the outside through the vent.

Cloacal sacs. Glands that open into the cloaca of snakes and some lizards and secrete an odorous liquid.

Constriction. In certain snakes called constrictors, a method of killing prey by compressing it in tight coils of the body.

Continental Divide. The crest that separates streams draining into the Pacific Ocean from those draining into the Atlantic Ocean.

Copulation. Sexual intercourse.

Cranial crests. Ridges that border the medial and posterior portion of the eyes in certain toads.

Cretaceous. The latest period of the Mesozoic era, about 135–65 million years ago.

Digit. Finger or toe.

Diploid. Possessing two copies of each type of chromosome (this is the usual condition in nearly all species).

Diurnal. Active during daylight hours.

Dorsal. Pertaining to, or situated on or near, the upper surface of an animal.

Dorsolateral folds. Ridges of skin along the side of the back in certain frogs.

Dorsum. The dorsal side, or back, of an animal.

Ectothermic. Deriving body heat from the external environment.

Eocene. An epoch of the Tertiary period, about 60–40 million years ago.

Extirpated. No longer extant in a particular area.

Fang. A long, sharp tooth, especially a hollow one modified for the conduction of venom.

Feces. Excrement.

Fossorial. Adapted for digging; living underground.

Frontoparietal bones. In spadefoot toads, the bones forming the top of the skull between the eyes.

Frontoparietal fontanelle. In spadefoot toads, the gap between the frontoparietal bones.

Gills. Feathery vascular structures through which certain amphibians (especially larvae) extract oxygen from the water.

Graben. A depression in the earth's crust between two parallel faults.

Habitat. The natural abode of an organism; the ecological situation in which it is commonly found.

Hibernaculum (plural, **hibernacula**). The place where an organism spends the winter or cold season.

Hibernate. To spend the winter in a lethargic, inactive state.

Hogback. A tilted, steep-sided, broken-edged ridge produced by the erosion of softer strata around harder strata.

Holocene. An epoch of the Quaternary period, from about 10,000 years ago to the present.

Home range. The area in which the daily activities of an individual occur.

Hormone. A chemical released into the blood that produces an effect on the activity of cells at a different location.

Igneous rock. Formed by the solidification of magma.

Interparietal scale, interparietal. In lizards, the rearmost large scale on the top of the head.

Invertebrates. Animals lacking a backbone.

Keeled scales. Scales with a straight, longitudinal ridge.

Kettle pond. A basin in a glacial deposit, generally a temporary body of water.

Labial scales, labials. The lip scales.

Labial tooth rows. Rows of tiny, horny, comblike teeth arranged in rows on the lips of anuran larvae. The designation "2/3" indicates that the upper lip usually has two rows of teeth and the lower lip has three.

Laramide. A mountain-building period that extended from the late Cretaceous to early Eocene.

Larva (plural, **larvae**). A gill-bearing, water-dwelling amphibian that has not metamorphosed.

Ligament. A tough band of tissue connecting different bones.

Medial. Toward or in the middle.

Mesozoic. The era between the Paleozoic and Cenozoic eras, about 230–65 million years ago.

Metamorphic rock. Rocks altered by great heat or pressure.

Metamorphosis. The change from the gill-bearing larval stage to the gill-less, more terrestrial stage characteristic of most amphibians.

Metapopulation. A group of populations that significantly interact with one another over a long period of time. For example, one population (subpopulation) may serve as an important source of individuals for recolonization of a habitat patch in which another population of the same species has been extirpated.

Miocene. An epoch of the Tertiary period, about 25–5 million years ago.

Monotypic. Represented by only one member (e.g., a family or genus with a single species is monotypic, as is a species with no subspecies).

Moraine. Rock debris deposited by a glacier.

Musk. A smelly substance secreted by glands at the sides of the shell of certain turtles.

Neonate. A newly born or hatched individual.

New World. The Western Hemisphere.

Nocturnal. Pertaining to, or active at, night.

Oligocene. An epoch of the Tertiary period, about 40–25 million years ago.

Omnivorous. Eating both plants and animals.

Oral papillae. Clusters of soft, nipplelike, sensory projections surrounding the mouth of certain anuran larvae.

Paleozoic. The era between the Precambrian and Mesozoic eras, about 570–230 million years ago.

Paravertebral. Adjacent to the vertebral (mid-dorsal) line.

Parietal scales, parietals. In snakes, a pair of enlarged scales on top of the head, just behind the eyes.

Parotoid gland. Aggregation of poison glands forming a lump on each side of the neck of certain toads.

Parturition. The act of giving birth.

Pers. comm. Personal communication; informal communication from the named person to the author.

Pers. obs. Personal observation; an observation by the author.

PIT. Passive integrated transponder; a small tagging device.

PL. Plastron length.

Plastron. The underside of the shell of a turtle.

Pleistocene. An epoch of the Quaternary period, about 2 million to 10,000 years ago; the "Ice Age."

Pliocene. An epoch of the Tertiary period, about 5–2 million years ago.

Precambrian. The era before the appearance of animals, more than 570 million years ago.

Prefrontal scales, prefrontals. In snakes, 2–4 enlarged scales on top of the head, just in front of the eyes.

Preocular scale, preocular. Scale bordering the front edge of the eye.

Quaternary. The period including the Pleistocene and Holocene (Recent) epochs, from about 2 million years ago to the present.

Sedimentary rock. Rocks consisting of (usually) layered deposits of fragments of earlier rock, animal shell, or precipitated material; for example, shale, sandstone, and limestone.

Subspecies. A formally named subdivision of a species.

Supraocular scales, supraoculars. Scales on top of the head, just above the eyes.

SVL (snout-vent length). The distance from the tip of the snout to the posterior end of the vent.

Syntopic. Occurring together in the same habitat in the same site.

Taxon (plural, **taxa**). A biological entity that has been given a scientific name.

Territory. Portion of the home range that is defended against other individuals of the same species.

Tertiary. The era between the Cretaceous and Quaternary periods, about 65–2 million years ago.

TL (total length). The distance from the tip of the snout to the tip of the tail in a fully extended individual.

Triploid. Possessing three copies of each type of chromosome.

Type specimen. Specimen upon which the name of a species or subspecies is based.

Upper labial scales, upper labials. Scales on the upper lips, not including the scale at the tip of the snout.

Vent. The external opening of the cloaca.

Vertebrate. Animal with a flexible column of cartilage or bones along the back, including fishes, amphibians, reptiles, birds, and mammals.

Wart. Glandular bump in the skin of toads.

References

Adler, K. 1979. *A brief history of herpetology in North America before 1900.* Society for the Study of Amphibians and Reptiles, Herpetological Circular No. 8.

———, ed. 1989. *Contributions to the history of herpetology.* Society for the Study of Amphibians and Reptiles, Contributions to Herpetology No. 5.

Aguirre, A. 1994. Declining toad populations. *Conservation Biology* 8:7.

Aird, S. D. 1984a. Morphological and biochemical differentiation of the western rattlesnake in Colorado, Wyoming and Utah. Ph.D. dissertation, Colorado State University, Fort Collins.

———. 1984b. Life history notes: *Crotalus viridis viridis* (prairie rattlesnake). *Herpetological Review* 15:18–19.

———. 1985. A quantitative assessment of variation in venom constituents within and between three nominal rattlesnake subspecies. *Toxicon* 23:1,000–1,004.

Aird, S. D., and I. I. Kaiser. 1985. Comparative studies on three rattlesnake toxins. *Toxicon* 23:361–374.

Aird, S. D., C. S. Seebart, and I. I. Kaiser. 1988. Preliminary fractionation and characterization of the venom of the Great Basin rattlesnake *(Crotalus lutosus lutosus). Herpetologica* 44:71–85.

Aldridge, R. D. 1979a. Seasonal spermatogenesis in sympatric *Crotalus viridis* and *Arizona elegans* in New Mexico. *Journal of Herpetology* 13:187–192.

———. 1979b. Female reproductive cycles of the snakes *Arizona elegans* and *Crotalus viridis. Herpetologica* 35:256–261.

———. 1982. The ovarian cycle of the watersnake *Nerodia sipedon,* and effects of hypophysectomy and gonadotropin administration. *Herpetologica* 38:71–79.

———. 1993. Male reproductive anatomy and seasonal occurrence of mating and combat behavior of the rattlesnake *Crotalus v. viridis. Journal of Herpetology* 27:481–484.

Aleksiuk, M., and P. T. Gregory. 1974. Regulation of seasonal mating behavior in *Thamnophis sirtalis parietalis. Copeia* 1974:681–689.

Alexander, C. F., and W. G. Whitford. 1968. Energy requirements of *Uta stansburiana. Copeia* 1968:678–683.

Allison, L. J., P. E. Brunkow, and J. P. Collins. 1994. Opportunistic breeding after summer rains by Arizona tiger salamanders. *Great Basin Naturalist* 54:376–379.

Altig, R. 1970. A key to the tadpoles of the continental United States and Canada. *Herpetologica* 26:180–207.

Anderson, B. L. 1979. Rocky Mountain wood frog habitat evaluation study 1978. Unpublished report, Colorado Division of Wildlife, Denver, May 4, 1979.

Anderson, J. D. 1970. Description of the spermatophore of *Ambystoma tigrinum. Herpetologica* 26:304–308.

Anderson, P. K. 1965. *The reptiles of Missouri.* University of Missouri Press, Columbia.

Anderson, R. A. 1993. An analysis of foraging in the lizard, *Cnemidophorus tigris.* Pages 83–116 in *Biology of whiptail lizards (genus* Cnemidophorus), J. W. Wright and L. J. Vitt, eds. Oklahoma Museum of Natural History, Norman.

———. 1994. Functional and population responses of the lizard *Cnemidophorus tigris* to environmental conditions. *American Zoologist* 34:409–421.

Anzalone, C. R., L. B. Kats, and M. S. Gordon. 1998. Effects of solar UV-B radiation on embryonic development in *Hyla cadaverina, Hyla regilla,* and *Taricha torosa. Conservation Biology* 12:646–653.

Applegarth, J. S. 1969. The variation, distribution, and taxonomy of the eastern fence lizard, *Sceloporus undulatus* Bosc in Latreille, in northeastern New Mexico. M.S. thesis, University of New Mexico, Albuquerque.

Armstrong, D. M. 1972. Distribution of mammals in Colorado. University of Kansas Museum of Natural History Monograph No. 3.

Arnold, S. J., and A. F. Bennett. 1984. Behavioural variation in natural populations. III: Antipredator displays in the garter snake *Thamnophis radix. Animal Behaviour* 32:1,108–1,118.

———. 1988. Behavioral variation in natural populations. V: Morphological correlates of locomotion in the garter snake *Thamnophis radix*. *Biological Journal of the Linnean Society* 34:175–190.

Arnold, S. J., and R. J. Wassersug. 1978. Differential predation on metamorphic anurans by garter snakes *(Thamnophis):* Social behavior as a possible defense. *Ecology* 59:1,014–1,022.

Ashton, K. G. 1998a. *Sceloporus undulatus elongatus* (northern plateau lizard): Mating behavior. *Herpetological Review* 29:102.

———. 1998b. Geographic distribution: *Spea multiplicata*. *Herpetological Review* 29:108.

———. 1998c. Natural history notes: *Pituophis melanoleucus deserticola* (Great Basin gopher snake). Regional heterothermy. *Herpetological Review* 29:170–171.

Ashton, K. G., and K. L. Ashton. 1998. Natural history notes: *Phrynosoma douglasi* (shorthorned lizard). Reproduction. *Herpetological Review* 29:168.

Ashton, K. G., and J. Johnson. 1998. Natural history notes: *Crotalus viridis concolor* (midget faded rattlesnake). Drinking from skin. *Herpetological Review* 29:170.

Ashton, K. G., H. M. Smith, and D. Chiszar. 1997. Geographic distribution: *Crotalus viridis viridis*. *Herpetological Review* 28:159.

Ashton, R. E., Jr., comp. 1976. *Endangered and threatened amphibians and reptiles in the United States*. Society for the Study of Amphibians and Reptiles, Herpetological Circular No. 5.

Asplund, K. K. 1974. Body size and habitat utilization in whiptail lizards *(Cnemidophorus)*. *Copeia* 1974:695–703.

Auffenberg, W. 1963. The fossil snakes of Florida. *Tulane Studies in Zoology* 10 (3):131–216.

Axtell, R. W. 1956. A solution to the long neglected *Holbrookia lacerata* problem and the description of two new subspecies of *Holbrookia*. *Bulletin of the Chicago Academy of Science* 10 (11):163–179.

———. 1961. *Eumeces epipleurotus* Cope, a revived name for the southwestern skink *Eumeces multivirgatus gaigei* Taylor. *Texas Journal of Science* 13:345–351.

———. 1972. Hybridization between western collared lizards with a proposed taxonomic rearrangement. *Copeia* 1972:707–727.

———. 1989. Interpretive atlas of Texas lizards. No. 8, *Crotaphytus collaris*. Privately published.

Bacchus, S. T., K. Richter, and P. Moler. 1993. Geographic distribution: *Xenopus laevis*. *Herpetological Review* 24:65.

Baeyens, D. A., M. W. Patterson, and C. T. McAllister. 1980. A comparative physiological study of diving in three species of *Nerodia* and *Elaphe obsoleta*. *Journal of Herpetology* 14:65–70.

Bagdonas, K. R. 1968. Variation in Rocky Mountain wood frogs. M.A. thesis, Colorado State University, Fort Collins.

———. 1971. Differentiation of western wood frogs. Ph.D. dissertation, Colorado State University, Fort Collins.

Bagdonas, K. R., and D. Pettus. 1976. Genetic compatibility in wood frogs. *Journal of Herpetology* 10:105–112.

Baird, S. F. 1859. Report on reptiles collected on the survey. Rep. Explor. and Surv. to ascertain the most practicable and economical route for a railroad from the Mississippi River to the Pacific Ocean 10, part 4 (3):17–20.

Baird, T. A., M. A. Acree, and C. L. Sloan. 1996. Age and gender-related differences in the social behavior and mating success of free-living collared lizards, *Crotaphytus collaris*. *Copeia* 1996:336–347.

Baker, S.C.F. 1968. Serum protein variation in leopard frogs. M.S. thesis, Colorado State University, Fort Collins.

Bakewell, G., J. M. Chopek, and G. L. Burkholder. 1983. Notes on reproduction of the side-blotched lizard *Uta stansburiana* in southwest Idaho. *Great Basin Naturalist* 43:477–482.

Ball, R. L. 1992. Geographic distribution: *Lampropeltis getula*. *Herpetological Review* 23:27.

Ballinger, R. E. 1974. Reproduction of the Texas horned lizard, *Phrynosoma cornutum*. *Herpetologica* 30:321–327.

———. 1977. Reproductive strategies: food availability as a source of proximal variation in a lizard. *Ecology* 58:628–635.

———. 1984. Survivorship of the tree lizard, *Urosaurus ornatus linearis*, in New Mexico. *Journal of Herpetology* 18:480–481.

Ballinger, R. E., D. L. Droge, and S. M. Jones. 1981. Reproduction in a Nebraska sandhills population of the northern prairie lizard *Sceloporus undulatus garmani*. *American Midland Naturalist* 106:157–164.

Ballinger, R. E., and T. G. Hipp. 1985. Reproduction in the collared lizard, *Crotaphytus collaris*, in west central Texas. *Copeia* 1985:976–980.

Ballinger, R. E., and S. M. Jones. 1985. Ecological disturbance in a sandhills prairie: Impact and importance to the lizard community on Arapaho Prairie in western Nebraska. *Prairie Naturalist* 17:91–100.

Ballinger, R. E., J. D. Lynch, and P. H. Cole. 1979. Distribution and natural history of amphibians and reptiles in western Nebraska with ecological notes on the herpetiles [*sic*] of Arapaho Prairie. *Prairie Naturalist* 11:65–74.

Ballinger, R. E., and C. O. McKinney. 1966. Developmental temperature tolerance of certain anuran species. *Journal of Experimental Zoology* 161:21–28.

Ballinger, R. E., and D. W. Tinkle. 1972. Systematics and evolution of the genus *Uta* (Sauria:

Iguanidae). *University of Michigan Museum of Zoology Miscellaneous Publications* 145:1–83.

Ballinger, R. E., and K. S. Watts. 1995. Path to extinction: Impact of vegetational change on lizard populations on Arapaho Prairie in the Nebraska Sandhills. *American Midland Naturalist* 134:413–417.

Baltosser, W. H., and T. L. Best. 1990. Seasonal occurrence and habitat utilization by lizards in southwestern New Mexico. *Southwestern Naturalist* 35:377–383.

Banta, B. H. 1964. A preliminary account of the herpetofauna of the Wet Mountains, Custer and Fremont Counties, Colorado. *Journal of the Colorado-Wyoming Academy of Science* 5 (5):49–50.

———. 1965. A preliminary report of the herpetofauna of a seven mile transect of the Black Forest, El Paso County, Colorado. *Journal of the Colorado-Wyoming Academy of Science* 5 (6):55–56.

———. 1968. The recent herpetofauna of the northern Wet Mountains, south-central Colorado. *Journal of Herpetology* 1:120.

Banta, B. H., and W. S. Brechbuhler. 1965. The recent herpetofauna of a transect of the northern Wet Mountains, Custer and Fremont counties, Colorado. *Journal of the Colorado-Wyoming Academy of Science* 5 (6):57.

Banta, B. H., and D. E. Hahn. 1966. Albinism in a Colorado garter snake. *Wasmann Journal of Biology* 24:249–250.

Banta, B. H., and P. Kimmel. 1965. A preliminary report upon the herpetofauna of Phantom Canyon, Pikes Peak Ranges, Teller and Fremont counties, Colorado. *Journal of the Colorado-Wyoming Academy of Science* 5 (6):56.

Banta, B. H., and C. A. Torbit, Jr. 1965. The herpetofauna of a four mile transect of prairie in El Paso County, Colorado, obtained in 1963 and 1964. *Journal of the Colorado-Wyoming Academy of Science* 5 (6):53.

———. 1966. An unusual tail regeneration in a Colorado skink (Reptilia: Lacertilia). *Wasmann Journal of Biology* 24:281–282.

Barbault, R., and M. E. Maury. 1981. Ecological organization of a Chihuahuan Desert lizard community. *Oecologia* 51:335–342.

Barry, L. T. 1932a. An extension of the range of four reptiles to include Colorado. *Copeia* 1932:103.

———. 1932b. Reptiles at the Colorado Museum of Natural History. *Journal of the Colorado-Wyoming Academy of Science* 1 (4):58.

———. 1933a. Notes on Colorado reptiles. *Copeia* 1933:99–100.

———. 1933b. Snakes of the Mesa Verde National Park. *Mesa Verde Notes* 4 (2):8–11.

———. 1934. A list of published recorded localities from which snakes and lizards have been taken in Colorado. Unpublished manuscript.

Bartelt, P. E. 1998. Natural history notes: *Bufo boreas* (western toad). Mortality. *Herpetological Review* 29:96.

Batson, R. 1949. Caesarean birth of a brood of *Natrix sipedon sipedon*. *Herpetologica* 5:147.

Bauerle, B. A. 1971. *Snakes and lizards of the Pawnee Site*. U.S. IBP Grasslands Biome Technical Report 120. Colorado State University, Fort Collins.

———. 1972a. *Biological productivity of snakes of the Pawnee Site, 1970–1971*. U.S. IBP Grasslands Biome Technical Report 207. Colorado State University, Fort Collins.

———. 1972b. Biological productivity of snakes of the Pawnee Site. D.A. thesis, University of Northern Colorado, Greeley.

Bauerle, B., and D. J. Spencer. 1971. *Environmental pollutants in two species of snakes from the Pawnee Site*. U.S. IBP Grasslands Biome Technical Report 137. Colorado State University, Fort Collins.

Bauerle, B., D. L. Spencer, and W. Wheeler. 1975. The use of snakes as a pollution indicator species. *Copeia* 1975:366–368.

Bauman, M. A., and D. E. Metter. 1977. Reproductive cycle of the northern water snake, *Natrix s. sipedon* (Reptilia, Serpentes, Colubridae). *Journal of Herpetology* 11:51–59.

Baur, B. E. 1986. Longevity of horned lizards of the genus *Phrynosoma*. *Bulletin of the Maryland Herpetological Society* 22:149–151.

Baxter, G. T. 1946. A study of the amphibians and reptiles of Wyoming. M.S. thesis, University of Wyoming, Laramie.

———. 1947. The amphibians and reptiles of Wyoming. *Wyoming Wildlife* 11 (August–October):11–34.

———. 1952. Notes on growth and the reproductive cycle of the leopard frog, *Rana pipiens* Schreber, in southern Wyoming. *Journal of the Colorado-Wyoming Academy of Science* 4 (4):91.

Baxter, G. T., and M. D. Stone. 1985. *Amphibians and reptiles of Wyoming*. 2nd ed. Wyoming Game and Fish Department, Cheyenne.

Beatson, R. R. 1976. Environmental and genetical correlates of disruptive coloration in the water snake, *Natrix s. sipedon*. *Evolution* 30:241–252.

Bechtel, H. B., and E. Bechtel. 1958. Reproduction in captive corn snakes, *Elaphe guttata guttata*. *Copeia* 1958:148–149.

Beidleman, R. G. 1954. Unusual occurrence of the tiger salamander in north-central Colorado. *Copeia* 1954:60–61.

Beiswenger, R. E. 1981. Predation by gray jays on aggregating tadpoles of the boreal toad *(Bufo boreas)*. *Copeia* 1981:459–460.

Belfit, S., and L. Nienaber. 1983. A dicephalic snake *(Lampropeltis getulus yumensis)* from Arizona. *Herpetological Review* 14:9

Benedict, A. D. 1991. *A Sierra Club naturalist's guide to the Southern Rockies.* Sierra Club Books, San Francisco.

Bennion, R. S., and W. S. Parker. 1976. Field observations on courtship and aggressive behavior in desert striped whipsnakes, *Masticophis t. taeniatus. Herpetologica* 32:30–35.

Berger, L., et al. 1998. Chytridiomycosis causes amphibian mortality associated with population declines in the rain forests of Australia and Central America. *Proceedings of the National Academy of Sciences* 95:9,031–9,036.

Bergman, E., S. Boback, B. Hill, J. Hobert, C. Montgomery, and S. P. Mackessy. 1996. Geographic distribution: *Pseudacris triseriata maculata. Herpetological Review* 27:209.

Bergman, E., B. Hill, C. Montgomery, T. Childers, J. D. Manzer, J. Sifert, and S. P. Mackessy. 1998. Geographic distribution: *Phrynosoma douglasii. Herpetological Review* 29:111.

Bergman, E., B. Hill, C. Montgomery, J. Hobert, S. Boback, and S. P. Mackessy. 1997a. Geographic distribution: *Chrysemys picta bellii. Herpetological Review* 28:49.

———. 1997b. Geographic distribution: *Tropidoclonion lineatum lineatum. Herpetological Review* 28:53.

Bergman, E., C. Montgomery, T. Childers, J. D. Manzer, J. Sifert, B. Hill, and S. P. Mackessy. 1998a. Geographic distribution: *Lampropeltis getula. Herpetological Review* 29:113.

———. 1998b. Geographic distribution: *Lampropeltis triangulum gentilis. Herpetological Review* 29:114.

Bernard, S. R., and K. F. Brown. 1977 (1978). Distribution of mammals, reptiles, and amphibians by BLM physiographic regions and A. W. Kuchler's associations for the eleven western states. U.S. Department of the Interior, Bureau of Land Management Tech Note 301, August 1977. Revised July 1978.

Berry, J. F., and C. M. Berry. 1984. A re-analysis of geographic variation and systematics of the yellow mud turtle, *Kinosternon flavescens* (Agassiz). *Annals of the Carnegie Museum of Natural History* 53:185–206.

Berven, K. A. 1990. Factors affecting population fluctuations in larval and adult stages of the wood frog *(Rana sylvatica). Ecology* 71:1,599–1,608.

Berven, K. A., and T. A. Grudzien. 1990. Dispersal in the wood frog *(Rana sylvatica):* Implications for genetic population structure. *Evolution* 44:2,047–2,056.

Best, T. L., and A. L. Gennaro. 1984. Feeding ecology of the lizard, *Uta stansburiana,* in southeastern New Mexico. *Journal of Herpetology* 18:291–301.

———. 1985. Food habits of the western whiptail lizard *(Cnemidophorus tigris)* in southeastern New Mexico. *Great Basin Naturalist* 45:527–534.

Best, T. L., and G. S. Pfaffenberger. 1987. Age and sexual variation in the diet of collared lizards *(Crotaphytus collaris). Southwestern Naturalist* 32:415–426.

Biesterfeldt, J. M., J. W. Petranka, and S. Sherbondy. 1993. Prevalence of chemical interference competition in natural populations of wood frogs, *Rana sylvatica. Copeia* 1993:688–695.

Birchard, G. F., and G. C. Packard. 1997. Cardiac activity in supercooled hatchlings of the painted turtle *(Chrysemys picta). Journal of Herpetology* 31:166–169.

Bird, I. L. 1879. *A lady's life in the Rocky Mountains.* John Murray, London.

Bishop, D. W., and R. Hamilton. 1947. Polydactyly and limb duplication occurring naturally in the tiger salamander, *Ambystoma tigrinum. Science* 106:641–642.

Bizer, J. R. 1977. Life history phenomena of *Ambystoma tigrinum.* Ph.D. dissertation, Washington University, St. Louis, Missouri.

———. 1978. Growth rates and size at metamorphosis of high elevation populations of *Ambystoma. Oecologia* 34:175–184.

Black, J. H., and R. B. Brunson. 1971. Breeding behavior of the boreal toad, *Bufo boreas boreas* (Baird and Girard) in western Montana. *Great Basin Naturalist* 31:109–113.

Blair, A. P. 1951. Note on the herpetology of the Elk Mountains, Colorado. *Copeia* 1951:239–240.

Blair, W. F. 1936. A note on the ecology of *Microhyla olivacea. Copeia* 1936:115.

Blair, W. F. 1976. Some aspects of the biology of the ornate box turtle, *Terrapene ornata. Southwestern Naturalist* 21:89–104.

Blake, I. H., and A. K. Blake. 1969. An ecological study of timberline and alpine areas, Mount Lincoln, Park County, Colorado. University of Nebraska Studies, New Series No. 40.

Blaker, A. A. 1976. *Field photography: Beginning and advanced techniques.* W. H. Freeman, San Francisco.

Blanchard, F., T. Arneill, L. Czupryna, D. Chiszar, and H. M. Smith. 1997. Geographic distribution: *Masticophis flagellum. Herpetological Review* 28:52.

Blanchard, F. N. 1921. A revision of the kingsnakes: genus *Lampropeltis.* Bulletin of the U.S. National Museum 114.

———. 1933. Eggs and young of the smooth green snake, *Liopeltis vernalis* (Harlan). Papers of the Michigan Academy of Science, Arts, and Letters 17:493–508.

———. 1938. Snakes of the genus *Tantilla* in the United States. Field Museum of Natural History, Zoological Series 20 (28):369–376.

———. 1942. The ring-neck snakes, genus *Diadophis. Bulletin of the Chicago Academy of Science* 7 (1):1–144.

Blanchard, F. N., M. R. Gilreath, and F. C. Blanchard. 1979. The eastern ringneck snake

(Diadophis punctatus edwardsii) in northern Michigan (Reptilia, Serpentes, Colubridae). *Journal of Herpetology* 13:377–402.

Blaney, R. M. 1977. Systematics of the common kingsnake, *Lampropeltis getulus* (Linnaeus). *Tulane Studies in Zoology and Botany* 19 (3–4):47–103.

Blaustein, A. R., B. Edmund, J. M. Kiesecker, J. J. Beatty, and D. G. Hokit. 1995. Ambient ultraviolet radiation causes mortality in salamander eggs. *Ecological Applications* 5:740–743.

Blaustein, A. R., P. D. Hoffman, D. G. Hokit, J. M. Kiesecker, S. C. Walls, and J. B. Hays. 1994. UV repair and resistance to solar UV-B in amphibian eggs: A link to population declines. *Proceedings of the National Academy of Sciences* 91:1,791–1,795.

Blaustein, A. R., D. G. Hokit, R. K. O'Hara, and R. A. Holt. 1994. Pathogenic fungus contributes to amphibian losses in the Pacific Northwest. *Biological Conservation* 67:251–254.

Blum, M. S., J. B. Byrd, J. R. Travis, J. F. Watkins II, and F. R. Gehlbach. 1971. Chemistry of the cloacal sac secretion of the blind snake *Leptotyphlops dulcis. Comparative Biochemistry and Physiology* 38B:103–107.

Boback, S., E. Bergman, C. Montgomery, J. Hobert, B. Hill, and S. P. Mackessy. 1997. Geographic distribution: *Gastrophryne olivacea. Herpetological Review* 28:48.

Boback, S., S. Link, E. Bergman, B. Hill, C. Montgomery, J. Hobert, and S. P. Mackessy. 1996. Geographic distribution: *Lampropeltis getula. Herpetological Review* 27:213.

Boback, S., S. Link, C. Montgomery, J. Hobert, E. Bergman, B. Hill, and S. P. Mackessy. 1996. Geographic distribution: *Chrysemys picta bellii. Herpetological Review* 27:210.

Boback, S., C. Montgomery, J. Hobert, E. Bergman, B. Hill, and S. P. Mackessy. 1996. Geographic distribution: *Thamnophis cyrtopsis crytopsis* [sic]. *Herpetological Review* 27:215.

Bobyn, M. L., and R. J. Brooks. 1994. Incubation conditions as potential factors limiting the northern distribution of snapping turtles, *Chelydra serpentina. Canadian Journal of Zoology* 72:28–37.

Bogan, M. A., S. J. Martin, and R. B. Bury. 1983. Baseline studies of riparian vertebrates of the Yampa and Green River corridors within Dinosaur National Monument, June and July 1982. Ecology Section, Denver Wildlife Research Center, U.S. Fish and Wildlife Service, Fort Collins, Colorado, in cooperation with the Rocky Mountain region of the U. S. National Park Service, Denver, Colorado.

Bona-Gallo, A., and P. Licht. 1983. Effects of temperature on sexual receptivity and ovarian recrudescence in the garter snake, *Thamnophis sirtalis parietalis. Herpetologica* 39:173–182.

Boreal Toad Conservation Strategy Team. 1997. Conservation strategy for the Southern Rocky Mountain population of the boreal toad *(Bufo boreas boreas).* Unpublished draft report.

Bound, V. 1977. Social structure of the side-blotched lizard, *Uta stansburiana,* in Colorado. M.S. thesis, Colorado State University, Fort Collins.

Bowker, R. G. 1993. The thermoregulation of the lizards *Cnemidophorus exsanguis* and *C. velox:* Some consequences of high body temperature. Pages 117–132 in *Biology of whiptail lizards (genus* Cnemidophorus*), J. W. Wright and L. J. Vitt, eds. Oklahoma Museum of Natural History, Norman.

Boykin, K., and N. Zucker. 1993. Winter aggregation on a small rock cluster by the tree lizard *Urosaurus ornatus. Southwestern Naturalist* 38:304–306.

Brackin, M. F. 1978. The relation of rank to physiological state in *Cnemidophorus sexlineatus* dominance hierarchies. *Herpetologica* 34:185–191.

———. 1979. The seasonal reproductive, fat body, and adrenal cycles of male six-lined racerunners *(Cnemidophorus sexlineatus)* in central Oklahoma. *Herpetologica* 35:216–22.

Bradford, D. F. 1989. Allotopic distribution of native frogs and introduced fishes in high Sierra Nevada lakes of California: Implication of the negative effect of fish introductions. *Copeia* 1989:775–778.

———. 1993. Winterkill, oxygen relations, and energy metabolism of a submerged dormant amphibian, *Rana muscosa. Ecology* 64:1,171–1,183.

Bragg, A. N. 1936. Notes on the breeding habits, eggs, and embryos of *Bufo cognatus* with a description of the tadpole. *Copeia* 1936:14–20.

———. 1937a. A note on the metamorphosis of the tadpoles of *Bufo cognatus. Copeia* 1937:227–228.

———. 1937b. Observations on *Bufo cognatus* with special reference to breeding habits and eggs. *American Midland Naturalist* 18 (2):273–284.

———. 1940a. Observations on the ecology and natural history of Anura. I. Habits, habitat and breeding of *Bufo cognatus* Say. *American Naturalist* 74: 322–349, 424–438.

———. 1940b. Observations on the ecology and natural history of Anura. II. Habits, habitat and breeding of *Bufo woodhousii woodhousii* (Girard) in Oklahoma. *American Midland Naturalist* 24:306–321.

———. 1941. Tadpoles of *Scaphiopus bombifrons* and *Scaphiopus hammondi. Wasmann Collector* 4 (3):92–94.

———. 1955-1956. In quest of the spadefoots. *New Mexico Quarterly* 25 (4):345–358.

———. 1957. Variation in colors and color patterns in tadpoles in Oklahoma. *Copeia* 1957:36–39.

———. 1962. Predator-prey relationship in two species of spadefoot tadpoles with notes on some other features of their behavior. *Wasmann Journal of Biology* 20:81–97.

———. 1964. Further study of predation and cannibalism in spadefoot tadpoles. *Herpetologica* 20:17–24.

———. 1966. Longevity of the tadpole stage in the plains spadefoot (Amphibia: Salientia). *Wasmann Journal of Biology* 24:71–73.

Bragg, A. N., and W. N. Bragg. 1958 [1959]. Variations in the mouth parts in tadpoles of *Scaphiopus (Spea) bombifrons* Cope (Amphibia: Salientia). *Southwestern Naturalist* 3:55–69.

Bragg, A. N., and M. Brooks. 1958. Social behavior in juveniles of *Bufo cognatus* Say. *Herpetologica* 14:141–147.

Bragg, A. N., and S. Hayes. 1963. A study of labial tooth rows in tadpoles of Couch's spadefoot. *Wasmann Journal of Biology* 21:149–154.

Bragg, A. N., and O. M. King. 1960. Aggregational and associated behavior in tadpoles of the plains spadefoot. *Wasmann Journal of Biology* 18:273–289.

Bragg, A. N., and C. C. Smith. 1942. Observations on the ecology and natural history of Anura. IX: Notes on breeding behavior in Oklahoma. *Great Basin Naturalist* 3:33–50.

Bramble, D. M. 1974. Emydid shell kinesis: Biomechanics and evolution. *Copeia* 1974:707–727.

Bramble, D. M., J. H. Hutchison, and J. M. Legler. 1984. Kinosternid shell kinesis: Structure, function and evolution. *Copeia* 1984:456–475.

Brattstrom, B. H. 1962. Thermal control of aggregation behavior in tadpoles. *Herpetologica* 18:38–46.

———. 1963. A preliminary review of the thermal requirements of amphibians. *Ecology* 44:238–255.

Breckenridge, W. J. 1960. A spiny softshell turtle nest study. *Herpetologica* 16:284–285.

Brekke, D. R., S. D. Hillyard, and R. M. Winokur. 1991. Behavior associated with the water absorption response by the toad, *Bufo punctatus. Copeia* 1991:393–401.

Brennan, L. A. 1934 [1936]. A check list of the amphibians and reptiles of Ellis County, Kansas. *Transactions of the Kansas Academy of Sciences* 37:189–191.

Britson, C. A., and W.H.N. Gutzke. 1993. Antipredator mechanisms of hatchling freshwater turtles. *Copeia* 1993:435–440.

Brodie, E. D., Jr., and D. R. Formanowicz, Jr. 1987. Antipredator mechanisms of larval anurans: Protection of palatable individuals. *Herpetologica* 43:369–373.

Brodie, E. D., Jr., R. A. Nussbaum, and R. M. Storm. 1969. An egg-laying aggregation of five species of Oregon reptiles. *Herpetologica* 25:223–227.

Brooks, R. J., M. L. Bobyn, D. A. Galbraith, J. A. Layfield, and E. G. Nancekivell. 1991. Maternal and environmental influences on growth and survival of embryonic and hatchling snapping

turtles *(Chelydra serpentina). Canadian Journal of Zoology* 69:2,667–2,676.

Brooks, R. J., G. P. Brown, and D. A. Galbraith. 1991. Effects of a sudden increase in natural mortality of adults on a population of the common snapping turtle *(Chelydra serpentina). Canadian Journal of Zoology* 69:1,314–1,320.

Brooks, R. J., D. A. Galbraith, E. G. Nancekivell, and C. A. Bishop. 1988. Developing management guidelines for snapping turtles. Pages 174–179 in *Management of amphibians, reptiles, and small mammals in North America,* R. C. Szaro, K. E. Severson, and D. R. Patton, eds. USDA Forest Service General Technical Report RM–166.

Brown, D. G. 1993. Habitat associations of prairie rattlesnakes *(Crotalus viridis)* in Wyoming. *Herpetological Natural History* 1:5–12.

Brown, E. R., J. W. Haberman, and J. K. Kappel. 1970. Productive collecting sites for *Sistrurus catenatus edwardsi/tergeminus* in southeast Colorado. *Journal of the Colorado-Wyoming Academy of Science* 7 (1):44.

Brown, G. P., C. A. Bishop, and R. J. Brooks. 1994. Growth rate, reproductive output, and temperature selection of snapping turtles in habitats of different productivities. *Journal of Herpetology* 28:405–410.

Brown, G. P., and R. J. Brooks. 1991. Thermal and behavioral responses to feeding in free-ranging turtles, *Chelydra serpentina. Journal of Herpetology* 25: 273–278.

———. 1993. Sexual and seasonal differences in activity in a northern population of snapping turtles, *Chelydra serpentina. Herpetologica* 49:311–318.

———. 1994. Characteristics of and fidelity to hibernacula in a northern population of snapping turtles, *Chelydra serpentina. Copeia* 1994:222–226.

Brown, G. P., R. J. Brooks, and J. A. Layfield. 1990. Radiotelemetry of body temperatures of free-ranging snapping turtles *(Chelydra serpentina)* during summer. *Canadian Journal of Zoology* 68:1,659–1,663.

Brown, G. P., R. J. Brooks, M. E. Siddall, and S. S. Desser. 1994. Parasites and reproductive output in the snapping turtle, *Chelydra serpentina. Copeia* 1994:228–231.

Brown, G. P., and P. J. Weatherhead. 1997. Effects of reproduction on survival and growth of female northern water snakes, *Nerodia sipedon. Canadian Journal of Zoology* 75:424–432.

Brown, H. A. 1976. The status of California and Arizona populations of the western spadefoot toads (genus *Scaphiopus*). *Los Angeles County Natural History Museum Contributions in Science* 286:1–15.

———. 1989. Tadpole development and growth of the Great Basin spadefoot toad, *Scaphiopus intermontanus,* from central Washington. *Canadian Field-Naturalist* 103:531–534.

Brown, H. A., R. B. Bury, D. M. Darda, L. V. Diller, C. R. Peterson, and R. M. Storm. 1995. *Reptiles of Washington and Oregon.* Seattle Audubon Society, Seattle, Washington.

Brown, L. E. 1970. Interspecies interactions as possible causes of racial size differences in the toads *Bufo americanus* and *Bufo woodhousei. Texas Journal of Science* 21:261–267.

———. 1973. Speciation in the *Rana pipiens* complex. *American Zoologist* 13:73–79.

———. 1992. *Rana blairi. Catalogue of American Amphibians and Reptiles* 536:1–6.

Brown, S.E.S. 1979. Reproductive and habitat ecology of two species of the genus *Helisoma* (Mollusca: Planorbidae). M.A. thesis, University of Colorado, Boulder.

Brown, W. S., and W. S. Parker. 1976. Movement ecology of *Coluber constrictor* near communal hibernacula. *Copeia* 1976:225–242.

———. 1982. Niche dimensions and resource partitioning in a Great Basin desert snake community. Pages 59–81 in *Herpetological communities,* N. J. Scott, ed. U.S. Fish and Wildlife Service, Wildlife Research Report 13.

———. 1984. Growth, reproduction and demography of the racer, *Coluber constrictor mormon,* in northern Utah. Pages 13–40 in *Vertebrate ecology and systematics: A tribute to Henry S. Fitch,* R. A. Siegel et al., eds. University of Kansas Museum of Natural History Special Publication 10:i–viii, 1–278.

Brown, W. S., W. S. Parker, and J. A. Elder. 1974. Thermal and spatial relationships of two species of colubrid snakes during hibernation. *Herpetologica* 30:32–38.

Brush, S. W., and G. W. Ferguson. 1986. Predation on lark sparrow eggs by a massasauga rattlesnake. *Southwestern Naturalist* 31:260–261.

Bunn, R. L. 1995. Geographic distribution: *Spea multiplicata. Herpetological Review* 26:42.

Burger, J., et al. 1988. Hibernacula and summer den sites of pine snakes *(Pituophis melanoleucus)* in the New Jersey pine barrens. *Journal of Herpetology* 22:425–433.

Burger, J., and R. T. Zappalorti. 1991. Nesting behavior of pine snakes *(Pituophis m. melanoleucus)* in the New Jersey pine barrens. *Journal of Herpetology* 25:152–160.

———. 1992. Philopatry and nesting phenology of pine snakes *Pituophis melanoleucus* in the New Jersey pine barrens. *Behavioral Ecology and Sociobiology* 30:331–336.

Burger, W. L. 1950a. Novel aspects of the life history of two ambystomas. *Journal of the Tennessee Academy of Science* 75:252–257.

———. 1950b. New, revised, and reallocated names for North American whiptailed lizards, genus *Cnemidophorus. Chicago Academy of Science, Natural History Miscellanea* 65:1–9.

Burger, W. L., Jr., and A. N. Bragg. 1947. Notes on *Bufo boreas* (B. and G.) from the Gothic region

of Colorado. *Proceedings of the Oklahoma Academy of Science* 27:61–65.

Burghardt, G. M., and H. W. Greene. 1988. Predator simulation and duration of death feigning in neonate hognose snakes. *Animal Behaviour* 36:1,842–1,843.

Burke, V. J., R. D. Nagle, M. Osentoski, and J. D. Congdon. 1993. Common snapping turtles associated with ant mounds. *Journal of Herpetology* 27:114–115.

Burkett, R. D. 1984. An ecological study of the cricket frog, *Acris crepitans.* Pages 89–103 in *Vertebrate ecology and systematics: A tribute to Henry S. Fitch,* R. A. Siegel et al., eds. University of Kansas Museum of Natural History Special Publication 10.

Burkholder, G. L., and W. W. Tanner. 1974. Life history and ecology of the Great Basin sagebrush swift, *Sceloporus graciosus graciosus* Baird and Girard, 1852. Brigham Young University Science Bulletin, Biology Series 19 (5):1–44.

Burkholder, G. L., and J. M. Walker. 1973. Habitat and reproduction of the desert whiptail lizard, *Cnemidophorus tigris* Baird and Girard in southwestern Idaho at the northern part of its range. *Herpetologica* 29:76–83.

Burnett, W. L. 1926. Notes on Colorado herpetology. *Occasional Papers of the Museum of Zoology and Entomology, Colorado State Agricultural College* 1 (1):1–3.

———. 1932. A new skink for Colorado. *Copeia* 1932:37.

Burt, C. E. 1928a. The synonomy, variation, and distribution of the collared lizards, *Crotaphytus collaris* (Say). *University of Michigan Museum of Zoology Occasional Papers* 196:1–19.

———. 1928b. Insect food of Kansas lizards with notes on feeding habits. *Journal of the Kansas Entomological Society* 1 (3):50–68.

———. 1929. The synonymy, variation, and distribution of the Sonoran skink, *Eumeces obsoletus* (Baird and Girard). *University of Michigan Museum of Zoology Occasional Papers* 201:1–12.

———. 1931. A study of the teiid lizards of the genus *Cnemidophorus* with special reference to their phylogenetic relationships. Bulletin of the U.S. National Museum 154.

———. 1932. Elimination of *Eumeces fasciatus* from the Colorado faunal list. *Copeia* 1932:104.

———. 1933a. Some lizards from the Great Basin of the West and adjacent areas, with comments on the status of various forms. *American Midland Naturalist* 14:228–250.

———. 1933b. Amphibians from the Great Basin of the West and adjacent areas (1932). *American Midland Naturalist* 14:350–354.

———. 1935. Further records of the ecology and distribution of amphibians and reptiles in the Middle West. *American Midland Naturalist* 16:311–336.

Burt, C. E., and M. D. Burt. 1929. Field notes and locality records on a collection of amphibians and reptiles chiefly from the western half of the United States. I. Amphibians, II. Reptiles. *Journal of the Washington Academy of Science* 19:428–434, 448–460.

Bury, R. B. 1977. *Amphibians and reptiles of the McElmo Rare Lizard and Snake Area in southwest Colorado.* Report to Bureau of Land Management, Montrose, Colorado.

———. 1983. Geographic distribution: *Elaphe guttata emoryi* (Great Plains rat snake). *Herpetological Review* 14:123.

Bury, R. B., and J. A. Whelan. 1984. Ecology and management of the bullfrog. U.S. Fish and Wildlife Service Resource Publication 155.

Bury, R. B., J. H. Wolfheim, and R. A. Luckenbach. 1979. Agonistic behavior in free-living painted turtles *(Chrysemys picta bellii). Biology of Behaviour* 4:227–239.

Busby, W. H., and J. R. Parmelee. 1996. Historical changes in a herpetofaunal assemblage in the Flint Hills of Kansas. *American Midland Naturalist* 135:81–91.

Caldwell, J. P. 1982. Disruptive selection: A tail color polymorphism in *Acris* tadpoles in response to differential predation. *Canadian Journal of Zoology* 60:2,818–2,827.

Campbell, J. B. 1970a. Food habits of the boreal toad, *Bufo boreas boreas,* in the Colorado Front Range. *Journal of Herpetology* 4:83–85.

———. 1970b. Hibernacula of a population of *Bufo boreas boreas* in the Colorado Front Range. *Herpetologica* 26:278–282.

———. 1970c. New elevational records for the boreal toad *(Bufo boreas boreas). Arctic and Alpine Research* 2:157–159.

———. 1970d. Life-history of *Bufo boreas boreas* in the Colorado Front Range. Ph.D. thesis, University of Colorado, Boulder.

———. 1971 [1972]. Reproduction and transformation of boreal toads in the Colorado Front Range. *Journal of the Colorado-Wyoming Academy of Science* 7:114.

———. 1976. Environmental controls on boreal toad populations in the San Juan Mountains. Pages 289–295 in *Ecological impacts of snowpack augmentation in the San Juan Mountains, Colorado,* H. W. Steinhoff and J. D. Ives, eds. Final Report, San Juan Ecology Project. Colorado State University Publications, Fort Collins.

Campbell, J. B., and W. G. Degenhardt. 1971. *Bufo boreas boreas* in New Mexico. *Southwestern Naturalist* 16:219.

Campbell, J. H. 1980. Edwin James's report on *Bipes* reconsidered. *Herpetological Review* 11:6–7.

Camper, J. D. 1996. *Masticophis taeniatus. Catalogue of American Amphibians and Reptiles* 639:1–6.

Camper, J. D., and J. R. Dixon. 1994. Geographic variation and systematics of the striped whipsnakes *(Masticophis taeniatus* complex; Reptilia: Serpentes: Colubridae). *Annals of the Carnegie Museum of Natural History* 63:1–48.

Canton, S. P. 1982. Comparative limnology and biota of mine spoils ponds in Colorado. *Southwestern Naturalist* 27:33–42.

Capron, M. 1987. Selected observations on south-central Kansas turtles. *Kansas Herpetological Society Newsletter* 67:13–15.

Carey, C. 1976. Thermal physiology and energetics of boreal toads, *Bufo boreas boreas.* Ph.D. dissertation, University of Michigan, Ann Arbor.

———. 1978. Factors affecting body temperatures of toads. *Oecologia* 35:197–219.

———. 1979a. Effect of constant and fluctuating temperatures on resting and active oxygen consumption of toads, *Bufo boreas. Oecologia* 39:201–212.

———. 1979b. Aerobic and anaerobic energy expenditure during rest and activity in montane *Bufo b. boreas* and *Rana pipiens. Oecologia* 39:213–228.

———. 1993. Hypothesis concerning the causes of the disappearance of boreal toads from the mountains of Colorado. *Conservation Biology* 7:355–362.

———. 1994. A matter of time: Response to Aguirre. *Conservation Biology* 8:7–8.

———. 1997. Disease, stress and amphibian declines. *Froglog* 22: 1.

Carpenter, C. C. 1958. Reproduction, young, eggs and food of Oklahoma snakes. *Herpetologica* 14:113–115.

———. 1959. A population of the six-lined racerunner *(Cnemidophorus sexlineatus). Herpetologica* 15:81–86.

———. 1960a. Aggressive behavior and social dominance in the six-lined racerunner *(Cnemidophorus sexlineatus). Animal Behaviour* 8:61–66.

———. 1960b. Reproduction in Oklahoma *Sceloporus* and *Cnemidophorus. Herpetologica* 16:175–182.

———. 1978. Comparative display behavior in the genus *Sceloporus* (Iguanidae). *Milwaukee Public Museum Contributions in Biology and Geology* 18:1–71.

———. 1981. *Trionyx spiniferus* (spiny softshell): Morphology. *Herpetological Review* 12:82.

———. 1982. The bullsnake as an excavator. *Journal of Herpetology* 16:394–401.

Carpenter, C. C., and J. C. Gillingham. 1975. Postural responses to kingsnakes by crotaline snakes. *Herpetologica* 31:293–302.

———. 1977. A combat ritual between two male speckled kingsnakes *(Lampropeltis getulus holbrooki:* Colubridae, Serpentes) with indications of dominance. *Southwestern Naturalist* 22:517–524.

Carpenter, G. C. 1995a. The ontogeny of a variable social badge: Throat color development in tree lizards *(Urosaurus ornatus). Journal of Herpetology* 29:7–13.

———. 1995b. Modeling dominance: The influence of size, coloration, and experience in tree lizards *(Urosaurus ornatus). Herpetological Monographs* 9:88–101.

Carr, A. F. 1952. *Handbook of turtles.* Cornell University Press, Ithaca, New York.

Carter, P. A. 1992. The evolutionary genetics of alcohol dehydrogenase in tiger salamanders. Ph.D. thesis, University of Colorado, Boulder.

Cary, M. 1911. A biological survey of Colorado. *North American Fauna* 33:1–256.

Cecil, S. G., and J. J. Just. 1979. Survival rate, population density and development of a naturally occurring anuran larvae *(Rana catesbeiana). Copeia* 1979:447–453.

Censky, E. J. 1986. *Sceloporus graciosus. Catalogue of American Amphibians and Reptiles* 386:1–4.

Censky, E. J., and C. J. McCoy. 1985a. Geographic distribution: *Heterodon nasicus nasicus. Herpetological Review* 16:60.

———. 1985b. Geographic distribution: *Tantilla nigriceps. Herpetological Review* 16:60.

Chadwick, L. E., and H. Rahn. 1954. Temperature dependence of rattling frequency in the rattlesnake, *Crotalus v. viridis. Science* 119:442–443.

Chantrell, C. J. 1965. A lower Miocene *Acris* (Amphibia: Hylidae) from Colorado. *Journal of Paleontology* 39:507–508.

Chapman, B. R., and S. D. Castro. 1972. Additional vertebrate prey of the loggerhead shrike. *Wilson Bulletin* 84:496–497.

Charland, M. B. 1989. Size and winter survivorship in neonatal western rattlesnakes *(Crotalus viridis). Canadian Journal of Zoology* 67:1,620–1,625.

Chenoweth, W. L. 1950. Records of amphibians and reptiles from New Mexico, Utah, and Arizona. *Transactions of the Kansas Academy of Sciences* 53:532–534.

Chiszar, D., and J. D. Drew. 1991. Geographic Distribution: *Pseudacris triseriata. Herpetological Review* 22:134.

Chiszar, D., J. D. Drew, and H. M. Smith. 1992. Geographic distribution: *Coluber constrictor flaviventris. Herpetological Review* 23:90.

———. 1993. A range extension of the Great Plains rat snake in eastern Colorado. *Bulletin of the Chicago Herpetological Society* 27 (8):165.

Chiszar, D., G. Hobika, H. M. Smith, and J. Vidaurri. 1991. Envenomation and acquisition of chemical information by prairie rattlesnakes. *Prairie Naturalist* 23:69–72.

Chiszar, D., V. Lipetz, K. Scudder, and E. Pasanello. 1980. Rate of tongue flicking by bull snakes and pine snakes *(Pituophis melanoleucus)* during exposure to food and non-food odors. *Herpetologica* 36:225–231.

Chiszar, D., L. J. Livo, R.R.J. Smith, and H. M. Smith. 1995. Geographic distribution: *Crotalus viridis. Herpetological Review* 26:156.

Chiszar, D., T. Melcer, R. Lee, C. W. Radcliffe, and D. Duvall. 1990. Chemical cues used by prairie rattlesnakes *(Crotalus viridis)* to follow trails of rodent prey. *Journal of Chemical Ecology* 16:79–86.

Chiszar, D., C. W. Radcliffe, H. M. Smith, and H. Bashinski. 1981. Effect of prolonged food deprivation on response to prey odors by rattlesnakes. *Herpetologica* 37:237–243.

Chiszar, D., K. Scudder, and L. Knight. 1976. Rate of tongue flicking by garter snakes *(Thamnophis radix haydeni)* and rattlesnakes *(Crotalus v. viridis, Sistrurus catenatus tergeminus,* and *Sistrurus catenatus edwardsi)* during prolonged exposure to food odors. *Behavioral Biology* 18:273–283.

Chiszar, D., K. Scudder, H. M. Smith, and C. W. Radcliffe. 1976. Observation of courtship behavior in the western massasauga *(Sistrurus catenatus tergeminus). Herpetologica* 32:337–338.

Chiszar, D., and H. M. Smith. 1991. Geographic distribution: *Masticophis flagellum testaceus. Herpetological Review* 22:67.

———. 1992. Geographic distribution: *Terrapene ornata ornata. Herpetological Review* 23:26.

———. 1993. Geographic distribution: *Crotalus viridis viridis. Herpetological Review* 24:156.

———. 1994a. Natural history notes: *Crotalus viridis viridis* (prairie rattlesnake). Record rattle-string. *Herpetological Review* 25:123.

———. 1994b. Geographic distribution: *Tantilla nigriceps. Herpetological Review* 25:168.

———. 1995a. Geographic distribution: *Spea multiplicata. Herpetological Review* 26:208.

———. 1995b. Geographic distribution: *Chelydra serpentina serpentina. Herpetological Review* 26:208.

Chiszar, D., H. M. Smith, and R. Defusco. 1993. *Crotalus viridis viridis* (prairie rattlesnake): Diet. *Herpetological Review* 24:106.

Chiszar, D., D. Theodoratus, and H. M. Smith. 1995. Geographic distribution: *Rana catesbeiana. Herpetological Review* 26:208.

Chopko, J. T. 1995. The Texas night snake *(Hypsiglena torquata)* in Las Animas County, Colorado. *Cold Blooded News* (Colorado Herpetological Society) 22 (1):4.

Christian, K. A. 1976. Ontogeny of the food niche of *Pseudacris triseriata.* M.S. thesis, Colorado State University, Fort Collins.

———. 1982. Changes in the food niche during postmetamorphic ontogeny of the frog *Pseudacris triseriata. Copeia* 1982:73–80.

Christian, K. A., and S. Waldschmidt. 1984. The relationship between lizard home range and body size: A reanalysis of the data. *Herpetologica* 40:68–85.

Christiansen, J. L., and J. W. Bickham. 1989. Possible historic effects of pond drying and winterkill on the behavior of *Kinosternon flavescens* and *Chrysemys picta*. *Journal of Herpetology* 23:91–94.

Christiansen, J. L., and R. R. Burken. 1979. Growth and maturity of the snapping turtle *(Chelydra serpentina)* in Iowa. *Herpetologica* 35:261–266.

Christiansen, J. L., J. A. Cooper, and J. W. Bickham. 1984. Reproduction of *Kinosternon flavescens* (Kinosternidae) in Iowa. *Southwestern Naturalist* 29:349–351.

Christiansen, J. L., J. A. Cooper, J. W. Bickham, B. J. Gallaway, and M. A. Springer. 1985. Aspects of the natural history of the yellow mud turtle *Kinosternon flavescens* (Kinosternidae) in Iowa: A proposed endangered species. *Southwestern Naturalist* 30:413–425.

Christiansen, J. L., and A. E. Dunham. 1972. Reproduction of the yellow mud turtle *(Kinosternon flavescens)* in New Mexico. *Herpetologica* 28:130–137.

Christiansen, J. L., and B. J. Gallaway. 1984. Raccoon removal, nesting success, and hatchling emergence in Iowa turtles with special reference to *Kinosternon flavescens* (Kinosternidae). *Southwestern Naturalist* 29:343–348.

Christiansen, J. L., and E. O. Moll. 1973. Latitudinal reproductive variation in a single subspecies of painted turtle, *Chrysemys picta bellii*. *Herpetologica* 29:152–163.

Chronic, H. 1980. *Roadside geology of Colorado*. Mountain Press Publishing, Missoula, Montana.

Chronic, J., and H. Chronic. 1972. Prairie, peak and plateau: A guide to the geology of Colorado. *Colorado Geological Survey Bulletin* 32.

Churchill, T. A., and K. B. Storey. 1992. Natural freezing survival by painted turtles *Chrysemys picta marginata* and *C. picta bellii*. *American Journal of Physiology* 262:R530–R537.

———. 1993. Dehydration tolerance in wood frogs: A new perspective on the development of amphibian freeze tolerance. *American Journal of Physiology* 265:R1,324–R1,332.

———. 1994. Metabolic responses to dehydration by liver of the wood frog, *Rana sylvatica*. *Canadian Journal of Zoology* 72:1,420–1,425.

Clark, D. R., Jr. 1974. The western ribbon snake *(Thamnophis proximus):* Ecology of a western population. *Herpetologica* 30:372–379.

———. 1976. Ecological observations on a Texas population of six-lined racerunners, *Cnemidophorus sexlineatus* (Reptilia, Lacertilia, Teiidae). *Journal of Herpetology* 10:133–138.

Clark, D. R., Jr., C. M. Bunck, and R. J. Hall. 1997. Female reproductive dynamics in a Maryland population of ringneck snakes *(Diadophis punctatus)*. *Journal of Herpetology* 31:476–483.

Clark, D. R., Jr., and C. S. Lieb. 1973. Notes on reproduction in the night snake *(Hypsiglena torquata)*. *Southwestern Naturalist* 18:248–252.

Clark, H. 1953. Eggs, egg-laying and incubation of the snake *Elaphe emoryi* (Baird and Girard). *Copeia* 1953:90–92.

Clark, T. W., T. M. Campbell III, D. G. Socha, and D. E. Casey. 1982. Prairie dog colony attributes and associated vertebrate species. *Great Basin Naturalist* 42:572–582.

Clarke, J. A., J. T. Chopko, and S. P. Mackessy. 1996. The effect of moonlight on activity patterns of adult and juvenile prairie rattlesnakes *(Crotalus viridis viridis)*. *Journal of Herpetology* 30:192–197.

Clarkson, R. W., and J. C. deVos, Jr. 1986. The bullfrog, *Rana catesbeiana* Shaw, in the lower Colorado River, Arizona-California. *Journal of Herpetology* 20:42–49.

Clarkson, R. W., and J. C. Rorabaugh. 1989. Status of leopard frogs *(Rana pipiens* complex: Ranidae) in Arizona and southeastern California. *Southwestern Naturalist* 34:531–538.

Clay, W. M. 1938. A synopsis of the North American water snakes of the genus *Natrix*. *Copeia* 1938:173–182.

Cockerell, T.D.A. 1910. Reptiles and amphibians of the University of Colorado expedition of 1909. *University of Colorado Studies* 7 (2):130–131.

———. 1927a. *Zoology of Colorado*. University of Colorado, Boulder.

———. 1927b. Natural history. Pages 139–200 in *History of Colorado*, J. H. Baker and L. R. Hafen, eds. Vol. I. Linderman, Denver.

Cocroft, R. B. 1994. A cladistic analysis of chorus frog phylogeny (Hylidae: *Pseudacris*). *Herpetologica* 50:420–437.

Cohen, A. C., and J. L. Cohen. 1990. Ingestion of blister beetles by a Texas horned lizard. *Southwestern Naturalist* 35:369.

Cohen, R. R. 1974. Geographic distribution: *Arizona elegans elegans*. *Herpetological Review* 5:21.

Cole, C. J. 1971. Karyotypes of five monotypic species groups of the lizards in the genus *Sceloporus*. *American Museum Novitates* 2,450:1–17.

———. 1972. Chromosome variation in North American fence lizards (genus *Sceloporus; undulatus* species group). *Systematic Zoology* 21:357–363.

Cole, C. J., and L. M. Hardy. 1981. Systematics of North American colubrid snakes related to *Tantilla planiceps* (Blainville). *Bulletin of the American Museum of Natural History* 171:199–284.

———. 1983. *Tantilla hobartsmithi*. Catalogue of American Amphibians and Reptiles 318:1–2.

Collins, J. P. 1979. Intrapopulational variation in the body size at metamorphosis and timing of metamorphosis in the bullfrog, *Rana catesbeiana*. *Ecology* 60:738–749.

———. 1981. Distribution, habitats and life history variation in the tiger salamander, *Ambystoma tigrinum,* in east-central and southeast Arizona. *Copeia* 1981:666–675.

Collins, J. P., and J. E. Cheek. 1983. Effect of food and density on development of typical and cannibalistic salamander larvae in *Ambystoma tigrinum nebulosum. American Zoologist* 23:77–84.

Collins, J. P., and J. R. Holomuzki. 1984. Intraspecific variation in diet within and between trophic morphs in larval tiger salamanders *(Ambystoma tigrinum nebulosum). Canadian Journal of Zoology* 62:168–174.

Collins, J. P., J. B. Mitton, and B. A. Pierce. 1980. *Ambystoma tigrinum:* A multi-species conglomerate? *Copeia* 1980:938–941.

Collins, J. T. 1973. A range extension and addition to the herpetofauna of Kansas. *Transactions of the Kansas Academy of Sciences* 76:88–90.

———. 1993. *Amphibians and reptiles in Kansas.* 3d ed., rev. University of Kansas Museum of Natural History, Public Education Series 13.

———. 1997. *Standard common and current scientific names for North American amphibians and reptiles.* 4th ed. Society for the Study of Amphibians and Reptiles, Herpetological Circular No. 25.

Colorado Herpetological Society. 1976. *A guide to the reptiles and amphibians of the Denver area.* Colorado Herpetological Society, Denver.

Colorado Natural Heritage Program. 1997. *Conservation status of the rare and imperiled vertebrates of Colorado.* Colorado State University, Fort Collins.

Conant, R., and J. T. Collins. 1991. *A field guide to reptiles and amphibians: Eastern and central North America.* Houghton Mifflin Company, Boston.

Conant, R., and A. Downs. 1940. Miscellaneous notes on the eggs and young of reptiles. *Zoologica* 25:33–48.

Congdon, J. D., G. L. Breitenbach, R. C. van Loben Sels, and D. W. Tinkle. 1987. Reproduction and nesting ecology of snapping turtles *(Chelydra serpentina)* in southeastern Michigan. *Herpetologica* 43:39–54.

Congdon, J. D., A. E. Dunham, and R. C. van Loben Sels. 1994. Demographics of common snapping turtles *(Chelydra serpentina):* Implications for conservation and management of long-lived organisms. *American Zoologist* 34:397–408.

Congdon, J. D., S. W. Gotte, and R. W. McDiarmid. 1992. Ontogenetic changes in habitat use by juvenile turtles, *Chelydra serpentina* and *Chrysemys picta. Canadian Field-Naturalist* 106:241–248.

Congdon, J. D., and D. W. Tinkle. 1982. Energy expenditure in free-ranging sagebrush lizards *(Sceloporus graciosus). Canadian Journal of Zoology* 60:1,412–1,416.

Conner, D. E. 1970. A confederate in the Colorado gold fields. D. J. Berthrong and O. Davenport, eds. University of Oklahoma Press, Norman.

Conners, J. S. 1986. A captive breeding of the Great Basin gopher snake, *Pituophis melanoleucus deserticola. Herpetological Review* 17:12–13.

Cook, F. R. 1964. Communal egg laying in the smooth green snake. *Herpetologica* 20:206.

Cooper, W. E., Jr. 1986. Chromatic components of female secondary sexual coloration: Influence on social behavior of male keeled earless lizards *(Holbrookia propinqua). Copeia* 1986:980–986.

Cope, E. D. 1900. *The crocodilians, lizards, and snakes of North America. Report of the U.S. National Museum for 1898,* pages 153–1270.

Corn, S. 1979. Size at metamorphosis and growth rates of juvenile frogs from montane populations of *Rana pipiens. Journal of the Colorado-Wyoming Academy of Science* 11 (1):90.

———. 1980. Polymorphic reproductive behavior in male chorus frogs *(Pseudacris triseriata). Journal of the Colorado-Wyoming Academy of Science* 12 (1):6–7.

Corn, P. S. 1981. Field evidence for a relationship between color and developmental rate in the northern leopard frog *(Rana pipiens). Herpetologica* 37:155–160.

———. 1982a. Natural selection in leopard frog *(Rana pipiens)* tadpoles. *Bulletin of the Ecological Society of America* 63:83.

———. 1982b. Ecological genetics of albino chorus frogs *(Pseudacris triseriata). Journal of the Colorado-Wyoming Academy of Science* 14 (1):57.

———. 1982c. Color and pattern polymorphism in anurans. *Bulletin of the Chicago Herpetological Society* 17 (3):57–68.

———. 1982d. Selection pressures affecting a dorsal color polymorphism in *Rana pipiens.* Ph.D. dissertation, Colorado State University, Fort Collins.

———. 1986. Genetic and developmental studies of albino chorus frogs. *Journal of Heredity* 77:164–168.

———. 1992. Laboratory and field evaluation of effects of PIT tags. *Froglog* 4:2.

———. 1993. Life history notes: *Bufo boreas* (boreal toad). Predation. *Herpetological Review* 24:57.

———. 1994. What we know and don't know about amphibian declines in the West. Pages 59–67 in *Sustainable ecological systems: Implementing an ecological approach to land management,* W. W. Covington and L. F. DeBano, eds. USDA Forest Service, Rocky Mountain Forest and Range Experimental Station, Fort Collins, Colorado, General Technical Report RM-247.

———. 1998. Effects of ultraviolet radiation on boreal toads in Colorado. *Ecological Applications* 8:18–26.

Corn, P. S., and R. B. Bury. 1986. Morphological variation and zoogeography of racers *(Coluber constrictor)* in the central Rocky Mountains. *Herpetologica* 42:258–264.

———. 1990. *Sampling methods for terrestrial amphibians and reptiles.* USDA Forest Service, General Technical Report PNW-GTR-256.

Corn, P. S., and J. C. Fogleman. 1984. Extinction of montane populations of the northern leopard frog *(Rana pipiens)* in Colorado. *Journal of Herpetology* 18:147–152.

Corn, P. S., M. L. Jennings, and E. Muths. 1997. Survey and assessment of amphibian populations in Rocky Mountain National Park. *Northwestern Naturalist* 78:34–55.

Corn, P. S., and L. J. Livo. 1989. Leopard frog and wood frog reproduction in Colorado and Wyoming. *Northwestern Naturalist* 70:1–9.

Corn, P. S., W. Stolzenburg, and R. B. Bury. 1989. *Acid precipitation studies in Colorado and Wyoming: Interim report of surveys of montane amphibians and water chemistry.* U.S. Fish and Wildlife Service Biological Report 80(40.26).

Corn, P. S., and F. A. Vertucci. 1992. Descriptive risk assessment of the effects of acid deposition on Rocky Mountain amphibians. *Journal of Herpetology* 26:361–369.

Corse, W. A., and D. E. Metter. 1980. Economics, adult feeding and larval growth of *Rana catesbeiana* on a fish hatchery. *Journal of Herpetology* 14:231–238.

Coss, R. G., and D. H. Owings. 1989. Rattler battlers. *Natural History* 98 (5):30–35.

Costanzo, J. P. 1985. The bioenergetics of hibernation in the eastern garter snake *Thamnophis sirtalis sirtalis. Physiological Zoology* 58:682–692.

———. 1988. Recovery from ice-entombment in garter snakes. *Herpetological Review* 19:76–77.

———. 1989a. Effects of humidity, temperature, and submergence behavior on survivorship and energy use in hibernating garter snakes, *Thamnophis sirtalis. Canadian Journal of Zoology* 67:2,486–2,492.

———. 1989b. A physiological basis for prolonged submergence in hibernating garter snakes *Thamnophis sirtalis:* Evidence for an energy-sparing adaptation. *Physiological Zoology* 62:580–592.

Costanzo, J. P., J. B. Iverson, M. F. Wright, and R. E. Lee, Jr. 1995. Cold hardiness and overwintering strategies of hatchlings in an assemblage of northern turtles. *Ecology* 76:1,772–1,785.

Costanzo, J. P., R. E. Lee, Jr., and P. L. Loritz. 1993. Glucose concentration regulates freeze tolerance in the wood frog *Rana sylvatica. Journal of Experimental Biology* 181:145–155.

Costello, D. F. 1969. *The prairie world.* Thomas Y. Crowell, New York.

Cottam, W. P. 1937. Copulation in the western blue racer. *Copeia* 1937:229.

Cousineau, M., and K. Rogers. 1991. Observations on sympatric *Rana pipiens, R. blairi,* and their hybrids in eastern Colorado. *Journal of Herpetology* 25:114–116.

Cowardin, L. M., V. Carter, F. C. Golet, and E. T. LaRoe. 1979. Classification of wetlands and deepwater habitats of the United States. U.S. Fish and Wildlife Service FWS/OBS-79/31.

Cowles, R. B. 1946. Carrion eating by a snake. *Herpetologica* 3:121–122.

Cowles, R. B., and E. S. Bakker. 1977. *Desert journal: Reflections of a naturalist.* University of California Press, Berkeley.

Cowles, R. B., and C. M. Bogert. 1936. The herpetology of the Boulder Dam region (Nev., Ariz., Utah). *Herpetologica* 1:33–42.

———. 1944. A preliminary study of the thermal requirements of desert reptiles. *Bulletin of the American Museum of Natural History* 83:261–296.

Cox, D. C., and W. W. Tanner. 1995. *Snakes of Utah.* Brigham Young University, Provo, Utah.

Crabtree, C. B., and R. W. Murphy. 1984. Analysis of maternal-offspring allozymes in *Crotalus viridis. Journal of Herpetology* 18:75–80.

Cragin, F. W. 1894. Herpetological notes from Kansas and Texas. *Colorado College Studies* 5:37–39.

Creusere, F. M., and W. G. Whitford. 1976. Ecological relationships in a desert anuran community. *Herpetologica* 32:7–18.

———. 1982. Temporal and spatial resource partitioning in a Chihuahuan Desert lizard community. Pages 121–127 in *Herpetological communities,* N. J. Scott, ed. U.S. Fish and Wildlife Service Research Report No. 13.

Crews, D., and W. R. Garstka. 1982. The ecological physiology of a garter snake. *Scientific American* 247:158–168.

Crews, D., and M. C. Moore. 1993. Psychobiology of reproduction of unisexual whiptail lizards. Pages 257–282 in *Biology of whiptail lizards (genus* Cnemidophorus), J. W. Wright and L. J. Vitt, eds. Oklahoma Museum of Natural History, Norman.

Criddle, S. 1937. Snakes from an ant hill. *Copeia* 1937:142.

Crites, J. 1985. The milk snake. *Colorado Outdoors* 34 (3):35–38.

Crowley, S. R. 1985a. Insensitivity to desiccation of sprint running performance in the lizard, *Sceloporus undulatus. Journal of Herpetology* 19:171–174.

———. 1985b. Thermal sensitivity of sprint-running in the lizard *Sceloporus undulatus:* Support for a conservative view of thermal physiology. *Oecologia* 66:219–225.

———. 1987. The effect of desiccation upon the preferred body temperature and activity level of the lizard *Sceloporus undulatus. Copeia* 1987:25–32.

Crowley, S. R., and R. D. Pietruszka. 1983. Aggressiveness and vocalization in the leopard lizard *(Gambelia wislizenii):* The influence of temperature. *Animal Behaviour* 31:1,055–1,060.

Cuellar, H. S. 1966. Delayed fertilization in the lizard *Uta stansburiana. Copeia* 1966:549–552.

Cuellar, H. S., and J. D. Fawcett. 1971. The male sexual cycle of the lesser earless lizard, *Holbrookia maculata maculata* (Reptilia: Iguanidae). *Journal of the Colorado-Wyoming Academy of Science* 7:111.

Cuellar, O. 1977. Genetic homogeneity and speciation in the parthenogenetic lizards *Cnemidophorus velox* and *C. neomexicanus:* Evidence from intraspecific histocompatibility. *Evolution* 31:24–31.

Cuellar, O., and J. W. Wright. 1992. Isogenicity in the unisexual lizard *Cnemidophorus velox. C.R. Society of Biogeography* 68:157–160.

Cunjak, R. A. 1986. Winter habitat of northern leopard frogs, *Rana pipiens,* in a southern Ontario stream. *Canadian Journal of Zoology* 64:255–257.

Cunningham, A. A. 1998. Disease and Pathology Working Group report: A breakthrough in the hunt for a cause of amphibian declines. *Froglog* 30:3.

Cunningham, G. R., S. M. Hickey, and C. M. Gowen. 1996. *Crotalus viridis viridis* (prairie rattlesnake): Behavior. *Herpetological Review* 27:24.

Curtis, B. F. 1960. Major geological features of Colorado. Pages 1–8 in *Guide to the geology of Colorado,* R. J. Weimer and J. D. Haun, eds. Geological Society of America, Rocky Mountain Association of Geologists, Colorado Scientific Society.

Dalrymple, G. H. 1979. Packaging problems of head retraction in trionychid turtles. *Copeia* 1979:655–660.

Dalrymple, G. H., and N. G. Reichenbach. 1984. Management of an endangered species of snake in Ohio, USA. *Biological Conservation* 30:195–200.

Dartt, M. 1879. *On the plains and among the peaks; or, how Mrs. Maxwell made her natural history collection.* Claxton, Remsen & Haffelfinger, Philadelphia.

Davenport, S. R., J. N. Stuart, and D. S. Sias. 1998. Geographic distribution: *Lampropeltis getula californiae. Herpetological Review* 29:53.

Davidson, C. 1996. *Frog and toad calls of the Rocky Mountains.* Library of Natural Sounds, Cornell Laboratory of Ornithology.

Davis, M. S. 1987. Acoustically mediated neighbor recognition in the North American bullfrog, *Rana catesbeiana. Behavioral Ecology and Sociobiology* 21:185–190.

Dean, N. K., and A. D. Stock. 1961. Amphibians and reptiles of the Navajo Reservoir basin. *University of Utah Anthropology Papers* 55:123–127.

Deboer, K. F. 1973. Neoteny in a population of *Ambystoma tigrinum nebulosum* in Gunnison County, Colorado. *Journal of the Colorado-Wyoming Academy of Science* 7 (4):7.

De Carvalho, A. L. 1954. A preliminary synopsis of the genera of American microhylid frogs. *University of Michigan Museum of Zoology Occasional Papers* 555:1–19.

DeFusco, R. P., D. Chiszar, and H. M. Smith. 1993. Geographic distribution: *Sceloporus undulatus erythrocheilus. Herpetological Review* 24:155.

———. 1994. Geographic distribution: *Liochlorophis vernalis blanchardi. Herpetological Review* 25:77.

Degenhardt, W. G., C. W. Painter, and A. H. Price. 1996. *Amphibians and reptiles of New Mexico.* University of New Mexico Press, Albuquerque.

Delson, J., and W. G. Whitford. 1973. Critical thermal maxima in several life history stages in desert and montane populations of *Ambystoma tigrinum. Herpetologica* 29:352–355.

DeMarco, V. G., R. W. Drenner, and G. W. Ferguson. 1985. Maximum prey size of an insectivorous lizard, *Sceloporus undulatus garmani. Copeia* 1985:1,077–1,080.

Densmore, L. D., III, J. W. Wright, and W. M. Brown. 1989. Mitochondrial-DNA analyses and the origin and relative age of parthenogenetic lizards (genus *Cnemidophorus*). II: *C. neomexicanus* and the *C. tesselatus* complex. *Evolution* 43:943–957.

de Queiroz, A. 1984. Effects of prey type on the prey-handling behavior of the bullsnake, *Pituophis melanoleucus. Journal of Herpetology* 18:333–336.

Derickson, W. K. 1976. Ecological and physiological aspects of reproductive strategies in two lizards. *Ecology* 57:445–458.

De Santis, B., B. Sheafor, H. M. Smith, and D. Chiszar. 1995. Geographic distribution: *Chelydra serpentina serpentina. Herpetological Review* 26:154.

Deslippe, R. J. 1989. Population structure, territoriality, and social behaviour of three species of iguanid lizards. M.S. thesis, University of Windsor, Ontario, Canada.

Deslippe, R. J., and R. T. M'Closkey. 1991. An experimental test of mate defense in an iguanid lizard *(Sceloporus graciosus). Ecology* 72:1,218–1,224.

Deslippe, R. J., R. T. M'Closkey, S. P. Dajczak, and C. P. Szpak. 1990a. Female tree lizards: Oviposition and activity patterns during the breeding season. *Copeia* 1990:877–880.

———. 1990b. A quantitative study of the social behavior of tree lizards, *Urosaurus ornatus. Journal of Herpetology* 24:337–341.

Dessauer, H. C., and C. J. Cole. 1989. Diversity between and within nominal forms of unisexual lizards. Pages 49–71 in *Evolution and ecology of unisexual vertebrates,* R. M. Dawley and J. P. Bogart, eds. Bulletin of the New York State Museum 466.

———. 1991. Genetics of whiptail lizards (Reptilia: Teiidae: *Cnemidophorus*) in a hybrid zone in southwestern New Mexico. *Copeia* 1991:622–637.

Devine, M. C. 1975. Copulatory plugs in snakes: Enforced chastity. *Science* 187:844–845.

———. 1977. Copulatory plugs, restricted mating opportunities and reproductive competition among male garter snakes. *Nature* 267:345–346.

Dickerson, M. C. 1906. *The frog book.* Doubleday, Page, New York.

Dillenbeck, T. 1988. Winter sightings. *Kansas Herpetological Society Newsletter* 71:12.

Diller, L. V. 1990. A field observation on the feeding behavior of *Crotalus viridis lutosus. Journal of Herpetology* 24:95–97.

Diller, L. V., and D. R. Johnson. 1988. Food habits, consumption rates, and predation rates of western rattlesnakes and gopher snakes in southwestern Idaho. *Herpetologica* 44:228–233.

Diller, L. V., and R. L. Wallace. 1986. Aspects of the life history and ecology of the desert night snake, *Hypsiglena torquata deserticola:* Colubridae, in southwestern Idaho. *Southwestern Naturalist* 31:55–64.

Dimmitt, M. A., and R. Ruibal. 1980a. Exploitation of food resources by spadefoot toads *(Scaphiopus). Copeia* 1980:854–862.

———. 1980b. Environmental correlates of emergence in spadefoot toads *(Scaphiopus). Journal of Herpetology* 14:21–29.

Dixon, J. R. 1959. Geographic variation and distribution of the long-tailed group of the glossy snake, *Arizona elegans* Kennicott. *Southwestern Naturalist* 4:20–29.

———. 1967. Aspects of the biology of the lizards of the White Sands, New Mexico. *Los Angeles County Museum of Natural History Contributions in Science* 129:1–22.

———. 1971. A noteworthy record of *Eumeces multivirgatus* from Texas. *Southwestern Naturalist* 15:502.

Dixon, J. R., and R. H. Dean. 1986. Status of the southern populations of the night snake (*Hypsiglena:* Colubridae) exclusive of California and Baja California. *Southwestern Naturalist* 31:307–318.

Dixon, J. R., and R. R. Fleet. 1976. *Arizona, Arizona elegans. Catalogue of American Amphibians and Reptiles* 179:1–4.

Dixon, J. R., and P. A. Medica. 1965. Noteworthy records of reptiles from New Mexico. *Herpetologica* 21:72–75.

———. 1966. Summer food of four species of lizards from the vicinity of White Sands, New Mexico. *Los Angeles County Museum of Natural History Contributions in Science* 121:1–6.

Dodd, C. K., Jr., and E. D. Brodie, Jr. 1975. Notes on the defensive behavior of the snapping turtle, *Chelydra serpentina. Herpetologica* 31:286–288.

Dodson, S. I., and V. E. Dodson. 1971. The diet of *Ambystoma tigrinum* from western Colorado. *Copeia* 1971:614–624.

Doles, M. W., C. W. Painter, and L. W. Gorum. 1996. Natural history notes: *Eumeces multivirgatus.* Clutch size. *Herpetological Review* 27:201.

Donaldson, W., A. H. Price, and J. Morse. 1994. The current status and future prospects of the Texas horned lizard *(Phrynosoma cornutum)* in Texas. *Texas Journal of Science* 46:97–113.

Donoho, R., J. Hobert, C. Montgomery, and S. P. Montgomery. 1996. Geographic distribution: *Eumeces obsoletus. Herpetological Review* 27:32.

Doroff, A. M., and L. B. Keith. 1990. Demography and ecology of an ornate box turtle *(Terrapene ornata)* population in south-central Wisconsin. *Copeia* 1990:387–399.

Douglas, C. L. 1966. Amphibians and reptiles of Mesa Verde National Park, Colorado. *University of Kansas Publications, Museum of Natural History* 15 (15):711–744.

———. 1967. New records of mammals from Mesa Verde National Park, Colorado. *Journal of Mammalogy* 48:322–323.

Dowling, H. G. 1952. A taxonomic study of the ratsnakes, genus *Elaphe* Fitzinger. IV: A check list of the American forms. *University of Michigan Museum of Zoology Occasional Papers* 541:1–12.

Droge, D. L., S. M. Jones, and R. E. Ballinger. 1982. Reproduction of *Holbrookia maculata* in western Nebraska. *Copeia* 1982:356–362.

Duellman, W. E., and R. G. Zweifel. 1962. A synopsis of the lizards of the *sexlineatus* group (genus *Cnemidophorus*). *Bulletin of the American Museum of Natural History* 123:155–210.

Dundee, H. A. 1947. Notes on salamanders collected in Oklahoma. *Copeia* 1947:117–120.

———. 1980. A comment on J. Howard Campbell's *Bipes* report. *Herpetological Review* 11:75–76.

———. 1996. Some reallocations of type localities of reptiles and amphibians described from the Major Stephen H. Long Expedition to the Rocky Mountains, with comments on some of the statements made in the account written by Edwin James. *Tulane Studies in Zoology and Botany* 30:75–89.

Dundee, H. A., and D. A. Rossman. 1989. *The amphibians and reptiles of Louisiana.* Louisiana State University Press, Baton Rogue.

Dunham, A. E. 1981. Populations in a fluctuating environment: The comparative population ecology of the iguanid lizards *Sceloporus merriami* and *Urosaurus ornatus. University of Michigan Museum of Zoology Miscellaneous Publications* 158:1–62.

———. 1982. Demographic and life-history variation among populations of the iguanid lizard *Urosaurus ornatus:* Implications for the study of life-history phenomena in lizards. *Herpeto-logica* 38:208–221.

———. 1990. An experimental study of interspecific competition between the iguanid lizards *Sceloporus merriami* and *Urosaurus ornatus. Ecological Monographs* 50:309–330.

Dunlap, D. G. 1977. Wood and western spotted frogs (Amphibia, Anura, Ranidae) in the Big Horn Mountains of Wyoming. *Journal of Herpetology* 11:85–87.

Dunlap, D. G., and K. C. Kruse. 1976. Frogs of the *Rana pipiens* complex in the northern and central plains states. *Southwestern Naturalist* 20:559–571.

Duvall, D., S. J. Arnold, and G. W. Schuett. 1992. Pitviper mating systems: ecological potential, sexual selection, and microevolution. Pages 321–336 in J. A. Campbell and E. D. Brodie Jr., editors. *Biology of Pitvipers.* Selva, Tyler, Texas.

Duvall, D., M. J. Goode, W. K. Hayes, J. K. Leonhardt, and D. Brown. 1990. Prairie rattlesnake vernal migrations: Field experimental analyses and survival value. *National Geographic Research* 6:457–469.

Duvall, D., B. M. Graves, and G. C. Carpenter. 1987. Visual and chemical composite signaling effects of *Sceloporus* lizard fecal boli. *Copeia* 1987:1,028–1,031.

Duvall, D., M. B. King, and K. J. Gutzwiller. 1985. Behavioral ecology and ethology of the prairie rattlesnake. *National Geographic Research* 1:80–111.

Easterla, D. A. 1975. Reproductive and ecological observations on *Tantilla rubra cucullata* from Big Bend National Park, Texas (Serpentes, Colubridae). *Herpetologica* 31:234–236.

Eaton, T. H., Jr. 1935. *Report on amphibians and reptiles of the Navajo Country.* Rainbow Bridge-Monument Valley Expedition Bulletin 3. Berkeley, California.

Ecology Consultants, Inc. 1976. *Final report on flora and terrestrial vertebrate studies of the Grand Valley unit.* Report to U.S. Bureau of Reclamation, Grand Junction, Colorado, and Salt Lake City, Utah.

Edgren, R. A. 1955. The natural history of the hog-nosed snakes, genus *Heterodon:* A review. *Herpetologica* 11:105–117.

Ehrlich, D. 1979. Predation by bullfrog tadpoles *(Rana catesbeiana)* on eggs and newly hatched larvae of the plains leopard frog *(Rana blairi). Bulletin of the Maryland Herpetological Society* 15:25–26.

Eichholz, M. W., and W. D. Koenig. 1992. Gopher snake attraction to birds' nests. *Southwestern Naturalist* 37:293–298.

Ellis, M. M., and J. Henderson. 1913. The Amphibia and Reptilia of Colorado, Part I. *University of Colorado Studies* 10:39–129.

———. 1915. The Amphibia and Reptilia of Colorado, Part II. *University of Colorado Studies* 15:253–263.

Ellis, S. L., T. Shoemaker, and R. Sanz. 1979. Inventories of plants, birds, mammals, reptiles, and amphibians of the Unaweep Canyon Springs, Mesa County, Colorado. Unpublished report to Colorado Natural Areas Program, Department of Natural Resources, Denver, Colorado.

Ellner, L. R., and W. H. Karasov. 1993. Latitudinal variation in the thermal biology of ornate box turtles. *Copeia* 1993:447–455.

Emlen, S. T. 1968. Territoriality in the bullfrog, *Rana catesbeiana. Copeia* 1968:240–243.

———. 1976. Lek organization and mating strategies in the bullfrog. *Behavioral Ecology and Sociobiology* 1:283–313.

———. 1977. "Double clutching" and its possible significance in the bullfrog. *Copeia* 1977:749–751.

Emory, W. H. 1848. *Notes of a military reconnaissance, from Fort Leavenworth, in Missouri, to San Diego, in California, including parts of the Arkansas, Del Norte, and Gila rivers.* H. Long & Brother, New York.

Engeman, R. M. 1994. Geographic distribution: *Apalone spinifera. Herpetological Review* 25:162.

Engeman, R. M., and R. W. Connell. 1990. Boreal toad in Clear Creek County, Colorado. *Northwestern Naturalist* 71:98.

Engeman, R. M., and J. J. Delutes III. 1994. Natural history notes: *Pituophis melanoleucus deserticola* (Great Basin gopher snake). Behavior. *Herpetological Review* 25:125.

Engeman, R. M., and E. M. Engeman. 1996. Longevity of Woodhouse's toad in Colorado. *Northwestern Naturalist* 77:23.

Engeman, R. M., and A. Hannes. 1988. Life history notes: *Sceloporus undulatus elongatus* (eastern fence lizard, northern plateau lizard). Behavior. *Herpetological Review* 19:34–35.

Engeman, R. M., T. A. Scrips, and T. G. Bonzer. 1984. Life history notes: *Coluber constrictor mormon* (western yellow-belly racer): Behavior. *Herpetological Review* 15:112.

Ernst, C. H. 1992. *Venomous reptiles of North America.* Smithsonian Institution Press, Washington, D.C.

Ernst, C. H., and R. W. Barbour. 1989. *Snakes of eastern North America.* George Mason University Press, Fairfax, Virginia.

Ernst, C. H., J. E. Lovich, and R. W. Barbour. 1994. *Turtles of the United States and Canada.* Smithsonian Institution Press, Washington, D.C.

Etchberger, C. R., M. A. Ewert, B. A. Raper, and C. E. Nelson. 1992. Do low incubation temperatures yield females in painted turtles? *Canadian Journal of Zoology* 70:391–394.

Etheridge, K., and L. C. Wit. 1982. *Cnemidophorus sexlineatus* (six-lined race-runner): Cannibalism. *Herpetological Review* 13:19.

Evans, H. E., and K. M. O'Neill. 1986. Wasps of the grasslands. *Colorado Outdoors* 35 (6):22–24.

Evans, L. T. 1959. A motion picture study of maternal behavior of the lizard *Eumeces obsoletus* Baird and Girard. *Copeia* 1959:103–110.

Everett, C. T. 1971. Courtship and mating of *Eumeces multivirgatus* (Scincidae). *Journal of Herpetology* 5:189–190.

Ewert, M. A. 1979. The embryo and its egg: Development and natural history. Pages 333–413 in *Turtles: Perspectives and research*, M. Harless and H. Morlock, eds. John Wiley & Sons, New York.

Fair, W. S., and S. E. Henke. 1997a. Efficacy of capture methods for a low density population of *Phrynosoma cornutum*. *Herpetological Review* 28:135–137.

———. 1997b. Effects of habitat manipulations on Texas horned lizards and their prey. *Journal of Wildlife Management* 61:1,366–1,370.

Fawcett, J. D., and J. W. Ferner. 1971. Femoral pores in *Sceloporus undulatus* (Reptilia: Iguanidae). *Journal of the Colorado-Wyoming Academy of Science* 7:110.

Feder, M. E., J. F. Lynch, H. B. Shaffer, and D. B. Wake. 1982. Field body temperatures of tropical and temperate zone salamanders. *Smithsonian Herpetological Information Service* 52:1–23.

Fenneman, N. M. 1931. *Physiography of western United States.* McGraw-Hill, New York.

Fenton, M. B., and L. E. Licht. 1990. Why rattle snake? *Journal of Herpetology* 24:274–279.

Ferguson, G. W. 1969. Interracial discrimination in male side-blotched lizards, *Uta stansburiana*. *Copeia* 1969:188–189.

———. 1970. Mating behavior of the side-blotched lizards of the genus *Uta* (Sauria: Iguanidae). *Animal Behaviour* 18:65–72.

———. 1971a. Observations on the behavior and interactions of two sympatric *Sceloporus* in Utah. *American Midland Naturalist* 86:190–196.

———. 1971b. Variation and evolution of push-up displays of the side-blotched lizard genus *Uta* (Iguanidae). *Systematic Zoology* 20:79–101.

———. 1972. Species discrimination by male side-blotched lizards *Uta stansburiana* in Colorado. *American Midland Naturalist* 87:523–524.

———. 1973. Character displacement of the push-up displays of two partially-sympatric species of spiny lizards, *Sceloporus* (Sauria: Iguanidae). *Herpetologica* 29:281–284.

———. 1976. Color change and reproductive cycling in female collared lizards *(Crotaphytus collaris). Copeia* 1976:491–494.

Ferguson, G. W., C. H. Bohlen, and H. P. Wooley. 1980. *Sceloporus undulatus:* Comparative life history and regulation of a Kansas population. *Ecology* 61:313–322.

Ferguson, G. W., and T. Brockman. 1980. Geographic differences of growth rate of *Sceloporus* lizards (Sauria: Iguanidae). *Copeia* 1980:259–264.

Ferguson, G. W., K. L. Brown, and V. G. DeMarco. 1982. Selective basis for the evolution of variable egg and hatchling size in some iguanid lizards. *Herpetologica* 38:178–188.

Ferguson, G. W., and S. F. Fox. 1984. Annual variation of survival advantage of large juvenile side-blotched lizards, *Uta stansburiana:* Its causes and evolutionary significance. *Evolution* 38:342–349.

Ferguson, G. W., J. L. Hughes, and K. L. Brown. 1983. Food availability and territorial establishment of juvenile *Sceloporus undulatus*. Pages 143–148 in *Lizard ecology: Studies of a model organism*, R. B. Huey, E. R. Pianka, and T. W. Schoener, eds. Harvard University Press, Cambridge, Massachusetts.

Ferguson, G. W., and H. L. Snell. 1986. Endogenous control of seasonal change of egg, hatchling, and clutch size of the lizard *Sceloporus undulatus garmani*. *Herpetologica* 42:185–191.

Fernandez, P. J., Jr., and J. P. Collins. 1988. Effect of environment and ontogeny on color pattern variation in Arizona tiger salamanders (*Ambystoma tigrinum nebulosum* Hallowell). *Copeia* 1988:928–938.

Ferner, J. W. 1970a. Home range ecology of *Sceloporus undulatus erythrocheilus* Maslin (Reptilia, Iguanidae). *Journal of the Colorado-Wyoming Academy of Science* 7 (1):43–44.

———. 1970b. Home range of *Sceloporus undulatus erythrocheilus* Maslin. *Herpetological Review* 2:6.

———. 1972. An ecological study of *Sceloporus undulatus erythrocheilus* (Reptilia, Iguanidae) in Colorado. Ph.D. thesis, University of Colorado, Boulder.

———. 1973. Notes on lip coloration in *Sceloporus undulatus erythrocheilus* (Reptilia: Iguanidae). *Journal of the Colorado-Wyoming Academy of Science* 7 (2):75.

———. 1974. Home-range size and overlap in *Sceloporus undulatus erythrocheilus* (Reptilia: Iguanidae). *Copeia* 1974:332–337.

———. 1976. Notes on natural history and behavior of *Sceloporus undulatus erythrocheilus* in Colorado. *American Midland Naturalist* 96:291–302.

———. 1979. A review of marking techniques for amphibians and reptiles. Society for the study of Amphibians and Reptiles. *Herpetological Circular* No. 9.

Fetkavich, C., and L. J. Livo. 1998. Late-season boreal toad tadpoles. *Northwestern Naturalist.* 79:120–121.

Fetkavich, C., L. J. Livo, and H. M. Smith. 1997. Geographic distribution: *Pseudacris triseriata*. *Herpetological Review* 28:93.

Fiero, M. K., M. W. Siefert, T. J. Weaver, and C. A. Bonilla. 1972. Comparative study of juvenile and adult prairie rattlesnake *(Crotalus viridis viridis)* venoms. *Toxicon* 10:81–82.

Finkler, M. S., and D. L. Claussen. 1997. Use of the tail in terrestrial locomotor activities of juvenile *Chelydra serpentina*. *Copeia* 1997:884–887.

Finley, R. B., Jr. 1953. A northern record of *Hyla arenicolor* in western Colorado. *Copeia* 1953:180.

———. 1958. The wood rats of Colorado: Distribution and ecology. *University of Kansas Publications, Museum of Natural History* 10:213–552.

Fisher, R. N., and H. B. Shaffer. 1996. The decline of amphibians in California's Great Central Valley. *Conservation Biology* 10:1,387–1,397.

Fitch, H. S. 1940. A biogeographical study of the *ordinoides* artenkreis of garter snakes (genus *Thamnophis*). *University of California Publications in Zoology* 44:1–150.

———. 1955. Habits and adaptations of the Great Plains skink *(Eumeces obsoletus)*. *Ecological Monographs* 25:59–83.

———. 1956a. A field study of the Kansas ant-eating frog, *Gastrophryne olivacea*. *University of Kansas Publications, Museum of Natural History* 8:275–306.

———. 1956b. Early sexual maturity and longevity under natural conditions in the Great Plains narrow-mouthed frog. *Herpetologica* 12:281–282.

———. 1956c. Temperature responses in free-living amphibians and reptiles of northeastern Kansas. *University of Kansas Publications, Museum of Natural History* 8:417–476.

———. 1956d. An ecological study of the collared lizard *(Crotaphytus collaris)*. *University of Kansas Publications, Museum of Natural History* 8:213–274.

———. 1958. Natural history of the six-lined racerunner *(Cnemidophorus sexlineatus)*. *University of Kansas Publications, Museum of Natural History* 11:11–62.

———. 1963. Natural history of the racer *Coluber constrictor*. *University of Kansas Publications, Museum of Natural History* 15:351–468.

———. 1965. An ecological study of the garter snake, *Thamnophis sirtalis*. *University of Kansas Publications, Museum of Natural History* 15:493–564.

———. 1970. Reproductive cycles of lizards and snakes. *University of Kansas Museum of Natural History Miscellaneous Publication* 52:1–247.

———. 1978. Sexual size differences in the genus *Sceloporus*. *University of Kansas Science Bulletin* 51 (13):441–461.

———. 1980. *Thamnophis sirtalis*. Catalogue of American Amphibians and Reptiles 270:1–4.

———. 1981. Sexual size differences in reptiles. *University of Kansas Museum of Natural History Miscellaneous Publication* 70:1–71.

———. 1982. Resources of a snake community in prairie-woodland habitat of northeastern Kansas. Pages 83–97 in *Herpetological communities*, N. J. Scott, ed. U.S. Fish and Wildlife Service, Wildlife Research Report (13):1–239.

———. 1983. *Thamnophis elegans*. Catalogue of American Amphibians and Reptiles 320:1–4.

———. 1985a. Variation in clutch and litter size in New World reptiles. *University of Kansas Museum of Natural History Miscellaneous Publication* 76:1–76.

———. 1985b. Observations on rattle size and demography of prairie rattlesnakes *(Crotalus viridis)* and timber rattlesnakes *(Crotalus horridus)* in Kansas. University of Kansas Museum of Natural History Occasional Papers 118:1–11.

Fitch, H. S., W. S. Brown, and W. S. Parker. 1981. *Coluber mormon*, a species distinct from *C. constrictor*. *Transactions of the Kansas Academy of Sciences* 84:196–203.

Fitch, H. S., and R. R. Fleet. 1970. Natural history of the milk snake *(Lampropeltis triangulum)* in northeastern Kansas. *Herpetologica* 26:387–396.

Fitch, H. S., and T. P. Maslin. 1961. Occurrence of the garter snake, *Thamnophis sirtalis*, in the Great Plains and Rocky Mountains. *University of Kansas Publications, Museum of Natural History* 13:289–308.

Fitch, H. S., and H. W. Shirer. 1971. A radiotelemetric study of spatial relationships in some common snakes. *Copeia* 1971:118–128.

Fitch, H. S., and W. W. Tanner. 1951. Remarks concerning the systematics of the collared lizards, *Crotaphytus collaris*, with description of a new subspecies. *Transactions of the Kansas Academy of Sciences* 54:548–559.

Fleet, R. R., and J. R. Dixon. 1971. Geographic variation within the long-tailed group of the glossy snake, *Arizona elegans* Kennicott. *Herpetologica* 27:295–302.

Fleharty, E. D. 1967. Comparative ecology of *Thamnophis elegans*, *T. cyrtopsis*, and *T. rufipunctatus* in New Mexico. *Southwestern Naturalist* 12:207–230.

Flowers, M. A., and B. M. Graves. 1995. Prey selectivity and size-specific diet changes in *Bufo cognatus* and *B. woodhousii* during early postmetamorphic ontogeny. *Journal of Herpetology* 29:608–612.

Fogleman, J. C. 1974. The distribution and inheritance of a dorsal color polymorphism in the leopard frog, *Rana pipiens*. M.S. thesis, Colorado State University, Fort Collins.

Fogleman, J. C., P. S. Corn, and D. Pettus. 1980. The genetic basis of a dorsal color polymorphism in *Rana pipiens*. *Journal of Heredity* 71:439–440.

Fogleman, J. C., and D. Pettus. 1974. The inheritance and distribution of a dorsal color polymorphism in leopard frogs, *Rana pipiens. Journal of the Colorado-Wyoming Academy of Science* 7 (5):73.

Fontenot, L. W., G. P. Noblet, and S. G. Platt. 1994. Rotenone hazards to amphibians and reptiles. *Herpetological Review* 25:150–153, 156.

Foote, R., and J. A. Macmahon. 1977. Electrophoretic studies of rattlesnake *(Crotalus & Sistrurus)* venom: Taxonomic implications. *Comparative Biochemistry and Physiology* 57B:235–241.

Force, E. R. 1935 [1936]. The relation of the knobbed anal keels to age and sex in the lined snake *Tropidoclonion lineatum* (Hallowell). *Papers of the Michigan Academy of Science, Arts and Letters* 21:613–617.

———. 1936. Notes on the blind snake, *Leptotyphlops dulcis* Baird and Girard in northeastern Oklahoma. *Proceedings of the Oklahoma Academy of Science* 16:24–26.

Ford, N. B. 1982. Species specificity of sex pheromone trails of sympatric and allopatric garter snakes *(Thamnophis). Copeia* 1982:10–13.

Ford, N. B., and V. Cobb. 1992. Timing of courtship in two colubrid snakes of the southeastern United States. *Copeia* 1992:573–577.

Ford, N. B., and C. W. Schofield. 1984. Species specificity of sex pheromone trails in the plains garter snake, *Thamnophis radix. Herpetologica* 40:51–55.

Forester, D. C. 1969. Reproductive isolation and hybridization between the spadefoot toads *Scaphiopus bombifrons* and *Scaphiopus hammondii* in West Texas. M.S. thesis, Texas Tech University, Lubbock.

———. 1973. Mating call as a reproductive isolating mechanism between *Scaphiopus bombifrons* and *S. hammondii. Copeia* 1973:60–67.

Forester, D. C., and D. V. Lykens. 1988. The ability of wood frog eggs to withstand prolonged terrestrial stranding: An empirical study. *Canadian Journal of Zoology* 66:1,733–1,735.

Forstner, M.R.J., S. K. Davis, and E. Arevalo. 1995. Support for the hypothesis of anguimorph ancestry for the suborder Serpentes from phylogenetic analysis of mitochondrial DNA sequences. *Molecular Phylogenetics and Evolution* 4 (1):93–102.

Fouquette, M. J., Jr. 1954. Food competition among four sympatric species of garter snakes, genus *Thamnophis. Texas Journal of Science* 6:172–188.

Fowler, J. A. 1966. A communal nesting site for the smooth green snake in Michigan. *Herpetologica* 22:231.

Fox, W. 1956. Seminal receptacles of snakes. *Anatomical Record* 124:519–540.

Frazer, N. B., J. L. Greene, and J. W. Gibbons. 1993. Temporal variation in growth rate and age at maturity of male painted turtles, *Chrysemys picta. American Midland Naturalist* 130:314–324.

Freddy, D. J., and J. L. Kogutt. 1978. Geographic distribution: *Crotalus viridis. Herpetological Review* 9:108.

Frost, D. 1983a. Past occurrence of *Acris crepitans* (Hylidae) in Arizona. *Southwestern Naturalist* 28:105.

Frost, D. R. 1983b. *Sonora semiannulata.* Catalogue of American Amphibians and Reptiles 333:1–4.

Frost, D. R., and J. T. Collins. 1988. Nomenclatural notes on reptiles of the United States. *Herpetological Review* 19:73.

Frost, D. R., and R. Etheridge. 1989. A phylogenetic analysis and taxonomy of iguanian lizards (Reptilia: Squamata). *University of Kansas Museum of Natural History Miscellaneous Publication* 81:1–65.

Frost, D. R., and D. M. Hillis. 1990. Species in concept and practice: Herpetological applications. *Herpetologica* 46:87–104.

Frost, D. R., and T. R. Van Devender. 1979. The relationship of the groundsnakes *Sonora semiannulata* and *S. episcopa* (Serpentes: Colubridae). Louisiana State University Museum of Zoology Occasional Papers 52:1–9.

Frost, D. R., and J. W. Wright. 1988. The taxonomy of uniparental species, with special reference to parthenogenetic *Cnemidophorus* (Squamata: Teiidae). *Systematic Zoology* 37:200–209.

Fuller, H. M., and L. R. Hafen, eds. 1957. *The journal of Captain John R. Bell. Official journalist for the Stephen H. Long expedition to the Rocky Mountains, 1820.* Far West and the Rockies History Series. Arthur H. Clark, Glendale, California.

Funk, R. S., and J. K. Tucker. 1978. Variation in a large brood of lined snakes, *Tropidoclonion lineatum* (Reptilia, Serpentes, Colubridae). *Journal of Herpetology* 12:115–117.

Furry, K., T. Swain, and D. Chiszar. 1991. Strike-induced chemosensory searching and trail following by prairie rattlesnakes *(Crotalus viridis)* preying upon deer mice *(Peromyscus maniculatus):* Chemical discrimination among individual mice. *Herpetologica* 47:69–78.

Galbraith, D. A., and R. J. Brooks. 1989. Age estimates for snapping turtles. *Journal of Wildlife Management* 53:502–508.

Galbraith, D. A., R. J. Brooks, and M. E. Obbard. 1989. The influence of growth rate on age and body size at maturity in female snapping turtles *(Chelydra serpentina). Copeia* 1989:896–904.

Galbraith, D. A., M. W. Chandler, and R. J. Brooks. 1987. The fine structure of home ranges of male *Chelydra serpentina:* Are snapping turtles territorial? *Canadian Journal of Zoology* 65:2,623–2,629.

Galbraith, D. A., C. J. Graesser, and R. J. Brooks. 1988. Egg retention by a snapping turtle, *Che-*

lydra serpentina, in central Ontario. *Canadian Field-Naturalist* 102:734.

Galbraith, D. A., B. N. White, R. J. Brooks, and P. T. Boag. 1993. Multiple paternity in clutches of snapping turtles *(Chelydra serpentina)* detected using DNA fingerprints. *Canadian Journal of Zoology* 71:318–324.

Gamow, R. I., and J. F. Harris. 1973. The infrared receptors of snakes. *Scientific American* 228 5:94–100.

Gannon, V.P.J., and D. M. Secoy. 1984. Growth and reproductive rates of a northern population of the prairie rattlesnake, *Crotalus v. viridis. Journal of Herpetology* 18:13–19.

———. 1985. Seasonal and daily activity patterns in a Canadian population of the prairie rattlesnake, *Crotalus viridis viridis. Canadian Journal of Zoology* 63:86–91.

Gans, C., and T. Papenfuss. 1980. There is no evidence that *Bipes* occurs in the U.S. *Herpetological Review* 11:74.

Garland, T., Jr. 1993. Locomotor performance and activity metabolism of *Cnemidophorus tigris* in relation to natural behaviors. Pages 163–210 in *Biology of whiptail lizards (genus* Cnemidophorus*)*, J. W. Wright and L. J. Vitt, eds. Oklahoma Museum of Natural History, Norman.

Garstka, W. R., B. Camazine, and D. Crews. 1982. Interactions of behavior and physiology during the annual reproductive cycle of the red-sided garter snake *(Thamnophis sirtalis parietalis). Herpetologica* 38:104–123.

Garstka, W. R., and D. Crews. 1981. Female sex pheromone in the skin and circulation of a garter snake. *Science* 214:681–683.

Garton, J. D., and H. R. Mushinsky. 1979. Integumentary toxicity and unpalatability as an antipredator mechanism in the narrow mouthed toad, *Gastrophryne carolinesis. Canadian Journal of Zoology* 57:1,965–1,973.

Gartside, D. F., J. S. Rogers, and H. C. Dessauer. 1977. Speciation with little genic and morphological differentiation in the ribbon snakes *Thamnophis proximus* and *T. sauritus* (Colubridae). *Copeia* 1977:697–705.

Gehlbach, F. R. 1956. Annotated records of southwestern amphibians and reptiles. *Transactions of the Kansas Academy of Sciences* 59:364–372.

———. 1965. Herpetology of the Zuni Mountains region of northwestern New Mexico. *Proceedings of the U.S. National Museum* 116:243–332.

———. 1970. Death-feigning and erratic behavior in leptotyphlopid, colubrid, and elapid snakes. *Herpetologica* 26:24–34.

———. 1974. Evolutionary relations of southwestern ringneck snakes *(Diadophis punctatus). Herpetologica* 30:140–148.

Gehlbach, F. R., and R. S. Baldridge. 1987. Live blind snakes *(Leptotyphlops dulcis)* in eastern screech owl *(Otus asio)* nests: A novel commensalism. *Oecologia* 71:560–563.

Gehlbach, F. R., and B. B. Collette. 1959. Distributional and biological notes on the Nebraska herpetofauna. *Herpetologica* 15:141–143.

Gehlbach, F. R., J. F. Watkins II, and H. W. Reno. 1968. Blind snake defensive behavior elicited by ant attacks. *BioScience* 18:784–785.

Gelatt, T. S., and J. D. Kelley. 1995. Western painted turtles, *Chrysemys picta bellii,* basking on a nesting common loon, *Gavia immer. Canadian Field-Naturalist* 109:456–458.

Gennaro, A. L. 1974. Growth, size, and age at sexual maturity of the lesser earless lizard, *Holbrookia maculata maculata,* in eastern New Mexico. *Herpetologica* 30:85–90.

Genter, D. L. 1984. Life history notes: *Crotalus viridis* (prairie rattlesnake): Food. *Herpetological Review* 15:49–50.

Geraghty, C. 1992. Current habitat status of and anthropogenic impacts on the tiger salamander, *Ambystoma tigrinum nebulosum.* Master's thesis, University of Illinois, Chicago.

Geraghty, C., and R. Willey. 1992. Current habitat status of and anthropogenic impacts on the tiger salamander, *Ambystoma tigrinum nebulosum.* Abstract, *6th Annual Meeting of the Society for Conservation Biology.*

Gern, W. A., and K. F. Deboer. 1973. Life patterns of neotenic *Ambystoma tigrinum nebulosum* in a moderate altitude pond. *Journal of the Colorado-Wyoming Academy of Science* 7 (4):7.

Gern, W. A., K. F. Deboer, G. L. Pepperd, R. A. Ponsford, and J. Ponsford. 1974. Difference in the egg size between neotenic and adult *Ambystoma tigrinum. Journal of the Colorado-Wyoming Academy of Science* 7 (5):67–68.

Gerrard, A. M. 1973. Observations on body proportions and habits of *Thamnophis radix haydeni. Journal of the Colorado-Wyoming Academy of Science* 7 (4):42.

Gibbons, J. W. 1968. Reproductive potential, activity, and cycles in the painted turtle, *Chrysemys picta. Ecology* 49:399–409.

Gibbs, H. L., K. A. Prior, P. J. Weatherhead, and G. Johnson. 1997. Genetic structure of populations of the threatened eastern massasauga rattlesnake, *Sistrurus c. catenatus:* Evidence from microsatellite DNA markers. *Molecular Ecology* 6:1,123–1,132.

Gillingham, J. C. 1979. Reproductive behavior of the rat snakes of eastern North America, genus *Elaphe. Copeia* 1979:319–331.

Gillis, J. E. 1975a. Characterization of a hybridizing complex of leopard frogs. Ph.D. dissertation, Colorado State University, Fort Collins.

———. 1975b. Geographic distribution: *Thamnophis elegans vagrans. Herpetological Review* 6:45.

———. 1979. Adaptive differences in the water economics of two species of leopard frogs from eastern Colorado. *Journal of Herpetology* 13:445–450.

Gillis, R. 1989. Selection for substrate reflectance-matching in two populations of red-chinned lizards *(Sceloporus undulatus erythrocheilus)* from Colorado. *American Midland Naturalist* 121:197–200.

———. 1991. Thermal biology of two populations of red-chinned lizards *(Sceloporus undulatus erythrocheilus)* living in different habitats in southcentral Colorado. *Journal of Herpetology* 25:18–23.

Gillis, R., and R. E. Ballinger. 1992. Reproductive ecology of red-chinned lizards *(Sceloporus undulatus erythrocheilus)* in southcentral Colorado: Comparisons with other populations of a wide-ranging species. *Oecologia* 89:236–243.

Gilmore, R. J. 1924. Notes on the life history and feeding habits of the spadefoot toad of the western plains. Colorado College Publications, General Series 129 (Science Series 13, No. 1):1–12.

———. 1929. Life history and feeding habits of the spadefoot toad. *Journal of the Colorado-Wyoming Academy of Science* 1 (1):41.

———. 1934. The tadpole of the spadefoot toad. *Journal of the Colorado-Wyoming Academy of Science* 1 (6):76.

Glaw, F., and J. Kohler. 1998. Amphibian species diversity exceeds that of mammals. *Herpetological Review* 29:11–12.

Gleason, R. L., and T. H. Craig. 1979. Food habits of burrowing owls in southeastern Idaho. *Great Basin Naturalist* 39:274–276.

Glenn, J. L., and R. Straight. 1977. The midget faded rattlesnake *(Crotalus viridis concolor)* venom: Lethal toxicity and individual variability. *Toxicon* 15:129–133.

Glissmeyer, H. R. 1951. Egg production of the Great Basin rattlesnake. *Herpetologica* 7:24–27.

Gloyd, H. K. 1928. The amphibians and reptiles of Franklin County, Kansas. *Transactions of the Kansas Academy of Sciences* 31:115–141.

———. 1937. A herpetological consideration of faunal areas in southern Arizona. *Bulletin of the Chicago Academy of Science* 5:79–136.

———. 1940. *The rattlesnakes, genera* Sistrurus *and* Crotalus: *A study in zoogeography and evolution.* Chicago Academy of Science Special Publication 4.

———. 1955. A review of the massasaugas, *Sistrurus catenatus,* of the southwestern United States (Serpentes: Crotalidae). *Bulletin of the Chicago Academy of Science* 10 (6):83–98.

Goebel, A. M. 1996. Systematics and conservation of bufonids in North America and in the *Bufo boreas* species group. Ph.D. dissertation, University of Colorado, Boulder.

Goettl, J. P., Jr., ed. 1997. *Boreal toad* (Bufo boreas boreas) *(Southern Rocky Mountain population) recovery plan.* Colorado Division of Wildlife, Denver.

Goldberg, S. R. 1971. Reproduction in the short-horned lizard *Phrynosoma douglassi* in Arizona. *Herpetologica* 27:311–314.

Goldberg, S. R., C. R. Bursey, and H. Cheam. 1998. Helminths of two native frog species *(Rana chiricahuensis, Rana yavapaiensis)* and one introduced frog species *(Rana catesbeiana)* (Ranidae) from Arizona. *Journal of Parasitology* 84:175–177.

Goldsmith, G. W. 1926. Habits and reactions of *Scaphiopus hammondi. Carnegie Institute Yearbook* 25:369–370.

Goode, M. J., and D. Duvall. 1989. Body temperature and defensive behaviour of free-ranging prairie rattlesnakes, *Crotalus viridis viridis. Animal Behaviour* 38:360–362.

Gorman, W. L. 1986. Patterns of color polymorphism in the cricket frog, *Acris crepitans,* in Kansas. *Copeia* 1986:995–999.

Gorman, W. L., and M. S. Gaines. 1987. Patterns of genetic variation in the cricket frog, *Acris crepitans. Copeia* 1987:352–360.

Gotte, S. W. 1992. Life history notes: *Chrysemys picta picta* (eastern painted turtle): Predation. *Herpetological Review* 23:80.

Gracie, A. E., and R. W. Murphy. 1986. Life history notes: *Gambelia wislizenii* (leopard lizard): Food. *Herpetological Review* 17:47.

Graham, T. B. 1995. Sympatric occurrence of Eubranchiopoda in ephemeral pools: A comment. *American Midland Naturalist* 133:371–372.

Graham, T. E., and A. A. Graham. 1991. Life history notes: *Trionyx spiniferus spiniferus* (eastern spiny softshell): Burying behavior. *Herpetological Review* 22:56–57.

———. 1997. Ecology of the eastern spiny softshell, *Apalone spinifera spinifera,* in the Lamoille River, Vermont. *Chelonian Conservation and Biology* 2 (3):63–369.

Graves, B. M. 1989a. Life history notes: *Crotalus viridis viridis* (prairie rattlesnake). Predation. *Herpetological Review* 20:71–72.

———. 1989b. Defensive behavior of female prairie rattlesnakes *(Crotalus viridis)* changes after parturition. *Copeia* 1989:791–794.

———. 1991. Consumption of an adult mouse by a free-ranging neonate prairie rattlesnake. *Southwestern Naturalist* 36:143.

Graves, B. M., and D. Duvall. 1987. An experimental study of aggregation and thermoregulation in prairie rattlesnakes *(Crotalus viridis viridis). Herpetologica* 43:259–264.

———. 1988. Evidence of an alarm pheromone from the cloacal sacs of prairie rattlesnakes. *Southwestern Naturalist* 33:339–345.

———. 1990. Spring emergence patterns of wandering garter snakes and prairie rattlesnakes in Wyoming. *Journal of Herpetology* 24:351–356.

———. 1993. Reproduction, rookery use, and thermoregulation in free-ranging, pregnant *Crotalus v. viridis. Journal of Herpetology* 27:33–41.

Graves, B. M., C. H. Summers, and K. L. Olmstead. 1993. Sensory mediation of aggregation among postmetamorphic *Bufo cognatus*. *Journal of Herpetology* 27:315–319.

Green, G. A., R. E. Fitzner, R. G. Anthony, and L. E. Rogers. 1993. Comparative diets of burrowing owls in Oregon and Washington. *Northwest Science* 67:88–93.

Greene, H. W. 1973. Defensive tail display by snakes and amphisbaenians. *Journal of Herpetology* 7:143–161.

———. 1984. Taxonomic status of the western racer, *Coluber constrictor mormon*. *Journal of Herpetology* 18:210–211.

———. 1990. A sound defense of the rattlesnake. *Pacific Discovery* 43 (4):10–19.

———. 1992. The ecological and behavioral context for pitviper evolution. Pages 107–117 in *Biology of the pitvipers*, J. A. Campbell and E. D. Brodie, Jr., eds. Selva, Tyler, Texas.

———. 1997. *Snakes: The evolution of mystery in nature*. University of California Press, Berkeley.

Greene, H. W., and G. V. Oliver, Jr. 1965. Notes on the natural history of the western massasauga. *Herpetologica* 21:225–228.

Greenwald, O. E. 1971. The effect of body temperature on oxygen consumption and heart rate in the Sonora gopher snake, *Pituophis melanoleucus affinis* Hallowell. *Copeia* 1971:98–106.

———. 1974. Thermal dependence of striking and prey capture by gopher snakes. *Copeia* 1974:141–148.

———. 1978. Kinematics and time relations of prey capture by gopher snakes. *Copeia* 1978:263–268.

Gregory, P. T. 1975. Aggregations of gravid snakes in Manitoba, Canada. *Copeia* 1975:185–186.

———. 1977. Life history observations of three species of snakes in Manitoba. *Canadian Field-Naturalist* 91:19–27.

Gregory, P. T., J. M. Macartney, and D. H. Rivard. 1980. Small mammal predation and prey handling behavior by the garter snake *Thamnophis elegans*. *Herpetologica* 36:87–93.

Gregory, P. T., and K. W. Stewart. 1975. Long-distance dispersal and feeding strategy of the red-sided garter snake *(Thamnophis sirtalis parietalis)* in the Interlake District of Manitoba. *Canadian Journal of Zoology* 53:238–245.

Grieb, J. R. 1952. Waterfowl production studies. Federal Aid Game Research Report 10:69. Colorado Department of Game and Fish.

Grimpe, R. D., and G. E. Benefield. 1981. *Lampropeltis g. holbrooki* (speckled kingsnake): Reproduction. *Herpetological Review* 12:80.

Grismer, L. L. 1994. Three new species of intertidal side-blotched lizards (genus *Uta*) from the Gulf of California, Mexico. *Herpetologica* 50:451–474.

Grismer, L. L., and J. A. McGuire. 1996. Taxonomy and biogeography of the *Sceloporus magister* complex (Squamata: Phrynosomatidae) in Baja California, Mexico. *Herpetologica* 52:416–427.

Grobman, A. B. 1941. A contribution to the knowledge of variation in *Opheodrys vernalis* (Harlan), with the description of a new subspecies. *University of Michigan Museum of Zoology Miscellaneous Publications* 50:1–38.

———. 1989. Clutch size and female length in *Opheodrys vernalis*. *Herpetological Review* 20:84.

———. 1992. Metamerism in the snake *Opheodrys vernalis*, with a description of a new subspecies. *Journal of Herpetology* 26:175–186.

———. 1990. The effect of soil temperatures on emergence from hibernation of *Terrapene carolina* and *T. ornata*. *American Midland Naturalist* 124:366–371

Grogan, W. L., Jr. 1974. Effects of accidental envenomation from the saliva of the eastern hognose snake, *Heterodon platyrhinos*. *Herpetologica* 30:248–249.

Grogan, W. L., Jr., and W. W. Tanner. 1974. Range extension of the long-nosed snake, *Rhinocheilus l. lecontei*, into east-central Utah. *Great Basin Naturalist* 34:238–240.

Grover, M. C. 1996. Microhabitat use and thermal ecology of two narrowly sympatric *Sceloporus* (Phrynosomatidae) lizards. *Journal of Herpetology* 30:152–160.

Gubanyi, J. A. 1990. Geographic distribution: *Arizona elegans* (glossy snake). *Herpetological Review* 21:41.

Guilette, L. J., Jr., R. E. Jones, K. T. Fitzgerald, and H. M. Smith. 1980. Evolution of viviparity in the lizard genus *Sceloporus*. *Herpetologica* 36:201–215.

Gutzke, W.H.N., and G. C. Packard. 1987. Influence of the hydric and thermal environments on eggs and hatchlings of bull snakes *Pituophis melanoleucus*. *Physiological Zoology* 60:9–17.

Gutzke, W.H.N., G. L. Paukstis, and L. L. McDaniel. 1985. Skewed sex ratios for adult and hatchling bullsnakes, *Pituophis melanoleucus,* in Nebraska. *Copeia* 1985:649–652.

Gutzke, W.H.N., G. L. Paukstis, and G. C. Packard. 1984. Pipping versus hatching as indices of time of incubation in reptiles. *Journal of Herpetology* 18:494–496.

Haenel, G. J. 1997. Mitochondrial DNA variation in populations of the tree lizard, *Urosaurus ornatus*. *Copeia* 1997:174–178.

Hahn, D. E. 1968. A biogeographic analysis of the herpetofauna of the San Luis Valley, Colorado. M.S. thesis, Louisiana State University, Baton Rouge.

———. 1979. *Leptotyphlops dulcis*. Catalogue of American Amphibians and Reptiles 231:1–2.

Hall, J. A. 1998. *Scaphiopus intermontanus*. Catalogue of American Amphibians and Reptiles 650:1–17.

Hall, J. A., J. H. Larsen, Jr., and R. E. Fitzner. 1997. Postembryonic ontogeny and larval behavior of the spadefoot toad, *Scaphiopus intermontanus* (Anura: Pelobatidae): External morphology. *Herpetological Monographs* 11:124–178.

Hall, R. J. 1971. Ecology of a population of the Great Plains skink *(Eumeces obsoletus). University of Kansas Science Bulletin* 48:357–388.

———. 1972. Food habits of the Great Plains skink *(Eumeces obsoletus). American Midland Naturalist* 87:258–263.

———. 1976. *Eumeces obsoletus. Catalogue of American Amphibians and Reptiles* 186:1–3.

Hall, R. J., and H. S. Fitch. 1972. Further observations on the demography of the Great Plains skink *(Eumeces obsoletus). Transactions of the Kansas Academy of Sciences* 74:93–98.

Hallowell, E. 1852 [1853]. On a new genus and three new species of reptiles inhabiting North America. *Proceedings of the Academy of Natural Sciences of Philadelphia* 6:206–209.

———. 1857 [1858]. Description of several new North American reptiles. *Proceedings of the Academy of Natural Sciences of Philadelphia* 9:215–216.

Halpin, Z. T. 1983. Naturally occurring encounters between black-tailed prairie dogs *(Cynomys ludovicianus)* and snakes. *American Midland Naturalist* 109:50–54.

Hamilton, R. 1948. The egg-laying process in the tiger salamander. *Copeia* 1948:212–213.

Hamilton, R. S. 1949. Natural history of the Rocky Mountain tiger salamander *Ambystoma tigrinum* and the occurrence of polydactylism in a local population. M.A. thesis, University of Colorado, Boulder.

Hamilton, W. J., Jr. 1941. A note on the food of the western burrowing owl. *Condor* 43:74.

Hammer, D. A. 1969. Parameters of a marsh snapping turtle population, Lacreek Refuge, South Dakota. *Journal of Wildlife Management* 33:995–1,005.

Hammerson, G. A. 1977. Head-body temperature differences monitored by telemetry in the snake *Masticophis flagellum piceus. Comparative Biochemistry and Physiology* 57A:399–402.

———. 1980. Geographic distribution: *Gastrophryne olivacea. Herpetological Review* 11:13–14.

———. 1981. An ecogeographic analysis of the herpetofauna of Colorado. Ph.D. dissertation, University of Colorado, Boulder.

———. 1982a. The first record of *Rana sylvatica* from the Southern Rocky Mountains and other early collections of Arthur E. Beardsley. *Herpetological Review* 13:10.

———. 1982b. Amphibian and reptile distribution in Colorado: Corrections of erroneous records. *Herpetological Review* 13:53–54.

———. 1982c. *Amphibians and reptiles in Colorado.* Colorado Division of Wildlife, Denver.

———. 1982d. Bullfrog eliminating leopard frog in Colorado? *Herpetological Review* 13:115–116.

———. 1983. Geographical ecology and variation in the lizard *Sceloporus undulatus* in Colorado. *Journal of the Colorado-Wyoming Academy of Science* 15:48–49.

———. 1984. More corrections of erroneous amphibian and reptile records from Colorado. *Herpetological Review* 15:21–22.

———. 1987. Thermal behavior of the snake *Coluber constrictor* in west-central California. *Journal of Thermal Biology* 12:195–197.

———. 1988. *A field survey of Colorado's rarest reptiles and amphibians.* Report to Colorado Division of Wildlife, Denver.

———. 1989a. *A field survey of amphibians in the Rocky Mountains of Colorado, August 1989.* Report to Colorado Division of Wildlife, Denver.

———. 1989b. Effects of weather and feeding on body temperature and activity in the snake *Masticophis flagellum. Journal of Thermal Biology* 14:219–224.

———. 1992. Field surveys of amphibians in the mountains of Colorado, 1991. Report to the Colorado Division of Wildlife and Colorado Field Office of The Nature Conservancy.

Hammerson, G. A., and A. D. Benedict. 1998. Geographic distribution: *Tantilla hobartsmithi. Herpetological Review* 29:55.

Hammerson, G. A., and D. Langlois. 1981. Colorado amphibian and reptile distribution latilong study. Colorado Division of Wildlife, Denver.

Hammerson, G. A., and B. P. Lapin. 1980. Geographic distribution: *Sceloporus undulatus elongatus. Herpetological Review* 11:115.

Hammerson, G. A., and L. J. Livo. 1999. Conservation status of the northern cricket frog *(Acris crepitans)* in Colorado and adjacent areas at the northwestern extent of the range. *Herpetological Review* 30:78–80.

Hammerson, G. A., and H. M. Smith. 1991. The correct spelling of the name of the short-horned lizard of North America. *Bulletin of the Maryland Herpetological Society* 27:121–127.

———. 1993a. Geographic distribution: *Rana pipiens. Herpetological Review* 24:154.

———. 1993b. Geographic distribution: *Thamnophis sirtalis. Herpetological Review* 24:157.

Hammerson, G. A., L. Valentine, and L. J. Livo. 1991a. Geographic distribution: *Leptotyphlops dulcis. Herpetological Review* 22:103.

———. 1991b. Geographic distribution: *Bufo debilis. Herpetological Review* 22:64.

———. 1991c. Geographic distribution: *Bufo punctatus. Herpetological Review* 22:64.

———. 1991d. Geographic distribution: *Spea intermontana. Herpetological Review* 22:64.

———. 1991e. Geographic distribution: *Kinosternon flavescens. Herpetological Review* 22:64–65.

———. 1991f. Geographic distribution: *Gambelia wislizenii. Herpetological Review* 22:65–66.

———. 1991g. Geographic distribution: *Arizona elegans*. *Herpetological Review* 22:66.

———. 1991h. Geographic distribution: *Coluber constrictor*. *Herpetological Review* 22:67.

———. 1991i. Geographic distribution: *Crotalus viridis*. *Herpetological Review* 22:67.

———. 1991j. Geographic distribution: *Masticophis flagellum*. *Herpetological Review* 22:67–68.

———. 1991k. Geographic distribution: *Rhinocheilus lecontei*. *Herpetological Review* 22:68.

———. 1991m. Geographic distribution: *Tantilla hobartsmithi*. *Herpetological Review* 22:69.

———. 1991n. Geographic distribution: *Tantilla nigriceps*. *Herpetological Review* 22:69.

———. 1991o. Geographic distribution: *Lampropeltis getula*. *Herpetological Review* 22:67.

———. 1991p. Geographic distribution: *Sistrurus catenatus*. *Herpetological Review* 22:68.

Haney, B. J., and J. H. Bushnell. 1985. Cutaneous myiasis in the box turtle, *Terrapene ornata ornata*. *Journal of the Colorado-Wyoming Academy of Science* 17 (1):22.

———. 1986. The prevalence and nature of myiasis in the box turtle, *Terrapene ornata*. *Journal of the Colorado-Wyoming Academy of Science* 18 (1):51.

Harding, J. H. 1997. *Amphibians and reptiles of the Great Lakes region*. University of Michigan Press, Ann Arbor.

Hardy, D. F. 1962. Ecology and behavior of the six-lined racerunner *Cnemidophorus sexlineatus*. *University of Kansas Science Bulletin* 43:3–73.

Hardy, R. 1939. An annotated list of reptiles and amphibians of Carbon County, Utah. *Proceedings of the Utah Academy of Sciences, Arts and Letters* 15:99–102.

Harestad, A. S. 1985. Life history notes: *Scaphiopus intermontanus* (Great Basin spadefoot toad). Mortality. *Herpetological Review* 16:24.

Harris, A. H. 1963. Ecological distribution of some vertebrates in the San Juan Basin, New Mexico. *Museum of New Mexico Papers in Anthropology* 8:1–63.

Hart, D. R. 1979. Niche relationships of *Thamnophis radix haydeni* and *Thamnophis sirtalis parietalis* in the Interlake District of Manitoba. *Tulane Studies in Zoology and Botany* 21 (2):125–140.

Hart, S., and S. Manchester. 1993. Geographic distribution: *Elaphe guttata emoryi*. *Herpetological Review* 24:156.

Harte, J., and E. Hoffman. 1989. Possible effects of acidic deposition on a Rocky Mountain population of the tiger salamander *Ambystoma tigrinum*. *Conservation Biology* 3 (2):149–158.

———. 1994. Acidification and salamander recruitment. *BioScience* 44:125–126.

Haverly, J. E., and K. V. Kardong. 1996. Sensory deprivation effects on the predatory behavior of the rattlesnake, *Crotalus viridis oreganus*. *Copeia* 1996:419–428.

Hawley, A.W.L., and M. Aleksiuk. 1975. Thermal regulation of spring mating behavior in the red-sided garter snake *(Thamnophis sirtalis parietalis)*. *Canadian Journal of Zoology* 53:768–776.

———. 1976. Sexual receptivity in the female red-sided garter snake *(Thamnophis sirtalis parietalis)*. *Copeia* 1976:401–404.

Hayes, F. E. 1985. Life history notes: *Hypsiglena torquata deserticola* (desert night snake). Behavior. *Herpetological Review* 16:79, 81.

Hayes, W. K. 1990. Prey handling and envenomation behavior of prairie and midget-faded rattlesnakes. *Journal of the Colorado-Wyoming Academy of Science* 22 (1):6.

———. 1992. Prey-handling and envenomation strategies of prairie rattlesnakes *(Crotalus v. viridis)* feeding on mice and sparrows. *Journal of Herpetology* 26:496–499.

Hayes, W. K., and D. Duvall. 1991. A field study of prairie rattlesnake predatory strikes. *Herpetologica* 47:78–81.

Hayes, W. K., D. Duvall, W. A. Gern, and G. T. Baxter. 1990. Geographic distribution: *Tantilla nigriceps nigriceps*. *Herpetological Review* 21:24.

Hayes, W. K., D. Duvall, and G. W. Schuett. 1992. A preliminary report on the courtship behavior of free-ranging prairie rattlesnakes, *Crotalus viridis viridis* (Rafinesque), in south-central Wyoming. Pages 45–48 in *Contributions in herpetology*, P. D. Strimple and J. L. Strimple, eds. Greater Cincinnati Herpetological Society.

Hayes, W. K., P. Lavín-Mucio, and K. V. Kardong. 1995. Northern Pacific rattlesnakes *(Crotalus viridis oreganus)* meter venom when feeding on prey of different sizes. *Copeia* 1995:337–343.

Haynes, C. M., and S. D. Aird. 1981. *The distribution and habitat requirements of the wood frog (Ranidae: Rana sylvatica Le Conte) in Colorado*. Colorado Division of Wildlife, Wildlife Research Section, Special Report 50.

Heath, A. G. 1975. Behavioral thermoregulation in high altitude tiger salamanders, *Ambystoma tigrinum*. *Herpetologica* 31:84–93.

Hecnar, S. J., and R. T. M'Closkey. 1997. Changes in the composition of a ranid frog community following bullfrog extinction. *American Midland Naturalist* 137:145–150.

Hedges, S. B. 1986. An electrophoretic analysis of Holarctic hylid frog evolution. *Systematic Zoology* 35:1–21.

Heger, N. A., and S. F. Fox. 1992. Viability of lizard *(Sceloporus undulatus)* eggs exposed to simulated flood conditions. *Journal of Herpetology* 26:338–341.

Heinrich, M. L. 1985. Life history notes: *Pseudacris triseriata triseriata* (western chorus frog). Reproduction. *Herpetological Review* 16:24.

Heinrich, M. L., and D. W. Kaufman. 1985. Herpetofauna of the Konza Prairie Research Natural Area, Kansas. *Prairie Naturalist* 17:101–112.

Henderson, R. W. 1970. Feeding behavior, digestion, and water requirements of *Diadophis punctatus arnyi* Kennicott. *Herpetologica* 26:520–526.

Hendricks, F. S., and J. R. Dixon. 1984. Population structure of *Cnemidophorus tigris* (Reptilia: Teiidae) east of the Continental Divide. *Southwestern Naturalist* 29:137–140.

Hendricks, P. 1996. Geographic distribution: *Thamnophis elegans vagrans. Herpetological Review* 27:89.

Henke, S. E., and M. Montemayor. 1997. Natural history notes: *Phrynosoma cornutum* (Texas horned lizard). Growth. *Herpetological Review* 28:152.

———. 1998. Diel and monthly variations in capture success of *Phrynosoma cornutum* via road cruising in southern Texas. *Herpetological Review* 29:148–150.

Hernandez-Juviel, J. M., D. J. Morafka, I. Delgado, G. D. Scott, and R. W. Murphy. 1992. Effect of enzyme dilution on the relative electrophoretic mobility of glutamate dehydrogenase isozymes in the prairie rattlesnake, *Crotalus viridis viridis. Copeia* 1992:1,117–1,119.

Herreid, C. F. 1961. Snakes as predators of bats. *Herpetologica* 17:271–272.

Herrington, B. 1985. Another reason for herpetologists to pick up their beer cans. *Herpetological Review* 16:113.

Herrmann, S. J. 1970. Systematics, distribution, and ecology of Colorado Hirudinea. *American Midland Naturalist* 83:1–37.

Hersek, M. J., D. H. Owings, and D. F. Hennessy. 1992. Combat between rattlesnakes *(Crotalus viridis oreganus)* in the field. *Journal of Herpetology* 26:105–107.

Hess, J. 1969a. Changes in frequency of the green-spot phenotype in piedmont populations of the chorus frog. Ph.D. dissertation, Colorado State University, Fort Collins.

Hess, J. B. 1969b. Genetic differences in duration of breeding season in chorus frogs. *Journal of Herpetology* 3:194.

Hews, D. K. 1988. Alarm response in larval western toads, *Bufo boreas:* Release of larval chemicals by a natural predator and its effect on predator capture efficiency. *Animal Behaviour* 36:125–133.

Heyer, W. R., M. A. Donnelly, R. W. McDiarmid, L. C. Hayek, and M. S. Foster, eds. 1994. Measuring and monitoring biological diversity: standard methods for amphibians. Smithsonian Institution Press, Washington, D.C.

Heyl, D. H., and H. M. Smith. 1957. Another unicolor many-lined skink from Nebraska. *Herpetologica* 13:12–14.

Hibbard, C. W. 1937. *Hypsiglena oncorhynchus* in Kansas and additional notes on *Leptotyphlops dulcis. Copeia* 1937:234.

———. 1964. A brooding colony of the blind snake, *Leptotyphlops dulcis dissecta* Cope. *Copeia* 1964:222.

———. 1970. Pleistocene mammalian local faunas from the Great Plains and central lowland provinces of the United States. Pages 395–433 in *Pleistocene and Recent environments of the central Great Plains,* W. Dort, Jr., and J. K. Jones, Jr., eds. University of Kansas Department of Geology Special Publication 3.

Hibbard, C. W., and D. W. Taylor. 1960. Two late Pleistocene faunas from southwestern Kansas. *Contributions of the University of Michigan Museum of Paleontology* 16 (1):1–223.

Hibbitts, T. 1992. Life history notes: *Hypsiglena torquata* (night snake): Predation. *Herpetological Review* 23:120.

Highton, R. 1991. Molecular phylogeny of plethodontine salamanders and hylid frogs: Statistical analysis of protein comparisons. *Molecular Biology and Evolution* 8:796–818.

Hill, B., E. Bergman, C. Montgomery, J. Hobert, S. Boback, and S. P. Mackessy. 1997. Geographic distribution: *Rhinocheilus lecontei tessellatus. Herpetological Review* 28:52.

Hill, S. 1943. Rattlesnakes of northwestern Colorado and southern Wyoming. *Trail and Timberline* 293:59–61.

Hillis, D. M. 1981. Premating isolating mechanisms among three species of the *Rana pipiens* complex in Texas and southern Oklahoma. *Copeia* 1981:312–319.

Hirth, H. F., R. C. Pendleton, A. C. King, and T. R. Downard. 1969. Dispersal of snakes from a hibernaculum in northwestern Utah. *Ecology* 50:332–339.

Hobert, J., E. Bergman, C. Montgomery, B. Hill, S. Boback, and S. P. Mackessy. 1996. Geographic distribution: *Rana catesbeiana. Herpetological Review* 27:209.

Hobert, J., S. Boback, C. Montgomery, E. Bergman, B. Hill, and S. P. Mackessy. 1997. Geographic distribution: *Sistrurus catenatus edwardsii. Herpetological Review* 28:52.

Hobert, J., R. Donoho, C. Montgomery, K. Waldron, and S. P. Mackessy. 1996. Geographic distribution: *Coluber constrictor flaviventris. Herpetological Review* 27:33.

Hobert, J., C. Montgomery, T. Childers, J. D. Manzer, E. Bergman, J. Sifert, B. Hill, and S. P. Mackessy. 1998. Geographic distribution: *Chelydra serpentina serpentina. Herpetological Review* 29:109.

Hobert, J., B. Quinn, R. Donoho, C. Montgomery, K. Waldron, and S. P. Mackessy. 1996. Geographic distribution: *Arizona elegans elegans. Herpetological Review* 27:33.

Hobert, J. P. 1997. The massasauga rattlesnake *(Sistrurus catenatus)* in Colorado. M.A. thesis, University of Northern Colorado, Greeley.

Hoddenbach, G. A. 1966. Reproduction in western Texas *Cnemidophorus sexlineatus* (Sauria, Teiidae). *Copeia* 1966:110–113.

Holland, R. L. 1965. A comparative study of morphology and plasma proteins of the blood in the lizard species *Cnemidophorus tesselatus* (Say) (Reptilia: Teiidae) from Colorado and New Mexico. M.A. thesis, University of Colorado, Boulder.

———. 1977. Geographic distribution: *Masticophis taeniatus taeniatus*. *Herpetological Review* 8:13.

Holland, R. L., D. Chiszar, C. Ristau, and H. M. Smith. 1994a. Geographic distribution: *Chrysemys picta bellii*. *Herpetological Review* 25:163.

———. 1994b. Geographic distribution: *Nerodia sipedon sipedon*. *Herpetological Review* 25:168.

Holland, R. L., and H. M. Smith. 1993a. Geographic distribution: *Eumeces obsoletus*. *Herpetological Review* 24:66.

———. 1993b. Geographic distribution: *Sceloporus undulatus garmani*. *Herpetological Review* 24:155.

———. 1994a. Geographic distribution: *Terrapene ornata ornata*. *Herpetological Review* 25:163.

———. 1994b. Geographic distribution: *Eumeces obsoletus*. *Herpetological Review* 25:164.

Holomuzki, J. R. 1986. Predator avoidance and diel patterns of microhabitat use by larval tiger salamanders. *Ecology* 67:737–748.

Holycross, A. T. 1995. Natural history notes: *Crotalus viridis* (western rattlesnake): Phenology. *Herpetological Review* 26:37–38.

Hopey, M. E., and J. W. Petranka. 1994. Restriction of wood frogs to fish-free habitats: How important is adult choice? *Copeia* 1994: 1,023–1,025.

Hoppe, D. M. 1978. Thermal tolerance in tadpoles of the chorus frog *Pseudacris triseriata*. *Herpetologica* 34:318–321.

Hoppe, D. M., and D. Pettus. 1984. Developmental features influencing color polymorphism in chorus frogs. *Journal of Herpetology* 18:113–120.

Horstman, G. P. 1995a. Geographic distribution: *Sceloporus graciosus graciosus*. *Herpetological Review* 26:45.

———. 1995b. Geographic distribution: *Pituophis catenifer deserticola*. *Herpetological Review* 26:47.

———. 1995c. Geographic distribution: *Pseudacris triseriata*. *Herpetological Review* 26:208.

Houseal, T. W., J. W. Bickham, and M. D. Springer. 1982. Geographic variation in the yellow mud turtle, *Kinosternon flavescens*. *Copeia* 1982:567–580.

Hovingh, P. 1986. Biogeographic aspects of leeches, mollusks, and amphibians in the intermountain region. *Great Basin Naturalist* 46:736–744.

Hovingh, P., B. Benton, and D. Bornholdt. 1985. Aquatic parameters and life history observa-

tions of the Great Basin spadefoot toad in Utah. *Great Basin Naturalist* 45:22–30.

Howard, C. W. 1974. Comparative reproductive ecology of horned lizards (genus *Phrynosoma*) in southwestern United States and northern Mexico. *Journal of the Arizona Academy of Science* 9:108–116.

Howard, R. D. 1978. The evolution of mating strategies in bullfrogs, *Rana catesbeiana*. *Evolution* 32:850–871.

———. 1980. Mating behaviour and mating success in woodfrogs, *Rana sylvatica*. *Animal Behaviour* 28:705–716.

Hoyt, J.S.Y. 1941. High speed attained by *Cnemidophorus sexlineatus*. *Copeia* 1941:180.

Hubbard, J. D. 1972. Some aspects of geographic variation in the boreal toad, *Bufo boreas boreas*. *Journal of the Colorado-Wyoming Academy of Science* 7 (2):65–66.

Hubbs, C., and N. E. Armstrong. 1961. Minimum developmental temperature tolerance of two anurans, *Scaphiopus couchi* and *Microhyla olivacea*. *Texas Journal of Science* 13:358–362.

Hudson, G. E. 1942. The amphibians and reptiles of Nebraska. *Nebraska Conservation Bulletin* 24:1–146.

Hughes, N. 1965. Comparison of frontoparietal bones of *Scaphiopus bombifrons* and *S. hammondii* as evidence of interspecific hybridization. *Herpetologica* 21:196–201.

Hulse, A. C. 1985. Home range size in *Holbrookia maculata* (Iguanidae) from southeastern Arizona. *Southwestern Naturalist* 30:608–610.

Humphrey, F. 1956. The gestation and incubation period of an Arizona kingsnake. *Herpetologica* 12:311.

Humphrey, R., D. Chiszar, and H. M. Smith. 1995. Geographic distribution: *Chelydra serpentina*. *Herpetological Review* 26:106.

Hunsicker, G. R. 1987. Biosystematics of *Sceloporus orcutti* and *Sceloporus magister* complexes (Reptilia: Iguanidae). Ph.D. dissertation, Loma Linda University, Loma Linda, California.

Hunt, R. H. 1980. Toad sanctuary in a tarantula burrow. *Natural History* 89: 45–53.

Hutchison, V. H., A. Vinegar, and R. J. Kosh. 1966. Critical thermal maxima in turtles. *Herpetologica* 22:32–41.

Imler, R. H. 1945. Bullsnakes and their control on a Nebraska wildlife refuge. *Journal of Wildlife Management* 9:265–273.

Irschick, D. J., and H. B. Shaffer. 1997. The polytypic species revisited: morphological differentiation among tiger salamanders *(Ambystoma tigrinum)* (Amphibia Caudata). *Herpetologica* 53:30–49.

Iverson, J. B. 1979. A taxonomic reappraisal of the yellow mud turtle, *Kinosternon flavescens* (Testudines: Kinosternidae). *Copeia* 1979:212–225.

———. 1989. The Arizona mud turtle, *Kinosternon flavescens arizonense* (Kinosternidae), in

Arizona and Sonora. *Southwestern Naturalist* 34:356–368.

———. 1990a. Nesting and parental care in the mud turtle, *Kinosternon flavescens. Canadian Journal of Zoology* 68:230–233.

———. 1990b. Sex ratios in snakes: A cautionary note. *Copeia* 1990:571–573.

———. 1991. Life history and demography of the yellow mud turtle, *Kinosternon flavescens. Herpetologica* 47:373–395.

———. 1992. *A revised checklist with distribution maps of the turtles of the world.* Privately printed, Richmond, Indiana.

———. 1995. Natural history notes: *Heterodon nasicus* (western hognose snake). Reproduction. *Herpetological Review* 26:206.

Iverson, J. B., H. Higgins, A. Sirulnik, and C. Griffiths. 1997. Local and geographic variation in the reproductive biology of the snapping turtle *(Chelydra serpentina). Herpetologica* 53:96–117.

Iverson, J. B., H. Higgins, A. G. Sirulnik, and C. A. Young. 1995. *Coluber constrictor flaviventris* (eastern yellow-bellied racer): Nesting. *Herpetological Review* 26:147–148.

Iverson, J. B., and P. E. Moler. 1997. The female reproductive cycle of the Florida softshell turtle *(Apalone ferox). Journal of Herpetology* 31:399–409.

Iverson, J. B., and G. R. Smith. 1993. Reproductive ecology of the painted turtle *(Chrysemys picta)* in the Nebraska Sandhills and across its range. *Copeia* 1993:1–21.

Jackson, M. K., and H. W. Reno. 1975. Comparative skin structure of some fossorial and subfossorial leptotyphlopid and colubrid snakes. *Herpetologica* 31:350–359.

Jacob, J. S., and C. W. Painter. 1980. Overwinter thermal ecology of *Crotalus viridis* in the north-central plains of New Mexico. *Copeia* 1980:799–805.

Jaeger, E. C. 1955. *A source-book of biological names and terms.* 3d ed. Charles C. Thomas, Springfield, Illinois.

Jaggi, D., M. Cage, M. C. Mulvaney, R. Guese, Y. Cage, S. Sasman, and P. P. Mulvaney. 1983. Geographic distribution: *Leptotyphlops dulcis dissectus. Herpetological Review* 14:123–124.

James, E. 1823. *Account of an expedition from Pittsburgh to the Rocky Mountains, performed in the years 1819, 1820. By order of the Hon. J. C. Calhoun, Secretary of War, under the command of Maj. S. H. Long, of the U. S. Top. Engineers. Compiled from the notes of Major Long, Mr. T. Say, and other gentlemen of the party.* Vol. 1. London: Longman, Hurst, Rees, Orme, and Brown.

James, M. T., and T. P. Maslin. 1947. Notes on myiasis of the toad, *Bufo boreas boreas* Baird and Girard. *Journal of the Washington Academy of Science* 37 (10):366–368.

Jameson, E. W. 1947. The food of the western cricket frog. *Copeia* 1947:212.

Janos, M., and D. Guadagno. 1997. Delta area. Pages 247–255 in *A birder's guide to Colorado,* H. R. Holt, ed. American Birding Association, Colorado Springs, Colorado.

Jansen, D. W. 1987. The myonecrotic effect of Duvernoy's gland secretion of the snake *Thamnophis elegans vagrans. Journal of Herpetology* 21:81–83.

Jennings, W. B., D. F. Bradford, and D. F. Johnson. 1992. Dependence of the garter snake *Thamnophis elegans* on amphibians in the Sierra Nevada of California. *Journal of Herpetology* 26:503–505.

Johnson, D. R. 1966. Diet and estimated energy assimilation of three Colorado lizards. *American Midland Naturalist* 76:504–509.

Johnson, T. B. 1982. Ash-throated flycatcher takes sagebrush lizard. *Southwestern Naturalist* 27:222.

Jones, K. B. 1990. Habitat use and predatory behavior of *Thamnophis cyrtopsis* (Serpentes: Colubridae) in a seasonally variable aquatic environment. *Southwestern Naturalist* 35:115–122.

Jones, K. B., and W. G. Whitford. 1989. Feeding behavior of free-roaming *Masticophis flagellum:* An efficient ambush predator. *Southwestern Naturalist* 34:460–467.

Jones, M. S., and J. P. Goettl. 1998. Henderson/Urad boreal toad studies. In *Boreal toad research progress report 1995–1997.* M. S. Jones, J. P. Goettl, K. L. Scherff-Norris, S. Brinkman, L. J. Livo, and A. M. Goebbel. Colorado Division of Wildlife, Denver.

Jones, S. M., and R. E. Ballinger. 1987. Comparative life histories of *Holbrookia maculata* and *Sceloporus undulatus* in western Nebraska. *Ecology* 68:1,828–1,838.

Jones, S. M., R. E. Ballinger, and J. W. Nietfeldt. 1981. Herpetofauna of Mormon Island Preserve, Hall County, Nebraska. *Prairie Naturalist* 13 (2):33–41.

Jones, S. M., R. E. Ballinger, and W. P. Porter. 1987. Physiological and environmental sources of variation in reproduction: Prairie lizards in a food rich environment. *Oikos* 48:325–335.

Jones, S. M., and D. L. Droge. 1980. Home range size and spatial distributions of two sympatric lizard species *(Sceloporus undulatus, Holbrookia maculata)* in the Sand Hills of Nebraska. *Herpetologica* 36:127–132.

Jones-Burdick, W. H. 1939. Guide to the snakes of Colorado. University of Colorado Museum Leaflet 1:1–11.

———. 1949. Guide to the snakes of Colorado. University of Colorado Museum Leaflet 5:1–23.

Jorgensen, C. D., and W. W. Tanner. 1963. The application of density probability function to determine the home ranges of *Uta stansburiana*

stansburiana and *Cnemidophorus tigris tigris*. *Herpetologica* 19:105–115.

Jung, R. E. 1993. Blanchard's cricket frogs *(Acris crepitans blanchardi)* in southwest Wisconsin. *Transactions of the Wisconsin Academy of Sciences, Arts and Letters* 81:79–87.

Justus, J. T., M. Sandomir, T, Urquhart, and B. O. Ewan. 1977. Developmental rates of two species of toads from the desert southwest. *Copeia* 1977:592–594.

Kappel, J. K. 1977a. *Lampropeltis getulus holbrooki*, a new species record for Colorado. *Journal of the Colorado-Wyoming Academy of Science* 9 (1):45.

———. 1977b. Geographic distribution: *Lampropeltis getulus holbrooki*. *Herpetological Review* 8:84–85.

Kardong, K. V. 1986. The predatory strike of the rattlesnake: When things go amiss. *Copeia* 1986:816–820.

Kardong, K. V., and S. P. Mackessy. 1991. The strike behavior of a congenitally blind rattlesnake. *Journal of Herpetology* 25:208–211.

Kasper, S., and S. N. Kasper. 1997. *Thamnophis elegans vagrans*: Paralysis. *Herpetological Review* 28:46.

Kassing, E. F. 1961. A life history study of the Great Plains ground snake, *Sonora episcopa episcopa* (Kennicott). *Texas Journal of Science* 13:185–203.

Kats, L. B., J. W. Petranka, and A. Sih. 1988. Antipredator defenses and the persistence of amphibian larvae with fishes. *Ecology* 69:1,865–1,870.

Kay, F. R., R. Anderson, and C. O. McKinney. 1973. Notes on activity patterns of two species of *Cnemidophorus* (Sauria: Teiidae). *Herpetologica* 29:105–107.

Keefer, S. D., and C. W. Loeffler. 1998. Geographic distribution: *Kinosternon flavescens flavescens*. *Herpetological Review* 29:50.

Kehmeier, J., C. Wagner, and L. J. Livo. 1996. Geographic distribution: *Pseudacris triseriata*. *Herpetological Review* 27:150.

Kenney, J. W., and F. L. Rose. 1974. Oxygen requirements and activity rhythms of the tiger salamander, *Ambystoma tigrinum* (Amphibia: Caudata). *Herpetologica* 30:333–337.

Keogh, J. S. 1996. Evolution of the colubrid snake tribe Lampropeltini: A morphological perspective. *Herpetologica* 52:406–416.

Kerfoot, W. C. 1962. An unusually large desert short-horned lizard (*Phrynosoma douglassi ornatissimum*—Iguanidae) from Colorado. *Southwestern Naturalist* 7:78–79.

———. 1968. Geographic variability of the lizard, *Sceloporus graciosus* Baird and Girard, in the eastern part of its range. *Copeia* 1968:139–152.

Kiesecker, J. 1996. pH mediated predator-prey interactions between *Ambystoma tigrinum* and *Pseudacris triseriata*. *Ecological Applications* 6 (4):1,325–1,331.

Kiesecker, J. M. 1991. Acidification and its effects on amphibians breeding in temporary ponds in montane Colorado. Master's thesis, University of Northern Colorado, Greeley.

Kiesecker, J. M., and A. R. Blaustein. 1997. Population differences in responses of red-legged frogs *(Rana aurora)* to introduced bullfrogs. *Ecology* 78:1,752–1,760.

King, M., and D. Duvall. 1990. Prairie rattlesnake seasonal migrations: Episodes of movement, vernal foraging, and sex differences. *Animal Behaviour* 39:924–935.

King, O. M. 1960. Notes on Oklahoma toads. *Southwestern Naturalist* 5:102–103.

Kingery, H. E., editor. 1998. *Colorado breeding bird atlas*. Colorado Bird Atlas Partnership, Denver, Colorado.

Klauber, L. M. 1935. A new subspecies of *Crotalus confluentus* Say, with remarks on related species. *Transactions of the San Diego Society of Natural History* 8:75–90.

———. 1936. A statistical study of the rattlesnakes. I. Introduction. II. Sex ratio in rattlesnake populations. III. Birth rate. *San Diego Society of Natural History Occasional Papers* 1:1–24.

———. 1937. A statistical study of the rattlesnakes. IV. The growth of the rattlesnake. *San Diego Society of Natural History Occasional Papers* 3:1–56.

———. 1939. A statistical study of the rattlesnakes. VI. Fangs. *San Diego Society of Natural History Occasional Papers* 5:1–61.

———. 1940a. A statistical study of the rattlesnakes. VII. The rattle (Part 1). *San Diego Society of Natural History Occasional Papers* 6:1–62.

———. 1940b. The worm snakes of the genus *Leptotyphlops* in the United States and northern Mexico. *Transactions of the San Diego Society of Natural History* 9 (18):87–162.

———. 1941. The long-nosed snakes of the genus *Rhinocheilus*. *Transactions of the San Diego Society of Natural History* 9 (29):289–332.

———. 1946. The glossy snake, *Arizona*, with descriptions of new subspecies. *Transactions of the San Diego Society of Natural History* 10 (17):311–398.

———. 1947. Classification and ranges of the gopher snakes of the genus *Pituophis* in the western United States. *Bulletin of the Zoological Society of San Diego* 22:1–81.

———. 1972. *Rattlesnakes: Their habits, life histories, and influence on mankind*. 2d ed. University California Press, Berkeley.

Knight, A., D. Styer, S. Pelikan, J. A. Campbell, L. D. Densmore III, and D. P. Mindell. 1993. Choosing among hypotheses of rattlesnake phylogeny: A best-fit rate test for DNA sequence data. *Systematic Biology* 42:356–367.

Knight, J. L. 1986. Variation in snout morphology in the North American snake *Pituophis melan-*

oleucus (Serpentes: Colubridae). *Journal of Herpetology* 20:77–79.

Knight, J. L., and J. T. Collins. 1977. The amphibians and reptiles of Cheyenne County, Kansas. *Report of the State Biological Survey of Kansas* 15:1–18.

Knight, T. W., J. A. Layfield, and R. J. Brooks. 1990. Nutritional status and mean selected temperature of hatchling snapping turtles *(Chelydra serpentina):* Is there a thermophilic response to feeding? *Copeia* 1990:1,067–1,072.

Knopf, G. N. 1966. Reproductive behavior and ecology of the unisexual lizard, *Cnemidophorus tesselatus* Say. Ph.D. dissertation, University of Colorado, Boulder.

Knowlton, G. F. 1934. Lizards as a factor in the control of range insects. *Journal of Economic Entomology* 28:998–1,004.

———. 1937. Notes on three Utah lizards. *Herpetologica* 1:109–110.

Knowlton, G. F., and M. J. Janes. 1933. Lizards as predators of the beet leafhopper. *Journal of Economic Entomology* 26:1,011–1,016.

Knowlton, G. F., and W. P. Nye. 1946. Lizards feeding on ants in Utah. *Journal of Economic Entomology* 39:546–547.

Knowlton, G. F., and W. L. Thomas. 1934. Notes on some insectivorous Utah lizards. *Utah Academy of Arts, Science and Letters* 11:257–259.

———. 1936. Food habits of Skull Valley lizards. *Copeia* 1936:64–66.

Kocher, T. D. 1986. Genetic differentiation during speciation in the *Rana pipiens* and *Ambystoma tigrinum* species complexes. Ph.D. dissertation, University of Colorado, Boulder.

Koerwitz, F. L. 1973. Ecology and reproduction of selected species of Anostraca in Colorado. D.A. dissertation, University of Northern Colorado, Greeley.

Korky, J. K. 1978. Differentiation of the larvae of members of the *Rana pipiens* complex in Nebraska. *Copeia* 1978: 455–459.

Kreba, R. 1977. Probable case of death-feigning by wood frog. *Blue Jay* 35:148.

Krohmer, R. W., and R. D. Aldridge. 1985a. Male reproductive cycle of the lined snake *(Tropidoclonion lineatum)*. *Herpetologica* 41:33–38.

———. 1985b. Female reproductive cycle of the lined snake *(Tropidoclonion lineatum)*. *Herpetologica* 41:39–44.

Krohmer, R. W., and D. Crews. 1989. Control of length of the courtship season in the red-sided garter snake, *Thamnophis sirtalis parietalis:* The role of temperature. *Canadian Journal of Zoology* 67:987–993.

Kroll, J. C. 1971. Combat behavior in male Great Plains ground snakes *(Sonora episcopa episcopa)*. *Texas Journal of Science* 23:300.

———. 1976. Feeding adaptations of hognose snakes. *Southwestern Naturalist* 20:537–557.

———. 1977. Self-wounding while death feigning by western hognose snakes *(Heterodon nasicus)*. *Copeia* 1977:372–373.

Krupa, J. J. 1986. Multiple clutch production in the Great Plains toad. *Prairie Naturalist* 18:151–152.

———. 1990. Advertisement call variation in the Great Plains toad. *Copeia* 1990:884–886.

———. 1994. Breeding biology of the Great Plains toad in Oklahoma. *Journal of Herpetology* 28:217–224.

———. 1995. Natural history notes: *Bufo woodhousii* (Woodhouse's toad). Fecundity. *Herpetological Review* 26:142, 144.

Kruse, K. C. 1981. Phonotactic responses of female northern leopard frogs *(Rana pipiens)* to *Rana blairi,* a presumed hybrid, and conspecific mating trills. *Journal of Herpetology* 15:145–150.

Kruse, K. C., and D. G. Dunlap. 1976. Serum albumins and hybridization in two species of the *Rana pipiens* complex in the north central United States. *Copeia* 1976:394–396.

Kupferberg, S. J. 1997. Bullfrog *(Rana catesbeiana)* invasion of a California river: The role of larval competition. *Ecology* 78:1,736–1,751.

Kuzarn, E. 1995. Treed. *Wyoming Wildlife* 59 (5):26–27.

Lambert, S., and G. M. Ferguson. 1985. Blood ejection frequency by *Phrynosoma cornutum* (Iguanidae). *Southwestern Naturalist* 30:616–617.

Lang, J. W. 1969 [1970]. Hibernation and movements of *Storeria occipitomaculata* in northern Minnesota. *Journal of Herpetology* 3:196–197.

Langlois, D. 1978. *Colorado reptile and amphibian distribution latilong study.* Colorado Division of Wildlife, Denver.

Lannoo, M. J., editor. 1998. *Status and conservation of Midwestern amphibians.* University of Iowa Press, Iowa City.

Lannoo, M. J., and M. D. Bachmann. 1984a. On flotation and air breathing in *Ambystoma tigrinum* larvae: Stimuli for and the relationship between these behaviors. *Canadian Journal of Zoology* 62:15–18.

———. 1984b. Aspects of cannibalistic morphs in a population of *Ambystoma t. tigrinum* larvae. *American Midland Naturalist* 112:103–109.

Lannoo, M. J., K. Lang, T. Waltz, and G. S. Phillips. 1994. An altered amphibian assemblage: Dickinson County, Iowa, 70 years after Frank Blanchard's survey. *American Midland Naturalist* 131:311–319.

Lapin, B. P., and G. A. Hammerson. 1982. Geographic distribution: *Leptotyphlops dulcis.* *Herpetological Review* 13:82.

Lardie, R. L. 1975. Courtship and mating behavior in the yellow mud turtle, *Kinosternon flavescens flavescens. Journal of Herpetology* 9:223–227.

———. 1983. Aggressive interactions and territoriality in the yellow mud turtle, *Kinosternon flavescens flavescens* (Agassiz). *Bulletin of the Oklahoma Herpetological Society* 8:68–83.

Larsen, K. W. 1987. Movements and behavior of migratory garter snakes, *Thamnophis sirtalis*. *Canadian Journal of Zoology* 65:2,241–2,247.

Larson, E. E., M. Ozima, and W. C. Bradley. 1975. Late Cenozoic volcanism in northwestern Colorado and its implications concerning tectonism and the origin of the Colorado River system. Pages 155–178 in *Cenozoic history of the Southern Rocky Mountains*, B. F. Curtis, ed. Geological Society of America Memoir 144.

Lavín-Murcio, P. A., and K. V. Kardong. 1995. Scents related to venom and prey as cues in the poststrike trailing behavior of rattlesnakes, *Crotalus viridis oreganus*. *Herpetologica* 51:39–44.

Lavín-Murcio, P. A., B. G. Robinson, and K. V. Kardong. 1993. Cues involved in relocation of struck prey by rattlesnakes, *Crotalus viridis oreganus*. *Herpetologica* 49:463–469.

Lawson, P. A. 1989. Orientation abilities and mechanisms in a northern migratory population of the common garter snake *(Thamnophis sirtalis)*. *Musk-Ox* 37:110–115.

Lawson, R. 1983. Life history notes: *Opheodrys vernalis* (smooth green snake): Reproduction. *Herpetological Review* 14:20.

———. 1987. Molecular studies of thamnophiine snakes: 1. The phylogeny of the genus *Nerodia*. *Journal of Herpetology* 21:140–157.

Lawson, R., and H. C. Dessauer. 1979. Biochemical genetics and systematics of garter snakes of the *Thamnophis elegans-couchii-ordinoides* complex. *Louisiana State University Museum of Zoology Occasional Papers* 56:1–24.

Layne, J. R., Jr., J. P. Costanzo, and R. E. Lee, Jr. 1998. Freeze duration influences postfreeze survival in the frog *Rana sylvatica*. *Journal of Experimental Zoology* 280:197–201.

Layne, J. R., Jr., and R. E. Lee, Jr. 1987. Freeze tolerance and the dynamics of ice formation in wood frogs *(Rana sylvatica)* from southern Ohio. *Canadian Journal of Zoology* 65:2,062–2,065.

———. 1995. Adaptations of frogs to survive freezing. *Climate Research* 5:53–59.

Legler, J. M. 1960a. Amphibians and reptiles of Flaming Gorge. *University of Utah Anthropology Papers* 48:177–183.

———. 1960b. Natural history of the ornate box turtle, *Terrapene ornata ornata* Agassiz. *University of Kansas Publications, Museum of Natural History* 11:527–669.

Lemos Espinal, J. A., D. Chiszar, C. Henke, and H. M. Smith. 1998. Natural history notes: *Phrynosoma cornutum* (Texas horned lizard): Predation. *Herpetological Review* 29:168.

Leuck, B. E. 1982. Comparative burrow use and activity patterns of parthenogenetic and bisexual whiptail lizards (*Cnemidophorus*: Teiidae). *Copeia* 1982:416–424.

———. 1985. Comparative social behavior of bisexual and unisexual whiptail lizards *(Cnemidophorus)*. *Journal of Herpetology* 19:492–506.

———. 1993. The effect of genetic relatedness on social behavior in the parthenogenetic whiptail lizard, *Cnemidophorus tesselatus*. Pages 293–317 in *Biology of whiptail lizards (genus Cnemidophorus)*, J. W. Wright and L. J. Vitt, eds. Oklahoma Museum of Natural History, Norman.

Levi, H. W., and L. R. Levi. 1955. Neotenic salamanders, *Ambystoma tigrinum*, in the Elk Mountains of Colorado. *Copeia* 1955:309.

Lewis, W. M. 1962. Stomach contents of bullfrogs *(Rana catesbeiana)* taken from a minnow hatchery. *Transactions of the Illinois State Academy of Science* 55:80–83.

Lewis, W. M., and D. R. Helms. 1964. Vulnerability of forage organisms to largemouth bass. *Transactions of the American Fisheries Society* 93:315–318.

Lewke, R. E. 1979. Neck-biting and other aspects of reproductive biology of the Yuma kingsnake *(Lampropeltis getulus)*. *Herpetologica* 35:154–157.

Licht, L. E. 1967. Growth inhibition in crowded tadpoles: Intraspecific and interspecific effects. *Ecology* 48:736–745.

———. 1968. Unpalatability and toxicity of toad eggs. *Herpetologica* 24:93–98.

———. 1969. Palatability of *Rana* and *Hyla* eggs. *American Midland Naturalist* 82:296–298.

Lillywhite, H. B. 1970. Behavioral temperature regulation in the bullfrog, *Rana catesbeiana*. *Copeia* 1970:158–168.

———. 1985. Trailing movements and sexual behavior in *Coluber constrictor*. *Journal of Herpetology* 19:306–308.

Lillywhite, H. B., and R. J. Wassersug. 1974. Comments on a postmetamorphic aggregation of *Bufo boreas*. *Copeia* 1974:984–986.

Lindeman, P. V. 1991. Survivorship of overwintering hatchling painted turtles, *Chrysemys picta*, in northern Idaho. *Canadian Field-Naturalist* 105:263–266.

———. 1996. Comparative life history of painted turtles *(Chrysemys picta)* in two habitats in the inland Pacific Northwest. *Copeia* 1996:114–130.

Lindeman, P. V., and F. W. Rabe. 1990. Effect of drought on the western painted turtle, *Chrysemys picta belli*, in a small wetland ecosystem. *Journal of Freshwater Ecology* 5:359–364.

Lindquist, S. B., and M. D. Bachmann. 1982. The role of visual and olfactory cues in the prey catching behavior of the tiger salamander, *Ambystoma tigrinum*. *Copeia* 1982:81–90.

Ling, R. W., J. P. VanAmberg, and J. K. Werner. 1986. Pond acidity and its relationship to larval development of *Ambystoma maculatum* and *Rana sylvatica* in upper Michigan. *Journal of Herpetology* 20:230–236.

Lipman, P. W., and H. H. Mehnert. 1975. Late Cenozoic basaltic volcanism and development of the Rio Grande depression in the Southern Rocky Mountains. Pages 119–154 in *Cenozoic history of the Southern Rocky Mountains,* B. F. Curtis, ed. Geological Society of America Memoir 144.

Littlejohn, M. J., and R. S. Oldham. 1968. *Rana pipiens* complex: Mating call structure and taxonomy. *Science* 162:1,003–1,005.

Livezey, R. L., and A. H. Wright. 1947. A synoptic key to the salientian eggs of the United States. *American Midland Naturalist* 37:179–222.

Livo, L. J. 1977. An addition to the herpetofauna of Colorado. *The Colorado Herpetologist* 3 (1):1.

———. 1981a. Geographic distribution: *Scaphiopus couchi. Herpetological Review* 12:83.

———. 1981b. Leopard frog *(Rana pipiens)* reproduction in Boulder County, Colorado. M.A. thesis, University of Colorado, Denver.

———. 1985. Notes on the lined snake, *Tropidoclonion lineatum,* in Colorado. *Journal of the Colorado-Wyoming Academy of Science* 17 (1):36.

———. 1988. Distributional records of amphibians and reptiles from Colorado. *Herpetological Review* 19:61.

———. 1989. Life history notes: *Eumeces obsoletus* (Great Plains skink). Escape behavior. *Herpetological Review* 20:70–71.

———. 1990. Life history notes: *Bufo cognatus* (Great Plains toad). Microhabitat selection. *Herpetological Review* 21:58.

———. 1993. Spiny softshell turtle distribution in Colorado. *Prairie Naturalist* 25 (4):355–357.

———. 1994a. Geographic distribution: *Rana pipiens. Herpetological Review* 25:75.

———. 1994b. Geographic distribution: *Masticophis taeniatus taeniatus. Herpetological Review* 25:77.

———. 1995a. Amphibian surveys in Boulder, Clear Creek, and Gilpin counties, Colorado, 1994. Unpublished report, Colorado Division of Wildlife, Denver.

———. 1995b. *Identification guide to montane amphibians of the Southern Rocky Mountains.* N.p.

———. 1998a. Predators of larval *Bufo boreas. Journal of the Colorado-Wyoming Academy of Science* 38 (1):32.

———. 1998b. Creepy crawlies. *Colorado Outdoors* 47 (4):8–12.

Livo, L. J., and D. Chiszar. 1994. Geographic distribution: *Crotalus viridis cerberus. Herpetological Review* 25:76.

Livo, L. J., D. Chiszar, and H. M. Smith. 1995. Geographic distribution: *Pseudacris triseriata. Herpetological Review* 26:208.

———. 1996. Geographic distribution: *Liochlorophis (= Opheodrys) vernalis. Herpetological Review* 27:154.

———. 1997. Natural history notes: *Spea multiplicata* (New Mexico spade foot). Defensive posture. *Herpetological Review* 28: 148.

Livo, L. J., G. A. Hammerson, and H. M. Smith. 1998. Summary of amphibians and reptiles introduced into Colorado. *Northwestern Naturalist* 79:1–11.

Livo, L. J., G. A. Hammerson, H. M. Smith, D. Chiszar, and S. P. Mackessy. 1998. Status of chorus frogs (genus *Pseudacris*) in southeastern Colorado. *Bulletin of the Maryland Herpetological Society* 34:22–28.

Livo, L. J., and D. Yeakley. 1997. Comparison of current with historical elevational range in the boreal toad, *Bufo boreas. Herpetological Review* 28:143–144.

Lockwood, S. 1883. Maternal anxiety in a horned toad. *American Naturalist* 17:682–683.

Lombard, J. 1949. Notes on the desert whiptail lizard in Utah. *Copeia* 1949:234.

Long, D. R. 1985. Lipid utilization during reproduction in female *Kinosternon flavescens. Herpetologica* 41:58–65.

———. 1986a. Clutch formation in the turtle, *Kinosternon flavescens* (Testudines, Kinosternidae). *Southwestern Naturalist* 31:1–8.

———. 1986b. Lipid content and delayed emergence of hatchling yellow mud turtles. *Southwestern Naturalist* 31:244–246.

———. 1988. Mullerian ducts in male *Bufo woodhousei. Southwestern Naturalist* 33:240–243.

———. 1989. Energetics and reproduction in female *Scaphiopus multiplicatus* from western Texas. *Journal of Herpetology* 23:176–179.

Lopez, T. J., and L. R. Maxson. 1990. Life history notes: *Rana catesbeiana* (bullfrog). Polymely. *Herpetological Review* 21:90.

Loughry, W. J. 1989. Discrimination of snakes by two populations of black-tailed prairie dogs. *Journal of Mammalogy* 70:627–630.

Lowe, C. H., Jr. 1955a. A new species of whiptailed lizard (genus *Cnemidophorus*) from the Colorado Plateau of Arizona, New Mexico, Colorado, and Utah. *Breviora (Harvard University Museum of Comparative Zoology)* 47:1–7.

———. 1955b. The evolutionary relationships of the narrow-lined skinks of the inland southwest, *Eumeces taylori, E. gaigei,* and *E. multivirgatus. Herpetologica* 11:233–235.

———. 1966. The prairie lined racerunner. *Journal of the Arizona Academy of Science* 4:44–45.

Lowe, C. H., C. R. Schwalbe, and T. B. Johnson. 1986. *The venomous reptiles of Arizona.* Arizona Game and Fish Department, Phoenix.

Ludlow, M. E. 1981. Observations on *Crotalus v. viridis* (Rafinesque) and the herpetofauna of the Ken-Caryl Ranch, Jefferson County, Colorado. *Herpetological Review* 12:50–52.

Ludwig, D. R., M. Redmer, R. Domazlicky, S. Kobal, and B. Conklin. 1992. Current status of amphibians and reptiles in DuPage County, Illinois. *Transactions of the Illinois State Academy of Science* 85:187–199.

Luepschen, L. K. 1981. Life history notes: *Bufo punctatus* (red-spotted toad). Larval coloration. *Herpetological Review* 12:79.

Lutterschmidt, W. I., G. A. Marvin, and V. H. Hutchison. 1996. *Rana catesbeiana:* Record size. *Herpetological Review* 27:74–75.

Lynch, J. D. 1978. The distribution of leopard frogs *(Rana blairi* and *Rana pipiens)* (Amphibia, Anura, Ranidae) in Nebraska. *Journal of Herpetology* 12:157–162.

———. 1985. Annotated checklist of the amphibians and reptiles of Nebraska. *Transactions of the Nebraska Academy of Science* 13:33–57.

Mabry, C. M., and J. L. Christiansen. 1991. The activity and breeding cycle of *Scaphiopus bombifrons* in Iowa. *Journal of Herpetology* 25:116–119.

Macartney, J. M., P. T. Gregory, and M. B. Charland. 1990. Growth and sexual maturity of the western rattlesnake, *Crotalus viridis,* in British Columbia. *Copeia* 1990:528–542.

MacCulloch, R. D., and D. M. MacCulloch. 1983. Demography, growth, and food of western painted turtles, *Chrysemys picta bellii* (Gray), from southern Saskatchewan. *Canadian Journal of Zoology* 61:1,499–1,509.

Macey, J. R., A. Larson, N. B. Ananjeva, and T. J. Papenfuss. 1997. Evolutionary shifts in three major structural features of the mitochondrial genome among iguanian lizards. *Journal of Molecular Evolution* 44:660–674.

Mackessy, S. P. 1988. Venom ontogeny in the Pacific rattlesnakes *Crotalus viridis helleri* and *C. v. oreganus. Copeia* 1988:92–101.

———. 1996. A survey of the herpetofauna of southeastern Colorado with a focus on the current status of two candidates for protected species status: The massasauga rattlesnake and the Texas horned lizard. Preliminary report to the Colorado Division of Wildlife. Unpublished report.

———. 1998. A survey of the herpetofauna of southeastern Colorado with a focus on the current status of two candidates for protected species status: The massasauga rattlesnake and the Texas horned lizard. Final report to the Colorado Division of Wildlife. Unpublished report.

Mackessy, S. P., R. Donoho, J. Hobert, C. Montgomery, and K. Waldron. 1996. Geographic distribution: *Pseudacris triseriata maculata. Herpetological Review* 27:30.

Mackessy, S. P., J. Hobert, R. Donoho, C. Montgomery, and K. Waldron. 1996. Geographic distribution: *Sistrurus catenatus. Herpetological Review* 27:36.

Mahmoud, I. Y. 1969. Comparative ecology of the kinosternid turtles of Oklahoma. *Southwestern Naturalist* 14:31–66.

———. 1997. Seasonal changes in gonadal activity and the effects of stress on reproductive hormones in the common snapping turtle, *Chelydra serpentina. General and Comparative Endocrinology* 107:359–372.

Mahrt, L. A. 1996. Natural history notes: *Urosaurus ornatus* (tree lizard): Autohemorrhaging. *Herpetological Review* 27:21–22.

———. 1998. Territorial establishment and maintenance by female tree lizards, *Urosaurus ornatus. Journal of Herpetology* 32:176–182.

Malmos, K., R. Reed, and B. Starret. 1995. Hybridization between *Bufo woodhousii* and *Bufo punctatus* from the Grand Canyon region of Arizona. *Great Basin Naturalist* 55:368–371.

Marco, A., J. M. Kiesecker, and D. P. Chivers. 1998. Sex recognition and mate choice by male western toads, *Bufo boreas. Animal Behaviour* 55:1,631–1,635.

Marr, J. C. 1944. Notes on amphibians and reptiles from the central United States. *American Midland Naturalist* 32:478–490.

Marti, C. D. 1974. Feeding ecology of four sympatric owls. *Condor* 76:45–61.

Martin, R. F. 1973a. Osteology of North American *Bufo:* The *americanus, cognatus,* and *boreas* species groups. *Herpetologica* 29:375–387.

———. 1973b. Reproduction in the tree lizard *(Urosaurus ornatus)* in central Texas: Drought conditions. *Herpetologica* 29:27–32.

———. 1977. Variation in reproductive productivity of range margin tree lizards *(Urosaurus ornatus). Copeia* 1977:83–92.

Martins, E. P. 1991. Individual and sex differences in the use of the push-up display by the sagebrush lizard, *Sceloporus graciosus. Animal Behaviour* 41:403–416.

Martof, B. S. 1970. *Rana sylvatica. Catalogue of American Amphibians and Reptiles* 86:1–4.

Martof, B. S., and R. L. Humphries. 1959. Geographic variation in the wood frog, *Rana sylvatica. American Midland Naturalist* 61:350–389.

Maslin, T. P. 1947a. Range extensions of three reptiles in Colorado. *Copeia* 1947:138.

———. 1947b. Guide to the lizards of Colorado. University of Colorado Museum Leaflet 3:1–14.

———. 1947c. *Rana sylvatica cantabrigensis* Baird and Girard in Colorado. *Copeia* 1947:158–162.

———. 1950. Herpetological notes and records from Colorado. *Herpetologica* 6:89–95.

———. 1953. The status of the whipsnake *Masticophis flagellum* (Shaw) in Colorado. *Herpetologica* 9:193–200.

———. 1956. *Sceloporus undulatus erythrocheilus* ssp. nov. (Reptilia, Iguanidae), from Colorado. *Herpetologica* 12:291–294.

———. 1957. Notes on the lizard *Eumeces multivirgatus gaigeae* from Colorado and Utah. *Herpetologica* 13:87–90.

———. 1959. *An annotated check list of amphibians and reptiles of Colorado.* University of Colorado Studies, Series in Biology 6.

———. 1962. All-female species of the lizard genus *Cnemidophorus,* Teiidae. *Science* 135:212–213.

———. 1964. Amphibians and reptiles of the Boulder area. Pages 75–80 in Natural history of the Boulder area, H. G. Rodeck, ed. University of Colorado Museum Leaflet No. 13.

———. 1965. The status of the rattlesnake *Sistrurus catenatus* (Crotalidae) in Colorado. *Southwestern Naturalist* 10:31–34.

———. 1966. The sex of hatchlings of five apparently unisexual species of whiptail lizards (*Cnemidophorus,* Teiidae). *American Midland Naturalist* 76:369–378.

———. 1967. Skin grafting in the bisexual teiid lizard *Cnemidophorus sexlineatus* and in the unisexual *C. tesselatus. Journal of Experimental Zoology* 166:137–149.

———. 1971. Conclusive evidence of parthenogenesis in three species of *Cnemidophorus* (Teiidae). *Copeia* 1971:156–158.

Maslin, T. P., and W. S. Koster. 1954. *Tropidoclonion lineatum* (Hallowell) in New Mexico. *Herpetologica* 10:172.

Matthews, T. C. 1968. Some evolutionary aspects of color polymorphism in a population of boreal chorus frogs. Ph.D. dissertation, Colorado State University, Fort Collins.

———. 1971. Genetic changes in a population of boreal chorus frogs *(Pseudacris triseriata)* polymorphic for color. *American Midland Naturalist* 85:208–221.

Matthews, T. C., and D. Pettus. 1966. Color inheritance in *Pseudacris triseriata. Herpetologica* 22:269–275.

Mauer, E. F. 1995. Natural history notes: *Chrysemys picta belli* (western painted turtle). Feeding behavior. *Herpetological Review* 26:34.

Mautz, W. J. 1982. Observations on an oviposition site of the side blotched lizard, *Uta stansburiana. Journal of Herpetology* 16:331–332.

Mayhew, W. W. 1965. Adaptations of the amphibian, *Scaphiopus couchi,* to desert conditions. *American Midland Naturalist* 74:95–109.

McAlister, W. H. 1963. Evidence of mild toxicity in the saliva of the hognose snake *(Heterodon). Herpetologica* 19:132–137.

McAllister, C. T., and S. P. Tabor. 1985. Life history notes: *Gastrophryne olivacea* (Great Plains narrowmouth toad). Coexistence. *Herpetological Review* 16:109.

———. 1983. Life history notes: *Crotaphytus collaris collaris* (eastern collared lizard). Hibernacula. *Herpetological Review* 14:73–74.

———. 1984. Life history notes: *Crotaphytus collaris collaris* (eastern collared lizard). Reproduction. *Herpetological Review* 15:48.

———. 1985. Food habits and feeding behavior of *Crotaphytus collaris collaris* (Iguanidae) from Arkansas and Missouri. *Southwestern Naturalist* 30:597–619.

———. 1987. Life history notes: *Crotaphytus collaris collaris* (eastern collared lizard). Seasonal activity. *Herpetological Review* 18:15.

McAllister, C. T., et al. 1991. Helminth parasites of unisexual and bisexual whiptail lizards (Teiidae) in North America. V. *Mesocestoides* sp. Tetrathyridia (Cestoidea: Cyclophyllidea) from four species of *Cnemidophorus. Journal of Wildlife Diseases* 27:494–497.

McAuliffe, J. R. 1978. Seasonal migrational movements of a population of the western painted turtle, *Chrysemys picta bellii* (Reptilia, Testudines, Testudinidae). *Journal of Herpetology* 12:143–149.

McClelland, B. E., and W. Wilczynski. 1989. Release call characteristics of male and female *Rana pipiens. Copeia* 1989:1,045–1,049.

McCoy, C. J., Jr. 1961. Distribution of the subspecies of *Sceloporus undulatus* (Reptilia: Iguanidae) in Oklahoma. *Southwestern Naturalist* 6:79–85.

———. 1962a. Noteworthy amphibians and reptiles from Colorado. *Herpetologica* 18:60–62.

———. 1962b. Herpetofaunal dispersal in the Grand Valley of Colorado. *Journal of the Colorado-Wyoming Academy of Science* 5 (3):41.

———. 1965. Life history and ecology of *Cnemidophorus tigris septentrionalis.* Ph.D. dissertation, University of Colorado, Boulder.

———. 1966. An annotated list of the amphibians and reptiles of Black Canyon of the Gunnison National Monument. National Park Service. Mimeograph.

———. 1967. Natural history notes on *Crotaphytus wislizeni* (Reptilia: Iguanidae) in Colorado. *American Midland Naturalist* 77:138–147.

———. 1974. Communal hibernation of the lizard *Cnemidophorus tigris* (Teiidae). *Southwestern Naturalist* 19:218.

———. 1975. Notes on Oklahoma reptiles. *Proceedings of the Oklahoma Academy of Science* 55:53–54.

McCoy, C. J., and F. R. Gehlbach. 1967. Cloacal hemorrhage and the defense display of the colubrid snake *Rhinocheilus lecontei. Texas Journal of Science* 19:349–352.

McCoy, C. J., and G. A. Hoddenbach. 1966. Geographic variation in ovarian cycles and clutch size in *Cnemidophorus tigris* (Teiidae). *Science* 154:1,671–1,672.

McCoy, C. J., G. N. Knopf, and J. M. Walker. 1964. The snake *Tantilla utahensis* Blanchard: An addition to the fauna of Colorado. *Herpetologica* 20:135–136.

McCoy, C. J., H. M. Smith, and J. A. Tihen. 1967. Natural hybrid toads, *Bufo punctatus* x *Bufo woodhousei,* from Colorado. *Southwestern Naturalist* 12:45–54.

McCoy, J. K., H. J. Harmon, T. A. Baird, and S. F. Fox. 1997. Geographic variation in sexual dichromatism in the collared lizard, *Crotaphy-*

tus collaris (Sauria: Crotaphytidae). *Copeia* 1997:565–571.

McCranie, J. R. 1988. Description of the hemipenis of *Sistrurus ravus* (Serpentes: Viperidae). *Herpetologica* 44:123–126.

McCrystal, H. K. 1982. Life history notes: *Elaphe guttata emoryi* (Great Plains rat snake). Food. *Herpetological Review* 13:46–47.

McGinnis, S. M., and M. Falkenstein. 1971. Thermoregulatory behavior in three sympatric species of iguanid lizards. *Copeia* 1971:552–554.

McGuire, J. A. 1996. Phylogenetic systematics of crotaphytid lizards (Reptilia: Iguania: Crotaphytidae). *Bulletin of Carnegie Museum of Natural History* 32:1–143.

McKnight, C. M., and W.H.N. Gutzke. 1993. Effects of the embryonic environment and of hatchling housing conditions on growth of young snapping turtles *(Chelydra serpentina)*. *Copeia* 1993:475–482.

M'Closkey, R. T., and K. A. Baia. 1990. Recolonization of a habitat by tree lizards. *Journal of Herpetology* 24:325–327.

M'Closkey, R. T., K. A. Baia, and R. W. Russell. 1987. Tree lizard *(Urosaurus ornatus)* territories: Experimental perturbation of the sex ratio. *Ecology* 68:2,059–2,062.

M'Closkey, R. T., S. J. Hecnar, D. R. Chalcraft, J. E. Cotter, J. Johnston, and R. Poulin. 1997. Colonization and saturation of habitats by lizards. *Oikos* 78:283–290.

Mecham, J. S. 1957. The taxonomic status of some southwestern skinks of the *multivirgatus* group. *Copeia* 1957:111–123.

———. 1967. Polymorphic *Eumeces multivirgatus* from the Texas High Plains. *Southwestern Naturalist* 12:104–105.

———. 1968. Studies on evolutionary effects of isolation in the *Rana pipiens* complex. *Yearbook of the American Philosophical Society* 1968:314–316.

———. 1980. *Eumeces multivirgatus. Catalogue of American Amphibians and Reptiles* 241:1–2.

Mecham, J. S., M. J. Littlejohn, R. S. Oldham, L. E. Brown, and J. R. Brown. 1973. A new species of leopard frog (*Rana pipiens* complex) from the plains of the central United States. *Texas Tech University Museum Occasional Papers* 18:1–11.

Medica, P. A. 1975. *Rhinocheilus lecontei. Catalogue of American Amphibians and Reptiles* 175:1–4.

———. 1980. Locality records of *Rhinocheilus lecontei* in the United States and Mexico. *Herpetological Review* 11:42.

Medica, P. A., and F. B. Turner. 1976. Reproduction by *Uta stansburiana* (Reptilia, Lacertilia, Iguanidae) in southern Nevada. *Journal of Herpetology* 10:123–128.

———. 1984. Natural longevity of iguanid lizards in southern Nevada. *Herpetological Review* 15:34–35.

Medica, P. A., F. B. Turner, and D. D. Smith. 1973. Hormonal induction of color change in female leopard lizards, *Crotaphytus wislizenii. Copeia* 1973:658–661.

Metcalf, A. L., and E. Metcalf. 1978. An experiment with homing in ornate box turtles (*Terrapene ornata ornata* Agassiz). *Journal of Herpetology* 12:411–412.

Metcalf, E. L., and A. L. Metcalf. 1970. Observations on ornate box turtles. *Transactions of the Kansas Academy of Sciences* 73:96–117.

———. 1979. Mortality in hibernating ornate box turtles, *Terrapene ornata. Herpetologica* 35:93–96.

———. 1985. Longevity in some ornate box turtles *(Terrapene ornata ornata). Journal of Herpetology* 19:157–158.

Meylan, P. A. 1987. The phylogenetic relationships of soft-shelled turtles (family Trionychidae). *Bulletin of the American Museum of Natural History* 186:1–101.

Michel, L. 1976. Reproduction in a southwestern New Mexican population of *Urosaurus ornatus. Southwestern Naturalist* 21:281–289.

Miller, A. H., and R. C. Stebbins. 1964. *The lives of desert animals in Joshua Tree National Monument.* University of California Press, Berkeley.

Miller, K. 1993. The improved performance of snapping turtles *(Chelydra serpentina)* hatched from eggs incubated on a wet substrate persists through the neonatal period. *Journal of Herpetology* 27:228–233.

Miller K., G. F. Birchard, M. J. Packard, and G. C. Packard. 1989. *Trionyx spiniferus* (spiny softshell turtle): Fecundity. *Herpetological Review* 20:56.

Miller, P. H. [1961?]. An annotated list of the amphibians and reptiles of Colorado National Monument. National Park Service Leaflet. Mimeograph.

Miller, P. H. 1977. A demographic study of the chorus frog, *Pseudacris triseriata.* M.S. thesis, Colorado State University, Fort Collins.

Milne, L. J. 1938. Mating of *Phrynosoma cornutum. Copeia* 1938:200–201.

Milstead, W. W. 1953a. Geographic variation in the garter snake, *Thamnophis cyrtopsis. Texas Journal of Science* 5:348–379.

———. 1953b. Ecological distribution of the lizards of the La Mota Mountain region of Trans-Pecos Texas. *Texas Journal of Science* 5:403–415.

———. 1965. Changes in competing populations of whiptail lizards *(Cnemidophorus)* in southwestern Texas. *American Midland Naturalist* 73:75–80.

Minton, S. A., Jr. 1958 [1959]. Observations on amphibians and reptiles of the Big Bend region of Texas. *Southwestern Naturalist* 3:28–54.

———. 1972. *Amphibians and reptiles of Indiana.* Indiana Academy of Science, Indianapolis.

———. 1978. Beware: Nonpoisonous snakes. *Natural History* 87:56–61.

Minx, P. 1996. Phylogenetic relationships among the box turtles, genus *Terrapene. Herpetologica* 52:584–597.

Mitchell, J. C. 1984. Observations on the ecology and reproduction of the leopard lizard, *Gambelia wislizenii* (Iguanidae) in southeastern Arizona. *Southwestern Naturalist* 29:509–511.

———. 1985. Life history notes: *Hypsiglena torquata ochrorhyncha* (spotted night snake). Behavior. *Herpetological Review* 16:54, 56.

Mitchell, S. L. 1990. The mating system genetically affects offspring performance in Woodhouse's toad *(Bufo woodhousei). Evolution* 44:502–519.

Mittleman, M. B. 1942. A summary of the iguanid genus *Urosaurus. Bulletin of the Museum of Comparative Zoology, Harvard University* 91:103–181.

Moll, D. 1979. Subterranean feeding by the Illinois mud turtle, *Kinosternon flavescens spooneri. Journal of Herpetology* 13:371–373.

Moll, E. O. 1979. Reproductive cycles and adaptations. Pages 305–331 in *Turtles: Perspective and research,* M. Harless and H. Morlock, eds. John Wiley & Sons, New York.

Montanucci, R. R. 1967. Further studies on leopard lizards, *Crotaphytus wislizeni. Herpetologica* 23:119–126.

———. 1978. Dorsal pattern polymorphism and adaptation in *Gambelia wislizenii* (Reptilia, Lacertilia, Iguanidae). *Journal of Herpetology* 12:73–81.

———. 1981. Habitat separation between *Phrynosoma douglassi* and *P. orbiculare* (Lacertilia: Iguanidae) in Mexico. *Copeia* 1981:147–153.

———. 1996. Morphological variation in the gular fold in the horned lizard genus, *Phrynosoma* (Iguania: Phrynosomatidae). *Herpetologica* 52:46–55.

Montanucci, R. R., and B. E. Baur. 1982. Mating and courtship-related behaviors of the short-horned lizard, *Phrynosoma douglassi. Copeia* 1982:971–974.

Montgomery, C. E. 1998. The natural history of the Texas horned lizard *(Phrynosoma cornutum)* in Colorado with notes on clinal variation throughout its range. M.A. thesis, University of Northern Colorado, Greeley.

Montgomery, C., T. Childers, E. Bergman, J. D. Manzer, J. Sifert, B. Hill, and S. P. Mackessy. 1998a. Geographic distribution: *Lampropeltis triangulum gentilis. Herpetological Review* 29:114.

———. 1998b. Geographic distribution: *Rhinocheilus lecontei tessellatus. Herpetological Review* 29:116.

———. 1998c. Geographic distribution: *Sistrurus catenatus edwardsii. Herpetological Review* 29:116.

Montgomery, C., T. Childers, J. D. Manzer, E. Bergman, J. Sifert, B. Hill, and S. P. Mackessy.

1998b. Geographic distribution: *Phrynosoma cornutumi. Herpetological Review* 29:110.

———. 1998b. Geographic distribution: *Elaphe obsoleta lindheimerii* (Texas rat snake). *Herpetological Review* 29:112.

Montgomery, C., L. Compton, T. Childers, E. Bergman, J. D. Manzer, J. Sifert, B. Hill, and S. P. Mackessy. 1998. Geographic distribution: *Elaphe guttata emoryi. Herpetological Review* 29:112.

Montgomery, C., J. Hobert, E. Bergman, B. Hill, S. Boback, and S. P. Mackessy. 1997. Geographic distribution: *Lampropeltis triangulum gentilis. Herpetological Review* 28:52.

Montgomery, C., J. Sifert, B. Hill, T. Childers, J. D. Manzer, E. Bergman, and S. P. Mackessy. 1998. Geographic distribution: *Scaphiopus couchii. Herpetological Review* 29:108.

Montgomery, C., K. Waldron, J. Hobert, R. Donoho, and S. P. Mackessy. 1996a. Geographic distribution: *Diadophis punctatus arnyi. Herpetological Review* 27:33.

———. 1996b. Geographic distribution: *Tantilla nigriceps nigriceps. Herpetological Review* 27:36.

Moore, R. G., and B. A. Moore. 1980. Observations on the body temperature and activity in the red-spotted toad, *Bufo punctatus. Copeia* 1980:362–363.

Moritz, C. C., J. W. Wright, and W. M. Brown. 1989. Mitochondrial-DNA analyses and the origin and relative age of parthenogenetic lizards (genus *Cnemidophorus*). III. *C. velox* and *C. exsanguis. Evolution* 43:958–968.

Morris, M. A. 1985. Envenomation from the bite of *Heterodon nasicus* (Serpentes: Colubridae). *Herpetologica* 41:361–363.

Morrison, R. L., M. S. Rand, and S. K. Frost-Mason. 1995. Cellular basis of color differences in three morphs of the lizard *Sceloporus undulatus erythrocheilus. Copeia* 1995:397–408.

Morrison, R. L., W. C. Sherbrooke, and S. K. Frost-Mason. 1996. Temperature-sensitive, physiologically active iridophores in the lizard *Urosaurus ornatus:* An ultrastructural analysis of color change. *Copeia* 1996:804–812.

Mosauer, W. 1932. The amphibians and reptiles of the Guadalupe Mountains of New Mexico and Texas. University of Michigan Museum of Zoology Occasional Papers 246:1–18.

Mourning, T. 1997. *Amphibian and reptile survey, north portion of West Region, 1994–1996.* Final report, Colorado Division of Wildlife. Unpublished report.

Mueller, C. F. and R. E. Moore. 1969. Growth of the sagebrush lizard, *Sceloporus graciosus,* in Yellowstone National Park. *Herpetologica* 25:35–38.

Munger, J. C. 1984a. Home ranges of horned lizards *(Phrynosoma):* Circumscribed and exclusive? *Oecologia* 62:351–360.

———. 1984b. Optimal foraging? Patch use by horned lizards (Iguanidae: *Phrynosoma*). *American Naturalist* 123:654–680.

———. 1984c. Long-term yield from harvester ant colonies: Implications for horned lizard foraging strategy. *Ecology* 65:1,077–1,086.

———. 1986. Rate of death due to predation for two species of horned lizard, *Phrynosoma cornutum* and *P. modestum. Copeia* 1986:820–824.

Murphy, M. B. 1953. Some observations on the neoteny and metamorphosis of races of *Ambystoma tigrinum* in two local populations. M.A. thesis, University of Colorado, Boulder.

Mushinsky, H. R. 1979. Mating behavior of the common water snake, *Nerodia sipedon sipedon,* in eastern Pennsylvania (Reptilia, Serpentes, Colubridae). *Journal of Herpetology* 13:127–129.

Muths, E., and P. S. Corn. 1997. Basking by adult boreal toads *(Bufo boreas boreas)* during the breeding season. *Journal of Herpetology* 31:426–428.

Nelson, C. E. 1972. Systematic studies of the North American microhylid genus *Gastrophryne. Journal of Herpetology* 6:111–137.

Nevo, E. 1973. Adaptive variation in size in cricket frogs. *Ecology* 54:1,271–1,281.

Newman, R. A. 1987. Effects of density and predation on *Scaphiopus couchi* tadpoles in desert ponds. *Oecologia* 71:301–307.

———. 1989. Developmental plasticity of *Scaphiopus couchii* tadpoles in an unpredictable environment. *Ecology* 70:1,775–1,787.

Newman, R. A., and A. E. Dunham. 1994. Size at metamorphosis and water loss in a desert anuran *(Scaphiopus couchii). Copeia* 1994:372–381.

Nieuwolt, P. M. 1996. Movement, activity, and microhabitat selection in the western box turtle, *Terrapene ornata luteola,* in New Mexico. *Herpetologica* 52:487–495.

Nieuwolt-Dacanay, P. M. 1997. Reproduction in the western box turtle, *Terrapene ornata luteola. Copeia* 1997:819–826.

Niewiarowski, P. H. 1995. Effect of supplemental feeding and thermal environment on growth rates of eastern fence lizards, *Sceloporus undulatus. Herpetologica* 51:487–496.

Niewiarowski, P. H., J. D. Congdon, A. E. Dunham, L. J. Vitt, and D. W. Tinkle. 1997. Tales of lizard tails: Effects of tail autotomy on subsequent survival and growth of free-ranging hatchling *Uta stansburiana. Canadian Journal of Zoology* 75:542–548.

Niewiarowski, P. H., and W. Roosenburg. 1993. Reciprocal transplants reveal sources of variation in growth rates of the lizard *Sceloporus undulatus. Ecology* 74:1,992–2,002.

Norris, D. O. 1973. Some aspects of reproduction in a population of neotenic tiger salamanders, *Ambystoma tigrinum. Journal of the Colorado-Wyoming Academy of Science* 7 (4):39.

———. 1989. Seasonal changes in diet of paedogenetic tiger salamanders *(Ambystoma tigrinum mavortium). Journal of Herpetology* 23:87–89.

Norris, D. O., E. J. Clark, and T. Kellogg. 1994. Geographic distribution: *Rana catesbeiana. Herpetological Review* 25:161.

Northen, P. T. 1970. The geographic and taxonomic relationships of the Great Basin spadefoot toad, *Scaphiopus intermontanus,* to other members of the subgenus *Spea.* Ph.D. dissertation, University of Wisconsin, Madison.

Nussbaum, R. A., and L. V. Diller. 1976. The life history of the side-blotched lizard, *Uta stansburiana* Baird and Girard, in north-central Oregon. *Northwest Science* 50:243–260.

Nyman, S. 1986. Mass mortality in larval *Rana sylvatica* attributable to the bacterium, *Aeromonas hydrophila. Journal of Herpetology* 20:196–201.

Obbard, M. E., and R. J. Brooks. 1980. Nesting migrations of the snapping turtle, *Chelydra serpentina. Herpetologica* 36:158–162.

———. 1981. A radio-telemetry and mark-recapture study of activity in the common snapping turtle, *Chelydra serpentina. Copeia* 1981:630–637.

O'Connell, D. J. 1997. Natural history notes: *Chelydra serpentina* (common snapping turtle). Reproduction. *Herpetological Review* 28:86.

Oldfield, B., and J. J. Moriarty. 1994. *Amphibians and reptiles native to Minnesota.* University of Minnesota Press, Minneapolis.

Oldham, J. C., and H. M. Smith. 1991. The generic status of the smooth green snake, *Opheodrys vernalis. Bulletin of the Maryland Herpetological Society* 27 (4):201–215.

Oldham, M. J., and C. A. Campbell. 1990. Status report on the cricket frog *Acris crepitans* in Canada. Unpublished report, Committee on the Status of Endangered Wildlife in Canada.

Olson, D. H., W. P. Leonard, and R. B. Bury, editors. 1997. *Sampling amphibians in lentic habitats.* Society for Northwestern Vertebrate Biology, Northwest Fauna 4.

Osborne, S. T. 1984. Life history notes: *Rhinocheilus lecontei antonii* (Mexican long-nosed snake): Behavior. *Herpetological Review* 15:50.

Pack, H. J. 1922. *Bufo cognatus cognatus* (Say) in Utah. *Copeia* 1922:8.

Pack, L. E., Jr., and W. W. Tanner. 1970. A taxonomic comparison of *Uta stansburiana* of the Great Basin and the Upper Colorado River basin in Utah, and a description of a new subspecies. *Great Basin Naturalist* 30:71–90.

Packard, G. C. 1997. Temperatures during winter in nests with hatchling painted turtles *(Chrysemys picta). Herpetologica* 53:89–95.

Packard, G. C., S. L. Fasano, M. B. Attaway, L. D. Lohmiller, and T. L. Lynch. 1997. Thermal environment for overwintering hatchlings of the painted turtle *(Chrysemys picta). Canadian Journal of Zoology* 75:401–406.

Packard, G. C., and M. J. Packard. 1987. Water relations and nitrogen excretion in embryos of the oviparous snake *Coluber constrictor. Copeia* 1987:395–406.

Packard, G. C., M. J. Packard, and G. F. Birchard. 1989. Sexual differentiation and hatching success by painted turtles incubating in different thermal and hydric environments. *Herpetologica* 45:385–392.

Packard, G. C., M. J. Packard, T. J. Boardman, and M. D. Ashen. 1981. Possible adaptive value of water exchanges in flexible-shelled eggs of turtles. *Science* 213:471–473.

Packard, G. C., M. J. Packard, and W. H. Gutzke. 1985. Influence of hydration of the environment on eggs and embryos of the terrestrial turtle *Terrapene ornata. Physiological Zoology* 58:564–575.

Packard, G. C., M. J. Packard, and K. Miller. 1990. *Chelydra serpentina* (common snapping turtle): Fecundity. *Herpetological Review* 21:92.

Packard, G. C., G. L. Paukstis, T. J. Boardman, and W.H.N. Gutzke. 1985. Daily and seasonal variation in hydric conditions and temperature inside nests of common snapping turtles *(Chelydra serpentina). Canadian Journal of Zoology* 63:2,422–2,429.

Packard, G. C., K. A. Ruble, and M. J. Packard. 1993. Hatchling snapping turtles overwintering in natural nests are inoculated by ice in frozen soil. *Journal of Thermal Biology* 18:185–188.

Packard, G. C., T. L. Taigen, T. J. Boardman, M. J. Tracy, and C. R. Tracy. 1979. Changes in mass of softshell turtle *(Trionyx spiniferus)* eggs incubated on substrates differing in water potential. *Herpetologica* 35:78–86.

Packard, G. C., T. L. Taigen, M. J. Packard, and T. J. Boardman. 1981. Changes in mass of eggs of softshell turtles *(Trionyx spiniferus)* incubated under hydric conditions simulating those of natural nests. *Journal of Zoology* 193:81–90.

Packard, G. C., T. L. Taigen, M. J. Packard, and R. D. Shuman. 1979. Water-vapour conductance of testudinian and crocodilian eggs (class Reptilia). *Respiratory Physiology* 38:1–10.

Painter, C. W. 1985. Herpetology of the Gila and San Francisco river drainages of southwestern New Mexico. Unpublished report. New Mexico Department of Game and Fish, Santa Fe.

———. 1993. Life history notes: *Apalone spinifera emoryi* (Texas spiny softshell): Coloration. *Herpetological Review* 24:148.

Painter, C. W., and T. J. Hibbitts. 1997. Natural history notes: *Lampropeltis triangulum celaenops* (New Mexico milk snake). Maximum size. *Herpetological Review* 28:90.

Painter, C. W., B. R. Tomberlin, and J. H. Gee. 1997. Natural history notes: *Tantilla hobartsmithi* (Southwestern black-headed snake) and *Tantilla nigriceps* (plains black-headed snake). Coloration. *Herpetological Review* 28:91.

Parker, W. S. 1972. Ecological study of the western whiptail lizard, *Cnemidophorus tigris gracilis,* in Arizona. *Herpetologica* 28:360–369.

———. 1973a. Notes on reproduction of some lizards from Arizona, New Mexico, Texas, and Utah. *Herpetologica* 29:258–264.

———. 1973b. Natural history notes on the iguanid lizard *Urosaurus ornatus. Journal of Herpetology* 7:21–26.

———. 1974. Comparative ecology of two colubrid snakes, *Masticophis t. taeniatus* (Hallowell) and *Pituophis melanoleucus deserticola* Stejneger, in northern Utah. Ph.D. thesis, University of Utah, Salt Lake City.

———. 1976. Population estimates, age structure, and denning habits of whipsnakes, *Masticophis t. taeniatus,* in a northern Utah *Atriplex-Sarcobatus* community. *Herpetologica* 32:53–57.

———. 1982. *Masticophis taeniatus. Catalogue of American Amphibians and Reptiles* 304:1–4.

———. 1994. Demography of the fence lizard, *Sceloporus undulatus,* in northern Mississippi. *Copeia* 1994:136–152.

Parker, W. S., and W. S. Brown. 1972. Telemetric study of movements and oviposition of two female *Masticophis t. taeniatus. Copeia* 1972:892–895.

———. 1973. Species composition and population changes in two complexes of snake hibernacula in northern Utah. *Herpetologica* 29:319–326.

———. 1974. Mortality and weight changes of Great Basin rattlesnakes *(Crotalus viridis)* at a hibernaculum in northern Utah. *Herpetologica* 30:234–239.

———. 1980. Comparative ecology of two colubrid snakes, *Masticophis t. taeniatus* and *Pituophis melanoleucus deserticola,* in northern Utah. *Milwaukee Public Museum Publications in Biology and Geology* 7:i–vii, 1–104.

Parker, W. S., and E. R. Pianka. 1973. Notes on the ecology of the iguanid lizard, *Sceloporus magister. Herpetologica* 29:143–152.

———. 1975. Comparative ecology of populations of the lizard *Uta stansburiana. Copeia* 1975:615–632.

———. 1976. Ecological observations on the leopard lizard *(Crotaphytus wislizeni)* in different parts of its range. *Herpetologica* 32:95–114.

Parmenter, R. R. 1981. Digestive turnover rates in freshwater turtles: The influence of temperature and body size. *Comparative Biochemistry and Physiology* 70A:235–238.

Parris, L. E. 1973. *Caves of Colorado.* Pruett Publishing Company, Boulder, Colorado.

Paulissen, M. A. 1987a. Diet of adult and juvenile six-lined racerunners, *Cnemidophorus sexlineatus* (Sauria: Teiidae). *Southwestern Naturalist* 32:345–397.

———. 1987b. Optimal foraging and intraspecific diet differences in the lizard *Cnemidophorus sexlineatus. Oecologia* 71:439–446.

———. 1988a. Ontogenetic and seasonal comparisons of daily activity patterns of the six-lined racerunner, *Cnemidophorus sexlineatus* (Sauria: Teiidae). *American Midland Naturalist* 120:355–361.

———. 1988b. Ontogenetic and seasonal shifts in microhabitat use by the lizard *Cnemidophorus sexlineatus. Copeia* 1988:1,021–1,029.

———. 1988c. Ontogenetic comparison of body temperature selection and thermal tolerance of *Cnemidophorus sexlineatus. Journal of Herpetology* 22:473–476.

Paulissen, M. A., and B. C. Harvey. 1985. *Cnemidophorus sexlineatus* (prairie lined racerunner): Arboreality. *Herpetological Review* 16:27.

Paulissen, M. A., J. M. Walker, J. E. Cordes, and H. L. Taylor. 1993. Diet of diploid and triploid populations of parthenogenetic whiptail lizards of the *Cnemidophorus tesselatus* complex (Teiidae) in southeastern Colorado. *Southwestern Naturalist* 38:377–381.

Paulson, B. K., and V. H. Hutchison. 1987. Origin of the stimulus for muscular spasms at the critical thermal maximum in anurans. *Copeia* 1987:810–813.

Pederson, S. C. 1988. Cranial osteology of the cannibal morph in tiger salamanders, *Ambystoma tigrinum.* M.A. thesis, University of Colorado, Boulder.

———. 1991. Dental morphology of the cannibal morph in the tiger salamander, *Ambystoma tigrinum. Amphibia-Reptilia* 12:1–14.

Pegler, S. T., D. Chiszar, and H. M. Smith. 1995. Geographic distribution: *Sistrurus catenatus tergeminus* x *edwardsii. Herpetological Review* 26:47.

Pennock, L. A. 1960. Ontogenetic changes in the feeding habits of the wandering garter snake, *Thamnophis elegans vagrans* (Baird and Girard). M.S. thesis, University of Colorado, Boulder.

Perrill, S. A., and L. C. Lower. 1994. Advertisement call discrimination by female cricket frogs *(Acris crepitans). Journal of Herpetology* 28:399–400.

Perrill, S. A., and M. Magier. 1988. Male mating behavior in *Acris crepitans. Copeia* 1988:245–248.

Perry, T. W., and G. Hauer. 1996. Natural history notes: *Tantilla nigriceps* (plains black-headed snake). Maximum size and size variation. *Herpetological Review* 27:205–206.

Peslak, J., Jr. 1986. An observation on the social interaction of Texas horned lizards *(Phrynosoma cornutum). Southwestern Naturalist* 31:552.

Peterson, C. R. 1974. A preliminary report on the amphibians and reptiles of the Black Hills of South Dakota and Wyoming. M.A. thesis, University of Illinois, Urbana-Champaign.

———. 1987. Daily variation in the body temperatures of free-ranging garter snakes. *Ecology* 68:160–169.

Petokas, P. J., and M. M. Alexander. 1980. The nesting of *Chelydra serpentina* in northern New York. *Journal of Herpetology* 14:239–244.

Petranka, J. W., M. E. Hopey, B. T. Jennings, S. D. Baird, and S. J. Boone. 1994. Breeding habitat segregation of wood frogs and American toads: The role of interspecific tadpole predation and adult choice. *Copeia* 1994:691–697.

Pettit, K. E., C. A. Bishop, and R. J. Brooks. 1995. Home range and movements of the common snapping turtle, *Chelydra serpentina serpentina,* in a coastal wetland of Hamilton Harbour, Lake Ontario, Canada. *Canadian Field-Naturalist* 109:192–200.

Pettus, D., and G. M. Angleton. 1967. Comparative reproductive biology of montane and piedmont chorus frogs. *Evolution* 21:500–507.

Pettus, D., and D. D. Post. 1969. Genetic discontinuity of leopard frogs of Colorado. *Journal of Herpetology* 3:193–194.

Pettus, D., and A. W. Spencer. 1964. Size and metabolic differences in *Pseudacris triseriata* (Anura) from different elevations. *Southwestern Naturalist* 9:20–26.

Peyton, M. M. 1991. Geographic distribution: *Tantilla nigriceps. Herpetological Review* 22:26.

Pfennig, D. 1990. The adaptive significance of an environmentally-cued developmental switch in an anuran tadpole. *Oecologia* 85:101–107.

Pfennig, D. W. 1992a. Polyphenism in spadefoot toad tadpoles as a locally adjusted evolutionarily stable strategy. *Evolution* 46:1,408–1,420.

———. 1992b. Proximate and functional causes of polyphenism in an anuran tadpole. *Functional Ecology* 6:167–174.

Pfennig, D. W., S. G. Ho, and E. A. Hoffman. 1998. Pathogen transmission as a selective force against cannibalism. *Animal Behaviour* 55:1,255–1,261.

Pfennig, D. W., A. Mabry, and D. Orange. 1991. Environmental causes of correlations between age and size at metamorphosis in *Scaphiopus multiplicatus. Ecology* 72:2,240–2,248.

Pfennig, D. W., M.L.G. Loeb, and J. P. Collins. 1991. Pathogens as a factor limiting the spread of cannibalism in tiger salamanders. *Oecologia* 88:161–166.

Phelan, R. L., and B. H. Brattstrom. 1955. Geographic variation in *Sceloporus magister. Herpetologica* 11:1–14.

Phillips, C. A., W. W. Dimmick, and J. L. Carr. 1996. Conservation genetics of the common snapping turtle *(Chelydra serpentina). Conservation Biology* 10:397–405.

Phillips, J. A., and H. J. Harlow. 1981. Elevation of upper voluntary temperatures after shielding the parietal eye of horned lizards *(Phrynosoma douglassi). Herpetologica* 37:199–205.

Pianka, E. R. 1970. Comparative autecology of the lizard *Cnemidophorus tigris* in different parts of its geographic range. *Ecology* 51:703–720.

Pierce, B. A. 1980. The relationship of electrophoretically detectable protein variation to morphological and life history characteristics in the tiger salamander, *Ambystoma tigrinum*. Ph.D. dissertation, University of Colorado, Boulder.

Pierce, B. A., and J. B. Mitton. 1980. Patterns of allozyme variation in *Ambystoma tigrinum mavortium* and *A. t. nebulosum*. *Copeia* 1980:594–605.

Pierce, J. R. 1976. Distribution of two mating call types of the plains spadefoot, *Scaphiopus bombifrons*, in southwestern United States. *Southwestern Naturalist* 20:578–582.

Pietruszka, R. D., J. A. Wiens, and C. J. Pietruszka. 1981. Leopard lizard predation on *Perognathus*. *Journal of Herpetology* 15:249–250.

Pilz, W. R. 1983. Nesting ecology and diet of Swainson's hawks in the Chihuahuan Desert, south-central New Mexico. M.S. thesis, New Mexico State University, Las Cruces.

Pinou, T., C. A. Hass, and L. R. Maxson. 1995. Geographic variation of serum albumin in the monotypic snake genus *Diadophis* (Colubridae: Xenodontinae). *Journal of Herpetology* 29:105–110.

Platt, D. R. 1969. Natural history of the hognose snakes *Heterodon platyrhinos* and *Heterodon nasicus*. *University of Kansas Publications, Museum of Natural History* 18:253–420.

———. 1983. *Heterodon. Catalogue of American Amphibians and Reptiles* 315:1–2.

———. 1984. Growth of bullsnakes *(Pituophis melanoleucus sayi)* on a sand prairie in south central Kansas. Pages 41–55 in *Vertebrate ecology and systematics: A tribute to Henry S. Fitch*, R. A. Siegel et al., eds. University of Kansas Museum of Natural History Special Publication 10.

Platt, S. G., and C. G. Brantley. 1991. Life history notes: *Apalone spinifera* (spiny softshell). Behavior. *Herpetological Review* 22:57.

Platz, J. E. 1989. Speciation within the chorus frog *Pseudacris triseriata*: Morphometric and mating call analyses of the boreal and western subspecies. *Copeia* 1989:704–712.

Plummer, M. V., and J. C. Burnley. 1997. Behavior, hibernacula, and thermal relations of softshell turtles *(Trionyx spiniferus)* overwintering in a small stream. *Chelonian Conservation and Biology* 2:489–493.

Plummer, M. V., and J. D. Congdon. 1994. Radiotelemetric study of activity and movements of racers *(Coluber constrictor)* associated with a Carolina Bay in South Carolina. *Copeia* 1994:20–26.

———. 1996. Rates of metabolism and water flux in free-ranging racers, *Coluber constrictor. Copeia* 1996:8–14.

Plummer, M. V., and N. E. Mills. 1996. Observations on trailing and mating behaviors in hognose snakes *(Heterodon platyrhinos)*. *Journal of Herpetology* 30:80–82.

Plummer, M. V., N. E. Mills, and S. L. Allen. 1997. Activity, habitat, and movement patterns of softshell turtles *(Trionyx spiniferus)* in a small stream. *Chelonian Conservation and Biology* 2:514–520.

Plumpton, D. L., and R. S. Lutz. 1993. Prey selection and food habits of burrowing owls in Colorado. *Great Basin Naturalist* 53:299–304.

Porter, K. R. 1969a. Evolutionary status of the Rocky Mountain population of wood frogs. *Evolution* 23:163–170.

———. Description of *Rana maslini*, a new species of wood frog. *Herpetologica* 25:212–215.

Porter, K. R., and D. E. Hakanson. 1976. Toxicity of mine drainage to embryonic and larval boreal toads (Bufonidae: *Bufo boreas*). *Copeia* 1976:327–331.

Post, D. D. 1972. Species differentiation in the *Rana pipiens* complex. Ph.D. dissertation, Colorado State University, Fort Collins.

Post, D. D., and D. Pettus. 1966. Variation in *Rana pipiens* (Anura: Ranidae) of eastern Colorado. *Southwestern Naturalist* 11:476–482.

———. 1967. Sympatry of two members of the *Rana pipiens* complex in Colorado. *Herpetologica* 23:323.

Pough, F. H. 1976. Multiple cryptic effects of crossbanded and ringed patterns of snakes. *Copeia* 1976:834–836.

———. 1978. Ontogenetic changes in endurance in water snakes *(Natrix sipedon):* Physiological correlates and ecological consequences. *Copeia* 1978:69–75.

Powell, G. L., and A. P. Russell. 1984. The diet of the eastern short-horned lizard *(Phrynosoma douglassi brevirostre)* in Alberta and its relationship to sexual size dimorphism. *Canadian Journal of Zoology* 62:428–440.

———. 1985a. Growth and sexual size dimorphism in Alberta populations of the eastern short-horned lizard, *Phrynosoma douglassi brevirostre. Canadian Journal of Zoology* 63:139–154.

———. 1985b. Field thermal ecology of the eastern short-horned lizard *(Phrynosoma douglassi brevirostre)* in southern Alberta. *Canadian Journal of Zoology* 63:228–238.

———. 1991. Parturition and clutch characteristics of short-horned lizards *(Phrynosoma douglassii brevirostre)* from Alberta. *Canadian Journal of Zoology* 69:2,759–2,764.

———. 1992. *Status report on the short-horned lizard* Phrynosoma douglassii *in Canada*. Committee on the Status of Endangered Wildlife in Canada.

Powell, R. 1982. Life history notes: *Thamnophis proximus* (western ribbon snake). Reproduction. *Herpetological Review* 13:48.

Preest, M. R., D. G. Brust, and M. L. Wygoda. 1992. Cutaneous water loss and the effects of temperature and hydration state on aerobic metabolism of canyon treefrogs, *Hyla arenicolor*. *Herpetologica* 48:210–219.

Price, A. H. 1987. Life history notes: *Hypsiglena torquata jani* (Texas night snake). Behavior. *Herpetological Review* 18:16.

———. 1990. *Phrynosoma cornutum. Catalogue of American Amphibians and Reptiles* 469:1–7.

———. 1992. Comparative behavior in lizards of the genus *Cnemidophorus* (Teiidae), with comments on the evolution of parthenogenesis in reptiles. *Copeia* 1992:323–331.

Price, A. H., and J. L. LaPointe. 1981. Structure–functional aspects of the scent gland in *Lampropeltis getulus splendida*. *Copeia* 1981:138–146.

———. 1990. Activity patterns of a Chihuahuan desert snake community. *Annals of the Carnegie Museum of Natural History* 59:15–23.

Pryor, G. S. 1996. Observations of shorebird predation by snapping turtles in eastern Lake Ontario. *Wilson Bulletin* 108:190–192.

Punzo, F. 1974a. Comparative analysis of the feeding habits of Arizona blind snakes, *Leptotyphlops h. humilis* and *Leptotyphlops d. dulcis*. *Journal of Herpetology* 8:153–156.

———. 1974b. A qualitative and quantitative study of the food items of the yellow mud turtle, *Kinosternon flavescens* (Agassiz). *Journal of Herpetology* 8:269–271.

———. 1991. Feeding ecology of spadefooted toads *(Scaphiopus couchi* and *Spea multiplicata)* in western Texas. *Herpetological Review* 22:79–80.

Purgue, A. P. 1997. Tympanic sound radiation in the bullfrog *Rana catesbeiana. Journal of Comparative Physiology* A 181:438–445.

Putman, J. A., R. R. Wright, W. H. Traher, and J. P. Boone. 1964. Zoology exhibits. *Denver Museum of Natural History Annual Report* 1963:30–35.

Puttmann, S. J., and K. J. Kehmeier. 1994. Rocky Mountain wood frog *(Rana sylvatica)* recovery plan. Colorado Division of Wildlife, Fort Collins. Unpublished report.

Radaj, R. H. 1981. Life history notes: *Opheodrys v. vernalis* (smooth green snake). Reproduction. *Herpetological Review* 12:80.

Radow, T. 1975. The reptiles and amphibians of Hovenweep National Monument. Field checklist. Mesa Verde Museum Association.

Rahn, H. 1942a. Effect of temperature on color change in the rattlesnake. *Copeia* 1942:178.

———. 1942b. The reproductive cycle of the prairie rattler. *Copeia* 1942:233–240.

Ramotnik, C. A. 1998. First record of the round-tailed horned lizard, *Phrynosoma modestum*, in Colorado. *Southwestern Naturalist* 43:497–498.

Ramsey, L. W. 1953. The lined snake, *Tropidoclonion lineatum* (Hallowell). *Herpetologica* 9:7–24.

———. 1956. Nesting of Texas horned lizards. *Herpetologica* 12:239–240.

Rand, M. S. 1990. Polymorphic sexual coloration in the lizard *Sceloporus undulatus erythrocheilus. American Midland Naturalist* 124:352–359.

———. 1991. Behavioral function and hormonal control of polymorphic sexual coloration in the lizard *Sceloporus undulatus erythrocheilus.* Ph.D. dissertation, University of Colorado, Boulder.

———. 1992. Hormonal control of polymorphic and sexually dimorphic coloration in the lizard *Sceloporus undulatus erythrocheilus. General and Comparative Endocrinology* 88:461–468.

Raymond, L. R., and L. M. Hardy. 1983. Taxonomic status of the corn snake, *Elaphe guttata* (Linnaeus) (Colubridae), in Louisiana and eastern Texas. *Southwestern Naturalist* 28:105–107.

Reeder, T. W., and J. J. Wiens. 1996. Evolution of the lizard family Phrynosomatidae as inferred from diverse types of data. *Herpetological Monographs* 10:43–84.

Reese, R. W. 1969. The taxonomy and ecology of the tiger salamander *(Ambystoma tigrinum)* of Colorado. Ph.D. dissertation, University of Colorado, Boulder.

———. 1972 [1973]. The taxonomy and distribution of the tiger salamander in Colorado. *Transactions of the Kansas Academy of Sciences* 75:128–140.

———. 1975. The "cannibals" of the tiger salamander. *Bulletin of the Maryland Herpetological Society* 11 (4):180–184.

Reeve, W. L. 1952. Taxonomy and distribution of the horned lizard genus *Phrynosoma. University of Kansas Science Bulletin* 34 (2):817–960.

Reichenbach, N. G., and G. H. Dalrymple. 1986. Energy use, life histories, and the evaluation of potential competition in two species of garter snake. *Journal of Herpetology* 20:133–153.

Reichling, S. B. 1995. The taxonomic status of the Louisiana pine snake *(Pituophis melanoleucus ruthveni)* and its relevance to the evolutionary species concept. *Journal of Herpetology* 29:186–198.

Reid, J. R., and T. E. Lott. 1963. Feeding of *Leptotyphlops dulcis dulcis* (Baird and Girard). *Herpetologica* 19:141–142.

Reid, W. H., and H. J. Fulbright. 1981. Impaled prey of the loggerhead shrike in the northern Chihuahuan Desert. *Southwestern Naturalist* 26:204–205.

Reinert, H. K. 1981. Reproduction by the massasauga *(Sistrurus catenatus catenatus). American Midland Naturalist* 105:393–395.

Reinert, H. K., and W. R. Kodrich. 1982. Movements and habitat utilization by the massasauga, *Sistrurus catenatus catenatus. Journal of Herpetology* 16:162–171.

Resetarits, W. J. 1983. Life history notes: *Thamnophis proximus proximus* (western ribbon snake). Food. *Herpetological Review* 14:75.

Reynolds, T. D. 1979. Response of reptile populations to different land management practices on the Idaho National Engineering Laboratory site. *Great Basin Naturalist* 39:255–262.

Robertson, I. C., and P. J. Weatherhead. 1992. The role of temperature in microhabitat selection by northern water snakes *(Nerodia sipedon)*. *Canadian Journal of Zoology* 70:417–422.

Robertson, S. L., and E. N. Smith. 1982. Evaporative water loss in the spiny soft-shelled turtle *Trionyx spiniferus*. *Physiological Zoology* 55:124–129.

Robinson, K. M., and G. C. Murphy. 1978. The reproductive cycle of the eastern spiny softshell turtle *(Trionyx spiniferus spiniferus)*. *Herpetologica* 34:137–140.

Roble, S. M. 1985. Observations on satellite males in *Hyla chrysoscelis, Hyla picta,* and *Pseudacris triseriata. Journal of Herpetology* 19:432–436.

Rockwell, R. B. 1911. Nesting notes on the ducks of the Barr Lake region, Colorado. Part II. *Condor* 13:186–195.

Rodda, G. 1975. The life history of the tiger salamander, *Ambystoma tigrinum,* from three foothills ponds near Boulder, Colorado. *Journal of the Colorado-Wyoming Academy of Science* 7 (6):32.

Rodeck, H. G. 1936. Colorado records. *Copeia* 1936:70.

———. 1943. Guide to the Amphibia of Colorado. University of Colorado Museum Leaflet 2:1–8.

———. 1948. The turtles of Colorado. *Journal of the Colorado-Wyoming Academy of Science* 3 (6):54.

———. 1949. Notes on box turtles in Colorado. *Copeia* 1949:32–34.

———. 1950. Guide to the turtles of Colorado. University Colorado Museum Leaflet 7:1–9.

Roessler, M.K.P., H. M. Smith, and D. Chiszar. 1990. Bidder's organ: Bufonid by-products of the evolutionary loss of hyperfucundity. *Amphibia-Reptilia* 11:225–235.

Rogers, K. L. 1985. Facultative metamorphosis in a series of high altitude fossil populations of *Ambystoma tigrinum* (Irvingtonian: Alamosa County, Colorado). *Copeia* 1985:926–932.

Rogers, K. L., and L. Harvey. 1994. A skeletochronological assessment of fossil and Recent *Bufo cognatus* from south-central Colorado. *Journal of Herpetology* 28:133–140.

Romspert, A. P., and L. L. McClanahan. 1981. Osmoregulation of the terrestrial salamander, *Ambystoma tigrinum,* in hypersaline media. *Copeia* 1981:400–405.

Rose, F. L. 1980. Turtles in arid and semi-arid regions. *Bulletin of the Ecological Society of America* 61 (2):89.

Rose, F. L., and D. Armentrout. 1976. Adaptive strategies of *Ambystoma tigrinum* (Green) inhabiting the Llano Estacado of West Texas. *Journal of Animal Ecology* 45:713–729.

Rose, F. L., M.E.T. Scioli, and M. P. Moulton. 1988. Thermal preferentia of Berlandier's tortoise *(Gopherus berlandieri)* and the ornate box turtle *(Terrapene ornata). Southwestern Naturalist* 33:357–390.

Rose, S. M. 1960. A feedback mechanism of growth control in tadpoles. *Ecology* 41:188–199.

Rosen, P. C. 1991. Comparative field study of thermal preferenda in garter snakes *(Thamnophis). Journal of Herpetology* 25:301–312.

Rosen, P. C., and C. R. Schwalbe. 1995. Bullfrogs: Introduced predators in southwestern wetlands. Pages 452–454 in *Our living resources,* E. T. Laroe et al., eds. USDI National Biological Service, Washington, D.C.

Rosine, W. N. 1952. Notes on the occurrence of polydactylism in a second species of Amphibia in Muskee Lake, Colorado. *Journal of the Colorado-Wyoming Academy of Science* 4 (4):100.

Ross, D. A., T. C. Esque, R. A. Fridell, and P. Hovingh. 1995. Historical changes, current status, and a range extension of *Bufo boreas* in Utah. *Herpetological Review* 26:187–189.

Ross, D. A., and R. A. Fridell. 1997. Distribution and status of the boreal toad *(Bufo boreus)* in Utah: new toads of the purple sage. *Proceedings of the Desert Fishes Council* 28:75.

Ross, P., Jr., and D. Crews. 1978. Stimuli influencing mating behavior in the garter snake, *Thamnophis radix. Behavioral Ecology and Sociobiology* 4:133–142.

Rossi, J. V., and R. Rossi. 1994. Geographic distribution: *Diadophis punctatus punctatus* (southern ringneck snake). Anti-ophiophagous behavior. *Herpetological Review* 25:123.

Rossman, D. A. 1962. *Thamnophis proximus* (Say), a valid species of garter snake. *Copeia* 1962:741–748.

———. 1963. The colubrid snake genus *Thamnophis:* A revision of the *sauritus* group. *Bulletin of the Florida State Museum* 7 (3):99–178.

Rossman, D. A., and W. G. Eberle. 1977. Partition of the genus *Natrix,* with preliminary observations on evolutionary trends in natricine snakes. *Herpetologica* 33:34–43.

Rossman, D. A., N. B. Ford, and R. A. Seigel. 1996. *The garter snakes: Evolution and ecology.* University of Oklahoma Press, Norman.

Roth, J. J., and D. Chiszar. 1992. Geographic distribution: *Coluber constrictor mormon. Herpetological Review* 23:90–91.

Roth, J. J., B. J. Johnson, and H. M. Smith. 1989. The western hognose snake, *Heterodon nasicus,* west of the Continental Divide in Colorado, and its implications. *Bulletin of the Chicago Herpetological Society* 24 (9):161–163.

Roth, J. J., E. C. Roth, and H. M. Smith. 1991. The minimal transformation size in the salamander *Ambystoma tigrinum. Bulletin of the Chicago Herpetological Society* 26 (12):269.

Roth, J. J., and H. M. Smith. 1990a. Geographic distribution: *Pituophis melanoleucus deserticola. Herpetological Review* 21:41.

———. 1990b. The milksnake, *Lampropeltis triangulum*, in northwest Colorado. *Bulletin of the Chicago Herpetological Society* 25 (1):6–7.

Rouse, B., D. Chiszar, and H. M. Smith. 1995. Geographic distribution: *Terrapene ornata ornata. Herpetological Review* 26:209.

Routman, E. 1993. Population structure and genetic diversity of metamorphic and paedomorphic populations of the tiger salamander, *Ambystoma tigrinum. Journal of Evolutionary Biology* 6:329–357.

Rowe, C. L., O. M. Kinney, A. P. Fiori, and J. D. Congdon. 1996. Oral deformities in tadpoles *(Rana catesbeiana)* associated with coal ash deposition: Effects on grazing ability and growth. *Freshwater Biology* 36:723–730.

Rowe, J. W. 1994a. Egg size and shape variation within and among Nebraskan painted turtle *(Chrysemys picta bellii)* populations: Relationships to clutch and maternal body size. *Copeia* 1994:1,034–1,040.

———. 1994b. Reproductive variation and the egg-size–clutch size trade-off within and among populations of painted turtles *(Chrysemys picta bellii). Oecologia* 99:35–44.

———. 1995. Hatchling size in the turtle *Chrysemys picta bellii* from western Nebraska: Relationships to egg and maternal body size. *Journal of Herpetology* 29:73–79.

Ruben, J. A. 1976. Aerobic and anaerobic metabolism during activity in snakes. *Journal of Comparative Physiology* 109B:147–157.

———. 1977. Morphological correlates of predatory modes in the coachwhip *(Masticophis flagellum)* and rosy boa *(Lichanura roseofusca). Herpetologica* 33:1–6.

Rundquist, E. M., E. Stegall, D. Grow, and P. Gray. 1978. New herpetological records from Kansas. *Transactions of the Kansas Academy of Sciences* 81:73–77.

Ruthven, A. G. 1908. Variations and genetic relationships of the garter snakes. *Bulletin of the U.S. National Museum* 61.

Ryan, M. J. 1978. A thermal property of the *Rana catesbeiana* (Amphibia, Anura, Ranidae) egg mass. *Journal of Herpetology* 12:247–248.

———. 1980. The reproductive behavior of the bullfrog *(Rana catesbeiana). Copeia* 1980:108–114.

Rybak, J., L. J. Livo, D. Chiszar, and H. M. Smith. 1996. Geographic distribution: *Hypsiglena torquata loreala. Herpetological Review* 27:213.

Rybak, J. A., H. M. Smith, and D. Chiszar. 1995. Geographic distribution: *Rana catesbeiana. Herpetological Review* 26:208.

Ryder, R. A. 1951. Waterfowl production in the San Luis Valley, Colorado. M.S. thesis, Colorado Agricultural and Mechanical College (Colorado State University), Fort Collins.

Sabath, M., and R. Worthington. 1959. Eggs and young of certain Texas reptiles. *Herpetologica* 15:31–32.

Saiff, E. 1975. Preglottal structures in the snake family Colubridae. *Copeia* 1975:589–592.

Sanders, O. 1986. The heritage of *Bufo woodhousei* Girard in Texas. Baylor University, Occasional Papers, Strecker Museum 1:1–28.

———. 1987. Evolutionary hybridization and speciation in North American indigenous bufonids. Available from the Strecker Museum, Baylor University, Waco, Texas.

Sanders, O., and H. M. Smith. 1951. Geographic variation in toads of the *debilis* group of *Bufo. Field and Lab* 19:141–160.

Sattler, P. W. 1980. Genetic relationships among selected species of North American *Scaphiopus. Copeia* 1980:605–610.

———. 1985. Introgressive hybridization between the spadefoot toads *Scaphiopus bombifrons* and *Scaphiopus multiplicatus* (Salientia: Pelobatidae). *Copeia* 1985:324–332.

Schaefer, K., D. Chiszar, and H. M. Smith. 1995. Geographic distribution: *Leptotyphlops dulcis dissectus. Herpetological Review* 26:110.

Schall, J. J. 1977. Thermal ecology of five sympatric species of *Cnemidophorus* (Sauria: Teiidae). *Herpetologica* 33:261–272.

———. 1978. Reproductive strategies in sympatric whiptail lizards *(Cnemidophorus):* Two parthenogenetic and three bisexual species. *Copeia* 1978:108–116.

———. 1993. Community ecology of *Cnemidophorus* lizards in western Texas: A test of the weed hypothesis. Pages 319–343 in *Biology of whiptail lizards (genus* Cnemidophorus*),* J. W. Wright and L. J. Vitt, eds. Oklahoma Museum of Natural History, Norman.

Scherff-Norris, K. L. 1997. *Hatchery manual for the rearing and propagation of captive boreal toads,* Bufo boreas. Colorado Division of Wildlife, Denver.

Schmidt, K. P. 1921. New species of North American lizards of the genera *Holbrookia* and *Uta. American Museum Novitates* 22:1–6.

———. 1922. A review of the North American genus of lizards *Holbrookia. Bulletin of the American Museum of Natural History* 46:709–725.

Schmidt, P. J., W. C. Sherbrooke, and J. O. Schmidt. 1989. The detoxification of ant *(Pogonomyrmex)* venom by a blood factor in horned lizards *(Phrynosoma). Copeia* 1989:603–607.

Schuett, G. W. 1994. Geographic distribution: *Lampropeltis triangulum. Herpetological Review* 25:167.

Schuett, G. W., D. L. Clark, and F. Kraus. 1984. Feeding mimicry in the rattlesnake, *Sistrurus catenatus*, with comments on the evolution of the rattle. *Animal Behaviour* 32:625–626.

Schuett, G. W., and F. Kraus. 1982. Life history notes: *Crotalus viridis concolor* (midget faded rattlesnake). Coloration. *Herpetological Review* 13:17–18.

Schuett, G. W., P. A. Buttenhoff, and D. Duvall. 1993. Corroborative evidence for the lack of spring-mating in certain populations of prairie rattlesnakes *(Crotalus viridis)*. *Herpetological Natural History* 1:101–106.

Schulz, K. 1996. *A monograph of the colubrid snakes of the genus* Elaphe *Fitzinger.* Koeltz Scientific Books, Czech Republic.

Schwalbe, C. R., and P. C. Rosen. 1988. Preliminary report on effect of bullfrogs on wetland herpetofauna in southeastern Arizona. Pages 166–173 in *Management of amphibians, reptiles, and small mammals in North America,* R. C. Szaro, K. E. Severson, and D. R. Patton, eds. USDA Forest Service General Technical Report RM-166.

Schwammer, H. 1983. Herpetologische beobachtungen aus Colorado/USA> Aasfressen bei *Sistrurus catenatus edwardsi/tergeminus* und verhaltensmimikry bei *Pituophis melanoleucus. Aquaria* 30:90–93.

Schwenk, K. 1985. Occurrence, distribution and functional significance of taste buds in lizards. *Copeia* 1985:91–101.

Scott, C. No date [1977 or 1978]. Study of wood frog distribution for the Colorado Division of Wildlife. Unpublished report, Colorado Division of Wildlife, Denver.

Scott, G. R. 1975. Cenozoic surfaces and deposits in the Southern Rocky Mountains. In *Cenozoic history of the Southern Rocky Mountains,* B. F. Curtis, ed. Geological Society of America Memoir 144.

Scott, J. R. 1977. Seasonal shift in the temperature preferendum of the wandering garter snake. *Herpetological Review* 8 (supplement):16.

———. 1978. Thermal biology of the wandering garter snake. Ph.D. dissertation, Colorado State University, Fort Collins.

Scott, J. R., and D. Pettus. 1979. Effects of seasonal acclimation on the preferred body temperature of *Thamnophis elegans vagrans. Journal of Thermal Biology* 4:307–309.

Scott, J. R., C. R. Tracy, and D. Pettus. 1982. A biophysical analysis of daily and seasonal utilization of climate space by a montane snake. *Ecology* 63:482–493.

Scott, N. J., Jr., and R. D. Jennings. 1985. The tadpoles of five species of New Mexican leopard frogs. *Occasional Papers of the Museum of Southwestern Biology* 3:1–21.

Seale, D. B. 1982. Physical factors influencing oviposition by the woodfrog, *Rana sylvatica,* in Pennsylvania. *Copeia* 1982:627–635.

Secor, S. M. 1983. Life history notes: *Lampropeltis getulus holbrooki* (speckled kingsnake). Reproduction. *Herpetological Review* 14:20.

———. 1987. Courtship and mating behavior of the speckled kingsnake, *Lampropeltis getulus holbrooki. Herpetologica* 43:15–28.

———. 1995. Ecological aspects of foraging mode for the snakes *Crotalus cerastes* and *Masticophis flagellum. Herpetological Monographs* 9:169–186.

Secoy, D. M. 1970. Aberrant head scalation in *Thamnophis radix haydeni* (Kennicott). *Journal of Herpetology* 4:91–92.

Secoy, D. M., and W. M. Brown. 1968. New county records in the herpetofauna of Colorado. *Southwestern Naturalist* 13:105–106.

Seely, J. A., G. P. Zegers, and A. Asquith. 1989. Use of digger bee burrows by the tree lizard *(Urosaurus ornatus)* for winter retreats. *Herpetological Review* 20:6–7.

Seibert, H. C. 1950. Population density of snakes in an area near Chicago. *Copeia* 1950:229–230.

Seibert, H. C., and C. W. Hagen. 1947. Studies on a population of snakes in Illinois. *Copeia* 1947:6–22.

Seigel, R. A. 1986. Ecology and conservation of an endangered rattlesnake, *Sistrurus catenatus,* in Missouri, USA. *Biological Conservation* 35:333–346.

Seigel, R. A., and H. S. Fitch. 1985. Annual variation in reproduction in snakes in a fluctuating environment. *Journal of Animal Ecology* 54:497–505.

Semmler, R. C. 1979. Spatial and temporal activities of the yellow mud turtle, *Kinosternon flavescens,* in eastern New Mexico. M.S. thesis, University of New Mexico, Albuquerque.

Sena, A. P. 1978. Temperature relations and the critical thermal maximum of *Holbrookia maculata maculata* (Reptilia: Iguanidae). *Southwestern Naturalist* 23:41–50.

Sexton, O. J. 1979. Remarks on defensive behavior of hognose snakes, *Heterodon. Herpetological Review* 10:86–87.

Sexton, O. J., R. M. Andrews, and J. E. Bramble. 1992. Size and growth rate characteristics of a peripheral population of *Crotaphytus collaris (Sauria: Crotaphytidae). Copeia* 1992:968–980.

Sexton, O. J., and J. R. Bizer. 1978. Life history patterns of *Ambystoma tigrinum* in montane Colorado. *American Midland Naturalist* 99:101–118.

Sexton, O. J., and K. R. Marion. 1974. Probable predation by Swainson's hawks on swimming spadefoot toads. *Wilson Bulletin* 86:167–168.

———. 1981. Experimental analysis of movements by prairie rattlesnakes, *Crotalus viridis,* during hibernation. *Oecologia* 51:37–41.

Seymour, R. S. 1995. Oxygen uptake by embryos in gelatinous egg masses of *Rana sylvatica:* The roles of diffusion and convection. *Copeia* 1995:626–635.

Shaffer, D. T., Jr., and W. G. Whitford. 1981. Behavioral responses of a predator, the round-tailed horned lizard, *Phrynosoma modestum* and its prey, honey pot ants, *Myrmecocystus* spp. *American Midland Naturalist* 105:209–216.

Shaffer, H. B., and M. L. McKnight. 1996. The polytypic species revisited: genetic differentiation and molecular phylogenetics of the tiger salamander *Ambystoma tigrinum* (Amphibia: Caudata) complex. *Evolution* 50:419–433.

Shaw, C. E. 1952. Notes on the eggs and young of some United States and Mexican lizards. Part I. *Herpetologica* 8:71–79.

Shaw, C. E., and S. Campbell. 1974. *Snakes of the American West*. Alfred A. Knopf, New York.

Sheffield, S. R., and N. Carter. 1994. Natural history notes: *Phrynosoma cornutum* (Texas horned lizard): Arboreal behavior. *Herpetological Review* 25:65–66.

Sherbrooke, W. C. 1981. *Horned lizards: Unique reptiles of western North America*. Southwest Parks and Monuments Association, Globe, Arizona.

———. 1987. Defensive head posture in horned lizards (*Phrynosoma*: Sauria: Iguanidae). *Southwestern Naturalist* 32:512–515.

Sherbrooke, W. C. 1990a. Predatory behavior of captive greater roadrunners feeding on horned lizards. *Wilson Bulletin* 102:171–174.

———. 1990b. Rain-harvesting in the lizard, *Phrynosoma cornutum:* Behavior and integumental morphology. *Journal of Herpetology* 24:302–308.

———. 1991. Behavioral (predator-prey) interactions of captive grasshopper mice *(Onychomys torridus)* and horned lizards *(Phrynosoma cornutum* and *P. modestum). American Midland Naturalist* 126:187–195.

Sherbrooke, W. C., and R. R. Montanucci. 1988. Stone mimicry in the round-tailed horned lizard, *Phrynosoma modestum* (Sauria: Iguanidae). *Journal of Arid Environments* 14:275–284.

Shine, R. 1991. Intersexual dietary divergence and the evolution of sexual dimorphism in snakes. *American Naturalist* 138:103–122.

Shipley, B., C. Henke, T. Morris, D. Chiszar, and H. M. Smith. 1996. Geographic distribution: *Thamnophis cyrtopsis cyrtopsis. Herpetological Review* 27:215.

Shirose, L. J., R. J. Brooks, J. R. Barta, and S. S. Desser. 1993. Intersexual differences in growth, mortality, and size at maturity in bullfrogs in central Ontario. *Canadian Journal of Zoology* 71:2,363–2,369.

Simon, H. 1979. *Easy identification guide to North American snakes*. Dodd, Mead, New York.

Simovich, M. A. 1994. The dynamics of a spadefoot toad *(Spea multiplicata* and *S. bombifrons)* hybridization system. Pages 167–182 in *Herpetology of the North American deserts: Proceedings of a symposium*, P. R. Brown and J. W. Wright, eds. Southwestern Herpetologists' Society Special Publication 5.

Sisk, N. R., and J. F. Jackson. 1997. Tests of two hypotheses for the origin of the crotaline rattle. *Copeia* 1997:485–495.

Sites, J. W., Jr., J. W. Archie, C. J. Cole, and O. F. Villela. 1992. A review of phylogenetic hypotheses for lizards of the genus *Sceloporus* (Phrynosomatidae): Implications for ecological and evolutionary studies. *Bulletin of the American Museum of Natural History* 213:1–110.

Skelly, D. K. 1996. Pond drying, predators, and the distribution of *Pseudacris* tadpoles. *Copeia* 1996:599–605.

Slowinski, J. B., and S. L. Rasmussen. 1985. Life history notes: *Crotalus viridis viridis* (prairie rattlesnake). Coloration. *Herpetological Review* 16:29.

Small, M. F., S. P. Tabor, and C. Fazzari. 1994. Natural history notes: *Masticophis flagellum* (western coachwhip). Foraging behavior. *Herpetological Review* 25:28.

Smith, A. G. 1949. The subspecies of the plains garter snake, *Thamnophis radix. Bulletin of the Chicago Academy of Science* 8:285–300.

Smith, A. K. 1976. Incidence of tail coiling in a population of ringneck snakes *(Diadophis punctatus). Transactions of the Kansas Academy of Sciences* 77:237–238.

———. 1977. Attraction of bullfrogs (Amphibia, Anura, Ranidae) to distress calls of immature frogs. *Journal of Herpetology* 11:234–235.

Smith, B. D., and H. M. Smith. 1972. Bipedalism in the lizard *Sceloporus undulatus erythrocheilus*, and other notes on Wyoming herpetozoa. *Journal of Herpetology* 6:81–82.

Smith, C. C., and A. N. Bragg. 1949. Observations on the ecology and natural history of Anura. VII. Food and feeding habits of the common species of toads in Oklahoma. *Ecology* 30:333–349.

Smith, D. D. 1983. Life history notes: *Crotaphytus collaris* (collared lizard). Reproduction. *Herpetological Review* 14:46.

———. 1985. Life history notes: *Ambystoma tigrinum* (tiger salamander). Behavior. *Herpetological Review* 16:77.

Smith, D. D., D. J. Pflanz, and R. Powell. 1993. Observations of autohemorrhaging in *Tropidophis haetianus, Rhinocheilus lecontei, Heterodon platirhinos*, and *Nerodia erythrogaster. Herpetological Review* 24:130–131.

Smith, D. G., and J. R. Murphy. 1973. Breeding ecology of raptors in the eastern Great Basin of Utah. *Brigham Young University Science Bulletin, Biology Series* 18:1–76.

Smith, G. R. 1996. Habitat use and its effect on body size distribution in a population of the tree lizard, *Urosaurus ornatus. Journal of Herpetology* 30:528–530.

Smith, G. R., and R. E. Ballinger. 1994a. Thermal tolerance in the tree lizard *(Urosaurus ornatus)* from a desert population and a low montane population. *Canadian Journal of Zoology* 72:2,066–2,069.

———. 1994b. Variation in individual growth rates in the tree lizard, *Urosaurus ornatus:* Effects of food and density. *Acta Oecologica* 15:317–324.

———. 1995a. Temperature relationships of the tree lizard, *Urosaurus ornatus,* from desert and low-elevation montane populations in the southwestern USA. *Journal of Herpetology* 29:126–129.

———. 1995b. Female reproduction in *Urosaurus ornatus* from the Chiricahua Mountains of southeastern Arizona. *Herpetological Natural History* 3:183–186.

Smith, G. R., and J. B. Iverson. 1993. Reactions to odor trails in bullsnakes. *Journal of Herpetology* 27:333–335.

Smith, H. M. 1934. The amphibians of Kansas. *American Midland Naturalist* 15:377–528.

———. 1938. Remarks on the status of the subspecies of *Sceloporus undulatus,* with descriptions of new species and subspecies of the *undulatus* group. *University of Michigan Museum Zoology Occasional Papers* 387:1–17.

———. 1946. *Handbook of lizards.* Comstock Publishing, Ithaca, New York.

———. 1956. *Handbook of amphibians and reptiles of Kansas.* 2d ed. University of Kansas Museum Natural History Miscellaneous Publication 9:1–356.

———. 1957. Curious feeding habit of a blind snake, *Leptotyphlops. Herpetologica* 13:102.

———. 1963. The taxonomic status of the Black Hills population of smooth greensnakes. *Herpetologica* 19:256–261.

———. 1971. Distribution of the racer *Coluber constrictor* in Mexico. *Journal of Herpetology* 5:212–214.

———. 1977. Phenological and other data for the plains red king snake. *The Colorado Herpetologist (Colorado Herpetological Society)* 3 (1):2–3.

———. 1978. *Amphibians of North America.* Golden Press, New York.

———. 1990. Robert William Reese, 1917–1990. *Bulletin of the Maryland Herpetological Society* 26:116–121.

———. 1991. Three new records of lizards in Ouray County, Colorado. *Bulletin of the Chicago Herpetological Society* 26 (10):223.

Smith, H. M., and E. D. Brodie, Jr. 1982. *Reptiles of North America.* Golden Press, New York.

Smith, H. M., and D. Chiszar. 1981. An observation on winter emergence of a garter snake, *Thamnophis radix. Bulletin of the Maryland Herpetological Society* 17:107–109.

———. 1988. Some overlooked early records for Colorado reptiles. *Colorado Herpetological Society Newsletter* 3 (March): 3–5.

———. 1989. The subspecific identity of the population of *Sceloporus undulatus* sympatric with *S. occidentalis. Bulletin of the Maryland Herpetological Society* 25:143–150.

———. 1993. Apparent intergradation in Texas between the subspecies of the Texas blind snake *(Leptotyphlops dulcis). Bulletin of the Maryland Herpetological Society* 29:143–155.

———. 1994a. Variation in the lined snake *(Tropidoclonion lineatum)* in northern Texas. *Bulletin of the Maryland Herpetological Society* 30:6–14.

———. 1994b. Geographic distribution: *Tropidoclonion lineatum. Herpetological Review* 25:35.

———. 1995. Geographic distribution: *Chrysemys picta bellii. Herpetological Review* 26:154.

———. 1996. Further evidence of the importance of the Wyoming Corridor in herpetozoan distribution. *Bulletin of the Maryland Herpetological Society* 32:28–31.

Smith, H. M., D. Chiszar, E. Evanoff, and J. B. Mitton. 1993. The range of the so-called relictual intergrades between the lizards *Sceloporus undulatus garmani* and *S. u. erythrocheilus. Bulletin of the Maryland Herpetological Society* 29:30–36.

Smith, H. M., D. Chiszar, and R. R. Montanucci. 1997. Subspecies and classification. *Herpetological Review* 28:13–16.

Smith, H. M., D. Chiszar, and J. J. Roth. 1996. Geographic distribution: *Urosaurus ornatus wrighti. Herpetological Review* 27:211–212.

Smith, H. M., D. Chiszar, J. R. Staley II, and K. Tepedelen. 1994. Populational relationships in the corn snake *Elaphe guttata* (Reptilia: Serpentes). *Texas Journal of Science* 46:259–292.

Smith, H. M., and K. T. Fitzgerald. 1983. Trauma-induced developmental vertebral displacement (rhoecosis) in a garter snake. *Herpetological Review* 14:69, 71–72.

Smith, H. M., G. A. Hammerson, D. Chiszar, and C. Ramotnik. 1993a. Geographic distribution: *Bufo cognatus. Herpetological Review* 24:152–153.

———. 1993b. Geographic distribution: *Rana pipiens. Herpetological Review* 24:153.

———. 1993c. Geographic distribution: *Pseudacris triseriata. Herpetological Review* 24:153.

———. 1993d. Geographic distribution: *Eumeces multivirgatus multivirgatus. Herpetological Review* 24:154.

———. 1993e. Geographic distribution: *Crotalus viridis viridis. Herpetological Review* 24:156.

———. 1993f. Geographic distribution: *Nerodia sipedon sipedon. Herpetological Review* 24:156.

———. 1993g. Geographic distribution: *Tantilla nigriceps. Herpetological Review* 24:157.

Smith, H. M., G. A. Hammerson, J. J. Roth, and D. Chiszar. 1991. Distributional addenda for the smooth green snake *(Opheodrys vernalis)* in western Colorado, and the status of its subspecies. *Bulletin of the Maryland Herpetological Society* 27:99–106.

Smith, H. M., and R. L. Holland. 1981. Still more on *Bipes. Herpetological Review* 12:8–9.

———. 1993. Geographic distribution: *Eumeces multivirgatus multivirgatus. Herpetological Review* 24:66.

———. 1993. Geographic distribution: *Eumeces obsoletus. Herpetological Review* 24:66.

Smith, H. M., D. C. Kritsky, and R. L. Holland. 1969. Reticulate melanism in the painted turtle. *Journal of Herpetology* 3:173–176.

Smith, H. M., M. Laverty, and D. Chiszar. 1995. Geographic distribution: *Pseudacris triseriata. Herpetological Review* 26:208.

Smith, H. M., T. P. Maslin, and R. L. Brown. 1965. Summary of the distribution of the herpetofauna of Colorado. *University of Colorado Studies, Series in Biology* 15:1–52.

Smith, H. M., C. A. Pague, and D. Chiszar. 1996. A brood of lined snakes *(Tropidoclonion lineatum)* from southeastern Colorado. *Bulletin of the Maryland Herpetological Society* 32:24–27.

Smith, H. M., M. S. Rand, J. D. Drew, B. D. Smith, D. Chiszar, and C. M. Dwyer. 1991. Relictual intergrades between the northern prairie lizard *(Sceloporus undulatus garmani)* and the red-lipped plateau lizard *(S. u. erythrocheilus)* in Colorado. *Northwestern Naturalist* 72:1–11.

Smith, H. M., and R. W. Reese. 1968. A record tiger salamander. *Southwestern Naturalist* 13:371–372.

———. 1970. Polychromatism, polymorphism and possible cryptic speciation in the tiger salamander *(Ambystoma tigrinum)* group of northeastern Colorado. *Journal of the Colorado-Wyoming Academy of Science* 7:10–11.

Smith, H. M., C. Ristau, T. Bell, M. Bell, and D. Chiszar. 1995. Geographic distribution: *Lampropeltis triangulum multistriata* x *taylori. Herpetological Review* 26:210.

Smith, H. M., P. Somers, and D. Chiszar. 1975 [1976]. Another albinistic wandering garter snake. *Utah Herpetologists' League Journal* 2 (2):1–3.

Smith, H. M., and D. Thompson. 1993. Four reptiles newly recorded from Ouray County, Colorado. *Bulletin of the Chicago Herpetological Society* 28 (4):78–79.

Smith, H. M., and F. N. White. 1955. Adrenal enlargement and its significance in the hognose snakes *(Heterodon). Herpetologica* 11:137–144.

Smith, H. M., and K. L. Williams. 1962. The nomen oblitum rule of the 1961 International Code of Zoological Nomenclature. *Herpetologica* 18:11–13.

Smith, J. M., and N. Zucker. 1997. Do female tree lizards, *Urosaurus ornatus,* exhibit mate choice? *Journal of Herpetology* 31:179–186.

Smith, N. M. 1974. Observation of voice in the western collared lizard *Crotaphytus collaris bicinctores. Great Basin Naturalist* 34:276.

Smith, P. W. 1956. The status, correct name, and geographic range of the boreal chorus frog.

Proceedings of the Biological Society of Washington 69:169–176.

Smith, R. 1980. *Empire Magazine, Denver Post,* March 16, 1980, 41.

Snow, G. E. 1978. Largest reported tiger salamander. *Bulletin of the Maryland Herpetological Society* 14:89–90.

Snyder, G. K., and G. A. Hammerson. 1993. Interrelationships between water economy and thermoregulation in the canyon tree-frog *Hyla arenicolor. Journal of Arid Environments* 25:321–329.

Snyder, J. D. 1972. An ecological investigation of sympatric populations of the lizards *Crotaphytus collaris* and *C. wislizeni.* M.A. thesis, San Francisco State University.

Snyder, R. C. 1952. Quadrupedal and bipedal locomotion of lizards. *Copeia* 1952:64–70.

Soltesz, K. L., and J. D. Holmes. 1977. Geographic distribution: *Tantilla nigriceps nigriceps. Herpetological Review* 8:14.

Somers, P. 1976. *Fauna inventory of the Animas–La Plata Project Area.* Final report.

Somers, P., G. E. Nichols, and R. W. Stransky. 1980. *Baseline ecological study of Narraguinnep Research Natural Area, San Juan National Forest.* Final report.

Somers, P. H., L. J. Livo, R.R.J. Smith, D. Chiszar, and H. M. Smith. 1995. Geographic distribution: *Coluber constrictor mormon. Herpetological Review* 26:156.

Spencer, A. W. 1964a. The relationship of dispersal and migration to gene flow in the boreal chorus frog. Ph.D. dissertation, Colorado State University, Fort Collins.

———. 1964b. Movement in a population of *Pseudacris triseriata. Journal of the Colorado-Wyoming Academy of Science* 5 (5):44.

———. 1964c. An unusual phoretic host for the clam *Pisidium. Journal of the Colorado-Wyoming Academy of Science* 5 (5):43–44.

———. 1971. Boreal chorus frogs *(Pseudacris triseriata)* breeding in the alpine in southwestern Colorado. *Arctic and Alpine Research* 3:353.

———. 1974. First record of the kingsnake *Lampropeltis getulus* in Colorado. *Journal of the Colorado-Wyoming Academy of Science* 7 (5):79–80.

Sperger, R. H., R. Humphrey, D. Chiszar, and H. M. Smith. 1995a. Geographic Distribution: *Chelydra serpentina serpentina. Herpetological Review* 26:43.

———. 1995b. Geographic Distribution: *Chrysemys picta bellii. Herpetological Review* 26:43.

———. 1995c. Geographic Distribution: *Coluber constrictor flaviventris. Herpetological Review* 26:46.

Sprules, W. G. 1972. Effects of size-selective predation and food competition on high altitude zooplankton communities. *Ecology* 53:375–386.

Stabler, R. M. 1948. Prairie rattlesnake eats spade-foot toad. *Herpetologica* 4:168.

Starrett, P. H., and L. S. Bazilian. 1996. Inheritance of the call of the bullfrog, *Rana catesbeiana*. *Bulletin of the Southern California Academy of Sciences* 95:83–87.

St. Clair, R. C., and P. T. Gregory. 1990. Factors affecting the northern range limit of painted turtles *(Chrysemys picta):* Winter acidosis or freezing? *Copeia* 1990:1,083–1,089.

St. Clair, R., P. T. Gregory, and J. M. Macartney. 1994. How do sexual differences in growth and maturation interact to determine size in north-ern and southern painted turtles? *Canadian Journal of Zoology* 72:1,436–1,443.

Stebbins, R. C. 1951. *Amphibians of western North America.* University of California Press, Berkeley.

———. 1954. *Amphibians and reptiles of western North America.* McGraw-Hill, New York.

———. 1985. *A field guide to western reptiles and amphibians.* 2d ed. Houghton Mifflin, Boston.

Steven, T. A. 1975. Middle Tertiary volcanic field in the Southern Rocky Mountains. Pages 75–94 in B. F. Curtis, editor. Pages 75–94 in *Cenozoic history of the Southern Rocky Mountains,* B. F. Curtis, ed. Geological Society of America Memoir 144.

Stevenson, R. D., C. R. Peterson, and J. S. Tsuji. 1985. The thermal dependence of locomo-tion, tongue flicking, digestion, and oxygen consumption in the wandering garter snake. *Physiological Zoology* 58:46–57.

Stickel, W. H. 1938. The snakes of the genus *Sonora* in the United States and Lower Califor-nia. *Copeia* 1938:182–190.

Stille, B. 1987. Dorsal scale microdermaglyph-ics and rattlesnake *(Crotalus* and *Sistrurus)* phylogeny (Reptilia, Viperidae: Crotalinae). *Herpetologica* 43:98–104.

Stille, W. T. 1954. Observations on the reproduction and biology of the green snake, *Opheodrys vernalis* (Harlan). *Natural History Miscellanea,* 127:1–11.

Stock, A. D. 1962. Amphibians and reptiles of the Curecanti area of Colorado. *University of Utah Anthropology Papers* 59:191–193.

Stone, P. A., J. L. Dobie, and R. P. Henry. 1992a. Cutaneous surface area and bimodal respiration in soft-shelled *(Trionyx spiniferus),* stinkpot *(Sternotherus odoratus),* and mud turtles *(Kinosternon subrubrum). Physiological Zool-ogy* 65:311–330.

———. 1992b. The effect of aquatic O_2 levels on diving and ventilatory behavior in soft-shelled *(Trionyx spiniferus),* stinkpot *(Sternotherus odoratus),* and mud turtles *(Kinosternon subru-brum). Physiological Zoology* 65:331–345.

Storey, J. M., and K. B. Storey. 1985. Triggering of cryoprotectant synthesis by initiation of ice nucleation in the freeze tolerant frog, *Rana sylvatica. Journal of Comparative Physiology* 156:191–195.

Straight, R. C., and J. L. Glenn. 1993. Human fatalities caused by venomous animals in Utah, 1900–1990. *Great Basin Naturalist* 53:390–394.

Streubel, D. P. 1975. Behavioral features of sym-patry of *Spermophilus spilosoma* and *Spermo-philus tridecemlineatus* and some aspects of the life history of *S. spilosoma.* A.D. dissertation, University of Northern Colorado, Greeley.

Stuart, J. N. 1988. Life history notes: *Hypsiglena torquata jani* (Texas night snake). Behavior. *Herpetological Review* 19:84–85.

———. 1995. Natural history notes: *Rana cates-beiana* (bullfrog). Diet. *Herpetological Review* 26:33.

———. 1998a. *Cnemidophorus velox. Catalogue of American Amphibians and Reptiles* 656:1–6.

———. 1998b. Reticulate melanism in south-western populations of *Chrysemys picta bellii* (Testudines: Emydidae). *Herpetological Review* 29:80–82.

Stuart, J. N., and C. W. Painter. 1993a. Life history notes: *Rana catesbeiana.* Cannibalism. *Herpe-tological Review* 24:103.

———. 1993b. Notes on hibernation of the smooth green snake *Opheodrys vernalis,* in New Mex-ico. *Bulletin of the Maryland Herpetological Society* 29:140–142.

Stull, O. G. 1932. An annotated list of the forms of the genus *Pituophis. University of Michi-gan Museum of Zoology Occasional Papers* 250:1–5.

———. 1940. Variations and relationships in the snakes of the genus *Pituophis. Bulletin of the U.S. National Museum* 175:1–225.

Stumpel, A.H.P. 1995. Natural history notes: *Masticophis taeniatus taeniatus* (desert striped whipsnake). Elevation record. *Herpetological Review* 26:102.

Sullivan, B. K. 1982a. Male mating behavior in the Great Plains toad *(Bufo cognatus). Animal Behaviour* 30:939–940.

———. 1982b. Significance of size, temperature and call attributes to sexual selection in *Bufo woodhousei australis. Journal of Herpetology* 16:103–106.

———. 1984. Advertisement call variation and observations on breeding behavior of *Bufo debilis* and *B. punctatus. Journal of Herpetol-ogy* 18:406–411.

———. 1985a. Male calling behavior in response to playback of conspecific advertisement call in two bufonids. *Journal of Herpetology* 19:78–83.

———. 1985b. Sexual selection and mating system variation in anuran amphibians of the Arizo-na-Sonoran Desert. *Great Basin Naturalist* 45:688–696.

———. 1986. Intra-populational variation in the intensity of sexual selection in breeding aggregations of Woodhouse's toad *(Bufo woodhousei). Journal of Herpetology* 20:88–90.

———. 1989. Interpopulational variation in vocalizations of *Bufo woodhousii. Journal of Herpetology* 23:368–373.

———. 1990. Natural hybrid between the Great Plains toad *(Bufo cognatus)* and the red-spotted toad *(Bufo punctatus)* from central Arizona. *Great Basin Naturalist* 50:371–372.

Sullivan, B. K., R. W. Bowker, K. B. Malmos, and E.W.A. Gergus. 1996. Arizona distribution of three Sonoran Desert anurans: *Bufo retiformis, Gastrophryne olivacea,* and *Pternohyla fodiens. Great Basin Naturalist* 56:38–47.

Sullivan, B. K., K. B. Malmos, and M. F. Given. 1996. Systematics of the *Bufo woodhousii* complex (Anura: Bufonidae): Advertisement call variation. *Copeia* 1996:274–280.

Swain, T. A., and H. M. Smith. 1978. Communal nesting in *Coluber constrictor* in Colorado (Reptilia: Serpentes). *Herpetologica* 34:175–177.

Sweet, S. S. 1985. Geographic variation, convergent crypsis and mimicry in gopher snakes *(Pituophis melanoleucus)* and western rattlesnakes *(Crotalus viridis). Journal of Herpetology* 19:55–67.

Sweet, S. S., and W. S. Parker. 1990. *Pituophis melanoleucus. Catalogue of American Amphibians and Reptiles* 474:1–8.

Swenson, L. E., and H. G. Rodeck. 1948. Notes on Colorado herpetology. *Journal of the Colorado-Wyoming Academy of Science* 3 (6):53–54.

Taggart, T. W. 1992a. Geographic distribution: *Lampropeltis getula. Herpetological Review* 23:91.

———. 1992b. Observations on Kansas amphibians and reptiles. *Kansas Herpetological Society Newsletter* 88:13–15.

Tanner, V. M. 1928. Distributional list of the amphibians and reptiles of Utah. No. 2. *Copeia* 166:23–28.

———. 1929. A distributional list of the amphibians and reptiles of Utah. No. 3. *Copeia* 171:46–52.

———. 1931. A synoptical study of Utah Amphibia. *Utah Academy of Science* 8:159–198.

———. 1939. A study of the genus *Scaphiopus:* the spade-foot toads. *Great Basin Naturalist* 1:3–20 + 3 plates.

———. 1942. Notes on the birth and growth of horned lizards. *Great Basin Naturalist* 3:60.

———. 1949a. Notes on the number, length, and weight of young garter snakes. *Great Basin Naturalist* 9:51–54.

———. 1949b. Amphibians and reptiles contributed to Brigham Young University by Owen Bryant. *Great Basin Naturalist* 9:47–49.

Tanner, V. M., and C. L. Hayward. 1934. A biological study of the La Sal Mountains, Utah. Report No. 1 (Ecology). *Utah Academy of Sciences, Arts and Letters* 11:209-[?].

Tanner, W. W. 1940. Notes on herpetological specimens added to the Brigham Young University vertebrate collection during 1939. *Great Basin Naturalist* 1:138–146.

———. 1941. A study of the variation in the less common snakes of Utah. *Great Basin Naturalist* 2:16–28.

———. 1944 [1946]. A taxonomic study of the genus *Hypsiglena. Great Basin Naturalist* 5:25–92.

———. 1949. Food of the wandering garter snake, *Thamnophis elegans vagrans* (Baird & Girard), in Utah. *Herpetologica* 5:85–86.

———. 1950. Variation in the scale and color pattern of the wandering garter snake in Utah and southern Idaho. *Herpetologica* 6:194–196.

———. 1953. Notes on the life history of *Phrynosoma d. hernandesi. Herpetologica* 9:140.

———. 1954. Herpetological notes concerning some reptiles of Utah and Arizona. *Herpetologica* 10:92–96.

———. 1955. A new *Sceloporus magister* from eastern Utah. *Great Basin Naturalist* 15(1–4):32–34.

———. 1957a. A new skink of the *multivirgatus* group from Chihuahua. *Great Basin Naturalist* 17(3,4):111–117.

———. 1957b. A new *Xantusia* from southeastern Utah. *Herpetologica* 13:5–11.

———. 1958a. Herpetological range extensions. *Herpetologica* 14:195.

———. 1958b. Herpetology of Glen Canyon of the Upper Colorado River Basin. *Herpetologica* 14:193–195.

———. 1966. A re-evaluation of the genus *Tantilla* in the southwestern United States and northwestern Mexico. *Herpetologica* 22:134–152.

———. 1972. Notes on the life history of *Uta s. stansburiana* Baird and Girard. *Brigham Young University Science Bulletin, Biology Series* 15:31–39.

———. 1978. Zoogeography of reptiles and amphibians in the intermountain region. Great Basin Memoirs 2 (Intermountain biogeography: a symposium):43–53.

———. 1989. Status of *Spea stagnalis* Cope (1875), *Spea intermontanus* [sic] Cope (1889), and a systematic review of *Spea hammondii* Baird (1839) (Amphibia: Anura). *Great Basin Naturalist* 49:503–510.

Tanner, W. W., and D. F. Avery. 1964. A new *Sauromalus obesus* from the upper Colorado basin of Utah. *Herpetologica* 20:38–42.

Tanner, W. W., and B. H. Banta. 1962. The distribution of *Tantilla utahensis* Blanchard. *Great Basin Naturalist* 22:116–118.

———. 1963. The systematics of *Crotaphytus wislizeni,* the leopard lizards. Part 1: A redescription of *Crotaphytus wislizeni wislizeni* Baird and Girard, and a description of a new subspecies from the upper Colorado River basin. *Great Basin Naturalist* 23(3,4):129–148.

———. 1977. The systematics of *Crotaphytus wislizeni*, the leopard lizards. Part III: The leopard lizards of the Great Basin and adjoining areas, with a description of a new subspecies from the Lahontan Basin. *Great Basin Naturalist* 37:225–240.

Tanner, W. W., D. L. Fisher, and T. J. Willis. 1971. Notes on the life history of *Ambystoma tigrinum nebulosum* Hallowell in Utah. *Great Basin Naturalist* 31:213–222.

Tanner, W. W., and J. E. Krogh. 1973. Ecology of *Sceloporus magister* at the Nevada Test Site, Nye County, Nevada. *Great Basin Naturalist* 33:133–146.

Tanner, W. W., and J. W. Heinrichs. 1964. An extension of *Arizona e. philipi* and *Rhinocheilus l. lecontei* into southcentral Utah. *Southwestern Naturalist* 9:40–49.

Tanner, W. W., and J. E. Krogh. 1974a. Ecology of the leopard lizard, *Crotaphytus wislizeni* at the Nevada Test Site, Nye County, Nevada. *Herpetologica* 30:63–72.

———. 1974b. Variations in activity as seen in four sympatric lizard species of southern Nevada. *Herpetologica* 30:303–308.

Tanner, W. W., and R. B. Loomis. 1957. A taxonomic and distributional study of the western subspecies of the milk snake, *Lampropeltis doliata*. *Transactions of the Kansas Academy of Sciences* 60:12–42.

Tanner, W. W., and J. R. Ottley. 1981. Reproduction in *Hypsiglena*. *Great Basin Naturalist* 41:310.

Taylor, E. H. 1935a. A taxonomic study of the cosmopolitan scincoid lizards of the genus *Eumeces* with an account of the distribution and relationships of its species. *University of Kansas Science Bulletin* 23:1–643.

———. 1935b. A new species of genus *Eumeces* from New Mexico. *University of Kansas Science Bulletin* 22:219–223.

Taylor, H. L. 1982. *Holbrookia maculata* (lesser earless lizard): Coloration. *Herpetological Review* 13:95.

———. 1983. Geographic patterns of variation in the teiid lizards *Cnemidophorus tigris septentrionalis* and *C. t. gracilis* and their systematic relationships. Ph.D. thesis, University of Colorado, Boulder.

———. 1988. A morphological analysis of intergradation between the teiid lizards *Cnemidophorus tigris tigris* and *C. tigris septentrionalis*. *Herpetologica* 44:176–185.

Taylor, H. L., and D. Buschman. 1993. A multivariate analysis of geographic variation in the teiid lizard *Cnemidophorus tigris septentrionalis*. *Herpetologica* 49:42–51.

Taylor, H. L., C. R. Cooley, R. A. Aguilar, and C. J. Obana. 1992. Factors affecting clutch size in the teiid lizards *Cnemidophorus tigris gracilis* and *C. t. septentrionalis*. *Journal of Herpetology* 26:443–447.

Taylor, H. L., C. Currie, and J. J. Baker. 1989. The mode of origin for males collected from natural clones of parthenogenetic lizards *(Cnemidophorus):* Cytological evidence. *Journal of Herpetology* 23:202–205.

Taylor, H. L., L. A. Harris, and G. L. Burkholder. 1994. Relationship of clutch size to body size and elevation of habitat in three subspecies of the teiid lizard, *Cnemidophorus tigris*. *Copeia* 1994:1,047–1,050.

Taylor, H. L., R. L. Holland, R. L. Humphrey, and H. M. Smith. 1996. Geographic distribution: *Sceloporus magister cephaloflavus*. *Herpetological Review* 27:87–88.

Taylor, H. L., and J. M. Walker. 1996. Application of the names *Cnemidophorus tigris disparilis* and *C. t. punctilinealis* to valid taxa (Sauria: Teiidae) and relegation of the names *C. t. gracilis* and *C. t. dickersonae* to appropriate synonymies. *Copeia* 1996:140–148.

Taylor, H. L., J. M. Walker, and J. E. Cordes. 1996. Systematic implications of morphologically distinct populations of parthenogenetic whiptail lizards: *Cnemidophorus tesselatus* pattern class D. *Herpetologica* 52:254–262.

———. 1997. Reproductive characteristics and body size in the parthenogenetic teiid lizard *Cnemidophorus tesselatus:* comparison of sympatric color pattern classes C and E in De Baca County, New Mexico. *Copeia* 1997:863–868.

Taylor, H. L., J. M. Walker, and P. A. Medica. 1967. Males of three normally parthenogenetic species of teiid lizards (genus *Cnemidophorus*). *Copeia* 1967:737–743.

Taylor, R. B. 1975. Neogene tectonism in south-central Colorado. Pages 211–226 in *Cenozoic history of the Southern Rocky Mountains*, B. F. Curtis, ed. Geological Society of America Memoir 144.

Tennant, A. 1984. *The snakes of Texas*. Texas Monthly Press, Austin, Texas.

Tevis, L. 1966. Unsuccessful breeding by desert toads *(Bufo punctatus)* at the limit of their ecological tolerance. *Ecology* 47:766–775.

Thomas, B. O., R. E. Cameron, and J. D. Holmes. 1970. The importance and role of amphibians and reptiles in grassland ecosystems. Pages 307–23 in *The grassland ecosystem: A preliminary synthesis. A supplement*, R. L. Dix and R. G. Beidleman, eds. Range Science Department, Science Series No. 2 (supplement). Colorado State University, Fort Collins.

Thomas, R., and F. H. Pough. 1979. The effect of rattlesnake venom on prey digestion. *Toxicon* 17:221–228.

Thompson, C. W., I. T. Moore, and M. C. Moore. 1993. Social, environmental and genetic factors in the ontogeny of phenotypic differentiation in a lizard with alternative male reproductive strategies. *Behavioral Ecology and Sociobiology* 33:137–146.

Thompson, C. W., and M. C. Moore. 1991a. Syntopic occurrence of multiple dewlap color morphs in male tree lizards, *Urosaurus ornatus. Copeia* 1991:493–503.

———. 1991b. Throat color reliably signals social status in male tree lizards, *Urosaurus ornatus. Animal Behaviour* 42:745–753.

Thompson, P., and J. W. Sites, Jr. 1986a. Two aberrant karyotypes in the sagebrush lizard *(Sceloporus graciosus):* Triploidy and a "supernumerary" oddity. *Great Basin Naturalist* 46:224–227.

———. 1986b. Comparison of population structure in chromosomally polytypic and monotypic species of *Sceloporus* (Sauria: Iguanidae) in relation to chromosomally-mediated speciation. *Evolution* 40:303–314.

Thornbury, W. D. 1965. *Regional geomorphology of the United States.* John Wiley and Sons, New York.

Thornton, W. A. 1960. Population dynamics in *Bufo woodhousei* and *Bufo valliceps. Texas Journal of Science* 12:176–299.

Thorp, T. J., and L. S. Clark. 1994. Common snapping turtle eats duck eggs. *Wilson Bulletin* 106:416.

Tiebout, H. M., III, and J. R. Cary. 1987. Dynamic spatial ecology of the water snake, *Nerodia sipedon. Copeia* 1987:1–18.

Tiekotter, K. L. 1977. A study of trematodes collected from toads of a Colorado alpine meadow. *Proceedings of the Nebraska Academy of Science and Affiliated Societies* 1977:22.

Tierney, L. 1859. *History of the gold discoveries on the South Platte River.* Pacific City, Iowa.

Tihen, J. A. 1937 [1938]. Additional distributional records of amphibians and reptiles in Kansas counties. *Transactions of the Kansas Academy of Sciences* 40:401–409.

Tihen, J. A., and D. B. Wake. 1981. Vertebrae of plethodontid salamanders from the Lower Miocene of Montana. *Journal of Herpetology* 15:35–40.

Tinkle, D. W. 1957. Ecology, maturation and reproduction of *Thamnophis sauritus proximus. Ecology* 38:69–77.

———. 1959. Observations on the lizards *Cnemidophorus tigris, Cnemidophorus tessellatus,* and *Crotaphytus wislizeni. Southwestern Naturalist* 4:195–200.

———. 1967. The life and demography of the side-blotched lizard. *University of Michigan Museum of Zoology Miscellaneous Publication* 132:1–182.

———. 1969. Evolutionary implication of comparative population studies in the lizard *Uta stansburiana.* In *Systematic Biology.* Publication of the National Academy of Science (1692):133–160.

———. 1972a. The dynamics of a Utah population of *Sceloporus undulatus. Herpetologica* 28:351–359.

———. 1972b. The role of environment in the evolution of life history differences within and between lizard species. *University of Arkansas Museum Occasional Paper* 4:77–100.

———. 1973. A population analysis of the sagebrush lizard, *Sceloporus graciosus* in southern Utah. *Copeia* 1973:284–296.

———. 1976. Comparative data on the population ecology of the desert spiny lizard, *Sceloporus magister. Herpetologica* 32:1–6.

———. 1982. Results of experimental density manipulation in an Arizona lizard community. *Ecology* 63:57–65.

Tinkle, D. W., and R. E. Ballinger. 1972. *Sceloporus undulatus:* A study of the intraspecific comparative demography of a lizard. *Ecology* 53:570–584.

Tinkle, D. W., J. D. Congdon, and P. C. Rosen. 1981. Nesting frequency and success: Implications for the demography of painted turtles. *Ecology* 62:1,426–1,432.

Tinkle, D. W., and A. E. Dunham. 1983. Demography of the tree lizard, *Urosaurus ornatus,* in central Arizona. *Copeia* 1983:585–598.

Tinkle, D. W., A. E. Dunham, and J. D. Congdon. 1993. Life history and demographic variation in the lizard *Sceloporus graciosus:* a long-term study. *Ecology* 74:2,413–2,429.

Tinkle, D. W., and N. F. Hadley. 1975. Lizard reproductive effort: Caloric estimates and comments on its evolution. *Ecology* 56:427–434.

Tinkle, D. W., H. M. Wilbur, and S. G. Tilley. 1970. Evolutionary strategies in lizard reproduction. *Evolution* 24:55–74.

Tinkle, D. W., and D. W. Woodward. 1967. Relative movements of lizards in natural populations as determined from recapture radii. *Ecology* 48:166–168.

Tocque, K. 1993. The relationship between parasite burden and host resources in the desert toad *(Scaphiopus couchii),* under natural environmental conditions. *Journal of Animal Ecology* 62:683–693.

Toliver, M. E., and D. T. Jennings. 1975. Food habits of *Sceloporus undulatus tristichus* Cope (Squamata: Iguanidae) in Arizona. *Southwestern Naturalist* 20:1–11.

Tonn, R. J. 1961. On the distribution and size variations of *Phyllodistomum bufonis. Journal of Parasitology* 47:841.

Torbit, C. A., Jr. 1964. A preliminary report on the herpetofauna of a section of prairie in El Paso County, Colorado. *Journal of the Colorado-Wyoming Academy of Science* 5 (5):51.

Tordoff, W. 1967. Microgeographic variation in gene frequencies of the chorus frog. M.S. thesis, Colorado State University, Fort Collins.

———. 1971. Environmental factors affecting gene frequencies in montane populations of the chorus frog, *Pseudacris triseriata.* Ph.D. dissertation, Colorado State University, Fort Collins.

Tordoff, W., III. 1969. Gene frequency differences among semi-isolated proximate populations of chorus frogs *(Pseudacris). Journal of Herpetology* 3:194.

———. 1980. Selective predation of gray jays, *Perisoreus canadensis,* upon boreal chorus frogs, *Pseudacris triseriata. Evolution* 34:1,004–1,008.

Tordoff, W., III, and D. Pettus. 1977. Temporal stability of phenotypic frequencies in *Pseudacris triseriata* (Amphibia, Anura, Hylidae). *Journal of Herpetology* 11:161–168.

Tordoff, W., III, D. Pettus, and T. C. Matthews. 1976. Microgeographic variation in gene frequencies in *Pseudacris triseriata* (Amphibia, Anura, Hylidae). *Journal of Herpetology* 10:35–40.

Tracy, C. R. 1980. Water relations of parchment-shelled lizard *(Sceloporus undulatus)* eggs. *Copeia* 1980:478–482.

Trauth, S. E. 1978. Ovarian cycle of *Crotaphytus collaris* (Reptilia, Lacertilia, Iguanidae) from Arkansas with emphasis on corpora albicantia, follicular atresia, and reproductive potential. *Journal of Herpetology* 12:461–470.

———. 1979. Testicular cycle and timing of reproduction in the collared lizard *(Crotaphytus collaris)* in Arkansas. *Herpetologica* 35:184–192.

Trauth, S. E., and C. T. McAllister. 1996. *Cnemidophorus sexlineatus. Catalogue of American Amphibians and Reptiles* 628:1–12.

Trauth, S. E., J. D. Wilhide, L. C. Hunt, A. Holt, T. L. Klotz, and S. A. Woolbright. 1996. Natural history notes: *Cnemidophorus sexlineatus* (six-lined racerunner). Aquatic behavior. *Herpetological Review* 27:20–21.

Travis, C. A., D. Chiszar, and H. M. Smith. 1996. Geographic distribution: *Heterodon nasicus. Herpetological Review* 27:212.

Tucker, J. K., and F. J. Janzen. 1997. Incidence of twinning in turtles. *Copeia* 1997:166–173.

Tucker, M. 1989. Life history notes: *Masticophis flagellum* (coachwhip). Behavior. *Herpetological Review* 20:72.

Tuma, M. W. 1993. Life history notes: *Kinosternon flavescens* (yellow mud turtle). Multiple nesting. *Herpetological Review* 24:31.

Turner, F. B. 1959. Some features of the ecology of *Bufo punctatus* in Death Valley, California. *Ecology* 40:175–181.

Turner, F. B., G. D. Hoddenbach, P. A. Medica, and J. R. Lannom, Jr. 1970. The demography of the lizard *Uta stansburiana* Baird and Girard in southern Nevada. *Journal of Animal Ecology* 39:505–519.

Turner, F. B., J. R. Lannom, Jr., P. A. Medica, and G. A. Hoddenbach. 1969. Density and composition of fenced populations of leopard lizards *(Crotaphytus wislizenii)* in southern Nevada. *Herpetologica* 25:247–257.

Turner, F. B., P. A. Medica, K. W. Bridges, and R. I. Jenrich. 1982. A population model of the lizard *Uta stansburiana* in southern Nevada. *Ecological Monographs* 52:243–259.

Turner, F. B., P. A. Medica, J. R. Lannom, Jr., and G. A. Hoddenbach. 1969. A demographic analysis of fenced populations of the whiptail lizard, *Cnemidophorus tigris,* in southern Nevada. *Southwestern Naturalist* 14:189–202.

Turner, W. T. 1974. Ecological relationships between two sympatric species of *Sceloporus* lizards. M.S. thesis, Colorado State University, Fort Collins.

Tweto, O. 1975. Laramide (late Cretaceous–early Tertiary) orogeny in the Southern Rocky Mountains. Pages 1–44 in *Cenozoic history of the Southern Rocky Mountains,* B. F. Curtis, ed. Geological Society of America Memoir 144.

———. 1979. The Rio Grande rift system in Colorado. Pages 33–56 in *Rio Grande rift: Tectonics and magmatism,* R. E. Riecker, ed. American Geophysical Union, Washington, D.C.

Tyler, J. D. 1978. Bullfrog observed eating Blanchard's cricket frog. *Bulletin of the Oklahoma Herpetological Society* 3 (4):68–69.

Ultsch, G. R. 1985. The viability of nearctic freshwater turtles submerged in anoxia and normoxia at 3 and 10 C. *Comparative Biochemistry and Physiology* 81A:607–611.

Ultsch, G. R., R. W. Hanley, and T. R. Bauman. 1985. Responses to anoxia during simulated hibernation in northern and southern painted turtles. *Ecology* 66:388–395.

Ultsch, G. R., C. V. Herbert, and D. C. Jackson. 1984. The comparative physiology of diving in North American freshwater turtles. I. Submergence tolerance, gas exchange, and acid-base balance. *Physiological Zoology* 57:620–631.

U.S. Fish and Wildlife Service (USFWS). 22 July 1994. 90-day finding and commencement of status review for a petition to list the Southern Rocky Mountain population of boreal toad as endangered. *Federal Register* 59 (140):37,439–37,441.

———. 23 March 1995. 12-month finding for a petition to list the Southern Rocky Mountain population of boreal toad as endangered. *Federal Register* 60 (56):15,281–15,283.

———. 2 February 1996. Export of box turtles from the United States in 1996. *Federal Register* 61 (23):3,894–3,898.

van Breukelen, F., J. Roth, D. Chiszar, and H. M. Smith. 1997. Geographic distribution: *Sceloporus undulatus elongatus. Herpetological Review* 28:158.

Van Devender, T. R., and W. Van Devender. 1975. Ecological notes on two Mexican skinks (genus *Eumeces). Southwestern Naturalist* 20:279–282.

Van Loben Sels, R. C., and L. J. Vitt. 1984. Desert lizard reproduction: Seasonal and annual variation in *Urosaurus ornatus* (Iguanidae). *Canadian Journal of Zoology* 62:1,779–1,787.

Van Riper, W. 1955. How a rattlesnake strikes. *Natural History* 64:308–311.

Vanzolini, P. E. 1974. Climbing habits of Leptotyphlopidae (Serpentes) and Walls' theory of the evolution of the ophidian eye. *Papeis Avulsos Zool* 23:13–16.

Vaughan, R. K., J. R. Dixon, and R. A. Thomas. 1996. A reevaluation of populations of the corn snake *Elaphe guttata* (Reptilia: Serpentes: Colubridae) in Texas. *Texas Journal of Science* 48:175–190.

Vaughan, T. A. 1961. Vertebrates inhabiting pocket gopher burrows in Colorado. *Journal of Mammalogy* 42:171–174.

Veer, V., D. Chiszar, and H. M. Smith. 1997. Natural history notes: *Sonora semiannulata* (ground snake). Antipredation. *Herpetological Review* 28:91.

Vertucci, F. A., and P. S. Corn. 1994. A reply to Harte and Hoffman, acidification and salamander recruitment. *BioScience* 44:126.

———. 1996. Evaluation of episodic acidification and amphibian declines in the Rocky Mountains. *Ecological Applications* 6:449–457.

Vitt, L. J. 1974. Winter aggregations, size classes, and relative tail breaks in the tree lizard, *Urosaurus ornatus* (Sauria, Iguanidae). *Herpetologica* 30:182–183.

———. 1975. Observations on reproduction in five species of Arizona snakes. *Herpetologica* 31:83–84.

———. 1977. Observations on clutch and egg size and evidence for multiple clutches in some lizards of southwestern United States. *Herpetologica* 33:333–338.

Vitt, L. J., and G. L. Breitenbach. 1993. Life histories and reproductive tactics among lizards in the genus *Cnemidophorus* (Sauria: Teiidae). Pages 211–243 in *Biology of whiptail lizards (genus* Cnemidophorus*)*, J. W. Wright and L. J. Vitt, eds. Oklahoma Museum of Natural History, Norman.

Vitt, L. J., J. D. Congdon, A. C. Hulse, and J. E. Platz. 1974. Territorial aggressive encounters and tail breaks in the lizard *Sceloporus magister*. *Copeia* 1974:990–993.

Vitt, L. J., and R. D. Ohmart. 1974. Reproduction and ecology of a Colorado River population of *Sceloporus magister* (Sauria: Iguanidae). *Herpetologica* 30:410–417.

———. 1977. Ecology and reproduction of lower Colorado River lizards. II. *Cnemidophorus tigris* (Teiidae), with comparisons. *Herpetologica* 33:223–234.

Vogt, R. C. 1981. *Natural history of amphibians and reptiles of Wisconsin*. Milwaukee Public Museum, Milwaukee, Wisconsin.

Vogt, R. C., and J. J. Bull. 1982a. Temperature controlled sex-determination in turtles: Ecological and behavioral aspects. *Herpetologica* 38:156–164.

———. 1982b. Genetic sex determination in the spiny softshell *Trionyx spiniferus* (Testudines: Trionychidae) (?). *Copeia* 1982:699–700.

Vogt, R. C., J. J. Bull, C. J. McCoy, and T. W. Houseal. 1982. Incubation temperature influences sex determination in kinosternid turtles. *Copeia* 1982:480–482.

Voris, H. K., and J. P. Bacon, Jr. 1966. Differential predation on tadpoles. *Copeia* 1966:594–598.

Waldman, B. 1982. Adaptive significance of communal oviposition in wood frogs *(Rana sylvatica)*. *Behavioral Ecology and Sociobiology* 10:169–174.

Waldman, B., and M. J. Ryan. 1983. Thermal advantages of communal egg mass deposition in wood frogs *(Rana sylvatica)*. *Journal of Herpetology* 17:70–72.

Waldron, K., C. Montgomery, J. Hobert, R. Donoho, and S. P. Mackessy. 1996. Geographic distribution: *Rhinocheilus lecontei tessellatus*. *Herpetological Review* 27:36.

Waldschmidt, S. 1980. Orientation to the sun by the iguanid lizards *Uta stansburiana* and *Sceloporus undulatus*: Hourly and monthly variations. *Copeia* 1980:458–462.

Waldschmidt, S., and C. R. Tracy. 1983. Interactions between a lizard and its thermal environment: Implications for sprint performance and space utilization in the lizard *Uta stansburiana*. *Ecology* 64:476–484.

Waldschmidt, S. R. 1978. Monthly variation in thermoregulatory behaviors and space utilization in the lizards *Uta stansburiana* and *Sceloporus undulatus*. M.S. thesis, Colorado State University, Fort Collins.

———. 1979. The effect of statistically based models on home range size estimate in *Uta stansburiana*. *American Midland Naturalist* 101:236–240.

———. 1983. The effect of supplemental feeding on home range size and activity patterns in the lizard *Uta stansburiana*. *Oecologia* 57:1–5.

Walker, A. L. 1965. Reproduction in the little earless lizard, *Holbrookia maculata maculata*. M.S. thesis, Texas Tech University, Lubbock.

Walker, J. M. 1980. Accessory femoral pores in a colony of the collared lizard, *Crotaphytus collaris* in Texas. *Journal of Herpetology* 14:417–418.

Walker, J. M., and J. E. Cordes. 1998. Parthenogenetic *Cnemidophorus tesselatus* complex (Squamata: Teiidae) at Higbee, Otero County, Colorado: Research between 1950 and 1998. *Bulletin of the Chicago Herpetological Society* 33 (4):75–84.

Walker, J. M., J. E. Cordes, and H. L. Taylor. 1996. Extirpation of the parthenogenetic lizard *Cnemidophorus tesselatus* from historically significant sites in Pueblo County, Colorado. *Herpetological Review* 27:16–17.

———. 1997. Parthenogenetic *Cnemidophorus tesselatus* complex (Sauria Teiidae): A neotype for diploid *C. tesselatus* (Say, 1823), redescription of the taxon, and description of a new triploid species. *Herpetologica* 53:233–259.

Walker, J. M., E. D. Parker, Jr., H. L. Taylor, J. E. Cordes, and R. M. Abuhteba. 1990. Hybridization between all-female *Cnemidophorus tesselatus* and gonochoristic *Cnemidophorus sexlineatus. Journal of Herpetology* 24:388–396.

Walker, J. M., H. L. Taylor, and J. E. Cordes. 1994. Hybrid *Cnemidophorus* (Sauria: Teiidae) in Ninemile Valley of the Purgatoire River, Colorado. *Southwestern Naturalist* 39:235–240.

———. 1995. Parthenogenetic *Cnemidophorus tesselatus* complex at Higbee, Colorado: Resolution of 30 years of controversy. *Copeia* 1995:650–658.

Walker, J. M., H. L. Taylor, J. E. Cordes, and M. A. Paulissen. 1997. Distributional relationships and community assemblages of three members of the parthenogenetic *Cnemidophorus tesselatus* complex and *C. sexlineatus* (Squamata: Teiidae) at Higbee, Otero County, Colorado. *Herpetological Natural History* 5:69–78.

Walls, J. G. 1997. *Pantherophis guttatus?* It's time to split the genus *Elaphe. Reptile Hobbyist* 2 (10):52–57.

Walls, S. C., S. S. Belanger, and A. R. Blaustein. 1993. Morphological variation in a larval salamander: Dietary induction of plasticity in head shape. *Oecologia* 96:162–168.

Wasserman, A. O. 1957. Factors affecting interbreeding in sympatric species of spadefoots (genus *Scaphiopus*). *Evolution* 11:320–338.

Watkins, J. F., II, F. R. Gehlbach, and R. S. Baldridge. 1967. Ability of the blind snake, *Leptotyphlops dulcis,* to follow pheromone trails of army ants, *Neivamyrmex nigrescens* and *N. opacithorax. Southwestern Naturalist* 12:455–462.

Watkins, J. F., II, F. R. Gehlbach, and J. C. Kroll. 1969. Attractant-repellent secretions in the intra- and interspecific relations of blind snakes *(Leptotyphlops dulcis)* and army ants *(Neivamyrmex nigrescens). Ecology* 50:1,098–1,102.

Watkins, J. F., II, F. R. Gehlbach, and R. W. Plsek. 1972. Behavior of blind snakes *(Leptotyphlops dulcis)* in response to army ant *(Neivamyrmex nigrescens)* raiding columns. *Texas Journal of Science* 23:556–557.

Watson, D. 1939. Susie, Harry and Oscar. *Mesa Verde Notes* 9 (1):12–15.

Waye, H. L., and C. H. Shewchuk. 1995. Natural history notes: *Scaphiopus intermontanus* (Great Basin spadefoot). Production of odor. *Herpetological Review* 26:98–99.

Weatherhead, P. J., and K. A. Prior. 1992. Preliminary observations of habitat use and movements of the eastern massasauga rattlesnake *(Sistrurus c. catenatus). Journal of Herpetology* 26:447–452.

Weatherhead, P. J., and I. C. Robertson. 1992. Thermal constraints on swimming performance and escape responses of northern water snakes *(Nerodia sipedon). Canadian Journal of Zoology* 70:94–98.

Webb, R. G. 1962. North American Recent softshelled turtles (family Trionychidae). *University of Kansas Publications, Museum of Natural History* 13:429–611.

———. 1970. *Reptiles of Oklahoma.* University of Oklahoma Press, Norman.

———. 1973. *Trionyx spiniferus. Catalogue of American Amphibians and Reptiles* 140:1–4.

———. 1990. *Trionyx. Catalogue of American Amphibians and Reptiles* 487:1–7.

Webster, C. 1986. Substrate preference and activity in the turtle, *Kinosternon flavescens flavescens. Journal of Herpetology* 20:477–482.

Weiner, N. J., and H. M. Smith. 1965. Comparative osteology and classification of the crotaphytaform lizards. *American Midland Naturalist* 73:170–187.

Weinstein, S. A., C. F. DeWitt, and L. A. Smith. 1992. Variability of venom-neutralizing properties of serum from snakes of the colubrid genus *Lampropeltis. Journal of Herpetology* 26:452–461.

Weintraub, J. D. 1974. Movement patterns of the red-spotted toad, *Bufo punctatus. Herpetologica* 30:212–215.

Weir, J. 1993. The taxonomic status of *Elaphe guttata intermontana*—the intermountain ratsnake (Woodbury & Woodbury, 1942). *Herptile* 18 (4):167–179.

———. 1994. The successful propagation of *Elaphe guttata intermontana* (Woodbury & Woodbury 1942) (= *E. g. emoryi*)—the intermountain ratsnake, in captivity. *Litteratura Serpentium, Utrecht* 14 (2):57–61.

Weldon, P. J., and G. M. Burghardt. 1979. The ophiophage defensive response in crotaline snakes: Extension to new taxa. *Journal of Chemical Ecology* 5:141–151.

Weller, W. F., and D. M. Green. 1997. Checklist and current status of Canadian amphibians. In Amphibians in decline: Canadian studies of a global problem, D. M. Green, ed. *Herpetological Conservation* No. 1: xiii + 338 pp.

Wendelken, P. W. 1978. On prey-specific hunting behavior in the western ribbon snake, *Thamnophis proximus* (Reptilia, Serpentes, Colubridae). *Journal of Herpetology* 12:577–578.

Werler, J. E. 1951. Miscellaneous notes on the eggs and young of Texan and Mexican reptiles. *Zoologica* 36:37–48.

Werner, E. E. 1994. Ontogenetic scaling of competitive relations: Size-dependent effects and responses in two anuran larvae. *Ecology* 75:197–213.

Werner, E. E., G. A. Wellborn, and M. A. McPeek. 1995. Diet composition in postmetamorphic bullfrogs and green frogs: Implications for interspecific predation and competition. *Journal of Herpetology* 29:600–607.

Wever, E. G., M. G. Hepp-Reymond, and J. A. Vernon. 1966. Vocalization and hearing in the leopard lizard. *Proceedings of the National Academy of Science* 55:98–106.

Whitaker, J. O., Jr., D. Rubin, and J. R. Munsee. 1977. Observations on food habits of four species of spadefoot toads, genus *Scaphiopus*. *Herpetologica* 33:468–475.

White, C. A. 1878. Note on the garter snake. *American Naturalist* 12:53.

Whiteman, H. H. 1997. Maintenance of polymorphism promoted by sex-specific fitness payoffs. *Evolution* 51:2,039–2,044.

Whiteman, H. H., S. A. Wissinger, and A. J. Bohonak. 1994. Seasonal movement patterns in a subalpine population of the tiger salamander, *Ambystoma tigrinum nebulosum. Canadian Journal of Zoology* 72:1,780–1,787.

Whiteman, H. H., S. A. Wissinger, and W. S. Brown. 1996. Growth and foraging consequences of facultative paedomorphosis in the tiger salamander, *Ambystoma tigrinum nebulosum. Evolutionary Ecology* 10:433–446.

Whitford, W. B., and W. G. Whitford. 1973. Combat in the horned lizard, *Phrynosoma cornutum. Herpetologica* 29:191–192.

Whitford, W. G., and M. Bryant. 1979. Behavior of a predator and its prey: The horned lizard *(Phrynosoma cornutum)* and harvester ants *(Pogonomyrmex* spp.). *Ecology* 60:686–694.

Whitford, W. G., and F. M. Creusere. 1977. Seasonal and yearly fluctuations in Chihuahuan Desert lizard communities. *Herpetologica* 33:54–65.

Whitford, W. G., and K. H. Meltzer. 1976. Changes in O₂ consumption, body water and lipid in burrowed desert juvenile anurans. *Herpetologica* 32:23–25.

Whiting, M. J., and J. R. Dixon. 1996. *Phrynosoma modestum. Catalogue of American Amphibians and Reptiles* 630:1–6.

Whiting, M. J., J. R. Dixon, and R. C. Murray. 1993. Spatial distribution of a population of Texas horned lizards (*Phrynosoma cornutum:* Phrynosomatidae) relative to habitat and prey. *Southwestern Naturalist* 38:150–154.

Whiting, M. J., B. D. Greene, J. R. Dixon, A. L. Mercer, and C. C. Eckerman. 1992. Observations on the foraging ecology of the western coachwhip snake, *Masticophis flagellum testaceus. The Snake* 24:157–160.

Widmer, E. A. 1967. Helminth parasites of the prairie rattlesnake, *Crotalus viridis* Rafinesque, 1818, in Weld County, Colorado. *Journal of Parasitology* 53:362–363.

Wiens, J. J. 1989. Ontogeny of the skeleton of *Spea bombifrons* (Anura: Pelobatidae). *Journal of Morphology* 202:29–51.

Wiens, J. J., and T. W. Reeder. 1997. Phylogeny of the spiny lizards *(Sceloporus)* based on molecu-lar and morphological evidence. *Herpetological Monographs* 11:1–101.

Wiens, J. J., and T. A. Titus. 1991. A phylogenetic analysis of *Spea* (Anura: Pelobatidae). *Herpetologica* 47:21–28.

Wiese, R. J. 1985. Ecological aspects of the bullfrog in northeastern Colorado. M.S. thesis, Colorado State University, Fort Collins.

———. 1990. Genetic structure of native and introduced populations of the bullfrog, a successful colonist. Ph.D. dissertation, Colorado State University, Fort Collins.

Wiese, R. J. No date [1989 or 1990]. Survey of the bullfrog along the Front Range and in eastern Colorado, 1989. Unpublished report to the Colorado Division of Wildlife.

Wilhoft, D. C., M. G. Del Baglivo, and M. D. Del Baglivo. 1979. Observations on mammalian prediation [*sic*] of snapping turtle nests (Reptilia, Testudines, Chelydridae). *Journal of Herpetology* 13:435–438.

Wilhoft, D. C., E. Hotaling, and P. Franks. 1983. Effects of temperature on sex determination in embryos of the snapping turtle, *Chelydra serpentina. Journal of Herpetology* 17:38–42.

Wilbur, H. M. 1977. Propagule size, number, and dispersion pattern in *Ambystoma* and *Asclepias. American Naturalist* 111:43–68.

Will, B. D., D. Chiszar, and H. M. Smith. 1995. Geographic distribution: *Chelydra serpentina serpentina. Herpetological Review* 26:208.

Willard, D. E. 1977. Constricting methods of snakes. *Copeia* 1977:379–382.

Willey, R. L. 1990. *Proposed monitoring of tiger salamander* (Ambystoma tigrinum nebulosum) *populations in western Colorado with emphasis on populations containing neotenic morphs.* Report to the Colorado Natural Areas Program. Unpublished report.

Williams, K. L. 1959. Nocturnal activity of some species of horned lizards, genus *Phrynosoma. Herpetologica* 15:43.

———. 1988. *Systematics and natural history of the American milk snake,* Lampropeltis triangulum. 2d ed. Milwaukee Public Museum, Milwaukee, Wisconsin.

———. 1994. *Lampropeltis triangulum. Catalogue of American Amphibians and Reptiles* 594:1–10.

Williams, T. A., and J. L. Christiansen. 1981. The niches of two sympatric softshell turtles, *Trionyx muticus* and *Trionyx spiniferus,* in Iowa. *Journal of Herpetology* 15:303–308.

Wilson, B. S. 1990. Life history notes: *Uta stansburiana* (side-blotched lizard). Cannibalism. *Herpetological Review* 21:61–62.

———. 1991. Latitudinal variation in activity season mortality rates of the lizard *Uta stansburiana. Ecological Monographs* 61:393–414.

Wilson, L. D. 1970. The coachwhip snake, *Masticophis flagellum* (Shaw): Taxonomy and distribution. *Tulane Studies in Zoology* 16:31–99.

———. 1973. *Masticophis flagellum. Catalogue of American Amphibians and Reptiles* 145:1–4.

———. 1978. *Coluber constrictor. Catalogue of American Amphibians and Reptiles* 218:1–4.

Wissinger, S. A., and H. H. Whiteman. 1992. Fluctuation in a Rocky Mountain population of salamanders: Anthropogenic acidification or natural variation? *Journal of Herpetology* 26:377–391.

Witschi, E. 1929. Studies on sex differentiation and sex determination in amphibians. II. Sex reversal in female tadpoles of *Rana sylvatica* following the application of high temperatures. *Journal of Experimental Zoology* 52:267–291.

Wood, W. F. 1935. Encounters with the western spadefoot, *Scaphiopus hammondii*, with a note on a few albino larvae. *Copeia* 1935:100–102.

Woodbury, A. M. 1928. The reptiles of Zion National Park. *Copeia* 166:14–21.

Woodbury, A. M., and R. M. Hansen. 1950. A snake den in Tintic Mountains, Utah. *Herpetologica* 6:66–70.

Woodbury, A. M., and D. M. Woodbury. 1942. Studies of the rat snake, *Elaphe laeta*, with description of a new subspecies. *Proceedings of the Biological Society of Washington* 55:133–142.

Woodbury, A. M., et al. 1951. Symposium: A snake den in Tooele County, Utah. *Herpetologica* 7:1–52.

Woodbury, M., and A. M. Woodbury. 1945. Life history studies of the sagebrush lizard *Sceloporus g. graciosus* with special reference to cycles in reproduction. *Herpetologica* 2:175–196.

Woodin, W. H. 1950. Notes on Arizona species of *Thamnophis. Herpetologica* 6:39–40.

Woodward, B. D. 1982a. Sexual selection and nonrandom mating patterns in desert anurans *(Bufo woodhousei, Scaphiopus couchi, S. multiplicatus,* and *S. bombifrons). Copeia* 1982:351–355.

———. 1982b. Persistence and male mating success in *Bufo woodhousei. Ecology* 63:583–585.

———. 1984a. Operational sex ratios and size biased mortality in *Scaphiopus* (Pelobatidae). *Southwestern Naturalist* 29:232–233.

———. 1984b. Arrival to and location of *Bufo woodhousei* in the breeding pond: Effect on the operational sex ratio. *Oecologia* 62:240–244.

———. 1987a. Intra- and interspecific variation in spadefoot toad *(Scaphiopus)* clutch parameters. *Southwestern Naturalist* 32:127–156.

———. 1987b. Clutch parameters and pond use in some Chihuahuan Desert anurans. *Southwestern Naturalist* 32:13–19.

Woodward, B. D., and S. Mitchell. 1990. Predation on frogs in breeding choruses. *Southwestern Naturalist* 35:449–450.

Woodward, B. D., S. L. Mitchell, and J. Kiesecker. 1990. Fairy shrimp–predator interactions in northern Colorado. *Journal of the Colorado-Wyoming Academy of Science* 22 (1):8.

Woody, J. R. 1967. Study of certain meteorological influences on the emergence and breeding with notes on the embryology of the plains spadefoot toad, *Scaphiopus bombifrons*. M.A. thesis, University of Northern Colorado, Greeley.

Woody, J. R., and B. O. Thomas. 1966. Preliminary studies of the *Scaphiopus bombifrons* in northeastern Colorado. *Journal of the Colorado-Wyoming Academy of Science* 5 (7):11–12.

———. 1968. Study of certain meteorological influences on the emergence and breeding of the palins [*sic*] spadefoot toad, *Scaphiopus bombifrons. Journal of the Colorado-Wyoming Academy of Science* 6 (1):11.

Worthington, R. D. 1972. Density, growth rates and home range sizes of *Phrynosoma cornutum* in southern Dona Ana County, New Mexico. *Herpetological Review* 4:128.

———. 1982. Dry and wet year comparisons of clutch and adult body sizes of *Uta stansburiana stejnegeri. Journal of Herpetology* 16:332–334.

Worthington, R. D., and M. D. Sabath. 1966. Winter aggregations of the lizard *Urosaurus ornatus ornatus* (Baird and Girard) in Texas. *Herpetologica* 22:94–96.

Worthylake, K. M., and P. Hovingh. 1989. Mass mortality of salamanders *(Ambystoma tigrinum)* by bacteria *(Acinebacter)* in an oligotrophic seepage mountain lake. *Great Basin Naturalist* 49:364–372.

Wright, A. H., and A. A. Wright. 1957. *Handbook of snakes of the United States and Canada.* Cornell University Press, Comstock Publishing Associates, Ithaca, New York.

Wright, B. A. 1941. Habit and habitat studies of the massasauga rattlesnake (*Sistrurus catenatus catenatus* Raf.) in northeastern Illinois. *American Midland Naturalist* 25:659–672.

Wright, D. L., K. V. Kardong, ad D. L. Bentley. 1979. The functional anatomy of the teeth of the western terrestrial garter snake, *Thamnophis elegans. Herpetologica* 35:223–228.

Wright, J. W. 1978. Parthenogenetic lizards. *Science* 202:1,152–1,154.

———. 1993. Evolution of the lizards of the genus *Cnemidophorus*. Pages 27–81 in *Biology of whiptail lizards (genus* Cnemidophorus*),* J. W. Wright and L. J. Vitt, eds. Oklahoma Museum of Natural History, Norman.

Wright, J. W., and C. H. Lowe. 1967. The evolution of alloploid parthenospecies *Cnemidophorus tesselatus* (Say). *Mammalian Chromosome Newsletter* 8:95–98.

———. 1968. Weeds, polyploids, parthenogenesis, and the geographical and ecological distribution of all-female species of *Cnemidophorus. Copeia* 1968:128–138.

Wunder, M. B., J. L. Siemers, and A. E. Ochs. 1998. Geographic distribution: *Spea bombifrons. Herpetological Review* 29:50.

Yancy, F. D., II. 1997. Natural history notes: *Hypsiglena torquata jani* (Texas night snake). Maximum size. *Herpetological Review* 28:205.

Yarrow, H. C. 1875. *Report upon the collections of batrachians and reptiles made in portions of Nevada, Utah, Colorado, New Mexico, and Arizona, during the years 1871, 1872, 1873, and 1874. Report upon the Geography & Geology of the Exploration & Survey west of the 100th Meridian (Wheeler Survey).* Vol. 5, chap. 4:509–584.

———. 1882. Checklist of North American reptiles and batrachia. *Bulletin of the U.S. National Museum* 24 (30):vi, 3–249.

Yedlin, I. N., and G. W. Ferguson. 1973. Variation in aggressiveness of free-living male and female collared lizards, *Crotaphytus collaris*. *Herpetologica* 29:268–275.

Yntema, C. L. 1976. Effects of incubation temperature on sex differentiation in the turtle, *Chelydra serpentina*. *Journal of Morphology* 150:453–462.

Young, B. A. 1997. On the absence of taste buds in monitor lizards *(Varanus)* and snakes. *Journal of Herpetology* 31:130–137.

Zamudio, K. R., K. B. Jones, and R. H. Ward. 1997. Molecular systematics of short-horned lizards: Biogeography and taxonomy of a widespread species complex. *Systematic Biology* 46:284–305.

Zeyl, C. 1993. Allozyme variation and divergence among populations of *Rana sylvatica*. *Journal of Herpetology* 27:233–236.

Zortman, R. D. 1968. Natural areas in Colorado, their administration by the Bureau of Land Management. M.S. thesis, Colorado State University, Fort Collins.

Zucker, N. 1989. Dorsal darkening and territoriality in a wild population of the tree lizard, *Urosaurus ornatus. Journal of Herpetology* 23:389–398.

Zucker, N., and W. Boecklen. 1990. Variation in female throat coloration in the tree lizard *(Urosaurus ornatus):* Relation to reproductive cycle and fecundity. *Herpetologica* 46:387–394.

Zucker, N., and L. J. Guillette, Jr. 1985. *Urosaurus ornatus* (tree lizard): Reproduction. *Herpetological Review* 16:28.

Zug, G. R. 1978. Anuran locomotion—structure and function. 2. Jumping performance of semiaquatic, terrestrial, and arboreal frogs. Smithsonian Contributions to Zoology No. 276.

Zweifel, R. G. 1956. Two pelobatid frogs from the Tertiary of North America and their relationship to fossil and Recent forms. *American Museum Novitates* 1,762:1–45.

———. 1961. Larval development of the tree frogs *Hyla arenicolor* and *Hyla wrightorum. American Museum Novitates* 1,813:1–19.

———. 1965. Variation in and distribution of the unisexual lizard, *Cnemidophorus tesselatus. American Museum Novitates* 2,235:1–49.

———. 1968. Reproductive biology of anurans of the arid southwest, with emphasis on adaptation of embryos to temperature. *Bulletin of the American Museum of Natural History* 140 (1):1–64.

———. 1970. Descriptive notes on larvae of toads of the *debilis* group, genus *Bufo. American Museum Novitates* 2,407:1–13.

———. 1980. Aspects of the biology of a laboratory population of kingsnakes. In *Reproductive biology and diseases of captive reptiles,* J. B. Murphy and J. T. Collins, eds. Society for the Study of Amphibians and Reptiles Contributions to Herpetology No. 1:i–x, 1–277.

———. 1981. Color pattern morphs of the kingsnake *(Lampropeltis getulus)* in southern California: Distribution and evolutionary status. Bulletin of the Southern California Academy of Science 80 (2):70–81.

———. 1997. Alternating use of hemipenes in the kingsnake, Lampropeltis getula. Journal of Herpetology 31:459–461.

Index

Note: Species accounts are cited in **boldface.** Citations followed by the letters m, f, t, and p denote maps, figures, tables, and photos respectively.